Literature

Literature

An Introduction to Theory and Analysis

**Edited by
Mads Rosendahl Thomsen,
Lasse Horne Kjældgaard,
Lis Møller, Dan Ringgaard,
Lilian Munk Rösing, and
Peter Simonsen**

Bloomsbury Academic
An imprint of Bloomsbury Publishing Inc

B L O O M S B U R Y
LONDON · OXFORD · NEW YORK · NEW DELHI · SYDNEY

Bloomsbury Academic

An imprint of Bloomsbury Publishing Plc

50 Bedford Square	1385 Broadway
London	New York
WC1B 3DP	NY 10018
UK	USA

www.bloomsbury.com

BLOOMSBURY and the Diana logo are trademarks of Bloomsbury Publishing Plc

First published 2017

© Mads Rosendahl Thomsen, Lasse Horne Kjældgaard, Lis Møller, Dan Ringgaard, Lilian Munk Rösing, Peter Simonsen, and contributors, 2017

British Library Cataloguing-in-Publication Data

A catalogue record for this book is available from the British Library.

ISBN:	HB:	978-1-4742-7197-4
	PB:	978-1-4742-7196-7
	ePDF:	978-1-4742-7199-8
	ePub:	978-1-4742-7198-1

Library of Congress Cataloging-in-Publication Data

A catalog record for this book is available from the Library of Congress.

Cover design: Jason Anscomb

Typeset by Integra Software Services Pvt. Ltd.
Printed and bound in Great Britain

Contents

Part II Contexts

Part III Practices

Foreword

J. Hillis Miller

This wonderfully useful, readable, and wide-ranging book will tell students and teachers, as well as general readers, most of what they need to know about the important topics in literary theory and analysis in Europe and America today. The book consists of thirty-three short chapters, each by a different specialist and each on a different topic in literary study. Each chapter is a survey of its topic with references to the major theorists on the subject. Each also shows how attention to that topic is useful by reading a carefully chosen example, Thomas Pynchon's *The Crying of Lot 49* for "Books," Shakespeare's *A Midsummer Night's Dream* for "Quality," and so on. Some chapters have more than one example from literature. In addition, each entry has an extremely helpful list of further readings on the topic in question.

The book is divided into three parts that move outward from literary texts (for example "Plot," "Narrator," and "Character") to their contexts (for example "History," "Ethics," and "Nature") to adjacent important concepts in literary study (for example "Archives," "Performance," and "Translation"). As is appropriate for today's dominant forms of literary study, attention to literature as such broadens out as the book progresses toward what is today called "cultural studies." The chapter called "Nature," though it uses Donne's "The Sun Rising" and Mary Shelley's *Frankenstein* as examples, is really about today's "ecocriticism." It is impossible in a short foreword, however, to do justice to the scope and brilliance of the various chapters or to their variety.

Literature: An Introduction to Theory and Analysis is based on a highly successful volume published in Danish and in Swedish translation in 2012 and used as a textbook in all five major Danish universities. This English version, however, has nineteen new chapters written by American, British, and European scholars. All the other chapters have been modified for the larger intended audience. It is now a genuinely international book, suitable for use in courses taught in English anywhere in the world.

Though this book is primarily intended for use in first and second year college and university courses in introduction to literature, it will also be useful for advanced literature courses, even postgraduate ones, or as a great resource for teachers of literature, or as a valuable resource for ordinary readers who may want to know something about what is meant by the "narrator" of a novel, or by "ethnicity" in literature, and so on. I'll use the book myself, as a resource tool, as a place to begin with a given topic. If I want to know, to take one example more or less at random, what is meant by "hermeneutics," the entry in this book on "Interpretation," by Jesper Gulddal of the University of Newcastle in Australia, will give me the basic facts, illustrated in this case by a discussion of Ibsen's *Pillars of Society* (1877).

As Dryden said of Chaucer's *The Canterbury Tales*, so I say of this book: "here is God's plenty".

Introduction

Mads Rosendahl Thomsen, Lasse Horne Kjældgaard, Lis Møller, Dan Ringgaard, Lilian Munk Rösing, and Peter Simonsen

---

Chapter Outline

There is no exact way to study literature, no fail-safe method, and no way to prove that one was right. This may be one reason why we often underestimate how complex literary studies are. Reading a text and forming an opinion about it is easy. Being able to look at a text from many different angles, making perspectives meet, seeing it in relation to other texts and contexts while maintaining a self-critical view of one's own approach require a number of skills, a great deal of knowledge and above all analytical practice. And there is a clear bonus: a deeper engagement with analyzing literature makes it possible to appreciate how mesmerizing texts can be as one is stuck in a stanza, thrown off by a metaphor (if it really is a metaphor), or befuddled by trying to figure out how the quintessential traits of a character can best be expressed.

Twentieth-century literary criticism was to some degree dominated by a relatively small number of schools or approaches such as New Criticism, Structuralism, and Deconstruction. Recent decades in literary studies have been marked by a welcome move toward pluralism that has striven to bring out the values in the large reservoir of theories that can help make sense of literature. Pluralism does not mean that anything goes, but that the critical engagement with texts and theories will have to prove itself in each new meeting. It is also a recurrent experience that the use of different approaches to literary works not only produces better and more nuanced analyses but also heightens the regard for those texts that seem to be able to respond to the various angles from which they are approached.

In thirty-three chapters, this book moves from definitions of literature and essentials of textual theory to contextualizing theories and perspectives on the uses of literature. Rather than giving priority to schools of criticism, as introductions to literary studies often do, *Literature: An Introduction to Theory and Analysis* seeks to clarify how to engage fruitfully with recurrent topics in literary criticism. The first part "Texts" takes up fundamental analytical terms such as interpretation, genre, characters, narrative, tropes, and intertextuality, all part of an indispensable vocabulary in literary analysis. The second part "Contexts" engages with the vast array of themes literature addresses such as politics, gender, ethnicity, and memory. But rather than being merely excuses for doing thematic studies, the chapters show how form and content work together. Finally, the third part "Practices" shows how the uses of literature cannot be separated from the study of literature. Adaptation, translation, and judgment of quality are among the terms that define the circulation of literary works which includes the capacity for critical writing and judgment of quality.

How to use this book

Literature: An Introduction to Theory and Analysis can be read in many ways. It can be the cornerstone of an introductory course to literary studies. The chapters in the book could then profitably be read along with the primary texts referred to and some of the critical texts, which each chapter refers to. The three parts of the book suggest one order but there are many ways the book could find use in a course. It can be read from start to finish, if there is enough time, but most instructors will find their own way, also dependent on course requirements.

The book can also be used as a handbook that delivers sharp perspectives on thirty-three different themes in literary studies, and which does so not in the abstract but in the interplay with literary works and the most important scholarly contributions to each theme.

And the book may be handy for readers of literature who would like to expand their vocabulary for the experience of literature, essentially the same thing an introductory course would do, maybe a bit more regulated but hopefully not less joyfully.

Part I

Texts

1

Literature

Lasse Horne Kjældgaard and Peter Simonsen

What if literature did not exist? This thought experiment has, of course, been carried out not in life but in literature. Ray Bradbury's novel *Fahrenheit 451* (1953) takes place in a future society where literature has been abolished, and where firemen are not fighting fires, but burning books. In Aldous Huxley's future-fiction novel *Brave New World* (1932), literature is also a thing of the past and replaced by extremely lifelike moving and tactile images, so-called feeling pictures. More recently, Alena Graedon's novel *The Word Exchange* (2014) has presented us with a world where books have disappeared, and where everybody is completely attached to their handheld digital devices, called Memes, which anticipate all wishes and desires of the user, while also creating and trading language itself on the so-called Word Exchange.

What all these novels about the future share is that they are the opposite of utopias: They are dystopias that depict conditions which probably only a few of us would ever find desirable. Another shared trait is that it is not only literature that has been eradicated or made redundant but also basic human and humanistic values, such as individual freedom, family, friendship, a deeper understanding of the past, and a dynamic view of the future. Societal phenomena that we normally think of as constants appear in the novels as variables, which are linked—in one way or another—to that variable we call literature.

In this way, the novels stage the importance of literature, by relating it to vital features of life that virtually no one would wish to go without. They bring to life living conditions that many of us would hesitate to call human. The novels even do so with a device that is pronouncedly, but not exclusively, literary, by asking, "what if?" In one of the first books written about literature, Aristotle's *Poetics* (c. 335 BC), the Greek philosopher declared that "the poet's job is saying not what did happen but the sort of thing that would happen, that is, what can happen in a strictly probable or necessary sequence" (Aristotle 1987, 547). This is exactly what these novels speculate upon: What may happen? What is possible?

The question about what a world without literature would be like is, indeed, a hypothetical question. Much less speculative, but not less daunting, is the question of what literature actually is. What are we talking about when we talk about literature?

Literature then and now

Not one thing, but many. The word itself comes from the Latin *litterātūra*, meaning writing or incorporated knowledge. Literature, Raymond Williams points out in *Keywords*, "is a difficult word" (183). Its difficulty stems in no small part from the fact that it refers both narrowly to literary works of art (in a modern sense that emerged after 1800) and broadly to all written, printed works (in an older sense). To add to this complexity, once upon a time literature was not even something you would read, but something you did or had. The Roman rhetorician Quintilian used the word *litteratura* about the ability to read and write (*Institutio Oratio*, Book 2, chapter 1, section 4), and until the second century literature was what you possessed in the form of wisdom and scientific training, it named an individual's collective knowledge or book learning (close to what we today would call literacy).

In English, according to the *Oxford English Dictionary* (*OED*, 3rd edition 2011), the word entered the language in 1460 in this now obsolete sense: "Familiarity with letters or books; knowledge acquired from reading or studying books, esp. the principal classical texts associated with humane learning; literary culture; learning, scholarship." This is the only sense listed in Samuel Johnson's dictionary (1755), which in other words did not register the emergence of the more modern and restricted sense of literature as the "result or product of literary activity; written works considered collectively; a body of literary works produced in a particular country or period, or of a particular genre." This usage was first put into circulation by Lord Shaftesbury, who in *Characteristicks* (1711) talked about how, "In mere Poetry, and the Pieces of Wit and Literature, there is a Liberty of Thought and Easiness of Humour indulg'd to us" (quoted in *OED*). Thus, in one of the first treatises on what was to be known as "aesthetics," Shaftesbury identified a crucial element in the modern understanding of literature: it entails the freedom to think and speak otherwise, in new and often controversial ways in combination with pleasure derived from the aesthetic qualities of the work of art (Derrida 1992).

So weakly and broadly may literature be defined, but in everyday usage, at universities and other educational institutions, the definition is usually much more limited. Literary research and teaching generally concerns only a few forms of writing, primarily poetry, fictional prose, and drama that meet certain aesthetic requirements (see Chapter 33), and which is usually printed with ink on sheets of paper that have been folded and bound together in a book (see Chapter 26). It is not a coincidence that the burning of books equals the destruction of literature in general in Bradbury's *Fahrenheit 451*. Frequently, literature is used synonymously with printed books.

This usage of literature in a more restricted sense related to aesthetics led, via philosophers and critics working around 1800 such as Immanuel Kant, Friedrich Schiller and Samuel Taylor Coleridge, to the use of literature without the definite article in the sense of "written work valued for superior or lasting artistic merit" (*OED*). The *OED* registers the first such usage in 1852 by Andrew Edgar in *Tusculana* and it merits quotation: "Literature may be divided into two great classes, the popular, and the learned or exclusive. Many persons who consider the matter superficially will no doubt regard the former as a very insignificant division; but to us it appears to be by much the more important, and to be that which really and substantially constitutes literature" (quoted in *OED*).

This modern, narrow concept of literature tied to an exclusive sense of fine art emerged in an uneasy traction with notions of "the popular" in the course of the nineteenth century, and it is an opposition that still informs many discussions about what literature is. The most recent *OED* usage comes from a review from 2001 of a John Le Carré novel: "Le Carre …[is] a mystery writer who produces literature. At least what I consider to be literature. The argument about what constitutes literature will probably go on forever" (*OED*). We can only hope that this argument will go on forever to pay testimony to a persistent interest in thinking about what kind of a thing literature is (a thing that by its very definition cannot be defined and thus provokes endless but fruitful discussion).

Yet, already in 1976, Raymond Williams noted that the restricted sense of literature (according to which a genre writer like Le Carré could be thought of as beyond the pale of recognized good taste) in recent years had been "challenged … by concepts of *writing* and *communication* which seek to recover the most active and general senses of which the extreme specialization had seemed to exclude" (187). Originating with the Romantic idealists, the narrow notion of literature as a form of art that emanates from a genius' free imagination and presupposes a special attitude in the reader, who must read without having a practical purpose in mind, is indeed under pressure. As J. Hillis Miller among others has pointed out in *On Literature* (2002), this notion of literature was complexly related to the rise of the printing press, of universal literacy, democracy, universal education, the modern nation state and the modern university with its cherished ideas of *Bildung* & *Wissenschaft*, and the spread of freedom of speech. These complex processes are indicators of the modern world and are in turn complexly related to the emergence of a modern sense of self and subjectivity as grounded in a free individual's autonomy, agency and self-consciousness as citizen with rights. These phenomena are all variously under pressure from an emergent postmodern sense of the self as fluid and decentered, a weakening of the nation state in the age of globalization and corporate capitalism, the transformation of the university and the increasing disconcern about the making of a national ethos, and the rise of new digital storage and search possibilities that disconnect literature from the book and reading from a solitary individual looking at pages in a book.

Hillis Miller, on the one hand, declares literature dead and, on the other hand, says it is perennial. It is extinct as the study of material books understood to hold special values and be especially disposed to cultivating or in a sense "culturing" the reader. It is perennial insofar as it names "a certain use of words or other signs that exist in some form or other" (13), a use of words and other signs which "exploits a certain potentiality in human beings as sign-using animals" (15). This potentiality is the extraordinary power words have of "signifying in the total absence of any phenomenal referent" (16): literature names the generation of a "virtual reality" (17). The airy words of a literary work can create something from nothing: "Language in literature is derouted so that it refers only to an imaginary world" (20), writes Miller, and these imaginary worlds have the power to make things happen once we have entered them: "Literature is a use of words that makes things happen by way of its readers" (20). The historical archive where we study ourselves is largely textual and must be read (increasingly using new digital technologies that enable new ways of reading), yet the archive of the future where we will be studied and where our sense of who we are is currently being articulated is multimodal. All of this constitutes the object of study for literary studies.

In other words, while the narrow sense of literature became more and more widespread among critics and intellectuals during the nineteenth and twentieth centuries served to found modern literary studies at universities, most strongly institutionalized by American New Criticism after the Second World War, it nurtures an idea which is no longer widely held or defended in academic literary studies. In recent decades, these have often tended toward a more pragmatic, plural, eclectic, and use-oriented approach to the study of literature, where urgent questions are raised about what a given literary text's formal shape makes the reader see, sense, or think in new ways about political, ethical, and environmental issues and about the challenges of various identity formations and subject positions. Thus, while literature in the old sense tied to books and *Bildung* may have died, literature remains and can be fruitfully studied as a resource in which we can explore what it means to be human, to inhabit a body and mind in space and time, in as many senses as can be imagined (Mousley 2013).

There is no single firm definition embracing the many phenomena that can be called literature. There can be several reasons for this. One of them is that literature can be found far beyond the confines of the printed book. Prayers and children's songs that you remember by heart, for example, are also kinds of literature. Another reason is that literature is something that lies on the borders of other arts and genres, and that these boundaries are constantly exceeded or renegotiated (see Chapter 28). Comics or graphic novels, for example, narrate by using pictures, often accompanied by text, while Dadaist sound poetry tests the limits of language in the direction of the purely acoustic expression.

Generic boundaries are also tested and transgressed on a regular basis. Works such as Plato's *The Republic*, *The Bible*; Augustine's *Confessions*; or Montaigne's *Essays* are so well written and important and meaningful that they can easily sneak into the category of literature, even if they are read, and proposed to be read, as something else than literature—as political philosophy, Holy Scripture, meditations, or memoir. An oeuvre like Søren Kierkegaard's has moved into the house of literature in the twentieth century in the sense that people are increasingly reading his texts as literary constructions and not only as a theological or philosophical treatises, with a focus not only on what the works mean but also on how they are structured and how they affect the reader with aesthetic means.

A third reason is that literature is "related" to an array of other forms of human behavior. The house of the imagination has other rooms than fiction, and in night dreams, daydreams, and symbolic play we can find invented worlds and activities that are associated with fiction, and thus also with literature. Fourthly, and finally, the "literary" has broken loose from literature in the narrow sense and is disseminated, as a kind of stylistic category, in many corners of the experience economy, from movies and TV shows to touristic travels. In *Bring on the Books for Everybody: How Literary Culture Became Popular Culture* (2010), Jim Collins has shown how "the literary experience" has changed into something engendered also by film adaptations and consumer communities, for instance. This does not make it easier to agree on an exhaustive and sharply outlined definition of what literature is.

Yet the absence of a common denominator need not mean a rejection or a complete dilution of the concept of literature. One can also draw less radical conclusions from the observation that literature is probably not something crystallizable into a set of criteria, into a kind of checklist that can be deployed as a description for all purposes. One can say the same thing about literature as the philosopher Ludwig Wittgenstein said of different kinds of games in §66 of *Philosophical Investigations* (1953): "if you look at them you will not see something that is common to all, but similarities, relationships, and a whole series of them at that" (Wittgenstein 1958, 31). Correspondingly, you may not find common features, which all kinds of literature share, but characteristics distributed unevenly across the many species and variants of literature. This logic amounts to thinking in "family resemblances," as Wittgenstein also called it. A son may closely resemble his father, and the father his brother, while the uncle and the nephew do not need to have any features in common. Still, they form a family. Two texts can easily be literature without having anything in common.

A comparable logic is to approach literature in terms of its prototypes. Some kinds of literature seem more prototypical than others. The majority of nonprofessional readers will probably associate the word "literature" with a fictional narrative, usually in the form of a novel or short story, where the language, point of view, and way of telling do not hinder the reader's following the story, empathizing with the characters, and experiencing the world from their perspective. Yet, most people also know that other kinds of literature exist—difficultly accessible poetry and prose, for example, which uses language for other purposes than mirroring virtual worlds. It might not be these kinds of literature, which we first think of when we hear the word but we nevertheless subsume them under the concept of literature when encountering them.

That could be a reason for commencing the study of literature by analyzing prototypical literary texts—without ever forgetting the big insights that may be gained from studying less typical or nonliterary types of text with the same concentrated care and analytical skills. The expanded capacity for attention, developed by the careful reading of literature, can be employed for many other purposes than studying literature.

In a widely disseminated "manifesto" for a new approach to literary criticism, Rita Felski proposes four categories for what she terms "modes of textual engagement" (Felski 2008, 14) to account for what is involved in literary reading: recognition, enchantment, knowledge, and shock. These modes of textual engagement are grounded in what for Felski motivates "ordinary readers" as well as academic readers to read. We read for all kinds of reasons, but not least (1) in order to better understand ourselves through seeing ourselves in others who are like us (*recognition*), (2) in order to be carried, held, or swept away through intense involvement with a text to experience being enchanted in an increasingly disenchanted contemporary world (*enchantment*), (3) in order to learn about other places, peoples, cultures, events in the world that we didn't know about before reading (*knowledge*), (4) in order to be shocked, revolted, and disturbed by appalling subject matter or truly upsetting form and language (*shock*). By virtue of their special formal characteristics and often existentially probing contents, literary texts, for Felski, "are formative in their own right, as representations that summon up new ways of seeing rather than echoes or distortions of predetermined political truths" (9–10).

Though one might be weary of the polemical thrust of Felski's call for a "postcritical" criticism (Felski 2015) that does not meet literature skeptically with the presupposition that it is trying to mislead us, much is also gained from first registering what is happening in the work. Felski's is a study of the "uses of literature" in a nonrestrictive sense of "use." By "uses" she means that literary works purvey "epistemic insights, vocabularies of self-understanding, and affective states" (21)—and the literary is for her still tied to the study of canonical verbal texts; yet as she puts it: "If literary studies is to survive the twenty-first century, it will need to reinvigorate its ambitions and its methods by forging closer links to the study of other media rather than clinging to ever more tenuous claims to exceptional status" (21).

Jane Austen, for example

Consider for example Jane Austen's novel, *Northanger Abbey* (1818). Its protagonist Catherine Morland is a voracious reader who lets her sense of herself and the world around her and her manner of engaging and acting in the world around her be influenced by her reading of gothic novels (considered trash at the time). Any reader today with a vivid imagination who likes to read literature that authorities such as teachers or parents think are trash (who would prefer *Twilight* to Tolstoy) can surely *recognize* herself in Catherine's experience of being immersed in a virtual reality of reading. Reading Ann Radcliffe's gothic novel *The Mysteries of Udolpho*, Catherine was "lost for all worldly concerns of dressing and dinner" and other everyday routines and rituals of her social class, lovingly mocked by Austen's narrator (Austen 2003, 35). Yet this immersion, this transformative *enchantment* on Catherine's behalf, is portrayed as dangerous and something that must be sanctioned, she must be set straight and enlightened, indeed, "taught a lesson" (Sedgwick 1993, 113–26): *knowledge* must be imparted and romantic fiction overruled by factual reason.

The novel shows us how Catherine's manner of reading the world around her according to the conventions of gothic fiction was misguided: it made her incapable of understanding other's points of views and almost led to her ruin in missing the opportunity to marry the man she loves, Henry Tilney, whose father (General Tilney) Catherine (led by her reading) *shockingly* accuses of having murdered his wife. Thinking about General Tilney's presumed guilt and his remarkable ability to hide it behind a façade, she remembers many other examples (from fiction) and imagines going to see the dead body of Mrs. Tilney (which she in fact thinks may not be dead but kept imprisoned by her husband): "Catherine had read too much not to be perfectly aware of the ease with which a waxen figure might be introduced, and a supposititious funeral carried on" (140) to cover up the crime—a knowledge she has from Radcliffe's fiction. This quote is both an example of Catherine's dangerous propensity to read life as if it were literature in a rather too literal manner and an example of Jane Austen's revolutionary style of free indirect discourse whereby the voice of the character and that of the narrator are blended and we get both the naïve and foolish mind of the young teenager and the distanced, knowing, ironic voice and perspective of the mature narrator, who mocks (but also adores) this mind.

Realizing that she suspects his father of murder on literary grounds, Henry is shocked and sets her straight:

> If I understand you rightly, you had formed a surmise of such horror as I have hardly words to—Dear Miss Morland, consider the dreadful nature of the suspicions you have entertained. What have you been judging from? Remember the country and the age in which we live. Remember that we are English, that we are Christians. Consult your own understanding, your own sense of the probable, your own observation of what is passing around you—Does our education prepare us for such atrocities? Do our laws connive at them? Could they be perpetrated without being known, in a country like this, where social and literary intercourse is on such a footing; where every man is surrounded by a neighbourhood of voluntary spies, and where roads and newspapers lay every thing open? Dearest Miss Morland, what ideas have you been admitting? (145)

The prosaic world described by Henry is the world of the novel genre: everyday, ordinary, probable, observable by senses, ruled by law and order, and informed by gossip, infrastructure, and the news. Boring when you think about it. Austen indeed opens the next chapter: "The visions of romance were over. Catherine was completely awakened" (146) as she comes to realize that all her troubles (she thinks Henry will never show any affection for her now) seemed traceable "to the influence of that sort of reading which she had indulged" earlier at Bath (146).

However, "The liberty which her imagination had dared to take with the character" (146) of General Tilney as callous was in fact spot on: he tried to keep Henry from marrying Catherine when he realized she was not filthy rich as he thought when he invited her to stay at Northanger Abbey and he only agrees to their marriage when his daughter, Eleanor, finds a rich man in a far-fetched plot twist at the very end when the "tell-tale compression of the pages" (185) alerts us to the fact that we are near the end of the novel with a lot of things remaining to be tidied up for this to end happily (as it must). So Catherine, by virtue of not in spite of her gothic-fed imagination, got it right, in a manner of speaking: "in suspecting General Tilney of either murdering or shutting up his wife, she had scarcely sinned against his character, or magnified his cruelty" (183). Literature gave her this specific human knowledge and gift of insight into human character.

Northanger Abbey is both an example of prototypical literature (merging the eminently modern literary technique of free indirect discourse and the crucial theme of love, marriage, and individual freedom within the marriage institution) and about the example of literature, what kind of exemplarity a literary text can have in terms of shaping and guiding our reading of ourselves and our relations to the world and those around us. It warns and advices us to both trust the imaginary sources, to be enchanted by the text, and at the same time to be critical of hypocrisy and double-dealing in writings even by those we thought were our friends and allies. Having been set straight by Henry and apparently awoken from the dreams of romance into the reality of the novel, Catherine becomes a more critical reader, for example, of her alleged friend (but really enemy), Isabella, one of whose letters' hypocrisy Catherine penetrates with acumen, reflecting that "She [Isabell] must think me an idiot, or she could not have written so; but perhaps this has served to make her character better known to me than mine is to her" (161). The novel teaches "mind reading" (Vermeule 2010) by showing how hard and sometimes perhaps impossible this is except in literature's virtual reality, where the novel's intrusive and self-reflexive narrator takes us inside the mind and heart of Catherine as she struggles to figure out the minds and hearts of those around her, who themselves are engaged in just this activity. Literature—and the genre of the novel in particular—aspires to give us access to the mind of the individual. As Austen's narrator (affecting indifference with a teasing casual "only" while delivering a profound insight that is revolutionary given the novel's doubtful stature according to leading aesthetic thinkers such as Kant and Coleridge) indeed points out in *Northanger Abbey*: a novel is "only some work in which the greatest powers of the mind are displayed, in which the most thorough knowledge of human nature, the happiest delineation of its varieties, the liveliest effusions of wit and humour are conveyed to the world in the best chosen language" (24) even and in particular when the mind in question belongs to a naïve teenager with a lively imagination stimulated by literature and one of the most talented novelists in world literature.

And yet, at the same time literature gives us the opacity of others' minds, shows us how we time and again get it wrong and fail to understand and reach the minds and hearts of one another. But in this failure is also a direction and reason for reading. To be able to learn to live in the suspended position between knowing yourself through knowing someone else in a virtual reality, and at the same time knowing that the others don't know you and maybe couldn't care less if you live or die, is one of the many lessons to be had from the wonderland that is literature and that includes all the novels, films, and theme parks which the imagination of someone like Jane Austen made happen along with all the wild notions among us about love, marriage, and happiness as being within reach of us all and—perhaps, it's imaginable—not dependent on matters of social status, wealth, or education.

Further reading

Roman Ingarden's *Das literarische Kunstwerk* (1931, eng. 1973) is an important contribution to twentieth-century literary theory. It combines a philosophical phenomenology with a very thorough description of the literary work of art, in its many parts and particulars, and it has influenced the development of New Criticism (the chapter on the ontology of the literary work in René Wellek's and Austin Warren's *Theory of Literature* is directly derived from Ingarden) and reader-response theory (especially Wolfgang Iser). Raymond Williams provides, in *Marxism and Literature* (1977), a series of still usable historical-materialist explanations of what literature has been and is perceived as. Gérard Genette isolates, in *Fiction et diction* (1991, eng. 1993), a nonessentialist concept of literature that contains the concept of "literariness" stemming from formalism and structuralism as well as more recent theories of fictionality. In *The Singularity of Literature* (2004), Derek Attridge polemicizes against various instrumentalist views of literature, be they political or ethical, and promotes instead a concept of literature that draws inspiration from the deconstructive philosopher Jacques Derrida and rethinks literature in relation to traditional ideas about innovation and singularity. A useful very short introduction to the study of literature is provided by Andrew Bennett and Nicholas Royle in *This Thing Called Literature: Reading, Thinking, Writing* (2015), which is both theoretically sophisticated and aimed at the actual and practical work of reading considered also as a form of creative writing.

References

Aristotle (1987) *A New Aristotle Reader.* Ed. J. L. Ackrill, Princeton, NJ: Princeton University Press.

Attridge, Derek (2004) *The Singularity of Literature*, London and New York: Routledge.

Austen, Jane (2003) *Northanger Abbey, Lady Susan, The Watsons, Sandition.* Eds. James Kinsley and John Davie, Oxford: Oxford University Press.

Bennett, Andrew and Nicholas Royle (2015) *This Thing Called Literature: Reading, Thinking, Writing*, London and New York: Routledge.

Collins, Jim (2010) *Bring on the Books for Everybody: How Literary Culture Became Popular Culture*, Durham: Duke University Press.

Derrida, Jacques (1992) *Acts of Literature.* Ed. Derek Attridge, New York: Routledge.

Felski, Rita (2008) *Uses of Literature*, Oxford: Blackwell.

Felski, Rita (2015) *The Limits of Critique*, Chicago and London: Chicago Press.

Genette, Gérard (1991) *Fiction et diction*, Paris: Seuil.

Ingarden, Roman (1931) *Das literarische Kunstwerk*, Tübingen: Max Niemeyer Verlag.

Miller, J. Hillis (2002) *On Literature*, London and New York: Routledge.

Mousley, Andy (2013) *Literature and the Human: Criticism, Theory, Practice*, London and New York: Routledge.

Sedgwick, Eve Kosovsky (1993) "Jane Austen and the Masturbating Girl," in *Tendencies*, Durham: Durham University Press, 109–29.

Vermeule, Blakey (2010) *Why Do We Care About Literary Characters?* Baltimore: Johns Hopkins University Press.

Wellek, René and Austin Warren (1948) *Theory of Literature*, San Diego, CA: Harcourt, Brace and Co.

Williams, Raymond (1977) *Marxism and Literature*, Oxford: Oxford University Press.

Williams, Raymond (1988 [1976]) *Keywords: A Vocabulary of Culture and Society*, London: Flamingo.

Wittgenstein, Ludwig (1958) *Philosophical Investigations.* Trans. G. E. M. Anscombe, Oxford: Blackwell.

2

Interpretation

Jesper Gulddal

Interpretation in the context of literary studies can be defined as the methodologically reflected procedure we employ in order to understand a literary text. As such, interpretation is a response to the experience of textual complexity. In our everyday lives we are surrounded by information that is self-evident in the sense of being semantically transparent to such a degree that there is no need for a sustained effort of understanding. However, such self-evidence is rare in literature. Whether due to the historical or cultural distance that separates authors from readers or to the difficulty of literary language itself, the literary text tends to meet us with a certain degree of foreignness that sometimes makes us give up in frustration, but more often stimulates our curiosity and encourages further investigation. It is ultimately this encounter with incomprehensibility, which is central to the reading of literary texts, that forces us to reflect on the questions of interpretation and understanding.

If it is difficult to answer these questions definitively, it is due to the fact that literary interpretation is situated in a gray zone between subjectiveness and critical objectivity. On the one hand, interpretation always involves a selection and configuration of textual elements that may be more or less justified, yet cannot be derived exclusively from the text itself. On the other hand, interpretation is also bound by the textual evidence, and the scope for interpretative freedom is therefore not unlimited. As the concept itself implies, interpretation is not simply a matter of facts, but of perspectives supported by examples and arguments. There are no final answers in matters of interpretation, only good questions. These questions, however, are of fundamental importance in literary criticism: What are the contributions of, respectively, the author, the text, and the reader to the production of meaning? Can interpretation be neutral and objective, or are critics always tied to their historical or cultural coordinates—or to their gender, sexuality, race, social class, ideology, religion, or any other kind of individual situatedness? Should interpretation be guided only by the text itself, or should it aim to illuminate the text by foregrounding its links to a specific historical environment? How can interpretation address ironical, ambiguous, enigmatic, or wholly meaningless texts? How do we find the right interpretative pitch between over-interpretation, which sees deep meaning in obscure or isolated details, and under-interpretation, which overlooks aspects of the literary text that are evidently significant?

These questions revolve around a single fundamental problem: How can we distinguish right from wrong in matters of interpretation? Due to the precarious balancing act between the subjective and the objective, the theoretical debate surrounding the concept of interpretation has from the beginning aimed to establish criteria for interpretation and for what makes one interpretation more accurate and correct than another.

Hermeneutics

The philosophical discipline that analyzes understanding and interpretation is called hermeneutics. Hermeneutics first came into being in late Antiquity as a response to an experience of cultural and religious loss. The mythological literature of the past, not least the Homeric epics, were in this period still revered as culturally foundational texts, but the language was antiquated, the religious notions seemed naïve, and often the texts themselves had only survived in fragmented or corrupted versions. These factors meant that a systematic effort of interpretation was required in order to reconstruct the textual material and recover its meaning for later generations. This challenge led to the first attempts to establish methods and procedures to guide interpretation.

Originally, hermeneutics was concerned primarily with antique literature as well as religious and legal works—that is, older and difficult texts invested with a certain cultural and social centrality and therefore requiring ongoing reinterpretation in light of new historical experiences. Around 1800, however, the field of hermeneutics was drastically expanded. The influential German theologian and philosopher Friedrich Schleiermacher insisted that interpretation was necessary not only when dealing with a select class of culturally significant texts, but in all cases of written expression where authors are unable to correct misunderstandings by virtue of their personal presence. A century later, at the beginning of the 1900s, the philosopher Wilhelm Dilthey proposed another major expansion, namely from writing to human "expressions of life" in the broadest possible sense—from "the babblings of children to *Hamlet* or the *Critique of Pure Reason*" (Dilthey 1972, 232). This dramatic "universalisation" of hermeneutics profoundly changed the status of interpretation: from being an ancillary to the disciplines of philology, theology, and jurisprudence, hermeneutics was now increasingly seen as the primary methodology of the humanities. Where the sciences sought to *explain* the natural work in terms of underlying laws and regularities, the humanities aimed to *understand* and *interpret* the cultural world as an expression of the human mind.

Apart from initiating the expansion of hermeneutics in the course of the nineteenth century, Friedrich Schleiermacher was also instrumental in articulating the interpretative principle known as the *hermeneutic circle*. Hermeneutics describes interpretation as based on a circular relationship between the individual parts and the text as a whole. This relationship can best be understood as a process. When reading the first few pages of a novel, the critic quickly forms an idea of its style, characters, themes, and formal features. These first impressions constitute a first attempt to understand the text as a whole, which then guides the perception of all subsequent parts, yet is also continually revised and refined so as to take into account more and more information. This continuous alternation between the parts and the whole will always remain an incomplete process, yet ideally leads to an increasingly sophisticated understanding of the literary text.

However, the hermeneutic circle is not primarily a procedure, but above all a principle of interpretation that emphasizes internal consistency: hermeneutically speaking the correct—or most correct—interpretation is that capable of integrating and accounting for as many aspects of the text as possible within the framework of a holistic understanding. This does not imply that interpretation is a matter of ironing out the contradictions of the text and forcing all textual elements to fit together perfectly; on the contrary, hermeneutic critics from Friedrich Schlegel to Peter Szondi have repeatedly emphasized the need to respect the incomprehensible or irreducibly singular aspects of the individual text. The circle simply implies that the successful interpretation aims to explain as much as possible and as strongly as possible. It is the hallmark of over-interpretation that the interpretation is supported by isolated passages, but cannot account adequately and convincingly for the text as a whole.

In addition to this emphasis on the internal consistency of the interpretation (but not necessarily of the object of interpretation), the concept of the hermeneutic circle also refers to the context-dependency of meaning. Individual parts are always understood in light of the higher semantic order in which they participate.

This is true within the text itself where, for example, individual sentences are understood in relation to paragraphs while paragraphs are understood on the basis of sections or chapters whose meaning in turn is relative to the whole work. Yet, the work is not the upper limit for this hermeneutic interplay of parts and whole; on the contrary, the work is itself a part of even larger wholes. Older hermeneutic thinkers such as Schleiermacher typically point toward the *oeuvre* and the author's individuality as relevant frameworks of interpretation. More recent contributions prefer less subject-oriented framings, for example the literary genre of the work or the social or philosophical environment that it emerged from. However, in both cases interpretation is seen as a matter of enhancing our understanding by positioning the object of interpretation within a larger context.

Twentieth-century hermeneutics is split into two different schools with very different agendas. One school is represented by philosophers such as Martin Heidegger, Hans-Georg Gadamer, and Paul Ricœur. The shared contention of these philosophers is that interpretation is a process in which the interpreter is not just a passively observing subject, but an active participant in the production of meaning. The concept of the hermeneutic circle thereby acquires a new meaning: rather than an interdependence of part and whole, it now describes a circularity in the relationship between the interpreter and the object of interpretation. Being embedded in a specific historical and cultural location, the interpreter always encounters the text with a set of background assumptions that, on the one hand, guides the interpretation but, on the other hand, also renders aspects of the text invisible. Hermeneutic philosophy insists that it is not possible to bracket or sidestep these "prejudices," as Gadamer calls them, in favor of a neutral perspective. In the process of interpretation, however, the critic's prejudices are put in play, and the encounter with the text ideally makes them visible and allows them to be developed, revised, or rejected. Accordingly, interpretation is always also self-interpretation, at least in the sense that interpretation leads to a recognition of the tacit assumptions that inform our approach to literary texts.

The other school of twentieth-century hermeneutics has a more practical orientation and aims, as was the case with pre-modern hermeneutics, to establish rules of thumb and general guidelines for correct interpretation. The aim here is not so much to investigate the philosophical foundations of interpretation, but rather to develop methods and arguments in support of concrete acts of interpretation— as, for example, in the context of literature, in Peter Szondi's reflections on the use of parallels and textual variants in the interpretation of difficult passages (1986); in E.D. Hirsch's controversial insistence on the author's intentions as a criterion of correct interpretation (Hirsch 1967); or in Jean Starobinski's reframing of the hermeneutical circle as a double movement that simultaneously tries to eliminate and acknowledge the alterity of the text (Starobinski 1989). Although very different in outlook and objectives, these theoretical approaches remind us that hermeneutics is a flexible and historically conscious practice characterized by an endeavor to understand the individuality of the literary work. Hermeneutics in this sense is neither a fixed method nor a theoretical "school," but a jumbled toolbox of practical guidelines and interpretative tricks.

An example

Norwegian dramatist Henrik Ibsen's first modern play, *Pillars of Society* from 1877 (Ibsen 1991), has long caused interpretative controversy. The stone of contention is the reconciliatory ending, which not only appears to absolve the play's foremost example of bourgeois depravity, shipyard owner Karsten Bernick, and, most problematically, completely neglects to punish his most criminal deed, namely the disguised attempt to dispose of his brother-in-law Johan Tønnesen. Readers and spectators are presented here with a choice between taking the ending at face value (and hence reject the play as an aesthetic and moral failure) or alternatively read it ironically, as first suggested by James MacFarlane in a seminal article from 1966.

A traditional hermeneutical interpretation in the tradition from Schleiermacher would regard the ending as a single textual element which, according to the principle of the hermeneutical circle, needs to be interpreted as a part of a larger semantic whole, whether internally as part of the play in its entirety or externally as part of the Ibsen corpus and its historical context in the broadest sense of the word. The most correct interpretation is therefore the one best capable of integrating the chosen understanding of the ending within a convincing and evidence-based account of the whole—which does not rule out that the ending can be seen as a break or a deviation either within the text itself or in relation to what is the norm in the writings of Ibsen himself or his contemporaries.

A more philosophical form of hermeneutics would ask a further question regarding the perspective of the interpreter itself and its embeddedness in a specific historical and cultural situation. Accordingly, it is no coincidence that the interpretation of Ibsen's ending as ironical was suggested first in the 1960s, at a time when modernist literature had become an inescapable point of reference for literary studies. This choice of literary compass often involves taking over, consciously or unconsciously, modernism's predilection for the dissonant, unsentimental and ironical and applying these preferences to older literature as well. Our own modernist "prejudices" therefore make us prefer an ironic and forward-looking interpretation while, conversely, blinding us to the late-Romantic idealism that Ibsen has not yet abandoned completely when writing his modern breakthrough play. According to modern philosophical hermeneutics, the interpreter should strive, not to transcend all historical situatedness but to achieve a fuller understanding of the differences between the respective historical horizons of the interpreter and the object of interpretation, thereby ensuring that the interpretation respects the otherness of the text and avoids forcing upon it the ideas and norms of a later period. The exchange between these horizons is seen as a productive relation that leads to a better understanding of oneself as well as of the historical other.

Critique of hermeneutics and anti-hermeneutics

The strong theoretical orientation of literary studies from the 1960s to the 1990s led to a thorough critical re-examination of hermeneutics as the central methodology of the humanities. Seen in light of the elaborate theoretical edifices of this period, hermeneutics sometimes appeared naïve and unambitious, seemingly content to explain what was already known and possibly allied in surreptitious ways to the authoritarian ideologies that "theory" aimed to expose and eliminate. While some critics charged hermeneutics with subjectivism and lack of rigor, others questioned its endeavor to establish criteria for correct interpretation, suggesting that such criteria involved a problematic reduction of the semantic multiplicity of literary texts.

Being against hermeneutics and interpretation in general therefore became one of the most important trends in literary studies of the late twentieth century, and this trend included an array of classic theoretical positions: the early Umberto Eco's ideas of the "open work" that, rather than having just one meaning, is a matrix of potential signification (Eco 1989); Roland Barthes's theory of the "writerly" text that calls for joyful performance instead of reductive interpretation (Barthes 1991); Theodor W. Adorno's insistence on the "enigma character" through which true works of art resist interpretation (Adorno 2013); or Richard Rorty's pragmatic hermeneutics, which gives preference to "strong" over "correct" interpretations (Rorty 1982).

Within this large and diverse theoretical field it is possible to distinguish between two main pathways for critiquing hermeneutics with origins, respectively, in social science and linguistics.

The foremost representative of the social science-based form is German philosopher Jürgen Habermas, who in 1971 put forward an influential critique of Heidegger's and Gadamer's philosophical hermeneutics. The basic contention of this critique is that hermeneutics concerns itself exclusively with the *surface* of the text: it analyzes and interprets the actual statements, yet refrains from interrogating these statements as products of a specific social and psychological reality. Seen from Habermas's Marxist perspective, however, society is defined by inequality and repression. This means that the overt statements cannot always be taken at face value, but should be regarded instead as manifestations of "systematically distorted communication," that is, as expressions of deeper, often unconscious issues of a psychosocial nature. If one is not content with reproducing the distortions of society, which hermeneutics, according to Habermas, is at risk of doing, it is necessary to develop a "deep hermeneutics" that uses sociological and psychoanalytical models to uncover the hidden link between the statement and the social structures that conditions and distorts it. Hermeneutics itself is seen here as naïve and conservative insofar because it purports simply to listen to what the text is saying, yet neglects to ask what it might be concealing (Habermas 1985).

Rooted in linguistics and philosophy of language, the second major way of critiquing hermeneutics is expressed in exemplary form in the writings of French philosopher Jacques Derrida, the founder of deconstruction, and his more or less loyal followers especially in US-based literary studies programs in the 1970s and 1980s. Deconstruction was in its inception influenced by Swiss linguist Ferdinand de Saussure's philosophy of language whose basic contention is that language is a system of "differences *without positive terms*" (Saussure 1916, 862)—that is, a system where meaning does not emerge by virtue of necessary links between words and what they refer to, but rather as a result of the difference between words. Derrida's deconstruction expands this notion of the differential nature of language from the level of the sign to that of the text. This expansion undercuts the concepts of meaning and interpretation: since the text consists only of relations and references from one sign to another, it is never possible to establish a privileged perspective or achieve an integration of parts and whole in line with hermeneutic precepts. The meaning of the text thereby becomes indeterminable, and any attempt at reaching a final authoritative interpretation is undermined by its endless chains of signification and self-contradiction (Derrida 2001).

These theoretical positions have in common that they critique hermeneutics, yet without fundamentally questioning the hermeneutical project itself, which consists in interpreting texts with a view to accessing their meaning: as the concept itself suggests, Habermas's "deep hermeneutics" is conceived as a further development of hermeneutics, while deconstruction, in its attempt to overcome interpretation, remains committed itself to interpretative form of close reading that ponders endlessly on textual details and subtle contradictions. A different tendency, which has garnered widespread interest in recent years, goes one step further and questions the status of interpretation as a privileged approach to literature and cultural artifacts in general. Avowedly anti-hermeneutical rather than simply critical of hermeneutics, this more radical position is not interested in interpreting in new or better or less naïve ways, but aims to go beyond hermeneutics altogether by developing alternatives to what it regards as the cerebral and meaning-fixated myopia that characterizes interpretation.

An important precursor to this anti-hermeneutics is American essayist Susan Sontag. In the programmatic essay "Against Interpretation" from 1964 (Sontag 2009), Sontag contends that Western philosophy of art since antiquity has privileged the content of art at the expense of its form, and that this valorization, which she regards as constitutive also of contemporary art and literature criticism, has led to the predominance of interpretation as an approach to aesthetic objects. Yet, interpretation is an act of trespassing that tames and defuses the transgressive power of art. Moreover, interpretation is useless as an approach to the nonfigurative, nonrealistic, and nonsemantic modes of expression that characterize modernist arts and literature of the twentieth century. Sontag consequently argues that a new aesthetic sensibility is needed to highlight the sensual rather than the ideal aspects of the work of art: "In place of a hermeneutics we need an erotics of art" (Sontag 2009, 14).

Although Sontag's essay has inspired numerous other attempts at pushing beyond interpretation, the development of a genuine anti-hermeneutical philosophy is a relatively recent event and is due above all to German-American literary historian Hans Ulrich Gumbrecht. In *Production of Presence* (2004), Gumbrecht introduces a distinction between two basic dimensions of art, literature, and cultural phenomena in general: "meaning" understood as the semantic content and presence understood as physical tangibility. Each of these two dimensions is irreducible to the other and is never completely absent, yet different cultures and historical periods attribute different weightings to them. Like a number of non-Western societies today, the European Middle Ages, for example, were a "presence culture" in which the physicality of things often took precedence over their underlying meaning. Conversely, the modern Western world is a "meaning culture" that to some extent has forgotten about presence as a dimension of reality and instead privileges the semantic content of the surrounding world. In meaning cultures interpretation is the dominant approach to literature, and interpretation is cast as the act of penetrating the surface of linguistic signs so as to uncover the truth that these signs conceal. However, since interpretation is incapable of accounting for the presence dimension of the literary text, it is necessary to develop a complementary noninterpretative approach centered on the "materiality" of literature—that is, on its physical, acoustic, or visual dimensions, or on its "mood," as Gumbrecht has suggested in a later book (2012).

What Sontag and Gumbrecht have in common is that they struggle to define nonhermeneutical criticism positively as a method or procedure that can be brought to bear on works of art and literature. This difficulty can be explained in two opposite ways. A hostile take would be that the concept of interpretation already covers all the aspects of literature that can be discussed in a rational register, and that venturing beyond interpretation therefore leads either nowhere or to subjectivism or silence. More sympathetically, it can be argued, as the two authors themselves do, that interpretation has exercised such a long and complete dominance in the humanities that it requires a sustained effort of innovation to imagine alternative approaches.

Whatever the reason, Sontag and Gumbrecht represent a step beyond the simple critique of hermeneutics: not content with holding forth on the impossibility of interpretation and the indeterminacy of meaning, they argue for a clean break with interpretation in favor of a noninterpretative and ultimately "meaningless" approach to art and literature.

World literature and the return of interpretation

After decades of critique of both interpretation in general and hermeneutics in particular, it might seem as if interpretation is dead, and that the field has finally moved on. It is certainly true that a critical re-examination of hermeneutics was long overdue, not only as a counterpoint to the widespread, semi-paranoid forms of interpretation where critics find hidden meanings in the most minute textual details but also, more generally, to a long-standing tradition of overestimating interpretation as the primary way in which humans relate to the world. Interpretation can no longer meaningfully be regarded as the lead methodology of the humanities.

Yet, it would nevertheless be premature to dismiss interpretation altogether. Hermeneutics was from the outset a response to incomprehension in the face of foreign and difficult literary texts. Arguably, this experience has become more pronounced and prevalent in the contemporary world, partly because of mass education and a cultural climate primarily attuned to the visual and digital, but above all as a result globalization understood as a massive increase in cross-cultural interaction and communication. The ability to bridge the gap between cultural horizons is more relevant today than ever before. In literary studies, this renewed topicality of interpretation comes to the forefront, although not without anti-hermeneutical push-back, in the contemporary interest in world literature. As a manifestation of globalization in the broad sense of the word, this interest amounts to a comprehensive global reorientation of the field. Whereas literary studies traditionally focused on European literary history and its extensions on other continents, the new school of world literature seeks to overcome the Eurocentric limitations of this traditional view by calling attention to emerging literatures as well as to established non-Western literary traditions.

The global expansion of literary studies has required methodological innovation to prevent critics from being overwhelmed by the considerable linguistic and cultural distances or the virtually unlimited scope of world literature. An anti-hermeneutical direction pioneered by Franco Moretti claims that the global approach to literature can no longer rely on interpretative close reading of individual works, but must instead develop a "distant" reading practice that reads extensively, sometimes assisted by digital technologies, with a view to describing macro-structures and general connections within literature as a global phenomenon (Moretti 2000). However, an alternative approach developed by David Damrosch draws on and further develops a number of key hermeneutic ideas, above all the interpretative challenges that arise when a work of literature is read outside the national and cultural context in which it was written (Damrosch 2003). When literary texts cross national borders, Damrosch argues, they inevitably lose part of their original meaning, yet also acquire new meanings by being read from an outside perspective. The political and religious references in a classic Chinese novel such as Wu Cheng'en's *Journey to the West* (sixteenth century) are all but lost on nonspecialist Western readers who in turn are able to read this work from the vantage point of Western literary traditions such as the animal fable, the pilgrimage as a narrative model, or the history of the modern European novel; and the opposite is true when a Western work such as *Pillars of Society* is read in China where the Ibsen reception has a history of more than 100 years. The loss of meaning incurred by the literary work when it leaves its country of origin is therefore counterbalanced by the gain of meaning that results from the world-literary fusion of horizons.

The key point, however, is that world literature returns us to the core problem of interpretation, namely the encounter with cultural phenomena whose historical and cultural otherness call for a sustained and disciplined effort of understanding. In this situation, as was already the case in antiquity, interpretation becomes a means of overcoming the rift between different horizons and thereby replacing incomprehension with understanding. In this sense, world literature highlights the inevitability of interpretation. It reminds us that understanding is a transient phenomenon that corrodes with time and distance and must constantly be restored in new contexts.

Further reading

A range of seminal contributions to the German tradition of hermeneutics, including excerpts from Schleiermacher, Dilthey, Heidegger, Gadamer, and Habermas, are collected in *The Hermeneutics Reader: Texts of the German Tradition from the Enlightenment to the Present*, edited by Kurt Mueller-Vollmer (1985). The main works of the these authors, as well of other hermeneutic thinkers such as Paul Ricœur and Gianni Vattimo, have all been translated into English in their entirety. Gadamer's *Truth and Method* (1960) is particularly useful: It not only presents an ambitious philosophy of understanding and interpretation but also offers a summation of the history of hermeneutics up until the mid-twentieth century. Jens Zimmermann's *Hermeneutics: A Very Short Introduction* (2015) is concise and accessible and includes an annotated list of suggestions for further reading. Gumbrecht's *Production of Presence* (2004) eloquently attempts to situate historically and challenge the dominance of interpretation in the humanities while also sketching the outlines of a new, noninterpretative approach to art and literature. Finally, David Damrosch's *What Is World Literature?* (2003) is a key point of reference for the recent interest in world literature. Although this book makes its points by means of exemplary analyses rather than sustained theoretical argumentation, it clearly and usefully revitalizes some of the key issues of modern hermeneutics.

References

Adorno, Theodor W. (2013) *Aesthetic Theory* [2013]. Trans. Robert Hullot-Kentor, London and New York: Bloomsbury.

Barthes, Roland (1991) *S/Z* [1970]. Trans. Richard Miller, New York: Farrar, Straus & Giroux.

Damrosch, David (2003) *What Is World Literature?* Princeton, NJ and Oxford: Princeton University Press.

Derrida, Jacques (2001) *Writing and Difference* [1967]. Trans. Alan Bass, Milton Park, Abingdon and New York: Routledge.

Dilthey, Wilhelm (1972) "The Rise of Hermeneutics" [1900]. Trans. Fredric R. Jameson, *New Literary History*, 3 (2): 229–44.

Eco, Umberto (1989) *The Open Work* (1962), Cambridge, MA: Harvard University Press.

Gadamer, Hans-Georg (2004) *Truth and Method* [1960], London and New York: Bloomsbury.

Gumbrecht, Hans Ulrich (2004) *Production of Presence*, Stanford: Stanford University Press.

Gumbrecht, Hans Ulrich (2012) *Atmosphere, Mood, Stimmung. On a Hidden Potential of Literature* [2011]. Trans. Eric Butler, Stanford: Stanford University Press.

Habermas, Jürgen (1985) "On Hermeneutics' Claim to Universality" [1971], in Kurt Mueller-Vollmer (ed.), *The Hermeneutics Reader*. Trans. Jerry Dribble, 294–319, New York: Continuum.

The Hermeneutics Reader. Texts of the German Tradition from the Enlightenment to the Present (1985) Ed. Kurt Mueller-Vollmer, New York: Continuum.

Hirsch, E. D. (1967) *Validity in Interpretation*, New Haven and London: Yale University Press.

Ibsen, Henrik (1991) *Pillars of Society* [1877]. *Plays: Four*. Trans. Michael Meyer, London: Methuen Drama.

MacFarlane, James (1966) "Meaning and Evidence in Ibsen's Drama," *Contemporary Approaches to Ibsen*, 1: 35–50.

Moretti, Franco (2000) "Conjectures on World Literature," *New Left Review*, 1: 54–68.

Rorty, Richard (1982) "Nineteenth-Century Idealism and Twentieth-Century Textualism," in *Consequences of Pragmatism*, 139–59, Brighton: The Harvester Press.

Saussure, Ferdinand de (2010) "*From* Course in General Linguistics" (1916), in Vincent B. Leitch (ed.), *The Norton Anthology of Theory and Criticism*, 850–66, New York and London: W. W. Norton.

Sontag, Susan (2009) "Against Interpretation" [1964], in *Against Interpretation and Other Essays*, 3–14, London: Penguin.

Starobinski, Jean (1989) "The Interpreter's Progress" [1970], in *The Living Eye*. Trans. Arthur Goldhammer, 171–229, Cambridge, MA and London: Harvard University Press.

Szondi, Peter (1986) *On Textual Understanding and Other Essays*. Trans. Harvey Mendelson, Minneapolis: University of Minnesota Press.

Zimmermann, Jens (2015) *Hermeneutics. A Very Short Introduction*, Oxford: Oxford University Press.

3

Genre

Eva Hättner Aurelius

The genre concepts are one of the most powerful tools in literary criticism. The genres hold together form, subject, and function: in Aristotle's well-known description of the tragedy we find these three elements: imitation of dialogue (form) and action (subject) and the production of fear and compassion (function), thus effecting catharsis (purification, also function). But as concepts, that is, scientific terms, the genre terms are very difficult to handle. These difficulties are most clearly apprehended when you try to define a genre—is Augustine's *Confessiones* an autobiography? Is Truman Capote's *In Cold Blood* a novel?

For the sake of argument, let us say that you are on the point of defining a text, picking its genre. To do so, you will have to take a position on the question of *what* literary genres are. Are they scholarly terms? Are they a class of objects defined in such a way that those included in one class can be clearly distinguished from other objects. The qualities or attributes that define the object must be both necessary and sufficient. For an object to be included in a class, it would have to have *all* those properties or attributes, and, moreover, would be impossible to include in a different class of objects. This approach holds genre terms to be scholarly terms, and almost always to be part of a conceptual system, a taxonomy, a terminology. These types are usually called theoretical genres, because so often they stem from a theory of literature, with the genres derived from that theory. This is the pattern found in Aristotle's *Poetics*: this is a theory of literature as "imitation," where epic and tragedy imitate in different ways. The alternative is that genres are everyday vernacular terms, subject to the vagaries of man and time. If so, genres are then cultural or social conventions that contribute to, and even control, the production of (literary) texts, and equally contribute to, and even control, the reception of the (literary) texts. "Genre," as Alastair Fowler puts it, "is much less of a pigeonhole, than a pigeon" (1982, 37). His point is that definitions or descriptions of genres exist in order to identify genres, not to be theories about them. Genres of this kind—understood as cultural or societal facts—are usually referred to as *historical* or traditional genres. In this approach, the interesting question about genres is not primarily what they *are*, but what they *do*; their function in the production and reception of texts, or rather what texts (or writers and readers) use genres for (Bakhtin 1986, 79; Jauß 1972, 110; Fowler 1982, 37 *et passim*).

These two understandings of genre's logical nature—as a class or as a vernacular term—are essentially the answers to the question "What is a genre?" that has dominated the discussion of genre in recent decades. This chapter argues for historical genres, for reasons that are both logical and practical.

The theoretical concept of genre has come in for criticism, much of it predicated on the notion that genre is a shaping force in the creation and reception of texts. In other words, proponents of the theoretical definition have been brought to task for making a mistake in their categorization. Ironically enough it was Todorov (1973), the advocate of theoretical genres, who formulated the telling argument against them. To avoid paradoxes, the theoretical genres, which are logical classes, cannot contain statements about the classes themselves—object language and metalanguage cannot be mixed. However, this requirement makes it impossible in an intellectually defensible fashion to safely derive the historical classes from the theoretical genres, as Todorov would have us do. If the theory of a genre fails to match with any text, then we are on the wrong track, as he said. But do we really *know* that we are going off at a tangent? The undertaking to verify (or falsify) these derivations is inherently problematic, because the theory and the text are completely separate: the genre is a purely theoretical, abstract entity, while the text is a concrete thing. The text manifests a genre, but its genre is not *in* the text. That in turn means that no observation about a text can verify or falsify a theory about its genre in a logically compelling fashion. One cannot prove that a genre theory is unsuccessful (Todorov 1973, 21). This unconditional requirement not to confuse object language and metalanguage is impossible to satisfy in practice, for the simple reason that it is impossible, or at least very difficult, to establish a metalanguage within the natural languages (Russell 1962, ch. 4 & 5; Tarski 1986, 457; Schüttpelz 1995, 185–7; Schüttpelz 1995, 186–7). If, then, we strictly separate the theoretical genres' language from the object's language, this theoretical language by definition says nothing about the text's meaning, seen in historical or cultural terms. Secondly, it demonstrates with great clarity that genre studies are trapped in the same paradox that characterizes literary studies in general: the diachronic and the synchronic cannot in practice be separated. For example, classify a text as a parody and you must clarify what is being parodied—that is, you have to actualize its history, its tradition. Similarly, genre would seem to be the historical, traditional element in a text and the ahistorical, systematic element at one and the same time. This interweaving of history and system when it comes to genre is also reflected in the fact that the text can both *show* what is general (the genre) and *change* it.

How to define a historical genre, courtesy of realistic, pragmatic semantics

How best to define the historical genres? If they are not classes with well-defined boundaries, and they are mutable into the bargain, how can we establish them as concepts? Because somehow these genre terms *are* concepts, they are signs or words; and we use those words, and they are significant. As Todorov wrote, "Further, it is of the very nature of language to move within abstraction and within the 'generic'. The individual cannot exist *in* language" (1973, 7).

Before addressing this, though, there is the question of the type of semantic theory that would be most useful here. This is because many of the difficulties encountered when defining or describing a concept, especially a type concept, stem from the choice of theory of linguistic meaning. I am referring here to realistic semantics and pragmatic semantics, the two main approaches in the discussion of linguistic meaning (Kutschera 1974, 31–51, 132–51, 190–5).

The older of the theories is realistic semantics, "realism" here meaning that general concepts exist independently of the objects ranged under them. These theories take linguistic meaning to be conventional relations between linguistic signs (words) and concrete or conceptual entities that are a given, regardless of the linguistic signs. In order to ensure the exact meaning of the word, something has to be fixed. These entities—concrete objects (a chair) or qualities (being red), or actual states (it is raining) or abstract objects (love)—exist in reality, including in thought, and these entities are related to words. This relationship is called "naming," and the meaning is nothing other than this naming. A common-sense theory, yes, but a problematic one. The objection, of course, is that language does not represent or name reality in a simple fashion. Particularly difficult to handle in this theory are type concepts—it was to ensure their accuracy or correctness that pre-existing general concepts were "invented," type concepts among them. The reasoning is this. Whenever reality— for which read entities—defies precise, unambiguous meaning, then unambiguous meaning is what we "invent" with our general concepts. *Pace* the conceptualists, it is not wrong at this point to introduce "concept"—psychological properties between the words and realistic entities—and thus set up a semantic triangle (words, concepts, "things") or the concept of "sign" (*le signe*), which comprises a material part, the sound or image of the sound (*le signifiant*), and the concept or concepts (*le signifié*). The connection between the symbol and its concept is still elusive. This theory argues that somewhere just out of reach in our consciousness these properties exist, and they are, by definition, the mirror images of the words they explain.

The need for clear, precise depictive language seems to end in conceptual realism, which was Plato's solution. If not in nominalism, then the concept does not exist. Yet this is by no means a solution to the problem—we use words, and we understand them. To illustrate this impasse, I once met a theologian who argued that since it was impossible to define the phenomenon of "religion" then the phenomenon is non-existent. Genre theory has often been caught up in the twists and turns of conceptual realism, nominalism, and conceptualism, while genre has become a question of the existence of general concepts, with the text's relationship to genre thought subordinate to its logical class (Schaeffer 1986). Jacques Derrida succinctly outlined the consequences of this class logic and subordination in "The Law of Genre": "a text cannot belong to no genre, it cannot be without or less a genre. Every text participates in one or several genres, there is no genreless text; there is always a genre and genres, yet such participation never amounts to belonging" (1980, 212).

The dualism in the realistic theory of meaning, which pits language on the one hand against meaning, importance on the other, poses problems when the moment comes to define genre terms. In some contexts, and especially in the natural sciences, this way of thinking about meaning is not especially disruptive. However, it does lead to problems when it comes to (*i*) the words or concepts in everyday language that denote types, but have vague boundaries, and at the same time are expected to work in scholarly language—for example, the word "novel"—and (*ii*) words denote objects that are mutable, and in two ways at that, because they can change over time, mutating, or, like Cervantes's *Don Quixote*—which signals "this is a chivalric romance"–"this is not a chivalric romance"—they often use everyday language's capacity for self-referential statements to the full.

What of pragmatic semantics then? The dualism of semantic realism was criticized by Wittgenstein in his *Philosophischen Untersuchungen* (1953; Kutschera 1974, 132–203). It is not sufficient as a theory to relate an entity to a word, he argued: meaning is all about how the word is used. Meaning is nothing other than usage—a word in a dictionary has no real meaning, it is only when it is used that it has meaning. Wittgenstein is not alone in viewing linguistic meaning in this way—C. S. Peirce, William James, and James Dewey were also advocates of pragmatic semantics. In two important ways, pragmatic semantics differ from realistic semantics.

First, language is human behavior, part of the texture of human life. Language's function must always be analyzed with this in mind. And because language is used in any number of different situations, to any number of different ends, it is impossible to attribute to it only one function—the descriptive (which includes its scholarly function). There are countless language-games.

Second, it steps round the slew of terms that reflect the dualism of realistic semantics; the only thing that will register empirically is the use of language. This theory provides a theoretical foundation for the second answer to the question of what a genre is. Genres—the genres in texts, that is—can be understood as culturally controlled language-games, not scholarly terms or classes to be handled in a metalanguage. Bakhtin was adamant about the link between a pragmatic theory of meaning and genre theory, as here in his article "Speech Genres," where the term "utterances" should be understood as concrete speech acts, and not sentences in general:

> A study of the nature of the utterance and of the diversity of generic forms of utterances in various spheres of human activity is immensely important to almost all areas of linguistics and philology.... To ignore the nature of the utterance or to fail to consider the peculiarities of generic subcategories of speech in any area of linguistic study leads to perfunctoriness and excessive abstractness, distorts the historicity of the research, and *weakens the link between language and life*. After all, language enters life through concrete utterances (which manifest language) and life enters language through concrete utterances. (Bakhtin 1986, 62–3, my emphasis)

The pragmatic theory of meaning, in the Wittgensteinian version, emphasizes that language usage is not primarily a sociological, hypothetical phenomenon, in the sense that the majority of language users determine its meaning, but that each language-game adheres to certain rules, and that is because regularity is a precondition for communication. What then are the rules that determine the meaning of an utterance? In Bakhtin's theory, genre is one of the most important rules to span the grammatical level in language and the pragmatic level. Genres, in other words, *mediate* between language as systematic property (language as grammar) and language as concrete utterances in specific situations (language as pragmatics). This is a theory that confirms the duality of genre: it is in some sense both *in* the text and *beyond* the text.

How does genre work? The analytical practice

What are the rules? What are the elements that have to be incorporated in a genre that in effect determine the use of the word genre? First and foremost, because pragmatic theory has gone so far as to reject the notion that well-defined objects and properties exist as exact meanings, the only possible linguistic precision is a *contextually determined precision*, which in most cases is a historically determined precision. Fowler puts it like this, apropos the mutability of historical genres, with their changing repertoire of constitutive elements: "Strictly speaking, discussion of a generic repertoire takes for granted a previous exploration of the range of constituent features ... during the active life of the kind. A theory of possible constituents should be worked out for the period in question. This is no easy undertaking, when forms change so radically and rapidly" (Fowler 1982, 57). There is no absolute, timeless precision. It bears repeating, though, that this does not mean that the need for terminological precision has to be abandoned. Precisely determined, the rules for the use of a term can enable a researcher to see functions and meanings in the text that might otherwise not have been evident if they had not been adequately determined. The pragmatic theory of meaning comes down to this: language and life are two sides of the same coin, which in practice means that if a term is not used according to its standard use the word will not work, it has no effect, and the interaction between theory and practice does not take place, and nothing new or interesting transpires.

The second consequence of the pragmatic theory of meaning is, of course, the need to find proof or circumstantial evidence for each usage. Definitions or descriptions of a concept are only possible on the basis of its use. That use is not regulated by a given concept, as a concept "exists" only when a fixed usage exists. However, as I noted earlier, what makes it particularly tricky to pin down is that genre terms are largely part of everyday language, not merely an exclusive, scholarly idiom. This is one of the reasons genres are mutable, but it is also what makes them interesting as an analytical tool—their existence both in and outside the text makes it possible to interpret not only the text itself but also the text's position and function in culture and society. Since so few of the rules or conventions are formulated explicitly in a text—a knowledge of genre is to some extent a social or cultural competence, a sort of preknowledge or horizon—evidence of the existence of these genres has to be sought either in explicit formulations of the rules elsewhere—in poetics, in criticism, in reception studies, in aesthetic tracts, in other literary texts—or by tracing the imitations from text to text, following the chain of similar texts that make up the tradition (Fowler 1982, 52). Yet this does not mean that the text fails to signal its genre (or genres); if it did not signal its genre (or genres), the genre's mediation between the text and the text's production and reception would be virtually impossible. (Genre exists both in the text and outside the text, after all.) Over and above this relationship between text and genre (rules or conventions) is the framework generated by the *paratextual* signals— the material indications of genre given out by, say, the book's jacket or blurb (such as "novel") (Genette 1997)—and other types of socially or culturally determined frameworks, which primarily apply where the text has to function in specific communicative situations, such as speeches of various kinds (political, religious) or songs (hymns, national anthems). Jauß asks about genre's connection with history in genera—with the "geschichtlichen Alltag" of everyday life in the past, or with genre's social function (Jauß 1972, 129)—and argues that since genre is neither a "lebenssubjektive Schöpfungen der Dichter," a subjective creation of the poet, nor yet a straightforward retrospective classification, but rather a social phenomenon of the kind that impacts on the functioning of life situations (Jauß 1972, 129), information about genre's connectivity with this historical reality can be gleaned by observing the situation, the "life situation," in which the genre is used. The letter, the genre chosen here to exemplify its importance for the interpretation and function of a text, is indeed associated with a very specific type of communication situation, and it is to this possible connection, this mediation, between genre and history at large that we now turn.

Written by the greatest correspondent of all time, Marie de Rabutin-Chantal, madame de Sévigné (1626–1696), the communication in question is the famous letter she wrote to her cousin Philippe-Emmanuel, marquis de Coulanges, on Monday December 15, 1670. In it, Sévigné talks of the reaction in Parisian society to the news that the following Sunday "La Grande Mademoiselle" was to marry an impoverished nobleman five years her junior, monsieur de Lauzun; La Grande Mademoiselle, meanwhile, was Duchess of Montpensier, Louis XIV's cousin, daughter of Louis XIII's brother, and one of Europe's richest heiresses, who had commanded troops during the Fronde, and had turned down proposals of marriage from kings.

The letter's genre is clearly signaled by the formal properties of the text: the date and place, its structure as an item of correspondence. Letter theory, which had evolved during the Renaissance, defined the letter in terms of this structure, with a letter being a document that conveys what is on the writer's mind to absent people (Hansson 1988, 15). The paratextual elements include the letter's envelope—the place where the addressee is mentioned, as is the sender.

In France by this time, the use of the term "letter" (or the cultural conventions of the letter genre) had been codified in several letter-writing manuals from the Renaissance onward. This went with the writing of personal or familiar letters, which had developed into its own art form since Erasmus had formulated his theory of this type of letter in *Opus de conscribendis epistolis* in 1522. Erasmus advocated greater freedom for writers to structure and style letters as they wished and to be personal in address, far removed from the medieval *ars dictaminis*. Erasmus' interest in the freedom of the familiar letter was sparked by the principle of *infinitum*, the infinite variety in the correspondents' personalities and development and in the topics of their letters (Fumaroli 1978, 886–900; Müller 1980, 138–57; Löwendahl 2007, 4). In the late sixteenth century and in particular in the seventeenth century, Italy and France saw numerous such publications—letter-writing manuals (*manuels*) and collections (*recueils*) of authentic or fictional correspondence in which *familiar letters*, meaning letters to friends, family, or lovers, were discussed and dissected (Altman 1986, 17–62). There was any amount of advice and guidelines, models and patterns for how best to write familiar letters. In France, the familiar letter developed largely because it became the aristocracy's genre of choice, and because they chose to write not in Latin, but in French, in their own language. The French aristocracy wanted to distance themselves from all that was scholarly, pedantic, and rhetorical, and so the style and contents of their correspondence was not far removed from their elegant conversation, adhering to the ancient ideal that a letter should imitate a conversation (Goldsmith 1988, 28–40; Löwendahl 2007, 42). Their conversation, as Mireille Gérard writes, was notable for the purity of its language and articulation (they despised vulgar or provincial speech), for their skill in reading, recounting the news, and telling stories, and all adapted to their interlocutors—concurring, pleasing, making them laugh (1978, 961). Conversation was meant to seem natural and easy, but for most people such effortlessness was not innate, but was learned. The same ideals applied to the familiar letter, and, in due course, a subgenre of the familiar letter, the *lettre galante*, for both the ideal was exactly the same as for elegant or salon conversation. They were designed to please and entertain, not to bore the reader (Löwendahl 2007, 43). In the evolution of elegant conversation and the *lettre galante*, women writers played an important role, it being very much in keeping with the salon, where women set the tone, and which was to dominate France's cultural arena in the first half of the seventeenth century. Mireille Gérard singles out Madeleine de Scudéry (1607–1701), who was among the first to formulate a clear and influential ideal for both elegant conversation and the *lettre galante*. She did this above all in her novels, *Le grand Cyrus* (1653) and *Clélie* (1654–60). In *Clélie*, she described the *lettre galante* as seemingly free in all respects:

> How that may be, said Plotine, I do not understand: but for the *lettres galantes*, that I know admirably well. It is in them that wit rightly has its full scope; where the imagination can range freely, and where the judgement is never so severe as not to indulge in moments of pleasant folly among more serious matters. There one can rail ingeniously; praise and flattery find a pleasing place; one can speak on occasion of friendship, as if one speaks of love: one looks for news; one might even utter innocent lies; one tells news that one does not know; one passes freely from one thing to the next; and to speak truth, since such letters are a conversation with absent people, one must exert oneself to avoid that certain kind of wit that has forced a character, that reeks of books and study; and that is far removed from the gallantry which may be called the soul of such letters. This calls for a style that is all at once easy, natural, and noble; and one must not fail to practise that art which means that there is almost nothing that cannot be raised in letters of this nature, and everything from the most lowly proverb to the utterances of the Sibyls, for anything can serve a clever mind. Yet one must guard against using on such occasions too great an eloquence, which is more properly particular to harangues; and one must use another, less clamorous address to more pleasant effect; especially amongst women; since, in a word, the art of formulating trifles well is not one afforded all people. (Scudéry 1654–60, 1138–40)

From these descriptions one can extract a systematic description of the genre in its "thematic, formal and rhetorical dimensions" (Frow 2006, 74–76), in turn modeled on the three linguistic categories of semantics, grammar, and pragmatics. This threefold model corresponds to the three elements mentioned in the introduction (form, subject, function) and to what several genre theorists hold to be the common descriptive model for historical genres; what is special about this model, compared with other ways of describing types of texts (starting with the medium, for example, or the mode/tone), is that the vast majority of genres have to be described in terms of all three dimensions, and that each genre thus brings together those three dimensions. In this Fowler follows Austin Warren in arguing that a "generic grouping should be based 'upon both outer form (specific metre or structure) and ... upon inner form (attitude, tone, purpose—more crudely, subject and audience),'" although for him the significant thing is that genre definitions or genre descriptions comprise specific formal and rhetorical elements and content (Fowler 1982, 55). Schaeffer argues that genres are constituted from an assemblage of similarities—textual, formal, and, above all, thematic (1986, 186). Jauß provides an analysis in tabular form of the four types of elements included in the descriptions of the medieval genres of the epic, the romance, and the novella, and they can readily be subsumed into the formal, thematic, and rhetorical elements (Jauß 1972, 114–18). In the letter, as in the other genres that are clearly tied to specific communication situations, it is the third, rhetorical dimension that is central. The questions "Which utterance situation?" and "What is this type of text intended to achieve?," both of which raise the author's position vis-à-vis readers or listeners and the text's performativity (Velten 2002) are fundamental to these genres (Bossi 1986, 63–76; Porter 1986, 1–16; Barton and Hall 1999; Bazerman 1999). Carolyn Miller, in writing about the genres associated with specific communication situations, has pointed out

> that a rhetorically sound definition of genre must be centered not on the substance or the form of discourse, but on the action it is used to accomplish. ... the defining principle is based in rhetorical substance (semantics), form (syntactics),or the rhetorical action the discourse performs (pragmatics). A classifying principle based in rhetorical action seems most clearly to reflect rhetorical practice (especially since, as I will suggest later, action encompasses both substance and form). (1984, 151–67)

Different genres have different emphases; thus, the stress in a classical elegy is on the formal dimension, while in a romance it is the thematic dimension. It is also true that it is rare for the three dimensions to be sharply distinguished from one another, in the sense that for example the formal dimension impinges on the thematic and rhetorical dimensions, and vice versa.

What is it that sets the *lettre galante* apart, duly systematized both according to this model and in the historical record? In terms of *rhetoric*, it is important to the genre that this was a correspondence between equals, and not only that, but they were aristocrats, members of the high elite, and enjoyed considerable cultural and economic power. The letters were an important element in the aristocracy's cultural practices. Their importance to aristocratic culture and the fact that these were letters between equals meant that they demonstrated, and indeed presupposed, the existence of an entire aristocratic world (complete with mores, norms and values). Their primary purpose was to entertain and please—to be boring was a mortal sin. Ultimately, the letters were written to establish, strengthen, and maintain bonds, whether bonds of friendship, love, or kinship; they were simply a key element in what today would be called "networking." *Formally* the genre is clearly an imitation of elegant conversation, where the utmost consideration must be paid to the addressee, and the language and topics chosen accordingly. What Bakhtin would have as its dialogism (Bakhtin 1984; Morson and Emerson, 1990, ch. "Metalinguistic: The Dialogue of Authorship") is very evident. Stylistically it meant that the letter writers used vocative forms of address (questions, exclamations, exhortations, second person pronouns) and plain, even casual, language; refined language, to be sure, but certainly not artful, esoteric, or rhetorically elaborate ("all at once easy, natural, and noble"), while the composition is very free ("one passes freely from one thing to the next"), a freedom of form that is matched by its freedom in terms of *themes*. *One* important topic, however, were news and stories, even gossip, where the truth was not always a priority ("one looks for news; one might even utter innocent lies; one tells news that one does not know" and "where the imagination can range freely").

This is the historically defined description of the *lettre galante* genre, which it soon becomes apparent that Sévigné's letter has used:

> What I am about to communicate to you is the most astonishing thing, the most surprising, the most marvellous, the most miraculous, most triumphant, most baffling, most unheard of, most singular, most extraordinary, most unbelievable, most unforeseen, biggest, tiniest, rarest, commonest, the most talked about, the most secret up to this day, the most brilliant, the most enviable, in fact a thing of which only one example can be found in past ages, and, moreover, that example is a false one; a thing nobody can believe in Paris (how could anyone believe it in Lyons?).... I can't make up my mind to say it. Guess, I give you three tries. You give up? Very well, I shall have to tell you. M. de Lauzun is marrying on Sunday, in the Louvre—guess who? I give you four guesses, ten, a hundred. Mme de Coulanges will be saying: that's not so very hard to guess, it's Mlle de La Vallière. Not at all, Madame. Mlle de Retz, then? Not at all, you're very provincial. Of course, how silly we are, you say: it's Mlle Colbert. You're still further away. Then it must be Mlle de Créquy? You're nowhere near. I shall have to tell you in the end: he is marrying, on Sunday, in the Louvre with the King's permission, Mademoiselle, Mademoiselle de .... Mademoiselle ... guess the name. He's marrying Mademoiselle, of course! Honestly, on my honour, on my sworn oath! Mademoiselle, the great Mademoiselle, Mademoiselle, daughter of the late Monsieur, Mademoiselle, granddaughter of Henri

IV, Mademoiselle d'Eu, Mademoiselle de Dombes, Mademoiselle de Montpensier, Mademoiselle d'Orléans, Mademoiselle, first cousin of the King, Mademoiselle, destined for a throne, Mademoiselle, the only bride in France worthy of Monsieur∞. There's a fine subject for conversation. If you shout aloud, if you are beside yourself, if you say we have lied, that is false, that you have been taken in, that this is a fine old tale and too feeble to be imagined, if, in fine, you should even abuse us, we shall say you are perfectly right. (Sévigné 1982, 61–2)

Sévigné is here imitating the elegant idiom of court gossip. Hers is very much a *letter galante*. All the linguistic tools are there: the hyperbolic superlatives, the breaking off (aposiopesis), the form of address (exclamations, questions, exhortations), the implicit and explicit dialogue with the addressee, Coulanges ("You give up? Very well, I shall have to tell you"). The metaphor that Sévigné uses to ask Coulanges if he can guess who is getting married—"Devinez-la: je vous le donne en trois. Jetez-vous votre langue aux chiens?" ("Guess: I give you three tries. Do you throw your tongue to the dogs?")—is plainly an application of the Scudéry stylistic ideal, which called for everything from country proverbs to Sibylline verses. Broadly speaking, Sévigné's language, and especially her metaphors, can be said to stand out for "the rich use of popular and proverbial sayings" (Kögel 1937, 233). This "speaking" tone, with its simple but elegant language, closely corresponds to the letter's subject matter: la Grande Mademoiselle's imminent marriage with the impoverished Lauzun was a splendid court scandal. It can hardly be doubted that the letter amused and pleased its recipient, and thus met its purpose by performing the desired practice of reconfirming the social ties that existed between Sévigné and her correspondent, the Marquis de Coulanges, a cousin five years her junior, son of Sévigné's first guardian, and one of the closest members of her circle. She is addressing herself to an equal, a relative, and a close friend, making her letter all of a piece with the aristocracy's networking practices, with all that meant in terms of a strongly pragmatic dimension: it performs all the necessary actions by gossiping (passing on the news), telling a story, and entertaining and pleasing the recipient, and thus maintaining social ties. In this way, one can see that the genre of the *lettre galante*, as Bakhtin's theory of genres would have it, plainly *mediates* between language's systematic properties (language as grammar) and language as action in a specific communication situation (language as pragmatics). This mediating function of genre, put another way, means that genre expresses something about the text that the text itself does not communicate. Sévigné does not write "Now I'll entertain you," let alone "Now I will strengthen the ties between us." Knowledge of the unspoken is part and parcel of what is called cultural competence. It was Schaeffer who emphasized that genre is rarely signaled openly in a text: "while in the case of hypertextuality in Genette's sense one finds an explicit discursive strategy linking a hypertext to his hypotext, this does not hold true in the majority of generic relations between texts" (Schaeffer1986, p. 201), and Rosalie Colie points out that the comprehension and interpretation of texts requires knowledge of the unspoken (Colie 1973, 115). The genre of the *lettre galante* includes actions designed to entertain and please and to strengthen social ties—indeed, that much was silently understood by both the letter writer and the recipient. The genre thus *mediates* between the text as a grammatical fact and the pragmatic facts—it is proof of the action, or more correctly the effect, the performativity (Velten 2002), which the letter was expected to achieve. For the sake of clarity, we can distinguish between the speech acts that are immediately apparent—the business of telling a story, gossiping—and those that are not. The latter can also rightly be called the text's purpose. One expected purpose of the familiar (and *galante*) letter is to be the mirror of the writer's soul, revealing the self in an act that had long been codified in the Ancients' thinking about the familiar letter (Müller 1980, 138–57). How, then, does Sévigné reveal her "self" in her letter?

The genre's twofold mediation

This last question broadens our genre-based understanding of Sévigné's letter to encompass the letter's image of mankind and the world—the *lettre galante*'s world of human beings and their norms and values—and ultimately the question of the genre's mediation between text and society. The world in question was that of the French aristocracy in the second half of the seventeenth century, in the age of Louis XIV, and Sévigné outlines both a self and a world in her language and her norms and values. Her language plainly shows what she and posterity call her "negligence" (Duchêne 1976, 113–27), her carelessness, which, whether learned or genuinely innate, gives the impression of spontaneity. Her "sloppy," seemingly spontaneous, and thus authentic, style conveys her and her peers' views on the scandal, namely that it was a misalliance of catastrophic proportions. To that extent, Sévigné and her circle appear to be strongly class conscious, and what we know otherwise about her views on the subject do little to change that conclusion—she seems to have possessed all the crushing arrogance of the propertied aristocracy toward the people and the classes she regarded as her inferiors. Several of her letters are testimony to her effortless condescension toward her subordinates. Her letter to Coulanges also demonstrates that she and her circle thought the whole business of the marriage more than a little ridiculous; her whole attitude is slightly ironic. It might be stretching the point to say the letter bears traces of the French nobility's frustration that in the wake of the Fronde (1648–1653), Mazarin and Louis XIV had been able to deprive the high aristocracy of their political power, but Sévigné certainly moved in circles sympathetic to the Fronde. Whatever the case, her writing self shows scant loyalty to the king and his court; on the contrary, both here and in other letters Sévigné appears as a marginally more temperate answer to the Duke of Saint-Simon (1675–1755), that supremely caustic chronicler of Louis's court. Regardless, we can safely argue that there was considerable tension between the aristocracy, here in the shape of Sévigné and her correspondent Coulanges, and the Crown. This much is in line with Fredric Jameson's theory in *The Political Unconscious* (1981) on genre's mediation of text and society: "The strategic value of generic concepts for Marxism clearly lies in the mediatory function of the notion of a genre, which allows the coordination of immanent formal analysis of the individual text with the twin diachronic perspective of the history of forms and the evolution of social life" (Jameson 2002, 92). Jameson, for whom genres and their functions can only be understood historically, in terms of their original context, argues that genre in its strong, original form was an attempt to cope with a social dilemma (Jameson 2002, ch. "Magical Narratives"). What the *lettre galante* might conceivably have been intended to handle was the aristocracy's dilemma about the monarchy and the royal court: submit to the Crown, accept their loss of power and their reduction to glittering court backdrop, subordinate to the king and his bureaucracy; or retreat to a culturally brilliant, satirical, or ironic position outside the court.

The genre of the *lettre galante*, as codified by Scudéry just as the Fronde ended and the downfall of the French aristocracy was upon them, can thus be considered as mediating not only between the text's linguistic–grammatical and pragmatic levels (Bakhtin), but also between society and text (Jameson). The fact that we can use historical genres has everything to do with their being a feature of the writers' and readers' horizon, *and*, as part of that horizon, that genres exist both inside and outside the text, both as a term in a train of thought and as an essential part of the text itself.

Further reading

Introductions to the theory of genre can be found in John Frow's *Genre* (2006), and in Alastair Fowler's *Kinds of Literature: An Introduction to the Theory of Genres and Modes* (1982). Gérard Genette and Tzvetan Todorovs's *Théorie des genres* (1986) contains some of the classic articles in genre theory. In *Die Lehre von der Einteilung der Dichtkunst, vornehmlich vom 16. Bis 19 Jahrhundert: Studien zur Geschichte der poetischen Gattungen* (1940), Irene Behrens shows that the great "triad"—epic, tragedy and lyric—is an invention of the eighteenth century.

References

Altman, Janet Gurkin (1986) "The Letter Book as a Literary Institution 1539–1789. Toward a Cultural History of Published Correspondences in France," *Yale French Studies. Men/Women of Letters*, 71: 17–62.

Bakhtin, Mikhail M. (1984) *Problems of Dostoevsky's Poetics* (1963). Ed. and Trans. Caryl Emerson, Minneapolis: University of Minnesota Press.

Bakhtin, Mikhail M. (1986) "The Problem of Speech Genres" (1952–53), in C. Emerson and M. Holquist (eds), *Speech Genres & Other Late Essays*. Trans. Vern W. McGee, Austin: University of Texas Press Slavic Series 8, University of Texas Press, pp. 60–102.

Barton, David and Nigel Hall (1999) "Introduction," in *Letter Writing as a Social Practice*, Philadelphia: John Benjamins Publ., pp. 1–14.

Bazerman, Charles (1999) "Letters and the Social Grounding of Differentiated Genres," in *Letter Writing as a Social Practice*, Philadelphia: John Benjamins Publ., pp. 15–20.

Bossis, Mireille (1986) "Methodological Journeys Through Correspondences," *Yale French Studies*, 71: 63–76.

Colie, Rosalie (1973) *The Resources of Kind: Genre-Theory in the Renaissance*, Berkeley: University of California Press.

Derrida, Jacques (1980) "The Law of Genre ," in *Glyph 7*. Trans. Avital Ronell, 202–32.

Duchêne, Roger (1976) "Madame de Sévigné et le style négligé," *Oeuvres et critiques*, årg. 1, nr 2, J. M. Place: Paris.

Fowler, Alastair (1982) *Kinds of Literature. An Introduction to the Theory of Genres and Modes*, Oxford: Clarendon Press.

Frow, John (2006) *Genre*, London and New York: New Critical Idiom, Routledge.

Fumaroli, Marc (1978) "Genèse de l'Épistolographie classique. Rhétorique humaniste de la lettre, de Pétrarque a Juste Lipse," *Revue d'histoire littéraire de la France*: 78.

Genette, Gérard (1997) *Paratexts: Thresholds of Interpretation* (1987). Trans. Jane E. Lewin, Cambridge: Cambridge University Press.

Gérard, Mireille (1978) "Art épistolaire et art de la conversation. Les vertus de la familiarité," *Revue d'histoire littéraire de la France*: 6.

Goldsmith, Elizabeth C. (1988) *"Exclusive Conversations." The Art of Interaction in Seventeenth-Century France*, Philadelphia: University of Pennsylvania Press.

Hansson, Stina (1988) *Svensk brevskrivning. Teori och tillämpning* (Skrifter utg. av Litteraturvetenskapliga institutionen vid Göteborgs universitet 18), Göteborg.

Jameson, Fredric (2002) *The Political Unconscious. Narrative as a Socially Symbolic Act* (1981), London and New York: Routledge.

Jauß, Hans Robert (1972) "Theorie der Gattungen und Literatur des Mittelalters," in Generalites, utg. av H. R. Jauß and Erich Köhler, *Grundriß der romanischen Literaturen des Mittelalters*, vol. 1, 107–138, Heidelberg, also in *Théorie des genres*, serial Points, Paris: Éditions du Seuil, 1986.

Kögel, Therese (1937) *Bilder bei Mme de Sèvigné. (Metaphern und Vergleiche). Eine lexikographische Arbeit*, diss. Würzburg: Ludwig-Maximilians-Universität zu München.

von Kutschera, Franz (1974) *Sprachphilosophie*, 2nd edition, München: Wilhelm Fink Verlag.

Löwendahl, Marie (2007) *Min allrabästa och ömmaste vän! Kvinnors brevskrivning under svenskt 1700-tal*, Göteborg and Stockholm: Makadam.

Miller, Carolyn R. (1984) "Genre as Social Action," *Quarterly Journal of Speech*, 70.

Morson, Gary Saul and Caryl Emerson (1990) *Mikhail Bakhtin: Creation of a Prosaics*, Stanford: Stanford University Press.

Müller, Wolfgang G. (1979) "Der Brief als Spiegel der Seele. Zur Geschichte eines Topos der Epistolartheorie von der Antike bis zu Samuel Richardson," in *Antike und Abendland. Beiträge zum Verständnis der Griechen und Römer und ihrer Nachlebens*, vol. XXV, Berlin and New York: Walter der Gruyter.

Porter, Charles A. (1986) "Foreword," *Yale French Studies*, 71.

Russell, Bertrand (1962) *An Inquiry into Meaning and Truth. The William James Lectures for 1940 Delivered at Harvard University*, Harmonsworth: Penguin.

de Scudéry, Madeleine (1654–60) *Clélie, historie romaine*. Seconde partie, Livre III, Paris.

Schaeffer, Jean-Marie (1986) "Du texte au genre. Notes sur la problématique générique," *Poétique*, 53, 1983, also in *Théorie des genres*, serien Points, Éditions du Seuil.

Schüttpelz, Erhard (1995) "Objektsprache und Metasprache," in J. Fohrmann and H. Müller (red.), *Literaturwissenschaft*, München: Wilhelm Fink Verlag.

de Sévigné, Madame (1982 and later) *Selected Letters*. Trans., with an introduction by Leonard Tancock, 61–62. London: Penguin Books.

Tarski, Alfred (1986) "Der Wahrheitsbegriff in den formalisierten Sprachen," in K. Berka and L. Kreiser (ed.), *Logik—Texte*, Berlin: Akademie-Verlag.

Théorie des genres (1986) Gérard Genette and Tzvetan Todorov (eds), in the serial Points, Paris: Èditions du Seuil.

Todorov, Tzvetan (1973) *The Fantastic. A Structural Approach to a Literary Genre* (1970). Trans. Richard Howard, Ithaca, NY: Cornell University Press.

Velten, Hans Rudolf (2002) "Performativität. Ältere deutsche Literatur," in Claudia Benthien and Hans Rudolf Velten (eds), *Germanistik als Kulturwissenschaft*, Rowohlt: Reinbek bei Hamburg.

4

Narrative

Stefan Iversen

Narratives are everywhere, at least according to a kind of text that also seems to be everywhere: introductions to narratives. Most scientific disciplines, and not only within the humanities, contain subfields interested in aspects of the power and explanatory of narratives. Few would disagree with the observation that most forms of communication—from carefully constructed fictions to formulaic news reports to spontaneous conversation—contain acts of storytelling. To students of literature, this omnipresent interest in narrative is both a blessing and a curse. It is a blessing because many new tools and methods are being developed for analyzing narrative, and a curse because of the proliferation of the term challenges clear definitions and distinctions. What are we talking about when we talk about narrative in literature?

Zooming all the way out, one may, as De Fina and Georgakopoulou do in *Analyzing Narrative* (2012), distinguish between, on the one hand, approaches to narrative as a "type of text" and, on the other hand, approaches to narrative as "a *mode, epistemology and method*" (1). Put crudely, the former approaches, dominant in disciplines like literary study and film study, focus on narrative as a *thing*, typically in the form of an object such as a novel or a play. In contrast to this, the latter approaches, often found in psychology, philosophy and sociology, focus on narrative as a *way of thinking*, typically involved in meaning-making processes. Ideas about narrative as a way of thinking have a lot to offer scholars of narrative as objects;

however, it is the approaches to narrative as a thing that have generated the most influential and productive insights with regard to literature. Therefore, they inform most of what follows.

This initial narrowing down makes it possible to say something more specific about narrative in literature. Elaborating slightly on Porter Abbott's suggestion in *The Cambridge Introduction to Narrative* (2008), I would like to propose the following simple definition: a narrative is a representation of connected events. According to this uncontroversial take, in order for something to qualify as a narrative, it must contain acts of telling (the events are not actually taking place, but re-presented) and it must deal with changes (the events are not just happening, but linked, typically through causality). To some narratologists, this definition would be too narrow. The leading figure of rhetorical narratology, James Phelan, defines literary narrative as "somebody telling somebody else on some occasion and for some purpose(s) that something happened" (Phelan 2007, 3), taking into account many issues left out by our basic offering, most notably the elements of the communicative situation (the intentions of the author, the setting, and the audience). Cognitive approaches to literary narrative, such as the one developed by Monika Fludernik (2009), would place a stronger emphasis on the characters and on the acts of reception, stating that the reader's reconstructions of a character's experiences ("experientiality"), rather than linked events, are what make something into a narrative proper. As should be obvious, the term "narrative" has a tendency to subsume other terms of literary study under it: narrator, character, voice, reader, intention. By limiting our definition to representation of connected events, we are not claiming that concepts like narrator or character have no bearing on understanding stories in literary fiction but given the context of this chapter it makes sense to leave the discussion of these phenomena to others.

In the following, therefore, we present and discuss some of the conceptual tools developed in order to analyze and interpret represented connected events as they materialize in literature. This take on narrative in literature will, in other words, mainly focus on what is often referred to as "plot." "Plot," like the term "narrative," is multivalent and used differently in many contexts. In narrative theory as well as in everyday use, "plot" sometimes refer to a fixed structure, sometimes to a process that a reader goes through as she makes sense of the events of the story unfolding in the telling. As Karin Kukkonen states in her entry on "Plot" in *Handbook of Narratology* (2014): "plot is both the process that facilitates readers' engagement with a story and its target, a pattern of meaning" (708). We will use the substantive "plot" when addressing a structure of a narrative and the verbalized form "plotting" when addressing readerly dynamics.

Two main questions guide this chapter: How does something like a series of connected events (a plot) work in narrative fiction? Why are we continuously drawn toward plots (and plotting), even in cases where we are absolutely certain that they are made up? The answers to these questions are connected, but we will treat them separately as we investigate, first, literary narrative's *form* and, second, its *function*.

How do narratives work?

Human beings are fast learners when it comes to recognizing and evaluating even highly complex series of events, as anyone who has tried re-reading a story to a child will know. The ease with which we understand and judge narratives, however, stands in stark contrast to the challenges we face when trying to more precisely account for the workings of plots and plotting. Through what processes do singular, separated events turn into a more or less coherent, meaningful whole? Two aspects call for attention: the relations between parts and whole (event and plot) and the fact that the plot is established through acts of representation.

In order for something to become a plot, events need to exist, for instance, in the form of actions caused by the characters or by occurrences in the presented universe. These events are normally separated in time and connected through chains of causality; in a narrative a "then" is often also a "therefore." These ideas about temporality and change over time as what gets transformed into the coherent unit of a plot find their first formulations in Aristotle's *Poetics*, which is focused on the genre of tragedy but produces insights pertaining to most narrative texts. Tragedy is first and foremost "the imitation of an action" (Aristotle 1984, 2320), and plot (in Aristotelian terms) is seen as "the combination of the incidents." This combination of incidents must now form a "whole," defined as that which has a beginning ("that which is not necessarily after anything else, and which has naturally something after it"), a middle ("that which by nature is after one thing and has also another after it"), and an end ("that which is naturally after something itself [...] and with nothing else after it") (Aristotle 1984, 2321).

This three-part structure of the plot as containing beginning, middle, and end has since been expanded and adjusted for various genres and discourse types (for instance, in the form of Gustav Freitag's triangle from *Die Technik des Dramas* (1863)) but it remains the standard model for the overarching structure of a basic plot, even if many literary texts go to great lengths to challenge, subvert or mock it.

Agatha Christie's *The Murder of Roger Ackroyd* is a crime novel, first published in 1926. A short summary of the story will be hard pressed not to actualize the default three-part plot structure of beginning, middle, and end. The story takes place in the small village of King's Abbott and begins with the untimely death of the widow Mrs. Ferrars, a death that the local Dr. Sheppard (as well as his talkative sister Caroline with whom he lives) explains as a suicide. A new, strange foreigner, who used to be a detective, moves in next to Dr. Sheppard and sister, a dinner party is held at the place of the local, rich gentleman Roger Ackroyd, and the beginning of the story ends with the discovery of the body of Mr. Ackroyd. He is murdered in his own house on the evening of the dinner party and among his last actions is the reading of a letter given to him by the late Mrs. Ferrars with whom he had a secret affair. The letter contains information about someone blackmailing Mrs. Ferrars about this affair, which, along with feelings of guilt for having killed her husband a year before, is what pushed her into suicide. The blackmailing motif becomes a major lead in the following murder investigation, carried out by the police and the neighbor detective Hercule Poirot, who reluctantly interrupts his retirement to investigate the dramatic events transpiring around him. The ending of the story's middle marks the beginning of the end as Poirot brings together the suspects and announces that he knows who killed Ackroyd and will make the information public the following day. Immediately after, Poirot confronts only the alleged murderer with the result of the investigation, thereby giving the person a chance to avoid public disgrace by committing suicide, thus bringing closure to the plot through a repetition of the same type of event that marked the beginning.

Beginning with Aristotle, scholars on narrative structure have tried to explain the differences between, on the one hand, a mechanical placing of events one after another and, on the other hand, a coherent and engaging plot. Aristotle's own explanation was that the quality of a given plot should be judged according to the degree to which it manages to achieve *anagnorisis* (meaning recognition) and lead up to *peripeteia* (meaning turning point). The tragedy of Oedipus functioned particularly well precisely because Oedipus' recognition of the fact that his new wife is his mother stages a very strong moment of anagnorisis. This in turn leads straight to an equally powerful turn or peripeteia in the action, coloring everything after the anagnorisis in a completely different light. Speaking in a less normative vein, more recent theories about what transforms singular events into a coherent plot talk about tensions between specific events and a storyworld. In David Herman's *Basic Elements of Narrative* (2009), elaborating on ideas developed by Jerome Bruner (see, for instance, Bruner's *Acts of Meaning* (1990)), a breach to the canonical is what gives a plot momentum. Non-trivial acts set the narrative in motion and the goal of the plot is often to bring the non-trivial and the canonical into dialogue, by either assimilating or transforming the unruly event into normality or in a reverse move by having the event bring change to or even revolutionize the status quo.

We may use these ideas on the relationship between singular events and connected whole to elaborate our understanding of the plot in Christie's murder mystery. What would seem like a quiet, rural life in a small village represents the canonical while the breaching elements that set the plot in motion come in the genre-typical form of dead people. The murder investigation traces actions and motives ever further back in order to reconstruct the causal links that produced the breaches, thus giving the story its forward momentum. Ultimately, this leads to a restoration of normality through a purging of the person found to be responsible.

The event of anagnorisis, immediately followed by the peripeteia of the story, materializes toward the end of the narrative. Here, the murderer, much to the surprise of himself and (at least this) first-time reader, realizes that the many so far seemingly disparate clues, leads, and shady motives can be sorted in a way that makes the arrow of responsibility point in one direction only. True to genre-expectations, the enthusiastic detective Poirot emerges as the superior plotter, who takes it upon himself to lead both the alleged murderer and the confused reader "the way that I have travelled myself. Step by step you shall accompany me, and see for yourself that all the facts point indisputably to one person" (211). By selecting between important and less important signs he is able to configure a coherent whole out of the many events, besting both the alleged murderer (who thought the connections between events would remain hidden) and the first-time reader (who struggles to construct one and only one string of events).

These readerly struggles are not accidental, but intentional—the design of the narrative sets out to produce them. More precisely, the move from ever-increasing doubt to a final understanding results from the way in which the events and motives are conveyed to the reader by the narrative. With this observation we arrive at what we referred to as the second main aspect of narrative form: plots are established through acts of representation, stories are told.

While this might seem like an uncontroversial statement, its consequences are not to be underestimated. The most important consequence is that any narrative contains not one, but two series of events: the series of events as they are represented to us through the order of the narrative and the series of events as we imagine them to have taken place. The first systematic formulation of the distinction between these two series of events emerged in the works of the Russian formalists during the 1910s. They defined narrative as consisting of *sjuzhet* and *fabula*, where sjuzhet is the order of events as presented by the text and fabula the chronological order of events. French structuralism inherited the distinction in the form of *historie* and *discourse* and it remains one of the most important sets of concepts in contemporary narrative research, with the English terms *discourse* and *story* as the most widespread equivalent.

Discourse is a textual phenomenon in that it exists for all to see, in the material actualization of the narrative: on the very first page we read about the death of Mrs. Ferrars, and on a much later page we learn about who blackmailed her. Story, on the other hand, is a psychological or mental phenomenon. It is a virtual and dynamic chain of chronologically ordered events configured by the reader as the reading takes place. In a first-time reading of *The Murder of Roger Ackroyd*, the reader will, based on her own level of perception and meticulousness, perform plotting by constructing and continually adjusting hypotheses, reshufflings, and trial-and-error procedures, attempting to approach the level of plot-mastery demonstrated by Poirot in his final talk.

There are at least three reasons for paying close attention to the relationships between discourse and story when analyzing the forms of narrative in literature. The first has already been mentioned and that is the assumption that the discourse is produced by a teller, often referred to as the narrator. In *Discours du récit* (1972), Gérard Genette claimed that a narrator may be telling the story either from *inside* the world of the story, typically in the form of a character (also known as a first-person- or I-narrator) or from *outside* the world of the story, typically in the form of third-person- or he-narrator. Christie's murder mystery is told by Dr. Sheppard and therefore qualifies as a piece of character-narration. What makes it an unusual character-narrative—and a highly original piece of crime fiction— becomes clear only when the murder investigation ends: Poirot's accusing finger points, "indisputably" as it where, at no other than Dr. Sheppard, the very same person who from page one has been in charge of the discourse through which the reader has been trying to make sense of the murderous events in King's Abbott. Having a murder mystery told by someone inside the world is a fairly conventional strategy, for instance, when the story is told by the good-hearted assistant whose lack of deductive brilliance makes that of his master shine even brighter. Equally traditional is the idea of hiding the murderer in plain sight by making him too obvious to suspect, thus heightening the surprise of the peripetaia. What is unique in the setup of *The Murder of Roger Ackroyd* is that the text hides the murderer behind the murderer, as Pierre Bayard puts it in his *Who Killed Roger Ackroyd?* (2000). The discourse ends up as a manuscript in two parts, where our reading of the latter part transforms our understanding of the first. The first part is written during the time of the investigation and thus prior to Poirot's finger pointing. Through very carefully distributed omissions Dr. Sheppard, even while taking part in the investigation, succeeds in producing this first part as a text that completely hides his own complicity, thinking he will be able to outsmart the detective. The second, shorter part is written after the realization that he would not. It describes his decision to kill himself and while it does not contain an actual, verbatim confession, it strongly suggests Dr. Sheppard's guilt ("He [Ackroyd] knew danger was close at hand. And yet he never suspected *me*" (Christie 1974, 219)).

Such sophisticated and innovative uses of omissions and double meanings point toward the second reason why the distinction between discourse and story is useful when analyzing narrative fiction. With this distinction, it becomes possible to conduct investigations of the ways in which a piece of literature open a space in which the reader is invited to experiment with the creation of coherence and meaning: at times by aiding the reader, at times by obstructing, or playing with the reader, for instance, through omissions, tilted retellings, denouncements, or false hints. Any written narrative thus places the reader in a peculiar double position of both being subject to the discourse and the master of the plotting. The meaning of the plot emerges through acts of interpretation and while some types of literary narrative, for instance the typical crime novel, often rather heavy-handedly leads the reader both into and out of zones of undecidability, other types of literature are less interested in prescribing one reading as the right one. In *Who Killed Roger Ackroyd?*, Bayard takes the potential power of the reader to a highly interesting extreme in that he offers a remarkable reading of Christie's novel, based on the assumption that Dr. Sheppard did not kill Ackroyd. Through a very detailed close reading of the information offered in Dr. Sheppard's writing, which remains the only source to this particular universe, Bayard arrives at a different, and to some more convincing conclusion than the one presented by Poirot when stating that all things considered the most likely murderer is in fact not the doctor, but his sister, Caroline Sheppard.

Thirdly, our treatments so far of the relation between the discourse and the story have addressed this relation as a retrospective one. We recognize this retrospective logic from most instances of everyday storytelling: first, something happens, then we tell about it. When dealing with fictional narratives, however, this commonsensical retrospective thinking can be deceitful. Fiction is non-referential in the sense that a fictional narrative, as Dorrit Cohn argues in *The Distinction of Fiction* (1999), creates the world it refers to by referring to it. Even if most fictional narratives behave as if the events they refer to happened prior to the presentation of them in the discourse, the causal link between the telling and the event is strictly speaking reversed. Events in fiction happen only because they are told which in turn means an act of reading is required to make them emerge. Most narrative theories, both classical such as Genette's *Discours du récit* and *Nouveau discours du récit* (1983) and rhetorical and cognitive such as, respectively, Phelan's *Experiencing Fiction* (2007) and Herman's *Story Logic* (2002), treat fictional narratives as if they were retrospective narratives. Some literary narratives, however, exploit or experiment with their non-referential status and go against the mimetic grain by constructing anti-mimetic plots or plot elements, for instance, by having events both take place and not take place at the same time. Such tendencies have been pointed out and investigated by among others the subfield of unnatural narratology (see Nielsen: "The Impersonal Voice in First-Person Narrative Fiction" (2004) and Alber, Iversen, Nielsen and Richardson: "Unnatural Narratology, Unnatural Narratives: Beyond Mimetic Models" (2010)).

Why are we drawn to fictional narratives?

After having looked at plot as a shaping and linking of non-canonical events through the double logic of story and discourse, we now turn to the question of the function of narratives in literature. What is it that makes us spend so much of our precious time immersed in purely invented plots? Among the many attempts at answering this, we will focus our attention on two sets of explanations, psychological explanations and ethical explanations, respectively.

The first coherent psychological explanation of why (fictional) plots matter to us is to be found in the works of Aristotle. According to him, the movement from anagnorisis to peripeteia produces what he refers to as *catharsis* in the viewer. Catharsis designates a sort of emotional cleansing, provoked by the sudden turning points of the plot. The strength of a plot's catharsis is tied proportionally to the peripeteia: a more powerful and irreversible turning point equals a stronger psychological effect in the audience. The idea of catharsis marks the beginning of long tradition of linking the reader's psycho-dynamical reactions with the formal features of a narrative. The simultaneously pleasant and unpleasant experience of the catharsis-reversal ("Aha! So it was Dr. Sheppard who did it!/Oh no! Was it Dr. Sheppard who did it?) provides emotional and intellectual stimuli in the form of controlled chocks, designed to rust off our inner mental apparatus. Variations of this idea play a major role in the parts of contemporary narrative theory that are inspired by the cognitive sciences. In *Why We Read Fiction* (2006), Lisa Zunshine draws on insights from evolutionary psychology when she describes narrative fiction as a form of emotional boot camp. A virtual world consisting of thoughts and emotions the reader may use to mirror, train or challenge the inner life of ourselves and the selves of others.

Modern takes on the psychological impact of plot has worked toward more dynamic and flexible models in order to alleviate the slightly mechanical thinking present in Aristotle's ideas about turning points in the tragedy. Still, the dialectic relationship between the accumulation and release of psychological tensions is considered to be the main thrust behind plots and plotting. In a key text, *Reading for the Plot* (1984), Peter Brooks sets out to explain our desire for connected series of fictive events by drawing on a broader concept of what desire is. Inspired by psychoanalytic thinking, Brooks understands our desire for narrative as a lust for getting away from lust, a desire for getting to desire's end. The drive that brings us to a narrative as well as brings us through the often rather stressful plotting-exercises is teleological in nature. We desire the plot because we desire to be released from it, a release that an ending—that which has "nothing else after it"—can provide. The plot-structure of fictions becomes a prototypical model for a basic psychological set of experiences: desires and needs spring from lacks that can be temporally filled. We engage with invented plot-lines because they, even if only for a short, Poirot-infused while, let us master experiences of lack and confusion similar to the ones presented to us in real life.

A crime novel such as *The Murder of Roger Ackroyd* provides the paradigmatic form for seeing these ideas in action. Brooks' insights lend themselves very well to explaining both the plot structure and the plotting initiated as a quest for release from the tensions of uncertainty in the form of a closure that seems both surprising and fitting (expect, perhaps, for acutely aware readers such as Bayard). Other types of literature, most notably experimental types of writing from the early modernisms and onward, have a less intimate or natural relationship with endings (as well as with causal connections and at times even with events as such) as something that re-establishes order and canonicity. In such narratives, the teleological desire gets thwarted, subverted, or even mocked by the dilatory spaces of a middle that never really ends but rather propels the reader toward ever changing, incompatible interpretations. In *Loiterature* (1999), Ross Chambers suggests the term *digressions* for such challenges to more or less straight progressions. In a thinly veiled polemic gesture toward the teleological fixations of Brooks, Chambers uses the term digression to talk about a different type of desire for reading and plotting, a desire for being led astray, for being taken down dead ends or for simply loitering around a discursively produced landscape. Rather than treating the teleological and the digressive reading desires as opposites in an either/or construction, it is often more productive to see them as dependent upon each other and thus always to some degree at work in any type of plot. Not even the most experimental types of written fiction can fully annihilate our desire to follow a series of events from beginning through a challenging middle toward the right end and likewise: even the most formulaic plots rely heavily on digressions in order to tease, postpone, and trouble the process of plotting.

These psychological explanations of the reasons why we bother with narrative fiction have a lot to say about relationships between formal aspects and readerly reactions but less to say about the impact of the actual content of fictional narratives. Most connected series of events present us with more or less explicit conflicts between themes, ideas, and values about what it means to be human and to conduct a meaningful, proper or at least liveable life. By engaging with the progressions of a fictional narrative, we inevitably become engaged in a series of ethical judgments, some made by the fictional characters and the narrator of the fictive universe, others made by us as readers. Rhetorical narratology in the tradition from Wayne C. Booth's *The Rhetoric of Fiction* (1961) has developed a highly detailed set of tools for analyzing these judgments, based on the assumption that fictional narratives first and foremost are rhetorical acts: someone wants to get something across to someone else. The author, or as Booth would say: the implied author uses his fictional narrative to launch certain sets of ethical dilemmas that the reader then, through the formal qualities of the discourse, is invited to position herself in relation to. The claim is not that narrative fiction should strive for clear and unmistakable moral content, rather the contrary. According to Phelan, the aesthetical value of a text is proportional to its ethical complexity. In working with the ethical aspects of a narrative, Phelan suggests a useful distinction between judgments taking place inside the presented universe (*ethics of the told*) and judgments coming from the act of narration (*ethics of the telling*). The first set of judgments relate to the characters, while the second set relate to the implied author and to a character-narrator, if one is present in the narrative.

Further reading

The dialectics between discourse and story serve as an important site of inquiry and discovery for literary criticism and textual analysis, not the least because it integrates thematic and formal matters. While one is observing how a plot begins and progresses toward its closure, one can benefit tremendously from also observing the progression and developments in norms, values, and worldviews, both on the level of the telling and on the level of the told. By moving recursively between the thematic and the formal, a reading of plot and progression can function as a major part of a fuller, systematic understanding of any particular piece of narrative fiction.

As mentioned initially, the field of narrative research, even when restricted to researchers mainly interested in literature, is huge and expanding. In addition to the above-mentioned theoretical texts, who all contain substantial contributions to the study of narrative fiction, one may want to learn more about the notion of event by consulting Peter Hühn's "Event and Eventfullness" and more about what makes some narratives seem more narrative than others by reading Abbotts "Narrativity." Both texts can be found in the second version of *Handbook of Narratology* (2014), an excellent, comprehensive encyclopedia of the core terms of classical and postclassical narratology. The handbook also exists in a free, continuously updated online version, called *The Living Handbook of Narratology* (http://www.lhn.uni-hamburg.de/). Interesting discussions on the dynamic aspects of plot can be found in the 2002 anthology *Narrative Dynamics* (2002), edited by Brian Richardson. For a substantial debate, highlighting agreements and disagreements between influential recent positions in narratology, see *Narrative Theory. Core Concepts and Critical Debates* (2012). Recommended standard works on the concepts and methods of narrative theory are *Routledge Encyclopedia of Narrative Theory* (2005) and *A Companion to Narrative Theory* (2005).

References

Abbott, Porter (2014) "Narrativity," in Peter Hühn et al. (eds), *Handbook of Narratology*, 2nd edition, Grönningen: De Gruyter.

Alber, Jan, S. Iversen, H. S. Nielsen and B. Richardson (2010) "Unnatural Narratology, Unnatural Narratives: Beyond Mimetic Models," *Narrative*, 18: 2.

Aristotle (1984) "Poetics," in J. Barnes (ed.), *The Complete Works of Aristotle*, vol. 2, Princeton, NJ: Princeton University Press.

Bayard, Pierre (2000) *Who Killed Roger Ackroyd?* New York: The New Press.

Booth, Wayne C. (1983) *The Rhetoric of Fiction*, Chicago: University of Chicago Press.

Brooks, Peter (1984) *Reading for the Plot*, Oxford: Clarendon Press.

Bruner, Jerome (1990) *Acts of Meaning*, Harvard: Harvard University Press.

Chambers, Ross (1999) *Loiterature*, Lincoln: University of Nebraska Press.

Christie, Agatha (1974) *The Murder of Roger Ackroyd*, Glasgow: Fontana/Collins.

Cohn, Dorrit (1999) *The Distinction of Fiction*, Baltimore: Johns Hopkins University Press.

De Fina, Anne and Alexandra Georgakopoulou (2012) *Analyzing Narrative*, Cambridge: Cambridge University Press.

Fludernik, Monika (2009) *An Introduction to Narratology*, New York: Routledge.

Freytag, Gustav (1983). *Die Technik des Dramas*, Stuttgart: Philipp Reclam.

Genette, Gérard (1972) "Discourse de récit," in *Figures III*, Paris: Éditions du Seuil.

Genette, Gérard (1983) *Nouveau discours du récit*, Paris: Éditions du Seuil.

Herman, David (2002) *Story Logic: Problems and Possibilities of Narrative*, Lincoln: University of Nebraska Press.

Herman, David (2009) *Basic Elements of Narrative*, Singapore: Wiley-Blackwell.

Herman, David, Manfred Jahn and Marie-Laure Ryan (eds) (2005) *Routledge Encyclopedia of Narrative Theory*, London: Routledge.

Herman, D., J. Phelan, P. Rabinowitz, B. Richardson and R. Warhol (2012) *Narrative Theory. Core Concepts and Critical Debates*, Columbus: Ohio State University Press.

Hühn, Peter (2014) "Event and Eventfulness," in Peter Hühn et al. (eds), *Handbook of Narratology*, 2nd edition, Göttingen: De Gruyter.

Kukkonen, Karin (2014) "Plot," in Peter Hühn et al. (eds), *Handbook of Narratology*, 2nd edition, Göttingen: De Gruyter.

Nielsen, Henrik Skov (2004) "The Impersonal Voice in First-Person Narrative Fiction," *Narrative*, 12: 2.

Phelan, James (2007) *Experiencing Fiction: Judgments, Progressions, and the Rhetorical Theory of Narrative*, Columbus: Ohio State University Press.

Phelan, James and Peter J. Rabinowitz (ed.) (2005) *A Companion to Narrative Theory*, Singapore: Blackwell.

Richardson, Brian (ed.) (2002) *Narrative Dynamics. Essays on Time, Plot, Closure and Frames*, Columbus: Ohio State University Press.

Zunshine, Lisa (2006) *Why We Read Fiction. Theory of Mind and the Novel*, Columbus: Ohio State University Press.

5
Character

Lis Møller

An essential aspect of the literary experience is our involvement with fictional characters. Novelistic fiction in particular has supplied us with an abundance of memorable characters—characters we identify with, empathize with, or love to hate. During the act of reading, these fictional characters may seem to us more engaging than our fellow human beings in the "real" world, and when the last page has been turned they linger on in our minds, often outlasting our memory of plot details. Our reluctance to part with certain fictional characters may manifest itself in different ways, the modern phenomenon of *fan fiction* being one of the more extreme. Fan fiction is written by readers who expand on the lives of their favorite characters. However, professional writers may join in, too. In *Death Comes to Pemberley* (2011), the British writer of crime fiction P. D. James resurrects the characters of Jane Austen's *Pride and Prejudice* (1813), and in so doing transfers them from one genre (the novel of manners) to another (the murder mystery). Other writers have been compelled to revive characters of their own creation. Sherlock Holmes fell into the abyss of the Reichenbach Falls in a final struggle with his mortal enemy, Professor Moriarty. But Conan Doyle had to give in to the pressure of his readers and fetch his hero out of the abyss: it was not just more detective stories from Doyle's pen that the readers craved, but stories featuring *this* particular sleuth. Today, Sherlock Holmes has his own museum—at the fictitious address 221B Baker Street—and a recent survey has shown that more than 50 percent of British youngsters believe Sherlock Holmes to be a historical figure (only 80 percent thought the same thing about Winston Churchill). One should of course lament this lack of basic historical knowledge, but the survey also underscores the sway that fictional characters hold over our minds.

Character in literary theory

While general readers have never stopped caring about fictional characters, literary critics and theorists have thought differently. In the words of Baruch Hochman, character "has not fared well" in twentieth-century literary theory (Hochman 1985, 13). Like the idea of unitary selfhood, "character" was dismissed as an anachronism and "as much an ideological construct as other basic concepts of Western 'logocentrism'" (Hillis Miller 1992, 31). Generations of students have been taught that character analysis—in particular the sort of character analysis that deals with fictional characters as if they were real people—is, at best, a naively mimetic undertaking. According to Aristotle, who subordinates character to plot in his *Poetics*, structuralist narratology reduced fictional characters to surface manifestations of deep structure actants serving functional roles. Drawing on Russian formalist Vladimir Propp's seminal study on the *Morphology of the Folk Tale* ([1928] 1977), the French-Algerian structuralist A. J. Greimas ([1966] 1983) identified six actants organized in three binary pairs: subject/object; sender/receiver; helper/opponent. Poststructuralism and deconstruction turned against the static models of structuralism and its propensity for binary oppositions, but shared its suspicion of character. As pointed out by J. Hillis Miller, character is an illusion, a "phantasmal effect of the displacements and exchanges of language," and critics who adopt a mimetic approach to the study of fictional characters are a party to realistic fiction's "mystification" (1992, 33, 30).

But lately, the tide has turned, and character has once again become a legitimate object of critical and theoretical interest. In 2011, the esteemed journal *New Literary History* devoted an entire issue to character. Commenting on "the sudden revitalization" in the last decade of "a once moribund field," editor Rita Felski points to "the impact of cognitive science on the humanities" that has "triggered a new wave of interdisciplinary scholarship" (2011, v). Drawing on recent developments in cognitive science, works by Ralf Schneider (2001), Lisa Zunshine (2003), Suzanne Keen (2006), Blakey Vermeule (2010), and others have challenged the structuralist and poststructuralist doctrine that characters have nothing to do with people. As Vermeule aptly observes, no level of theoretical sophistication has so far succeeded in weaning readers from reacting to fictional characters as if they were real people. Rather than censuring readers' involvement with fictional characters, literary study should address that question which is also the title of Vermeule's book: *Why Do We Care About Literary Characters?* Why do we empathize with people whom we know to exist only in a book? In cognitive psychology *mind reading* (also known as the *Theory of Mind* [ToM]) denotes our ability to see bodies as animated by consciousness and to explain "people's behavior in terms of their thoughts, feelings, beliefs, and desires" (Zunshine 2003, 271; see also Keen 2006, 207; Vermeule 2010, 35ff). Research has demonstrated that our understanding of, and emotional involvement in, fictional characters presupposes a capacity for mind reading: people with autism who lack the ability to read others' minds to varying degrees show no interest in fiction and storytelling (Simon Baron-Cohn in Zunshine 2003, 272f.). But empirical studies have also suggested that the reading of characters in literary fiction may stimulate and improve people's ToM—and recently cognitive psychologists Jessica Black and Jennifer L. Barnes have shown that the viewing of fictional characters in film narratives has a similar effect (Black and Barnes 2015). From a cognitive perspective, then, fictional characters present us with a unique opportunity to rehearse and enhance our mind-reading capacity—and, consequently, to sharpen our ability to understand others' minds.

As cognitive studies of characters in literary fiction focus on readers' interaction with characters, they may intersect with reader-response theory and criticism. Ralf Schneider proposes to "conceive of literary character as a mental model that the reader construes in the reading process through a combination of information from textual and mental sources" (Schneider 2001, 608). Alan Palmer (2002; 2004) combines reader-response theory, cognitive approaches, and so-called postclassical narratology (i.e., developments in narratology after structuralism) in his study of the constructions of the minds of fictional characters. And Keen has called for a "revival of reader-response studies" in order to examine the shaping influence of actual readers (including actual readers' gender and class) on characters (Keen 2011, 295). Finally, the works of James Phelan deserve to be mentioned. Since the 1980s—well before the cognitive turn—Phelan has written extensively on fictional characters and narrator-characters, that is, narrators who are also characters, adopting a rhetorical approach to character as an integral part of narrative progression (Phelan 1989, 2005).

Taxonomies of character

In *Aspects of the Novel* (1927), the British author and critic E. M. Forster famously distinguished between *round* and *flat* characters. Round characters are like real people in the sense that they are complex and capable of developing, whereas flat characters are types or caricatures, that is, they are static and (in their purest form) "constructed round a single idea or quality" (Forster 2005, 35). Round characters surprise us in a convincing way; characters who never surprise are flat; and those who fail to convince us are flats pretending to be round (41). But surely there is more to be said about fictional characters. Hochman has proposed a sequence of eight binary oppositions that describe aspects of literary characters:

Stylization	Naturalism
Coherence	Incoherence
Wholeness	Fragmentariness
Literalness	Symbolism
Complexity	Simplicity
Transparency	Opacity
Dynamism	Staticism
Closure	Openness

(Hochman 1985, 89)

Each of these pairs defines extreme ends of a scale on which fictional characters can be placed, that is, a character can incline to a greater or lesser extent toward one of the two extremes. Hochman's sequence of categories permits the nuanced analysis of individual characters, but his taxonomy mixes categories that apply only to fictional characters with categories that apply to real people as well: a real person can also be said to be more or less complex or transparent, but only fictional characters may be stylized or symbolic. A rather different—and, in my opinion, more adequate— taxonomy has been suggested by Phelan (1989), who proposes to view fictional character as composed of three components: the *mimetic*, the *thematic*, and the *synthetic* (the synthetic refers to the fictional character as construct and artifice). At least in principle all three components are present in all characters, but the mimetic and thematic components may be more or less developed and the synthetic more or less foregrounded (Phelan 1989, 3).

In the following I propose to apply Phelan's taxonomy, but to replace "synthetic" with *functional*, that is, I suggest that we refer to the mimetic, thematic, and functional components of the fictional character. Characters are mimetic to the extent that they are like real people, or rather like possible people. As readers we relate to the mimetic component of character when we apply our mind-reading abilities in order to ponder characters' motives and give reasons for their actions, or when we empathize with them. The mimetic component is at stake when we ask ourselves whether a character is "plausible," that is, whether we believe that a person with *those* qualities and *that* background could act in just *that* way in *that* particular situation. All fictional characters (even the non-human) are mimetic, but to a greater or lesser degree, and some barely at all. Characters in allegory, for instance—characters who go by names such as Do-well, Do-better, and Do-best (William Langland, *Piers Plowman* [c. 1370–

1390])—are embodiments of a particular quality or idea rather than possible people. In these characters the thematic component is dominant and the mimetic merely a thin varnish. The thematic component concerns the representative dimension of character, the degree to which characters represent a certain type, figure, quality, or idea. In reading the thematic component of character, our everyday psychology and mind-reading skills are of little avail: knowledge of literature, mythology, symbolism, cultural codes, and generic conventions is more relevant. Forster's "flat" characters are predominately thematic, as are characters tending toward stylization and symbolism according to Hochman's taxonomy. Characters with pronounced mimetic traits do not necessarily have a less developed thematic component. Hedda Gabler in Henrik Ibsen's play *Hedda Gabler* (1891) is a highly complex, though not very likeable, possible person. But with her anachronistic ideal of "vine leaves in the hair" she is also a modern descendant of Diana, Roman goddess of the hunt and the moon, who has replaced Diana's attributes, the bow and the quiver, with her general father's pistols (Møller 2006). Finally, all characters have a functional component, that is, they are cogs in the machinery of the fictional text, agents that propel the plot. Some subordinate characters are primarily functional—they are merely "there" to perform a particular (and perhaps crucial) action—for instance, the sentry who reports to Creon that Antigone has defied his orders and buried her brother (Sophocles's *Antigone* [c. 441 BC]).

Mimetic, thematic, and functional character in *Atonement*

In Ian McEwan's novel *Atonement* (2001), two young people meet on a hot summer morning in 1935 by a fountain in the garden of a country estate. Cecilia Tallis, the oldest daughter of the house, and Robbie Turner, the gifted son of the Tallises' charlady, have recently graduated from Cambridge, he with a first and she with a disappointing third, and both feel that their lives are on hold. Having wavered between different options, Robbie has finally made up his mind to proceed to medical college; Cecilia's father has promised to support him financially, just as he has funded his Cambridge degree. Cecilia is still undecided as to her future. She is restless and knows full well that she ought to leave home, yet she lingers for reasons unknown to herself. On this particular day the Tallises are expecting Cecilia's older brother, who will bring a guest, a university friend, and on paper a suitable match for Cecilia. A bunch of flowers must be brought to the guest room, and it has occurred to Cecilia to fill the vase—an expensive family heirloom of great sentimental value— at the fountain in the garden where Robbie is working. Cecilia and Robbie grew up together and have been childhood friends, but now the spontaneity is gone and their meeting by the fountain is strained and awkward. Conversation flags, and as he grabs the vase, trying to help her fill it, things go completely wrong. The precious vase breaks, and pieces sink into the basin:

> He looked into the water, then he looked at back at her, and simply shook his head as he raised a hand to cover his mouth. By this gesture he assumed full responsibility, but at that moment, she hated him for the inadequacy of the response. He glanced toward the basin and sighed. [...] [H]e began to unbutton his shirt. Immediately she knew what he was about. Intolerable. He had come to the house and removed his shoes and socks—well, she would show him then. She kicked off her sandals, unbuttoned her blouse and removed it, unfastened her skirt and stepped out of it and went to the basin wall. He stood with hands on his hips and stared as she climbed into the water in her underwear. Denying his help, any possibility of making amends, was his punishment. The unexpectedly freezing water that caused her to gasp was his punishment. She held her breath, and sank, leaving her hair fanned out across the surface. Drowning herself would be his punishment. (McEwan 2002 [2001], 30)

The scene ends with Cecilia, sopping wet, marching back into the house with the broken vase while Robbie stands dumbfounded by the fountain.

Our primary concern as readers of this passage is probably with the *mimetic* component of the two characters. We respond to Cecilia and Robbie as possible people, bringing our real-life experience of human nature into play and adjusting it to information in the text on the actions, thoughts, and feelings of the characters in question. Important information is provided by a character's social context, in particular his or her interaction with and relation to other characters in the text. Cecilia dives into the fountain in order to challenge Robbie ("well, she would show him then") and to punish him, but why, and for what? Both Cecilia and Robert are Cambridge graduates and thus equals, but they belong to different social classes. The son of a charlady and supported financially by Cecilia's father, Robbie is (by British 1935 standards) socially inferior to upper-class Cecilia. Robbie's decision to spend his summer vacation working on the Tallis estate is (or so it seems to Cecilia) a way of taking on this inferior position and emphasizing class barriers. But Cecilia suspects that Robbie is merely acting the part of the humble servant—and that he is deliberately overacting in order to taunt her for her privileges, for instance, by taking off his shoes and socks before entering the "big house." When Robbie begins to unbutton his shirt in order to dive into the fountain and fetch the broken pieces, she sees it as yet another gesture of assumed servility designed to humiliate her. Thus Cecilia is engaged in a complicated mind reading of Robbie: *she* thinks that *he* intends that *she* shall feel... etc. Their conversation leading up to the vase incident has been about literature, a seemingly innocent topic. Cecilia has declared that she much prefers Fielding to Richardson's *Clarissa*, a remark which she instantly regrets: "He might be thinking she was talking to him in code, suggestively conveying her taste for the full-blooded and sensual. That was a mistake, of course, and she was discomfited and had no idea how to put him right" (25). *She* fears that *he* shall think that *she* intended to send an erotically inviting signal that *he* should respond to. Even when a character is lost in his or her private thoughts, these thoughts are socially situated, constituting an extension of the character's interaction with other characters. The mind is *dialogic*, to borrow Mikhail Bakhtin's term (Bakhtin 1996). We relate to Cecilia's dialogic mind as we seek to understand her motives, and we will probably suspect what Cecilia herself has not yet realized: that she is in love with Robbie.

When Cecilia takes off her clothes and dives into the fountain, she displays a hitherto unseen aspect of her personality. Her spontaneous stripping is thus a mimetic feature: it tells us something about her as a possible person and makes her a more "round" character capable of surprising us. But undressing is also an *act* and as such it is part of this character's *functional* component. As anyone who has read McEwan's novel would know, this act will start a veritable chain reaction; in fact it will set the plot going. Within the space of the next twenty-four hours Robbie and Cecilia will make passionate declarations of love—and they will be brutally torn apart when Robbie is arrested and charged with a rape which he did not commit. None of this would have happened if Cecilia had not taken off her clothes. *Atonement* is about the false accusation of rape as a crime against Robbie and Cecilia and about the (im)possibility of atoning for this crime. But McEwan's novel is also about love. Reading the two characters, Robbie and Cecilia, we do not merely relate to them as possible people demanding our empathy, but also perceive them as representatives of a literary theme, that is, as *thematic* characters. We recognize the young couple from literature as well as from "life." The entire scene by the fountain deliberately bears the stamp of romantic cliché—Rich Girl Meets Poor Boy—just as the motif of the broken vase is a recurrent sexual symbol in art and literature (see Brooks 1993, 158f.). The fact that Cecilia's thirteen-year-old sister Briony has just completed a romantic melodrama about "spontaneous Arabella" eloping with a poor young doctor (who turns out to be a prince) throws the cliché into relief.

Inner life

What Cecilia and Robbie do not know is that the incident by the fountain is being watched by a third party. From her window (where she can see, but not hear what is going on in the garden), Briony witnesses a scene which she—an imaginative child teetering on the brink of adolescence—understands better than the couple in the garden *and* gets completely wrong. Briony's first instinct is that Robbie is about to propose to her sister. This interpretation is in a way quite correct: the scene is about an erotic attraction which the couple by the fountain have not yet acknowledged. But Cecilia's stripping is an unexpected turn, which does not fit into the framework of romance. Briony's perception of Robbie as a fairy-tale hero boldly asking the princess's hand in marriage collapses, and instead she construes him as the villain of the piece:

> Robbie imperiously raised his hand now, as though issuing a command which Cecilia dared not disobey. It was extraordinary that she was unable to resist him. At his insistence she was removing her clothes, and at such a speed. She was out of her blouse, now she had let her skirt drop to the ground and was stepping out of it, while he looked on impatiently, hands on hips. What strange power did he have over her. Blackmail? Threats? (38)

In real life we are left to read the minds of other people by way of their actions and utterances, the tone of their voices, their gestures and facial expressions, their interaction with other people, etc. In short, we are in the same boat as Robbie, Cecilia and Briony in their storyworld, and we run a similar risk of getting it wrong—perhaps with grave consequences for everyone. In McEwan's novel Briony's misconception of the scene by the fountain is the first link in a chain of erroneous deductions that leads her to falsely accuse Robbie of rape.

However, Briony is not just a child who has not yet quite grasped the mysteries of adult sexuality. She is also an aspiring writer of fiction, and to the young author the scene by the fountain is something of a revelation:

> As she stood in the nursery waiting for her cousins' return she sensed that she could write a scene like the one by the fountain and she could include a hidden observer like herself. [...] She could write the scene three times over, from three points of view [...]. There did not have to be a moral. She need only show separate minds, as alive as her own, struggling with the idea that other minds were equally alive. [...] [O]nly in a story could you enter these different minds and show how they had an equal value. That was the only moral a story need have. (40)

Only fictional narratives provide what real life denies us: immediate access to the minds of others, insight into their thoughts and feelings, and the possibility of perceiving the world as seen through their eyes. Literary fiction, then, gives us the experience of crossing a boundary which in real life remains a relentless barrier: the boundary between self and other. It is not least this possibility of entering different minds that provokes our emotional involvement with fictional characters and makes us think of them as "real people." A paradox begins to emerge: the mimetic component of character is largely due to an artifice which according to Dorrit Cohn is a distinguishing feature of fiction. As Cohn points out, it is by its potential for presenting the inner life of characters that fictional narrative "most radically severs its connections with the real life outside the text" and differentiates itself from non-fictional narrative discourse (Cohn 1999, 16).

As a literary construct character is bound up with the narrative situation, so the study of character is closely related to narratology. Cohn in particular has studied from a narratological perspective the techniques employed by fictional narrative for portraying the inner life of characters. In her seminal study *Transparent Minds: Narrative Modes for Presenting Consciousness in Fiction* (1978), she classifies different techniques available to homodiegetic and heterodiegetic narration. Whereas the homodiegetic (first-person) narrator in principle has only access to his or her own mind, the heterodiegetic (third-person) narrative situation allows for a wider spectrum of possibilities typologized by Cohn as *Psycho-Narration, Quoted Monologue,* and *Narrated Monologue.* Psycho-narration is the narrator's presentation of the inner life of a character. The voice of the narrator is clearly distinguished from the thoughts and mind-set of the character in question, making psycho-narration the technique that involves more distance between narrator and character than the other two techniques. The strength of psycho-narration is that it can present those feelings and intimations which the character is unable to put into words. Quoted (inner) monologue is the narrator's quotation (with or without quotation marks) of a character's thoughts—as in *stream of consciousness.* Finally, narrated (inner) monologue hovers between psycho-narration and quoted monologue. Coinciding with *free indirect discourse,* narrated monologue presents the thoughts of a character in the character's own idiom, but using the grammar and syntax of the narrator (third person and usually past tense). Narrated monologue is a recurrent device in the passages from *Atonement* cited above, for instance: "Immediately she knew what he was about. Intolerable. He had come to the house and removed his shoes and socks—well, she would show him then" (30). As Cohn has observed, an utterance such as "well, she would show him then" (Cecilia's words, but narrator's syntax) is literally an unheard-of departure from standard grammatical norms (Cohn 1999, 24). One would never hear it spoken in real life. Narrated monologue, then, is the most "literary" and artificial of the three forms; yet as readers we do not experience it as "unnatural." On the contrary, narrated monologue gives us a sense of immediacy, which we readily embrace. Furthermore, narrated monologue allows for a seamless transition into psycho-narration. In the passages quoted above, the inner life of Briony is presented in a mixture of narrated monologue and psycho-narration. The narrator not only provides us with a direct access to Briony's melodramatic imagination and vocabulary ("Blackmail? Threats?" [38]), but also puts into words what thirteen-year-old Briony only dimly senses.

Character and ethics

As most fiction readers would agree, the experience of entering characters' minds is highly addictive, but does the presentation of inner life have an ethical perspective as well—as Briony vaguely suspects? The relationship between ethics and character is certainly well established: the word "ethics" is affiliated with "ethos," meaning character or personality. In classical rhetoric, ethos is one of three forms of appeal. To appeal by means of one's ethos implies that the speaker seeks to win the audience over by appealing to his or her character, say, to his or her personal integrity. Ethos is a key concept in Wayne C. Booth's book *The Company We Keep*, which carries the subtitle: *An Ethics of Fiction* (1988). Booth's topic is not just the ethos of fictional characters, but also (and foremost) the readers' ethos. His argument is that the imaginary company one keeps does indeed influence the ethos that one develops. In the past (that is, before the twentieth century), it was taken for granted that fiction could corrupt as well as improve readers' morality and that characters could be classified as good or bad role models. Literary history boasts famous examples of characters who have got themselves into bad imaginary company: Miguel de Cervantes's Don Quixote, for one—and Gustave Flaubert's Emma Bovary, who was denounced herself by contemporary critics as bad company. Booth's intention is certainly not to revive this kind of moralistic criticism. Nevertheless, he believes that the fictional characters that readers encounter somehow influence the ethos that we form.

But the question of the relationship between character and ethics could also be rephrased: Does the unique possibility offered by narrative fiction—the possibility of accessing characters' inner life—*per se* present an ethical perspective in the sense that it promotes the conception of the other as animated by a consciousness like one's own? If this is the case, ethics is not just about the personality (ethos) of fictional characters, but about ways in which characters are narrated. This in fact is Briony's intuition as she reflects on the scene by the fountain. She does not need to cast her characters as heroes or villains or supply a moral, because to "show separate minds, as alive as her own" would do the trick: "only in a story could you enter these different minds and show how they had an equal value. That was the only moral a story need have" (40). What Briony has discovered are the techniques of internal focalization ("points of view," 40) and narrated monologue. Some years later, eighteen-year-old Briony takes the step into twentieth-century modernism when she, inspired by Virginia Woolf, writes a short story based on the scene by the fountain and rejects the characterization of the nineteenth-century novel in favor of modernist stream of consciousness. But Briony is herself a character in a novel which owes a great deal to nineteenth-century psychological realism. Or so it seems. In the fourth and final part of McEwan's novel, Briony is revealed to be the author of the three previous parts. *Atonement* thus changes into a postmodern meta-novel, a novel about the novel which Briony has written in order to atone for her crime against Cecilia and Robbie. And Cecilia and Robbie? As readers we must face the fact that the two young people who have demanded our undivided sympathy are, as it were, fictions of the second degree: their thoughts, feelings, and perceptions have largely been imaginary constructions created by another fictional character.

Does the postmodern ending of McEwan's novel pull the carpet from under character as a novelistic device? Yes and no. The novel-in-the-novel brings into focus the relationship between fiction and reality and reminds us that access to inner life other than our own is *always* an illusion. As soon as the historian begins to initiate us into Napoleon's thoughts before the battle of Waterloo, he or she has stepped into the realm of fiction. But this implies that *only* narrative fiction can give us the experience of entering other people's minds. Literary fiction can teach us to imagine other people as animated by a mind "as alive as [our] own" (40). *Atonement* is about this unique power of literary fiction. If ethics (as McEwan has suggested elsewhere [Finney 2004, 80]) has to do with the ability to put oneself in the other's place, then literary fiction is *always* ethical, no matter how immoral it may be.

Further reading

W. J. Harvey's *Character and the Novel* is from 1965, but provides a wealth of literary examples and is still worth reading. As an antidote to Harvey's humanistic approach to character, one might read Thomas Docherty's *Reading (Absent) Character* (1983). Docherty's book addresses (the deconstruction of) character in French *nouveau roman* and postmodern fiction. For in-depth analyses of particular characters, see *Bloom's Major Literary Characters,* a series of anthologies edited by Harold Bloom. The series includes volumes on characters as diverse as Huck Finn (2004) and Satan (2005), and has prefaces by Bloom on character and the analysis of character. Among the works mentioned in this chapter I particularly recommend Hochman (1985), Phelan (1989), and Cohn (1978). For recent developments in cognitive approaches to character, see the special issue of *New Literary History* on character (number 42, 2011).

References

Bakhtin, Mikhail M. (1996 [1981]) *The Dialogic Imagination.* Ed. Michael Holquist, Austin: University of Texas Press.

Black, Jessica and Jennifer L. Barnes (2015) "Fiction and Social Cognition: The Effect of Viewing Award-Winning Television Dramas on Theory of Mind," *Psychology of Aesthetics, Creativity, and the Arts,* 9 (4): 423–9.

Bloom, Harold (ed.) (2004) *Huck Finn,* Philadelphia: Chelsea House.

Bloom, Harold (ed.) (2005) *Satan,* Philadelphia: Chelsea House.

Booth, Wayne C. (1988) *The Company We Keep. An Ethics of Fiction,* Berkeley: University of California Press.

Brooks, Peter (1993) *Body Work. Objects of Desire in Modern Narrative*, Cambridge, MA: Harvard University Press.

Cohn, Dorrit (1978) *Transparent Minds. Narrative Modes for Presenting Consciousness in Fiction*, Princeton, NJ: Princeton University Press.

Cohn, Dorrit (1999) *The Distinction of Fiction*, Baltimore: Johns Hopkins University Press.

Docherty, Thomas (1983) *Reading (Absent) Character. Towards a Theory of Characterization in Fiction*, Oxford: Clarendon.

Felski, Rita (2011) "Introduction," *New Literary History*, 42: v–ix.

Finney, Brian (2004) "Briony's Stand Against Oblivion: The Making of Fiction in Ian McEwan's Atonement," *Journal of Modern Literature*, 27 (3): 68–82.

Forster, E. M. (2005) "Flat and Round Characters," in Michael J. Hoffman and Patrick D. Murphy (eds), *Essentials of the Theory of Fiction*, 35–41, Durham and London: Duke University Press.

Greimas, Algirdas Julien (1983) *Structural Semantics. An Attempt at a Method*. Trans. Daniele McDowell, Ronald Schleifer, and Alan Velie. Lincoln, Nebraska: University of Nebraska Press.

Harvey's, W. J. (1965) *Character and the Novel*, New Haven: Yale University Press.

Hochman, Baruch. 1985. *Character in Literature*. Itacha and London: Cornell University Press.

Keen, Suzanne (2006) "A Theory of Narrative Empathy," *Narrative*, 14 (3): 207–36.

Keen, Suzanne (2011) "Reader's Temperaments and Fictional Character," *New Literary History*, 42 (2): 295–314.

McEwan, Ian (2002 [2001]) *Atonement*, London: Vintage.

Miller, J. Hillis (1992) *Ariadne's Thread. Story Lines*, New Haven and London: Yale University Press.

Møller, Lis (2006) "Artemiskomplekset. *Hedda Gabler* læst med Brandes," in Astrid Søther et al. (eds), *Ibsen og Brandes. Studier i et forhold*, 240–62, Oslo: Gyldendal.

Palmer, Alan (2002) "The Construction of Fictional Minds," *Narrative*, 10 (1): 28–46.

Palmer, Alan (2004) *Fictional Minds*, Lincoln and London: University of Nebraska Press.

Phelan, James (1989) *Living to Tell About It. A Rhetoric and Ethics of Character Narration*. Itacha and London: Cornell University Press.

Phelan, James (2005) "Narrative Judgments and the Rhetorical Theory of Narrative: Ian McEwan's Atonement," in James Phelan and Peter Rabinowitz (eds), *A Companion to Narrative Theory*, 322–36, Malden, MA: Blackwell Publishing.

Propp, Vladimir (1977) *Morphology of the Folk Tale*, Austin: University of Texas Press.

Schneider, Ralf (2001) "Toward a Cognitive Theory of Literary Character: The Dynamics of Mental-Model Construction," *Style*, 35 (4): 607–40.

Vermeule, Blakey (2010) *Why Do We Care About Literary Characters?* Baltimore: Johns Hopkins University Press.

Zunshine, Lisa (2003) "Theory of Mind and Experimental Representations of Fictional Consciousness," *Narrative*, 11 (3): 270–91.

6

The Narrator

Jan Alber

This chapter provides an overview of the most important ways of classifying narrators. In addition, it illustrates these taxonomies by means of examples. According to James Phelan and Wayne C. Booth, "the narrator is the agent or, in less anthropomorphic terms, the agency or 'instance' that tells or transmits everything—the existents, states, and events—in a narrative to a narrate" (Booth 2005, 388). While readers typically assume the existence of a mediating narrator in prose narratives (novels and short stories) and narrative poetry, the concept does not easily translate to other narrative media or genres (such as drama or film).

Traditional typologies of narrators in prose fiction

In *A Theory of Narrative* (1984), Franz K. Stanzel presents his three prototypical narrative situations, and he sees them as descriptions of basic possibilities of rendering what he calls the "mediacy" of narration. Stanzel proceeds from three pairs of oppositions arranged as scaled categories of *person*, *perspective*, and *mode*. Person, the first element of the narrative situation, is based on the relationship between the narrator and the characters, and it ranges from identity (first-person reference) to non-identity (third-person reference) of the realms of existence of the narrator and the characters. Perspective concerns the way in which the fictional world is perceived, extending from *internal* to *external*. The internal perspective involves a limited perception and is located inside the main character or at the center of the events; the external perspective, on the other hand, implies omniscience—including "unlimited insight into the thoughts and feelings of the characters" (Stanzel 1984, 126). Mode, finally, breaks down into the overt mediacy of narration in the teller mode and the covert mediacy which produces the illusion of immediacy in the reflector mode.

The first-person narrative situation combines a character-narrator with the internal perspective and the teller mode. In Dickens's *Great Expectations* (1860–1861), for instance, Pip serves as the first-person narrator and we are limited to his perception of the world. More specifically, the older Pip (the narrating I) tells us what happened to him when he was younger (the experiencing I). Also, Pip is a narrator who actively mediates and comments on the story:

> My first most vivid and broad impression of the identity of things seems to me to have been gained on a memorable raw afternoon towards evening. At such a time I found out for certain that this bleak place overgrown with nettles was the churchyard; and that Philip Pirrip, late of this parish, and also Georgiana wife of the above, were dead and buried; and that Alexander, Bartholomew, Abraham, Tobias, and Roger, infant children of the aforesaid, were also dead and buried; and that the dark flat wilderness beyond the churchyard, intersected with dikes and mounds and gates, with scattered cattle feeding on it, was the marshes; and that the low leaden line beyond was the river; and that the distant savage lair from which the wind was rushing was the sea; and that the small bundle of shivers growing afraid of it all and beginning to cry, was Pip. (Dickens 1996, 23–4)

The authorial narrative situation, on the other hand, features a third-person narrator as well as the external perspective and the teller mode. Fielding's *Tom Jones* (1749), for example, is narrated by an omniscient narrator who has an Olympian view on the storyworld (including access to the thoughts and feelings of the characters). Furthermore, the third-person narrator frequently intrudes and comments on the narrative. In the following passage, he describes the character of Allworthy in great detail. Later on, he tells us that Tom Jones thinks of his beloved Sophia before having sexual intercourse with Molly Seagrim:

> In that part of the western division of this kingdom which is commonly called Somersetshire, there lately lived, and perhaps lives still, a gentleman whose name was Allworthy, and who might well be called the favourite of both nature and fortune; for both of these seem to have contended which should bless and enrich him most. In this contention, nature may seem to some to have come off victorious, as she bestowed on

him many gifts, while fortune had only one gift in her power; but in pouring forth this, she was so very profuse, that others perhaps may think this single endowment to have been more than equivalent to all the various blessings which he enjoyed from nature. From the former of these, he derived an agreeable person, a sound constitution, a solid understanding, and a benevolent heart; by the latter, he was decreed to the inheritance of one of the largest estates in the county. [...] In this scene, so sweetly accommodated to love, he [Tom Jones, J. A.] meditated on his dear Sophia. While his wanton fancy roved unbounded over all her beauties, and his lively imagination painted the charming maid in various ravishing forms, his warm heart melted with tenderness; and at length, throwing himself on the ground, by the side of a gently murmuring brook, he broke forth into the following ejaculation [...]. (Fielding 1974, 210)

The figural narrative situation, finally, combines a (barely perceptible) third-person narrator with the internal perspective, while the narrative is dominated by one or several reflectors, that is, characters that think, feel, and perceive but do not mediate the story like a teller figure. The following passage from Woolf's *Mrs. Dalloway* (1925), for instance, is narrated by a covert third-person narrator, while the passage is dominated by the thoughts and sense impressions of Septimus Warren Smith, a shell-shocked First World War veteran who suffers from hallucinations:

Men must not cut down trees. There is a God. (He noted such revelations on the backs of envelopes.) Change the world. No one kills from hatred. Make it known (he wrote it down). He waited. He listened. A sparrow perched on the railing opposite chirped Septimus, Septimus, four or five times over and went on, drawing its notes out, to sing freshly and piercingly in Greek words how there is no crime and, joined by another sparrow, they sang in voices prolonged and piercing in Greek words, from trees in the meadow of life beyond a river where the dead walk, how there is no death. There was his hand; there the dead. White things were assembling behind the railings opposite. But he dared not look. Evans was behind the railings! "What are you saying?" said Rezia suddenly, sitting down by him. Interrupted again! She was always interrupting. (Woolf 2000, 21)

In contrast to Stanzel's three prototypical narrative situations, Gérard Genette's taxonomy is based on the cross-tabulation of heterodiegetic and homodiegetic forms of narration and three types of focalization (1988, 121; see also 1980, 189–94; 245). Homodiegetic narrators exist within the same ("homo") fictional realm ("diegesis") as the characters do, while heterodiegetic narrators exist in a different ("hetero") fictional world ("diegesis"). Focalization, on the other hand, concerns the restriction of the information provided by the narrator. In cases of *internal* focalization, the narrative focuses on thoughts and feelings; in cases of *external* focalization, the narrative restricts itself to behavior, action, and settings; and in cases of *zero* focalization (which Genette equates with "omniscience" [1980, 189]), there is no restriction of the information that is provided (however, since every narrative implies some kind of restriction, such a scenario is strictly speaking impossible).

For Genette, this taxonomy is an improvement on Stanzel's because it does not only focus on prototypical forms of narrative, but it also includes less common narrative forms. Beckett's *Malone Dies* (1951), for instance, features homodiegetic narration with internal focalization. The first-person narrator focuses exclusively on his suffering and he excludes external happenings:

> I shall soon be quite dead at last in spite of all. Perhaps next month. Then it will be the month of April or of May. For the year is still young, a thousand little signs tell me so. [...] I could die to-day, if I wished, merely by making a little effort, if I could wish, if I could make an effort. But it is just as well to let myself die, quietly, without rushing things. Something must have changed. I will not weigh upon the balance any more, one way or the other. I shall be neutral and inert. (Beckett 1959, 179)

Furthermore, Hemingway's "The Killers" (1927) combines heterodiegetic narration with external focalization (the neutral subtype in Stanzel [1955, 93]). The third-person narrator concentrates on external processes; he does not tell us what the characters think or feel:

> The door of Henry's lunchroom opened and two men came in. They sat down at the counter. "What's yours?" George asked them. "I don't know," one of the men said. "What do you want to eat, Al?" "I don't know," said Al. "I don't know what I want to eat." Outside it was getting dark. The street-light came on outside the window. The two men at the counter read the menu. From the other end of the counter Nick Adams watched them. He had been talking to George when they came in. (Hemingway 1973, 45)

Such cases of third-person neutral narrative have also been termed "camera-eye narration" because we observe scenarios of things evolving as if by themselves, in a direct, unmediated way (Stanzel 1984, 294–9; Genette 1988, 120–1).

Moreover, Genette argues that Camus's *L'Étranger* (1942) features homodiegetic narration with external focalization. In the following passage, Meursault, the first-person narrator, tells us in a rather detached manner how he killed another person:

> Tout mon être s'est tendu et j'ai crispé ma mains sur le revolver. La gâchette a cédé, j'ai touché le ventre poli de la crosse et c'est là, dans le bruit à la fois sec et assourdissant que tout a commencé. J'ai secoué la sueur et le soleil. [...] Alors, j'ai tiré encore quatre fois sur un corps inerte où les balles s'enfonçaient sans qu'il y parût. (Camus 1957, 95)

The most prominent feature of first-person neutral narratives (such as Robbe-Grillet's *La Jalousie* [1957] and Auster's *Moon Palace* [1989]) is the narrator's refusal or inability to inform the readers about her inner life.

Melville's *Moby-Dick; or, the Whale* (1851), finally, combines homodiegetic narration with zero focalization. Henrik Skov Nielsen writes the following about *Moby-Dick*: "After long passages in which internal focalization occurs through Ishmael, the narrative suddenly provides extended access to the thoughts of other characters. This is especially true for chapters 37–39" (2004, 138). The idea of an "omniscient" first-person narrator allows for various different interpretations. From my vantage point, Saleem Sinai, the telepathic first-person narrator of Rushdie's *Midnight's Children* (1981), also qualifies as an example:

> I was a radio receiver, and could turn the volume down or up; I could select individual voices; I could even, by an effort of will, switch off my newly-discovered inner ear. [...] My voices, far from being sacred, turned out to be as profane, and as multitudinous, as dust. Telepathy, then; the kind of thing you're always reading about in the sensational magazines. But I ask for patience—wait. Only wait. It was telepathy; but also more than telepathy. Don't write me off too easily. Telepathy, then: the inner monologues of all the so-called teeming millions, of masses and classes alike, jostled for space within my head. (Rushdie 1981, 162–7)

However, first-person narrators do not usually display the same degree of omniscience that many authorial narrators possess (on the limitations of the latter see Füger 1978). Further examples of homodiegetic narration with zero focalization are discussed by Nielsen (2004) and Heinze (2008).

As far as narrative levels are concerned, Genette argues that "*any event a narrative recounts is at a diegetic level immediately higher than the level at which the narrating act producing this narrative is placed*" (1980, 228; italics in original). He distinguishes between an *extradiegetic* narrator (such as Chaucer, the first-person narrator of *The Canterbury Tales*) who produces a first narrative which constitutes an *intradiegetic* (or *diegetic*) level (such as the story about the pilgrims riding toward Canterbury), in which an (intra)diegetic character (such as the nun's priest) might appear, who, in turn, might become the (intra)diegetic narrator of a *metadiegetic* narrative (such as "The Nun's Priest's Tale") about a metadiegetic character (such as Chauntecleer), who, in turn, might become the metadiegetic narrator of a *meta-metanarrative*, and so forth (1980, 228; 1988, 85). In contrast to Genette, Mieke Bal (1981, 43) states that *hypo-* (from Greek "under") is a more adequate prefix than *meta-* (from Greek "on, between, with") to refer to what are after all subordinate narratives.

Seymour Chatman (1990, 115) discriminates between "overt narrators," who communicate directly to the reader (as in Stanzel's first-person and the authorial narrative situation) and "covert narrators," who remain hidden in the discursive shadows (as in Stanzel's figural narrative situation or cases of external focalization). Interestingly, covert narrators often become more overt during the course of the narrative. In *Mrs. Dalloway*, for instance, the neutral narrator at one point engages in moral commentary so that we can picture her as a human being with ethical principles (Woolf 2000, 84–5). Hemingway's "The Killers" likewise features a passage in which the presence of a human narrator can be felt. At one point, the narrative voice states that "in their tight overcoats and derby hats [Al and Max] looked *like a vaudeville team*" (Hemingway 1973, 52; my italics, J. A.). This comparison has to be made by a human being—a camera is not able to compare two entities to one another.

I would like to mention two extensions of these traditional narrator typologies. Monika Fludernik (1996, 43–4) argues that these classification systems are ultimately derived from "natural" narratives, that is, instances of spontaneous oral storytelling in the actual world. She thus reconceptualizes these taxonomies on the basis of familiar real-world cognitive frames such as telling (which plays a role in the authorial as well as the first-person narrative situation), viewing (which is relevant in cases of external focalization), experiencing (which plays a role in reflector-mode narratives), and reflecting (which is relevant with regard to self-reflexive postmodernist narrators).

Moreover, in contrast to Stanzel, Genette, and Chatman, who argue that every narrative has to have a narrator, Richard Walsh suggests eradicating all third-person narrators. For him, "the narrator is always either a character who narrates, or the author" (2007, 78). Walsh writes that "extradiegetic heterodiegetic narrators [...] who cannot be represented without thereby being rendered homodiegetic or intradiegetic, are in no way distinguishable from authors" (2007, 84). Liesbeth Korthals Altes, on the other hand, feels that Walsh's proposal to replace all third-person narrators with authors is overly hasty. For her, there might be interpretive reasons why a critic wants to posit an authorial narrator or a covert narrative medium (2014, 146). For instance, the authorial narrator of Thackeray's *Vanity Fair* (1848) at one point appears in the world of his characters, and he describes this encounter as follows: "it was at the little comfortable Ducal town of Pumpernickel [...] that I first saw Colonel Dobbin" (Thackeray 2001, 729). It would arguably be odd to say that the actual author here appears in the storyworld.

Unreliable narrators and experimental storytelling scenarios

Narrators are of course not necessarily credible speakers. One of Booth's most significant contributions to narrative theory is the concept of the unreliable narrator. According to Booth, a narrator "is reliable when he or she speaks for or acts in accordance with the norms of the work (which is to say, the implied author's norms), unreliable when he does not" (1983, 158–9). Humbert Humbert, the first-person narrator of Nabokov's *Lolita* (1955), who fabricates a specific version of his pedophile desires for Lolita, is often considered to be unreliable in this sense. Ansgar Nünning provides a list of textual signals of narratorial unreliability. For him, "two of the most prominent of these are internal contradictions within the narrator's discourse and discrepancies between his or her utterances and actions" (1997, 96). One important question in this context is whether unreliability presupposes a first-person speaker or whether cases of unreliable third-person narration exist as well.

James Phelan has refined Booth's concept on the basis of the narrator's three tasks: narrators may be unreliable by misreporting, misinterpreting, and misevaluating, as well as by underreporting, underreading, or underevaluating (Phelan 2005, 51). In the first three cases, the reader has to reject the narrator's version of the story, whereas in the latter three cases, she needs to supplement it. Phelan also distinguishes between estranging and bonding types of unreliability. In the first case, the narrator's unreliability "underlines or increases the distance" between narrator and reader, whereas in the second case, it "reduces the distance" between the two (2007, 222–3).

More experimental narratives play around with the traditional human narrator in a wide variety of ways. Novels such as J. M. Coetzee's *Waiting for the Barbarians* (1980), Bret Easton Ellis's *American Psycho* (1991), and Dennis Cooper's *My Loose Thread* (2001), for instance, confront us with scenarios in which a first-person narrator renders her story in the present tense ("simultaneous narration"). While first-person narratives typically involve the distinction between the narrating I and the experiencing I, the two are fused in cases of simultaneous narration: the narrator narrates exactly while experiencing. Dorrit Cohn describes the "fictional present" as the "narrator's 'impossible' verbal stance," and argues that such narratives have "the advantage of dislocating the narrative text from a temporally fixed point of origin" (1999, 105–6). Some (but not all) forms of simultaneous narration produce impossible sentences. *Waiting for the Barbarians*, for instance, features a passage in which the narrator narrates while sleeping: "Face down, pressed so tightly between the floor and the slats of the bed that when I move my shoulders the bed lifts, I try to compose myself for a day of hiding. I doze and I wake, drifting from one formless dream to another" (Coetzee 1980, 93).

There are also storytelling scenarios (such as those in you-, we-, and they-narratives) which completely transcend the traditional typologies by Stanzel, Genette, and Chatman. In you-narratives, for instance, a covert narrative voice addresses the central protagonist in the second-person singular, and tells this character a story that happened to her (see Bonheim 1983; Fludernik 1994a, b, 2011; Richardson 2006, 17–36; Alber 2016, 84–7). Jay McInerney's *Bright Lights, Big City* (1984), for example, begins as follows:

> You are not the kind of guy who would be at a place like this at this time of the morning. But here you are, and you cannot say that the terrain is entirely unfamiliar, although the details are fuzzy. You are at a nightclub talking to a girl with a shaved head. The club is either Heartbreak or the Lizard Lounge. All might come clear if you could just slip into the bathroom and do a little more Bolivian Marching Powder. Then again, it might not. (McInerney 1984, 1)

You-narratives are unnatural; they only exist in the world of fiction because in non-fictional discourse we cannot tell our addressees in great detail what they experience, think, or feel. Second-person narratives radicalize tendencies inherent in language, and widen the scope of what is possible in the world of fiction by moving beyond standard human limitations. The same is, incidentally, true of Stanzel's authorial and the figural narrative situation (see Alber 2013) as well as Genette's homodiegetic narration with internal focalization (see Nielsen 2004). Like you-narratives, these three constellations involve extensions of real-world possibilities. The major difference between these three cases is that the former two have already been turned into literary conventions we are now familiar with, whereas the third case arguably still strikes readers as being odd, weird, or defamiliarizing.

We-narratives (such as Ayi Kwei Armah's *Two Thousand Seasons* [1973], John Barth's *Sabbatical: A Romance* [1982], or Joan Chase's *During the Reign of the Queen of Persia* [1983]) are narrated in the first-person plural. It is either the case that a narrator speaks for a whole group, or readers are presented with the group's collective narrative (Margolin 1996; 2000; Marcus 2008a, b, c; Fludernik 2011; Alber 2015b; Richardson 2015a). In we-narratives, "multiple agents are subsumed under the heading of shared worldviews, assumptions, intentions, or thought processes. Either the speaker speaks for him- or herself and somebody else or we listen to a collective voice, which consists of several speakers at the same time" (Alber 2015b, 213).

They-narratives (such as Joseph Conrad's *The Nigger of the "Narcissus"* [1899], the first three-quarters of D. H. Lawrence's "Things" [1928], Georges Perec's *Les choses* [1965], and two chapters of Maxine Swann's *Flower Children* [2007]) involve a situation in which a narrator refuses to use the proper names of the characters. One important question in the context of narration in the third-person plural is why the narrator does not refer to the figures individually and instead subsumes them within the roles and functions they perform (see Fludernik 2011; Richardson 2015a; Alber forthcoming).

Genette notes that "in fiction, nothing prevents us from entrusting" the role of the narrative agent "to an animal [...] or indeed to an 'inanimate' object" (1980, 244, n74). Indeed, narrative fiction teems with impossible (or unnatural) narrators that would never be able to speak in the real world (see Richardson 2006, 2015b; Alber 2015a, 2016, 61–103). The narrator can, for example, be a baby without a brain (Jenny Diski's *Like Mother* [1989]), a huge female breast (Philip Roth's *The Breast* [1972]), an animal (Robert Olen Butler's "Jealous Husband Returns in Form of Parrot" [1996]), a tree (Ursula Le Guin's "Direction of the Road" [1975]), a coach (Dorothy Kilner's *The Adventures of a Hackney Coach* [1781]), or even an atom (Tobias Smollett's *The History and Adventures of an Atom* [1769]). In other cases, the narrator has already died (Samuel Beckett's "The Calmative" [1954] and Alice Sebold's *The Lovely Bones* [2002]) or is still unborn (the musing sperm in John Barth's "Night-Sea Journey" [1968]). *The Adventures of a Hackney Coach*, for instance, begins as follows: "This is the most fashionable Coach on the stand, says a pretty young lady, *stepping into me*" (Kilner 1781, 1; my italics, J. A.).

Given this range of different narrators, some narratologists have pointed out that the narrator does not necessarily have to be human or humanlike. Mieke Bal, for example, de-anthropomorphizes the narrator in general and uses the pronoun "it" whenever she refers to the narrative instance. She notes that the term "narrator" refers to "the linguistic subject, a function and not a person, which expresses itself in the language that constitutes the text" (Bal 1997, 16; see also Culler 2004, 30). Similarly, Marie-Laure Ryan writes that readers may sometimes get the impression that the narrative discourse does not spring "from the mind of an individuated, anthropomorphic being and does not express a narratorial personality." She thus reminds us of the fact that "the narrator is a theoretical fiction, and that the human-like, pseudonatural narrator is only one of its many possible avatars" (Ryan 2001, 152).

Narrators in other media

Narrative poems are also narrated by narrators who can be homo- or heterodiegetic, overt or covert, and more or less reliable. The narrator of Wordsworth's *Prelude* (1805), for instance, is homodiegetic, while the narrator of Pope's *The Rape of the Lock* (1712–1717) is heterodiegetic. An unreliable narrator can be found in Browning's dramatic monologue "My Last Duchess" (1842). The situation is slightly more complicated in film. David Bordwell argues that film has narration but no narrator (1985, 61). According to Bordwell, cinematic narration is created by the *viewer*, who uses cognitive schemata to transform the film's images and sounds into a series of perceptible configurations, which she then interprets as a story. In contrast to Bordwell, Chatman states that films are narrated by a *cinematic narrator*. Chatman defines this narrator in terms of "the organizational and sending agency" (1990, 127) behind the film. Theoreticians such as George Wilson (1986, 135) and Berrys Gaut (2004, 248), on the other hand, write that it is *the implied filmmaker* who mediates the film as a whole, guides us through it, and directs our attention to important issues. Booth defines the implied filmmaker as "a creative voice uniting all the choices" (2002, 125), whereas Manfred Jahn radically de-anthropomorphizes this agent and speaks of a "filmic composition device (FCD)," which he defines as "the theoretical agency behind a film's organization and arrangement." The FCD "need not be associated with any concrete person or character, particularly neither the director nor a filmic narrator" (Jahn 2003, F4.1.2–F4.1.3).

Since there can be no discrepancy between the film narrator and the implied filmmaker or FCD (all three are covert arranger functions responsible for the organization or total showing of the film), Jan Alber proposes doing away with the concept of the cinematic narrator (2010, 169). He also follows Jerrold Levinson (1996, 229) who redefines the implied author or filmmaker as a construct created in the recipient's mind on the basis of cues in the narrative. Alber thus argues that films are mediated by what he calls the "hypothetical filmmaker," a term which denotes "the single entity to which the viewer ascribes conscious or unconscious motivations that actuated the professionals who were responsible for the making of the film in question" (2010, 167–8).

The concept of the dramatic narrator is also highly contested. While Stanzel (1984, 65), Genette (1988, 16–17), and Keir Elam argue that drama "is without narratorial mediation" (1980, 119), Manfred Jahn writes that plays "are structurally mediated by a first-degree narrative agency which, in a performance may either take the totally unmetaphorical shape of a vocally and bodily present narrator figure [...] or remain an anonymous and impersonal narrative function in charge of selection, arrangement, and focalization" (2001, 674). Patrick Colm Hogan likewise posits a non-personified narrator as the source of dramatic emplotment (2013, 40–1). According to Ansgar Nünning and Roy Sommer, mimetic narrativity usually prevails in drama: plays represent storyworlds which are populated with characters to whom something happens, and no deictic or expressive markers exist that would warrant the existence of a dramatic narrator. However, there are numerous instances in which plays do actually represent acts of narration and thus display a certain degree of diegetic narrativity. Examples are prologues, epilogues, asides, soliloquies, direct audience address, narrator figures such as the stage manager in Thornton Wilder's *Our Town* (1938) or Henry Carr in Tom Stoppard's *Travesties* (1974), verbal summaries of offstage action, the play within the play, metanarrative commentary, and stage directions (2008, 337–8; 340–1).

But what or who mediates the play as a whole? Monika Fludernik argues that this is done by the performance level of the staging. More specifically, she associates the script and the stage directions with Genette's narrative discourse and the actual performance with the process of narrating (Genette 1980, 27; 1988, 13):

> The selection of scenes, the temporal arrangements and the *mise en scène*, in so far as they are provided in the stage directions, form part of the discourse level, which can then be read off the playscript. By contrast, the visual qualities of the staging, the director's choice of props and costumes, the inclusion of music and of superimposed visual elements as well as the actors' interpretation of the characters and plot are equivalent to the narrational level, and this narrational level is in fact a *performative* level. (Fludernik 2008, 363)

Alternatively, one might argue that the play as a whole is mediated by a "hypothetical author/dramatist"—in analogy with Alber's concept of the hypothetical filmmaker (2010, 167–8).

Further reading

Ultimately, it is of course up to the recipient to decide if her specific reading strategy demands a mediating narrator or not. The most pressing question in this context is whether the concept of the narrator helps us come up with better readings or interpretations. Following Korthals Altes's recent metahermeneutic reconceptualization of narratology (2014), critics are invited to ponder and explicate the reasons why they want (or do not want) to posit a narrator. Most readers still assume the existence of a narrator in the case of prose narratives (for alternative views see Banfield 1982 and Walsh 2007). However, the role of mediacy in drama and film remains open to study: is it in any sense helpful to posit a dramatic or cinematic narrator or should we simply assume that plays and films are mediated by hypothetical authors or filmmakers (see Hühn and Sommer 2014; Kuhn and Schmidt 2014)? Finally, it is also necessary to investigate the question of whether it makes sense to posit a narrator in other media or genres (such as paintings, computer games, dance performances, hypertext narratives, and apps) (see Ryan and Thon 2014).

References

Alber, Jan (2010) "Hypothetical Intentionalism: Cinematic Narration Reconsidered," in Jan Alber and Monika Fludernik (eds), *Postclassical Narratology: Approaches and Analyses*, 163–85, Columbus: Ohio State University Press.

Alber, Jan (2013) "Pre-Postmodernist Manifestations of the Unnatural: Instances of Expanded Consciousness in 'Omniscient' Narration and Reflector-Mode Narratives," *Zeitschrift für Anglistik und Amerikanistik*, 61 (2): 137–53.

Alber, Jan (2015a) "Innovative Eighteenth-Century Fiction: The Case of the Speaking Objects in Circulation Novels," in Rainer Emig and Jana Gohrisch (eds), *Anglistentag 2014 Hannover: Proceedings*, 187–202, Trier: WVT.

Alber, Jan (2015b) "The Social Minds in Factual and Fictional We-Narratives of the Twentieth Century," *Narrative*, 23 (2): 212–25.

Alber, Jan (2016) *Unnatural Narrative: Impossible Worlds in Fictiona and Drama*, Lincoln: University of Nebraska Press.

Alber, Jan (forthcoming) "They-Narratives," in Alison Gibbons and Andrea Macrae (eds), *Pronoun Use in Literature*, London: Palgrave Macmillan.

Bal, Mieke (1981) "Notes on Narrative Embedding," *Poetics Today*, 2 (2): 41–59.

Bal, Mieke (1997) *Narratology: Introduction to the Theory of Narrative* [1985], Toronto: University of Toronto Press.

Banfield, Ann (1982) *Unspeakable Sentences: Narration and Representation in the Language of Fiction*, Boston: Routledge & Kegan Paul.

Beckett, Samuel (1959) *Molloy, Malone Dies, The Unnamable*, London: Calder.

Bonheim, Helmut (1983) "Narration in the Second Person," *Recherches anglaises et americaines*, 16 (1): 69–80.

Booth, Wayne C. (1983) *The Rhetoric of Fiction* [1961], Chicago: University of Chicago Press.

Booth, Wayne C. (2002) "Is There an 'Implied' Author in Every Film?" *College Literature*, 29 (2): 124–31.

Bordwell, David (1985) *Narration in the Fiction Film*, London: Routledge.

Camus, Albert (1957) *L'étranger*, Paris: Minuit.

Chatman, Seymour (1978) *Story and Discourse: Narrative Structure in Fiction and Film*, Ithaca, NY: Cornell University Press.

Chatman, Seymour (1990) *Coming to Terms: The Rhetoric of Narrative in Fiction and Film*, Ithaca, NY: Cornell University Press.

Coetzee, J. M. (1980) *Waiting for the Barbarians*, London: Secker & Warburg.

Cohn, Dorrit (1999) *The Distinction of Fiction*, Baltimore, MD: Johns Hopkins University Press.

Culler, Jonathan (2004) "Omniscience," *Narrative*, 12 (1): 22–34.

Dickens, Charles (1996) *Great Expectations* [1860–61]. Ed. Janice Carlisle, Boston: Bedford Books.

Elam, Keir (1980) *The Semiotics of Theatre and Drama*, London: Methuen.

Fielding, Henry (1974) *The History of Tom Jones: A Foundling* [1749], London: Collins.

Fludernik, Monika (1994a) "Introduction: Second-Person Narrative and Related Issues," *Style*, 28 (3): 281–311.

Fludernik, Monika (1994b) "Second-Person Narrative as a Test Case for Narratology: The Limits of Realism," *Style*, 28 (3): 445–79.

Fludernik, Monika (1996) *Towards a 'Natural' Narratology*, London and New York: Routledge.

Fludernik, Monika (2008) "Narrative and Drama," in John Pier and José Ángel García Landa (eds), *Theorizing Narrativity*, 355–83, Berlin and New York: de Gruyter.

Fludernik, Monika (2011) "The Category of 'Person' in Fiction: *You* and *We* Narrative-Multiplicity and Indeterminacy of Reference," in Greta Olson (ed.), *Current Trends in Narratology*, 101–41, Berlin: De Gruyter.

Füger, Wilhelm (1978), "Das Nichtwissen des Erzählers in Fieldings *Joseph Andrews*. Baustein zu einer Theorie negierten Wissens in der Fiktion," *Poetica*, 10 (2–3): 188–216.

Gaut, Berys (2004), "The Philosophy of the Movies: Cinematic Narration," in Peter Kivy (ed.), *The Blackwell Guide to Aesthetics*, 230–53, Malden, MA: Blackwell.

Genette, Gérard (1980) *Narrative Discourse: An Essay in Method* [1972]. Trans. Jane E. Lewin, Ithaca, NY: Cornell University Press.

Genette, Gérard (1988) *Narrative Discourse Revisited* [1983]. Trans. Jane E. Lewin, Ithaca, NY: Cornell University Press.

Heinze, Rüdiger (2008) "Violations of Mimetic Epistemology in First-Person Narrative Fiction," *Narrative*, 16 (3): 279–97.

Hemingway, Ernest (1973) "The Killers [1927]," in *The Nick Adams Stories*, 45–60, New York: Bantam Books.

Hogan, Patrick Colm (2013) *Narrative Discourse: Authors and Narrators in Literature, Film, and Art*, Columbus: Ohio State University Press.

Hühn, Peter and Roy Sommer (2014) "Narration in Poetry and Drama," in Peter Hühn et al. (eds), *The Handbook of Narratology. Vol. I*, 419–34, Berlin: De Gruyter.

Jahn, Manfred (2001) "Narrative Voice and Agency in Drama: Aspects of a Narratology of Drama," *New Literary History*, 32: 659–79.

Jahn, Manfred (2003) "A Guide to Narratological Film Analysis," January 4, 2016.
    www.uni-koeln.de/~ame02/pppf.htm

Kilner, Dorothy (1781) *The Adventures of a Hackney Coach*, Dublin: C. Jackson and
    P. Byrne.

Korthals Altes, Liesbeth (2014) *Ethos and Narrative Interpretation: The Negotiation of
    Values in Fiction*, Lincoln: University of Nebraska Press.

Kuhn, Markus and Johann G. Schmidt (2014) "Narration in Film," in Peter Hühn et al.
    (eds), *The Handbook of Narratology. Vol. I*, 384–405, Berlin: De Gruyter.

Levinson, Jerold (1996) "Messages in Art," in Jerrold Levinson (ed.), *The Pleasures
    of Aesthetics: Philosophical Essays*, Ithaca and London: Cornell University Press,
    224–41.

Marcus, Amit (2008a) "A Contextual View of Narrative Fiction in the First Person
    Plural," *Narrative*, 16 (1): 46–64.

Marcus, Amit (2008b) "Dialogue and Authoritativeness in 'We' Fictional Narratives:
    A Bakhtinian Approach," *Partial Answers*, 6 (1): 135–61.

Marcus, Amit (2008c) "We Are You: The Plural and the Dual in 'We' Fictional
    Narratives," *Journal of Literary Semantics*, 37 (1): 1–21.

Margolin, Uri (1996) "Telling Our Story: On 'We' Literary Narratives," *Language and
    Literature*, 5 (2): 115–33.

Margolin, Uri (2000) "Telling in the Plural: From Grammar to Ideology," *Poetics Today*,
    21 (3): 591–618.

McInerney, Jay (1984) *Bright Lights, Big City*, New York: Vintage.

Nielsen, Henrik Skov (2004) "The Impersonal Voice in First-Person Narrative Fiction,"
    Narrative, 12 (2): 133–50.

Nünning, Ansgar (1997) "'But why will you say that I am mad?' On the Theory, History,
    and Signals of Unreliable Narration in British Fiction," *Arbeiten aus Anglistik und
    Amerikanistik*, 22 (1): 83–105.

Nünning, Ansgar and Roy Sommer (2008) "Diegetic and Mimetic Narrativity: Some
    Further Steps Towards a Narratology of Drama," in John Pier and José Ángel García
    Landa (eds), *Theorizing Narrativity*, 331–54, Berlin and New York: De Gruyter.

Phelan, James (2005) *Living to Tell About It: A Rhetoric and Ethics of Character
    Narration*, Ithaca, NY: Cornell University Press.

Phelan, James (2007) "Estranging Unreliability, Bonding Unreliability, and the Ethics of
    Lolita," *Narrative*, 15 (2): 222–38.

Phelan, James and Wayne C. Booth (2005) "Narrator," in David Herman, Manfred Jahn,
    and Marie-Laure Ryan (eds), *Routledge Encyclopedia of Narrative Theory*, 388–92,
    London: Routledge.

Richardson, Brian (2006) *Unnatural Voices: Extreme Narration in Modern and
    Contemporary Fiction*, Columbus: Ohio State University Press.

Richardson, Brian (2015a) "Representing Social Minds: 'We' and 'They' Narratives,
    Natural and Unnatural," *Narrative*, 23 (2): 200–12.

Richardson, Brian (2015b) *Unnatural Narrative: Theory, History, and Practice*,
    Columbus: Ohio State University Press.

Rushdie, Salman (1981) *Midnight's Children*, London: Jonathan Cape.

Ryan, Marie-Laure (2001) "The Narratorial Function: Breaking Down a Theoretical Primitive," *Narrative*, 9 (2): 146–52.

Ryan, Marie-Laure and Jan-Noël Thon (eds) (2014) *Storyworlds Across Media: Toward a Media-Conscious Narratology*, Lincoln: University of Nebraska Press.

Stanzel, Franz Karl (1955) *Die typischen Erzählsituationen im Roman: Dargestellt an Tom Jones, Moby-Dick, The Ambassadors, Ulysses u. a.*, Vienna: Braumüller.

Stanzel, Franz Karl (1984) *A Theory of Narrative* [1982]. Trans. C. Goetsche, Cambridge: Cambridge University Press.

Thackeray, William Makepeace (2001) *Vanity Fair: A Novel Without a Hero* [1848]. Ed. John Carey, London: Penguin.

Walsh, Richard (2007) *The Rhetoric of Fictionality: Narrative Theory and the Idea of Fiction*, Columbus: Ohio State University Press.

Wilson, George (1986) *Narration in Light: Studies in Cinematic Point of View*, Baltimore and London: Johns Hopkins University Press.

Woolf, Virginia (2000) *Mrs. Dalloway* [1925]. Ed. David Bradshaw, Oxford: Oxford University Press.

7
Style

Lilian Munk Rösing

Chapter Outline

The attention to style is a distinctive mark of literary language and literary analysis. Even if a text has no style, that is, its author has tried to make it as close to ordinary, non-literary language as possible, this is a stylistic choice and has important consequences to its effect and meaning.

In pragmatic, communicative language, style is not necessarily a part of the message. In a food recipe or a letter from your lawyer, the arrangement, rhythm, and sound of the words do not necessarily influence the message—in literary language they do. Attention to style is attention to the verbal material from which literature is made, on the level of letters, words, and sentences—what do they look and sound and feel like, how are they arranged? Style is about the texture of the text.

Stylistic devices can roughly be divided into "tropes" and "figures." Tropes are substitutive or alternative nominations to the plain or normal ones. A metaphor is a trope. Figures, on the other hand, are about the composition of words and letters, the patterns in which the text arranges them. Repetition is a figure. Assonance (repetition of sound, mostly vowel) and alliteration (repetition of initial sound) are figures. Also the syntax of the text, the length of the sentences, and the order of words belong to the side of figure. When you focus on the figures of the text you focus on words and letters as building blocks or sounds that can be put together in different patterns. Roughly, figures are about the words' positions and poses, whereas tropes are about their substitutions.

Style is also, of course, about vocabulary: Is the vocabulary large and varied, or narrow and monotonous, is the text marked by a certain sociolect or dialect, etc.? And style is about grammar: What classes of words are dominating or absent from the text (are there, for instance, many adjectives or not)? What grammatical form (tense, aspect, case) do the words have (are the verbs for instance past or presence tense)?

Defined as the tropes, figures, and grammar of the text, style is quite concrete, quite analyzable. Pure detection and identification of the tropes and figures of a text is not very interesting to literary studies, though, unless it is combined with interpretation, that is, unless you ask: What is the effect of those tropes and figures, how do they contribute to the signification of the text?

Details and whole

Contrary to the concrete, technical understanding of style that you find in classical stylistics, you will also find definitions of style as something much more abstract, as the ungraspable X factor of a text or an author; this "je-ne-sais-quoi" that gives to the text a certain and inimitable individuality, like when you talk about a person's style. "Le Style, c'est l'homme même"—the style is the man, thus wrote the French rhetorician Buffon in 1753.

The French literary scholar Gérard Genette, who generally defines style as the "perceptible" aspect of the text, at a moment speaks of style as "the manner of holding a paintbrush, a bow, a racket, or a loved one" (Genette 1993, 131). To define style as the way you hold your pencil is in accordance with the etymology of the word, coming from Latin "stylus," meaning pen. But Genette's expansion of the list of things to hold brings us to the gesture, "the manner of holding," as a metaphor for style. In its more abstract and expressive definition, style is compared to gesture, attitude, tone, and voice, and like those metaphors it has a quality of surplus, excess, something hard to define exactly and exhaustingly.

The abstract definition of style locates it in the text as a whole, as something emanating from, and even exceeding, the text in its totality. The concrete definition of style locates it in the details of the text, its figures, and tropes. This is a recurring discussion in stylistic theory: Can you really grasp style by nearsighted close reading of stylistic details? Again, just observing and identifying the stylistic figures does not bring your literary analysis very far. But if you are able to connect the microstructure of the stylistic characteristics to the macrostructure of the text's worldview, you are on your way. This is for instance what Proust does in his essay on Flaubert's style (Proust 1920). Here Proust points to Flaubert's use of "l'imparfait," the French past tense that is used to describe (repetitive or enduring) states, whereas "passé simple" is used to describe actions and events. Proust talks of Flaubert's "eternal imparfait" which emphasizes the situation of his characters: They are stuck in states and repetitions rather than being the subjects of actions or the objects of events. On the other hand, Flaubert may connect the tense that marks action to non-human things: "La colline s'abaissa," he writes, "the hill went down," but in the tense that makes of this an action, as if the hill had an agency. What should have been a part of the scenography becomes an actor. If we take Proust's analysis update and connect it to the eco-critical point that deconstructs the distribution of nature and human to background and foreground, we may suggest that Flaubert hereby takes nature to the foreground.

The connection between "style" as the overall attitude or atmosphere of the text, and style as stylistic details can be made, as does Proust, by way of deduction from details to whole, but also by way of induction from general impression to details—how does the text as a whole "feel" (solemn, cool, humoristic, angry, obscure, etc.), and can I point to the stylistic details that produce this effect?

Perceptibility and exemplification

Let us return to Gérard Genette's basic definition of style as the perceptible aspect of the text, or that which constitutes the text's "perceptibility": "Style is nothing but the aspect—let us call it perceptible—that constitutes what [Roman] Jakobson called a text's 'perceptibility'" (Genette 1993, 113). This is a way of saying that style is what the text "feels like" to the reader, but also a way to differentiate between those textual details that are relevant to stylistic analysis, and those that are not. To have a stylistic effect, a detail must be within the scope of the reader's perception. For instance, the "L" in "Love's Labour Lost" makes itself perceivable by close repetition (alliteration)—whereas it would have no meaning to talk of stylistic effect or alliteration when observing three words starting with L spread in a whole page of prose. This is put to the point by Michael Riffaterre when he defines style as "an emphasis drawing the reader's attention to certain elements of the linguistic sequence" (Riffaterre 1971, 30). A further clarification has been made by Laurent Jenny, who, departing from Genette, defines style as "a differentiation of the text's perceptible qualities" (Jenny 2000, 100). Style is not just the fact that verbal language has perceptible qualities (sound, rhythm, graphics, temporal sensation, mood, etc.), but that those qualities are differentiated, patterned, drawing our attention to some of them and not to other ones.

Style is a name for the fact that literary texts are not just something that we intellectually decode, but also something that we perceive through our senses—concretely we sense the patterns of words and sound, both graphically and phonetically; mentally we sense the images (and even smells, sounds, feelings, sounds) that the text provokes.

You may also say that the text does not only signify what it means, it also "exemplifies" it. A composition of words and letters may be not only a representation, but also an instance of something. "The wind whistling" does not only refer to the sound of the wind, it is an "exemplification" of this sound ("wee-wiz"). The concept of "exemplification" in this sense was coined by the American philosopher Nelson Goodman and taken over by Genette. Goodman and Genette distinguish between a linguistic sign's "denotation" (its signification as given in a dictionary) and its "exemplification"—the meaning that it *evokes* by being itself an instance of it. Genette relates this distinction to Sartre's distinction between "signification" and "sense." The siglum "XVII" *signifies* a certain century, writes Sartre, but the *sense* of this century "clings like a veil, like a spider's web, to the curls of a wig, escapes in whiffs from a sedan chair" (Sartre 1952, 304). The wig or the sedan chair evokes or exemplifies what "XVII" does only signify or denote. Like the wig and the sedan chair, words are also things; they have material qualities that *evoke* a meaning instead of denoting it. Genette points to the French word "nuit" that "sparkles or resounds like a thing" (Genette 1993, 98), and thus actually exemplifies the opposite of its signification.

In his sonnet 129 Shakespeare writes this about "the expense of spirit in a waste of shame" (which roughly means ejaculation):

> Past reason hunted, and no sooner had
> Past reason hated, as a swallowed bait
> On purpose laid to make the taker mad

Here the poem by its rhyming does what it tells: it lays out a "bait," as it lays out the rhyme word "laid" where you would not expect to find it, in the middle of the next line. This could actually make the "taker" of the rhyme, the reader, quite mad, or at least somehow disturbed.

Figures and tropes

Like style is suspended between something abstract and diffuse on the one hand, and the concreteness of stylistic figures on the other hand, it is suspended between deviation and norm, intention and non-intention. Style may be something prescribed, the fulfillment of a stylistic norm, like classic poetics prescribing hexameters for the epos, or "high style" for elevated subjects and "low style" for baser ones. Or style may be the individual author's singular signature, as it would tend to be in a modern poetics of deviation. But even the modern author ("modern" here meaning from Shakespeare and onwards) is directed not only by his singular personality when writing, but also by established genres and forms, not to speak of language itself as a material that may develop in ways and form patterns that exceed the author's intention.

Stylistic analysis is basically about focusing your attention on the text's material of words and letters, identifying its figures, tropes, syntax, and grammar, and considering their meaning and effect.

Figures are patterns of words and letters. Roughly they can be divided into figures of repetition and figures of opposition. Basic figures of repetition are anaphora, chiasm, parallelism, and pleonasm. Anaphora is the repetition of the same word(s) in the beginning of a verse or sentence. Like when the ghost in Shakespeare's *Hamlet* laments his destiny: "Of life, of crown, of queen at once dispatched" (I, sc. 5, v 75), by anaphora augmenting his loss and making of the loss of queen its peak. Chiasm is a reversed repetition, following the pattern A-B-B-A, like when Hamlet after having unintentionally murdered Polonius exclaims that heaven has pleased "to punish me with this and this with me" (III, sc. 4, v 176). Here chiasm installs a false symmetry, as if Hamlet's "punishment" (being a murderer) is symmetrical to Polonius's (being murdered). Parallelism is when two verses or sentences have the same syntactical structure. Like when Hamlet lists the things that cannot truly denote his grief: "Nor customary suits of solemn black/ Nor windy suspiration of forc'd breath" (I, sc. 2, v 78). Pleonasm is not repetition of the same word, but a redundancy of meaning. Hamlet practices pleonasm when talking about his mother's desire: "As if increase of appetite had grown/ by what it fed on." To say that an increase has grown is a pleonasm, as growth is already implied in increase (and vice versa). Pleonasm is the figure of "too much," and this is exactly the problem that Hamlet has with his mother's desire: it is too much to him.

To say that appetite grows when fed is of course also a *paradox*, which brings us to the figures of opposition. Besides paradox, basic figures of opposition are antithesis and oxymoron. Antithesis is simple opposition, and perhaps the most famous antithesis in Western literary history is to be found in *Hamlet*: "To be or not to be," showing Hamlet as the one who thinks in oppositions. Oxymoron originally means "sharp-dull" and is thus itself an oxymoron: a figure in which the clash of opposition is between closely related clauses, often adjective and substantive ("black milk," Celan), like when Claudius speaks of "wisest sorrow" (I, sc. 2, v 5), thus linking an overwhelming feeling (sorrow) to an adjective denoting control and reflection (wise).

There are also figures defined not so much by their position as by their pose; those are the so-called dramatic figures, for instance apostrophe, which is the phenomenon of the text addressing itself to someone or something dead, absent, or non-human ("Oh, wild west wind, thou breath of autumn's being").

The basic tropes are metaphor and metonymy. In metaphor there is a relation of likeness between vehicle and tenor (like when Ophelia calls Hamlet "the rose of this fair state," III, sc. 1, v 154). In metonymy there is no relation of likeness, but of contiguity. The most common form of metonymy is synecdoche, part for whole (like when Hamlet's father calls himself "the whole ear of Denmark," I, sc. 5, v 36). Analyzing tropes implies identifying what (tenor: Hamlet) is compared to what (vehicle: rose), and what is their common denominator (beauty, pride, but in the context of Ophelia's line also something that withers). For a further introduction to tropes, see Christoph Bode's chapter in this volume.

Claudius: To be and not to be

Let us take a closer look at one specific scene in Shakespeare's *Hamlet* and see how the play's stylistic texture is decisive to its overall structure. We shall enter the play just before Hamlet enters it, the second scene in the first act. In the first scene the ghost of Hamlet's father has appeared to the sentinels and Hamlet's friend Horatio on the battlement of the castle in the night. The second scene shows the newly crowned and newlywed king Claudius, the brother and murderer of Hamlet's father, giving audience with Queen Gertrude, Hamlet's mother, by his side. This is how he handles the situation in his opening lines:

Claudius:

> Though yet of Hamlet our **d**ear brother's **d**eath
> The memory **be gr**een and that it us befitted
> To **b**ear our hearts in **gr**ief, and our whole kingdom
> To be contracted in **one brow of woe**,
> Yet so **fa**r hath discretion **fo**ught with nature
> That **we** with **wi**sest sorrow think on him
> Together **wi**th remembrance of ourselves. (I, 2, v.1–7)
> Therefore our sometime sister, now our queen,
> Th'imperial jointress to this warlike state
> Have we, as 'twere with a defeated joy,
> With an auspicious and a dropping eye,
> With **mir**th in funeral and with **dir**ge in marriage,
> In Equal scale weighing **d**elight and **d**ole
> Taken to wife. […] (I, 2, v. 8–14; my emphasis)

As for the "perceptible" side of the text, it is hard not to perceive the excess of alliteration and assonance: dear death, be green bear grief, we with wisest, mirth dirge, delight dole. This consonance reaches a climax with "one brow of woe" which is like a soup of w- and o-sounds, hard to pronounce, as the distinction between the words is almost dissolved.

This is what Claudius's language does: It blurs out distinctions, dissolves semantic oppositions in the consonance of sounds. "Green," connoting hope, and "grief," a quite opposite feeling, are melted together by way of alliteration. So are the opposites "delight" and "dole," whereas "mirth" (joy) and "dirge" (lament) are melted together by way of assonance.

The figure of melting together opposites is also present as oxymoron: "wisest sorrow," "mirth in funeral," "dirge in marriage" are all oxymora, blurring the distinction between strategy and feeling, grief and joy.

Syntactically, Claudius's lines are characterized by joining clauses without marking their difference or opposition; the juncture is "and," "together with," or just a comma where one would expect to find "but." Claudius does not say "We must grief the king," *but* "we must also think of ourselves," he says: "Sorrow […] *together with* remembrance of ourselves." He does not say that Gertrude was once his sister, *but* now she is his queen—"sister" and "queen" are joined by a simple comma. He does not say: I feel delight, but also dole; he says: "delight and dole." The oxymora "Mirth in funeral" and "dirge in marriage," being in themselves figures joining opposites, are also joined simply by an "and." So are the "auspicious" and the "dropping" eye, suggesting a rather grotesque image of a face in which one eye is looking up to the sky, while the other one is looking down in sorrow. If the play's most famous line "to be or not to be" was pronounced by Claudius, he would probably say "to be and not to be," replacing the conjunction of opposition by the conjunction of simple juncture. To be and not to be—what's the problem?

Even of Gertrude he makes a "jointress," which is quite ironical: the dead king and his murderer-brother are joined by having the same wife. As the purpose of these lines is to declare that he has married Gertrude, the simple juncture of "sister" and "queen" becomes symptomatic. To turn one's sister into one's wife is incestuous. The whole rhetoric of Claudius is incestuous: it is blurring the distinction between opposites, symptomatically also the distinction between sister and wife that is the prohibition against incest that is constitutive of the Law.

Remembering Nelson Goodman's concept of "exemplification" we may say that Claudius' style, his figures and syntax "exemplify" the incestuous blurring of distinctions that he has enacted by murdering his brother and marrying his sister-in-law. When Claudius addresses himself to Hamlet, it is also by putting an "and" where a conjunction of opposition would be expected:

But now, my cousin Hamlet, and my son (I, 2, v. 64)

Again, like in the simple junction of "sister" and "queen," what is blurred is a distinction of kinship. Claudius covers the distinction between "cousin" and "son" by presenting it as a simple junction.

Hamlet 1: The son in the sun

Let us now see what Hamlet answers. This is actually his very first line in the play:

A little more than kin, and less than kind (I, 2, v. 65)

The meaning of this line is most ambiguous. Hamlet may say that he is a little too much related to Claudius to be friendly. Or he may say that he is both too much and too little related to him. Meaning among other things that Claudius, as his uncle, is too much of a relative to marry his mother and become his father.

Stylistically, Hamlet's line is dominated by the pun (kin/kind—both words meaning both friendly and related by family). The pun is a figure drawing our attention to the materiality of the word—the same verbal material can have different meanings. Whereas Claudius joins opposite words, Hamlet by punning points to the difference within a single word. If we focus on the materiality, the letter substance, of the words "kin" and "kind," Hamlet's line reads like a puzzle: What is more than k-i-n and less than k-i-n-d? It must be k-i-n plus half a letter … Thus Hamlets' line insists on subtle differences, the difference within the same word, the difference of half a letter. Whereas Claudius's style blurs opposition, Hamlet's insists on difference.

Claudius goes on:

How is it that the clouds still hang on you? (I, 2, v. 66)

Here Claudius lances a trope: the clouds as a metaphor for Hamlet's mood. Hamlet answers, partly by accepting Claudius's game of metaphors, partly by rejecting it:

Not so, my lord, I am too much in the sun. (I, 2, v. 67)

By the word "sun" Hamlet joins Claudius's meteorological metaphor, but he also does another thing: he rhymes. "Sun" rhymes with the last word in Claudius's first address to Hamlet: "son." It is what you call an identical rhyme. "Sun" and "son" are homophone: they sound exactly the same, but mean two different things. The rhyme with "son" makes us aware that Hamlet's line may also mean that he is too much a son, which may again have several meanings, one of them being that Claudius has too much made him his son. Again we have a pun, again an insistence on subtle difference, and again our attention is drawn to the materiality of the words, their "perceptible" side. This attention casts light back on Claudius's metaphor "clouds," making us aware that this word has a certain substance of letters in common with the name "Claudius." What hangs on Hamlet may be Claudius as much as his grief. The "sun" in his answer if we read it as a metaphor, also be Claudius, his (illegitimate) sovereignty as a king shining "too much" on Hamlet. Finally, the meteorological metaphors also have a reference to the medical tradition of regarding madness as caused by either too much moonlight or too much sun.

Hamlet 2: To be or not to be

If Claudius's style exemplifies his position of blurring oppositions, Hamlet's style exemplifies a position of insisting on subtle difference. But this is only one of Hamlet's positions, forming when he gives himself into puns and verbal virtuosity, as he shall later do when playing "mad." In his soliloquys the style is different, dominated by antitheses and pleonasms. After his dialogue with Claudius Hamlet has his first long soliloquy, raging about his mother's wedding:

> But two months dead—nay, not so much, not two—
> So excellent a king, that was to this
> Hyperion to a satyr, so loving to my mother
> That he might not beteem the winds of heaven
> Visit her face too roughly. Heaven and earth,
> Must I remember? Why, she should hang on him
> As if increase of appetite had grown
> By what it fed on; and yet within a month—
> Let me not think on't—Frailty, thy name is woman— (I, 2, v.138–46)

Here, in a clear-cut antithesis, Hamlet compares his dead father to Hyperion (the sun god) and Claudius to a satyr (half beast). Then he breaks into pleonasm, the growing increase, and paradox, appetite growing when being fed. The lines are furthermore marked by dramatic figures: Aposiopesis (interrupting oneself, marked by the hyphens) and apostrophe (addressing non-persons: "Heaven and earth," "Frailty"). Those figures give a certain temper, a certain pathos to the lines, showing Hamlet as upset, not to say pathetic.

What makes way for Hamlet's famous misogynous exclamation, "Frailty, thy name is woman," is thus his opposing the good father figure to the bad one (antithesis) and the too-much-ness of his mother's desire (pleonasm). The exclamation exceeds the meter; it breaks with the blank verse, making it impossible to stress every second syllable, as the iambic pentameter would have it. Thus, metrically, the exclamation is in itself "too much"; it exemplifies the too-much-ness of which it complains.

Thus Hamlet has different styles, forming different positions: on the one hand the insistence on subtle difference marked by puns and figures, on the other hand a splitting in which difference is staged as opposition, marked by antithesis and pleonasm. Both positions can be seen as alternative to Claudius's blurring of distinctions, only the "punning" Hamlet's alternative is subtle difference, whereas the "pathetic" Hamlet's is antithesis.

Hamlet's most famous line is pure antithesis: "To be or not to be." The fundamental antithesis to Hamlet is the one between life and death. But perhaps this difference is not as antithetical as the Hamlet of soliloquy would have it; perhaps it could be thought more in the style of the punning Hamlet, as a scale of subtle differences.

Perhaps you could learn to live while recognizing death, perhaps there is such a thing as ghosts, something neither dead nor alive.

Antithesis or difference

In a rare case of collective incorrect remembrance we all think that Hamlet pronounces his famous line while holding Yorrick's skull. This is not so. Hamlet's address to the skull is apparently about something quite different; it is about women's makeup:

> Now get you to my ladies chamber and tell her, let her paint an inch thick, to this favour she must come. Make her laugh at that. (V, sc. 1, v 186–188)

Hamlet has a problem with women's makeup; at a moment he even gives this as the reason for his madness: "God hath given you one face, and you make yourselves another […] it hath made me mad" (III, sc. 1, v 144–149). In his address to Yorrick's skull the loathing of women's makeup, a great source of Hamlet's misogyny, is connected to the antithesis between life and death, which partly legitimates the faulty idea of Hamlets' saying "To be or not to be" while holding the skull.

The antithetical Hamlet is also the misogynist Hamlet. One difference that poses a problem to him, and might perhaps be cleverer thought as subtle difference than antithesis, is sexual difference. If Hamlet were a baroque poet, he would not use the skull to insult his lady, but to seduce her. To the antithetical Hamlet, the life-or-death-Hamlet, the skull is the ultimate signification of life, which hereby becomes unbearable. To the baroque poet it is not the ultimate signification, but rather in itself a signifier, a *memento mori* signifying *carpe diem*: now is the time to love.

To put it roughly, *Hamlet* is a play about blurring and remarking distinctions. The villain, Claudius, has blurred out distinctions; the law and the state vacillate. A remarking of distinction is needed. Hamlet's different styles suggest different ways of remarking: difference or antithesis. In the end Hamlet goes with the antithesis; he opposes Claudius and kills him by his sword. But what happens is tragically that the sword does not remark the lost distinction, it rather blurs it completely, fulfilling the very incestuous logic that it should fight. What is blurred out is not least the distinction between tragedy and comedy; if it was not so sad it would be a comedy of mistaken identity: Hamlet mistakes Laertes's sword for his, Gertrude mistakes Hamlet's cup for hers; at the most odd moment the English ambassador enters to declare the death of Rosencrantz and Guildenstern. Laertes, Hamlet, and Claudius are slain by the same poison-dipped sword; Gertrude and Claudius both drink from Hamlet's poisoned cup, everyone dies in this collective murder that actually has the structure of an incestuous orgy. The final scene shows that antithesis does not save Hamlet from incest, on the contrary. I would suggest Hamlet's other style, his punning wit, to be a better alternative to the blurring of distinctions than pure antithesis, opposing the bad father to the good one, man to woman, and finally ending up in a lethal lack of differentiation.

Even the problem of the ghost could be viewed as a problem defying the logic of antithesis. The ghost disturbs the antithesis of death and life, being something in between. To put it more philosophically, its ontological state is uncertain. Hamlet has problems handling this uncertainty, and it is only by forcing it to be a certainty that he can interpret its command to kill Claudius ("Revenge this foul and most unnatural murder") as something that should be taken literally and obeyed. The conventional interpretation of *Hamlet* goes with his interpretation of the ghost: Its command is certain, and Hamlet's problem is that he thinks and talks too much instead of obeying it.

But if we, following the logic of the style and the plot, problematize the life-death-antithesis, other interpretations of the ghost are made possible. Perhaps it is not an authority speaking from a certain, paternal place (something like the Freudian superego), but rather an ontologically uncertain voice speaking from a place hard to locate (something like the Freudian subconscious).

Thus, stylistic analysis is not only descriptive, but a way into a text's basic conflicts and ideas. Shakespeare's style, the perceptible side of his language, has led us to the central structures in *Hamlet*. The figures, tropes, and syntax have shown to exemplify the positions around which the central conflict revolves, but also helped us to define this central conflict in another way than the conventional one, as a matter of difference versus antithesis rather than acts versus words. Style matters; we cannot grasp the text's subject matter without being sensitive to its materiality.

Further reading

The reach and limits of stylistic analysis are discussed in Michael Riffaterre's polemic article "Describing Poetic Structures: Two Approaches to Baudelaire's 'Les Chats.'" Here he criticizes Roman Jakobson and Claude Lévi-Strauss for their extremely close stylistic reading of Baudelaire's poem "Les chats." In the history of literary theory stylistic attention has been the hallmark of the formalist schools from the first half of the twentieth century: Russian Formalism and New Criticism, and later of Deconstruction. In "A Postscript to the Discussion on Grammar of Poetry" (1980) Roman Jakobson pinpoints the importance of attention to the linguistic devices of the literary text. In *The Structure of the Artistic Text* (1977) Jurij Lotman writes about literary language as the language in which the materiality of words and letters has a semantic value. The close readings of the New Critics are still inspiring as for their sense of style; for instance, William K. Wimsatt: *The Verbal Icon* (1954). So are Paul De Man's deconstructive close readings (for instance, in *Blindness and Insight* 1971/1983). Whereas New Criticism insists on the organic unity of style and content, deconstruction rather points to the places where style contradicts content. Helen Vendler's "The Art of Shakespeare's Sonnets" (1997) offers exemplary stylistic points. In "Hamlet: letters and spirits" (1995) Margaret Ferguson combines stylistic close reading with clever interpretation. Readers and handbooks include Lambrou and Stockwell: *Contemporary Stilistics* (2007) and *The Bloomsbury Companion to Stylistics* (ed. Sotirova, 2015).

References

Brooks, Peter (1984) "Narrative Desire," in *Reading for the Plot*, Cambridge, MA: Harvard University Press.

De Man, Paul (1983) *Blindness and Insight*, 2nd edition, revised, London: Routledge.

Ferguson, Margaret W. (1995) "Hamlet: Letters and Spirits," in David Scott Kastan (ed.), *Critical Essays on Shakespeare's Hamlet*, New York: G. K. Hall & co., 139–155.

Genette, Gérard (1993) *Fiction and Diction*. Trans. Catherine Porter, Ithaca and London: Cornell University Press.

Goodman, Nelson (1968) *Languages of Art*, Idianapolis/Cambridge: Hackett Publishing.

Jakobson, Roman (1980) "A Postscript to the Discussion on Grammar of Poetry," *Diacritics*, 10 (1): 22.

Jakobson, Roman and Claude Lévi-Strauss (1962) "Les Chats de Charles Baudelaire," *L'Homme*, 2.

Jenny, Laurent (2000) "Du style comme pratique," *Littérature*, 118.

Lambrou, Marina and Peter Stockwell (eds) (2007) *Contemporary Stylistics*, London: Continuum.

Lotman, Jurij (1977) *The Structure of the Artistic Text*. Trans. Lenhoff and Vroon, Michigan Slavic Contributions No 7.

Proust, Marcel (1920) "A propos du 'style' de Flaubert," *La Nouvelle revue française*, 1er mars 1920, 72–90.

Riffaterre, Michael (1966) "Describing Poetic Structures: Two Approaches to Baudelaire's 'Les Chats,'" *Yale French Studies*, 36–37.

Riffaterre, Michael (1971) *Essais de stylistique structural*, Paris: Flammarion.

Sartre, Jean-Paul (1952) *Saint Genet*, Paris: Gallimard.

Shakespeare, William (1982) *Hamlet*. Ed. Harold Jenkins. The Arden Shakespeare, London: Thomson Learning.

Sotirova, Violeta (ed.) (2015) *The Bloomsbury Companion to Stylistics*, London: Bloomsbury.

Vendler, Helen (1997) *The Art of Shakespeare's Sonnets*, Cambridge, MA: Harvard University Press.

8

Sensation

Isak Winkel Holm

Art is a "bloc of sensations, that is to say, a compound of percepts and affects," according to *What Is Philosophy?* by Gilles Deleuze and Félix Guattari (1994, 164). That a visual artwork or movie can be said to constitute a "bloc of sensations" does indeed seem quite apparent; yet, according to Deleuze and Guattari the definition applies to all types of artworks, including works of literature: "Whether through words, colors, sounds, or stone, art is the language of sensations" (176). That this is so seems less apparent. We are used to viewing the work of literature as either a representation of real things and events (*mimesis*) or as a word-construction (*poesis*), but Deleuze and Guattari compel us to add a third possible conceptual matrix: To see art as a configuration of sensations (*aiesthesis*). From this point of view, the important thing is not how human beings act in or speak of the world but, rather, how they *sense* the world.

Jens Peter Jacobsen (1847–1885) was a Danish writer of considerable international fame, inspiring authors like D. H. Lawrence and Rainer Maria Rilke. His short story "Mrs Fönns" (1882) opens with a sizeable bloc of sensations. Mrs. Paula Fönns, a widow, and her daughter Ellinor sit together on a bench and find themselves puzzled that the dull landscape they are watching really is the fabled Provence:

> And this really was the Provence! A clayey river with flakes of muddy sand, and endless shores of stone-gray gravel; pale-brown fields without a blade of grass, pale-brown slopes, pale-brown hills and dust-colored roads, and here and there near the white houses, groups of black trees, absolutely black bushes and trees. Over all this hung a whitish sky, quivering with light, which made everything still paler, still dryer and more wearily light; never a glimmer of luxuriant, satiated hues, nothing but hungry, sun-parched colors; not a sound in the air, not a scythe passing through the grass, not a wagon rattling over the roads; and the town stretching out on both sides was also as if built of silence with all the streets still as at noon time, with all the houses deaf and dumb, every shutter closed, every blind drawn, each and every one; houses that could neither see nor hear. (Jacobsen 1921, 123–4)

The mother shows but a "resigned smile" at the lifeless monotony of the landscape; as a young woman she did not get the man she loved, and the man she eventually did end up with died while the children were still very young. The daughter is "mournful and weary" from just having been rejected by a man over another woman. The sensations of the two women are distinctly influenced by their respective states of mind and the text does therefore not describe the "real" Provence as much as it describes a perceived Provence; not a landscape *an sich*, but a landscape as it comes to appear to and through the senses of the two women. Thus, when reading the short story, the reader not so much sees a landscape as she sees someone *else* seeing a landscape. This fact is emphasized a couple of pages further into the story when Ellinor's big brother Tage arrives at the same bench with the lovely Ida and her father: "the newcomers were tired from a little railway excursion they had taken into the Provence with its blooming roses" (125). To the love-struck Tage, Provence is a region of blooming roses; for the solitary women, Provence is barren and pale-brown.

After having related the story of Ellinor's unrequited love, the narrator speculates on how all of this connects to Provence: "And what had all that to do with the region here? The blow had fallen upon her far from here amid the surroundings of her home, by the edge of a sound with changing waters, under pale green beech-trees. Yet it hovered on the lips of every pale brown hill, and every green-shuttered house stood there and held silence concerning it" (121). The blow, then, is connected to the region because sensations are inherently connected to one's frame of mind. Deleuze and Guattari define art as a "bloc de sensations," and as in English, the French word "sensation" not only refers to how one senses the outside world but also to one's inner feelings. Art, therefore, is a configuration of both percepts and affects. This duality is decisive not only for Jacobsen's short story specifically but also for literature at large: Blooming roses and pale-brown landscape, dust-colored roads and stone-gray gravel, but also enthrallment and boredom, love and despair.

This chapter suggests a reading of Jacobsen's short story as a bloc of outer and inner sensations; as percepts and affects.

Emotional piling up

Jacobsen learned the technique of making the fictional world appear through his characters' external and internal sensations from Gustave Flaubert. Due to this stylistic feature, Flaubert has long been a central point of attention in scholarly discussions of sensations in literature, with German Romanist Erich Auerbach being the first to identify and describe this specific feature of his style. In an article on *Madame Bovary*—published when Auerbach was in exile in Istanbul in 1937 and later added to his famous *Mimesis* (1945)—Auerbach analyzes the description of the Bovary couple's sad dinner tables during the first years of their marriage. On one side of the table sits the mediocre and boring Charles who seems to forever eating; on the other side sits Emma, slowly withering away in silent despair.

Auerbach comments on what he calls Flaubert's "pictures" of these dinner tables the following way:

> But the picture is not presented *an sich*; it is subordinated to the dominant subject, Emma's despair ... [T]he reader first sees Emma, who has been much in evidence in the preceding pages, and he sees the picture first through her; directly, he sees only Emma's inner state; he sees what goes on at the meal indirectly, from within her state, in the light of her feeling [*ihres Empfindens*]. (Auerbach 2003, 483, translation modified)

Auerbach's comment is readily transferable from Flaubert to Jacobsen: It is through Paula Fönns and Ellinor, from their state of mind and in light of their feelings that we come to see the landscape of Southern France as monochrome and barren.

It is important to realize that Auerbach's stylistic analysis is not just focusing on the question of *voice*. According to Auerbach, Flaubert's way of depicting Emma's despair cannot be reduced to a version of what we in narratology normally refer to as *free indirect discourse*. As readers, we read about the "emotional piling up of the causes that time and again bring Emma's aversion to her husband to the boiling point" (485), but at no point do we hear Emma vocalize these causes herself; the disordered affective material is not organized by Emma's voice, but rather by the "the ordering hand of the writer," as Auerbach puts it (485). The "pictures" of the dinner tables therefore seem to describe something prior to language, a sort of "mind-stuff" that the voice of the narrator cannot just quote (Cohn 1978, 11). We could even go so far as to call it free indirect sensation rather than free indirect style: We see the world through Emma's eyes, not through her language. While the French term "style indirect libre" does include this stylistic feature, the German term "erlebte Rede" does not, hence Auerbach's point. And the former is what is at play in Jacobsen's short story: It is not Paula Fönnss' or Ellinor's voices which come to affectively color the detailed descriptions of the landscape; rather, this coloring takes place on a deeper level of consciousness where primary sensation and not language reigns.

We should add that the stylistic analysis suggested by Auerbach is also not just focusing on *tropes* and *figures*. A rhetorical analysis of the opening pages of the short story would show that the dominant trope is personification, albeit an unusual type of personification where it is not human qualities that are projected onto the landscape, but, instead, a *lack* of human qualities (paleness, silence, dumbness) (Johansen 2003, 209). A rhetorical analysis would also show that the dominating rhetorical figures are different types of repetitions, most saliently anaphoric parallelisms (pale-brown fields... pale-brown slopes... pale-brown hills... etc.). To be sure, these rhetorical features contribute to the construction of the bloc of sensation insofar as the tropes underline highlight the lifelessness and the figures emphasize the monotony. In the section after the description of Provence we are told that Ellinor is "mournful and weary, as one often becomes after many days of rain, when all one's gloomy thoughts seem to pour down upon one with the rain; or as at the idiotically consoling tick-tack of a clock" (Jacobsen 1921, 120). In the description of Provence, the idiotic tick-tack is present in the text as a series of explicitly repetitive anaphoras. But even though the rhetorical features give shape to the sensations of the two women, the rhetoricity of language is only secondary to the materiality of sensation. The description of Provence is not first of all a matter of voices, of tropes and figures, but of the two women's sensations and states of mind.

Thus, the opening sequence of "Mrs Fönss" shows how linguistically centered analyses of style, either narratological or rhetorical, must be supplemented by a phenomenological stylistic analysis which does not primarily concern itself with linguistic meaning, but pre-linguistic sensation. In his classic article "Linguistics and Poetics" (1957), Roman Jakobson outlines a program for how to analyze literary style. This program focuses on the uncovering of certain constitutive parallelisms within poetic language, that is patterns of mirroring and parallelisms which exist on "all linguistic levels—phonological, morphological, syntactic, and lexical" (Jakobson 1987, 83). When we investigate a work of literature as a bloc of sensations, we are also looking for patterns of mirrorings and parallelisms, just not on the level of language, but on the level of sensations.

The spider's web

Patterns of sensations were the decisive concern for a school of literary studies which developed in a number of francophone countries at the time of Auerbach's exile in

Istanbul. This school is known under various names: The Geneva School, thematic critique or phenomenological critique. As opposed to the structuralists, the group of thematic critics was seldom concerned with formulating theoretical programs or adopting polemic positions, but spent their time performing highly intricate and thorough readings of literature instead. One of the very few theoretical works appearing from the Geneva School, *La conscience critique* (The Critical Consciousness) by Georges Poulet, was published as late as 1969 and appears in hindsight more as a sort of summing up *post festum* than as an actual program for the school, seeing as thematic critique had already been sidetracked by structuralism. In the introduction to the book, Poulet demonstrates a number of marked differences between the various thematic critics, but emphasizes the fact that the "homogeneity of the group springs from a common interest in phenomena of the human consciousness" (Poulet 1971, 9). The members of the group, that is, agreed that human consciousness is not directed toward the book as a physical object *in* the world, but as an experience *of* the world. A literary work is, according to Poulet, "a rational being ... a consciousness; the consciousness of another ... in this case the consciousness is open to me, welcomes me, lets me look deep inside itself, and even allows me, with unheard-of license, to think what it thinks and feel what it feels" (Poulet 1969, 54). In this quote, Poulet not only suggests that a work of literature lets the reader think what is being thought by the work but also that the work lets the reader sense what it senses. As a phenomenon of the consciousness the literary work, then, is not only cognition but also perception: a sort of prosthetic sense which enables the reader to sense the world through the consciousness of another: "My consciousness behaves as though it were the consciousness of another" (56).

The consciousness of another? Poulet is adamant in pointing out that this concept is not to be confused with the consciousness of the actual author. Rather, it is a "consciousness inherent in the work," an organizing center "ensconced in the heart of the work" (59). But even though Poulet distances himself from biographical readings, he keeps on referring to concepts such as the center and the heart of the work. The evocation of a "subjective principle" at the very center of any literary text was what structuralism and, later, deconstruction would find questionable about thematic critique. "[T]here is no spider-web without a center which is the spider," writes Poulet in what is probably a polemic against the structuralism of his day (67), a structuralism which seemed to have succeeded in analyzing cultural spider-webs as if they had been purged chemically of any and all spiders.

This is not the place to discuss whether spiders do or do not exist in works of literature; instead, I want to focus on the space in which the spider's web is suspended. A real spider weaves its web in a specific biotope, for example on a lawn, in a forest, or in a basement, and the same goes for literature. Whether literature is perceived to be a bloc, a pattern, or a web of sensations, we must, when we read it, retain a certain idea about the space in which this configuration of sensations located. The different suggestions as to the nature of this space have determined the discussions of the role of sensation in literature in the latter part of the twentieth century. The spider's web has, put very schematically, been suggested to exist in four different biotopes: That of the subject, that of the act of sensation, that of the work of literature, and that of culture.

The space of the subject

Jean-Pierre Richard's debut book on Stendhal and Flaubert, *Littérature et sensation* (Literature and Sensation, 1954), written fifteen years before Poulet's theoretical summary, is strongly inspired by the French philosopher Gaston Bachelard, according to whom one cannot see a landscape without first having dreamt it. In his reading of Flaubert, Richard sets out to investigate in which ways Flaubert "dreams" the physical world in order to be able to see it. Specifically, Richard establishes a series of dominant sensations which run through Flaubert's authorship as a whole— the visual sensation of interacting colors and of melting ice, the feeling of entrapment and of masochistic pleasure, and the feeling of dissolving and being dispersed as liquid across a surface. The latter feeling finds one of its many expressions when Emma Bovary's young lover Léon observes her in the hotel room and appears to be transformed into a gelatinous, spineless blob of consciousness, or even a sort of ejaculate which "spread out like a wave over the contours of her head, and was then drawn down into the whiteness of her breast" (Flaubert 2004, 265). This same liquid-like movement is also manifest in the last pages of the novel where Emma runs home after a failed attempt at getting Rodolphe, another lover, to assist her economically, and the "ground beneath her feet felt more unresisting than water, the furrows looked to her like vast, dark breakers, unfurling" (279). Yet, Richard does not only investigate the patterns of liquid-like dispersion in *Madame Bovary* but also how these patterns extend beyond the confines of the novel and penetrate into other works and, as is documented in letters and other philological sources, even Flaubert's life. Richard for instance recounts how Flaubert was very fond of long, warm baths, thereby indicating that it was actually Flaubert himself who possessed an empty, gelatinous *I* and who fought to gain a firm foothold in the world. Thus, unlike Poulet's later book, Richard does not distinguish between the "subjective principle," the organizing center "ensconced in the heart of the work," and the empirical and historical subject Gustave Flaubert.

If we apply Richard's approach to Jacobsen's "Mrs Fönss," we find ourselves honing in on the monotonous time experienced by the mournful and weary Ellinor, an experience which comes to define the equally monotonous rhythm permeating the descriptions of Provence. This, as we have already seen, is a way of experiencing time which happens after many days of rain, when all one's gloomy thoughts seem to pour down upon one with the rain; or as at the idiotically consoling tick-tack of a clock, when one sits and grows incurably tired of one's self; or at watching the flowers of the wall-paper, when the same chain of worn-out dreams clanks about against one's will in the brain and the links are joined and come apart and in a stifling endlessness are united again.

Like Richard, one could trace this pattern of sensations beyond the boundaries of the particular short story and try to find it in other works of Jacobsen, and even in his biography. In the novel *Marie Grubbe*, for instance, where the "sum of time seemed to be counted out with hours for pennies; at every stroke of the clock one fell rattling at her feet, crumbled and was dust" (Jacobsen 1918, 121), or in Jacobsen's other novel, *Niels Lyhne*, when Niels hears a mantel clock "ticking out its 'once-again, once-again', dropping the empty seconds, one by one, in the chalice of the day and filling it full" (Jacobsen 1919, 94).

These patterns of sensation exist in a space that remains delimited by the individual subject. They are, in Richard's own words, characteristic of "Flaubert's sensuality" and of "the Flaubertian being." Richard is a masterful text reader, but he inevitably ends up cataloging his observations as peculiarities that depend on the author as biographical subject: Flaubert and Jacobsen as private individuals. By this token, the integrity of the literary works as works of art is dissolved and they, instead, become nothing but symptoms of a single individual's psychological make-up.

The space of sensation

Georges Poulet's chapter on Flaubert from *Les métamorphoses du cercle* (The Metamorphoses of the Circle, 1961), published six years after Richard's *Littérature et sensation*, has as its starting point Auerbach's observations regarding Emma and Charles Bovary's sad dinner tables. Following Auerbach's lead, Poulet chooses to focus on the appearance of the scene as it is shaped by the mental state of Emma. Yet, it is not so much the content of Emma's sensations which interest Poulet as it is their form, a form specifically identified by Poulet as circular. When it is written about Emma that "all the bitterness of life was served up to her on her plate" (Flaubert 2004, 59), Poulet finds it significant that the sentence performs a concentric movement. Prior to this sentence, Flaubert described the oven, the door and the walls, elements which together form a sad periphery around the dinner table, and in the above-quoted sentence the text suddenly goes from horizon to center, literally serving the whole sad situation on a circular platter (Poulet 1961, 373). In the proceeding sentence, the reader is presented with a movement in the opposite direction, a zoom out and up from dinner plate to world which follows the steam from the hot food: "along with the gusts of steam rising from the boiled beef, she could feel a kind of stagnant dreariness rising from the depths of her soul" (Flaubert 2004, 59). Poulet demonstrates convincingly that such movements of expansion and contraction between smaller and larger circular forms play an important structuring role in Flaubert's descriptions of his fictional characters' acts of sensation. Poulet concludes: "All these texts show that what Flaubert had discovered and put into words was a new way of presenting the relations between human beings and their objects, a truer way, or at least a more concrete way, a more *sensate* way" (Poulet 1961, 390).

Applying Poulet's approach to "Mrs Fönss" means focusing on how Jacobsen presents the sense acts of his fictional characters. An example of such a sense act is the aforementioned "negative" personification from the description of Provence, which in fact is not merely negative personification but also negative description in the sense of it being a meticulous enumeration of absent sense impressions ("never a glimmer... not a sound... not a scythe... not a wagon") (Jacobsen 1921, 120). Here, the sense act does not swing to the rhythm of expansion and contraction, as was the case with Flaubert, but rather back and forth between anticipation and disappointment. An anticipated pleasurable sensation collides with an actual disappointing sensation when Paul Fönss and Ellinor contemplate the view of Provence: "And this really was the Provence!" (119). We find a surprisingly similar grammatical structures, juxtaposing anticipation and disappointment, in many other of Jacobsen's blocs of sensation, most famously in the short story with the title "There should have been roses"(Jacobsen 1921, 115).

These types of sensational patterns are located in a space defined by the meeting between the subject and the world in the sense act. They do not relate to the sensibility of the biographical Flaubert or Jacobsen but, rather, to more abstract ways in which human consciousness can react or be moved when confronted with the world. Poulet writes about the "Flaubertian imagination" and the "Flaubertian spirit", and when doing so he does not refer to the psychology of the biographical Flaubert, but to his specific way of presenting the act of sensation.

The space of the work of literature

Like Poulet, Jean Starobinski also starts off from Auerbach's reading of Charles and Emma's dinner tables as he tries to hone in on the role of sensations in *Madame Bovary*. In his essay "L'échelle de températures" (The Scale of Temperatures, 1983), Starobinski starts out by showing how "we see and sense through his [Charles'] sensations," which means that Flaubert's text is to be understood as a "representation of the act of sensation" (Starobinski 1983, 45). But while Auerbach was mostly interested in Emma, Starobinski chooses to focus on Charles for whom the act of sensation is not disturbed by any thought activity whatsoever. Charles, in other words, is so stupid that subjectivity as such is reduced to a bare minimum and thinking is substituted for unprocessed bodily sensations: Warmth, coldness, the clucking of the hens in the courtyard, blood's rhythmic thumbing through the ears. We could say that Starobinski uses Charles as a sort of cognitive deadweight which enables him to penetrate the surface layers of consciousness and investigate the nature of pre-linguistic sensation.

In order to map out how these thoughtless streams of sensation are being presented in the novel, Starobinski employs structuralism's distinction between a horizontal and vertical axis in language. In the terms used by Roman Jakobson in his "Linguistics and Poetics," the horizontal axis is the combinatory axis where words follow each in other in the speech chain, while the vertical axis is the axis of selection from which the speaker selects between semantically cognate words (Jakobson 1987, 71). Since Starobinski's interest is not in words as such but, rather, in patterns of sensation, he transfers Jakobson's two axes from the field of linguistics to that of phenomenology. On the horizontal axis we now find syntagmatic series of sensations as they unfold in the novel; on the vertical axis we find different qualities of sensations (Starobinski 1983, 51). The title of this essay on Flaubert is "The Scale of Temperatures" because Starobinski here focuses on the vertical axis stretched out between the fictional character's sensations of heat and cold.

If we apply Starobinski's approach to Jacobsen's "Mrs Fönss," we have to focus on scales of color rather than on scales of temperature. Chromatic sensations dominate the universe of the short story and these sensations are distributed along an axis stretched out between the, on the one hand, pale-white and sunless colors seen by Paula Fönss and Ellinor and, on the other, the blooming roses seen by Tage. When mother and daughter take in Provence from a bench, they do not see "a glimmer of luxuriant, satiated hues" but only "hungry, sun-parched colors" (Jacobsen 1921, 120). The contrast between satiated and "hungry" colors reoccurs in the portraiture of the two women's faces: The "strong, fine lines of her [the mother's] features were accentuated by the darker more deeply colored complexion which the years had given her" (124), whereas Ellinor is described as a "pale child whose features she [the mother] could only dimly distinguish under the faint yellow glow of the night lamp" (137). The series of chromatic perceptions featured in the short story are clearly not on a spectrum of contrast colors such as red and green. In the terminology of digital image processing we could say that it is not about contrast or brightness, but about saturation.

The contrast between saturated and pale colors is also at the center of the short story's second large bloc of sensation, a bloc which conveys to the reader an image of the courtyard in front of the Avignon museum. The day after the events described above, Paula Fönss and her son Tage have taken a stroll to visit the museum, and at their destination Paula meets her teenage sweetheart, Emil Thorbrögger:

> The gateway, however, gave admission to the not specially large court which was surrounded by a freshly white-washed arcade whose short squat columns had black iron bars between them.

> They walked about and looked at the objects placed along the wall: Roman sepulchral monuments, pieces of sarchophagi, a headless draped figure, the dorsal vertebrae of a whale, and a series of architectural details.
>
> On all the objects of interest there were fresh traces of the mason's brushes.
>
> By now they had come back to their starting point.
>
> Tage ran up the stairs to see if there might not be people somewhere in the house, and Mrs Fönss in the meantime walked up and down the arcade.
>
> As she was now on the turn toward the gate a tall man with a bearded, tanned face, appeared at the end of the passage directly in front of her. (128)

The description of the museum courtyard begins at the nonsaturated end of the chromatic scale thanks to the white-washed arcade, the black iron bars, the white marble statues, the fresh traces of the mason's brush, and the white vertebrae from a whale. But when Thorbrögger finally enters the scene his tanned faced grinds against the general chromatic paleness. And after the short conversation between the teenage sweethearts, the chromatic saturation of the scene is boosted significantly: "In that way they went on talking for a while. At last the custodian appeared, hot and out of breath, with heads of lettuce under his arms and a bunch of scarlet tomatoes in his hand" (130). Characteristically, red and green—normally contrast colors—are on the same end of this specific scale; together, scarlet red and bright green form a contrast to the paleness.

In connection with his analysis of the temperature scale in Flaubert's writings, Starobinski emphasizes that the meaning of the sensations is not just literal, but also figurative. Temperatures are obviously something one measures with a thermometer, and as such the question of temperature is part of the "real" landscape of *Madame Bovary*. But temperatures are also part of the imaginary landscape of the novel, seeing as the oscillations between coolness and heat take on "symbolic value" as a movement between death and life, between deprivation and desire (Starobinski 1983, 60). In Jacobsen's short story we find that the chromatic sensations are suspended in the same way between literal and figurative meaning. The pale-white museum courtyard appears mostly as a mausoleum, filled with bones, sarcophagi and lime-white tombs, but as soon as more saturated colors return to the scene life returns as well: Thorbrögger's tanned face signals maturity and experience, and the salad and the tomatoes connote fertility. Furthermore, Tage's attempt at ringing the museum doorbell in the beginning of the scene is described as "fruitless" [*frugtesløst*], an ambiguous word which should be understood somewhere between the literal and the figurative, at the same time futile and fruit-less.

Sensational patterns of this type belong in a space strictly contained by the borders of the literary work itself. Starobinski does not locate the series of perceptions or the phenomenological axes in the "Flaubertian being" or in the "Flaubertian imagination." Instead, he maps these cobweb-like structures of perception in order to understand how the novel constructs a fictional universe which is both sensate and symbolic.

The space of culture

Like the francophone critics from the thematic school, Swedish literary scholar Sara Danius is occupied with the way the world becomes visible in the writings of Flaubert. In *The Prose of the World* (2006), Danius makes clear that it is not just the objective world but also the subjective act of seeing that is the issue in *Madame Bovary* (Danius 2006, 83). Yet, as opposed to Auerbach and the school of thematic critique, Danius emphasizes that sensations in Flaubert's writing tend to detach themselves from any actual human being: "Sights are related to seers, and everything that is seen is always perceived by someone. And yet the perspective implied is not reducible to any one character" (66). Detached sensations are *nobody's* sensations; they are rather "highly impersonal" and "autonomous visual event[s]" (67, 89). Emma, for instance, becomes such a visual event when she is gazed upon by all the novel's covetous men. This event is autonomous because it does not make sense to follow it back to each of the men and their specific psychological make-up: Charles, Léon, and Rodolphe all see Emma in roughly the same way. Through the generic gaze of masculine desire, Emma comes to appear as a passive object rather than as a subject, as so many delicate visual details rather than as a self-enclosed individual. In the terminology of Danius, the men in the novel not only share Emma they also share their "modes of perception" (92). They share a cultural, ideological, and misogynist template for how to view women and without this template as their visual-phenomenological filter Emma would literally be invisible to them.

If we should apply Danius's approach to "Mrs Fönss," we could hone in on Paula Fönss' highly developed sense of decorum. Her awareness of her age and social status becomes apparent in a "thousand movements, in expressions and gestures, in the way in which she would respond to a hint, in the fashion in which she would smile at an answer" (Jacobsen 1921, 139). Here, Jacobsen does not describe a particular sensation of Mrs. Fönss' body but, rather, the general rules that govern the public appearance of a forty-year-old widow. A similar example can be found in Jacobsen's meticulous description of the female character Edele in the novel *Niels Lyhne*. Over the better part of two pages, Edele's appearance is described exhaustively, from her thick, heavy hair to her tall, slender figure, and in finishing off this description Jacobsen adds: "This was the way people saw Edele Lyhne" (Jacobsen 1919, 31). It is, then, not so much *us*, the readers, that see Edele directly; instead, we see how *people* (i.e., the middle-aged, bourgeois men of Copenhagen) see Edele.

The patterns of sensation investigated by Danius cannot be located in one specific subject (Richard), in one specific writer (Poulet), or in one specific work of literature (Starobinski). Rather, they exist in the cultural space at large. As such, they are part of a collective "representational economy" which serves to define how women can become visible within a given historical period.

Summing up, we can outline at least two important things to keep in mind when dealing with sensations in literature. First, that sensations are not necessarily contingent upon a sensing subject. In the words of Deleuze and Guattari, the aim of art is "[b]y means of the material" to "wrest the percept from perceptions of objects and the states of a perceiving subject, to wrest the affect from affectations as the transition from one state to another" (Deleuze and Guattari 1994, 167). A percept is a perception which has been torn loose from a particular subject and a particular place in the social order; an affect is a detached and—in the words of affect theorist Sara Ahmed—a "nonresiding" emotion (Ahmed 2004a, 119). Danius' concept of the "representational economy" can thus be seen as another version of Ahmed's theory on the "affective economy": A term describing particular ways in which detached and de-subjectivized affects circulate or are distributed across a social field (Ahmed 2004b, 8).

The second thing to keep in mind is that sensation and affect are related. The economies of perception and affect are two sides of the same social field. Jacobsen's description of Provence is therefore not either a bloc of pure sensations of the outer world *or* a bloc of pure internal affect; in the words of Auerbach, the landscape is seen *in light of* an affect. We usually understand feelings as belonging to the inner world of the subject and not as enabling the subject to navigate in the outer world. But distinguishing too sharply between inside and outside makes it impossible to get a proper grip on how sensations function in works of literature. In coupling detached percepts and affects, a short story like "Mrs Fönss" demonstrates how sensations are fundamental to literature's exploration of the ways of world-making.

Further reading

As quoted in the above article, Georges Poulet states that homogeneity of the group of thematic critics "springs from a common interest in phenomena of the human consciousness." Hereby, he acknowledges the group's substantial inspiration from the philosophical movement of phenomenology. Founded by the German philosopher Edmund Husserl, phenomenology is the study of "phenomena," that is things as they appear in human consciousness. For introductions to classical and contemporary phenomenology, see Dermot Moran, *Edmund Husserl: Founder of Phenomenology* and Dan Zahavi, *The Oxford Handbook on Contemporary Phenomenology*. Compared to Husserl, many French phenomenologists are characterized by their anti-intellectualism, seeing consciousness not as synonymous with the clear light of reason, but, rather, as mixed up with unclear sensations and indistinct images. For the group of thematic critics, the important figures are Maurice Merleau-Ponty and Gaston Bachelard. Merleau-Ponty explores the role of the body for the way things appear in human consciousness; for a recent introduction, see Taylor Carman,

Merleau-Ponty (2008). Bachelard, on the other hand, investigates the role of fantasy and imagination in experience; for an introduction, see Cristina Chimisso, *Gaston Bachelard: Critic of Science and the Imagination* (2001).

Translation: Jens Christian Borrebye Bjering

References

Ahmed, Sara (2004a) "Affective Economies," *Social Text*, 22/2 (79): 117–39.

Ahmed, Sara (2004b) *The Cultural Politics of Emotion*, Edinburgh: Edinburgh University Press.

Auerbach, Erich (2003) *Mimesis: The Representation of Reality in Western Literature*. Trans. Willard R. Trask, Princeton, NJ and Oxford: Princeton University Press.

Carman, Taylor (2008) *Merleau-Ponty*, London: Routledge.

Chimisso, Cristina (2001) *Gaston Bachelard: Critic of Science and the Imagination*, London: Routledge.

Cohn, Dorrit Claire (1978) *Transparent Minds: Narrative Modes for Presenting Consciousness in Fiction*, Princeton, NJ: Princeton University Press.

Danius, Sara (2006) *The Prose of the World: Flaubert and the Art of Making Things Visible*, *Historia litterarum*, Uppsala: Acta Universitatis Upsaliensis.

Deleuze, Gilles and Félix Guattari (1994) *What Is Philosophy?* London: Verso.

Flaubert, Gustave (2004) *Madame Bovary: Provincial Manners*. Trans. Margaret Mauldon, Oxford: Oxford University Press.

Jacobsen, J. P. (1918) *Marie Grubbe*. Trans. Hanna Astrup Larsen, New York: Boni and Liverlight.

Jacobsen, J. P. (1919) *Niels Lyhne*. Trans. Hanna Astrup Larsen, Oxford: Oxford University Press.

Jacobsen, J. P. (1921) *Mogens and Other Stories*. Trans. Anna Grabow, New York: Nicholas L. Brown.

Jakobson, Roman (1987) *Language in Literature*, Cambridge, MA: Belknap Press.

Johansen, Jørgen Dines (2003) *Litteratur og begær. Ti studier i dansk og norsk 1800-tals litteratur*, Odense: Syddansk Universitetsforlag.

Moran, Dermot (2005) *Edmund Husserl: Founder of Phenomenology*, Cambridge and Malden, MA: Polity Press.

Poulet, Georges (1961) *Les métamorphoses du cercle*, Paris: Plon.

Poulet, Georges (1969) "Phenomenology of Reading," *New Literary History*, 1 (1): 53–68.

Poulet, Georges (1971) *La conscience critique*, Paris: Librairie José Corti.

Starobinski, Jean (1983) "L'échelle des températures," in Raymonde Debray-Genette (ed.), *Travail de Flaubert*, 238p, 45–78. Paris: Éditions du Seuil.

Zahavi, Dan (2012) *The Oxford Handbook of Contemporary Phenomenology*, Oxford: Oxford University Press.

9
Rhythm

Dan Ringgaard

The German romanticist poet Friedrich Hölderlin is reported to have said, "all is rhythm, the entire destiny of human kind is one heavenly rhythm, just as every single work of art is one sole rhythm" (Arnim 1920, 344). What Hölderlin might be saying is that life as well as art is immersed in rhythms, such as the rhythm of life and death, day and night, sorrow and joy, the beating of the waves, the rhythm of the heartbeat, of the working day, and in art: the beat, the brush stroke, the breath.

Rhythm can be perceived in two ways: as structure and as emergence. Hölderlin points to the latter, while we are accustomed to the first. As soon as something repeats itself in sufficiently regular intervals, there is rhythm. It is a rhythm that can be counted. In music you can count the beats and the length of the tones and the pauses. But it is far from certain that we hear music in that way. Rather than listening to a row of tones and pauses, we may perceive a movement from one tone to the next. Something occurs and fades away. In that case, we hear the music as emergence, not as structure. The ancient Greeks had two words for forms that correspond to these two perceptions of rhythm: *Morphé* means a punched out and finished form, *rhythmos* designates a form that is coming into being and an uninterrupted movement.

The French linguist Emil Benveniste has explained *rhythmos* as the realization of form in time (Benveniste 1975). Rhythm is the manner in which something takes shape over time. If we turn this wording around, it means that rhythm is the shape of time, and that time is inconceivable without rhythm. It also implies that the rhythm of, for instance, a poem is an expression of a particular experience of time. Understood as *rhythmos* Hölderlin's statement isn't that mysterious after all.

Within literature one may point to three fields of interest to a rhythm analysis. First, there is *the represented world*, the world that a text depicts and the reader coproduces imaginatively. Just like the world in which we live this world has a large number of interlaced rhythms. Second, there is *the progression of the text*, the rhythm in which themes, motifs, metaphors, and a number of other textual elements materialize, are developed, and then disappear. And finally there are the realm of *the verbal signifiers*, the sound, stress, and graphic expression of each word. The classic field of metrics or prosody resides within this third field, in all three fields though rhythm is at work, in prose as in poetry.

The represented world and the progression of the text

Throughout his writings Friedrich Nietzsche returned to rhythm as an organizing force of life. He might hail it as an instrument of civilization, something that gives shape to the individual life, or criticize it as a power of oppression. In light of his idea of the eternal return, rhythm is assigned a third meaning. The eternal return might be described as a notion of a cosmic, relentlessly returning rhythm of life that one must acknowledge and surrender to in order not to become its victim. Such a notion is not entirely foreign to Hölderlin's statement.

Nietzsche's idea about the existence of more or less hidden rhythms of society that rule our lives is an important point of departure for the rhythm analysis of French sociologist Henri Lefebvre (Lefebvre 2004). Lefebvre is interested in the rhythms that produce the spaces we live in. He lines up a number of basic rhythmic elements such as repetition/variation, mechanic/organic, cyclic/linear, continuity/rupture, and arrhythmic/eurhythmic/polyrhythmic, and he suggests that in all the spaces where there is rhythm there will be types of repetition, processes that will interrupt or change these repetitions, and arcs of suspension, sequences with a beginning, a middle and an end. Just look out your window, he suggests, and down on the street, and you will discover all sorts of rhythms, visible as audible, slow and quick, that emerge, refract and participate in sequences: pedestrian crossings, traffic lights, shadows and weather, different kinds of road users, the course of the day, the workings of time on the houses.

A literary text, however, does not confine itself to mirror the lived world; it is also a world in its own right. In a small essay entitled "Poetry and Music" from 1932, the Swedish modernist poet Gunnar Ekelöf insists that the rhythm of a poem cannot be consigned to the verbal signifiers; it is present on all levels of the poem:

> An art form whose dimension is time should of course have a time bound inner form of the same sort as music, a form that works with repetitions, modulations and implementations of themes. (Ekelöf 1992, 333)

In "Music and Poetry" from 1945, T. S. Eliot speaks along the exact same lines about implementations of themes, transitions between movements and contrapuntal arrangements of subject matter. According to Eliot what poetry and music have in common cannot be narrowed down to melody, and it does not exist independently of subject matter (Eliot 1957). Ekelöf as well as Eliot imagines the poem as a sequence and point to analogies with music. Due to the fact that language proceeds in time, all that is part of a text will be shaped in time and take part in the rhythm of the text. That goes for themes and motifs, figures and tropes, characters, actions and places, narrators and focalizations, tone, syntax and choice of words. Therefore a rhythm analysis of the progression of the text must consider the entire text as a shaping of words in time and set out to recognize the patterns that might appear.

To a woman passing by

Let us take a closer look at how to analyze the rhythm of the represented world of the text and the progression of the text. Here is Charles Baudelaire's sonnet "À une passante" from *Les fleurs du mal*, Flowers of Evil, 1857, followed by James McGowan's translation from 1993 into English:

À une passante
La rue assourdissante autour de moi hurlait.
Longue, mince, en grand deuil, douleur majestueuse,
Une femme passa, d'une main fastueuse
Soulevant, balançant le feston et l'ourlet;

Agile et noble, avec sa jambe de statue.
Moi, je buvais, crispé comme une extravagant,
Dans son œil, ciel livide où germe l'ouragan,
La douceur qui fascine et le plaisir qui tue.

Un éclair … puis la nuit !—Fugitive beauté
Dont le regard m'a fait soudainement renaitre,
Ne te verrai-je plus que dans l'éternité?

Ailleurs, bien loin d'ici ! trop tard ! *jamais* peut-être!
Car j'ignore où tu fuis, tu ne sais où je vais,

Ô toi que j'eusse aimée, ô toi qui le savais!
To a Woman Passing By

Around me roared the nearly deafening street.
Tall, slim, in mourning, in majestic grief,
A woman passed, with a glittering hand
Raising, swinging the hem and flounces of her skirt;

Nimble and stately, statuesque of leg.
I, shaking like an addict, from her eye,
Black sky, spawner of hurricanes, drank in
Sweetness that fascinates, pleasure that kills.

One lightning flash … then night! Sweet fugitive
Whose glance has made me suddenly reborn,
Will we not meet again this side of death?

Far from this place! too late! *never* perhaps!
Neither one knowing where the other goes,
O you I might have loved, as well you know!

Haussmann began the construction of the Parisian boulevards in 1853, so one might imagine the scene to take place on one of these, at the time, astonishingly modern venues. The poem opens with what Lefebvre would call an arrhythmic space. The speaker of the poem is surrounded by the cacophonic soundscape of the big city. Things move around him making the dominant rhythm of the city circular. Out of the crowd, like an apparition, steps a woman in mourning raising her skirt with complete ease, apparently untouched by the turmoil. We see her all the more clearly because the world around her is unseen, it is mere noise. Words like majestic, lifting, balancing and agile (to use the direct translations from French) and the comparison with the statue underscores her progress as unhindered by the crowded street. If the street is arrhythmic and cyclical, her movement is eurhythmic and linear; she strives in a harmonious and unhindered pace. She is emergence and pure flow; she is *rhythmos*. This is the first rupture of the poem: from the gyre of the city to the flow of the woman. The second rupture is stronger in the original due to the verb "crispé," a contraction of muscles caused by a sensation or an emotion. The poet suffers a physical shock; he literally cracks down as he sees the woman, creating this exact moment of shock in the middle of the boisterous vertigo of the street. Here is the epicenter of the sonnet, the heart and force of the singular experience, turning the rupture into the major rhythmical figure of the sonnet. From this second rupture comes the opposition of the remaining sonnet between fleeting beauty and eternity. The poet is reborn in her brief gaze; he sees eternity through the moment as if the sudden breach in time was the doorway to nontime. It is the aftermath and consequences of this brief touch of the two temporal dimensions that resounds throughout the tercets.

If we proceed to the progression of the text, it is striking how the sentences and with them the different phases of the poem does not coincide with the composition of the sonnet. The city space is introduced in the first verse and by the first sentence. Then the apparition of the woman unfolds from verse two and spills over in the first verse of the second quatrain whose last three verses along with the third sentence of the sonnet deals with the reaction of the poet. This reaction, however, is prolonged metaphorically in the first tercet where lighting strikes and all becomes night. So not only is there another spill over between the stanzas, but the traditional tipping point of the sonnet from description to reflection, from image to thought, in the beginning of the first tercet, is postponed for half a verse; and it is further disturbed by the 13th verse where the woman reappears as she is fleeing, as if the poet catches a last glimpse of her, a reverberation or an echo that throws him, and the reader, back into the streets. The strict order of the sonnet is lapsing, or cracking down, perhaps as a result of the chaotic surroundings and as a repercussion of the disturbing encounter.

This leaves us with two notable rhythmical events. There is the twofold rupture leading to the opposition of the moment and eternity, and there is the slippage between sentence and sonnet, a transgression of borders and with it the repercussion of the event within the afterthought. Taken as a whole it is a polyrhythmic poem addressing a vertiginously complex experience of exterior and interior time. However, if rhythmic space consists of repetition, interruption, and suspension, as Lefebvre suggested, the dominant mode of Baudelaire's sonnet is one of interruption, or as Walter Benjamin (Benjamin 1999) would have it in a famous reading of the sonnet, of shock. At its center stand the apparition of the woman and the eruption of the physical shock.

The verbal signifiers and the hesitation of the verse

All texts of literature need to have rhythm, especially poems. A poem doesn't have a thing if it hasn't got rhythm. This goes for rhythm in the broad sense in which I have used it so far, and it particularly goes for the verbal signifiers of the poem, the rhythm that can be heard when it is read aloud, or the rhythm the reader hears with the inner ear. When the verbal signifiers of a poem, the audible and graphical side of it, gain in importance, a tension arises between what the words mean and how they sound, subsequently look like on the page. The attention of the reader is split between sound and meaning. Poems thrive on this tension. The French poet Paul Valéry has called poetry "this prolonged hesitation between the sound and the meaning" (Valéry 1958, 73).

This hesitation of Valéry's occurs by way of a stylization of the signifiers of everyday language. The language we speak in ordinary situations is also rhythmical, although vaguely, and it is this rhythm that the poetic language stylizes. In a literary text, the rhythm of the verbal signifiers is produced as an interplay between three levels: (1) the stress, number of syllables, length and sound of the words, (2) the syntactical and rhetorical figures of the sentence, and (3) the graphical layout of the text. There is *metrical verse* and *free verse*. Metrical verse are comparatively highly stylized on the level of the single word, in Germanic languages according to the stress of the words, in Roman languages primarily by way of the number of syllables, and in Latin and ancient Greek it is the length of the words that counts. Rhyme may function as a further means of stylization. The free verse is not so tightly organized, it typically works through repetitions and variations of phrases, sound effects, syntactical and rhetorical figures and graphic patterning; in short what we might term *parallelisms*. While the metrical verse is repeatable because the exact same pattern is filled in by different words, the free verse is by definition unrepeatable since it establishes and dissolves the patterns as it goes along. Historically the metrical verse outnumbers the free verse, but the free verse has been around for a long time. It got its name in eighteenth-century Germany, was rebooted in late nineteenth-century France, and became the dominant verse form of the twentieth century and still is, perhaps more in Continental Europe than in Anglophone literature.

Verse stems from the Latin *versus* which means "turn." The basic experience when you read a poem is that it turns and begins again, as opposed to prose that, from the Latin *prorsus*, means "straight." A poem has two duelling forms of organization, the verse and the sentence; prose only has one, the sentence. The verse is organized around the verbal signifiers; the sentence is a carrier of meaning. This is why it makes sense to say that the poem hesitates between sound (the verse) and meaning (the sentence). It becomes all the more obvious when the sentence doesn't stop when the verse does, but proceeds on down to the next verse. This is called an *enjambment*. The enjambment works in two directions. On the one hand, it ties the verses together because the meaning continues beyond the limit of the verse. On the other, it creates this hesitation between the verse that the reader looks back on, and the sentence that needs to be followed beyond the verse limit. In free verse, this tension between verse and sentence, and with it the enjambment, becomes even more important because the verse, or perhaps more appropriately the line, often is defined entirely by the line break.

In metrical verse, the metrical pattern emerges as the complex stresses of the words are reduced to either stress or unstressed. This binary system is organized in units, or *feet*, of typically two or three syllables, and a certain number of units form a verse. Verses often come in stanzas, and together they constitute the poetic forms alongside less formal elements such as composition, theme and motif. The issue of the formal or signifying elements of poetry again leads to the question of meaning. What in the formal description of the poem is important to pay attention to and what isn't? On a macrolevel, the meter and form of a poem articulates the poetic tradition. A poem echoes a specific tradition once it makes use of a particular meter and a specific form, and it might choose to concur with or deviate from it. The hexameter, for instance, belongs to the ancient epic, and the blank verse owes its worldwide fame to Shakespeare's plays. On a microlevel, another type of deviation may take place, one between the meter and the other elements that constitute the rhythm of a poem. The rhythm of a poem is as mentioned not just made up by the meter, usually more complex patterns and stronger dynamics will occur once you compare the stresses that is given to the words by the meter to their ordinary stress and to the other rhythmic elements of the poem. In free verse, the tension between meter and rhythm is weakened or completely gone, and the dynamics must be located among the other rhythmic elements not least in the graphic arrangement of the line versus the sentence. In prose, this latter tension also disappears.

There are basically two strategies when it comes to attributing meaning to rhythmical form. One is to emphasize the ruptures, shifts, and repetitions; the other is to point to notable similarities and differences between the signifiers and the signified. If an otherwise regular meter changes abruptly or a phrase returns after a long absence, it calls attention to itself. What is said at that particular spot grows in importance. Alternatively if a poem about inner peace is written in calm and simple rhythms and harmonious sounds (like a lullaby), it is probably fair to say that the signifiers mime the signified. On the other hand, a tight classic form, say like the sonnet, might function as a contrast to turbulent modern experiences. The first strategy is *structural*; it is concerned with the patterns of the text. The other strategy is *mimetic*; it deals with possible reflections between form and subject matter.

Back to Baudelaire

Baudelaire's sonnet is written in the by far most common French verse, the Alexandrine, a twelve-syllable verse form with a *caesura* (a brief pause) after the sixth syllable. Let me just point to three central issues regarding the verbal signifiers in this rich and complex poem: the mimetic quality of sound and syntax, the dynamics of the enjambment and the caesura, and the semantics of the rhyme. Isn't there a distinct onomatopoetic quality in the first verse ("La rue assourdissante autour de moi hurlait"), as if it calls forth the rumble and the clamor of the street? And doesn't the change in sound and syntactical rhythm in the beginning of verse two, the prolonged syllables ("Longue, mince") underscore the grace and the completely different pace of the woman? Just as the interruptions in the beginning of the first tercet ("Un éclair … puis la nuit !—Fugitive beauté") seem to simulate the speechlessness and physical shock already alluded to by the out of breath and apoplectic sound of "crispé"? Sounds and rhythms on their own rarely signifies anything particular, but within a semantic context and as part of a poetic tradition they tend to emphasize, or contradict for that matter, the represented emotions, thoughts and perceptions of the text. Here they primarily reinforce the two ruptures already present in the rhythm of the represented world.

There are two enjambments in the poem which is quite bold for a French sonnet at this time: "d'une main fastueuse/Soulevant …" ("a glittering hand/Raising") and "Fugitive beauté/Dont le regard" ("Sweet fugitive/Whose glance"). They strengthen the spillover effect already encountered between the syntax of the poem and the form of the sonnet. The displacement of the caesura in verse 5, 6, and 9 to the, respectively, 5th, 4th, and 7th syllable works along the same lines underscoring the ruptures of the poem and straining the classic form to its limit as a possible effect of the fluidity of modernity. This opposition is put to the fore as the poem rhymes "Fugitive beauté" (fleeting beauty) on "l'éternité" (eternity) and by doing so singles out the intersection of the two dominant temporalities of the poem: the moment of rupture as the possible escape from time. These sparse observations among the verbal signifiers of the poem only strengthen the impression encountered earlier on of an extremely dynamic and temporally complex poem of conflicting motions as well as emotions, highly strung as its speaker between form and chaos, rupture and release, mind and body, reverberating with an overflow, not just of powerful feeling as William Wordsworth would have it (Wordsworth 2014, 79), but an overflow of the outside world, of modernity.

The poetic function and defamiliarization

The Czech linguist Roman Jakobson has developed a theory that further explains Valéry's hesitation between sound and meaning, most elaborately in the lecture "Linguistics and Poetics" from 1960 (Jakobson 2010). Language is organized in time, and the words follow each other in certain combinations. For this reason, Jakobson speaks about an axis of combination that is syntactically organized, and imagines it as the horizontal axis in a system of coordinates. Each word on this axis is chosen among words of similar meaning in order to take its proper place in the chain of words. The number of possible words that we choose between, Jakobson places on what he calls the axis of selection which is semantically organized and make up the vertical axis of the system of coordinates. Here we choose the word that is the most fitting with regard to what we have to say. In literature however, and especially in poetry, the time in which language unfolds, needs form, in effect rhythm, and for that reason other qualities than meaning begins to matter. The choice of words is no longer entirely a matter regarding the axis of selection. Instead words are chosen according to how they might fit into rhythmical and no longer strictly syntactical patterns on the axis for combination.

When this rhythmical principle asserts itself what Jakobson calls the *poetic function* of language is heightened. In the poetic function the medium is the message. And the media is language itself. It isn't like that in everyday language. There language is a fairy invisible vehicle of meaning, like a window to the world. But once language is organized according to its rhythms and sounds the window itself becomes visible, as if somebody breathed on it, and we discover a gap between language and the world. We see that the words are not just signs, but things, that they are a material that can be sensed and shaped. To Jakobson poetic language, primarily though not exclusively, points to itself thus questioning its relation to reality and the meanings it bestows upon it. Jakobson's model emphasizes the dynamic and creative relationship between sound and meaning. The rhythmical stylization brings forth the sensual qualities of the words, or the aspect of the signifier, but by doing that it also produces new meaning because it molds the language through which we ordinarily consider things in new and surprising ways. The demand for a particular form redirects the habitual meanings and makes us see the world in a new way.

To understand how the poetic function alters our experience of language and reality better, one might turn to another key concept of the formalist movement that Jakobson is a late member of *ostranenie* or *defamiliarization*. The concept is discussed by the Russian Viktor Shklovsky in an article from 1916 called "Art as Technique" (Shklovsky 1994). Here Shklovsky argues that our perception of reality is automatized. We see what we expect to see, and that makes us blind to what is actually going on right in front of our eyes. However, by referring to ordinary objects and actions in unusual ways, art can de-automatize our perception. It can be done by referring to an object by way of its function instead of its name, by describing a familiar situation from an odd perspective, and in many other ways. Speaking about things in verse instead of prose may also do the trick. Speaking in verse makes things weird. By pointing toward the materiality of the words verse de-familiarizes the automatic relation between signs and things. This explains why poems can seem magical, eye opening, but also enigmatic and difficult. Poetry returns us to a sensual world in the shape of sensual words and rhythms. Rhythm always involves the body, it works along lines that does not involve meaning, which was an important issue to the formalists for whom aesthetics (issues of sensualities) were prior to hermeneutics (issues of interpretation). Without the prober tools to comprehend sound and rhythm in a poem, we not only risk missing the hesitation between sound and meaning which is so essential to a poem, we also tend to overlook the sensual world that the poem brings us into contact with on the field of representation as well as the field of presentation.

Further reading

For further reading, first consult the many relevant entries in *The Princeton Encyclopedia of Poetry and Poetics*. You will find a rich and informed discussion of several of the issues only touched upon in this essay in David Attridge's *Moving Words: Forms of English Poetry*. In *Musicalization of Fiction: A Study of the Theory and History of Intermediality* Werner Wolf conducts a thorough discussion of the relationship between literature and music. For a more philosophical approach to prosody, read Giorgio Agamben's essays in *The End of the Poem*. On the particular subject of the verse of Baudelaire from the vantage point of an English-speaking audience, a good pick is Clive Scott's *A Question of Syllables: Essays in Nineteenth-Century French Verse*.

References

Agamben, Giorgio (1999) *The End of the Poem*, Stanford: Stanford University Press.

Arnim, Bettina von (1920) *Die Günderode*, Berlin: Propyläen-Verlag.

Attridge, David (2015) *Moving Words: Forms of English Poetry*, Oxford: Oxford University Press.

Baudelaire, Charles (1968) *Oeuvres Completes*, Paris: Seuils.

Baudelaire, Charles (1993) *The Flowers of Evil*. Trans. James McGowan, Oxford: Oxford University Press.

Benjamin, Walter (1999) "On some Motifs in Baudelaire," in *Illuminations*, London: Pimlico.

Benveniste, Emil (1975) "La notion de 'rythme' dans son expression linguistique," in *Problemes de linguistique générale*, vol. 1, Paris: Gallimard.

Ekelöf, Gunnar (1992) "Dikt och musik," in *Skrifter*, vol. 7, Stockholm: Bonniers.

Eliot, T. S. (1957) "The Music of Poetry," in *On Poetry and Poets*, London: Faber and Faber.

Greene, Roland (ed.) (2012) *The New Princeton Encyclopedia of Poetry and Poetics*, 4th edition, Princeton, NJ: Princeton University Press.

Jakobson, Roman (2010) "Linguistics and Poetics," in Vincent B. Leitch (ed.), *The Norton Anthology of Theory and Criticism*, 2nd edition, New York and London: W. W. Norton & Company.

Lefebvre, Henri (2004) *Rhythmanalysis. Space, Time and Everyday Life*, London and New York: Continuum.

Scott, Clive (1986) *A Question of Syllables: Essays in Nineteenth-Century French Verse*, Cambridge: Cambridge University Press.

Shklovsky, Viktor (1988) "Art as Technique," in David Lodge (ed.), *Modern Criticism and Theory*, 16-30. London and New York: Longman.

Valéry, Paul (1958) "Poetry and Abstract Thought," in *The Art of Poetry*, New York: Pantheon.

Wolf, Werner (1999) *The Musicalization of Fiction: A Study in the Theory and History of Intermediality*, Amsterdam-Atlanta: Editions Rodopi B. V.

Wordsworth, William (2014) *Wordsworth's Poetry and Prose*, New York and London: W. W. Norton & Company.

10

Tropes

Christoph Bode

According to a useful handbook definition, a *trope* "is a figure of speech that uses a word or phrase in a sense other than what is proper to it" (Greene 2012, 1463). Tropes are the building blocks of *figurative* language (as opposed to the *literal* meaning of words) and some believe that tropes are therefore the hallmark of literature and of poetry in particular. The most widely known trope is *metaphor*— meaning "transference" or "carrying across": the idea being that a word is transferred from its proper realm to where it doesn't belong. But this is most puzzling: obviously, definitions of "trope" and "metaphor" cannot do without using tropes and metaphors themselves (like "figure" or "carrying across"). But how can you then speak of a "proper" use of language, from which the figurative use *deviates*? Surely, the above definitions do not strike us as particularly poetic—or do they?

It seems this problem has haunted Western Philosophy ever since it began to think about language: philosophers like Aristotle warned against an overuse of metaphor as "alien" or even "barbaric," while their very warnings were riddled with metaphors and other instances of tropical speech. Maybe the most famous example of this is a passage from John Locke's *Essay Concerning Human Understanding* (1690, chapter 10 of Book 3, "Of the Abuse of Words"), in which he warns that the figurative use of words is only good to "insinuate wrong *ideas*, move the passions, and thereby mislead the judgement" (quoted in Paul de Man in Sacks [ed.] 1979, 13); if one wanted truth, Locke says, one had to steer clear of the figurative use of language. But then John Locke is mostly known for his phrase that the mind of a newborn child is like a tablet of wax on which nothing is yet written—*tabula rasa*—before the first sense impressions leave their traces. So, ironically, and against his own warnings, he used a metaphor to illustrate his most central philosophical insight. What is more: in the larger context of the above quote, Locke suggests that eloquence, "like the fair sex," has many beauties, but is deceptive, only to add that some men "find pleasure to be deceived." This is most interesting from the point of view of Gender Studies: figurative language is said to be dangerous and it is associated with the female sex— but in this male truth-discourse it pops up time and again, like the return of the irrepressible.

That is my main point before I enter upon a discussion of tropes in literature: not only literature, but human language in general is absolutely permeated with tropes. They are not in any way "added" to it (in the last sentence, "enter" and "permeated" are, strictly speaking, metaphors). From which it follows that figurative language does not in any way "deviate" from anything. After all, you can't deviate from yourself. Figurative language as such is definitely not specific to literature—you can find it everywhere—let alone to poetry. So if in the following I take my examples exclusively from poetry, this is only for reasons of economy—and because I am too lazy to make up examples of my own. But also, admittedly, because the uses of tropes in poetry can show us, like under a magnifying glass, *how they work*. Because that should be our prime interest: *What do they do? How do they function? What do they do* to us *and to our way of looking at the world? What difference do they make?*

Classical rhetoric identifies a number of kinds of tropes. The most important ones are *simile, metaphor, metonymy, symbol,* and *allegory*. And as I take you through them, the above questions will be leading us. Because it is definitely not enough just to be able to identify a particular trope—you want to know what it is good for.

Metaphor and metonymy

The simplest trope is the explicit comparison by way of "like" or "as." That is called a *simile*. When Robert Burns writes, "O My Luve's like a red, red rose/That's newly sprung in June" (all quotes of primary literature are taken from the *Norton Anthology of English* or *American Literature*, respectively), then everybody will understand that the poet does not *identify* his love with a rose, he just compares her to this flower in one or more respects, although these respects are not spelt out. Freshness? Youth? Red cheeks? Red lips? Fragrance? Everybody can make up their own mind. It's enough for the simile to work if you can come up with *one* possible similarity.

Some poems are about finding the right kind of simile. In sonnet no. 18, William Shakespeare rejects a first idea, because the comparison is ludicrously inadequate:

Shall I compare thee to a summer's day?
Thou art more lovely and more temperate;
Rough winds do shake the darling buds of May,
And summer's lease hath all too short a date.
Sometime too hot the eye of heaven shines
And often is his gold complexion dimmed;
And every fair from fair sometimes declines,
By chance or nature's changing course untrimmed.
But thy eternal summer shall not fade
Nor lose possession of that fair thou ow'st,
Nor shall death brag thou wander'st in his shade,
When in eternal lines to time thou grow'st.
So long as men can breathe or eyes can see,
So long lives this, and this gives life to thee.

It is striking—is it not?—that when the third quatrain begins (with a typical *volta*, or turn-about), "But thy eternal summer …," we are puzzled that the poet, hitherto ultra-realistic in his rejection of exaggerated claims, is now making exactly such claims, because how can he possibly say that his lover will neither age nor die? But if we understand that in the final line "this" refers to the very poem we've just read, then we realize this is no hyperbole at all: this poem cannot die (we still read it today …), and *in this* the lover will live on. Nice move, eh? It is not the worst poetry that rejects clichés and stereotypes.

In contrast to simile, *metaphor* suggests a similarity without using "like" or "as." When it is said about Achilles (or was it Hector after all?) that he was a lion in battle, the "normal" expression "great warrior" is *substituted* by the figurative "lion," because—or so says classical rhetoric—these two ideas (mind you, not the *words*!) have something in common that allows the substitution of the one by the other. Just like in Burns's rose example, we may wonder what exactly that *tertium comparationis* (the third that allows a comparison and then a substitution) might exactly be. Valor? Strength? Majesty? The great thing is that we do not have to choose, we do not have to go for just one point of comparison—just like the simile, the metaphor may evoke a whole host of connotations. But in any case, the word we read is called the *vehicle* of the metaphor, whereas what it signifies (Achilles) is called the *tenor* of the metaphor. The vehicle always comes from "elsewhere." Its meaning is transferred. That is why the trope is called a *metaphor* (transference) in the first place.

But here lurks a larger problem: similes may be fortunate or unfortunate, depending on how plausible a comparison is, but we can't argue with them from a logical point of view. When we read, in T. S. Eliot's "The Love Song of J. Alfred Prufrock,"

> Let us go then, you and I,
> When the evening is spread out against the sky
> Like a patient etherized upon a table [.],

then we will wonder in which respect an evening *can* be like a patient (well, maybe calm like under anaesthetics?), but at least that's not an illogical proposition. But to say that Achilles *is* a lion is a patent falsehood. Minimal as the leaving out of "like" or "as" may seem, its consequences in terms of logic, semantics, and epistemology are momentous: *metaphors lie*. And therefore, the more unusual a metaphor is, the more it stops us in the tracks, because we have to reconstruct from the vehicle—which is the only thing that is given—what the tenor might possibly be. And even if we find a satisfactory one (in the case of Achilles, we do not have far to go), there is still that discontent that what the metaphor suggested wasn't "true." That is, good metaphors affect our habitual way of structuring the world, of understanding it, because they ask us to modify our *frames of reference*, to question how "true" our established way of processing the world really is. Metaphors are an invitation to *see "this" in terms of "that"*. Unusual metaphors do not only call up a knowledge we already possess—rather, they are *productive of meaning* and *productive of knowledge* in a way a pure substitution theory of metaphor may have difficulty to explain.

Human language is full of *dead metaphors*, that is metaphors that nobody (except linguists and literary scholars) recognizes as metaphors any longer. When you say "at the foot of the mountain," do you really imagine the mountain as a live being? When you say you "surf the Internet," do your really imagine yourself as a beach boy (or surfer girl, respectively)? Through overusage, these metaphors have lost their power to let us see the world in a new light. So, metaphors have their use-by date. After that, we no longer "buy" them. We crave for new ones. If the vehicle of a new one comes from afar, we speak of a *bold metaphor*. If it is very difficult or next to impossible to make out what exactly its tenor might be, then we speak of an *absolute metaphor*.

So every metaphor makes a proposal to see a section of the world differently, to imagine *x in terms of y*. Take, for instance, Ezra Pound's imagist poem "In a Station of the Metro" (arguably the shortest poem in the English language):

> The apparition of these faces in the crowd;
> Petals on a wet, black bough.

That is the whole poem. Pound claims he compressed it, in one and a half years, from thirty lines to just these two. If you can imagine the emergence of these faces *as* petals on a wet, black bough, then the metaphor has done its work. There is certainly more than just one *tertium comparationis*. But you do not have to enumerate them to acknowledge that waiting in a station of the metro will never be the same for you, never ever. (There is so much more to this poem, like: think about the function of the semi-colon. How is it better than a simple comma? Or a full stop? And what about the three stressed syllables at the end of the second line? Ah, but I'm digressing—our theme is tropes.)

The ancients knew that metaphor is the most important and the most dynamic of tropes. Metaphors can really challenge and revolutionize our established view of the world. The same cannot be said of *metonymy*. Metonymy is a trope that substitutes one expression by another, if the two objects or ideas (mind you, not the *words*!) stand in some relation of proximity to one another (spatial, temporal, or causal). "Washington announces" is a metonymy for "the current administration of the United States of America," for that is where it is. To decode a metonymy, you just need some kind of cultural knowledge. Metaphors can be about *finding out*, metonymy is always about *calling up* a knowledge you already have. Small surprise: the relationship between the two parts of a metonymy does *exist* in reality before it is mentioned; in metaphor, this relationship is often only *created* when it is suggested. It is therefore not surprising that while children can only use and process metaphors from the age of 10 onwards, they use and understand metonymy far earlier (see Gardner and Winner in Sacks).

Allegory and symbol

Two more tropes to go, *allegory* and *symbol*. They can be treated in conjunction, in a contrastive way. *Allegory* can best be defined as a systematized metaphor; that is, you do not only look for one point of similarity only, but for a whole *series* of similarities, for example A stand to B, B to C, C to D, and D to E in the same relationship as V to W, W to X, X to Y, and Y to Z. Allegory is used for *mapping* one system onto another. Take this poem by Sir Walter Raleigh, "What Is Our Life?," in which he compares life to a play in the theater, point by point:

> What is our life? A play of passion,
> Our mirth the music of division.
> Our mothers' wombs the tiring-houses be,
> Where we are dressed for this short comedy.
> Heaven the judicious sharp spectator is,
> That sits and marks still who doth act amiss.
> Our graves that hide us from the searching sun
> Are like drawn curtains when the play is done.
> Thus march we, playing, to our latest rest,
> Only we die in earnest, that's no jest.

Allegory, like its sister *personification*, is always asking for re-translation: take, for instance, the allegorical personification of Justice—a lady (because of Latin *justitia*), blindfolded (because she is said to pass judgment irrespective of who stands before her), with a sword in her hand (because she also executes the verdict). It is as if the semiotic power of metaphor were tamed in allegory by the sheer number of correspondences—it is tied down, like Gulliver in Lilliput. It must mean *one* thing. Or two *in one*. But it doesn't really provoke a lot of creative guessing or presuppose an unfettered imagination.

That is different with *symbol*. There are many different definitions of "symbol" (some of them conflicting), but I have always preferred Goethe's, who said that if you try to illustrate the general with the particular, then you are working allegorically, but if you give the reader something concrete and particular that only *implies* the general, then you work symbolically (cf. Goethe 1982, 471). The two processes mirror each other (in each case, you are given something concrete or particular and expected to see something behind it), but with a fundamental difference: allegory is just an illustration of a *known*, whereas a symbol is an invitation to explore the *unknown* possible meaning(s) implied. (Curiously enough, in this respect symbol resembles metaphor, whereas allegory—as systematized metaphor—more resembles metonymy.) Allegory (Greek "to say something differently") *can* say something differently, while symbol seems only able to express itself in *this* particular way. And if the symbol sends you on a never-ending quest, it coincides with the *absolute metaphor* mentioned earlier on: it is *implied* that it means more than it says, but it cannot be made out what exactly that might be—still, you are provoked into looking for it.

What I just said about symbols is, of course, not true for *conventionalized* symbols, like the Red Cross, the peace dove, the bleeding heart. No difficult decoding there. Here, however, we're talking about non-conventionalized symbols (yes, in literary texts …), which have not yet solidified into easily decipherable chiffres, so that you can look them up in a symbol dictionary. We are talking about *nonce* symbols: symbols that are created for only one occasion, in this one particular text. When do we think we're confronting such a symbol anyway? That is an easy one. If an expression or image is used over and over again in such a conspicuous way that we begin to wonder, could it be this means something else, in addition to just being this? My favorite example—to use a novel for once—is E. M. Forster's *A Room with a View* (1908). Throughout the novel, this topos—a room with a view—is used with such frequency that readers soon understand this is not only about a hotel room with a view over the river Arno, but it is about the heroine's desire to break free from her restricting British views: the novel is about her arduous emancipation.

Do tropes create meaning?

Let us look a bit closer at this question of whether tropes just *reproduce* a knowledge that you already have or are themselves *productive* of knowledge and new meaning.

In the eighteenth century there was a controversy between the Neo-classicists and the Romantics about the nature of poetic language. In his *Essay on Criticism* (1709/11), Alexander Pope formulated the Neo-classicist position:

> True wit is nature to advantage dressed,
> What oft was thought, but ne'er so well expressed[.]
> [...]
> Expression is the dress of thought [...]. (Part 2, 297/298, 318)

So you can have an idea and express it differently, clothe in different expressions, but it will still be the "same" idea. The Romantics, like William Wordsworth and Samuel Taylor Coleridge, were deeply critical of this: language, they argued, is not extraneous to thought. If you express an idea differently, it becomes a different idea. Moreover, if you follow Pope's precept, you think first and then you *translate* your idea into a sort of "poetic" language, but that means that your "same" idea could just as well have been expressed in prose—no? But if something can be translated back into prose *without any loss*, then it's not really poetry—is it? Rather, the thing to do, they argued, would be to think *poetically*, to use language as a *tool* to explore unknowns, to say things that could not be expressed in any other way (the main sources for this summary are Wordsworth's *Essays upon Epitaphs* [Wordsworth 1988, 322–71] and Coleridge's *Biographia Literaria* ([Coleridge 1984, chapter 1]). Not coincidentally, Pope's view is characteristic of an ideology that sees the world as static and harmonious, while the Romantics' view is that the world is dynamic, evolving, and potentially full of contradictions.

Now, let me return to what is, in many respects, the most interesting of tropes, metaphor. Let us investigate once more how metaphors behave with regard to this larger question of whether tropes are simply affirmative or transcending and transformative. Here are two examples of how fog is metaphorically presented. The first poem, "The Fog," is by Carl Sandburg:

> The fog comes
> on little cat feet.
>
> It sits looking
> over harbor and city
> on silent haunches
> and then moves on.

At roughly the same time—around 1916—T. S. Eliot writes this in his Modernist "The Love Song of J. Alfred Prufrock" (from which I have already quoted earlier on):

> The yellow fog that rubs its back upon the windowpanes,
> The yellow smoke that rubs its muzzle on the windowpanes
> Licked its tongue into the corners of the evening,
> Lingered upon the pools that stand in drains,

Let fall upon its back the soot that falls from chimneys,
Slipped by the terrace, made a sudden leap,
And seeing that it was a soft October night,
Curled once about the house, and fell asleep.

The contrast is striking, is it not? Sandburg's metaphor rests upon one *tertium comparationis* alone: silently, like on cat's paws. But Eliot takes this only as a starting point and then unfolds the whole package of "fog like cat" and makes the fog behave in very surprising ways indeed ("Licked its tongue into the corners of the evening," "made a sudden leap")—the vehicle has radically modified the tenor, because that is definitely not the way we usually think of fog. That's what this passage is about: imagine. See this as that, even beyond the obvious similarities.

The ubiquity of tropes

But if language is tropical, or figurative, through and through and if thinking takes place in language, how can we then say that one expression is more adequate than another, or, to formulate it more radically, where do we find truth? Is truth only in language, within a particular way of talking, a discourse? In his essay "Über Wahrheit und Lüge im außermoralischen Sinne," the philosopher Friedrich Nietzsche argued that this was exactly the case:

> What, then, is truth? A mobile army of metaphors, metonyms, and anthropo-morphisms—in short, a sum of human relations which have been enhanced, transposed, and embellished poetically and rhetorically, and which after long use seem firm, canonical, and obligatory to a people: truths are illusions about which one has forgotten that this is what they are; metaphors which are worn out and without sensuous power; coins which have lost their pictures and now matter only as metal, no longer as coins.

So, people tend to forget that all language is figurative, and once tropes are no longer seen as tropes, people regard them as "truth" and believe in them, while at the same time they become deeply suspicious of the figurative use of language (like Locke), which they suspect of being "deceiving." But all we ever have is interpretation, because of the tropical nature of language. All expression is necessarily figurative, because there is no other, "pure" language. But there is, of course, one type of language use in which this figurative, or tropical, dimension of language is often (though not always) *highlighted* in a conspicuous way, by the introduction of new and unusual tropes: *literature*, and poetry in particular.

I will return to that "though not always" in a moment, but let me first address another interesting question that has to do with tropes and truth and discourse: if it is true that all truth that can be spoken about can only be found *within* a discourse, is then all truth that cannot be spoken about (supposing there is such a thing) irrelevant? John Keats's "On First Looking into Chapman's Homer" sonnet gives an interesting answer:

> Much have I travelled in the realms of gold,
> And many goodly states and kingdoms seen;
> Round many western islands have I been
> Which bards in fealty to Apollo hold.
> Oft of one wide expanse had I been told
> That deep-browed Homer ruled as his demesne:
> Yet did I never breathe its pure serene
> Till I heard Chapman speak out loud and bold:
> Then felt I like some watcher of the skies
> When a new planet swims into his ken;
> Or like stout Cortez, when with eagle eyes
> He stared at the Pacific—and all his men
> Looked at each other with a wild surmise—
> Silent, upon a peak in Darien.

We need only some additional information to "place" this poem: John Keats knew no Greek and Chapman's translation of Homer was hard to come by when Keats lived. When he had the chance to read it (for one night only), he was bowled over and found he had made a major discovery. Keats probably wrote this sonnet while walking home from his friend's. Now, the striking thing about the sestet is that the speaker of the poem compares his feelings with the feelings of two discoverers (one astronomer, one *conquistador*) whose response to their respective discoveries was— silence. That's odd, for the poem implies: the adequate response to my discovery would have been to remain silent. But then this poem would not exist. The poem is not itself the adequate response—it can only point toward it. It points to a truth that is not directly expressible. The real thing would be—silence. This kind of move, when a text admits of its own necessary inadequacy, is called Romantic irony. It is a case of language pointing to its limitations, by way of a trope, the simplest ever: a (double) simile.

To wind up and return once more to the unavoidable tropicality of human language: if language is permeated with tropes and if one of the functions of literature is to remind us of this fact, why did I say earlier on that it is *not always* that the tropical dimension of language is highlighted in literature? Robert Frost's "The Road Not Taken" is an intriguing case:

> Two roads diverged in a yellow wood,
> And sorry I could not travel both
> And be one traveler, long I stood
> And looked down one as far as I could
> To where it bent in the undergrowth;

Then took the other, as just as fair,
And having perhaps the better claim,
Because it was grassy and wanted wear;
Though as for that the passing there
Had worn them really about the same,

And both that morning equally lay
In leaves no step had trodden black.
Oh, I kept the first for another day!
Yet knowing how way leads on to way,
I doubted if I should ever come back.

I shall be telling this with a sigh
Somewhere ages and ages hence:
Two roads diverged in a wood, and I—
I took the one less traveled by,
And that has made all the difference.

As far as I can see, there is no single metaphor here, no simile, no metonymy, no symbol—nothing that would indicate, on a merely linguistic level, that this is anything other than the description of a simple, everyday situation of choice, in a matter of little consequence. True: we learn something about the character of the speaker—the fact that he took the road *less* traveled by is a telling detail. And the five-line stanzas are nicely wrought, with their slight preponderance of one rhyme over the other, they mimetically mirror the *little* difference between the two roads. But the mere fact that by its textual organization as a *poem* (and maybe by the "all" in the final line), we are provoked to look for a tropical, figurative meaning *behind* the obvious, literal one. That is the way we are set up as signifying animals, that is the way we have been culturally conditioned to decode this special kind of text, which is flagged out for special processing by its mere typographical arrangement. Most readers do not have any difficulty in reading this poem about a situation in the woods as an *allegory* of the choices that you make in your life—this way or that way, at first it doesn't seem to make a big difference, but in the long run it does. But you can't go back again, in life. That is where the comparison with the situation in the woods stops. No comparison runs on all fours.

But my main point obviously is: we are so crazy for tropes, that even at the slightest provocation we start looking for them. As long as it's flagged out as "that" kind of discourse, we do not even need any tropes *within* the text to set us going—we then simply take the whole text as a trope and read it allegorically, as "saying something differently." We are like that—we cannot help it. And that is a very comforting idea, is it not? Looking for tropes and decoding them, as well as *producing* them in reading or writing, is something that comes quite naturally to us. Don't fear tropes— love them.

Further reading

If you want to explore further what different tropes there are, you should definitely consult the latest edition of *The Princeton Encyclopedia of Poetry and Poetics* (ed. Roland Greene). It is an invaluable mine of information about all kinds of tropes. An extremely helpful reader is *On Metaphor* by Sheldon Sacks. It contains Paul De Man's critique of Locke and others ("The Epistemology of Metaphor"), also formidable essays by Donald Davidson ("What Metaphors Mean") and by Howard Gardner and Ellen Winter ("The Development of Metaphoric Competence"). Three classics on the workings of tropes are Wordsworth's "Essays on Epitaphs" (in Wordsworth 1988), the first chapter of Coleridge's *Biographia Literaria*, and what is one of the most radical takes on the tropicality of language, Nietzsche's "On Truth and Lie in an Extra-moral Sense." Paul Ricœur's *The Rule of Metaphor: The Creation of Meaning in Language* is also strongly recommended: going back to Aristotle, it reconstructs the way in which philosophy has always struggled with the productive potential of metaphor.

References

Coleridge, Samuel Taylor (1984) *Biographia Literaria* [*Collected Works* 7], 2 vols. in 1. Eds. James Engell and Walter Jackson Bate. Princeton, NJ: Princeton University Press.

Goethe, Johann Wolfgang von (1982) "Maximen und Reflexionen," in *Werke* (Hamburg Edition), 365–471, Munich: dtv.

Greene, Roland (ed.) (2012) *The Princeton Encyclopedia of Poetry and Poetics: Fourth Edition*, Princeton, NJ: Princeton University Press.

Nietzsche, Friedrich (1873) "On Truth and Lie in an Extra-moral Sense," http://oregonstate.edu/instruct/phl201/modules/Philosophers/Nietzsche/Truth_and_Lie _in_an_Extra-Moral_Sense.htm (accessed February 18, 2016).

The Norton Anthology of American Literature: Sixth Edition (2003). 5 vols. Ed. Nina Baym. New York/London: Norton.

The Norton Anthology of English Literature: Seventh Edition (2000). 2 vols. Ed. M. H. Abrams. New York/London: Norton.

Ricœur, Paul (2003) *The Rule of Metaphor: The Creation of Meaning in Language*, London: Routledge.

Sacks, Sheldon (ed.) (1979) *On Metaphor*, Chicago and London: University of Chicago Press.

Wordsworth, William (1988) *Selected Prose*. Ed. John O. Hayden, Harmondsworth: Penguin.

11

Intertextuality

Elisabeth Friis

Good writers are also good readers. You are definitely less than certain of becoming a good writer, even though you may be a very assiduous reader. But if a writer has never opened a book, it is doubtful whether she would ever be capable of writing so much as a single line of literature for which others would care in the least. Because writers read, their texts are always connected to other texts, and this is what is usually called the intertextuality of the text. Texts written previously are active in the texts that succeed them. And as T. S. Eliot has noticed, this effect is reciprocal. Each time we read a new text, it will influence our reading of every text we have ever read before. This is a staggering perspective. And in any work one does in textual analysis the necessity of reflecting upon the intertextual dimensions of the text, of qualifying and categorizing these, is evident. Now what does it mean from a philosophical and theoretical perspective that the text is not an isolated fact, and how do we actually discover those other texts with whom it is upholding a conversation?

Intertextuality as philosophy of the text

The intertextual in which every text is held, it itself being the text-between of another text, is not to be confused with some origin of the text: to try to find the "sources", the "influences" of a work, is to fall in with the myth of filiation. (Barthes 1977, 160)

When Roland Barthes rejects the "myth of filiation" as a basis for the theory of intertextuality, he points to a central problem that haunts the relation between texts within the field of literary studies: the relationship between a text and its sources. *Filios* means "son," and what Barthes terms the "myth of filiation" refers to the notion that any connection between a text and its repetition, its prolongation or simply its discrete presence in a posterior text will mime the relationship between a father (its author, its original source) and his son (the successor, the imitator).

In Harold Bloom's theory of the "Anxiety of Influence," the tale of the mutual relations between texts is precisely a tale of "fathers and sons": A "poet son" reacts to a "poet father" who precedes him, for instance by mocking, ridiculing, exalting, ignoring, or mimicking the literary production of this "poet father." In this manner Bloom turns the question of literary influence into a question of oedipal psychology. Bloom's viewpoint has been subject to heavy criticism, among others from Sandra Gilbert and Susan Gubar, who judge the patriarchal joust between father and son to be excluding women authors, and who talk instead of an "Anxiety of Authorship"—the female writer's basic fear of taking on the (authoritative) author's voice.

But to Barthes the gender question is not at all relevant. Innumerable other texts are streaming through *any* text, so that the very idea of tracing the "origin" of a text, *its paternal or its maternal source*, by tracing its connections to previous sources is plainly false: The source material of any text is multiple as the sand—a text never has just one origin, one pedigree—it is a bastard. To Barthes the inexhaustible intertextuality is a quality in any text. This contention stands in direct continuation of Barthes' contemporary and colleague Julia Kristeva's notion of what kind of phenomenon a *text* is (in terms of the philosophy of the text).

Inspired by the Russian theoretician Mikhail Bakhtin, Kristeva toward the end of the 1960s begins to use the term "intertextuality" in order to describe what she sees as a constitutive trait of the very phenomenon "a text." To Kristeva, all texts—

and this equally means all *types* of texts, whether poetry or prose, whether written or oral, whether fictional or referential—have been created from already existing discourses. No author writes in an original manner—what the author does is to put together bits and pieces (for instance, phonemes, morphemes, paradigms, syntagms) from the infinite mass of text, which is constituted by everything that may and ever will be collected under the name of *culture*. Kristeva simply defines "the text" as "productivity":

> The text is [...] a productivity, and this means: first, that its relationship to the language in which it is situated is redistributive (destructive-constructive), and hence can be better approached through logical categories rather than linguistic ones; and second, that it is a permutation of texts, an intertextuality in the space of a given text, several utterances, taken from other texts, intersect and neutralize one another. (Kristeva 1980, 36)

Intertextuality as a theory of the text

When a new book carries the designation "fiction" or "poetry," these are not terms that the publisher has just invented. The fact that literature is still related to certain *genres* is perhaps the simplest example of how texts speak to other texts, or rather: Of how a text is connected to other texts, of what its inter-textual relations are (*inter* meaning "between" in Latin).

Besides *genre*, the marked *quotation* is another immediately visible form of intertextuality, an exact or at least unmistakably recognizable rendering of something that has already been said or written in another context. A more difficult, and therefore a more controversial, form of intertextuality is that of the *allusion*. In the case of quotations, the text itself marks its source: In Marcel Proust's *Remembrance of Things Past*, the French seventeenth-century author Madame de Sévigné is constantly quoted by name. But in the case of allusions the reader will only understand that the text is referring to another text if the reader is already familiar with that other text. In the case of James Joyce's novel *Ulysses*, it will be clear to many readers that the novel might bear some kind of relationship to the Greek hero Ulysses. That is, if they know in advance that such a hero does exist. And when, in *Ulysses*, the sea is referred to as "the snotgreen sea," it is necessary to have read Homer's *Odyssey* quite carefully in order to be able to catch the humorous allusion to the standard English rendering of one of the Homeric epithets: *The Wine-dark sea*.

Tracing the intertextual relations of a text (for instance, the genre to which it belongs, quotations that name their sources) may be so banal an operation that you may not realize that this is what you are actually doing: If a book carries the designation "a novel," then it entertains some kind of intertextual relation to the genre of "the novel." On the other hand, an intertextual reference may demand rather a great amount of advance knowledge in order to become visible to the reader. One does not understand an allusion without some degree of familiarity with the text to which it alludes. In order to take heed of the intertextual aspects of a text—something which is necessary if a literary analysis is to keep abreast of the text it analyzes—it is first of all necessary to read a lot and all of the time, and secondly to read annotated editions. When reading Shakespeare it is of no use reading cheap paperbacks without any notes in them. It takes for instance an Arden Critical Edition to have any chance of catching all of Shakespeare's allusions and puns, etc. And even then you will time and again find that something did elude you anyway.

So what matters is to sharpen your attention toward the different ways in which intertextuality operates. You simply have to establish a checklist. For that purpose one may use the French literary theoretician Gérard Genette's theory of different kinds of intertextuality (his is a theory of textual analysis). Genette operates with five different categories of basic intertextual forms: Intertextuality, paratextuality, metatextuality, hypertextuality, and architextuality. It is important not to let oneself be confused by the fact that Genette's most general category does not go by the name of "intertextuality," but by that of "transtextuality" ("intertextuality" being just one of the specific subcategories of "transtextuality"). This is important to bear in mind all through the following account, where I shall begin by defining the five basic forms of transtextuality and then use them as a checklist when focusing on the presence of other texts in Paul Celan's poem *Death Fugue*.

Intertextuality

Genette defines intertextuality as "a relationship of co-presence between two texts or among several texts: The actual presence of one text within another." This form of intertextuality has already been discussed. It is mainly a matter of quotations and allusions. But a third form of intertextuality also belongs in this category, namely that of *plagiarism*, which has been defined by Genette as "undeclared but literal borrow." As far as academic texts are concerned, plagiarism is dealt with harshly. It would for instance be a case of plagiarism if somebody translated an excerpt from an article that was written in French and let it slide into that somebody's own text, unmarked. But would it also be a case of plagiarism if an author borrowed a metaphor from someone else? The line between plagiarism and quotation is very fine indeed, and it could be argued that literary texts are allowed to plunder at will. When the American poet Juliana Spahr constructs an entire poetic suite in her volume *thisconnectionofeveryonewithlungs* [2005] around the repetition of the word "exists," some would say this was a plagiarism of the Danish poet Inger Christensen's repetition of the word "exists" (in Danish: *findes*) in her volume *Alfabet* from 1981 [Eng. trans.: *Alphabet*, 2001]. And others would say that Spahr is simply continuing the great text that is the world. But we shall return to the question of plagiarism in connection with the analysis of Celan.

Paratextuality

That a text contains paratextuality means that it is supplied with information that transcends the frame of the text itself. The paratext is going to form or direct how the text is received—the way in which the text's readers will see it. In Genette's expression, the paratext lies at the *threshold* of the text. Genette has written an entire book dedicated to the phenomenon of paratext. The French title is *Seuils* (1987), which precisely means *thresholds*. Herein he distinguishes paratext as *peritext* from paratext as *epitext*.

The peritext (i.e., the paratext which has physical contact with the text) comprises, for instance, the titles of books, their subtitles, epigraphs, dedications, notes, and covers. The epitext (the paratext that has no physical contact with the text) comprises, for instance, other texts written by the same author, interviews with the author, the author's letters, and just any public statement that both relates to the text and may be connected to the author. This means that the epitext does not comprise the text's reception in the broadest sense ("the critics"), though it does include any attempt by the author to influence how the text will be received.

Metatextuality

A metatext is a text that can be read as a direct comment upon another text. The metatext connects a given text to another text, the text of which it speaks, without necessarily quoting this last text. Perhaps without even mentioning the text upon which it is a comment. In that case the reader will very often need to consult some epitextual information. Literary criticism is of course a metatext. The book that you are reading right now is metatextual.

Hypertextuality

The largest book written by Genette on intertextuality is called *Palimpsestes: La littérature au second degré* (1982). The book on palimpsests is mainly the study of a single one of the five types of intertextuality pointed out by Genette: Hypertextuality. Hypertextuality is defined by Genette as "any relationship uniting a text B (hypertext) to an earlier text A (hypotext)." Here, too, etymology can be of assistance: *Hyper* means "above," while *hypo* means "beneath." The palimpsest is Genette's highly illustrative metaphor for the relationship between hypertext and hypotext. A palimpsest is a document in which the original text has been wiped out or scratched off in order to make space for a new text. This is a practice dating from Antiquity, the practical purpose of which was to recycle expensive and scarce papyrus. The word *palimpsest* in Ancient Greek simply means scraping again. *Palimpsestes* is primarily about three different genres: Parody, travesty, and pastiche, these three genres being prototypical examples of hypertextual relationships. Without a hypotext like Samuel Richardson's *Pamela: or, Virtue Rewarded* (1740), we would not have had Henry Fielding's wonderful parody of that work, the hypertext *An Apology for the Life of Mrs. Shamela Andrews* (1741).

Hypertextuality, though, by no means limits itself to comical or satirical genres. It forms the nucleus of a long tradition within the history of literature: that of epic poetry. The *Aeneid* of Virgil combines the Homeric epics *The Iliad* and *The Odyssey* while imitating the Homeric structures, themes, motifs, meters, and poetic figures. The art of imitation (*imitatio*) is a refined craft that more or less disappears with Romanticism, and which has got nothing to do with plagiarism. Imitatio is simply a prototypically hypertextual form. For a hypertextual relationship is an intended and self-conscious relationship between text A and text B, and in Genette's terminology it is precisely the imitation of another specific text—and not the imitation of generic models (for instance genres)—which defines the relationship as a hypertextual one. Once more, advance knowledge of the specific hypotext to which the hypertext refers is necessary. And it is exactly this specificity that sets the hypertext apart from the last of Genette's types of intertextual relationship, namely architextuality, which is by definition generical.

Architextuality

Architextuality designates the text's relationship to formal categories of texts—first and foremost *genres*. The architext may simply be defined as the sum total of the general or transcendent categories—types of discourse, modes of enunciation or literary genres—from which each text emerges. One example of a type of discourse might be that of the satirical poem. One example of a mode of enunciation might be that of apostrophe. The architextual relationship may be very close—like the relationship between a sonnet by Petrach and a sonnet by Shakespeare. Or a little less close—like the relationship between Sir Arthur Conan Doyle's *The Hound of the Baskervilles* and Edgar Allan Poe's criminalistic short stories: the texts share certain traits. They have certain generical principles in common. But when a text draws upon architextuality, it is not in the process of rewriting any specific text—that would be the domain of hypertextuality. Architextuality by the way represents Genette's first attempt at making a classificatory statement about intertextuality. The concept is developed in *Introduction à l'architexte* (1979).

A transtextual reading of *Death Fugue*

Paul Celan was a German-speaking Romanian of Jewish descent. He was born in 1920 in the city of Czernowitz. His parents were deported in 1942 and both died. In 1970, Celan killed himself. His body was found in the river Seine. Celan's poem "Death Fugue" is without doubt the most well-known and most recognized post-war poem about the Holocaust. Here it is in the translation of Michael Hamburger:

Death Fugue

Black milk of daybreak we drink it at sundown
we drink it at noon in the morning we drink it at night
we drink it and drink it
we dig a grave in the breezes there one lies unconfined
A man lives in the house he plays with the serpents
he writes
he writes when dusk falls to Germany your golden
hair Margarete
he writes it and steps out of doors and the stars are
flashing he whistles his pack out
he whistles his Jews out in earth has them dig for a
grave
he commands us strike up for the dance

Black milk of daybreak we drink you at night
we drink you in the morning at noon we drink you at
sundown
we drink and we drink you
A man lives in the house he plays with the serpents
he writes
he writes when dusk falls to Germany your golden hair
Margarete
your ashen hair Sulamith we dig a grave in the breezes
there one lies unconfined

He calls out jab deeper into the earth you lot you
others sing now and play
he grabs at the iron in his belt he waves it his
eyes are blue
jab deper you lot with your spades you others play
on for the dance

Black milk of daybreak we drink you at night
we drink you at noon in the morning we drink you
at sundown
we drink and we drink you
a man lives in the house your golden hair Margarete
your ashen hair Sulamith he plays with the serpents

He calls out more sweetly play death death is a master
from Germany
he calls out more darkly now stroke your strings then
as smoke you will rise into air
then a grave you will have in the clouds there one
lies unconfined

Black milk of daybreak we drink you at night
we drink you at noon death is a master from Germany
we drink you at sundown and in the morning we drink
and we drink you
death is a master from Germany his eyes are blue
he strikes you with leaden bullets his aim is true
a man lives in the house your golden hair Margarete
he sets his pack on to us he grants us a grave in
the air
He plays with the serpents and daydreams death is
a master from Germany

your golden hair Margarete
your ashen hair Shulamith

It is a distinctive feature of Celan's poem that it is built from material that was already at hand, but which has been arranged in an original fashion. Thus, the formal mode of this poem is predominantly transtextual.

Intertextuality II

In line with the order in which Genette proceeds, we shall—with assistance of John Felstiners seminal work *Paul Celan: Poet, Survivor, Jew*—begin by looking at the *intertextual* elements that are used by the poem: Are quotations, allusions, or plagiarism present in the poem? The answer to which is: Maybe, yes, and yes.

If we begin by the question of plagiarism, Celan himself never mentioned the fact that the poem was written with a point of departure in the poem "ER" (English "HE") by his Czernowitz colleague, Immanuel Weissglas. It goes as follows:

ER

Wir heben Gräber in die Luft und siedeln
Mit Weib und Kind an dem gebotnen Ort.
Wir schaufeln fleißig, und die andern fiedeln,
Man schafft ein Grab und fährt im Tanzen fort.

ER will, daß über diese Därme dreister
Der Bogen strenge wie sein Antlitz streicht:

Spielt sanft vom Tod, er ist ein deutscher Meister,
Der durch die Lande als ein Nebel schleicht.

Und wenn die Dämmrung blutig quillt am Abend,
Öffn' ich nachzehrend den verbissnen Mund,
Ein Haus für alle in die Lüfte grabend:
Breit wie der Sarg, schmal wie die Todesstund.

ER spielt im Haus mit Schlangen, dräut und dichtet,
In Deutschland dämmert es wie Gretchens Haar.
Das Grab in Wolken wird nicht eng gerichtet:
Da weit der Tod ein deutscher Meister war.

The fact that Weissglas's text is present in Celan's text is beyond doubt. But this is not a piece of information to be found in the most common editions of Celan's poetry. It is necessary to take a look at research articles like that of Leonard Forster. Forster shows how Celan's poem borrows several motifs directly from the poem "ER": Digging a grave in the breezes, the daybreak, death being a German master, "his" playing with serpents, furthermore the name Margarete, which is present in Weissglas's text as the diminutive "Gretchen," alongside this Gretchen's hair, which makes even clearer the allusion to Margarete/Gretchen in Goethe's *Faust*.

Even though Celan's poem is in a way written "on top of" Weissglas's poem, the relation between the poems is not a hypertextual one, in which Weissglas's text would be the hypotext, and Celan's text its hypertext. We remember that the relationship between hypotext and hypertext must always be explicit. The question, then, is whether we may say that Celan quotes or alludes to Weissglas's poem. And the answer is probably a "no," since the connection remains so hidden. Weissglas's poem most certainly has not been well known. At a certain level this is a case of plagiarism, which is not a moral judgment, of course, but one of textual theory. But Celan's poem is also replete with allusions, for instance, in the form of "Schwarze Milch/Black Milk." The black milk is an oxymoron that Celan may have borrowed from another Czernowitz colleague, the poet Rose Ausländer. But similar images may be found in other German poets such as Georg Trakl or Franz Werfel. And then black milk carries the following evident affinity to a very powerful and uncanny passage from *Lamentations*:

Her Nazarites were purer than snow, they were whiter than milk, they were more ruddy in body than rubies, their polishing was of sapphire: Their visage is blacker than a coal; they are not known in the streets: their skin cleaveth to their bones; it is withered, it is become like a stick. (*KJV*, 4, 7–8)

The coupling of "black" with "milk" evidently *also* carries an allusion to *Lamentations*. An allusion, that entails quite a lot: It is a reference to the Jewish canon (the Old Testament), and the image could easily be a description of starving concentration camp prisoner. Besides, the rhythm of *Lamentations* is paratactical (as goes for so many of the texts of the Old Testament), as is the case for "Death Fugue."

The allusions in Celan's text are not only *literary* ones. If, employing an expression that Umberto Eco has used in several contexts, we regard the "Holocaust" in its capacity of a "cultural unit," the poem's strategy is that of an intensifying repetition of metonymical signs (i.e., signs based on a relation of contiguity), related to German Nazism and to the Holocaust. "Your golden hair" and "his eyes are blue" allude to both Heinrichs Heine's *Lorelei* and the racial doctrines of Nazism, and "hair" is an allusion to the shaved heads of the camp inmates: The hair which the Nazis used for making fabric and other things, and of which heaps still remain at Auschwitz, "a grave in the breezes" and "a grave in the air," may be read as metonymies for the smoke from the crematoriums, "ashen" as a metonymy for the remains from the crematoriums, and "master from Germany" and "fugue" as metonymies for German high culture ("the old masters") just as the aforementioned "Margarete" is an allusion to Gretchen in Goethe's *Faust*. "Sulamith" is a figure in the Song of Songs and functions in the poem as an allusion to the Jewish people. We may, however, also choose to regard the name of Sulamith as a direct *quotation* from the Song of Songs, which would make all three forms of intertextuality: plagiarism, allusion, and quotation, present in Celan's poem.

Paratextuality II

"Death Fugue" is also a poem that very much relates to information that transcends, peritextually or epitextually, the borders of the text itself. A peritextul element could be the history of the poem's publication. According to Celan himself he wrote the poem in Bucarest in 1945. Nevertheless, it was not published until 1947, in a Romanian version carrying the title "Tangoul mortii" [Death Tango] in the magazine *Contemporanul*. In 1948, Celan publishes his first volume of poetry in German, *Der Sand aus den Urnen*, and here *Todesfuge* appears under its definitive title. Why the fugue was originally a tango is a classical paratextual/epitextual question, to which there is a number of interesting answers. The peritextual elements of the paratext might bear upon Celan's own recital of the poem (Celan's recital, which can be heard on YouTube, is to a high degree an interpretation—for example the speed accelerates markedly during his reading, while slowing down toward the end) or the remarks he makes about the poem in his correspondence with the writer Ingeborg Bachmann. To her, for instance, he writes the following on November 12 1959:

> You know—nay, you knew—and so I have to remind you of this now, that the Death Fugue is also this to me: An epitaph and a grave. […] My mother, too, has only *this* grave.

> [Du weisst—nein, Du wusstest –, und so muss ich Dich jetxt daran erinnern, dass die Todesfuge auch dies für mich ist: eine grabschrift und ein Grab. […] Auch meine Mutter hat nur *dieses* Grab. (Bachmann and Paul 2009, 127)]

The fact that Celan calls the poem a grave and an epitaph—and in the same breath calls it his mother's grave—may open the reading of the poem towards Celan's biography. Or perhaps underline the poem's character of being literally a very palpable cenotaph for all of the disappeared and unburied victims of the Holocaust.

Metatextuality II

Celan's poem has given rise to a comprehensive metatextual production. It has generated lots of debate, and many critical readings. A very famous metatextual discourse in which Celan's poem is central is the debate as to whether writing poetry is still possible after the Holocaust. The instigator of the debate is the German philosopher Theodor W. Adorno, who in his text *Kulturkritik und Gesellschaft* ("Cultural Criticism and Society," 1955, Adorno, vol. 10, p. 30.) made the remark that "writing a poem after Auschwitz is barbarian." But it is furthermore the case that Adorno later, and influenced by precisely Celan's poetry, changes his original stance to this: "Celan's poems seek to speak ultimate terror through silence" ("Celans Gedichte wollen das äußerste Entsetzen durch Verschweigen sagen", Adorno, vol. 7 477).

Hypertextuality II

Celan's poem is no hypertext, since the text does not explicitly or clearly rewrite or imitate another text—see again the section on intertextuality. On the other hand, it has perhaps itself become a hypotext? Imre Kertész has, for instance, written the novel *Kaddish for an Unborn Child* (1980): A text about the Holocaust in which the reference to *Death Fugue* plays a significant role but this relation might also be described as a simple intertextual one. Furthermore poetic texts can be found which more or less explicitly use Celan's text as a hypotext, for instance, by following the poem's metrical pattern.

Architextuality II

Architextuality being "the entire set of general or transcendent categories—types of discourse, modes of enunciation, literary genres—from which emerges each singular text," we may begin by stating that Celan's poem belongs to the absurdly broad genre of *lyric poetry*. It is no novel, no short story, no drama. The text is rhythmical, it is densely populated with imagery, and it works through intensifying repetitions rather than by progression—all of those are very "lyrical" traits though they may also be found in novels, short stories, and drama. In other words we shall not be getting very far by looking into architextuality on such a broad (Aristotelian) level. As for lyric poetry, Aristotle's original definition of the genre indeed limits itself to saying that "lyric poetry is accompanied by the lyre."

But on a less general level we of course find another statement of genre, and indication of architextuality, in the poem's title, *fugue*. A fugue is a musical form—emblematically connected to the German composer Johann Sebastian Bach. A fugue has a melodic theme—called its subject—which is contrasted to one or more countersubjects, which may proceed in close order alongside the melodic theme and so form a counterpoint. It is possible to analyze the repetitions in Celan's poem in relation to the compositional technique of the fugue. In that case the "man playing with serpents" could form the poem's counterpoint. But considering the poem's syncopated form it makes just as much sense to compare it to a tango, corresponding to the poem's original title, which may indicate that the allusion to Bach (*The Art of the Fugue*, etc.) may be more central to Celan's poem than any wish to place it within the framework of any single musical genre.

Opening Celan's text toward its intertextual traits is—hopefully this is by now evident—an absolutely necessary operation if we are to give an analysis of the text. Such an analysis has not been given here. But the mere fact of checking it via Genette's categories has made some of the basic elements of the text appear. And whether we look upon intertextuality as a constitutive trait of the phenomenon "a text," alongside Barthes or Kristeva, or proceed in a more pragmatic fashion, isolating and discussing intertextuality in the more typological sense of Gérard Genette, one thing is clear: A text is never a closed space, and we must always be attentive as to how and why it establishes inter-textual relations.

Further reading

In *Intertextuality*, Graham Allen gives a clear account of the central theories of intertextuality: from Bakhtin to Genette. *Palimpsestes: La littérature au second degré* is Genette's great book on hypertextuality. It contains a short introduction in which Genette sums up all of his intertextual categories. Mary Orr's *Intertextuality: Debates and Contents* sticks to Kristeva, Barthes, Bloom, and Genette and is of special interest to those seeking to acquaint themselves with Kristeva's concept of intertextuality without reading French.

References

Adorno, Theodor W. (1973a) *Ästhetische Theorie. Bind 7, Gesammelte Schriften in zwanzig Bänden*, Frankfurt a. M.: Suhrkamp.

Adorno, Theodor W. (1973b) *Kulurkritik und Gesellschaft. Bind 10, Gesammelte Schriften in zwanzig Bänden*, Frankfurt a. M.: Suhrkamp.

Allen, Graham (2000) *Intertextuality. The New Critical Idiom*, London: Routledge.

Barthes, Roland (1977) "From Work to Text," in *Image Music Text*, Essays selected and translated by Stephen Heath, London: Fontana Press.

Barthes, Roland (1984) "De l'oeuvre au texte," in *Le bruissement de la langue*, Paris: Seuil.

Bloom, Harold (1973) *Anxiety of Influence: A Theory of Poetry*, Oxford: Oxford University Press.

Celan, Paul (1958) "Todesfuge," i *Mohn und Gedächtnis*, Deutsche Verlags-Anstalt.

Felstiner, John (1995) *Paul Celan: Poet, Survivor, Jew*, New Haven: Yale University Press.

Forster, Leonard (1985) "Todesfuge: Paul Celan, Immanuel Weissglas and the Psalmist," *German Life and Letters*, 39: 1.

Genette, Gérard (1979) *Introduction à l'architexte*, Paris: Seuil [*The Architext: An Introduction*, University of California Press, 1992].

Genette, Gérard (1982) *Palimpsestes: La littérature au second degree*, Paris: Seuil [*Palimpsests: Literature in the Second Degree*, University of Nebraska Press, 1997].

Genette, Gérard (1987) *Seuils*, Paris: Seuil [*Paratexts. Thresholds of Interpretation*, Cambridge University Press, 1997].

Gilbert, Sandra og Susan Gubar (1979/2000) *The Madwoman in the Attic. The Woman Writer and the Nineteenth-Century Literary Imagination*, New Haven: Yale University Press.

Ingeborg, Bachmann and Celan Paul (2009) *Herzzeit. Der Briefwechsel*, Frankfurt a. M.: Suhrkamp.

Kristeva, Julia (1969) *Sémiotikè, recherches pour une sémanalyse*, Paris: Seuil. "The Bounded Text" can be read in translation in *Desire in Language: A Semiotic Approach to Literature and Art*, Columbia University Press, 1980.

Kristeva, Julia (1980) *Desire in Language: A Semiotic Approach to Literature and Art*, Columbia University Press.

Orr, Mary (2003) *Intertextuality: Debates and Contexts*, London: Polity.

Part II

Contexts

Part II

Context

12
Author

Jon Helt Haarder

If you look at the state of the author in modern literary studies, the short version is that to leading literary scholars of the nineteenth century, the author was what both criticism and research was really about, whereas for leading scholars of the twentieth century, the watermark of true literary science was having the text in focus while keeping the author at arm's length.

One of the most influential critics in the first half of the nineteenth century was the Frenchman Charles-Augustin Sainte-Beuve. In an account of his famous—and later infamous—"biographical method" in 1862, he wrote, "Getting to know yet another person, and getting to know him well, is a matter of great importance that should not be disdained, especially if this person is prominent and famous" (Sainte-Beuve 1865). Works of literature were thus—notably along with, for example, private conversations, letters and knowledge of the author's maternal lineage—to him the way in which you found out more about another person.

Sainte-Beuve wrote, getting to know great and famous people through literature is not contemptible. But contempt for Sainte-Beuve and his biographical method was just what Marcel Proust displayed when he in 1908 slowly started to piece together one of the twentieth century's greatest novels. *In Search of Lost Time* was among other a product of the critical essays Proust wrote about Sainte-Beuve, later collected under the title *Against Sainte-Beuve* (1988).

The core of Proust's caustic criticism is that Sainte-Beuve was a deplorable reader of literature and his method no more than insipid gossip. The fact of the matter is that Sainte-Beuve was unable to distinguish between the author you might meet in a bar and the voice speaking through the text. Proust's reaction to Sainte-Beuve is typical of a major emphasis in twentieth-century literary discussions of the author: Literary studies should not be concerned with listening to the voice of the empirical author, but should decipher something else that is making itself heard in the text. A large number of the stances within literary theory agree on this point, but diverge when it comes to defining this something else, other texts, the unconscious, market power, colonial power structures, and so on.

Anti-author theories

The clash over the use and value of biography for literary studies, or Sainte-Beuve's method, was an extended affair. No sooner was the author declared unimportant than he or she returned in some form or another. The Anglo-American trend within literary theory known as New Criticism struggled to wrench reading free of the author to focus only on *the words on the page*.

In the essay "The Intentional Fallacy" from 1946 (revised in 1954), Monroe Beardsley and W. K. Wimsatt did away with the kind of criticism that focuses on the question: What did the author *really* mean? What the author meant is only interesting to the extent that his or her intention is realized in the completed work. It is quite simply a logical fallacy to look for an intention elsewhere than in the work itself.

In actual fact, Wimsatt and Beardsley do not write about the *interpretation* of text. They are concerned with the now almost forgotten question of text *evaluation* and deny that a work's aesthetic value can be measured on the basis of whether it can and how it does live up to the author's intention. However, their essay can be read in such a way that it is about interpretation; the idea is that a work's intention, what the work is supposed to mean, can be found in the work itself, not in the empirical author's opinions and intentions. And it is in this way that the essay has actually been read.

In the same period, structuralism successfully spread from linguistics to other areas of the humanities, including literary theory. Structuralism consolidated a general shift of focus within the humanities away from a nineteenth-century obsession with origins and grand historical narratives toward structural or systemic accounts. The idea of literary studies as a study of authorial intention and biographical background was laid to rest.

In conjunction with these—somewhat different—rejections of the author's relevance, purely textual concepts were developed for the text's sender function. Wayne Booth discussed what he termed the *implied author* in *The Rhetoric of Fiction* (1961), which is the image of the text's sender that the reader creates using the text. Booth in other words focused on the reader and thus distanced himself from both biographical criticism and New Criticism.

Even though these markedly anti-authorial theories successfully permeated Western literary studies, in 1968 Roland Barthes was still compelled, with a fury not unlike Marcel Proust's sixty years earlier, to state: "The image of literature to be found in ordinary culture is tyrannically centred on the author" (Barthes 1995, 126). Barthes struggled hard to liberate the text and us as readers from this tyranny and he and his fellow anti-author theorists were somewhat successful in this. It is nevertheless clear that my opening paragraph, in which I suggest that nineteenth-century literary research was centered on the author whereas in the twentieth century it was all about distancing the text from the author, is oversimplified.

The author returns

The main trend in modern literary *theory* (though not the only trend of course) seems to be based on the kind of reaction we encountered in Marcel Proust, the renunciation of Sainte-Beuve, but in actual practice there has also been a fair amount of literary research that has drawn the empirical author into consideration in various ways. Why does the author always make a comeback?

There are many answers to this question. One of them is that literature to some extent is communication. The human *default setting* for communication is presumably face-to-face conversation where the sender is present. Here the context—the speaker's body language and our own knowledge of the speaker—is relevant to decoding the message. This context is absent when we meet a written text.

One of narratology's founders, Gerard Genette, has suggested that our reading of Proust is unavoidably changed if we know that he was half-Jewish and homosexual. And then he adds:

> I am not saying that people must know those facts; I am saying only that people who do know them read Proust's work differently from people who do not and that anyone who denies the difference is pulling our leg. (Genette 1997, 8)

This is an important distinction. Genette writes that we *unavoidably* read biographically if we have any biographical knowledge. He does not expand on this, but it seems to me that this unavoidability—elsewhere I refer to it as *biographical irreversibility* (Haarder 2016)—must be anchored in the fact that we (both together and as individuals) learn to communicate verbally, through body language and using gestures before learning to write, and in this form of communication, knowledge of the sender is important, perhaps vitally so. But conversely, it is not the case that you *must* be aware of Proust's sexual preferences and ethnicity to understand and evaluate *In Search of Lost Time*, as Sainte-Beuve would have claimed.

On the contrary, to read a text, writes Paul Ricœur, is to consider the author dead and the text as posthumously published (Ricœur 1981, 137). Ricœur's point is that a text must not be considered written speech, but as writing, and that this basically involves (at least initially) setting the sender aside.

It is thus no wonder that the author exercises a certain force of attraction on us and always returns—it is something almost physical. Conversely, we must learn to communicate on writing's terms if we seriously want to be readers. Here we touch on the author issue's pedagogical aspect: literary studies should make us readers and thus enable us to choose between different types of reading with varying degrees and types of interest for the sender.

The above line of reasoning primarily concerns the reading situation as such and what can be called the phenomenology of "biographism." A question related to this is the existence not only of biographically oriented researchers, but entire research paradigms that, despite the anti-author theories, are in various ways interested in authors as part of scholarly dealings with literature.

This is not a field that will be discussed in more detail here, but it is generally made possible by the idea that the author in a specific historical context has created a piece of aesthetic communication. In our interpretation, we can therefore consider what is expressed in the work and the historical context in which it was written. If this—perfectly valid—perspective is *a priori* eliminated by a given theoretical foundation, what is built on it will be haunted by the author. Also for ethical reasons, to whom would the responsibility otherwise fall if, for example, a text advocated genocide or incest?

The author as a concept

Author can mean several things. Yet in a context such as the present the word "author" generally means a creator of fiction, that is someone who by virtue of the originality of his or her works of fiction own the copyright to them, and who with the help of printing technology can sell them in the market. This conception of authorship is connected to the multifaceted changes in Western societies from the eighteenth century onward. The medieval *auctor* had possessed an authority deriving from, in the last instance, divine revelation. The new author claimed this authority for himself and based it on the originality of his or her work (Pease 1995, 266).

In this transition, the author on the one hand was liberated not only from the constraints of the old genre system with its rules and the idea of imitation of the old masters but also from the constraints of society. In principle, authors were no longer bound by tradition, the church, the state, or the sciences. On the other hand, due to the same independent status, authors and artists in general were afforded enormous prestige in society. Artists became those most commonly able—and perhaps by virtue of Modernity's increasing specialization and waning influence of Christianity, also the last commonly able—to address wider contexts.

These notions stem directly from the varied changes around the year 1800, but go much further back on closer inspection (Minnis 1984; Chartier 1994). Conversely, they are no further away than some modern welfare states such as the Scandinavian ones. Here, artists, including literary authors, are paid to—somewhat independently of any particular interests—"put issues to debate," for the benefit of us all.

Roland Barthes was also interested in these historical contexts of the concepts of the author, but his issue with the author and his placing of the issue in a historical context are framed by a more general philosophical agenda. For Barthes and the entire idea complex that we refer to as post-structuralism (see An Overview of Schools of Criticism), the author is suspect because the author represents an incarnation of a particular subject philosophy that the author, paradoxically, is also against: the idea of the self-sufficient subject who by virtue of reason can see through the world and the self.

What is interesting now is that Barthes' and modern art's impersonalism with which he in his essay associates actually regurgitates medieval author theory (Burke 1995, xvii). Back then, the individual author—*auctor*—was perceived as a disseminator of God's creative power and authority—*auctoritas* (which nonetheless rubbed off on his *auctores*). If you take God out of the equation, you actually have the author theory that characterizes both modern art and large parts of modern literary theory.

"Je est un autre," poet Arthur Rimbaud wrote in a letter in 1871; you might translate it as "I is another" to reproduce the deliberate mistake. There is no empirical "I" speaking in the written word, but there is something else, something radically foreign and different that Barthes and many with him linked to language and literature itself, but which people in the Middle Ages just called God.

In light of this, modern discussions about the author are only the most recent examples of an ancient battle between situated and transcendental conceptions of the author, the battle between perceiving the author as a particular human being who has expressed himself or herself at a certain time in a certain context, and perceiving the author as an intermediate link to something else—God, inspiration, the instinctive, language, power. For the author of these lines, however, it seems most likely that the situated and the transcendental conception of the author complement one other. The fact that the writing process subjects the writer to forces greater and stronger than the individual does not render it meaningless to perceive any given piece of literature as a particular author's aesthetic communication with his or her readers. Any attempt to create meaning, including verbal masterpieces, is a clash between a desire to create meaning and powers greater than the subject. It is thus a practical and concrete question whether and how the author is to be seen as relevant to literary studies.

"Performative biographism"

Just like everything else from the real world, authors can appear in texts—their own, for example. They might use their name or prompt the reader to think about them in other ways. In this case, the author is perhaps perceived not so much as the originating subject of a text as a character in it, and reference to the author is a device within the larger context of the text. This aspect is all the more obvious with famous authors who can play on their celebrity in and around their works.

As early as 1923, Boris Tomashevsky pointed this out. Playing with the relationship between the text and the author's life can play a structural role in the work, he writes (Tomashevsky 1995, 89). Tomashevsky was a formalist and as such did not advocate this biographical approach. He had his sights set further back in literary history, but his idea has only gained currency since then. As is obvious, the emergence of new media has offered excellent platforms for continuing this game elsewhere.

I have referred to authors' conscious use of themselves or others as part of a literary work "performative biographism" (Haarder 2016), and we have seen a lot of this in the last twenty-odd years. Authors, for example, experiment artistically with their biography and with the public reaction to confessions of private embarrassments or accusations against others. These experiments are best understood as performance or conceptual art. The author conceptualizes his or her biography and sees what happens once it is rendered public.

Karl Ove Knausgård's *My Struggle* (2013–) looks like a traditional autobiographical novel in the Proust lineage, but if you read volume 2, you will find that it is actually based on a concept: a kind of dogma rule of writing a novel without using anything other than Knausgård's own life. The work gradually becomes a narrative documentation of the real-life consequences of its own project. The last line of *My Struggle* volume 6 is:

> Then we'll take the train to Malmö, then we'll get in the car and then we'll drive home to our house, and all the way there I'll enjoy—really enjoy—the thought that I'm no longer an author.

The irony is palpable. Whether Knausgård actually believes this or not, it is his work's reception history and individual readers that decide whether he is an author or not (and thus also whether his nearest and dearest will have to live with the consequences of his authorship in the long term). Knausgård will probably always be considered the author of *My Struggle*. The author cannot in fact decide what it means to be an author; the author can only partly decide what kind of author he or she is.

Author function, author image

In the essay "What Is an Author?" (1979), Michel Foucault investigates how the author concept, or rather the author discourse, limits what can be said, written, and thought about literature. He uses the term *author function* to describe the author as a discourse, or more specifically the author as a functional principle governing the relationship between the sender, text, recipient, and context.

Author functions are limiting for individual authors. What an author is is closely linked to the culture and the society in which the author operates. What are the consequences if the author in this form is permitted to return? We can read about this in book historian Roger Chartier's work. He writes in both critical and appreciative extension of Foucault:

> As he [the author] returns in literary criticism or literary sociology the author is both dependent and constrained. He is dependent in that he is not the unique master of the meaning of his text, and his intentions, which provided the impulse to produce the text, are not necessarily imposed either on those who turn his text into a book (bookseller–publishers or print workers) or on those who appropriate it by reading it. He is constrained in that he undergoes multiple determinations that organize the social space of literary production and, in a more general sense, determine the categories and the experiences that are the very matrices of writing. (Chartier 1994, 29)

An author is, as Pierre Bourdieu writes, "socially defined" (1969, 95). Here he considers that an author's work always somehow responds to the public's image of the author, and it is easy to connect Bourdieu's idea with Foucault's author function.

There are thus now two levels to the public co-determination of both the individual author and the concept of being an author at a given point in time. The *author function* is what Foucault and Chartier write about: namely the changing historical and discursive conditions for writing. These conditions are also contributory to the next level: the *author image* is the image of a particular author and his or her work that the public creates on the basis of both the work and the author's appearances in other media.

The point is that each individual author to a certain extent can influence this image—after all, it is largely formed from the author's texts. What Genette (1997) calls the paratext—book covers, media presence, and so on—can also be used to influence the author image. Conversely, no author is the sole creator of his or her author image. It is partly public, with everyone as co-author in principle, and partly subject to cultural stereotypes in the broadest sense, for example gender-specific stereotypes or the notion of the author as a bohemian who is critical of society. Fotis Jannidis (2002) suggests the term *author configuration* for the level of "social definition" between author function and author image.

The final level is the individual, empirical author, the living person, but this person is not independent of the other levels, even in private. The author thus embodies certain conditions relating to identity creation in general. Not only the author but the individual is to some extent socially defined, and the meeting between the author's creative urge, author function, and author image is in a sense the image of us all.

Authors on Facebook

To see identity at work as an author project, one only has to look at the Internet's social media. Here we work on composing the version of ourselves that we want others, and ourselves, to believe in. Here the conditions for our self-representation are clearly shaped on the one hand by the media and its functionalities—a kind of technological development of the author function—as well as by culturally active stereotypes on the level of author configurations. On the other hand, we are responding to (what we imagine are) the opinions of ourselves already in circulation, images that we thus develop further or try to change—corresponding to the level of author image.

The contemporary conditions for the formation of identity are linked to the digital revolution. On the one hand, we are still part of a book-printing culture and carry the bourgeois author concept with us. On the other hand, the computer is in the process of changing this culture. The computer is a writing machine that translates all information into the same binary alphabet, and in a sense, our otherwise visually dominated culture is a culture of writing to a greater extent than the previous two, which were based on manuscripts and the printed word, respectively.

The core of digitization is textualization—everything can be written as a code that can be manipulated. This has the profound significance that the relationship between information and the processor of information is not fixed. Consider the program Word, which I use to author this chapter. Both the text I am writing and the program that processes this text are ultimately written using the same binary alphabet. Interpreting the enormous consequences of this is outside of the scope of this chapter. We must be content simply to consider the author—and ourselves.

On the one hand, the bourgeois author function is carried on as long as the author is still considered a framework for the text. It is still the author's text in several senses of this ownership. On the other hand, this framework can be moved into the object field. This happens when some students copy and paste their assignments, and when in connection with blogs (and books based on blogs!) we attain a multi-sender relationship—and it also happens when authors such as Philip Roth, Michel Houellebecq, or Karl Ove Knausgård appear as authors in their texts and continue to discuss this appearance in new texts, be it those they write themselves or when they appear in the media to become the object of others' processing.

Working with the author

Given that texts are always written by someone, you can refer to them as an expression of one or more people's creative work in specific contexts—biographical, material historical, philosophical, media historical, and literary historical. It should also be obvious that selecting certain works and considering them an "oeuvre" because they are by the same author imply a biographical framework since the criterion for selecting the relevant texts is that they have the same sender.

The significance attributed to this varies. There is, to name just a few possibilities, a big difference between perceiving an author's texts as expressions of an empirical person's interpretation of his or her life, perceiving them as expressing a particular relationship with the world—as you do in the phenomenological tradition—and perceiving them as strategic input into the literary field at a certain point in time. Working with texts by involving the author—by using the concept of authorship, for example—can thus involve both well-known hermeneutical approaches and more performative approaches where one sees the writer as a character created by the text or the oeuvre.

You can also start by asking whether the author is directly present in the text. This may be more or less direct. Obvious indications include the use of the author's name, a function that especially in discussions of autobiography as a genre has played a central role. But it is easy for the relationship between text and sender to be put into play in other ways, for example by reproducing a sequence of events that readers will recognize from the extratextual world. The author can thus be a device in the text, and reference to the author today often serves the aesthetic function of leaving the reader on the threshold between irreconcilable relationships: Should this be enjoyed as art, or should I respond to this as an action within a community? This aesthetic of the threshold is the basis for major polemics around authors such as Houellebecq or Knausgård. What the texts in such cases mean thus also depends on what happens because they are published.

Translation: Siân Mackie

Further reading

Sean Burke's anthology *Authorship* (1995) is a good place to start. Here you will find the aforementioned classics and many more in addition to good introductions, comments, and bibliographies. Fotis Jannidis et al. (ed.): *Texte zur Theorie der Autorschaft* (2000) has a smaller selection of texts, some of which coincide with

Burke's anthology, and a pragmatic introduction that gives a good overview. Sean Burke's *The Death and Return of the Author* (3rd edition, 2008) is more advanced. Jones's "Autofiction: A Brief History of Neologism" (2010) gives a good overview of the history of the autofiction concept.

References

Barthes, Roland (1995) "Death of the Author," in Sean Burke (ed.), *Authorship. From Plato to the Postmodern. A Reader*, Edinburgh: Edinburgh University Press.

Bourdieu, Pierre (1969) "Intellectual Field and Creative Project," *Information sur les sciences sociales*, 8 (2): 89–119.

Burke, Sean (ed.) (1995) *Authorship. From Plato to the Postmodern. A Reader*, Edinburgh: Edinburgh University Press.

Burke, Sean (2008) *Death and Return of the Author. Criticism and Subjectivity in Barthes, Foucault and Derrida*, 3rd edition, Edinburgh: Edinburgh University Press.

Chartier, Roger (1994) *The Order of Books*, Stanford: Stanford University Press.

Foucault, Michel (1979) "What Is an Author?" in J. V. Harari (ed.), *Textual Strategies. Perspectives in Post-Structuralist Criticism*, Ithaca, NY: Metuen & Co. Ltd.

Genette, Gerard (1997) *Paratexts. Thresholds of Interpretation*, Cambridge: Cambridge University Press, pp. 101–29.

Haarder, Jon Helt (2016) "A Story We Are Part of: Introducing *Performative Biographism* by Way of Reading Karl Ove Knausgård's *My Struggle* (and vice versa)," in Henik Skov Nielsen (ed.), *Expectations*, Copenhagen: Medusa.

Jannidis, Fotis et al. (2000) *Texte zur Theorie der Autorschaft*, Stuttgart: Philipp Reclam jun.

Jannidis, Fotis (2002) "Autor, Autorbild und Autorintention," *edition*, 16.

Jones, E. H. (2010) "Autofiction: A Brief History of a Neologism," in R. Bradford (ed.), *Life Writing. Essays on Autobiography, Biography and Literature*, Basingstoke: Palgrave Macmillan, 174–84.

Minnis, Alistair J. (1984) *Medieval Theory of Authorship. Scholastic Literary Attitudes in the Later Middle Ages*, London: Scolar Press.

Pease, Donald (1995) "Author," in Sean Burke (ed.), *Authorship. From Plato to the Postmodern. A Reader*, Edinburgh: Edinburgh University Press.

Proust, Marcel (1988) *Against Sainte-Beuve and Other Essays*, London: Penguin Classics.

Ricœur, Paul (1981) *Hermeneutics and the Human Sciences. Essays on Language, Action and Interpretation*, Cambridge: Cambridge University Press, 263–76.

Sainte-Beuve, Charles-Augustin (1865) "Chateaubriand jugé par un ami intime en 1803. Suite et fin," in *Nouveaux Lundis*, Vol. III, Paris: Michael Lévy Freres. Available at http://obvil.paris-sorbonne.fr/corpus/critique/sainte-beuve_nouveaux-lundis-03/body-2 (accessed March 11, 2016).

Tomashevsky, Boris (1995) "Literature and Biography," in Sean Burke (ed.), *Authorship. From Plato to the Postmodern. A Reader*, Edinburgh: Edinburgh University Press, 81–9.

13
Reader

Winfried Fluck

Why can readers, even professional readers, never agree on the meaning of a literary text? When literary studies were institutionalized in higher education, scholars tried to solve this problem first by establishing the formalist doctrine of "close reading," assuming that interpretive disagreements were the result of sloppy readings, and then by creating theoretical and methodological surveys of literary analyses to help interpreters put their readings on a firm methodological ground. Neither strategy solved the problem of interpretive disagreements. Even interpreters who share the same theoretical position or interpretive method will come up with different readings of one and the same text. A literary text, no matter how conscientiously a close reading may be, cannot fully determine what the reader considers its meaning. It took literary studies some time to finally acknowledge that the problem must have something to do with another important actor in the reading process that had been neglected so far. In the mid-1960s, the concept of the reader finally began to gain critical prominence as a key concept in literary studies. This new focus on the reader did not lead to a common theoretical position or method but to a range of different approaches called—to name only the most important and influential ones—reception theory, reception aesthetics, reader response criticism, transactional criticism, or affective stylistics. All of these approaches agree that the reader plays an important role in any reading- and sense-making process and that "meaning has no effective existence outside of its realization in the mind of a reader" (Tompkins 1980, ix). But they differ in the conclusions that should be drawn from this basic insight.

The reader in the text

The literary scholars who were initially most influential in shifting attention to the reader were the members of the so-called Konstanz School of Reception Theory whose home base was the Universität Konstanz in Southern Germany. Their best known and internationally most influential representatives were Hans Robert Jauß and Wolfgang Iser whose major studies have become classics in the field. But they also demonstrate that the concept of the reader can be taken in different directions. For Jauß in his *Literaturgeschichte als Provokation*, different reader responses can be explained by the different horizons of expectations in which readers are positioned historically; reception theory here leads to reception history, a study of the historically changing frames of explanation that shape reception. In contrast, Iser in *The Implied Reader* and The Act of Reading focuses on the way in which the literary text itself, through its formal strategies, implies certain reading activities, for example, by suspended connectivities or blanks in the text that compel the reader to fill the gaps by means of his own imagination. Iser's key focus does not lie on historical readers but on an analysis of how the text manages to involve the reader and stimulate his active participation in the construction of the text's meaning. Iser's key term of an implied reader thus links text and reader. It "incorporates both the pre-structuring of the potential meaning of the text, and the reader's actualization of this potential through the reading process" (Iser 1974, xii).

When reception theory reached American soil it was subsumed under the term "reader response criticism." The term already indicates what would become the major point of criticism of the Konstanz School in American reception theory. Contrary to the promise of a shift from text to reader, suggested by labels like reception theory or reception aesthetics, critics argued that Iser does not really move over to the side of the reader. Instead of referring to actual readers he talks about a reader position inscribed in the text, the meaning of a text is therefore still crucially determined by the text itself, albeit in such a form that it takes the reader to bring it out. This can indeed explain a strong modernist bias in Iser's work, because the de-familiarizing and negating strategies of modernist literature require more reader involvement than does realism, for example, where the reader is not challenged to the same degree to become active in the construction of meaning.

Literature in the reader

One of the main critics of Iser was Stanley Fish whose attack may have been motivated in part by the fact that he himself had provided a study of reader activities in the interpretation of a text taken from an entirely different period. In his study, *Surprised by Sin: The Reader in "Paradise Lost,"* Fish, too, assigns reader activities a crucial role but they are of a different nature than Iser's. In his essay "Literature in the Reader: Affective Stylistics" (Fish 1967), Fish has provided a concise outline of his method, a method of interpretation in which sentences are read word by word in temporal sequence and "slow motion" in order to fully expose oneself to their affective potential. In reading words on the page, the reader forms hypotheses about meaning that may have to be revised already in reading the next word or sentence. Writing is designed to affect the reader and in response to these affective cues, the reader constantly has to reconsider and reorient his own attitudes toward the text, often literally from moment to moment. The task of reader response criticism is thus not to retrieve what the text means but to describe the developing reading process in order to show how it affects the reader in the course of reading. Thus, Fish "makes the crucial move in reader-oriented criticism by removing the literary text from the center of critical attention and replacing it with the reader's cognitive activity" (Tompkins 1980, xvii). Nevertheless, in the final analysis it is still the text that directs the responses of the reader. But how can Fish be sure that readers will respond in the manner pre-structured by the text? How can reader responses be avoided that go in other directions? Simply by positing a general linguistic and cultural competence that text and reader share and that provides a common basis for understanding.

This seemingly easy solution creates another problem, however: Who defines what counts as competence? The logic of his argument carries Fish to the concept of an interpretive community that sets limits to what kind of readings are considered valid or not on the basis of a set of assumptions that are taken for granted by all members of the community and that the reader therefore accepts as a given. His reading will be guided by this interpretive framework, and this means that idiosyncratic, wildly subjective readings are impossible. Fish's attempt to get away from the control of the text, while, at the same time, avoiding arbitrarily subjective readings, leads him to place all control over meaning on the side of a community of readers. But this approach discards the fact that interpretive disagreements do not only happen between different interpretive communities but also between members of the same community.

With Fish's interpretive community, reception theory has arrived at the other end of Iser's reception aesthetics: whereas in Iser's perspective one cannot describe reading activities properly, unless one has read the text carefully and grasped the formal strategies through which the text guides the reader's activities, the text has now become of secondary importance, because it is only the product of the interpretive framework of the reader. Textual facts, "rather than being the objects of interpretation, are its products" (Fish 1980, 9). The liberation of the reader from the text leads to a new kind of confinement. Sense-making is no longer determined by the text but by "a community whose assumptions about literature determine the kind of attention he pays and thus the kind of literature 'he' makes" (Fish 1980, 11). In their interpretations, readers merely reenact the premises of a community's view of literature. Interpretive disagreements are thus disagreements between different communities, not individual readers who are seen here exclusively as social actors.

The reader of the text

For Fish meaning may no longer be controlled by the text, yet is still controlled by a reading community. For Norman Holland, another influential scholar in reception theory whose work went through several stages, reader responses are not controlled or decisively shaped by a reading community, but by the personal history and identity of a reader who will make use of the text for his own psychological needs. Texts trigger personal associations that have their source in the psychological make-up of the reader. Although these associations are free and spontaneous, there will nevertheless also be a characteristic pattern of response. In a first phase of Holland's work, this pattern emerges from unconscious fantasies of the reader that are transformed in the reading process, so that the anxieties connected with them can be overcome. In a second phase, the pattern emerging in the act of reading reflects a central identity theme of the reader that lends unity to his very personal responses. In both phases, the reader's response recreates the text in terms of his own associations. Holland therefore calls his version of reader response criticism as transactional criticism. There can be no longer any significant interpretive debate about these readings, however, because one cannot argue with a reader's psychological needs, and if one is not a psychologist, one may not even be able to identify the reader's identity theme. In Holland's approach, reader response criticism has finally reached the point in which the reader's subjective response determines meaning completely.

A strong emphasis on the reader as the determining force in the relation between text and reader brings Holland already close to empirical reader research that wants to replace reception theories based on theoretical assumptions about meaning construction by stringent empirical studies of actual reader responses. It is impossible to do justice to the vast body of empirical studies here, but the result that stands out is that the reader's responses have an even more unpredictable and idiosyncratic quality than expected even by radical reception theorists. Even for Holland, the decidedly personal nature of a reader's response can still be tied to an identity theme or a particular psychological disposition, so that there is still a certain degree of consistency and predictability in the reader's response. But empirical studies often show reader responses to be even more unpredictable. A typical example, taken from their empirical research, is provided by Kuiken, Miall, and Sokora: " (…) one respondent reflecting on an orange colored patch was reminded of a medicine once taken and (…) was capable of fusing the emotional memory with the present color-impression. (…) In both cases, resonance occurs between explicitly recalled personal memories and some portion of the world of the aesthetic object" (Kuiken et al. 2004, 181–2). What empirical studies have shown again and again is that there is no reliably predictable pattern in the responses of readers and that all attempts to map the reader's flow of associations in any systematic fashion is doomed to failure.

Reading and interpretation

Where does this leave reader response criticism? The more focused and concrete studies of the role of the reader have become, the more, it seems, reader response criticism is drifting toward an acknowledgment of the uniqueness and singularity of any act of reading. In order to do full justice to this uniqueness of response, literary studies would have to produce an endless number of empirical studies and even those would run the danger of being reductionist in their generalizations. At this point, it seems useful to distinguish between two different kinds of reading activity that are often conflated in reader response criticism. For a non-professional reader, who is reading for fun, associations are free and, as empirical studies show, this is clearly one of the pleasures of reading. In contrast to this care-free, "irresponsible" reader, readers who do their reading in an institutional context—like the public sphere or educational institutions—have to justify their associations and connect them in meaningful and plausible ways to their object of analysis. There may be institutional pressure to do so, but the main reason is that interpretations are based on a premise of intersubjectivity. Interpretations are attempts to establish some kind of common ground for a debate over views and values.

A literary text may evoke all kinds of associations, emotions, and affects, but the task of literary studies is to determine which of these associations are culturally meaningful and/or aesthetically relevant. One does not have to be a humanist scholar to argue that there would be no need to institutionalize the study of literature in schools, colleges, and universities, if literary studies would not be considered to play an important part in the formation of cultural meanings and cultural values. For this purpose, it is not enough to simply register the seemingly limitless variety of reader responses; one also has to make choices and justify them. Reception theory, no matter what its particular theoretical position, therefore has to focus on reading as a form of interpretation, that is, it has to describe readers as interpreters in order to find out how they construe meaning and value. The purpose is to provide a better understanding of what is being read by focusing on how it is being read.

A transfer-model of reading

Reception theory, then, is part of a cultural dialogue about meanings and values, including aesthetic values. Its proper object of analysis is interpretations and not simply readings. At the same time, reception theory gained influence by drawing attention to the fact that the role of the reader has to be taken into account in these analyses. But what could an approach look like that takes its point of departure from the acknowledgment that the text cannot fully determine the readers' responses, so that readers can respond quite differently to one and the same text, but that, on the other hand, does not want to dissolve the text in an ocean of singular reader responses? The challenge is to take both sides into account. Interpretations may be tied to expectations of validity or plausibility but, as I said at the beginning, they nevertheless disagree constantly. How can these two seemingly contradictory aspects be brought together in one coherent perspective?

Partly in response to the critique of a tacit modernist bias of his reception aesthetics, Wolfgang Iser moved on in the later stages of his career to what he called a "literary anthropology." The reader still plays a central role, but the definition of the reading process moves from the textual construction of an implied reader position to the description of an elementary, "anthropological" constituent of the reading process, no matter what kind of text the reader encounters, realist or modernist, high or low. In order to make his point, Iser uses the example of reading *Hamlet*: "In this respect the required activity of the recipient resembles that of an actor, who in order to perform his role must use his thoughts, his feelings, and even his body as an analogue for representing something he is not. In order to produce the determinate form of an unreal character, the actor must allow his own reality to fade out. At the same time, however, he does not know precisely who, say, Hamlet is, for one cannot properly identify a character who has never existed" (Iser 1989, 244). Since the reader has never encountered Hamlet or Huckleberry Finn and does in fact know that neither one ever existed in real life, he has to come up with his own mental image of him. This mental process will proceed along textual lines but the reader will also have to draw on his own associations to bring the abstract letters on the page to life.

Thus, in the act of reading the text comes to represent two things at once: the world of the text and imaginary elements added to it by the reader—not because formal strategies challenge him to do so, or because it has been suggested by an interpretive community, but for the simple reason that the world described in the text has to be imagined by the reader, if he wants to make any sense of it. And in imagining the text, the reader must draw on his own store of experiences and associations. Critics do not disagree that Huck Finn is about twelve years old, illiterate, and speaks a colorful colloquial vernacular. Nevertheless, despite this factual basis the Huck Finn imagined by Wolfgang Iser will be different from the Huck Finn imagined by Winfried Fluck, because these two readers will draw on different imaginary resources in order to bring the figure of Huck to life. The basic point about the reading process is that, in order to become meaningful as an experience, it has to be brought to life by means of an imaginary transfer on the side of the reader. Reading literature thus puts us in a position "in-between." It allows us to enter imaginatively another person's world and perhaps even his or her body; on the other hand, we cannot and do not want to completely give up our own identity. As a result, we create other, more expressive versions of ourselves. As several scholars have stressed, this potential for imaginary self-extension is of special attraction for (not only young) readers in search of recognition (Brownstein 1982; Appleyard 1991; Fluck 2013a).

Another way of describing this phenomenon is to say that literary texts can function as a host for readers who make use of them for imaginative and emotional transfers of their own. After reunification in Germany, for example, there was a brief moment in which some East Germans compared themselves to the American South after the Civil War. In both cases, a "better" world seemed to have been conquered by a stronger, but inferior civilization—namely West Germany—with primarily materialistic values. Let us imagine that such an East German reader ran across the novel *Gone with the Wind* at the time. This East German had never been to the American South, in fact, hardly knew anything about it, except that it was considered racist. Had she still read the novel in the communist German Democratic Republic, this might have been her major focus. All of a sudden, however, she sees something else in the book, namely an analogy between what she considers the cruel fate of two supposedly superior civilizations. The imaginary and emotional elements she invests in the transfer that actualizes the novel may now be dominated no longer by feelings of superiority but by the theme of how to deal with humiliation and defeat. The meaning of the book has changed; it is no longer a book about racism but about how to preserve self-respect in defeat.

The important point here for understanding the reading process is that the transfer between two worlds that are far apart—that of a Southern belle of the nineteenth-century and that of a late twentieth-century reader in Leipzig—becomes possible through analogies. The relation of reader to text is established, not by identification with a particular figure, or by certain formal strategies, or by an identity theme, but in a much more open, unpredictable way: by establishing analogies between the world of the text and the world of the reader. These analogies can take their point of departure from any aspect of the text, including words, characters, spatial descriptions, plot patterns, as well as affects, feelings, moods, corporeal schemata, and so on. One can broadly distinguish between structural similarities and affective affinities, but within these categories the setting up of analogies does not show any predictable pattern. It will depend on many variants that include historical and social conditions, as well as psychological dispositions, but also identity markers such as gender, race, and sexual preferences (Flynn 1986). Yet the individual variation and unpredictability of reader responses go beyond such identity markers. (Members of these groups also disagree about a text's meaning.) There will always be new readings and responses emerging, not only in different historical periods but also among readers or viewers of the same period, society, class, gender, or racial formation, because the reader is free to respond to the text by establishing ever new analogies.

The central role of analogizing in the process of reading and the construction of meaning can explain phenomena in the reception of literature that have often been seen as puzzling. One is the seemingly paradoxical fact that figures like criminals, even murderers or monsters, which would be avoided and rejected in real life, can become attractive and popular figures in reading. The explanation is that, in encountering such figures in literature, readers do not identify with them, but focus on those aspects to which they can establish analogies: they relate positively to the defiant non-conformism of the gangster and ignore the criminal context. This freedom to construct meaning by segmented analogies is the reason why one and the same text can be praised as either subversive or ideologically affirmative, depending on the textual segment to which the reader establishes analogies. Even in the ideologically most conformist text, such as a domestic novel of the American antebellum period, there may be occasional rebellious acts by characters that the reader can activate for a transfer, although these characters may in the end submit to the patriarchal order. This is one of the paradoxes of reading: because of the reader's freedom to set up his own analogies between text and reader, the actual experience of reading a text may be quite different from its ideological project.

The fact that reading is a process that unfolds in a series of ongoing transfers between text and reader can also explain why readers can still relate to a text like *Huckleberry Finn*, although their own contemporary America is far removed from the pastoral idyll of the text. It can explain why readers in other countries can relate to the text, although life on the Mississippi has never been part of their cultural imaginary. It can explain why different readers, including critics and scholars, can read one and the same text differently and will often not be able to agree on the meaning of the text; their disagreements result from the fact that their interpretations are based on different analogies and different forms of analogizing. Finally, the fact that reading is based on transfers can also explain why we may read one and the same text differently at different times: simply put, the difference is produced by the discovery of new analogies in the act of reading that we may have overlooked or ignored before.

Analysis of a reader's response

How can such considerations help us to analyze and understand reader responses, for example, to a text like Mark Twain's *Adventures of Huckleberry Finn*? Although the novel had been popular from the start, it was not taken seriously by scholarly readers who long considered it a "boy's book." The transformation of the book into not only a "quintessentially American" novel but also one of the masterpieces of world literature can be traced to the end of the 1940s and to Lionel Trilling's introduction to the Rinehart College Edition of *Huckleberry Finn*. Before Trilling's introduction, the novel was an amusing trifle, after it became "one of the world's great books and one of the central documents of American culture" (Trilling 1950, 101).

In his analysis, Trilling is selective, ignoring aspects that have provoked others. The main significance of the novel for Trilling lies in Huck's moral struggle and, especially, in the scene in chapter 31 in which Huck, despite his internalization of Southern slave-holder morality, decides not to betray Jim, even if it means that he will have to "go to hell." With this moral choice, Huck transcends the popular bad boy genre and becomes a human character who has outgrown the bad boy stereotype. For Trilling, one of the major American critics of the 1950s, this scene is important for a special reason. Trilling was a critic of American left liberalism of the 1930s, and for this criticism, *Huckleberry Finn* provides a useful analogy: it lies in Huck's courage to go against the grain of convention and to be willing to face the consequences, even if it means to be damned. What Trilling admires about *Huckleberry Finn* is Huck's willingness (and ability) to resist the pressures of political and social orthodoxies. In *Huckleberry Finn* these orthodoxies are those of the Southern slave-holding society, in Trilling's world they are those of the Left intelligentsia in the 1930s, the so-called Red Decade, that prevented Leftist intellectuals and scholars from rebelling against the orthodoxies of Stalinism. Trilling's interpretation and praise of Twain's novel was thus based on an analogy and transfer between two scenes and situations that, for Trilling, seemed to possess striking structural similarities. From being a book against Southern slave-holding society, Trilling's *Huckleberry Finn* is transformed into a book against communist fellow travelership, and this transformation is made possible by a transfer based on a perceived similarity between two historically and ideologically different constellations. In yet another transfer, post-War American criticism then forgot about this political context and read the book in terms of a "typically American" innocence (exemplified by Huck) that is characterized by an inherent, intuitive morality. In other words, scholars now read the novel in terms of one of the key tenets of American exceptionalism. Reader responses can truly be amazing in their transformative powers: through a set of transfers, inspired and made possible by analogies others had ignored, a Victorian bad boy story can thus become a major literary manifestation of the idea of American exceptionalism.

This story puts an entirely new perspective on the problem with which we began, the conflict of interpretations. Seen from the perspective of reading as transfer, the phenomenon of interpretive disagreements is no longer an irritating disturbance that we should try to overcome but, on the contrary, an indispensable resource for cultural history, because, as the history of *Huck Finn*-criticism shows, reader responses can be invaluable documents of changes in views and values.

Further reading

Hans Robert Jauß in *Toward an Aesthetics of Reception*, focusing on historical processes of reception, and Wolfgang Iser's study *The Act of Reading*, focusing on the implied readers of literary texts, are two foundational texts of reception theory. Different schools of reception theory are well represented in the essay collections *The Reader in the Text*, ed. by Jane Tompkins and *The Reader in the Text*, eds by Susan Suleiman and Inge Crosman. For a survey of the role of gender in reading, see the essay collection *Gender and Reading*, eds by Elizabeth Flynn and Patricinio Schweickart. The book contains a very useful annotated bibliography. An excellent description of reading in different phases of life can be found in J. A. Appleyard's study *Becoming a Reader. The Experience of Fiction from Childhood to Adulthood*. My essays "The Imaginary and the Second Narrative" and "Reading for Recognition" attempt to redescribe the act of reading as a transfer between text and reader. Recent attempts to make use of Bruno Latour's Actor Network Theory for a description of the reading process are provided by Rita Felski, *The Limits of Critique*, Chicago, 2015, and David Alworth, *Site Reading: Fiction, Art, Social Form*, Princeton, 2016.

References

Appleyard, J. A. (1991) *Becoming a Reader: The Experience of Fiction from Childhood to Adulthood*, New York: Cambridge University Press.

Brownstein, Rachel M. (1982) *Becoming a Heroine*, New York: Penguin.

Fish, Stanley (1967) *Surprised by Sin: The Reader in "Paradise Lost,"* London: Macmillan.

Fish, Stanley (1980) *Is There a Text in This Class? The Authority of Interpretive Communities*, Cambridge: Harvard University Press.

Fluck, Winfried (2013a) "The Imaginary and the Second Narrative: Reading as Transfer," in Laura Bieger, Ramon Saldivar, and Johannes Voelz (eds), *The Imaginary and Its Worlds*, 237–64, Hanover: Dartmouth College Press.

Flynn, Elizabeth A. and Patrocinio P. Schweickart (1986) *Gender and Reading: Essays on Readers, Texts, and Contexts*, Baltimore: Johns Hopkins University Press.

Holland, Norman (2011) *The Nature of Literary Response: Five Readers Reading*, New Brunswick: Transaction Publishers.

Iser, Wolfgang (1974) *The Implied Reader: Patterns of Communication in Prose Fiction from Bunyan to Beckett*, Baltimore: Johns Hopkins University Press.

Iser, Wolfgang (1978) *The Act of Reading: A Theory of Aesthetic Response*, Baltimore: Johns Hopkins University Press.

Iser, Wolfgang (1989) *Prospecting: From Reader Response to Literary Anthropology*, Baltimore: Johns Hopkins University Press.

Jauß, Hans Robert (1982) *Toward an Aesthetic of Reception*, Minneapolis: University of Minnesota Press.

Kuiken, Don, David S. Miall and Shelley Sikora (2004) "Forms of Self-Implication in Literary Reading," *Poetics Today*, 25 (2): 171–203.

Tompkins, Jane P. (ed.) (1980) *Reader-Response Criticism: From Formalism to Post-structuralism*, Baltimore: Johns Hopkins University Press.

Trilling, Lionel (1950) "Huckleberry Finn," *The Liberal Imagination: Essays on Literature and Society*, 100–113, Garden City, NY: Doubleday.

14

History

Mads Rosendahl Thomsen

William Shakespeare's play *Othello* is the story of the Venetian general, Othello, who is framed by the jealous Iago, and kills his wife, Desdemona, convinced that she has been unfaithful. Presumably, the play was written in 1603, with inspiration from an Italian novella from 1565. The play premiered on November 1, 1604, in London, and was published in 1622. It has since been performed in theaters and made into numerous films. The play does not reveal exactly when the action is supposed to take place, but without being exact about this matter, there are references to events from the 1570s, making it unusually close to Shakespeare's own historical moment, compared to his other plays.

The many dates related to a play such as *Othello* demonstrate the complexity of literature's relations with the past, and the many ways in which a work of literature may be contextualized historically. First, there is the content of the work: How much should one consider how it relates to *historical events*? Does it make a difference whether the conflicts Shakespeare uses as the backdrop for his intimate drama are plausible, albeit not historically accurate? Secondly, there is the historical moment in which the play was written: How did *Shakespeare's own historical moment* influence the play? How does the language and culture of his present manifest themselves in the play? Thirdly, *literature has its own history*: How can Shakespeare's work be understood as part of a literary culture and tradition that has a limited autonomy, with respect to the rest of the world, and that cannot be understood solely as part of a broader cultural history? Fourthly, this history is connected to the *use* that has been made of the play ever since its first performance and its canonization in literary history, as an example of a key work addressing, among other things, an understanding of racism. Similarly, the emphasis on jealousy, as a theme that elevates the play beyond the confines of its own historical moment, also exemplifies a particular use and interpretation of the play that depends on historical shifts in context. Then, one has to decide whether the play's historical events and particulars are more or less important than the thematic content that continues to fascinate readers and spectators, or whether it is precisely the combination of historical distance and thematic universality that makes *Othello* and numerous other works part of a living literary culture.

Aristotle described the difference between history and poetry by claiming that "poetry deals with general truths; history with specific events" (Aristotle 1958, 18). But even if this distinction often holds, literature also deals with historical conditions and events that may be virtually impossible to ignore in an analysis. At other times, it is obvious that historical events are more or less contingent, but can readers just ignore their specificity? There is no one answer to this. One may grasp the world of *Othello* without comparing it to its historical setting or to Shakespeare's literary world, but one should realize that there may be something one misses from such an interpretive strategy. The problem is how to determine which elements situate the play in a significant relationship to its past, given that the play does not involve an exact, identifiable historical event, but instead has to do with roles in society and moral norms. However, one would probably read and watch *Othello* quite differently, if one found that nothing in the play had any similarity to history.

With *Othello* as the primary example, the following questions will be addressed: How can the culture of the past be included in the analysis of a text? How can a text's position in literary history be explained? And, is there a respectable approach to history that does not rely so much on understanding as on a fascination with a different era and being in contact with a time beyond one's own?

Historicism and New Historicism

American literary historian Stephen Greenblatt has argued that the ambition to include historical elements in the reading of literary works should not be abandoned, a move that was legitimized by New Criticism from the 1940s onward, and that seemed to be supported by the deconstructionism of 1970s by way of misunderstood catchphrases, such as "there is nothing outside the text." Greenblatt is critical of the more traditional historicism that he finds characterized by three conditions, according to *The American Heritage Dictionary*: that the individual has little influence on historical currents; that historians should avoid all value judgments in the study of the past; and that one should venerate history and tradition. Greenblatt suggests that one should examine the limits of action for the individual, and recognize that there is room for divergence and eventually, more profound change. Furthermore, one's own historical and cultural position should not be hidden, but used to bring perspective to current debates, for instance, in the way that the racism expressed in *Othello* can bring more nuance to current conditions. Finally, Greenblatt wants to bring in new material to stir conventional historical interpretations, and focus more on the conflict the artist may have had with his own epoch, rather than accepting him or her as being a genius that expresses the spirit of a past era.

Greenblatt used the term *New Historicism* to describe his approach to literary studies, but even though many scholars are described as new historicists, there is no general paradigm or school, but instead, a loose set of ideas regarding the understanding of the relation between history and literature (see "New Historicism" under An Overview of Schools of Criticism). Greenblatt's own contribution is dominated by developing an approach that does not nitpick historical facts, but focuses on underlying social structures in past societies that can reveal overlooked dimensions of a text, or support particular interpretations with reference to historical conditions. Greenblatt, among others, is inspired by the work of anthropologist Clifford Geertz, whose concept of *thick description* is founded on the argument that significant and important knowledge of norms and social structures may be extracted from seemingly insignificant events of daily life (Geertz 1973, 27). Although an anthropologist can access other cultures through fieldwork, it is not possible to travel back to c. 1600 and observe societies in the past. Instead, Greenblatt uses written sources, anecdotes, and stories that have been preserved and that describe circumstances in the past.

In his analysis of *Othello*, Greenblatt focuses on explorers' meetings with indigenous people, in particular the way in which they use their ability to understand and convey their empathy with indigenous people, and use this to their advantage (Greenblatt 1980, 228). Greenblatt sees the ability to improvise in response to an analysis of other people's actions as a characteristic way in which Western explorers and colonizers gained control of (usually) much larger groups of indigenous people. This insight is then turned on *Othello*, where its parallel in Iago's ability to understand Othello's emotions, and manipulate them with his perception of reality, enables him to set a trap for Othello. This leads to the tragic end of Desdemona, who cannot convince Othello of her innocence, and is killed by him. Greenblatt's thesis of the importance of improvisation is supported by key passages, as here where Iago in scene three of act one develops his plan in accordance with Othello's character:

I hate the Moor,
And it is thought abroad, that 'twixt my sheets
He has done my office: I know not if 't be true;
But I, for mere suspicion in that kind,

Will do as if for surety. He holds me well;
The better shall my purpose work on him.
Cassio's a proper man: let me see now;
To get his place and to plume up my will
In double knaver. How, how? Let's see.
After some time, to abuse Othello's ear
That he is too familiar with his wife.
He hath a person and a smooth dispose
To be suspected, framed to make women false.
The Moor is of a free and open nature,
That thinks men honest that but seem to be so,
And will as tenderly be led by the nose
As asses are. (Shakespeare 1994, 393–94)

The way Greenblatt connects the ability to improvise, as it appears in the play, with historical reports, is both convincing and seductive. A central aspect of New Historicism is the disclosure of analogies between social structures or conventions, and the literary text. The approach has been criticized for shifting focus from accomplishments, reducing Shakespeare to a mouthpiece for historical conditions, for example. But in the case of *Othello*, it is exactly the inspiration from historical sources that presents new facets in the work, which does not detract from the artistic value of his plays by showing their relationship to historical situations. A related criticism, which may be more significant, is that historical approaches to literature tend to be more interested in history than in literature, and thus, literature ends up serving historical interests. Ultimately, the New Historicist approach is dependent on its ability to make convincing connections between the world of the play and the historical world in a way that discloses qualities that would otherwise have been overlooked. Greenblatt is aware of the danger of seeing enchanted, almost magical, connections between texts and historical events. It is a fascination that he and Catherine Gallagher also find in one of their key inspirations, German literary historian Erich Auerbach:

> Auerbach knows perfectly well, of course, that an entire epoch cannot be adequately represented in a single text, let alone in a small textual fragment, but in his work we repeatedly glimpse what we regard as a quasi-magical effect: the conjuring of a complex, dynamic, historically specific spirit of representation out of a few paragraphs. (Gallagher and Greenblatt 2000, 37)

The relation between the part and the whole is, as in any interpretative practice, of great importance, and Greenblatt's approach also reflects his attitude toward literary history, as described above. History is not determined once and for all, but there are limits to what may be concluded from fragments of sources. This does not alter the fact that there is always an element of construction at work, when larger aspects of history and literary history are presented.

Periods

The periodization of history is one of the central tools for characterizing shared conditions over long periods of time. Terms such as Antiquity, the Middle Ages, and the Renaissance cover hundreds of years and there is always the risk of making generalizations that do not hold as they may be contradicted by specific works of literature that do not abide to the content of the periodizations. Other periods are very short, usually as the contemporary era is approached. Modernism and Postmodernism are often used to describe long stretches of twentieth-century literature, but each period may also be said to extend over a few decades, depending on how one defines them. French historian Fernand Braudel suggested using overlapping periodizations:

> The historians of the eighteenth and early nineteenth centuries had been attentive to the perspectives of the *longue durée* in a way in which, afterwards, only a few great spirits—Michelet, Ranke, Jacob Burckhardt, Fustel—were able to recapture. If one accepts that this going beyond the short span has been the most precious, because the most rare, of historiographical achievements during the past hundred years, then one understands the preeminent role of the history of institutions, of religions, of civilisations, and (thanks to archeology with its need for vast chronological expanses) the ground-breaking role of the studies devoted to classical antiquities. It was only yesterday that they proved the saviors of our profession. (Braudel 1980, 29)

There are changes that may make a shorter period distinct from another, such as Modernism and Postmodernism, but both these periods are part of a longer period that could be termed Modernity, with roots going back to Industrialization, at least. Sometimes, a few years make a huge difference. The perspective on a work written in 1938 and another written in 1948 may hardly be avoided, considering the Second World War and what it did to people's outlooks. As time passes such differences are often ignored, and the reading of Greek tragedies in the present usually takes into consideration only the events at the time of writing, as is the case with much of the reception of Shakespeare's work.

The sense of change over the long term, or *longue durée*, in Braudel's words, is a key aspect of the influence of Shakespeare's works. The transition from a medieval to a modern universe involves a conflict that is a subtle but important part of his works. The American critic Harold Bloom extravagantly claimed that Shakespeare created the modern human (Bloom 1994, 6), whereas Stephen Greenblatt notices the negotiation between worldviews in Shakespeare's drama (Greenblatt 1990, 20). From the Medieval faith in a world where God guaranteed coherence to the primate of humanity's own, self-doubting knowledge of the world is characteristic of the Renaissance.

In *Othello*, a difference in worldviews is embodied in Othello and Iago. Othello represents the perspective of the Middle Ages, which sees God's and the Devil's deeds as part of the world, whereas Iago plays along with these beliefs, but considers them to be nothing more than superstitions:

> Naked in bed, Iago, and not mean harm!
> It is hypocrisy against the devil:
> They that mean virtuously, and yet do so,
> The devil their virtue tempts, and they tempt heaven.

(Shakespeare 1994, 458)

Literary works often thrive on the tension between competing worldviews, and these can make their particular stories universal; Shakespeare's work is rife with examples. This is the case in several of his plays: in the tragedy caused by medieval codes of honor, in *Romeo and Juliet*, or in the recognition of the fact that words do not always fit the objects or ideas with which they are associated, as Prince Hamlet struggles to give up the idea of a God-given language. The French historian and philosopher Michel Foucault called the circumstance of what was previously considered certain being replaced by new views an "epistemic shift" (Foucault 1974, 346). It is precisely through their ability to capture the break between worlds that Shakespeare and his contemporaries, French essayist Michel de Montaigne, and the Spanish author of *Don Quixote,* Miguel de Cervantes, become both important and fascinating.

The literary historian and critic Frank Kermode argued that there are two basic ways of organizing literary history. One is through canon formations that emphasize certain authors at the cost of others, and in the case of Shakespeare that has happened to such an extent that some booksellers have sections devoted to this one author, and not to Renaissance drama. The other mode is to create periods that ascribe distinct qualities to a given time, as distinct from the preceding and following periods. According to Kermode, what is common to both approaches is that they tend to modernize the past and find values in it that resonate with the contemporary world. And there is no way around making history simpler and more manageable, because otherwise it would not be history, but the past itself. So although it is not possible to make any claim about the past, there is no definitive truth concerning it, there are only constructs that simplify and bring with them the values of the present:

> The last thing you can say about them [periods] is that in real use they are "value-free"; they not only impose valuations on particular works and particular periods, but they all tend more or less silently to place uniquely high value on our own period, since it is on behalf of that period that the valuations are made. We want to select from the past what is modern about it and assume that we have a very privileged view of the past that enables us to do so. In other words, periods are another way of making modern. (Kermode 1988, 123)

The literary historian David Perkins agrees with Kermode in many respects, but emphasizes the conflict between the desire to organize the past, and to comprehend it as broadly as possible. This is a conflict between complexity and coherence: if one wants to present the past as realistically and in as much detail as possible, one ends up with a high degree of complexity. If one wants to present the past in a focused and convincing way, one will seek coherence, knowing that nuances will be lost:

> Every theorist of literary history—every practical attempt in this genre—ultimately shatters on this dilemma. We must perceive a past age as relatively unified if we are to write literary history; we must perceive it as highly diverse if what we write is to represent it plausibly. (Perkins 1992, 27)

But that is always the condition of history, which may never be history itself, but a representation of it, which keeps evolving as new interpretations of it challenge or displace the existing ones. Shakespeare's work is not the whole story of what theater was in his day, but the dominance of his work by way of a long and often tumultuous process of canonization is more an expression of the current value of his authorship than a reflection of its initial importance to society. Similarly, the values of the Renaissance that are lauded in his plays, such as the individual's liberation from tradition, the secularization of the world, and the connection of high and low forms, from bad jokes to eloquent speech, are all definitely present in his work, but one could also present other descriptions of the world of the Renaissance that would elicit an admiration for Antiquity, and the kind of historicism against which Greenblatt warns.

A more recent example of the way in which literary history modernizes the past is apparent in the reception of James Joyce's *Ulysses* (2000). Brian McHale has argued that early criticism was first drawn to a new technique, the *stream-of-consciousness*, which provided the reader with a new sense of being inside the mind of another. It was also a technique that did not draw on historical models, but fitted well with other descriptions of Modernism and the break with the past. McHale's point is that later criticism, coinciding with the rise of Postmodernism, paid more attention to the pastiches of traditional genres Joyce wrote, and that gives the work a distinct polyphonic structure (McHale 1987, 153). McHale holds that *Ulysses* may be called both modernist and postmodernist, but the important point is that the latter interpretation became possible and accepted, as a new epoch cast its own distinct light on the work.

Both periodization and canonization express a certain consensus of ideas concerning what is of value in history, but they may also cover aspects that one will not see if one blindly trusts in their capacity to capture and frame the past.

History, understanding, and fascination

The preceding pages have primarily been concerned with the understanding of literary works in relation to history, or with how to understand literary history as a process where certain developments take place one after another. However, it is also possible to approach historical time with the idea that the primary objective is not to understand and order history with the goal of learning, but to capture the fascination the past has for the contemporary moment. The German-American literary historian Hans Ulrich Gumbrecht (also see Chapter 2) has argued for such an approach, where the fascination of being in contact with the past for a time is privileged over historical understanding. Or, as Stephen Greenblatt has summarized, one of his motivations for studying the past has to do with having a conversation with the dead (Greenblatt 1989, 1).

In Gumbrecht's book *In 1926: Living at the Edge of Time* (1997), a wide variety of sources concerning 1926 are included: not because 1926 was a particularly interesting year; the purpose is to show how close one can get to a different time through newspapers, books, silent movies, jazz records, and so on, to a sense of what it means to have been present in that year. The first part of the book is a catalogue of various objects and phenomena of the time—records, elevators, marathon dancing, bicycle races, and boxing matches—and how people experienced and wrote about them. There is no ambition to reveal a higher truth about, or coherent meaning of, 1926, but the primary intent is to bring the everyday life of that year a bit closer.

When Shakespeare's plays are performed in theaters rebuilt after the original architecture a similar desire is expressed, similar to when one admires or discusses the historical accuracy of the costumes and scenography in one of the many adaptations to film. The words in a modern performance of Shakespeare are the same as in an original one, but it is obvious that the desire for presence and authenticity means something in this situation, just as there is still a high demand for first editions of rare or not-so-rare books, where not a word is added, yet the book as an object carries a certain historical aura with it. However, in *In 1926* Gumbrecht goes beyond mere fascination, and in the final sections of the book he writes what he calls a "metaphysics of the everyday," identifying the dichotomies that guide people's ideas of the world: Do they think of center and periphery, or immanence and transcendence? Is the future welcoming or threatening? Is the past experienced as something that is lost, or something from which one has been emancipated? French sociologist Pierre Bourdieu attempts, in a different way, to describe the codes of the artistic field within the wider society in *The Rules of Art* (1996).

Both Gumbrecht and Bourdieu try to create a broader context around works, in order to understand the social space in which they came into being, but without pretending to fully explain the works against that background. To Gumbrecht, the question is one of acknowledging fascination beyond understanding as a legitimate way of addressing literature in history, along with the general classification into periods, the continuous discerning of what should be canonical or not, or attempts to explain fictional worlds by comparing them to the history and culture of their times.

Further reading

The Norton Critical Edition of Othello is a well-annotated version of the play, followed by several seminal articles. David Perkins' *Is Literary History Possible?* is a short, but wide-ranging reflection on literary history. Fernand Braudel's *On History* is recommended for a more general consideration of writing history. Stephen Greenblatt's and Catherine Gallagher's *Practicing New Historicism* is a good introduction to new historicism. John Guillory's *Cultural Capital: The Problem of Literary Canon Formation* is a well-argued investigation of the role of canons in the making of literary history. Ted Underwood's *Why Literary Periods Mattered* is a thoughtful examination of the uses of periodization with an outlook to how new digital approaches can further the understanding of historical change. Finally, Friedrich Nietzsche's *On the Use and Abuse of History for Life* is a key text on the importance of history to humanity.

References

Aristotle (1958) *On Poetry and Style*, New York: Liberal Arts Press.

Bloom, Harold (1994) *The Western Canon: The Books and Schools of the Ages*, New York: Harcourt Brace.

Bourdieu, Pierre (1996) *The Rules of Art*, Cambridge: Polity Press.

Braudel, Fernand (1980) *On History*, Chicago: University of Chicago Press.

Foucault, Michel (1974) *The Order of Things: An Archaeology of the Human Sciences*, London: Routledge.

Gallagher, Catherine and Stephen Greenblatt (2000) *Practicing New Historicism*, Chicago: University of Chicago Press.

Geertz, Clifford (1973) *The Interpretation of Cultures: Selected Essays*, New York: Basic Books.

Greenblatt, Stephen (1980) *Renaissance Self-Fashioning: From More to Shakespeare*. Chicago: University of Chicago Press.

Greenblatt, Stephen (1989) *Shakespearean Negotiations: The Circulation of Social Energy in Renaissance England*, Berkeley: University of California Press.

Greenblatt, Stephen (1990) "Resonance and Wonder," *Bulletin of the American Academy of Arts and Sciences*, 43: 4.

Guillory, John (1993) *Cultural Capital: The Problem of Literary Canon Formation*, Chicago: University of Chicago Press.

Gumbrecht, Hans Ulrich (1997) *In 1926: Living at the Edge of Time*, Cambridge: Harvard University Press.

Joyce, James (2000) *Ulysses*, London: Penguin.

Kermode, Frank (1988) *History and Value*, Oxford: Clarendon Press.

McHale, Brian (1987) *Postmodernist Fiction*, New York: Methuen.

Nietzsche, Friedrich (1995) *The Use and Abuse of History*, New York: Macmillan.

Perkins, David (1992) *Is Literary History Possible?* Baltimore: Johns Hopkins University Press.

Shakespeare, William (1994) *Four Tragedies*, London: Penguin.

Underwood, Ted (2015) *Why Literary Periods Mattered*, Stanford: Stanford University Press.

15
Ethics

Lasse Horne Kjældgaard

Do you become a good person by reading literature? Joseph Goebbels, who as a young scholar wrote a doctoral dissertation on the dramas of Wilhelm von Schütz, aspired to become a writer of novels, and later in life became Hitler's propaganda minister, did not. Goebbels's studies of German romanticism and his own literary publications did not refrain him from taking the lead in the Nazi genocide and crimes against humanity. Perhaps they even spurred him on?

The example is an extreme one, but it shows, at least, that we are dealing with a problem. The question—whether you become a better person by reading literature—necessarily implies the opposite option: that you may become a crueller person by reading literature. Plato introduced this argument already in the tenth book of *The Republic* (c. 380 BC), condemning the pernicious effects of poetry and proposing its banishment from his ideal state. His reaction shows that the notion of the benefits of literature goes hand in hand with the idea of its harmfulness. Both have been widely used to defend or attack literature, from ancient times until today.

The discussion is not just a theoretical one. The question whether literature in general or certain literary genres in particular improves or damages the moral of the readers can result in censorship or bans—or, vice versa, in various forms of preferential treatment in relation to other genres (for example, as a reason why teaching fiction is important in primary school and secondary education).

The discussion is not reserved for professional readers either. Ethical issues are very often at the heart of the matter when non-professional readers talk about (popular) fiction. Is it, for instance, all right that Lisbeth Salander turns into a vigilante avenger in Stieg Larsson's *Millennium* trilogy, paying back on the numerous men who hate women? Does E.L. James's *Fifty Shades of Grey* trilogy glorify abusive relationships and female submissiveness, or does it rather help readers escape sexual repression and encourage them to live out their fantasies? Questions like these show that the link between literature and ethics is strong among many types of readers, and that it concerns various types of literature.

A precarious relationship

In the twentieth century, literary theory and literary criticism have tended to exorcise fiction from the ethical domain. New Criticism, especially, made a point out of detaching the literary work both from the biographical author and from the emotional life that the work might inspire in the reader. The "intentional fallacy" was the name for the former analytical error. The "affective fallacy" was the name for the latter mistake. It was considered a psychological distraction to evaluate a literary work on the basis of feelings roused by reading, including moral feelings. Questions of human experience—and empathy—were bracketed, and this tendency was only furthered, at least to begin with, by the theoretical waves of structuralism, deconstruction, and post-structuralism, focusing on signs and structures rather than psychology and morality.

Historically, this is an important development. Until the eighteenth century, it was virtually impossible to evade ethical criteria when evaluating literature. Literary works were not primarily judged as "good" or "bad," in aesthetic terms, but rather in epistemological terms, as "true" or "false," or in ethical terms, as "moral" or "immoral." Literature was primarily seen as a didactic tool with an ultimate purpose of disseminating messages that were usually of a moral or religious kind.

The Danish author Ludvig Holberg, for example, wrote about his satirical fictional travelogue *Niels Klim* (1741) that the "whole story is of no importance, if it is not considered as an envelope around moral doctrines and considerations" (Holberg 1963, 180). This was how literature was generally regarded up until the eighteenth century: as a kind of verbal wrapping around maxims and moral precepts. Elsewhere, Holberg compared this literary approach to the practicing of medicine:

> As doctors gild bitter pills, to encourage patients to take them, so do philosophers follow their example, attracting the desire and attention of readers by several figures that they have put on this useful knowledge. Some have, in this respect, found it fit to unfold such morals in pleasant fables. (Holberg 1992, 10)

Like bad-tasting medications, moral instructions were sugar-coated with narratives and other literary devices in order to make them easier to swallow. "Sweetening the pill" could serve as a label for this literary theory, which was prevalent in the age of Enlightenment.

This began to change during the eighteenth century. Art and literature began to stand out from morality and religion and science, becoming, as it is often said, "autonomous," independent. Traditionally, this development is described as a process of liberation. The philosophical epitome of this process was Immanuel Kant's statement, in *The Critique of Judgement* (1790), "that the beautiful … is wholly independent of the representation of the good" (Kant 1952, 69). According to Kant, judgments of taste were fundamentally different from moral judgments due to the "disinterestedness" of the former. This word became a key concept to the foundation of a distinct way of thinking philosophically about literature and the fine arts, called "aesthetics."

Nevertheless, together with the "liberation" of art and literature came a new ban: against serving moral purposes. The relation between ethics and literature went from one normative extreme to another. Oscar Wilde concisely expressed this new condition in the preface to *The Picture of Dorian Gray* from 1891: "There is no such thing as a moral or an immoral book. Books are well written, or badly written. That is all" (Wilde 1999, 17). Questions of morality were, or ought to be, unrelated to the evaluation of literature.

This categorical view has been softened in literary critique and research in recent years. A number of developments have paved the way for a return to moral issues, and for a renewed theoretical awareness of the relationship between literature and ethics. That goes for the last thirty years of reader-response criticism and for the return to history and to questions of referentiality, which victim studies, feminism, post-colonialism, and new historicism have brought about. At the same time, advances in experimental psychology and brain research have facilitated more empirical approaches to the question of what happens in the brain when reading literature.

Finally, attention to the quite recently discovered genre of "witness literature" has created new interest in ethics and the ethical dimensions of reading and teaching literature. The Israeli philosopher Avishai Margalit has tried to formulate the hope that keeps writers of witness literature (Holocaust victims are the paradigmatic example) up under the most abandoned circumstances, namely the chance "that in another place or another time there exists, or will exist, a moral community that will listen to their testimony" (Margalit 2002, 155). Margalit's statement may serve as a description of the increased ethical importance, which reading and teaching literature assumes when dealing with witness literature. It obviously becomes an ethical deed, and an ethical challenge, in itself.

Ethical dimensions of literature

But why, one may ask, can it be tempting to regard literature as an ethical phenomenon? Several answers to this question are possible. The essential feature of poetry was, to Plato, its capacity to imitate (see *Mimesis*). Many discussions of the ethical implications of literature revolve around this ability. Literature offers us patterns of possible lives, which we, as readers, may engage in both mentally and sentimentally, with intellect as well as passion. These examples can be positive or negative, commendable or revolting. Literature shows us not only heroes, villains and fools, good deeds and vile misdeeds, noble emotions but also complex and unpleasant emotions. The examples may encourage us to consider how we want to be—and how we definitely do not want to be—as human beings. We are free to draw our own lessons from them.

Perhaps the possibility of ethical interpretations follows from the form of narrative in itself. "Could we ever narrativize without moralizing?," the American historian Hayden White has asked rhetorically (White 1987, 25). Supporting this hypothesis is the frequent use of the word "moral" about the lesson to be drawn from a story or an event or experience.

The word used by Ludvig Holberg and Hayden White, however, "moralizing," does not sound particularly fortunate in present-day English. Often, it is used as a derogatory term about the behavior of people who are (too) prone to make moral judgments about others. This pursuit is fit for "moralizers" but not for artists. Earlier, however, the word "moralize" had a different meaning, namely to indulge in moral consideration or discussion—and not necessarily to prescribe what is morally right or wrong. Nor does White use the word in the didactic or judgmental sense but rather in the sense of interpreting morally or symbolically. These differences of semantics and value point to the way in which high-quality—that is, complex—literary works often deal with ethical issues: not dogmatically, not prescriptive, but rather inquiring, investigative, and appraising. They show us the inadequacy of our moral concepts and judgments in the face of (imaginative) reality. Such works keep the reader ethically awake, you might say.

A number of mainly American lawyers, psychologists, and literary scholars have, over the last decades, taken a great interest in the ways in which literature may engage us in ethical problems and dilemmas, without specifying any simple solutions. This line of inquiry has led them to resume a concept from eighteenth-century philosophy, "moral imagination" (Himmelfarb 2006). The term itself transcends the sharp division between ethics and art. Moral imagination can be defined as the ability to analyze the complex relations between circumstances, motives, actions, and consequences of human behavior. This is something we do, or try to do, all the time in real life, but certainly not without making mistakes or doing harm to both others and ourselves.

Fiction, in contrast, can work as a kind of simulator, where one can practice, developing and maintaining one's moral imagination, free of costs, so to speak.

Another recurrent concept in the opening of literary studies to ethical concerns is "empathy." The word is etymologically related to the German word "Einfühlung" and is used about the ability to understand and appreciate another person's feelings, situation, experience, and so on.

A prominent advocate of both "moral imagination" and "empathy" is the American philosopher Martha Nussbaum. According to her, empathy is nurtured by the reading of literature, which "inspires intense concern with the fate of characters and defines those characters as containing a rich inner life, not all of which is open to view; in the process, the reader learns to have respect for the hidden contents of that inner world, seeing its importance in defining a creature as fully human" (Nussbaum 1997, 90). By reading literature, one can learn to put oneself in the place of others, and this—so the argument goes—guides the reader to behave less selfishly and become more considerate to others.

In addition, some scholars claim that literature can make the reader's empathy grow not only in the depth but also in scope. The expansion of understanding and compassion can also affect the limits of who, in general, is considered "human" at all. Thus, the American cultural historian Lynn Hunt has argued for a historical relation between the emergence of the idea of human rights and the simultaneous rise and success of the novel, especially the epistolary novel:

> In the eighteenth century, readers of novels learned to extend their purview of empathy. In reading, they empathized across traditional social boundaries between nobles and commoners, masters and servants, men and women, perhaps even adults and children. As a consequence, they came to see others—people they did not know personally—as like them, as having the same kinds of inner emotions. (Hunt 2007, 40)

For this reason, reading novels has helped to pave the way for human rights to be held as "self-evident truths," making a major contribution to a historical process that most people today consider a moral progress.

Precisely this expression, "moral progress," has been used by the American pragmatist philosopher Richard Rorty, about the effects of literature, as compared with philosophy. He too invoked the concept of "moral imagination":

> Literature is more important for moral progress, because it contributes to the widening of the moral imagination. It makes us more sensitive by deepening our understanding of the motivations of, and of the differences among, our fellow humans. Philosophy is useful for summarizing previous moral insights in the form of moral principles, but it does not do much creative work. For example, philosophical reflections did not do much to eliminate slavery, but narratives about the lives the slaves were living contributed a lot. (Rorty 2006, 67)

According to Rorty, causes of moral progress have gained traction because of the effects of literature rather than philosophical thinking. Literature has given millions of readers insight into what cruelty and suppression do to people, and it has facilitated understanding between people, of both their differences and their similarities. In this way, it can be said to have contributed to "moral progress."

The underlying assumption of this argument has been dubbed the "empathy-altruism hypothesis" by the American scholar Suzanne Keen. The hypothesis is certainly not unproblematic. First, it is difficult to clarify the causality and validity of the argument: "Do empathetic people make good readers, or do good readers become empathetic people? Both may be true without guaranteeing that novels routinely do more than entertain, inform, soothe, or excite their readers," Keen has objected (Keen 2007, xv). Second, it is difficult to infer unequivocally from ethical insights to ethical action. The habit of reading literature can also, some argue, lead to a blasé state of mind as well as indifference to real human suffering. Thirdly, the empirical examples of downright cruel literati, pushed to the extreme by the case of Joseph Goebbels, may also be employed to debunk the claim that reading literature necessarily makes people behave better in real life.

Another set of critical questions relates to the literary and medial scope of the claim that reading literature enhances the capacity to empathize and, furthermore, the ability to act ethically. Does it apply only to certain genres or categories of literature, as, for instance, Greek tragedies, Shakespeare's plays, and canonized novels? Or does it apply also to popular fiction and bestsellers, which may influence a much larger audience in moral or immoral directions?

Perhaps this question can only be meaningfully answered on the level of single works of literature? Some works seem so purposefully designed to elicit ethical reactions—to such a degree that it would be insufficient, and perhaps even offensive, to analyze them as mere formal artistry, without addressing their ethical implications. That might be the case for Shakespeare's tragic comedy *The Merchant of Venice* (c. 1596), for Fyodor Dostoevsky's novel *Crime and Punishment* (1886) or for Lars von Trier's motion picture *Dogville* (2003). Other works—such as Samuel Beckett's trilogy *Molloy, Malone Dies* and *The Unnammable* (1951–1953)—seem more resistant to ethical perspectives.

Finally, there is the question of whether literature has special abilities to handle ethical issues in comparison with fiction mediated on television, film, or the theater? Martha Nussbaum follows this line of argument in the quotation above, highlighting the privileged access to other people's inner life granted by literature. But is that really so?

Moreover, it would be relevant to address the question of the means used by literature to pursue these ends—what role does humor, irony, sarcasm, and perversion play to the ethical benefits of literature? Eighteenth-century satires, for instance, stage various forms of transgression, but often with an aim of raising awareness of—and confirming—certain virtues and moral values. This too can be argued in the case of a very different work, Brett Easton Ellis' scandalous novel *American Psycho* (1991), which also lends itself to moral interpretations as a modern satirical novel of manners.

Beyond moral judgment

That can hardly be said about the novel *Disgrace* (1999) by the South African writer and Nobel laureate John Coetzee. It may serve as a fairly recent example of a literary work, which poses ethical questions completely without lecturing or inducing anyone to believe in simple answers or, indeed, solutions.

Disgrace begins, seemingly facile, with a familiar motif from the campus novel tradition. A 52-year-old South African Professor of Literature, David Lurie, seduces a twenty-year-old college student, who attends one of his classes. Someone gossips, and the university initiates disciplinary proceedings against him. At a hearing, Lurie readily confesses, but that is not sufficient. His colleagues also demand that he should repent in a convincingly heartfelt way. Lurie refuses to do so. He walks out from the hearings and gets dismissed by the university. He refuses offers of psychological counselling, therapy, and reformation. Publically, he is scandalized and disgraced, and yet he holds on to his integrity and his honor. He remains true to his inner self, to which he denies his opponents access.

Throughout this part of the novel, we remain in a fairly safe and recognizable world, with relatively uncomplicated ethical issues. No, of course it is not morally acceptable to conflate power and sexuality, as Professor Lurie does when he seduces his student, whose exam he is responsible for—a practice, which is difficult not to perceive as an extension of his weekly visit with a prostitute. We can probably all agree to that. The affair is not harmless. It brings the young woman in an extremely difficult situation and leaves her on the verge of giving up her studies. It is reprehensible. On the other hand, there are, of course, also reservations to be made about the kind of atonement that the university demands of Lurie. He must not only distance himself from his actions, but do so with a sincerity that his colleagues will believe. This kind of punishment may also be disturbing to many of us.

But soon all moral agreement ends. David Lurie flees out of the city to the countryside, to his adult lesbian daughter Lucy, who runs a dog kennel in The Eastern Cape. Her neighbor, Petrus, belongs to the black majority, which her own white minority has dishonored for centuries. During the apartheid regime, he worked for her. Now that society has changed, she has sold him a plot of land, on which he has built his own home.

One Wednesday morning, when father and daughter are discussing morality and immorality in general, on the occasion of Lurie's deed, three men come to the house. They gain access by pretending that they need to use the phone to call for medical help for a childbirth. Then follows an orgy of violence. When it is over, David Lurie's eye, ear, and his entire scalp are damaged. And his daughter has been brutally beaten and raped by all three men, who have left the property in his car.

This is only the beginning. The event opens up a chasm between the two protagonists, father and daughter. David Lurie, through whom the entire novel is focalized, suffers from his inability to understand his daughter. She reports the theft, but not the gang rape, to the police. This causes her father to take her to school:

> Do you think that what happened here was an exam: if you come through, you get a diploma and safe conduct into the future, or a sign to paint of the door-lintel that will make the plague pass you by. That is not how vengeance works, Lucy. Vengeance is like a fire. The more it devours, the hungrier it gets […] Is it some form of private salvation you are trying to work out? Do you hope you can expiate the crimes of the past by suffering in the present? (Coetzee 2000, 112)

But his lecturing is lost on Lucy. She will not accept his terminology and refuses to talk about sin and atonement, plague and fire. She wants to communicate through her actions.

Petrus holds a party where David and Lucie recognize the youngest of the three perpetrators among the guests. David's suspicion that the neighbor has orchestrated the attack grows. He thinks his daughter should buy a gun and take shooting lessons. But she will not comply with his request. On the contrary, she forms closer bonds to the neighbor and to the boy, who may be the father of the child she carries. The rape has made her pregnant, and she is convinced that the sexual assault was the real objective of the criminals. For that reason, she is also convinced that the rape holds the key to the country's restoration.

So, the novel involves the reader in one kind of disgrace—David Lurie's shameful expulsion from the university, due to the sexual harassment case—upon which it introduces a new kind of disgrace, making the first one fade. After all, there is a long way from the "informed consent" of two adults, albeit intergenerational, to gang rape. And there is a vastly longer way between the professor's stubborn rejection of the imposed penance to his daughter's reaction to the injustice that has surpassed her: She not only accepts it but humbles herself even further. As her own Truth and Reconciliation Commission, she chooses the ultimate kind of tolerance, for the sake of peace: losing her honor.

Behind Coetzee's controversial novel about the process of dismantling apartheid in South Africa stands, like an after-image, the greatest historical icon of tolerance in the twentieth century, Nelson Mandela, who came out after twenty-six years of humiliating incarceration and held out his hand to his tormentors, saying: I condone you, we should all be here, because the alternative to tolerance is war. Coetzee depicts a similar gesture in *Disgrace*, from the other side of the great divide. It is a novel about ethical issues, which is not the slightest moralistic or didactic. It forces the reader to consider ethical issues that are extreme and complex and very diverse, showing that both sexual activities on campus and the challenges of racial desegregation are part of the same moral reality.

Disgrace may thus be regarded as a confirmation that the relationship between literature and ethics thrives on precariousness.

Further reading

A passionate defense of the ethical significance of reading literature, rich in examples and analyses, can be found in Wayne C. Booth's *The Company We Keep: An Ethics of Fiction*. Suzanne Keen's *Empathy and the Novel* provides a thorough examination of the history and current status of the concept of empathy in the theory of the novel. The anthology *Mapping the Ethical Turn. A Reader in Ethics, Culture, and Literary Theory*, edited by Todd F. Davis and Kenneth Womack, brings together several key contributions to the "ethical turn" in literary studies, including seminal texts by Martha Nussbaum, James Phelan, and J. Hillis Miller.

References

Coetzee, John (2000) *Disgrace*, London: Vintage.

Himmelfarb, Gertrude (2006) *The Moral Imagination: From Edmund Burke to Lionel Trilling*, Chicago: Ivan R. Dee.

Holberg, Ludvig (1963) *Ludvig Holbergs memoirer*, Copenhagen: Schønberg.

Holberg, Ludvig (1992) *Moralske Tanker*, Copenhagen: Det Danske Sprog- og Litteraturselskab.

Hunt, Lynn (2007) *Inventing Human Rights. A History*, New York and London: W. W. Norton.

Kant, Immanuel (1952) *The Critique of Judgement*. Trans. J. Creed Meredith. Oxford: Clarendon Press.

Keen, Suzanne (2007) *Empathy and the Novel*, Oxford and New York: Oxford University Press.

Margalit, Avishai (2002) *The Ethics of Memory*, Cambridge, MA: Harvard University Press.

Nussbaum, Martha C. (1997) *Cultivating Humanity. A Classical Defense of Reform in Liberal Education*, Cambridge, MA: Harvard University Press.

Rorty, Richard (2006) *Take Care of Freedom and Truth Will Take Care of Itself. Interviews with Richard Rorty*, Stanford: Stanford University Press.

White, Hayden V. (1987) *The Content of Form. Narrative Discourse and Historical Representation*, Baltimore: Johns Hopkins University Press.

Wilde, Oscar (1999) *Complete Works*, Glasgow: HarperCollins.

16
Politics

Jakob Ladegaard

"Politics," claims the narrator of Stendhal's novel *The Red and the Black* (1830), "is a stone tied round the neck of literature which submerges it in less than six months" (Stendhal 2012, 295). This notion of literature's tie to politics is shared by those who believe that good literature portrays the universal content of the human condition, rather than historical struggles. But a narrator's notion (especially one as ironic as Stendhal's) is sometimes contradicted by the very story he is telling. *The Red and the Black* portrays the young Julien, who moves from modest circumstances in the province to Paris, driven not only by love but also by ambition and a desire for social recognition that embody contemporary bourgeois ideals of individual freedom and social mobility. Along the way he meets noblemen and priests who defend the more static world of the *ancien régime*. Stendhal's description of these encounters adds up to a nuanced portrait of the tensions in French society that sparked the revolution in July 1830—a few months before *The Red and the Black* appeared with the subtitle *A Chronicle of the Nineteenth Century*.

Is *The Red and the Black* a political novel? Not in the sense implied by Stendhal's narrator, it is not burdened by accounts of the daily quarrels and concerns of parliaments and courts covered by the press and soon forgotten again. But politics in the age of modern democracies is not only a matter of the debates and decisions of those in power. It is also essentially about the experiences and possibilities of ordinary people like Julien. If Stendhal's novel is political, it is in this wider sense as a reflection on the opportunities of individuals and groups in a modern society with social, economic, and political conflicts and different moral, cultural, and religious ideals. While academic disciplines such as political science, sociology, economics, and law typically treat these phenomena separately, a novel like *The Red and the Black* provides insight into their relationships, not seen solely from the bird's-eye view of social science, but combining analysis of large-scale social constellations with the particularity of individual experience. And unlike other classical art forms, it does so in the common medium of political arguments and prevarications: language. These are some of the reasons why literature can provide unique insights into social and political conditions and sometimes cause readers to rise and defend or change them.

But there is a long tradition for debating exactly *what kinds* of political insight literature gives, *how* to analyze it correctly, and *what types* of literature are political in the "right" or "wrong" way. This chapter will present some of the most influential approaches to these questions from critics broadly related to the tradition of Marxist ideology critique. For practical reasons, the examples of this chapter are taken from modern Western literature. However, the methods and theories created by this critical tradition can also be and have been used to study literature from other times and places. The chapter first presents some common ideas in the ideology critical tradition, particularly as they are played out in the critique of the modern idea of autonomous literature. Then follows an exposition of three theories of political literature related to the Frankfurt School. Finally, the chapter discusses French philosopher Jacques Rancière's current exploration of political literature, which both draws on the tradition of ideology critique and criticizes it. All in an effort to show how some of the most influential critics of the last century have answered the question: What is political literature?

Ideology critique and modern literature

The concept of ideology critique was introduced by Karl Marx in *The German Ideology* (1845–1846) to criticize the idealist philosophy of history that found its most influential expression in the work of G. W. F. Hegel. In contrast to Hegel, Marx does not view the historical process as driven by Spirit, but by the economic and political contradictions between social classes. In modern times, the main struggle is that between the working class and the bourgeoisie. According to Marx, the latter's economic dominance is reflected in cultural, artistic, and philosophical production. Even if they present themselves as rational, natural, or God-given truths, Marx argues, an era's dominant ideas are those of its dominant class. *Ideology*, in Marx' sense, is thus a system of ideas that appears universal but in reality expresses the worldview and interests of the ruling class (Marx 2001, 92f.). An ideology critical analysis aims to reveal the function of such "truths" in the class struggle. Marx' main concern in this context was with philosophical and religious systems of ideas. It was not until the first decades of the twentieth century that systematic ideology critical approaches to modern literature and culture were developed. One of the early epicenters of this development was the group of Marxist cultural critics, social scientists, and philosophers that gathered around the Institute for Social Research in Frankfurt in the 1920s and 1930s. The work of the Frankfurt School studies how literary works and theories can promote dominant ideologies, but also how certain kinds of literature resist or subvert ideology. These two dimensions of the work of the School and its heirs are dealt with separately in this and the following sections. Let us first focus on the ideology critique of the modern idea of autonomous art.

In aesthetic philosophical terms, modern literature is heralded by the idea of the autonomous or self-reliant artwork. The idea is poignantly presented in the German philosopher Immanuel Kant's *Critique of Judgement* (1790). For Kant, artistic creation is essentially a work of freedom, which makes obsolete the rules of Classicist poetics. He further argues that the experience of beauty suspends habitual patterns of thinking and results in a feeling of harmony between the senses and consciousness (Kant 1974, 132). This is the background of the Romantic cult of artistic genius and art's freedom from prosaic life. At the turn of the eighteenth century, aesthetic theory thus establishes a separate sphere, where art is to be enjoyed for its own sake. This view of art is echoed in the narrator's rejection of political literature in *The Red and the Black* and has influenced Western conceptions of literature ever since (see Chapters 1, 15, and 28).

The idea of art's autonomy becomes an object of critical analysis in the Frankfurt School. In 1937, one of its key figures, Herbert Marcuse, thus denounces it for throwing a conciliatory veil over the conflicts of capitalist society. Autonomous art, he argues, provides only an illusory freedom that temporarily suspends the contradictions of modern existence and satisfies the longing for a better world. In doing this, art diverts the audience's critical energy from political reality and thus basically serves the existing order (Marcuse 1965, 66f.). The romantic view of art that arose when the bourgeoisie became the dominant class in Europe is, in other words, bourgeois ideology.

The later French sociologist Pierre Bourdieu refines Marcuse's analysis by drawing attention to the art institution that propagates the ideology of autonomous art in society through museums, universities, schools, and literary theory (Bourdieu is critical of formalist and hermeneutic approaches that tend to separate the meaning of art works from their social context). To be accepted in the art institution, a person must acquire the appropriate language, knowledge, and taste. For middle- and upper-class children such skills and tastes are often acquired in their upbringing and thus come to appear natural, while these codes will often seem alien to lower-class children who are not exposed to them in their homes. For Bourdieu, the idea of autonomous art is therefore not only ideological in the general sense that it glosses over the contradictions of capitalism but it also has the more precise function of establishing and naturalizing a social hierarchy of those with "good" taste who appreciate "fine" art, and those with "bad" taste who walk in the darkness of popular culture (Bourdieu 1996, 285–312).

Perhaps the lines between high and low culture cannot be drawn as sharply today as Bourdieu did in 1992. Over the last twenty years, the boundary between good and bad taste, high art and popular culture, has become still more blurry. But the notion that cultural products are not only enjoyed for their own sake but are also—consciously or not—used as a way of creating particular social identities is hardly obsolete. According to American sociologists Richard A. Peterson and Roger M. Kern, the line of cultural distinction is now increasingly drawn between a global elite that enjoys the best of all cultures and genres and a locally based underclass with an un-ironic penchant for kitsch (Peterson and Kern 1996).

Marcuse and Bourdieu's critique of art's autonomy is theoretical, but others have put it into analytical practice. One example of this is Marjorie Levinson's analysis of William Wordsworth's long poem "Lines written a few miles above Tintern Abbey: On Revisiting the Banks of the Wye during a Tour, July 13, 1798" (1798). In this poem, the lyrical I revisits the Wye River after an absence of five years and reflects on the changes he has gone through in the meantime. His first visit to the river bank was one of sensual rapture, but he has since become more self-conscious and cannot return to his former self-forgetfulness. Instead, he now finds a deeper pleasure in a vision of the connection between spirit and nature. The poem thereby recounts a typical romantic story of a development that begins with sensuous unity between man and nature, moves through a self-conscious separation, and ends with their spiritual reunion in and through poetic beauty.

Levinson begins with a question: How does the story of personal development relate to the place and historical moment that the title indicates so carefully? There seems to be no specific connection. Even the famous ruin of the Tintern Abbey monastery referred to in the title is not mentioned in the poem. The few traces of human activity are either depicted as harmoniously integrated in the landscape (such as the peasant houses with gardens and hedges in lines 11–18) or merely registered as sensual impressions whose causes are unknown (like the smoke rising from the woods in lines 18–23). This is not consistent with the actual appearance and function of the poem's locus that Levinson finds in historical sources. The river Wye was busy and contaminated as a result of the area's coal and iron industry; the monastery was a tourist attraction crowded with beggars who dwelled in the forests (hence the smoke); and the peasant houses were not "green to the very door" (Wordsworth 1971, 113) as a symbol of their inhabitant's harmony with nature, but because the common land, which had previously nourished many peasants, was being fenced and privatized (hence the poem's hedges), forcing people to cultivate their front yards (Levinson

2009, 29f.). Against that background, the poem's insight into spirit and nature is an idealized construction, which overlooks the fact that both landscapes and people are shaped by social and historical processes. This "sublimation of oversight into insight" (48) consists of a series of poetic reinterpretations of social phenomena. An example is the aforementioned smoke that Wordsworth at first vaguely ascribes to "vagrant dwellers" (Wordsworth 1971, 114), only to immediately present a more "poetic" alternative, "the hermit." By thus transforming the involuntary poverty of the real beggars living in the forests into the voluntary exile of a storybook hermit, the poem serves the interest of the ruling classes to suppress social problems whose solution could limit their power (Levinson 2009, 43).

This kind of ideology critical textual analysis and theory aim to unveil the historical reality and interests behind the "truths" disseminated in literature regardless of the topic, the author's stated intentions, and the fact that it was not written under external constraints like censorship. However, ideology critique's anchoring of literature in social reality can run a risk of turning into a straitjacket if historical explanations are elevated to objective truths. This sometimes happened in the 1970s in circles, where Marxism was considered a science and culture seen as a reflection of its material, social basis. As this view has been largely abandoned, it has given way to a broader and more nuanced understanding of ideology as a phenomenon that not only reflects bourgeois domination of workers but shapes social identities on all levels—gender, culture, ethnicity and so on—in conjunction with complex global economic and political processes. Michel Foucault's analysis of power and knowledge has been a major source of inspiration in this development. Often by way of Foucault, ideology criticism has become an inspiration for feminism, queer studies and post-colonialism's critique of social constructions of gender, sexuality, and ethnic identities. Another line of contemporary critical theory that in addition to the Marxist tradition draws on Hegel and Jacques Lacan, is the work of Slovenian philosophers Slavoj Žižek and Alenka Zupančič. The latter's *The Odd One In: On Comedy* (2008) is a rich, philosophical study of comedy as a genre that can both confirm social hierarchies and subvert them through a comic disjunction between the subject and her imaginary identification with a social role.

The critical potential of literature

As mentioned above, the Frankfurt School and its successors study not only ideological literature but also literature with a critical or even subversive potential. One of the significant theories of political literature that emerged from the circle was the Hungarian-born Georg Lukács' defense of realism. Unlike spiritually oriented movements like Romanticism, Realism deals with the material and social conditions of everyday life. In particular, Lukács praised Honoré de Balzac's novels for their realistic portraits of social types that condense the internal and external structures of an entire social milieu (Lukács 1989, 27ff.). Lukács' penchant for realism was shared by Stalin, who made socialist realism the official Soviet art doctrine. Although Lukács surpasses most of the doctrine's defenders in theoretical and analytical sophistication, his theory of realism shares some of the doctrine's weaknesses. First of all, it is in danger of falling into the determinist and reductive trap that I mentioned at the end of the last paragraph. Lukács posits an "objective" Marxist social analysis as a measure of the degree of literary realism. The truth about society therefore tends in his analysis to be given in advance; a novel can merely dramatize it more or less correctly.

Although few today adopt Lukács' orthodox class analysis, it remains a widely held view that social realism is a particularly political genre. And one can certainly argue that since realist fiction appeals to a wide audience, its often indignant depiction of the lives of marginalized persons and groups could have a certain impact. But it remains a tricky issue to determine whether a literary work portrays the oppressed "as they really are." One might be tempted to ask, where the feeling of recognition comes from among reviewers and readers who rarely move in the environments portrayed by social realist literature, if not from the media and mainstream culture? In that case, does Realism not tend to confirm the reader's preconceptions of the world—and thus the political *status quo*—rather than change it?

This type of criticism can be advanced with the support of another of the main figures of the Frankfurt School, Theodor W. Adorno, who sees a political potential in literary form rather than realist content. To understand this, one must return to his and Max Horkheimer's *Dialectic of Enlightenment* (1944), which criticizes the bourgeois Enlightenment tradition's faith in scientific rationality. Since reason works by subsuming individual phenomena to categorical concepts, according to the two authors Enlightenment rationality has a dogmatic tendency which in political terms contains the seeds of totalitarianism, which the two authors as Jews and non-dogmatic Marxists fled from in Nazi Germany and denounced in the Soviet Union (Adorno and Horkheimer 2002). Another similarity between modern bourgeois society and totalitarian regimes, according to the authors, is the use of popular movies, radio and music to discipline the masses (94–136). For Adorno, critical literature must reject the workings of the cultural industry by becoming more autonomous than bourgeois art, resisting mass consumption and total interpretations. Only then can art become "society's social antithesis" (Adorno 1980, 19), both a testament to society's injustices and a promise of justice. Adorno highlights modernists like Kafka and Beckett as authors whose formally experimental works portray society's violence against individuals without resolving contradictions into a redeeming totality (Adorno 1990).

Adorno's critics have accused his idea of political literature of being elitist. From Bourdieu's perspective, one can ask whether Adorno in fact contributes to increasing the division between high and low culture? One can also ask if political literature should not aim for a wide audience to be effective. For is it not only by activating the many that Adorno's hope for radical change could come true? Defenders of his position might answer the last question by noting that it is not Adorno's fault that Kafka and Beckett are not more widely read—that state of affairs is instead a testimony to the power of the cultural industry with which he will not compromise. For in his opinion, literature is not political in terms of its effect within the framework of the established political system but in terms of its potential to break this framework. Regarding the first question, one can point out that Adorno's preferred artists were not as canonized in the bourgeois art institution in 1962 as now. That they have since entered this canon could from Adorno's perspective be seen as a sign of capitalism's ability to transform counterculture to marketable mainstream. Nevertheless, the denunciation of popular culture does appear to be a blind spot in the culture critical field of vision of Adorno and likeminded literary critics like Fredric Jameson.

To support this line of criticism one can invoke Walter Benjamin, who was also associated with the Frankfurt School. He shared Adorno's skepticism about bourgeois Enlightenment and Lukács' "scientific" Marxism. This is evident in his cultural critical archival studies of nineteenth-century Paris. Instead of telling a story about the progress of modern bourgeois society or portraying culture as a result of the productive forces, he studies Charles Baudelaire's poems in conjunction with socio-economic and political phenomena like gambling, assembly line work, world fairs, barricades, and prostitution without having one determine the others. They are all born of and in turn shape the ideological and material structures particular to the modern experience of urban life. According to Benjamin, Baudelaire captures the ambivalences of that experience in condensed poetic images that combine fascination of the city's chaotic beauty with outrage over the degradation of its masses (Benjamin 1999, 2006).

As in Adorno's case, Benjamin often focuses on formal features like poetic images and verse form to tease out a poem's socio-critical function. But for Benjamin, this function does not amount to a rejection of modern society, but to an ability to capture its simultaneity of resistance and oppression, defeat, and hope. While Adorno's philosophical prose often draws the broad outlines of modern history, Benjamin finds inscriptions of its ambivalences in everyday materials and popular culture. He thus does not reject cinema as mere entertainment. He regrets the loss of unique, aesthetic aura caused by filmic art's mechanical reproduction of images (Benjamin 2008, 22–24), but believes that the mass dissemination that this mode of artistic production allows for makes cinema an ideal medium for political art (41f.). Benjamin's eye for the often overlooked meaning of mass culture, his probing style and feel for the small stories of resistance embedded in the great history of oppression, has made his work a benchmark for later culture critical literary research and inspired cultural studies across the globe.

In the 1930s, Benjamin studied Surrealism, in whose recycling of discarded everyday materials he saw a parallel to his own critical practice. Adorno was less favorably inclined toward the movement. The debate about the interwar avant-garde groups flared up again later when Peter Bürger in 1974 claimed that their goal was to unite everyday life and art and thereby realize the freedom that autonomous art only conjured up as illusion. Bürger describes this project as heroic but unsuccessful, and characterizes later movements such as Pop Art and Fluxus as vain repetitions (Bürger 1974, 78–80). Art historian Hal Foster reversely argued that Dadaist works like Marcel Duchamp's urinal and Hugo Ball's sound poems did not destroy, but merely expanded the limits of what the art institution defines as art, by bringing everyday life into art. The opposite movement from art to everyday life only happened with the 1960s Avant-garde's happenings and performances (Foster 1996, 15–20). However, such art forms also soon became common artistic forms of expression. Nevertheless, the direct approach of activist art may be effective in creating involvement in social issues. It often does so by being provocative and especially in recent times by blurring the line between artistic activity and social work. From Adorno's perspective, one could argue that art in the latter case loses its formal distance from capitalist consumer culture—and thereby sacrifices its true political potential. One could imagine a kind of compromise between the avant-garde dream of life become art and Adorno's insistence on aesthetic autonomy, a "compromise" in which art to be politically effective must maintain a certain aesthetic distance from the forms of the common world, while being oriented toward its political problems. Such a "compromise"—or more accurately, a clash that lives off the tension between the two poles—is found in French philosopher Jacques Rancière's theory of political literature.

Jacques Rancière and political literature

The aesthetic revolution promoted by Kant and the Romantics inaugurates what Rancière calls "the aesthetic regime of art." From the beginning, this regime is built on a paradox (Rancière 2004, 22ff.). On the one hand, as Bourdieu and Levinson argued, it declares art and the artist to be free. But on the other hand, already for Kant great works of art express more than the author's idiosyncrasies. They express something universal which Romanticism understands as the spirit of a people, society, or culture. The aesthetic regime thus combines an idea of the autonomy of art with an idea of its heteronomy: Art is free from society and necessarily tied to its forms of life (Rancière 2002, 133ff.).

According to Rancière, each of these two ideas is linked to a political principle. The idea of artistic freedom, which in principle makes all words aesthetically equal, is associated with an ideal of indefinite democratic equality and freedom. Conversely, the idea that literature is an expression of a certain social condition is tied to an ideal of a state where words directly express things and thoughts, where everything finds its proper place in the whole. Neither of the two principles can be realized in itself in literature or politics. But when they come together in a certain way, according to Rancière, the result can be political literature. For that to happen, the literary work must at once freely shape its material *and* evoke the dominant ideological patterns of discourse—the conventional ("natural," "true") relationships between words, things, and people that shape identities in the social order (149–51). Instead of realistically portraying the oppressed (and thus risking to confirm the popular opinion of them), literature may use its freedom to depict them in unfamiliar ways that challenge the ways they are habitually perceived and help pave the way for their political recognition. In his Benjamin-inspired archival study of nineteenth-century French workers' literature, Rancière thus argues that it was by writing books that broke with the elites' and socialist leaders' perception of the workers' "nature" that workers became visible in the social field as independent individuals with the right to have democratic rights (Rancière 1981).

Literature has also found more subtle ways of undermining the conventional meaning of modern political keywords like freedom, equality, and the people. According to Rancière, William Wordsworth does exactly this in his otherwise innocent-looking "I wandered lonely as a cloud" (1807) that has been memorized by generations of British schoolchildren. In the edition from 1815 the first stanza reads:

> I wandered lonely as a cloud
> That floats on high o'er vales and hills,
> When all at once I saw a crowd,
> A host of golden daffodils,
> Beside the lake, beneath the trees
> Fluttering and dancing in the breeze. (Wordsworth 1977, 619)

In the final stanza the lyrical I, lying on his couch in the "bliss of solitude," is reminded of the flowers "And then my heart with pleasure fills, / And dances with the Daffodils" (Wordsworth 1977, 620)—another romantic tale of an experience of nature's beauty, a later separation and a final spiritual reunion in which it would be hard with Levinson to find other signs of a social context than the I's couch, which if anything seems to associate him more with the elites than the people.

Is this poem really political? Yes, claims Rancière, for the free movements of the lyrical I "as a cloud" presuppose an experience of political liberation (Rancière 2004, 12f.). Wordsworth had such an experience when on July 13, 1790, during the French revolution, he landed in Calais to hike to the Alps. In his lyrical epic, *The Prelude* (1805), he describes the flower-decorated triumphal arches by the roads and the "merry crowd" who invited him to celebrate the anniversary of the fall of the Bastille with "dances of liberty" (Wordsworth 1979, 206). Here was freedom and equality come to life. But the happy experience of deep harmony between the liberated masses, the traveling poet and blooming nature was soon past. The revolution became bloodier and England joined the war against revolutionary France. On both sides of the Channel, words like nature, people, equality, and freedom were now used to justify nationalist militarism and vilify the enemy. In this situation, Wordsworth wrote "Tintern Abbey" and "I wandered lonely as a cloud." The "crowd" of dancing flowers the poet unexpectedly meets in the latter recalls the rejoicing Frenchmen he describes in *The Prelude*. Levinson would perhaps see the poetic conversion of revolutionaries into flowers as the fabrication of an ideological veil. But from Rancière's point of view, the poetic image reversely elevates the inconspicuous flowers to objects that contain and confirm the truth of the wanderer's early experience of emancipation and equality on the French roads at a time when war threatened to make lies out of revolutionary ideals. Wordsworth's simple verses about the shepherds and poor soldiers—voiceless victims of the war—he met on his many walks along the English roads tell the same story (Rancière 2004, 19f.). Perhaps "Tintern Abbey" could also be read as an attempt to preserve the belief that freedom and equality are not mere ideology, but a real experience that can be stored in a poem. In any case, it is striking that the title's date is the eighth anniversary of Wordsworth's first visit to France on 13 July.

From an ideology critical viewpoint like Levinson's, one might criticize Rancière for not taking sufficient account of the historical context. Conversely, from Rancière's viewpoint one can criticize Levinson for focusing so much on hidden inequality and lack of freedom that equality and freedom as real, if often short-lived, political experiences disappear out of view. A combination of the ideology critical insights into the history of power with Rancière's insistence that people sometimes break free of its grip is perhaps a way forward for ideology critical literary studies. In any case, it is a welcome contribution to the debate on political literature that can fill a rather sleep-inducing national treasure like "I wandered lonely as a cloud" with the noise of monumental democratic movements which like clouds know no borders.

Further reading

Pierre Bourdieu's *Rules of Art: Genesis and Structure of the Literary Field* is a classic work in the field of sociological literary theory, which in addition to aesthetic philosophical discussions includes literary readings of notably Gustave Flaubert and a study of the book market and literary institutions. Walter Benjamin's literary essays all exist in English translation. In addition to the fragmentary monument known as the *Arcades Project* and the essays discussed in this chapter, his original study of baroque literature and politics in *The Origin of German Tragic Drama* and essays such as "The Task of the Translator" continue to influence various strands of literary criticism today. In *The Flesh of Words: The Politics of Writing*, Jacques Rancière applies his philosophical reflections on politics and literature in readings of Wordsworth and a number of other writers from Cervantes to Proust. Finally, Terry Eagleton, who has written several excellent introductions to ideology criticism and literary theory, has edited with Drew Milne *Marxist Literary Theory: A Reader* (1996), an anthology with about thirty articles and excerpts from prominent ideology critical theorists from Marx to the present, including the most important figures in the Frankfurt School. The book gives a good overview of the ideology critical approach to literature.

References

Adorno, Theodor W. (1980 [1970]) *Ästhetische Theorie*, Frankfurt a. M.: Suhrkamp.

Adorno, Theodor W. (1990) "Commitment," in A. Arato and E. Gebhardt (eds), *The Essential Frankfurt School Reader*, New York: Continuum, 300–18.

Adorno, Theodor W. and Max Horkheimer (2002) *Dialectic of Enlightenment: Philosophical Fragments*. Trans. Edmund Jephcott, Stanford: Stanford University Press.

Benjamin, Walter (1999) "Paris, Capital of Nineteenth Century," *The Arcades Project*. Trans. Howard Eiland and Kevin McLaughlin, Cambridge, MA: Harvard University Press.

Benjamin, Walter (2006) "On Some Motifs in Baudelaire," *Selected Writings*, Volume 4: 1938–1940 (trans. Howard Eiland and Michael W. Jennings). Cambridge, MA: Harvard University Press.

Benjamin, Walter (2008) "The Work of Art in the Age of Its Technological Reproducibility," in Michael W. Jennings, Brigid Doherty and Thomas Y. Levin (ed.), *The Work of Art in the Age of Its Technological Reproducibility and Other Writings on Media*, Cambridge, MA: Harvard University Press, 19–55.

Bourdieu, Pierre (1996) *The Rules of Art: Genesis and Structure of the Literary Field*, Cambridge: Cambridge Polity Press.

Bürger, Peter (1974) *Theorie der Avantgarde*, Frankfurt a. M: Suhrkamp Verlag.

Foster, Hal (1996) *The Return of the Real—The Avant-garde at the End of the Century*, Cambridge, MA: MIT Press.

Kant, Immanuel (1974) *Kritik der Urteilskraft*, Werkausgabe (Red. Wilhelm Weischedel), vol. X, Frankfurt a. M: Suhrkamp Verlag.

Levinson, Marjorie (2009) [1986] *Wordsworth's Great Period Poems: Four Essays*, Cambridge: Cambridge University Press.

Lukács, Georg (1989) *Studies in European Realism: A Sociological Survey of the Writings of Balzac, Stendhal, Zola, Tolstoy, Gorki and Others*, London: Merlin Press.

Marcuse, Herbert (1965 [1937]) "Über den affirmativen Charakter der Kultur," *Kultur und Gesellschaft*, vol. I. Frankfurt a. M.: Suhrkamp Verlag.

Marx, Karl (2001) *The German Ideology*, Minneapolis: Electric Book Company.

Peterson, Richard A. and Roger M. Kern (1996) "Changing Highbrow Taste—From Snob to Omnivore," *American Sociological Review*, 5: 900–907.

Rancière, Jacques (1981) *La Nuit des Prolétaires—Archives du rêve ouvrier*, Paris: Fayard.

Rancière, Jacques (2002) "The Aesthetic Revolution and Its Outcomes—Emplotments of Autonomy and Heteronomy," *New Left Review*, March–April: 14.

Rancière, Jacques (2004) *The Flesh of Words—The Politics of Writing*, Stanford: Stanford University Press.

Stendhal (2012) *The Red and the Black: A Chronicle of 1830*. Trans. Horace B. Samuel, Dover Thrift Editions.

Wordsworth, William (1971 [1963]) "Lines Written a Few Miles Above Tintern Abbey: On Revisting the Banks of the Wye During a Tour, July 13, 1798," in W. Wordsworth and S. T. Coleridge (eds), *Lyrical Ballads* (Red. R.L. Brett and A.R. Jones), London: Methuen.

Wordsworth, William (1977) "I Wandered Lonely as a Cloud," in John O. Hayden (ed.), *The Poems, Vol. 1*, Harmondsworth: Penguin Books.

Wordsworth, William (1979) *The Prelude—1799, 1805, 1850* (Red. Jonathan Wordsworth et al.), New York: Norton.

Zupančič, Alenka (2008) *The Odd One In: On Comedy*, Cambridge, MA and London: MIT Press.

17

Gender

Lilla Tőke and Karen Weingarten

One of the first things people ask a visibly pregnant woman is "do you know the baby's gender?" The person asking is usually looking for one of two answers, girl or boy. In this context, gender is being used to demarcate biological sex: Will the baby be biologically male or female? However, most feminist theorists would explain that gender is a cultural construction. To speak of a fetus' gender makes no sense because it hasn't yet been subjected to our cultural norms that shape the construction of gender. While it's true that most children born female will become women, and most born male will become men, there are enough exceptions to this process that it makes little sense to label a newborn baby according to these categories.

What is gender? Referring to the *Oxford English Dictionary* only complicates the answer to this question, although the definition most commonly referenced by those working in the field can be found with some digging. It's "the state of being male or female as expressed by social or cultural distinctions and differences, rather than biological ones." This definition, like the one I reference above, positions gender in distinction to sex: gender is culturally determined and sex is biologically given. Yet feminist theorists like Judith Butler have questioned this distinction to argue that all identity is performed and based in language: sex, in other words, is always gendered. According to this line of argument, to be a woman or to be a man—indeed, to be female or male—is part of a social process that begins the moment we are born and named.

Women's studies, gender studies, and sexuality studies: Studying sex and gender in the academy

The concept of gender first transformed literary studies through scholars who were interested in thinking both about underrepresented women writers and representations of women in literature. Later these feminist approaches to literature turned to thinking about how sexuality, sex, queer identity, and gender identity shape our reading of a text. Feminist theorists influenced by fields like critical race theory, postcolonial studies, and poststructuralism also questioned whether the category "women" could be represented as one coherent and singular identity. The study of literature helped, in part, to show the often contradicting and plural forms of women's representations. (See, for example, Toril Moi's "What is a Woman?" and Gaytri Spivak's "Three Women's Texts and a Critique of Imperialism".)

The canon of British and American literature was originally conceived of as almost entirely composed of white, male authors. The explanation for this has historically been twofold: in a patriarchal society women were neither encouraged nor given the resources to become writers. The basis of patriarchy assumes that women are not only second-class citizens, but that they cannot compete with men intellectually, artistically, or politically because, innately, they are constructed for reproductive and domestic duties—and not for success in the social world. As Virginia Woolf explains this in *A Room of One's Own*, if Shakespeare had a sister with his talents she could have never achieved his fame simply because of the assumptions imposed on her sex. And those women who did manage to write, and even to publish, despite the constraints and hurdles, were often dismissed as "scribbling women," to use the phrase that the much lauded nineteenth-century American writer Nathaniel Hawthorne ascribed to the successful women writers of his time.

Starting in the 1960s and 1970s, feminist scholars, in what is called a "second wave of feminism," began doing recovery work that brought lost women writers back into publication. In the United States, writers such as Charlotte Perkins Gilman and Zora Neale Hurston were given renewed attention, and their works were seen as representative of American women in a particular era and as important contributions to the American literary canon. However, almost as soon as feminist scholarship emerged as an important voice in literary scholarship, there were also critiques of its myopic understanding of women's writing and the role of gender in reading literature. Critical race theorists and women of color rightly pointed out that much feminist scholarship that addressed the oppression of women assumed a white, Western, heterosexual, middle-class woman at the center of analysis. As a consequence, the experiences of black women, immigrant women, non-Western women, queer women, and trans women (to name just a few groups) were elided, and literature by women without the privilege of whiteness, wealth, and heterosexuality continued to be ignored. Kimberlé Crenshaw's development of the theory of intersectionality, among others, gave feminist literary theorists a language for describing how gender never functions as a identifying category without the influencing intersections of other identity categories. In other words, a black woman is shaped by the intersecting identities of being black and being a woman. To try to account for her experiences without an awareness of how *both* those identities shape her (and shape the identity categories themselves) would result in a limited understanding of a black woman's experience.

The "third wave of feminism" starting in the 1980s worked in conjunction with queer studies, and later transgender studies, to question the norms of women's sexual, reproductive, and biologic realities. Theorists such as Eve Kosofsky Sedgwick and Judith Butler, both of whom were influenced by Michel Foucault's writings on sexuality and the development of norms, shaped the way gender and sex were understood as contributing to the formation of identity (what they term subjectivity), and in turn, the reading of literature. Sedgwick, in particular, paved the way for queer studies in literary analysis through readings of texts that were imbued with what she called homoeroticism—sexual love between two men. Yet, she also showed how that love had to be directed through a woman because of prohibitions against same-sex relationships. Later she broadened her analysis to argue that all of Western literature is shaped by the cultural binary of homosexuality/heterosexuality. To put it differently, our embedded assumptions about heterosexuality and homosexuality as opposites—and believing that one constitutes normative behavior while the other does not—determine the way we read literature.

Sedgwick's theories fundamentally altered how we read literature today, whether or not we focus on sex and gender. She paved the way for critics like Jack Halberstam and Lee Edelman, who have expanded the definition of "queerness" and the ways in which it challenges the norms that have infiltrated our lives—from the assumptions we make about what it means to be a woman to the ways in which we privilege the child as the product of heterosexual love. To read literature through the lens of gender, then, is not only to think about the role of women in writing but to question the category of "woman" itself and how it intersects with sexuality, racial identity, physical ability, geography, class status, and normative constructions like femininity and masculinity. These intersections form the basis of our reading of Toni Morrison's novel *Beloved* below and demonstrate the workings of intersectionality.

Sex/Gender, feminism, and reading literature

As the section above suggests, a feminist approach to studying literature, one that places gender or sex at its center, can never be described as a singular method. It would be more accurate to say that there are feminist approaches, all influenced by different fields and methods. The French feminists, Hélene Cixous, Luce Irigaray, Julia Kristeva, and others, for example, emphasized attention to language and *how* gender norms are constructed and reinforced through both the written and spoken work. Cixous, in particular, coined the term *écriture feminine* to both challenge phallocentric language—texts that privilege male experience and authority— and call for a mode of writing that emerges out of and reflects women's bodily experiences, such as breastfeeding and menstruating. Cixous and other feminists influenced by this tradition contend that *écriture feminine* can be created by men as well. However, one of the most common critiques leveled at this argument is that it essentializes women's experiences and assumes a normative experience of womanhood shared by all people identifying as such. For many different reasons, not all women menstruate, not all women reproduce, and not all women breastfeed, and so to define women, and women's writing, through these kinds of experiences is always to exclude some.

In addition to the question of whether there can be such a category described as women's writing, or feminine writing, focusing on gender in literature also leads to the question of whether to do so is to take a feminist approach. And what does a feminist approach to the study of literature entail? Feminism advocates the belief that women are equal to men, and it works to expose the existing inequalities between men and women; or, in other words, it exposes how social inequality exists because of gender norms. Feminism is then not only concerned with the study of women but is also interested in how sexual and gender difference shape our lives. Therefore, a feminist approach to a text might be just as interested in examining constructions of masculinity in order to examine how certain gendered norms are constructed and privileged. To study a text through a feminist lens means to study both the representation of men and women and their relationality to each other—as well as to other identities such as race and class—to understand how gender and sex are dynamic and intersect with other forces to shape who we are.

Beloved and the intersections of sex, gender, and race

Toni Morrison's novel *Beloved* (1987) is most often referred to as a novel about the effects of slavery and its repercussions for racial relations in the United States. Yet, in addition to being a novel about race, it is rife with gender tensions that challenge patriarchal concepts about African American women, their sexuality, motherhood, and traditional family structures. A gendered reading of the novel therefore will draw on the theory of intersectionality, which helps us expose how the characters' identities and actions are rooted in complex interactions between their race, gender, and social position. *Beloved* takes place in 1873 in Cincinnati, Ohio, where Sethe, a former slave, lives with her daughter, Denver, after her mother-in-law Baby Suggs dies and her two sons run away. The narrative begins with the arrival of Paul D, whom Sethe has not seen in eighteen years, long after they worked together as slaves on Mr. Garner's plantation called "Sweet Home" in Kentucky. The arrival of Paul D to 124 Bluestone Road, the name Sethe uses to refer to her new home, sets a series of events into motion and also brings back important memories that help the reader understand Sethe's story. Through Sethe and Paul D's flashbacks, the narrative moves continuously between past and present to reveal their life on the plantation under the "gentle" mastery of the Garners and later the more typical, brutal treatment by Schoolteacher, the nephew who takes over after Mr. Garner's death. We find out about their attempt to escape, Sethe's dreadful journey to freedom, the help she receives from a young white girl, Amy, as well as the short period of happiness with her children and Baby Suggs that ends abruptly in horrific violence. When Schoolteacher discovers where Sethe and her children are hiding, and comes to take them back to Sweet Home, back to a life of slavery, she kills her older daughter out of desperation.

In the present moment of the novel, which takes place years after the death of Sethe's daughter, Sethe, Denver, and Paul D seem to come together as a family—that is, until a young woman appears unexpectedly on their porch calling herself "Beloved." At first, they welcome the stranger, but as times goes on, Beloved's strange behavior makes the women think that she is the embodied ghost of Sethe's lost daughter. Paul D is similarly suspicious. Beloved seems to manipulate all three characters in different ways: she demands Sethe's undivided attention, she develops a close, sisterly bond with Denver, and she seduces Paul D against his will. When Paul D finds out about Sethe's "rough choice"—her infanticide—he leaves 124, and from that moment on Sethe and Beloved's relationship intensifies and becomes more destructive. Beloved grows more and more abusive, while Sethe concentrates all her remaining energy on satisfying her demands as a way to compensate for killing her daughter in the face of a life that would return them to slavery. As the two women fall into a co-dependent and abusive relationship, Denver takes care of them for a while, but finally she leaves in order to seek help and to save herself. Shortly after, Beloved, pregnant and naked, disappears as the townsfolk come to rescue Sethe, but Sethe refuses their help and she lies down in Baby Sugg's bed to die.

Besides depicting the traumatic impact of slavery on African Americans and the institutional racism that shapes both their history and present, *Beloved* also destabilizes traditional gender models. The novel discloses a simultaneous desire and inability of black men and women to embody the free, white, patriarchal society's gender norms. Sethe and Paul D are the foremost examples of the struggle to come to terms with the detrimental impact that slavery had on their ability to fulfil traditional, patriarchal gender expectations.

First of all, their sexual and physical abuse and abandonment affect the female characters in especially detrimental ways that lead to a fundamental distrust toward all men, white or black. As Baby Suggs puts it, "A man ain't nothing but a man" (27), and Sethe immediately recognizes this with Paul D, who soon upon his arrival "ran her children out, and tore up the house" (26). Sethe gives voice to her frustration when, during an argument, Paul D insists that "I never mistreated a woman in my life." Sethe sarcastically responds, "That makes one in the world" (80). The normalcy of enslaved women's sexual and physical exploitation transpires also in the fact that Paul D takes special pride in the Sweet Home men restraining themselves and allowing Sethe to choose between them.

The characters' desire and inability to perform traditional gender roles is also reflected in their sexual practices, which can be effectively addressed through third-wave feminists theories that unveil and criticize a binary (normative versus nonnormative) categorization of sexuality. The above-mentioned difficulty to control male sexual desire makes sense since the world that the Sweet Home men inhabit does not regulate black sexuality as it considers it outside the human realm. In the same section, Paul D readily admits that Sweet Home men have "taken to calves" (12) in the absence of women and that during the "long year of yearning, rape seemed the solitary gift of life" (12). The sexual act between Paul D and Beloved is also problematic in several ways. "Fixed by a girl" (149), unable to resist a ghost who has taken the body of a young woman, Paul D gives in to Beloved's aggressive demand to "touch me on the inside part" (137). He simultaneously desires her waiting "in the cold room at night" (136) and feels a rage that "wanted to knock her down" (136). The sexual relation between Paul D and Beloved is beyond acceptable social norms in more than one way. First of all, it's potentially pedophiliac because of Beloved's seemingly young age and juvenile behavior. Moreover, it transgresses standard family structures that value monogamy since Paul D effectively cheats on Sethe by giving in to Beloved's aggressive sexual initiation and seduction, which in addition contradicts stereotypical view of active-male and passive-female sexual roles. Finally, Beloved's nonhuman, ghost-like character taints this sexual act even with a sense of necrophilia.

It is without a doubt that black women's bodies serve as a prize and consolation for *all* men in the novel. When Schoolteacher explains the animalistic and human characteristics of Sethe's body to his nephews, he dehumanizes her to a degree that the young boys "with mossy teeth" (83) feel entitled to take away her milk "one sucking on my breast the other holding me down while schoolteacher is watching and writing it up" (83). The scientific eye of Schoolteacher overlooks Sethe's rape, intensifying the cruelty and perversion of the nephews' act. However, as we find out later, Schoolteacher is not the only one witnessing Sethe's milk being taken away. Halle is also forced to watch the scene hiding in the hay above and unable to intervene. Thus, the joint gaze of the two men — master and slave — willingly or unwillingly, turns her abuse and violation into a derogatory, pornographic performance. Sethe's awareness of her humiliation and the outrage she feels over Halle's impotent behavior is clear in her question that, "He saw them boys do that to me and let them keep on breathing air? He saw? He saw? He saw?" (81).

However, what Sethe is most disturbed by in this violation of her body is "losing her milk." She speaks repeatedly in the novel about the importance of her milk for her baby, who she has sent ahead with her two boys, and of the need to "get my milk to my baby girl" (19). It is primarily her motherly instincts (the need to feed her baby) that drive Sethe to make the impossible journey to freedom despite being heavily pregnant and crippled by Schoolteacher's physical torture. Baby Suggs's experience of motherhood demonstrates very well that in a slave society "nobody stopped playing checkers just because the pieces included children" (28). She had eight children by six different men, none of whom stayed with her, except for Halle. Paul D also recognizes the slave mother's limited agency when he calls Sethe's love for her children "risky" because "for a used-to-be-slave woman to love anything that much was dangerous, especially if it was her children she had settled on to love" (54). The novel echoes Simone de Beauvoir's claim that women are defined by their reproductive and other physical characteristics. In this particular context, Baby Suggs, Sethe, and all black female characters are void of any agency over their laboring, reproductive, or sexual bodies in the institution of slavery.

As Paul D's statement above shows, besides the right over women's bodies as laborers and sexual instruments, the white masters also consider enslaved women to be reproductive tools to benefit from economically. Therefore, for Sethe, her breastmilk, which allows her to feed her baby, symbolizes nothing less than freedom itself. Loving her children boundlessly is her act of rebellion against a society that allows enslaved women "to love just a bit" (54). The freedom to be a mother is the only kind of freedom Sethe is able to achieve, and she is not about to give this up as Schoolteacher appears to take her and her children back to the plantation. Sethe's violent act, as horrific as it is, is a desperate statement of freedom. It means a refusal to hand over her maternal agency, the only one she has, to the white man. No doubt that, as Steven Daniels notes, the choices that "slavery is shown to allow, even oblige, are inevitably and necessarily unthinkable choices between bad alternatives" for women (363). However, under these unimaginable conditions women use the power they have—even if that means infanticide—to fight the sexual and reproductive bondage of slavery (Weinbaum 458).

The men of *Beloved* and gender relations

Women are not the only ones in the novel to have their gender roles circumscribed by slavery. The Sweet Home men's masculinity is shaped by slavery, as it has deprived them of the ability to protect their families, control their labor, and decide the fate of their bodies. Such emasculation and dehumanization drives Halle senseless and leaves Paul D frustrated and insecure. Halle's inability to interfere when he secretly witnesses Sethe's rape by Schoolteacher's nephews shatters his masculinity and sense of self to such an extent that he loses his sanity. However, Halle's powerlessness also results in a failure to show up according to the plan and to help Sethe, who is nine months pregnant, escape, thereby abandoning her. Similarly, Paul D suffers from his inability to live up to what a "man" is supposed to be. While he is proud of Sethe's strength, her independence makes him jealous. As the narrative explains when describing her escape on her own: "'All by yourself, too.' He was proud of her and annoyed by her. Proud she had done it; annoyed that she had not needed Halle or him in the doing" (9).

More than anything else, Paul D desires to restore his masculinity by trying to establish himself as an essential part of Sethe's life. However, his self-doubt and insecurity as a man is unceasing and he thinks that others, such as Sixo and Halle, "were men whether Garner said so or not. It troubled him that, concerning his own manhood, he could not satisfy himself on that point" (260). He continuously tries to "put his story next to hers" (322), to assert his subjectivity through paralleling his memories with hers in order to establish centrality in the narrative that seems to prefer Sethe's point of view that has "left him his manhood like that"(322).

Paul D is jealous of the intimate relationship between Denver and Sethe and is trying to carve a space for himself in the family structure, to return to some kind of patriarchal utopia. He begs Sethe to "leave it to me" (55), to let him take care of them. Slowly, Sethe agrees to "leave it to him," or at least "well, some of it" (55). The novel's nostalgia for a family that "could be" (57) peeks in the scene when Paul D takes Sethe and Denver to the carnival. This idyllic "family" afternoon, however, foreshadows the destruction that Beloved brings to both Paul D and Sethe as she appears on the porch when they get home. Beloved is the one who ultimately undermines Paul D's efforts to construct his masculinity. She pushes Paul D out of the house, humiliates him though seduction, and drags him around like a "rag doll" (261). In order to overcome his guilt of giving into Beloved's sexual allure and in a final desperate attempt to reassert his masculinity, Paul D tries to convince Sethe to have his child. This gesture moves far beyond validating his own reproductive ability. Becoming a father is Paul D's desperate attempt to save his shattered masculinity.

While Sethe and Paul D have an indestructible bond due to their past at Sweet Home, and while Paul understands Sethe better than anyone else because of their shared trauma, his solidarity fails when he reflects on Sethe's "rough choice" (212). His condemnation is quick and clear as he declares that, "You got two feet, Sethe, not four" (194), which is to say that he considers Sethe's act inhuman, unworthy of a woman and mother. Sethe's violent act offers an easy way out for Paul D. to move from "his shame to hers" (194); in other words, it becomes a way to rid himself of the guilt he feels for betraying Sethe by having sex with Beloved. Yet, his absolvement comes at the expense of Sethe's guilt as a mother. This moment in the novel has a larger significance as it shows that in *Beloved* ultimately gender tensions cut across racial solidarity and that despite everything they share, there is "a forest" dividing Paul D and Sethe (194).

Challenges to patriarchy in *Beloved*

However, the novel's feminist work does not stop at the level of female characterization. Toni Morrison's writing is an example of what French feminists would have described as *écriture feminine*. The novel presents experience as multiple, diverse, and often irreconcilably different through its linguistic and narrative complexity. The play between coherence and fragmentation on the level of sentences and narration (pp. 153–6) reflects the characters traumatized and disjointed self. It also represents the struggle to work through the past and create a coherent and sovereign subjectivity. The lack of linear narration also breaks traditional forms of storytelling in order to reproduce the workings of memory. Finally, *Beloved* presents multiple, sometimes indistinguishable narrative voices ("I am Beloved and she is mine" p. 249) in order to destabilize a phallocentric, dominant point of view in the text and to allow many different stories to emerge and experiences to exist next to each other. The novel's fragmented narrative structure opens up an important possibility for new, radical ways of telling and reading a woman's story.

At the same time, the unstable gender roles and the lack of established, patriarchal family structures also allow for new, radical ways of social bonding. Newly freed women in the novel become unusually strong and independent. Because "all their men—brothers, uncles, fathers, husbands, sons—had been picked off one by one by one" (63), women learn to escape and survive on their own, take care of themselves and their children, relying mostly on themselves and each other. The bond between Baby Suggs, Sethe, and Denver is a poignant example of such strength and solidarity. So is the short but intense encounter between Amy and Sethe during her escape to freedom. The women of Sweet Home gain social and financial independence under their new circumstances that is not determined by men. In Cincinnati, Baby Suggs becomes a matriarchal figure for the new black community, a healer and a preacher who teaches her people "that the only grace they could have is the grace they could imagine" (103) and to love themselves because no one else will love them. Sethe works as a cook, a job that she enjoys and takes pride in, and one that allows her to take care of her entire family. In the absence of men, black women find themselves empowered and they change how they see their gender role.

This change is most obvious in Sethe's behavior when she is willing to take Paul D as a partner, but refuses to hand over the responsibility of raising her children.

The new social conditions also produce maternal communities that cut across gender and racial divides. Instead of one mother (and one father) raising Denver, an interracial community of men and women contribute to her birth, her survival as an infant and her relatively successful upbringing. Most obviously, Baby Suggs and Sethe work as a tight unit raising all four of Sethe's children. They live in a house offered up by the Boldwins, an old white couple who later also try to help Sethe as she is losing herself to Beloved. Sethe also would not be able to make it to safety without Amy's help, who serves as a midwife as she gives birth to Denver by the river. Stamp Paid, an old formerly enslaved man, takes special care of the newborn as they cross the river to freedom and he continues to look out for Denver. It is Stamp Paid who takes her from Sethe's arms as she is driven mad by the possibility of becoming a slave again together with the children. Paul D also takes on the role of the father for Denver, at least for a while. Lady Jones, a mixed race teacher, welcomes Denver in her house when she runs away from the deteriorating conditions at 124. As this reading of *Beloved* demonstrates, decoding gender identity is only possible in relation to other segments of subjectivity as we try to think about the crippling physical and psychological effects of slavery on African American men and women. At the same time, our positional reading of gender also allows us to see that *Beloved* carries in it a message of resistance against white patriarchal oppression through strong female collectivity and interracial solidarity.

Gender never stands alone

Reading *Beloved* through the lens of gender relations helps us understand that gender identity never stands alone. Sethe's womanhood is bound up in her history of slavery, in what it meant to mother as a black woman—first under the conditions of slavery and then in the years shortly after—and in her relations with black men, who were emasculated during slavery and in the years after. Sethe's womanhood is tied to the history of African Americans, and therefore, to understand her experiences as a woman and as a mother is to understand the history of blacks in America. Even her crime, the killing of her daughter, which seems to break the laws of motherhood, must be read within this history. Similarly, Paul D's masculinity—his embodiment of gender norms that often violate the lives of women—must also be understood within the history of slavery and the treatment of African Americans in a country that has not been able to overcome institutional racism. His masculinity is directly tied to how both black women and men have been shaped by a history that devalues their relationships, their roles as parents, and their family structures. In other words, Sethe and Paul D, like all of us, have gendered identities that intersect and constantly shift, in relation to each other, to their histories, and to the people who come and go in their lives.

Further reading

Eagleton (2010) excerpts key texts in feminist theory and offers an introduction to how literature has been read through the lens of gender and sex. Butler (2006) questions the binary view of gender relations that divides human beings into two clear-cut groups, women and men and also argues that gender is something actively performed rather than given. Chodorow (1995) makes the case that gender, in addition to being culturally, linguistically, and politically construed, is also determined by personal and subjective psychological processes. De Beauvior's book (1961) is a groundbreaking feminist text and a pioneering study in the history of women's oppression. Haraway (1990) in her collection of essays explores how technology and the concept of the cyborg has the potential to eliminate any specific universal qualities of being a man or a woman. Anzaldua (1987), Davis (1981), and hooks (1999) offer an analysis of how race and gender intersect in the construction of identity. DuCille (1993) and Spillers (2003) are examples of how these theories inform the reading of literature. Halberstam (1998) and Kimmel (2000) provide starting points for discussions of masculinity and its role in feminist theory. Somerville (2000), Munoz (2009), and Edelman (2004) show how queer theory informs the reading of texts and cultural constructions.

References

Anzaldua, Gloria (1987) *Borderlands/La Frontera: The New Mestiza*. San Francisco: Aunt Lute Books.
Butler, Judith (2011) *Bodies That Matter: On the Discursive Limits of Sex*, New York: Routledge.
Chodorow, Nancy (1995) "Gender as a Personal and Cultural Construction," *Signs*, 20: 516–44.

Davis, Angela (1981) *Women, Race, and Class*, New York: Vintage Books.

De Beauvior, Simone (1961) *The Second Sex*, New York: Routledge.

duCille, Ann (1993) *The Coupling Convention: Sex, Text, and Tradition in Black Women's Fiction*, New York: Oxford University Press.

Eagleton, Mary (ed.) (2010) *Feminist Literary Theory: A Reader*, London: Wiley-Blackwell.

Edelman, Lee (2004) *No Future: Queer Theory and the Death Drive*, Durham: Duke University Press.

Halberstam, Judith (1998) *Female Masculinity*, Durham: Duke University Press.

Haraway, Donna (1990) *Simians, Cyborgs, and Women: The Reinvention of Nature*, New York: Routledge.

hooks, bell (1999) *Yearning: Race, Gender, and Cultural Politics*, New York: South End Press.

Kimmel, Michael S. (2000) *The Gendered Society*, New York and Oxford: Oxford University Press.

Morrison, Toni (1987) *Beloved*, New York: Vintage International.

Munoz, Jose Esteban (2009) *Cruising Utopia: The Then and There of Queer Futurity*, New York: New York University Press.

Somerville, Siobhan (2000) *Queering the Color Line: Race and the Invention of Homosexuality in American Culture*, Durham: Duke University Press.

Spillers, Hortense (2003) *Black, White, and in Color: Essays on American Literature and Culture*, Chicago: University of Chicago Press.

18

Ethnicity

Tabish Khair

"With notions of 'race' in public and scientific disrepute since 1945, ethnicity has obligingly stepped into the gap," notes Richard Jenkins in *Rethinking Ethnicity* (Jenkins 1997, 9). He goes on to develop his engagement with the term by way of Max Weber's *Economy and Society* (1922), in which Weber had differentiated between ethnicity and what he called "anthropological type" (race, phenotype, etc.). Weber had not only defined ethnicity as a belief in a common descent, no matter how remote, he had also stressed its predominantly political nature: "Weber seems to be suggesting that the belief in common ancestry is likely to be a *consequence* of collective political action rather than its *cause*; people come to see themselves as *belonging* together—coming from a common background—as a consequence of *acting* together" (Jenkins 1997, 10, *orig. it*).

Hence, right at the start "ethnicity"—a term that starts getting popular only in the 1960s—was and is situated between two stools: biological (not-race + almost-kin) and political. It shares aspects of both, and it veers slightly away from both: ethnicity is not race, but ethnicity is also not political solidarity/belonging of the sort that all Democrats or all Republicans have in the United States, at least in theory. Any bid to employ the term has to keep this in mind.

To begin with, let us look at a definition:

> Ethnicity is a concept that describes the real or imagined features of group membership, typically in terms of one or other combination of language, collective memory, culture, ritual, dress and religion, amongst other features. It is therefore a looser definition than "race," and the key distinction with other ways of conceiving groups is that it makes self-definition central. (Meer 2014, 37)

Despite being a comprehensive and standard definition of ethnicity, even this leaves various matters unresolved: one can argue that "race" was also a matter of "self-definition," at least for the "master races," and that so are other terms used interchangeably with ethnicity, such as "nationality" or "culture." One can also argue, from other perspectives, that none of these terms are matters of self-definition to some peoples.

Even though synonyms might be employed in common parlance, speakers who use the signifier "ethnic"—or its equivalents—often seem to refer to different signifieds. The most obvious difference is the one between signifiers like "ethnic cuisine" and "ethnic garments" on the one side, and signifiers like "ethnic community" and even "ethnicity" on the other. The first lot, for instance, are deeply "global": a cuisine becomes "ethnic" only when it leaves its region of origin and arrives, properly packaged, elsewhere. No one eats ethnic Danish cuisine in Denmark or ethnic Punjabi food in Punjab, though both might be available, if properly packaged, in London, or to tourists anywhere. On the other hand, the "ethnic Dane" is supposed to be rooted in a place called Denmark, with roots in the dark soil of "history," and this is true of the ethnic Punjabi in Punjab or the ethnic Scot in Scotland, even though, as scholars have noted, there is a tendency to refer to minority communities as "ethnic"—even when these communities are not "native" to the geographical space (see Craig et al. 2012). Jenkins devotes an entire chapter to debunking this tendency. The chapter, titled "Majority Ethnicity," starts with this necessary warning: "Ethnicity is not a particular attribute of minorities nor is it restricted to exotic Others" (Jenkins 1997, 90).

This is, of course, an erudite scholar speaking. In common parlance, the term "ethnic" is more likely to be applied to, say, Caribbean or Indian immigrants in England and Denmark, not to the "ethnic" English or the "ethnic" Dane. Obviously, as Friedman points out, ethnicity is the result of a process of "regionalisation" (in which case, it can be a "national" description), "ethnification of migrants and nationals" (in which case it is usually applied to minorities or immigrants) and "indigenisation" (in which case it can be both). In that sense, "ethnicity" is not as much a matter of "self-definition" as of the "definition of others," though again how can one talk of the self without reference to the other, or vice versa? Still, if twentieth-century ethnicity is a politer and more culture-inflected replacement of the nineteenth-century "race," then evidently not all "cousins" are called ethnic, though a difference seems to exist between the ethnicity of "cousins" and that of (say) "cuisines." Where on this continuum between ethnic cousins and ethnic cuisines does literature belong?

The difference between ethnic cuisines and ethnic cousins is not immaterial or incidental. Just as ethnic cuisines are sold across space (and time) on a narrative of coming from a *particular* geographical and historical space, ethnic cousins also come into existence only within narratives, as Weber had intuited almost a century ago when he stressed the political nature of "ethnicity." In recent years, "ethnicity," Blanton notes with reference to anthropological theory, has moved from a "Romantic" focus on "a people's shared origins and history, and an emotional attachment to their culture, language and local territory" to perspectives (including Blanton's) derived from Fredrik Barth's focus on social action as driving the formation to ethnic groups in order to organize interaction for social purposes. This is a version of the ethnic group building as a "signalling system" (Blanton 2015, 9176–7). Blanton notes that the Romantic "language of blood and kin" has also survived in altered forms, and I would add that it subtly dominates most public and political discourses today (and might even be returning to academia, where it has been marginal since the 1960s).

The imbrication of ethnicity with "race" and "nationality" has been widely noted, and scholars have observed that historically ethnicity was (and is) used as often "a euphemism for racism in general and cultural racism in particular" (Chattoo and Atkin 2012, 20)—with the focus slanted toward cultural and religious differences rather than biological ones. Both these trends noted by Blanton and others are obviously based on narratives—whether the stories being traced are those of blood and kinship or those of welfare or a Lockean commonwealth. In both cases, we have a set of narratives; however, the fact that ethnicity is based on narratives is not meant to suggest that it is necessarily an arbitrary construct or "false." Narratives can be of different sorts. While stories are inevitable, not all stories are the same—or effect reality in the same ways. We will return to this later, but by way of a text—a novel— written in the years when "ethnicity" was coming to replace the earlier prevalence of "race." This novel is rooted in a discursive culture of "race" (its narrative is not located in the present of the author; it's set further back in time), but, as we shall see, it engages exactly the problems that "ethnicity" addresses—or obscures, depending on how one uses the term. And as it is a novel, it is obviously about stories, narratives.

Jean Rhys' *Wide Sargasso Sea*

To begin with, Jean Rhys' *Wide Sargasso Sea* (1966) is a Gothic novel not just because it is "inspired" by the most Gothic of all elements in Charlotte Brontë's reluctantly Gothic and often anti-Gothic novel, *Jane Eyre*: the mad Creole woman in the attic, the secret of the Great Colonial House. "Creole," of course, is already a frayed term—and more so in the nineteenth century, where both the novels are set, when it was used to refer to any subject, white or black, *born* in the Caribbean. One can locate the germ of "ethnicity" in constructions like "creole"—and Rochester does so in *Wide Sargasso Sea*, for "creole" did not necessarily mean (as it often does today) "of mixed race" and yet the suspicion of such mixture lurked around it. The nineteenth-century Creole— like twenty-first century "ethnicity"—was *not* constructed of kinship and race, *not* constructed of space and nation, and *not* constructed of language and "culture," and yet it was constructed of all or some of these very non-elements. While both great novels contain "Gothic" secrets, the main secret in *Wide Sargasso Sea* is not that of a "creole madwoman in the attic": madness and depravity and intermarriage are not the main secrets of *Wide Sargasso Sea*. They are just rumors, mere symptoms of the great secret that even the narrative of *Wide Sargasso Sea* never fully acknowledges because it does not have the language to talk about it: I will call it the secret of the existence and elusiveness, the reality and falsehood, the objectivity and subjectivity of "ethnicity."

Wide Sargasso Sea is not primarily, as one (Penguin 2000) blurb puts it, the story of (a post-emancipation, nineteenth century) "Creole heiress Antoinette Cosway" who, born in "an oppressive colonialist society," meets "a young Englishman who is drawn to her innocent sensuality and beauty. After their marriage disturbing rumors begin to circulate, poisoning her husband against her. Caught between his demands and her own precarious sense of belonging, Antoinette is driven towards madness." There are minor simplifications in this "blurb" version of the novel: it is doubtful whether the Englishman ("Rochester") was ever in love with Antoinette and even more doubtful whether "sensuality" would be attractive to him, and it is definitely clear that he married her at least partly for her fortune. It is also unclear if Antoinette really goes "mad" in any simple sense of the word, at least not before she is carted off to England. However, these are minor matters.

What is more interesting is the way the blurb completely overlooks—with a simplistic gesture toward "oppressive colonialist society"—the great secret that haunts Antoinette, her mother and her family. This is rooted in the lesser secret of slavery. Antoinette and her mother belong to the disappearing old "plantation" families, the crumbling great houses that were built on the labor of slaves. Antoinette grows up in a period when slavery has been abolished—leading to the impoverishment of families like hers—but its memory is still fresh. This memory is used against her by both blacks and whites, especially the new white elite which despises the older slave-owners because its basis of profit, though as exploitative in many ways, is based on the obfuscating control of capital, not of human bodies directly. However, finally, as Antoinette realizes, control of capital translates into control of human bodies: she is rendered a captive in her marriage and made mad because her husband, not she, inherits her wealth.

Both Antoinette and her mother resent the new exploiters and their assumed moral superiority. They also see the reality of slave-holding in grey tones, rather than the black-and-white of the "new comers": this enables them to connect to some ex-slaves, such as Christophine and Caroline, in a way that the new whites, like Mr. Mason or Rochester, are simply incapable of. The "rumours" that, according to the blurb, poison Rochester's mind against Antoinette also arise due to the "paradigm" shift between the exploitation of slavery and the exploitation of high capital. Rochester cannot comprehend the ways in which some white slave owners used black women for sexual purposes (though he does go to bed with a colored women, who wants cash), and this lack of comprehension of the old relations of power is acerbated by his lack of connection to the place and the people. All this leads to suspicions of "racial contamination," miscegenation—he imagines Antoinette as being of mixed blood—and these suspicions conveniently mesh with his economic interests. But that is Rochester's story.

On their side, even though Antoinette and her mother can see the hypocrisy in the ways of the new comers, they cannot fully face their own past of slavery. They either tend to see it as largely benevolent, or simply overlook its oppressive and brutal faces. The latter occurs in a number of places in the novel, but I will confine myself to one instance. Antoinette is taking Rochester to her honeymoon island, called Massacre. Rochester asks, with a touch of moral and civilizational superiority,

> "And who was massacred here? Slaves?"
> "Oh no." She sounded shocked. "Not slaves. Something must have happened a long time ago. Nobody remembers now." (Rhys 2000, 39)

Antoinette is generally vague about the slaveholding part of Caribbean history, and in this case—as Angela Smith points out in the introduction to the edition of the novel that I have used—a precise answer is available. What is interesting is that this answer puts both Rochester and Antoinette in the dock. The massacre recorded in the name of the (actual) island took place in 1675, when one Colonel Philip Warner probably murdered his "mixed race" half-brother, Indian Warner, whom he had refused to recognize as being related to him. This "history" not only puts paid to Rochester's glib moral certainties about a place he hardly knows; it also forces Antoinette to face the brutality of a past she would prefer to see in softer colors.

Antoinette, as a Caribbean "Creole," has a different relationship to space (creole, in the nineteenth century sense), identity (color), terror (Obeah/Vodou), culture, and language than Rochester and people like him, who offer women like Antoinette the only option to a respectable future. *Wide Sargasso Sea* always struggles to tell a story that has more than one side to it. It lacks the language to do so. But the ostensible narrative—like the weeds on stretch of water referred to in the title of the novel—is deceptive, and the reader who takes the plain facts for reality is heading for a cold plunge. As Antoinette replies when Rochester asks her if there is another side to Daniel Cosway's story, "There is always the other side, always" (Rhys 2000, 82).

What is this other side that, Rhys suggests in *Wide Sargasso Sea*, can only be experienced, not narrated? In one sense, obviously, it is the other side of Antoinette's story. But to say so is to simplify the great complexity of this novel. One way to understand the depth of what Antoinette wants to narrate and cannot (and that Rhys can only narrate in negations, gaps, gestures, such as the ones examined below) is to focus on one scene, the scene that introduces us to Antoinette, now newly married to Rochester, and shows the first signs of the divide between them. We have already encountered the start of the scene, where Rochester asks an accusingly "civilised" question about the name of a place and Antoinette, immediately on the defensive, takes refuge in a vast forgetfulness. This is a question that divides the husband and the wife as coming to the same place from different histories: they are married, they are white and "English," and yet they are not the same. I will argue that what has cropped up is not "race" but what we now call ethnicity, and it comes from two different narratives about the same "race" and the same "place."

Rochester, freshly married to Antoinette in rich white colonial circles of Spanish Town, Jamaica, arrives with his beautiful white Creole bride to the island of "Massacre," whose history Rochester reduces and Antoinette refuses at the same time by refusing to face up (in very different ways) to its naming. Despite its name, this is also an island that holds Antoinette's best memories of growing up. Antoinette is eager to meet the "negro" (slave and now recently turned ex-slave) women from her childhood, who had served as her playmates, nurses, and, in one case, a foster mother. One such older woman is "Caro"—as Antoinette calls her—or Caroline. Rochester sees Caro as "a gaudy old creature in a brightly flowered dress, a striped head handkerchief and gold ear-rings." Obviously, though Rochester does not realize it, Caro is richer than most of the other ex-slaves on that little island. It is raining. Excited at seeing Caro, who responds with spontaneous warmth too (though Rochester manages to offend her a bit later), Antoinette rushes out to meet her. "You'll get soaked, Antoinette," says Rochester. "No, the rain is stopping," replies Antoinette. Then we have this description from Rochester:

> She held up the skirt of her riding habit and ran across the street. I watched her critically. She wore a tricorne hat which became her. At least it shadowed her eyes which are too large and can be disconcerting. She never blinks at all it seems to me. Long, sad, dark alien eyes. Creole of pure English descent she may be, but they are not English or European either. (Rhys 2000, 40)

Much has been left unsaid in this section, even pushed outside the consciousness of the characters (though not necessarily both of them at the same time): the complex relationship of the ex-slave owner and the ex-slave, which is primarily a physical relationship, not the abstract economic one that "new capitalists" like Rochester prefer; the cultural differences between Rochester's England, where a lady does not lift up her riding habit and run across the street in rain (and that too to greet a "gaudy" ex-slave) and the Caribbean, Antoinette's inability to face up to the inhumanity of slavery, at least in the face of Rochester's implicit civilizational accusation, and Rochester's refusal to see its "humanity;" the complicating matter of class and place, and so on. The list is long. All Antoinette gestures are at the same time illustrative of gaps between her and her husband, but they are also gaps in the narrative: silence, absence, or noise that cannot be filled with clear explanatory words, perhaps because such words cannot (yet?) come into existence in the historical and discursive context.

And thus begins a trail of suspicion—of Antoinette's "impurity," of which there is no proof though Rochester chooses to believe the rumors and innuendoes, and of miscegenation in general, of which there is ample proof, for the men in Antoinette's family in the past obviously used slave women for their pleasure, but this proof Antoinette is forced to ignore in order to stay "pure" in Rochester's eyes—which finally leads to the "madness" of Antoinette, returning the novel to the generic mad Creole in the attic of Bronte's *Jane Eyre*. It is a rich and revealing progression, but I do not have space to go into all of it. And it is not entirely necessary: the above extract is sufficient for our purposes. One can see what happens. Antoinette behaves in a way that Rochester does not associate with polite female behavior. He has already been provoked by the new space—"Massacre"—and its new relationships, which he cannot fully comprehend, as they are alien to him, and hence which he can only reduce to stereotypes. Then his beautiful white bride throws herself into this alien space. She is still as white, "English" and beautiful as she was in Spanish town, where Rochester married her, at least partly for her money, though now he will attribute it partially to being feverish. But she is not white or English as Rochester understands the terms. The difference of her upbringing—culture, "language use," space, relations, and so on—is one way in which ethnicity can be conceptualized, and often is. But it is not sufficient for Rochester. His mind immediately moves to "racial" differences: the "dark alien eyes," which lead on to the suspicion of miscegenation and what was seen as connected to it in the nineteenth century, madness; the fact that Antoinette does not seem to blink to Rochester is not understood, or not solely, as connected to the fact that she is used to the stronger sunshine. This initially subconscious suspicion of madness and miscegenation is to grow over the rest of the novel, and finally— through specific acts of interpellation by Rochester (such as addressing Antoinette by the name of her supposedly mad mother)—it engulfs and destroys Antoinette. And yet, the problem of ethnicity is not fully resolved for Rochester, as it isn't in most contemporary usages either: "Creole of pure English descent she may be, but they are not English or European either" (Rhys 2000, 40).

Antoinette might be "pure English," but she has "mixed cousins" (whom she tries to occlude). She has the albatross of "ethnic cousins" hanging around her visibly white neck, and civilized Rochester has not yet become a fan of ethnic cuisines. What is Antoinette then? Rhys knew the impossibility of asking (let alone answering) this question—also as a "colonial/postcolonial" writer before the term "postcolonial," like "ethnic cuisine," became established at least in some refined circles of the "West."

The state of the postcolonial

It is not as if Antoinette does not have other stories to tell, or that there are no other stories which can be used by her to shape herself, but Rochester's "story" about Antoinette still defines her future. Rochester's story need not be right or wrong. That is immaterial. It is hegemonic. Not just Antoinette, but even, to some extent, Rhys lacks the words that can empower Antoinette's and other stories. Antoinette is driven to silence, madness, and a ghostly conflagration; Rhys can suggest the other stories only through gaps, contradictions, noise, and silence. The Caribbean is *not* the Orient, and yet that was the essential and still relevant point of Edward Said's *Orientalism* (1978): the brunt of Said's critique of Orientalism was *not* that Europe or the "West" had cultural prejudices. All cultures have their prejudices, but the hegemony of Europe in the past few centuries turned many European perspectives, prejudiced or not, correct or not, into the main and at times the only—*definitive*—truth about complex non-European places, ideas, histories, customs, or peoples. The "Orient" might not have survived into the twenty-first century, except in inane media discourse at times, given the general chipping away at "grand narratives" in the second half of the twentieth century. But sometimes the smaller designations of ethnicities seem to serve a similar purpose. What is more interesting is that such definitions are also adopted by various "ethnicities" and applied to themselves. But then that was the case with the grand Oriental too, wasn't it? Remember the wise Oriental or the duplicitous Oriental?

Rhys' brilliant attempt at dealing with the Creole nature of Antoinette's realities (and stories) is a good indication of the problems of ethnicity in contemporary literature, and most contemporary writers do not have Rhys's incredible talent to help them face and tangentially overcome the problem. This is reflected in many current definitions, but I will look at it particularly in light of three terms used by literary criticism throughout the twentieth century: "national literature," "postcolonialism," and "multiculturalism." In some ways, all three terms can be discussed in light of the hidden relationship and the tension between ethnic cousins and ethnic cuisines today.

National literature is the easiest to tackle. Mostly nineteenth-century usages of "national literature" presumed a people united by the kinship of blood and language—if not a "race" then at least an ethnicity. Today, talk of "national literature" is not just rarer, but it also avoids any obvious ethnic overtone. And yet, "national literature," as a term, stays haunted by ethnicity, if not "race": that is the reason why Salman Rushdie, Monica Ali, Hanif Kureishi, Hari Kunzru et al.—either born and brought up in UK or born elsewhere but brought up in UK from a very early age—

are more likely to be discussed in "postcolonial" contexts (and journals) than those of *English* (national) literature. Sometimes, they might be incorporated into *"British literature"*—a roomier national description—but mostly when hyphenated with words like "Black," or "new" or "diasporic." On the other hand, writers of a certain ethnicity become "English" or "American" much faster: no one, after all, discusses Charles Bukowski as an "immigrant German" writer.

Postcolonialism and multiculturalism present other dimensions of this problem. Some questions will make it clear. Why is Salman Rushdie "postcolonial" but not Martin Amis? After all, whatever comes after or with colonization must affect the descendants of both the colonized and the colonizer? Again, why is Salman Rushdie studied as postcolonial but not, or not a tenth as often, Nirmal Verma or Ismat Chughtai? Related to this is the problem of "multiculturalism": I can be seen as "multicultural" because I speak English along with other Indian languages, but a Bihari working in Tamil Nadu and speaking three or four widely different languages (*but* no English or European language) will not usually register as "multicultural" in most discourses.

Similarly, in many European nations, regional versions of multicultural identities are ignored—so that "multiculturalism" becomes an issue to be lamented or celebrated only when Africans or Asians arrive on the ground. Werbner rightly distinguishes between multiculturalism from above and below: "[In Britain,] politicians tend to use multiculturalism as a euphemism for immigration or extremism [...] All they achieve by the failure-of-multiculturalism discourse is a growing sense of alienation among religious and ethnic minorities" (Werbner 2012, 207). One can argue, following the logic of Werbner's discussion that the naming of multiculturalism is not the same as the interculturality that exists and has always existed, though in differing permutations, in all spaces. Multiculturalism from below is always there, in all spaces, and it is doubtful that this is recognized by definitions of multiculturalism from above. Ethnicity, sometimes, seems to be a version of multiculturalism from above, but also when it seems to come from below, the problem remains: Who is defining a people from within? Is it an internal elite? Is it a new elite or a traditional one? Is it a reactionary or progressive definition? And, finally, do we have the language to comprehend "multiculturality" (or "ethnicity") from below, and is it not likely that any bid to define and tabulate it will be prescriptive at least to some extent?

It sometimes seems that we have come a long way from Antoinette's days—and to some extent we have, for we can now read *Wide Sargasso Sea* in its own literary and cultural context, something enabled by postcolonialism, and other literary developments. And yet, in many other ways we have not: for the mesh of differences and similarities that made Antoinette different—ethnically different maybe—is still not easy to negotiate and calibrate. To return to Weber's original perception and accent it a bit differently, there are still dominant narratives that impede or ignore some "collective political actions" and certain experiences of "acting together" while privileging others. Hence, the Antoinettes of today's world are still forced to assume certain consolidated ethnicities—whether in terms of kinship or culture, whether as cousins (as in certain discussions of aboriginality in postcolonialism) or as cuisines (as in certain discussions of hybridity in postcolonialism). The "concretisation of identities" that Friedman notes (Friedman 1997, 71) is obviously part of different narratives, but, as always, it also leaves some stories out of the pale of narration.

Further reading

Barth (1981) is a seminal text: a comprehensive attempt to define ethnicity in ways that did not reduce it biologically or dismiss it politically. Fenton (2010) gives a scholarly description of the term and its controversies, and Jenkins (1997) engages critically with the various ways in which "ethnicity" has been employed till date. Jenkins also provides some revealing "case studies." Both Fenton and Jenkins offer key understandings of the term and its complexities, and also situate it historically. Barot (1996) and Werbner and Modood (1997) contain papers by major scholars of ethnicity—or "race," "hybridity," "cultural identity," "nationalism," and "multiculturalism," which are all terms and definitions that any usage of ethnicity has perforce to engage with.

References

Barot, R. (ed.) (1996) *The Racism Problematic: Contemporary Sociological Theories of Race and Ethnicity*, Lampeter: Edwin Mellon Press.

Barth, F. (1981) *Process and Form in Social Life: Collected Essays of Frederik Barth*, vol. 1, London: Routledge and Kegan Paul.

Blanton, Richard E. (28 July 2015) "Theories of Ethnicity and the Dynamics of Ethnic Change in Multiethnic Societies," *PNAS*, 112 (30): 9176–81.

Chattoo, Sangeeta and Karl Atkin "Race, Ethnicity and Social Policy: Theoretical Concepts and the Limitations of Current Approaches to Welfare," in Craig, Gary, Karl Atkin, Sangeeta Chattoo and Ronny Flynn (eds) *Understanding "Race" and Ethnicity: Theory History, Policy, Practice*, 19–40, London: The Policy Press.

Craig, Gary, Karl Atkin, Sangeeta Chattoo and Ronny Flynn (eds) (2012) *Understanding "Race" and Ethnicity: Theory History, Policy, Practice*, London: The Policy Press.

Fenton, Steve (2010) *Ethnicity*, Cambridge: Polity Press.

Friedman, Jonathan (1997) "Global Crises, The Struggle for Cultural Identity and Intellectual Porkbarrelling: Cosmopolitans verse Locals, Ethnics and Nationals in an Era of De-Hegemonisation," in Pnina Werbner and Tariq Modood (eds), *Debating*

Cultural Hybridity: Multi-Cultural Identities and the Politics of Anti-Racism, 70–89, London and Jersey: Zed Books.

Jenkins, Richard (1997 [1998]) *Rethinking Ethnicity: Arguments and Explorations*, London and Delhi: Sage Publications.

Meer, Nasar (2014) *Key Concepts in Race and Ethnicity*, Los Angeles and London: Sage Publications Ltd.

Rhys, Jean (2000) *Wide Sargasso Sea* (1966). London: Penguin Books

Werbner, Pnina (2012) "Multiculturalism from Above and Below: Analysing a Political Discourse," *Journal of Intercultural Studies*, 33 (2): 197–209.

Werbner, P. and T. Modood (eds) (1997) *Debating Cultural Hybridity: Multi-Cultural Identities and the Politics of Anti-Racism*, London and Jersey: Zed Books.

19

Desire

Lilian Munk Rösing

Sexual desire is a common subject matter in literature, but desire is not only sexual and not only a subject matter. For instance, desire is also the desire to read. To interrogate into the desire of somebody or something is to ask what drives them. What drives the reader? What drives the text? What drives the fictional characters?

The theory that has thought the most about the problem of desire is psychoanalysis. Psychoanalysis defines the human subject as a being of language and desire, and desire as something else than need. A need can be satisfied, desire cannot, or only momentarily: as soon as it is satisfied, a new desire is born. Hunger, for instance, is a need; we have to eat to sustain our pure physical being. But the gastronomic want for well-prepared dishes and new, surprising sensations of taste is a desire. The human is the being that will always (or as soon as its needs are minimally satisfied) transform need into desire.

In this chapter, I shall try to explain desire according to psychoanalysis (here primarily Sigmund Freud and Jacques Lacan), and why desire is also a concept for that which drives language, literature, and the reader. I hope to show what it means to focus on the dynamics of desire when analyzing not only the story, but also the composition and implied reader of the text.

Desire, language, and separation

To psychoanalysis, desire comes into life at the same time as language. This view is implied in Freud's theory of the Oedipus complex and explicit with the French psychoanalyst Jacques Lacan who to a high degree regards the analysis of the psyche as an analysis of language. Lacan's famous saying "The unconscious is structured like a language" (Lacan 1977, 203) thus claims the same dynamics of difference and deference to be at work in the unconscious and in language.

Language and desire come into life at the moment that Freud calls the oedipal phase, while Lacan calls it "the name of the father" (Lacan 2006a) or "the symbolic castration" (for instance Lacan 2006b) or the child's entrance into "the symbolic order." The symbolic order is one of Lacan's three orders. The others are the imaginary and the real. Very shortly defined the symbolic order is the order of language, Law, and sociality. The imaginary order is the order where the fissures, lacks, and differences that characterize the symbolic order are imagined to be non-existent (like in romantic ideals). Finally, the real is the leftover that escapes the symbolic order, because it is too material, too amorphous, or too ungraspable to be put in words and concepts (skinless flesh, unarticulated sound, nameless affect, etc.) (Lacan 1982). Freud's well-known Oedipus-theory is the theory that the small (male) child desires his mother and wishes the father to die. But this desire for the mother implies a separation from the mother; you can only desire what you are not already one with. In the same way the verbal designation of a thing implies a separation, that between word and thing. Desire and language imply separation, and the original separation is that from the mother (happening already at birth).

In Freud's Oedipal triangle, the father is the one who has the function of separating the child from the mother and prohibit their union. This function is what Lacan calls the symbolic "castration." From this prohibition desire is born. Both the child's desire and the insight that also the desired other (prototypically the mother) is desiring something. In one and the same cut, child is separated from mother, the word (for instance "mother") from the thing itself (for instance the mother's body), desire from its object. This separation is at the same time a splitting within the subject, or the subject comes into being as this very splitting. Prohibition, naming, desire, and entrance into the symbolic order happen simultaneously.

The coincidence between prohibition and name is implied in Lacan's concept "le nom du père" which means "the name of the father," bur sounds just like "le non du père," "the no of the father." If the mother gives her body to bearing the child, the father (at least in patrilineal convention) gives his name to the child, and by this name the child is inscribed into the social order. The name, so to speak, removes the child from the maternal body and inscribes it into society.

Psychoanalysis has been criticized for basing itself on the model of the nuclear family, which is a historically and culturally limited social formation. In other times and cultures the child has been brought up differently, for instance in tribes or expanded families with other primary caregivers than the mother, and the father may be in close bodily contact with the infant. In societies such as the Scandinavian you might argue that it is the Day Care rather than the father that separates the child from its mother and inscribes it into the social order. But the point is that the (coincident) functions (of separating, naming, and inscribing into the social order) remain, even if they are filled out/incarnated by various instances and persons.

What is universal, beyond the relativity of history and culture, is that desire and language rest upon a separation and a prohibition coinciding with the child's inscription into the social order, and that the subject, understood as a being of language and desire, has a fissure or split, also within itself, as a fundamental condition.

Oedipality and triangles

The incitement of desire by prohibition is an initiating logic in many stories. We know it for instance from *Genesis* which would never have become a story, but a lyrical praising of the Garden of Eden, had there not been an inspiring prohibition against eating the fruit from the tree of knowledge. We know the logic also from many fairy tales: when there is a prohibition to open a certain door or enter a certain room, we can be completely sure that this prohibition will be transgressed.

The famous Greek tragedy that has given name to Freud's Oedipus complex has as its narrative dynamo the ignorant transgression of the fundamental prohibition, the prohibition against incest. The Oedipal triangle is to be found in innumerable stories in literary history. Just as famous as Oedipus (and just as much a source of inspiration for Freud) is Shakespeare's Hamlet who wants to kill his (step)father and calls on his mother in her bedroom.

If Hamlet's story is translated from Freudian Oedipality into a more Lacanian, structural conceptualization, his problem can be regarded as the corruption of the symbolic order (the court, the Law, the state of Denmark) by the murder of the paternal authority (the name of the father: old Hamlet) who has been replaced by an immoral drinking and fornicating tyrant (Claudius, whom Freud in his Oedipal interpretation understands as stand-in for the son, for young Hamlet). The initial situation is the suspension of the symbolic castration and the rule of incest. Hamlet now sees it as his task to reinstall the Law-funding divide and he thinks he can do this by obeying to his dead father's ghostly voice and kill Claudius. But the moment when he finally sticks his sword into Claudius becomes, in a tragic-ironic way, at the same time the moment where all characters are dissolved into one incestuous mass. Rather than becoming the instrument of division and distinction, the sword (and the poisoned cup) becomes the instrument that dissolves all divides and lets Hamlet, Claudius, Horatio, and Gertrude die in a pool of poison and blood. The killing sword is not able to install the order of language and desire that rests on the subject's taking on his own split and recognizing desire and split as fundamental conditions also for others (including the mother/ the woman). Therefore one could claim Hamlet's problem not to be his hesitation to kill Claudius, but rather his belief that through this murder he can install the divide that initiates language and desire, even if this divide is rather to be found in his own split and his giving himself away to the puns and wit of language.

Claudius could be seen as a variant of the figure that Freud calls the primal father: the father who does not respond to any Law and has unlimited access to enjoyment, drinking, eating, fornicating, killing at his will (Freud 1955a). This figure is inclined to appear when the symbolic paternal authority disappears—think for instance of the gang leaders in urban life today, or Dennis Hopper in David Lynch's *Blue Velvet* as the infantile sadist who takes command when the lawn-moving suburban father collapses from a heart attack.

The triangle as a fundamental figure for the structure of desire is further developed by the French anthropologist René Girard and his concept of "mimetic desire." Girard claims, based on his readings in European literary history, that our desire mimes the other's desire: We desire what the other desire. This way our relation to the other desiring is more primary than our relation to the one we desire. This figure shows itself for instance in triangles of two men or women desiring the same woman or man, their desire originating in their relation/rivalry rather than being inspired by its object. Following Girard, the queer theoretic Eve Kosovsky Sedgwick argues that the relation between the two men or women in this kind of triangles has a tinge of homoeroticism, for which the heterosexual desire of the third part is a cover-up. Thus, in *Gone with the Wind*, Sedgwick finds Scarletts desire for Ashley originating in her rivalry with Melanie, and Rhetts desire for Scarlett originating in his rivalry with Ashley (Sedgwick 1985).

The idea that desire is born from separation from the desired object and nourished by the prohibition to have it is what Lacan notes with his concept "*a*" or "object small a" ("objèt petit a"). That desire emanates from the social order is what he conceptualizes by claiming that it emanates from what he calls "A," ("L' Autre"), "the big Other."

Small a

"Object small a" is the fantasy of the completely satisfying object that the concrete phenomenal object can never fill out. It is Don Juans's fantasy of the perfect woman, a woman's fantasy of the perfect pair of shoes, a master chef's fantasy of the perfect meal, a nymphomaniac's or macho man's fantasy of eternal erection. It is "Maren" in Søren Kierkegaard's anecdote of the small child who cries for "Maren, Maren, Maren," but is disappointed when Maren appears: "It was not *that* Maren." It is the green color in August Strindberg's anecdote of the small boy who wants a green fishing net, but rejects it when he has it: "I did not want *that* green colour."

Object small a is the indeterminate "it" when you say "she's got *it*"; in modern media language it is called x-factor, in Lacanian it is called "that-in-you-more-than-yourself," "en-toi-plus-que-toi" (Lacan 1977, 263–76).

Object small a is desire's object as well as its cause; desire is initiated by this fantasy of some "it" that would really be "it," like in "this is it." The problem is that no concrete object is never completely "it" (even if commercials try to make us believe so: "Coke is it"), at best it gives us temporary satisfaction, but then leads to more desire (which is of cause what the whole capitalist economy of consumption is based on). Shakespeare has put this troubling logic of desire into verse when he lets Hamlet speak out his disgust for his mother's desire, her way of looking at her husband: "as if increase of appetite had grown by what it fed on." Desire is the appetite that grows when it is fed, desire is paradoxical and redundant, which here makes Hamlet produce a pleonasm; the verse actually does not say that appetite grows, but that the increase (of appetite) grows. Also in his sonnets Shakespeare puts this logic into verse: "My love is as a fever longing still/ for that which longer nourish the disease"— the object of desire is not the cure of desire, but its cause.

In Isak Dinesen's short story "The Blank Page" *object a* could be said to be the perfect story. In the frame at the beginning a storyteller ("an old, coffee-brown, black-veiled woman") is staged, and the want that initiates the story is made explicit in her first line: "You want a tale, sweet lady and gentleman?" The desire for stories is immediately connected to sexual desire, as the woman tells of her youth when she let young men tell her "tales of a red rose, two smooth lily buds, and four silky, supple, deadly entwining snakes." The anatomic connotations of rose, lily buds, and snakes (mouth, breasts, limbs) are here hardly to be ignored, thus giving us the image of the young woman being, as it were, inseminated with stories by the young men.

Instead of right away giving her audience a story, the storyteller seems to make a detour by starting to tell about the origin of her stories: they have been inseminated into her by young men, and they have been taught to her by her grandmother (who perhaps also has had them inseminated into her, at least she is predicated as "often-embraced").

The lesson that the storyteller quotes from her grandmother is the idea that the perfect story is told by silence: "Who tells a finer tale than any of us? Silence does. […] When a royal and gallant pen, in the moment of its highest inspiration, has written down its tale with the rarest ink of all, where, then, may one read a still deeper, sweeter, merrier and more cruel tale than that? Upon the blank page." The metaphor of insemination is still present (the "gallant pen" that writes "with the rarest ink of all"), but the object of desire, the object a, has been deferred from tale to silence, from the pen connoting insemination to the blank page connoting (at first sight) virginity.

By her detour the storyteller has augmented the audience's desire for her story (which is her merchandise; we are told from the beginning that she "made her living by telling stories") and emphasized the *object a* quality of the story by raising the question of "the finest tale of all" as well as the question of the story's origin.

Big O

One of Lacan's definitions of the big Other is "the subject supposed to know" (Lacan 1977, 232), that is the person or instance that we imagine to know the truth about our life, our identity, our desire. It may be God, it may be our parents, our partner, our psychoanalyst, the priest, a political party, an ideology, or a more diffuse sense of something or somebody knowing who I am, and what I should go for. To Lacan, the idea that someone or somebody has the truth is really just an idea, no truth. There is no metaphysical guarantee for the big Other, which Lacan puts in this way: "There is no Other for the Other."

The fact that the big Other is an idea, not a truth, does not make it less important in the formation of our consciousness. The big Other teaches us what to desire, or as Lacan puts it: "Desire is the desire of the big Other" (Lacan 1977, 235). In our society of consumption it is obvious that the advertising industry has the function of the big Other, telling us what to desire. But you can also think of enthusiastic adult faces bending over the infant who must think: "What do they want from me?" which at the same time is the question: "what do they want me to want?" This is the big Other's question to the subject: "What do you want?" Lacan puts it in Italian, quoting a line from Mozart's *Don Giovanni*: "Che vuoi?"

In "The Blank Page" the first line of the woman storyteller is actually a variant of "Che vuoi?": "You want a tale?" Thus, she is staged as the big Other to her audience ("sweet lady and gentleman," but also the reader), explicitly and immediately addressing their desire. As she is sitting silently, giggling, "munching with her toothless mouth" she has the enigmatic quality of the big Other, but when she talks her authority seems somewhat deferred: she refers to her own "big Other," her grandmother who again is referred to her "mother's mother" in this line of ancestors remarkably skipping every second link; the line goes from grandmother to granddaughter, but never from mother to daughter.

The deference of authority may seem to say that there is always a big Other to the big Other, but at the same time the story suggests this deference to be infinite which leads pretty much to the opposite and Lacanian conclusion: There is no Other to the Other; authority is always staged, contingently established, and has no absolute guarantee.

Seemingly setting off to satisfy her audience's desire for a tale, the old woman introduces other objects of desire: silence (as "the finest tale of all") and the origin of storytelling ("where do stories come from?"). Those questions seem to be of more interest to a storyteller than to a listener/reader, as they are kind of meta-questions, the old woman's investigation into her own art. The listeners' object of desire slides into the teller's object of desire. Desire is the desire of the big Other, meaning both that we come to desire what (we imagine that) the Other desires, and that we have a desire for the big Other, to know its want and solve its enigma.

So the frame of "The Blank Page" may be said to be framing the (explicit) listeners' or (implied) readers' desire, their want for a story. Within this frame (which is actually only there at the beginning of the text, not in the end) we get the story of "the blank page": In a Portuguese Carmelite convent the nuns grow flax and manufacture bridal sheets for the royal and noble families of Europe. After the wedding night the sheets are returned to the convent, and the central part with its blood stains is cut out and hung in a frame in the convent's gallery, which may thus be said to be a kind of proto-collection of women's body art.

The rite of hanging up the stained sheets is an inscription of the bride in the social and symbolic order. By being penetrated on the wedding night, she is symbolically castrated, inscribed into patriarchal society as her husband's wife, and her blood transformed from bodily materiality into a signifier.

The point of the story, though, is the fact that among the stained sheets there is a completely blank one. This is "the blank page," clearly established by the storyteller as an allegory of that silence that tells the finest tale of all: "It is in front of the blank page that old and young nuns, with the Mother Abbess herself, sink into deepest thought," thus the last words of the text.

The old and young nuns and the Mother Abbess at the end seem to mirror the storyteller and her female ancestors at the beginning, but the women have become silent contemplators instead of storytellers, they have turned their backs upon us, we are no longer confronted with the old woman's enigmatic face, but with the Abbess's back.

The begetting of stories

The nuns' fabrication of sheets and the storytelling women's fabrication of stories are thus analogized, and both are heavily interwoven with sexual metaphors. On the one hand, we have metaphors of insemination and penetration to explain the origin of both stories and sheets; on the other hand, we have images of something like a virgin birth: stories and sheets originating from pure female communities (the storytellers, the nuns), or from the untouched and unbroken (uncastrated) female body alone.

In the frame we have seen how the origin of stories is at once referred to insemination and to the purely matriarchal line of grandmothers and granddaughters, in which the maternal body is skipped, which saves us from the idea of a female body fissured by giving birth. In the central story this ambiguity is reoccurring: On the one hand, the flax is said to be conceived by "milk-white bullocks" and the nuns' "virginal hands;" on the other hand, the bullocks plow the field, and the nuns have "mould under the nails." The idea of virgin birth is most overtly present when the blue color of the flax is compared to the blue apron of Virgin Mary at the moment of the Annunciation, but once again the image of virginity is disturbed by the phallic image of the holy spirit as a dove with his "neck-feathers raised."

The flax may be cultivated and the linen woven by an all-female collective, but we are told, in yet another metaphor of insemination, that the very first linseed was brought to the convent by a man, a crusader from the holy land. The linseed may come from a field cultivated by a woman, Caleb's daughter, but we also hear how she has her field blessed by the springs of her father: "he gave her the upper springs and the nether springs" (ejaculation/insemination again).

Similarly the line of storytellers may be matriarchal and oral, but has had written text grafted unto it by a man, the Jewish rabbi who has taught quotes from the Bible to the storyteller's grandmother's grandmother. Throughout the story, writing and inscription is connected to the male, the phallic, whereas the female collectives are connected to blank paper (the nuns' linen) or oral storytelling. The product of purely female creativity is not written (upon). This mirrors a recurrent fantasy in Isak Dinesen's work: to be part of an oral storytelling tradition. But actually, Dinesen's work is written. The text before us is no pure linen, no blank page, no untouched body, it is stained from the ink of letters.

In one reading, the central symbol, the unstained sheet, may be interpreted as yet another version of some kind of "virgin" or purely female creativity, as the sign of a female body untouched by man, that is symbolically uncastrated. Such an image belongs to Lacan's imaginary order: the order in which the fissures and divisions of symbolic castration are imagined to be non-existent. By its reoccurring metaphors of insemination, penetration, and inscription, the text actually undermines this fantasy. In another reading, the sheet may rather be seen as an allegory of that which cannot be captured by the symbolic order (by the conventional inscription and sign value of the sheet), the left-over: The secret, intimate life of the body on the sheet. Meditating in front of the sheet, as do the princesses and nuns at the end of the story, in this interpretation has an affinity to wondering about "the primal scene," which is Freud's concept for the child's fantasy of the parents' coitus, and with Lacan becomes a more abstract concept for the scene of desire from which the subject is born. "What happened on the sheet between bride and groom?" might be seen as a version of the question: "What happened on the sheet between my parents?", or more abstractly: "From which desire am I born?"

The sexual metaphors and allusions thus finally analogize three kinds of activities: inventing stories, manufacturing linen, and having sex. And the unstained sheet becomes the ambiguous symbol of the secret, the enigma of all three activities. It becomes what Freud in his *Interpretation of Dreams* calls an "overdetermined" symbol, a concentrated image determined by many different treads of signification.

Narrative desire

One thing is to use the psychoanalytic concepts to analyze literature's stories of desire. Another thing is to ask for the desire at work not so much in the characters of the text, but in the text itself, and in the reader while consuming it. This desire is interrogated by Peter Brooks in his *Reading for the Plot* in which he reacts against structuralism's freezing of the text in static structures and insists on the reader's dynamic unfolding of the text, the pleasure taken from plot.

Leaning on Freud and Lacan Brooks understands desire (which can never be satisfied) as different from need (which can)—and as something thriving on hindrance. Desire neither can nor should be satisfied, its complete satisfaction is not only impossible, but would also be unbearable: If all hindrance for the satisfaction of desire is taken away, we shall die.

According to Brooks, this is the point in Balzac's story "La peau de chagrin." Here the protagonist Raphaël comes to own a talisman that can satisfy his desire, but the price is high: each time one of his desires is satisfied, his skin will shrink. Raphaël's possession of the talisman is immediately followed by the death of his father, which suspends the father's prohibition against gambling: the law of the father and the no of the father (le nom/non du père) are gone. Despite Raphaël's attempts to learn the impossible art of not desiring anything at all, he dies from the shrinking of his skin. Brooks interprets the story of Raphaël as developing from a powerless desire rebounding against its impregnable object (Raphaël's beloved Feodora who is without the fissures through which desire can find its way) to an inhibited desire the satisfaction of which implies death.

One of Brook's points is that desire is a general theme in narrative genres: "One could no doubt analyse the opening paragraph of most novels and emerge in each case with the image of a desire taking on shape, beginning to seek its objects, beginning to develop a textual energetics" (38).

This is true of "The Blank Page": it opens by the image of a desire taking shape, the desire of the lady and gentleman for a tale, the desire of the old woman to tell a very special tale (and be well paid). This meta-dimension of "The Blank Page" leads us to Brook's most important point: if narrative literature likes to tell stories about desire, it is because the dynamics of narrative itself is a dynamics of desire. The characters' desire runs parallel to the reader's desire (for solution, explanation, surprise, overview) and to the narrator's. To Brooks the narrator's desire is to suspend that satisfaction of narrative desire that coincides with death, just like Sehrazat (the storyteller in *One Thousand and One Nights*) saved her head night after night by suspending the satisfaction of the sultan's desire. The narrative (like the erotic) dynamics lives from the suspension of the satisfaction of desire.

In "The Blank Page" the reader's desire is stimulated by the storyteller's explicit addressing a want ("You want a tale?") and the detours by which she augments the object of desire from being just "a tale" to being the question of the story's origin and finally the finest tale of all. The frame establishes the storyteller as a somewhat coy mistress, delaying the moment when she starts to tell, playing reluctant by her claim that she risks her own credit ("we are somewhat averse to telling it, for it might well, among the uninitiated, weaken our own credit"). Finally starting to tell the story, the excursive detour stays her strategy, and only at the very end does she present to us the central theme of her story, announced already by the title of the whole text: "The Blank Page."

Thus the reader is incited to follow the storyteller right to the end, but what he gets at the end is actually—nothing, a blank page. What he gets is an allegory of ellipsis, of the moment when nothing is told and everything left to the listener's or reader's imagination. What he gets is an untold story of desire that may mean everything from the negation of desire to the excess of desire. The unstained sheet may mean that there was no desire on the wedding night (they did not have sex, for instance because the groom was impotent), or that there had been an excess of desire before (the bride was not a virgin), or that the newly wed found unconventional ways to satisfy their desire (they may have had other than genital sex, they may have had it other places than in bed). What we get is not an answer, but an enigma, suspended between a serious meta-narrative allegory and a vulgar joke, between refined poetics and witty obscenity.

Furthermore, if we take seriously the blank page as an allegory of the storyteller's poetics, we have to see the finest, deepest, merriest, most cruel tale of all not in the written text before our eyes, but in the silence after the text, the silence when we could expect to return to the frame, the old woman and her listeners, but never do. In the material body of the text, the blank page is not the image of the unstained sheet that it presents in its writing, but the white of the paper when the writing has stopped.

Desire beyond pleasure

Brooks leads the merciless logic of desire back to Freud's much debated essay *Beyond the Pleasure Principle* (1919, Freud 1955b). Freud here takes his point of departure in his observation of a compulsion to repeat which is at odds with the pleasure principle. Shell-shocked soldiers returned from the First World War, and in their dreams and memory they kept repeating the explosion that has traumatized them. This went against Freud's earlier thesis that the human psyche generally strives for pleasure, not in the sense of sexual orgasm (enjoyment), but rather in the sense of well-being. In his essay, Freud attempts to subsume the compulsion to repeat under the pleasure principle by understanding it as a retrospective training to master what was impossible to master when it happened. Freud compares the situation to his observation of his grandchild repeatedly throwing a wooden reel with a string attached to it and drawing it back, saying "o-o-o-oh" when the reel is gone, and "Da!" when he draws it back. Freud interprets the reel as a symbol of the mother, and the child's play as an attempt to master the shift between her presence and absence—of which he is actually the passive victim—through symbolization (gesticulation and linguistic sounds).

But next to his rational explanation of the compulsion to repeat, Freud launches the theory that its motor is the human drive toward an energetic stasis which is ultimately that of death.

What Freud discovers in *Beyond the Pleasure Principle* is that there is a drive in the human being that is stronger than pleasure and self-sustainment. It is here clear that psychoanalysis does not understand desire as a biologic or utilitarian drive to reproduce, but as a drive with no meaning or purpose. Its only purpose is to sustain itself (not the human being), and it is characterized by the paradox that it is annihilated when satisfied. To handle desire (in a way so it is neither annihilated, nor annihilates us) becomes to psychoanalysis a great existential task—and also a social one, inasmuch as the Law and the order of society are mechanisms to regulate desire. Literature is able not only to tell stories of desire's ways but also to launch desire's dynamic chain of signifiers (the chain of events of the plot, the chain of words of the sentence, the chain of letters of the word), so it does not lead too quickly to annihilation and death.

Further reading

Freud's *Interpretation of Dreams* is and stays a fundamental textbook not only in psychoanalysis but also in textual analysis, because you can here follow how Freud follows the traces of the signifiers in order to trace desire. As Lis Møller has pointed out in *The Freudian Reading* (which is also a must-read if you want to know more about the relation between psycho- and textual analysis), the most inspiring for the literary scholar is not what Freud *says* about interpreting dreams, but what he *does* when interpreting them. In *Literature and Psychoanalysis*, Shoshana Felman in an interesting way reflects on the relation between literature and psychoanalysis by talking about their mutual implication instead of the application (of psychoanalysis on literature). An introduction to Jacques Lacan is to be found in Dylan Evans: *An Introductory Dictionary of Lacanian Psychoanalysis*. Lacan has through the latest decades inspired a new wave of psychoanalytic critique of arts and culture, represented not least by the Slovenian philosopher Slavoj Žižek. Žižek's *Looking Awry* and *How to Read Lacan* may also serve as introductions to Lacanian theory, so may Lilian Munk Rösing: *Pixar with Lacan*. The most pedagogical introduction to Žižek's analytical method is Sophie Fiennes' film: *The Pervert's Guide to Cinema*, where Žižek analyzes a number of classical film scenes, in which he is simultaneously staged. Brilliant Lacanian literary analysis is to be found in Joel Fineman: *Shakespeare's Perjured Eye* (on Shakespeare's Sonnets) and Juliet Flower MacCannell: *The Hysteric's Guide to the Future Female Subject*.

References

Brooks, Peter (1984) "Narrative Desire," in *Reading for the Plot*, Cambridge, MA: Harvard University Press.

Dinesen, Isak (1957) "The Blank Page," in *Last Tales*, New York: Random House.

Evans, Dylan (1996) *An Introductory Dictionary of Lacanian Psychoanalysis*, London: Routledge.

Felman, Shoshana (ed.) (1982) *Literature and Psychoanalysis—The Question of Reading: Otherwise*, Baltimore: John Hopkins University Press.

Fiennes, Sophie (2006) *The Pervert's Guide to Cinema*, starring Slavoj Žižek.

Fineman, Joel (1985) *Shakespeare's Perjured Eye. The Invention of Poetic Subjectivity in the Sonnets*. Berkeley: University of California Press.

Freud, Sigmund (1953) *The Interpretation of Dreams* (1900), Standard Edition of the Complete Psychological Works of Sigmund Freud, vol. XIII. Trans. and ed. J. Strachey, London: The Hogarth Press.

Freud, Sigmund (1955a) *Totem and Taboo* (1912), Standard Edition of the Complete Psychological Works of Sigmund Freud, vol. XIII. Trans. and ed. J. Strachey, London: The Hogarth Press.

Freud, Sigmund (1955b) *Beyond the Pleasure Principle* (1919), Standard Edition of the Complete Psychological Works of Sigmund Freud, vol. XVIII. Trans. and ed. J. Strachey, London: The Hogarth Press.

Girard, René (1961) *Mensonge romantique, vérité romanesque*, Paris: Editions Grasset.

Lacan, Jacques (1977) *The Four Fundamental Concepts of Psychoanalysis*, The Seminar of Jacques Lacan, Book XI (1964). Trans. Alan Sheridan, New York: W. W. Norton & Company.

Lacan, Jacques (1982) "Le symbolique, l'imaginaire et le réel" (1953), in *Bulletin de l'Association Freudienne*, nr. 1. Paris.

Lacan, Jacques (2006a) "The Function and Field of Speech and Language in Psychoanalysis" (1953), in *Écrits*. Trans. Bruce Fink, New York: W. W. Norton & Company.

Lacan, Jacques (2006b) "The Subversion of the Subject and the Dialectic of Desire in the Freudian Unconscious" (1960), in *Écrits*. Trans. Bruce Fink, New York: W. W. Norton & Company.

MacCannell, Juliet Flower (1999) *The Hysteric's Guide to the Future Female Subject*, Minneapolis: University of Minnesota Press.

Møller, Lis (1991) *The Freudian Reading. Analytical and Fictional Constructions*, Philadelphia: University of Pennsylvania Press.

Rösing, Lilian Munk (2016) *Pixar with Lacan. The Hysteric's Guide to Animation*, London and New York: Bloomsbury.

Sedgwick, Eve Kosofsky (1985) *Between Men*, New York: Columbia University Press.

Shakespeare, William (1603) *Hamlet*. The Arden Shakespeare. Ed. Harold Jenkins, London: A & C Black Publishers (1990).

Žižek, Slavoj (1991) *Looking Awry. An Introduction to Lacan Through Popular Culture*, Cambridge, MA: MIT Press.

Žižek, Slavoj (2006) *How to Read Lacan*, London: Granta Books.

20

Nature

Peter Mortensen

According to Raymond Williams, the word "nature" is "perhaps the most complex word in the language" (Williams 1983, 219). To speak of "nature" in literary studies is to invoke a concept in and of crisis. As I write this, in December 2015, the world's leaders have again convened in an effort to keep the global temperature increase under two degrees centigrade, which is estimated to be the "tipping point" beyond which climate change becomes irreversible and uncontrollable. Biologists, however, report that climate change is already in full swing, and that we are on the threshold of the largest mass extinction since a meteor strike killed off the dinosaurs approximately 65 million years ago (Kolbert 2014). The planet's human population, however, has ballooned beyond seven billion and is expected to reach nine billion around 2050.

What compounds this crisis is the fact that the very concept at stake—nature—is notoriously slippery and riddled with ambiguity. In its broadest sense, "nature" refers to all aspects of the biophysical world including human creations such as iPods, nuclear plants, and airport landing strips. In its narrower and more familiar meaning, "nature" is used in distinction to what is artificial, cultural, or man-made, which often entails a privileging of some phenomena (such as elephants, daffodils, or waterfalls) over others (such as domestic chickens, wheat fields, or water reservoirs).

National parks such as Yellowstone (USA), Serengeti (Tanzania), and Fiordland (New Zealand) enclose and protect large areas of pristine and untrammeled wilderness, where poets, thrill-seekers, visionaries, and ordinary tourists can encounter nature in its purest crystallization. While densely populated and intensely cultivated countries like Denmark, Germany, and Britain have little if any wild nature left, however, they still possess old and powerful environmentalist traditions and organizations.

Literature explores the instabilities, uncertainties, and ambiguities of human–natural relations, and it has done so from the very beginning. The anonymous Sumerian epic *Gilgamesh* (c. 2000 BC), which is one of the oldest texts that we know, concerns urban–rural conflicts and has "the forest as its first protagonist" (Harrison 1993, 14). The nineteenth century saw the flourishing of the romantic pastoral, lyric nature poetry, regional writing, and the non-fictional prose genre known in the English-speaking world as "nature writing." At the other end of the historical spectrum, contributions to the burgeoning genres of "eco-horror" and "cli-fi," such as Margaret Atwood's *Oryx and Crake* (2003), Frank Schätzing's *The Swarm* (2007), and Paolo Bacigalupi's *The Wind-Up Girl* (2009), construct frightening visions of life on Earth in the human-dominated era that some geologists have begun to call "the Anthropocene" (Crutzen and Stoermer 2000).

"Ecocriticism," which is also sometimes known as "ecopoetics" (Bate 2000), "environmental criticism" (Buell 2005), and "green cultural criticism" (Coupe 2000), has been one of the fastest-growing trends in academic literary studies over the last twenty-five years. Ecocriticism can be defined as "the relationship between literature and the physical environment" (Glotfelty 1996, xviii), as the "study of the relationship between literature and the environment conducted in a spirit of commitment to environmentalist praxis" (Buell 1995, 430), or more simply as "literary and cultural criticism from an environmentalist viewpoint" (Kerridge 2006, 530). What is too often missing from public debates about issues like biodiversity loss, chemical pollution, climate change, ocean acidification, human population growth, and overconsumption is discussion of the human, cultural, and literary dimensions of environmental crisis. Ecocriticism is unlike other literary-critical schools in so far as ecocritics have neither a theoretical Bible nor a shared methodological approach nor even a commonly agreed upon set of terms and priorities. However, ecocritics believe that the environmental crisis is also and not least a crisis of human culture, human consciousness, and the human imagination. The environmental crisis, they assume, has to do not only with too much CO_2 in the atmosphere, too much plastic in the oceans, too many endangered species, or too few resources in the ground. Environmental questions and problems are interwoven with the beliefs that we hold, the traditions that we cherish, the metaphors that we use, the stories that we tell. Realizing this brings literary criticism into renewed focus as a genuine and potentially valuable way of confronting environmental crisis and working toward more sustainable relations with the more-than-human world.

In bed with John Donne

The relationship between literature and nature is as ambiguous as the term "nature" itself, for as a human construct literature simultaneously distances us from and brings us closer to the natural world. In the modern university, the study of plants, animals, and ecological relationships takes place in natural science departments, while literature programs and courses are usually placed under the humanities. The term "humanities" is related to "humanism," the philosophy that emphasizes the rationality, intelligence, and agency of human beings as distinct from the irrationality, non-intelligence, and passivity of non-human entities like machines, animals, and plants. A more critical or polemical stance toward human exceptionalism and universalism is implied when ecocritics speak of "anthropocentrism," which is the belief that the human being occupies the center of the universe, or when they refer to "speciesism," which is the assumption that the members of one species (our own) enjoy automatic privilege over all others because of some intrinsic quality variously defined as soul, reason, intelligence, self-awareness, language, altruism, consciousness of death, or the ability to use tools.

Both humanism and the idea of literature as a special imaginative discourse originated in the Renaissance, which saw the diminishing power of religious institutions, the invention of the printing press, the opening of the New World to European colonization, and the formulation of new dualistic, mechanistic, and materialistic philosophies that drove a wedge between man and the natural world. Literary texts, too, sometimes work to wrest human beings out of their kinship with the organic universe. The speaker of John Donne's poem "The Sun Rising," for example, gives us an expression of Renaissance anthropocentrism that is memorable for its hyperbolic audacity:

> Busy old fool, unruly Sun,
>   Why dost thou thus,
> Through windows, and through curtains, call on us?
> Must to thy motions lovers' seasons run?
>   Saucy pedantic wretch, go chide
>   Late school-boys and sour prentices,
>   Go tell court-huntsmen that the king will ride,
>   Call country ants to harvest offices;
> Love, all alike, no season knows nor clime,
> Nor hours, days, months, which are the rags of time.
>
>   Thy beams so reverend, and strong
>   Why shouldst thou think?
> I could eclipse and cloud them with a wink,
> But that I would not lose her sight so long.

If her eyes have not blinded thine,
Look, and to-morrow late tell me,
  Whether both th' Indias of spice and mine
  Be where thou left'st them, or lie here with me.
Ask for those kings whom thou saw'st yesterday,
And thou shalt hear, "All here in one bed lay."

She's all states, and all princes I;
    Nothing else is;
Princes do but play us; compared to this,
All honour's mimic, all wealth alchemy.
      Thou, Sun, art half as happy as we,
      In that the world's contracted thus;
    Thine age asks ease, and since thy duties be
    To warm the world, that's done in warming us.
Shine here to us, and thou art everywhere;
This bed thy center is, these walls thy sphere.
(Donne 2000, 92–3)

Donne's lyric cleverly mocks the popularity of courtly love poetry modeled on the Italian Francesco Petrarcha (Petrarch), by exchanging the voice of the sexually frustrated Petrarchan speaker for the voice of a cocky "I" who has clearly had his fill of erotic pleasure and seems to be addressing us in a state of post-coital bliss. In terms of literary history, Donne is often classified among the "metaphysical poets" (Eliot 1975, 59–67), a group of sophisticated urban wits who wrote experimental poems mixing erotic, religious, and scientific imagery in daring ways. Almost thirty years before Donne was born, Copernicus had published his theory proposing that the Earth revolves around the sun rather than vice versa. Many years before, around 1490, Leonardo da Vinci had produced the image known as "Vitruvian Man," which captures the humanist spirit by showing man at the center of all things. Donne's speaker bases his case for human exceptionalism neither on traditional Christian metaphysics nor on Aristotelian rationalism but on the claim that humans—and humans alone—possess the capacity to love. In other words, it is the transcendent power of *eros* that gives men and women their cosmologically privileged status in the world vis-à-vis all other biophysical entities.

Throughout his irreverent apostrophe, Donne's speaker baits, bullies, badgers, belittles, and ultimately (in his own mind at least) bests his natural antagonist. By the end of the poem, the human persona has emerged triumphant as the king of the world, somewhat like Leonardo DiCaprio's character in James Cameron's *Titanic*, while the sun has been relegated to a form of early retirement. "The Sun Rising" is often linked to the Catholic Donne's romance with the high-born Protestant Anne Moore, whom he courted and rather unwisely married in 1601. The poem can be taken as a celebration of love, showing how enraptured lovers come to form a microcosmic universe complete onto itself. Ecocritics, however, might find the poem's championing of human beings at the cost of every other thing to be somewhat reminiscent of what David Ehrenfeld (1978) calls "the arrogance of humanism." Environmental theorists have argued that humanist and anthropocentric assumptions permeate modern Western (and increasingly non-Western) societies and are partly responsible for our failure to break the vicious cycle of environmental destruction (White 1967; Merchant 1980; Plumwood 2002). Moreover, recent research in animal ethology complicates Donne's argument by demonstrating that humans are far from the only creatures who experience what we call love. The biologist Bernd Heinrich, for example, finds the long-term bonding behavior of ravens to be particularly like that of humans: "I suspect they [ravens] fall in love like we do," he writes, "simply because some kind of internal reward is required to maintain a long-term pair bond" (Heinrich 1999, 341).

Bad weather in *Frankenstein*

Literary texts express a wide range of emotions toward non-human nature, including pride, hatred, fear, and disgust but also compassion, love, admiration, and desire. Since the Renaissance, literature has played a key role in configuring and circumscribing *humanitas* as a realm of value and substance distinct from nonhuman nature. Yet literary texts also voice contextualizing counter-perspectives that bring us closer to nature and trouble our sense of difference and dominion.

Victor Frankenstein, the (anti-)hero of Mary Shelley's novel *Frankenstein* (1818), is heir to the Enlightenment project of dominating and alienating nature. Early scenes show Victor cavorting happily amidst the lakes and mountain tops of his Swiss home region. Later chapters, however, follow Victor's trajectory from Rousseauistic child of nature to science prodigy involved in obscure experimental research designed, as he puts it, to "penetrate into the recesses of nature, and shew how she works in her hiding places" (Shelley 1996, 28). However, nature strikes back in the form of terrible weather. Already in his first letter the explorer Robert Walton writes that he feels "a cold northern breeze play upon my cheek" and is drawn to the North Pole as "the seat of frost and desolation" (Shelley 1996, 7). As the narration is taken over first by Victor and then by his nameless creature, the novel continues to accumulate references to storm, thunder, fog, rain, snow, ice, and cold, as when Victor is surprised by a storm after seeking refuge in the French Alps:

> I quitted my seat, and walked on, although the darkness and storm increased every minute, and the thunder burst with a terrific crash over my head. It was echoed from Saleve, the Juras, and the Alps of Savoy; vivid flashes of lightning dazzled my eyes, illuminating the lake, making it appear like a vast sheet of fire; then for an instant everything seemed of a pitchy darkness, until the eye recovered itself from the

preceding flash. The storm, as is often the case in Switzerland, appeared at once in various parts of the heavens. The most violent storm hung exactly north of the town, over that part of the lake which lies between the promontory of Belrive and the village of Copet. Another storm enlightened Jura with faint flashes; and another darkened and sometimes disclosed the Mole, a peaked mountain to the east of the lake. (1996, 48)

Critics of novels have normally classified weather, wind, and other climatic and environmental factors as secondary and epiphenomenal compared to the human drama that is believed to drive fictional narratives. Along these lines, the frequent storms in *Frankenstein* can be interpreted as symbolic representations of the mental and emotional chaos that torments the Frankenstein family generally and the protagonist Victor Frankenstein specifically. Yet both Mary Shelley's letters and various historical sources confirm that the weather *was* extreme in the summer of 1816, which Mary and her husband Percy spent with their romantic poet friend Lord Byron in a large house on Lake Geneva in Switzerland. In that year, people in countries across the northern hemisphere experienced unusually cold, rainy, windy, and unstable weather conditions. Scientists have later established that the 1816 "year without a summer" was the result of a global climate catastrophe on the other side of the planet. In 1815, the Indonesian volcano Tambora erupted, killing some 80,000 people and spewing enormous quantities of ash into the atmosphere. These particles blocked out the rays of the sun, reduced air quality, and caused a long period of unstable weather in Europe and North America (Bate 2000, 96; Phillips 2006; Wood 2014).

Readers of *Frankenstein* will notice not only how often the bad weather is mentioned, but also how closely it is connected to a single character: Frankenstein's disowned and maligned Creature. As the Creature points out, he is resistant to extreme climate and temperatures: "The desert mountains and dreary glaciers are my refuge ... the caves of ice, which I only do not fear, are a dwelling to me" (Shelley 1996, 66). Other characters, however, experience the Creature as giving palpable shape to hostile climatic forces. When Victor first re-encounters his Creature, he reports that "a mist came over my eyes, and I felt a faintness seize me; but I was quickly restored by the cold gale of the mountains" (65). Later the two combatants meet on the Orkney islands amidst a desolate and appalling landscape' (113) before they pull each other to death in a final struggle on the ice-covered Arctic: "Follow me," the Creature challenges his creator: "I seek the everlasting ices of the north, where you will feel the misery of cold and frost to which I am impassive" (142).

Literature has the power to both conceal and reveal how closely we are bound up with nature. We are unaccustomed to thinking of wind and weather as central categories of literary analysis, but *Frankenstein* challenges us to consider wind, weather, climate, and other aspects of the physical environment as forces possessing a powerful and troubling agency rather than a mere backdrop to human decisions and actions. The weather makes a difference and plays a role in *Frankenstein*, as it increasingly does in our own climate-troubled age. Chakrabarty (2009) argues that anthropogenic (human-made) climate change dethrones the human being as the sole subject of history and forces us to realize how deeply and inextricably natural history is imbricated in human history and vice versa. Shelley's novel remains timely reading because it destabilizes traditional dichotomies and questions conventional understandings of what counts as important/unimportant, exterior/interior, or central/peripheral.

From Samsø to Ogoniland

Ecocritics debate and question the value, usefulness, multiple meanings, and possible pitfalls of concepts like "nature" and "environment." Some recommend abandoning the concept of nature altogether, because they think that it imprisons thinking in melancholy yearning for an unspoiled otherness that could never exist and probably never existed in the first place (Morton 2007; Žižek 2008). At the same time, there has been a broader shift toward the concepts of "sustainability" and "sustainable development," which was first defined by the Brundtland World Commission (1987) as "development that meets the needs of the present without compromising the ability of future generations to meet their own needs" (1987, 27).

There are different kinds of "green" literature informed by different understandings of nature. The Danish author Thorkild Bjørnvig (1918–2004) wrote both ecopoetry and ecocriticism before these became critical buzzwords. From his base on the rural island of Samsø, Bjørnvig commented and protested everything from nuclear power to industrial whaling, pesticide use, the building of motorways, vivisection, deforestation, and oil pollution. Here is a stanza from his well-known poem about the grebe (a freshwater diving bird) that is dying because its feathers are covered in a slick of waste oil:

It doesn't fly, as expected—
an oilclot on its breast
has softly infiltrated,
has lamed its faculties, its urge
to sing, to mate and multiply,
to swim, fly, and dive,
to hunt, catch, devour—
all the joys of its body;
has struck it down like a fatal illness:
a drop, a floating speck,
and mineral leprosy
mats its feathers like glue. (Bjørnvig 1987, 509)

Bjørnvig does not address the destruction of nature as a historically, culturally, and socially specific phenomenon. Instead he uses mythopoeic terms to diagnose a catastrophic mental, philosophical, and emotional collapse, which has fatally distorted modern Western man's being-in-the-world. It remains unclear when precisely the technology-obsessed Prometheus overpowered his more empathetic brother (Bjørnvig 1998, 459–64). But it is certain, as Bjørnvig points out in a polemic with his poet colleague Poul Henningsen, that the crisis of nature and the evils of modern civilization stem from our inability to understand and recognize that nature has its own life and does not exist as a resource that we can exploit at our pleasure: "For me nature ... is alive and mysterious, and whatever we do to it—or refrain from doing—we should do *also* for nature's sake" (Bjørnvig 1978, 35 [my translation]).

Rooted in romanticism, deep ecology, and animal rights discourse, Bjørnvig's writing resonates with what has been called ecocriticism's "first wave" (Buell 2005, 13–28), which concerned itself with literary revaluation and canon formation tended to see nature and human beings as opposed to one another, and held that the proper response of environmental criticism should be to help protect the natural environment from the despoliations of human culture. The Nigerian Ken Saro-Wiwa (1941–1995) was Africa's perhaps best-known nature writer and environmental activist. Saro-Wiwa led the Movement for the Survival of the Ogoni People (MOSOP) in its struggle to stop the poisoning of the Ogoni people's farm lands and fishing waters, which began with intensive oil extraction in the 1960s. In poetry, novels, plays, and TV series, Saro-Wiva exposed the complicity of multinational oil corporations (especially Shell and Chevron) in the social and environmental destruction of Ogoniland. Increasingly powerful and intolerable to the corrupt military regime, he was imprisoned, convicted, and finally hanged.

One of Saro-Wiwa's last texts is the poem "Ogoni! Ogoni!" (1995):

Ogoni is the land
The people, Ogoni
The agony of trees dying
In ancestral farmlands
Streams polluted weeping
Filth into murky rivers
It is the poisoned air
Coursing the luckless lungs
Of dying children
Ogoni is the dream
Breaking the looping chain
Around the drooping neck
Of a shell-shocked land. (Astley 2007, 80)

Both Bjørnvig's "The Grebe" and Saro-Wiwa's "Ogoni! Ogoni!" are works of "petromodernity" (LeMenager 2014, 67) lamenting the tragic consequences of the West's dependency on cheap fossil fuels. With images of a poisoned, impoverished, and diseased nature, these poems provide compatible yet different versions of "toxic discourse" (Buell 1998). Bjørnvig's speaker is shaken to his core when he sees how "mighty nature" is "reduced" (Bjørnvig 1987, 508) to an industrial waste product. In Saro-Wiwa's poem, the tone is more impassioned and the crisis more specific. The rivers, children, and ancestral agricultural lands in the Niger Delta did not contaminate themselves. "Shell-shocked land" is a suggestive, provocative, and potentially risky metaphor to end on, which almost explicitly identifies a guilty party well-known to the poem's Western readers.

Bjørnvig tends to regard nature as a pristine realm that is compromised by man's contaminating otherness, but Saro-Wiwa counters political corruption with the hope of other, more productive hybridizations. As emphasized by the poem's initial chiasmus, "Ogoni" is the name both of the land and of the people who inhabit the land, an ambiguous word that rhymes with "agony" but instills both pain and hope. From Saro-Wiwa's perspective, there is no sense in differentiating oil's polluting effect on nature from its socially, economically, and culturally destructive consequences, for they are inextricably interwoven aspects of the oil corporations' "deadly ecological war on the Ogoni" (Saro-Wiwa 1995, 13). Saro-Wiwa's poem gives us no reason to believe that there is, has been, or could ever be a nature in which man is not always already implicated.

What is at stake in the relationship between these writers, then, is different approaches to the endlessly problematic concept of nature, as well as different ways of engaging readers to practice on nature's behalf. Bjørnvig's nature poetry encourages us to consider how we can restore to nature a part of its lost autonomy, for example by withdrawing our sphere of activity and establishing sanctuaries in which nature can be itself without human interference. The problem in Saro-Wiwa's texts, by contrast, is not whether people have the right to use nature's resources, but rather how closely ecocide is bound up with social inequality, neo-colonialism, and transnational capitalism. Whereas Bjørnvig's poetry seems commensurable with traditional (and worthy) environmentalist causes like nature conservation and the protection of endangered species, Saro-Wiwa's texts orient their readers toward other constellations combining sustainability (a term that Saro-Wiva never uses) with environmental justice, minority rights, and socio-economic development.

Further reading

Among many anthologies of nature-oriented literature, books like *Wild Reckoning* (Burnside and Riordan 2004), *The Thunder Mutters* (Oswald 2006), and *Earthshattering* (Astley 2007) mix canonical and contemporary texts to show that nature poetry encompasses much more than simple lyrical celebration or finger-wagging didacticism. Bill McKibben's voluminous *American Earth* (2008) focuses on the US tradition of non-fictional nature writing. *Granta 102* (Cowley 2008) stimulated today's growing interest in "the new nature writing," which differs from the old nature writing by being less complacent and elitist, better informed by science, and more aware of social and ecological crisis.

In *The Future of Environmental Criticism* (2005), Lawrence Buell proposed dividing ecocriticism into two "waves," but Pippa Marland's (2013) three- or four-wave revision of this model shows how explosively ecocriticism has expanded and how stubbornly it now resists being surveyed or generalized. At the same time, the increasing academic visibility and respectability of ecocriticism mean that there are now numerous book-length introductions to nature-oriented literary and cultural study. Among these, the most useful is probably still Greg Garrard's *Ecocriticism* (2004/2011). *The Cambridge Companion to Literature and the Environment* (Westling 2013) includes student-friendly introductions to different topics, while *The Cambridge Introduction to Literature and the Environment* (Clark 2010) is written by a trained deconstructivist with a keen eye for irony and paradox.

Originating in the United States and to a lesser extent the United Kingdom, ecocriticism remains an English-dominated discourse, and many if not most nature-oriented studies of non-Anglophone writers and text are (like this essay) written in English. Patrick Murphy's early *Literature of Nature: An International Sourcebook* (1998) has essays on writers from countries like Germany, Malta, Romania, Japan, Korea, India, China, and Russia. Among more specialized studies, Axel Goodbody's *Nature, Technology and Cultural Change in Twentieth-Century German Literature* (2007) places Germany on the ecocritical map, while *The Natural World in Latin American Literatures* (Kane 2010) tries to do something similar for Latin America. The journal *Ecozon@* (www.ecozona.eu) publishes articles in German, French, Spanish, and Italian (but mostly in English). However, Asian ecocriticism is flourishing, and *East Asian Ecocriticisms: A Critical Reader* (Estok and Kim 2013) makes parts of it available (in English).

Anthropogenic climate change is ubiquitous in political and scientific debate, but until recently literary critics seemed slow or reluctant to tackle this wicked subject. Recently, however, this has begun to change with the appearance of both theoretical texts (Cohen 2012), general genre surveys (Trexler 2015), and specialized eco-historical studies (Wood 2014). The complexities and challenges of climate change far surpass those of all previous environmental problems, and it remains to be seen whether "global warming criticism" (Bate 2000, 245) will separate itself from the larger ecocritical field and establish itself as a critical domain in its own right.

References

Astley, Neil (ed.) (2007) *Earth Shattering: Ecopoems*, London: Bloodaxe.
Atwood, Margaret (2003) *Oryx and Crake*, London: Bloomsbury.

Bacigalupi, Paolo (2009) *The Wind-Up Girl*, New York: Nightshade.

Bate, Jonathan (2000) *The Song of the Earth*, London: Picador.

Bjørnvig, Thorkild (1978) *Også for naturens skyld: Økologiske essays*, Copenhagen: Gyldendal.

Bjørnvig, Thorkild (1987) "Poetry," Trans. Marilyn Nelson Waniek, *The Literary Review*, 30: 507–10.

Bjørnvig, Thorkild (1998) *Samlede digte*, Copenhagen: Gyldendal.

Buell, Lawrence (1995) *The Environmental Imagination: Thoreau, Nature Writing, and the Formation of American Culture*, Cambridge: Harvard University Press.

Buell, Lawrence (1998) "Toxic Discourse," *Critical Inquiry*, 24: 639–65.

Buell, Lawrence (2005) *The Future of Environmental Criticism: Environmental Crisis and Literary Imagination*, London: Blackwell.

Burnside, John and Maurice Riordan (ed.) (2004) *Wild Reckoning: An Anthology Provoked by Rachel Carson's "Silent Spring,"* London: Calouste Gulbenkian Foundation.

Chakrabarty, Dinesh (2009) "The Climate of History: Four Theses," *Critical Inquiry*, 35: 197–22.

Clark, Timothy (2010) *The Cambridge Introduction to Literature and the Environment*, Cambridge: Cambridge University Press.

Cohen, Tom (2012) *Telemorphosis: Theory in the Age of Climate Change*, Ann Arbor: Open Humanities Press.

Coupe, Lawrence (2000) *The Green Studies Reader: From Romanticism to Ecocriticism*, London: Routledge.

Cowley, Jason (ed.) (2008) *Granta 102: The New Nature Writing*, London: Granta.

Crutzen, Paul J. and E. F. Stoermer (2000) "The 'Anthropocene,'" *Global Change Newsletter*, 41: 17–18.

Donne, John (2000) *The Major Works*, Oxford: Oxford University Press.

Ehrenfeld, David (1978) *The Arrogance of Humanism*, New York: Oxford University Press.

Eliot, T. S. (1975) *Selected Prose*, New York: Harcourt Brace Jovanovich.

Estok, Simon C. and Won-Chung Kim (ed.) (2013) *East Asian Ecocriticisms: A Critical Reader*, London: Palgrave.

Garrard, Greg (2004/2011) *Ecocriticism*, London: Routledge.

Glotfelty, Cheryll (1996) "Introduction: Literary Studies in an Age of Environmental Crisis," in Cheryl Glotfelty and Harold Fromm (eds), *The Ecocriticism Reader: Landmarks in Literary Ecology*, Athens, Georgia: University of Georgia Press, xv–xxxvii.

Goodbody, Axel (2007) *Nature, Technology and Cultural Change in Twentieth-Century German Literature: The Challenge of Ecocriticism*, London: Palgrave.

Harrison, Robert Pogue (1993) *Forests: The Shadow of Civilization*, Chicago: University of Chicago Press.

Heinrich, Bernd (1999) *Mind of the Raven*, New York: HarperCollins.

Kane, Adrian Taylor (ed.) (2010) *The Natural World in Latin American Literatures: Ecocritical Essays on Twentieth Century Writings*, Jefferson: McFarland.

Kerridge, Richard (2006) "Environmentalism and Ecocriticism," in Patricia Waugh (ed.), *Literary Theory and Criticism: An Oxford Guide*, Oxford: Oxford University Press, 530–43.

Kolbert, Elizabeth (2014) *The Sixth Extinction: An Unnatural History*, London: Bloomsbury.

LeMenager, Stephanie (2014) *Living Oil: Petroleum Culture in the American Century*, Oxford: Oxford University Press.

Marland, Pippa (2013) "Ecocriticism," *Literature Compass*, 10: 846–68.

McKibben, Bill (ed.) (2008) *American Earth: Environmental Writing Since Thoreau*, New York: Library of America.

Merchant, Carolyn (1980) *The Death of Nature: Women, Ecology and the Scientific Revolution*, New York: HarperCollins.

Morton, Timothy (2007) *Ecology Without Nature*, Cambridge: Harvard University Press.

Murphy, Patrick (ed.) (1998) *Literature of Nature: An International Sourcebook*, New York: Fitzroy Dearborn.

Oswald, Alice (ed.) (2006) *The Thunder Mutters: 101 Poems for the Planet*, London: Faber and Faber.

Phillips, Bill (2006) "*Frankenstein* and Mary Shelley's 'Wet Ungenial Summer,'" *Atlantis*, 28: 58–68.

Plumwood, Val (2002) *Environmental Culture: The Ecological Crisis of Reason*, New York: Routledge.

Saro-Wiwa, Ken (1995) *A Month and a Day: A Detention Diary*, London: Penguin.

Schätzing, Frank (2007) *The Swarm*, London: William Morrow.

Shelley, Mary (1996) *Frankenstein*, New York: Norton.

Trexler, Adam (2015) *Anthropocene Fictions: The Novel in a Time of Climate Change*, Charlottesville: University of Virginia Press.

Westling, Louise (ed.) (2013) *The Cambridge Companion to Literature and the Environment*, Cambridge: Cambridge University Press.

White, Lynn Jr. (1967) "The Historical Roots of Our Ecologic Crisis," *Science*, 155 (3767): 1203–7.

Williams, Raymond (1983) *Keywords. A Vocabulary of Culture and Society*, Oxford: Oxford University Press.

Wood, Gillen D'Arcy (2014) *Tambora: The Eruption That Changed the World*, Princeton, NJ: Princeton University Press.

World Commission on Environment and Development (1987) *Our Common Future*, Oxford: Oxford University Press.

Žižek, Slavoj (2008) "Nature and Its Discontents," *SubStance*, 117: 37–72.

21

Place

Frederik Tygstrup

I would like there to exist places that are stable, unmoving, intangible, untouched and almost untouchable, unchanging, deep-rooted; places that might be points of reference, of departure, of origin:/My birthplace; the cradle of my family, the house where I may have been born, the tree that I might have seen grow (that my father may have planted the day I was born), the attic of my childhood filled with intact memories …/Such places don't exist, and it's because they don't exist that space becomes a question, ceases to be self-evident, ceases to be incorporated, ceases to be appropriated. Space is a doubt: I have constantly to mark it, to designate it. It's never mine, never given to me, I have to conquer it. (Perec 1999, 90–1)

This passage from Georges Perec's 1974 prose book *Species of Spaces and Other Places* is an exercise, and indeed a very erecian one, in reflexive nostalgia. The nostalgic longing for a sense of belonging, a sense of home, is not, according to Perec, directed toward an actual place or a specific moment in the past; rather it addresses an imaginary place, the place "where I may have been born," as it is characteristically put in a subjunctive mode. Perec does not express a longing for the place of his childhood and the attic replete with the stuff of memory, but a longing for the *idea* of the place of childhood and of an attic to explore. Perec sees nostalgia as a cultural fact rather than as an individual disposition. To his mind, it is a general condition that "such places don't exist" (even though he was perhaps particularly prone to see this, having grown up with distant relatives under a false name during the Second World War).

Nostalgia, in its reflective mode, is ambivalent, torn between two competing existential modalities. On the one hand, it nurtures the idea of home and the attachment to a specific place, while on the other it acknowledges to be subjected to an un-homely space that must be conquered anew in every moment, all while longing for the imaginary home. This distinction between a homely place and an un-homely space abounds in countless variants in modern cultural criticism and literary theory. Marc Augé, the prominent French anthropologist, has suggested the notion of "non-places" to characterize an array of modern social spaces as airports, shopping malls, corporate headquarters, and so on (Augé 1992). Nonplaces are anonymous, functionally optimized and thoroughly rational spaces designed to accommodate dwelling and passing in the most convenient way, dictated by the smoothness of transportation, consumption, production, or any other rationale. And it is precisely this focus on a single objective that confers the character of nonplaces on such spaces. Places proper are per contrast understood as intimate, complex, and saturated with significance, that is, evading the unilateral demand of goal-oriented rationality. Place, thus, appears as a specimen of provisory, protected enclosures of difference and autonomy vis-à-vis the dominant social spaces, as "other spaces" or what Michel Foucault notoriously baptized "heterotopies" in a talk given in 1967 (Foucault 1994). In this way, a distinction emerges between space as something rational and objective, a dominant ordering of the world according to clear and constraining rules, and place as something subjective and affective with no clear delimitation between outside and inside, between the body and it surrounding, between atmosphere and feeling.

In sociological parlance, the demise of such an originary experience of place in favor of a rational and efficient organization of space is a result of social modernization, the "disenchantment" of the world, as Max Weber suggestively put it. To this perspective, the nostalgia diagnosed by Perec appears not only as a longing for an imaginary home but also for a different age, where a more profound sense of continuity in the life of the individual would allegedly still be tangible, where the attic replete with tokens of childhood memories might exist somewhere, where the enchanted places of childhood could be revisited. Thus the nostalgic feeling reveals itself to be a threefold longing: for an idealized home, for a historical past, and indeed for an individual past entrenched in the former. This threefold longing is a prominent feature of modernity, a reaction to accelerated pace of transformation of social life, where traditional life forms are discarded and replaced by rational social bonds, where "everything solid melts into air," as Marx and Engels famously put it in *The Communist Manifesto*. And where we, consequently, dream of comforting and unchangeable places in utopian—or heterotopian—seclusion from the torrent of modernization.

The spatial turn

It has become a commonplace that a "turn" toward the question of space has occurred in the arts, sciences, and culture at large throughout the twentieth century, prompting a new set of problems pertaining to our understanding of space and our experience of space. The nineteenth century, per contrast, fashioned time, not least in the guise of different philosophies of history, abundantly producing histories of nature, of species, of nations, and of the lives of individuals. While time, and the quintessentially temporal nature of whatever exists, was scrutinized in so many innovative ways, space somehow appeared as a more immediately accessible resource—a wide and open field for new explorations, for imperialist ventures, for instructive traveling. This balance was gradually getting skewed throughout the twentieth century, and the accelerated process of modernization is not only rendering the comforting and traditional places of an inherited culture precarious, space now also appears as a *finite* resource in a new and problematic way. The enthusiastic measuring of the world in the romantic era, vividly described in Daniel Kehlmann's novel of that name from 2005, eventually came to an end; wars became world wars, societies became mass societies, and all of a sudden the globe itself shrank into an endangered and precarious place. The spatial turn appears in this context as an emerging sense that space is not a resource, but a problem, and that we consequently will have to rethink science, politics, and existence in different, now spatial terms. Marcel Proust opens *Remembrance of Things Lost* by letting his protagonist get lost in space. Halfway dozing, delicately balancing somewhere between sleep and wake, he lies in the dark and cannot determine where he actually is: if he is at home, perhaps traveling, or if he resides in one of the many rooms generously provided by onirism or by reminiscing. In this nebulous state he experiences, at is goes, "everything revolved around me in the darkness: things, places, years" (Proust 2015, 6).

The spatial turn betokens an increasing awareness that space is *complicated*, something that can no longer be evinced with any immediate certainty. As Perec remarks, "spaces have multiplied, been broken up and have diversified. There are spaces today of every kind and every size, for every use and every function. To live is to pass from one space to another, while doing your very best not to bump yourself" (Perec 1999, 6) Accordingly, the spatial turn has given rise to still more—and still more differentiated—ways of describing and understanding space.

Modernity's sense of space, as incepted in the Renaissance, is based on the idea of positionality: space is infinite, continuous, and homogenous, and every single thing and event in the world can be indexed by the unique position they occupy in this space. This view was afforded by the development of modern astronomy, as Galileo and Kepler described the planets precisely as moving bodies in space, and further developed in Newtonian physics, from where it was again extended into a general epistemological doctrine, as formulated in the Kantian critical philosophy, where it now becomes a general condition of possibility for any experience that the object of experience is situated in such a positional space.

This understanding of space is still with us, and by now there is no thing that we cannot pin down with utmost precision to its three coordinates (x, y, z). In this sense, there is a direct lineage from Galileo to GPS. There is no point that we cannot map, as there is indeed no place into which we cannot transport ourselves in a matter of the briefest time, we have indeed succeeded in making the globe a small and handy object. But at the same time, this increasing homogeneity notwithstanding, it is as if still more differences also crop up at the same time; it might well be that we are able to measure out space with still more accuracy, but we also seem to use the space in which we live in still more complex ways. The girl in the seat across from me in the commuter train is close by indeed, our knees almost touch, but she is engaged in a conversation with somebody in another country, and the guy next to her is streaming live television from a different continent, all while the mobile box in which we are sitting together takes us from one city to the next and I watch the birds outside. The use of space is a question of the *relations* that are being set up between different positions, and we forge such relations in still more complex ways and aided by still more advanced technologies. It might be, thus, that space is compressed and the globe is shrinking, but the spatial relations we activate, use, and participate in during the course of a day are becoming still more entrenched, an intricately braided network of relations.

Production of space

The spatial turn has brought a new and acute attention toward the use of space and the ways in which this usage can be described. Or put differently: toward space as a concrete network of relations between relative positions, rather than a system of absolute positions. The turn has perhaps most notably been conceptualized by French sociologist and urbanist, Henri Lefebvre. In his seminal book from 1974, *The Production of Space,* he argues that space should be described through those spatial practices that are particular to actual and historically specific societal formations. The organization of social production, as he programmatically put it, is not just something that takes place in a localized space; it is a historical production of space in its own right. And this production of space, in turn, takes place at a number of different levels at the same time: in the organization and manipulation of the material world, as we build space; in the social and cultural modes of understanding and forms of intuition, through which we verbalize and conceive of spatial relations; and in the organization of our social habits and routines that frame our experience of space. With Lefebvre, thus, we turn to the space that appears through actual human practice, on an individual level as well as for society at large.

In a philosophical perspective, Lefebvre's conceptual move had already been prepared by the phenomenological thinking of the early twentieth century and the way in which phenomenologists turned their interest toward the specificities of the everyday experience of the world. Against the classic modern idea of the abstract homogeneity of space, they argued that space always appears in a singular way, according to the context of the perceiving subject. Hence, the space of the world around us always comes with a perspectival distortion, distributing what can be seen and what remains invisible. This perspectival twist obviously pertains to the physical field of vision, but throughout the phenomenological tradition a set of further perspectival mechanisms has successively been recorded. Take for instance the peculiar character and quality of the attention we direct toward our surroundings: the architect, the shopper, the pickpocket, the lover, they all see different aspects of the city they pass through, they are attentive to different relational patterns that make up the spaces in which their distinct, individual experiences take place. Or take the moods and atmospheres of certain places, and indeed the way in which we might in some situations be attuned to such ineffable spatial presences, and in others not. So rather than talking about space tout court, we should distinguish between spaces of intuition, spaces of agency, spaces of moods, and many other spaces as well, as they appear according to different ways of being present in a situation. This is the basis on which Lefebvre can assert that it does not suffice to understand that human practice unfolds in space: this practice also and continuously creates, reproduces, and transforms a shared social space.

Representation of space

When Perec notes that "there are spaces today of every kind and every size, for every use and every function," what he designates is in fact this perspectival polyvalence that comes with the social production of space. *Species of Spaces* is organized accordingly. The book departs from the child's well-known, thoughtful fabulation on her address: Paris, France, Europe, The World, The Universe ... Perec then further details this series of convoluted spaces by taking his departure the same place as did Proust, namely the bed, and going from there to the room, the apartment, the house, the quarter, the city, the country, and so forth. The historian of ideas, Michel Serres, has noted that such an innocuous zoom from the close to the distant might once have been a simple and unproblematic gesture. Thus, Balzac could open a novel somewhere in the skies over France to end up by placing his protagonist on a street corner in Paris. In distinction, it seems to be a common experience to most writers of the twentieth century that this continuity has been disrupted, and that a new approach to description must be devised for every leap in scale. This is precisely what is at stake in Perec's novel as well, where the series of focalizations in passing from the bed to the universe gives rise to a number of conspicuously different descriptive modes.

Perec's take on this is, as always, experimental. The rule of this game is to come up with a new representational strategy for each new level of scale introduced. Perec is not a raconteur in any traditional sense, he confects conceptual artworks forged in language, always laying out meticulous rules, as when he wrote *La Disparition* (eng. *A Void*) with the one rule that the letter "e" were not to be used. The experiment conducted in *Species of Spaces* could perhaps similarly be conveyed as an attempt to draw a series of scale-specific maps in a medium not commonly used for this purpose, that is language. Every formation of space, every step en route from the bed to the universe, presents themselves to consciousness as distinctly different. The mood in a house, the rhythm of a street, the sound of a city—such different spatial phenomena testify to very different sorts of human practice, and they are consequently approached and captured through different literary strategies. This eventually gives a particularly playful note to the book, as Perec tests out a number of different writing strategies: scenic fragments, lists, notes, project blueprints, reflections, continuously on the watch for novel modes of description and perspectives on space. Every place in its particular language.

A long tradition, going back at least to Lessing' famous poetologic treatise from 1766, *Laookon*, has considered literature to be a predominantly temporal medium, in distinction to the allegedly more spatial order of the image. This of course hinges on the way in which we take in information through the two media: reading a text is a temporal process, while an image can be read in a single glance; the text appears as a sequence, the image as a composition. In keeping with this medial difference it has become common to extend this difference to also pertain to the content that they convey, and thus to consider literature as most apt for describing processes in time and images for depicting spatial matters. In the case of literature, this view has then usually been corroborated by focusing strongly on narrative as the main feature of literature, the plot as the centerpiece which can be assorted with necessary descriptions of places and persons.

If, however, one sets out to examine literature's power to describe space and spatial phenomena beyond what are mere accessories to a plot, there is in fact an entire panoply of forms of evoking space. First, there are all the different ways in which narrative and description actually intermingle. A location can be described by way of the narrative of an itinerary across it or within it, and more generally almost any narrative of some practice will implicitly set out some of the spatial particularities of the location of that practice. Inversely, there is no verbal description of any thing or any spatial environment that could not have been developed differently, with another approach, with an other perspective. One prominent force of the medium of the text—and generally an undertheorized one, really—is precisely this immense versatility in its approach to space; contrary to iconic descriptions, the text is able to focus in and highlight those specific relations that make up the particular qualities of a place, be it a specific mood, some unique sensual presence, an insight, an encounter that gives this place its very own signature. Once that we learn to appreciate the complex and multifaceted nature of spatial phenomena, that is that space is thus not a simple matter of positionality, but a hugely permutable environment formed by our individual and social agency and in turn forming the conditions of further agency, then we will be able to see how literature and more broadly textuality is an exquisite medium for the representation of space.

Cartography

To Perec, the text is a kind of map. Text allows you to plot and sketch spatial relations that can only difficultly be grasped in other media. Here Perec has retained another insight animating the turn toward space: that cartography is not only a matter of drawing visual, metric maps, but might include a wide range of other techniques as well. The traditional map charts one kind of spatial relations, those that can be plotted metrically, but many other relations may be just as relevant. In a famous essay on the Bonaventura hotel in Los Angeles, "Postmodernism, or the Cultural Logic of Late Capitalism," American literary scholar Fredric Jameson showed that this piece of postmodern architecture can actually only be rendered through a meticulous stitching together of experiential, imaginary, and speculative interactions and relations, a space that should be actually *read* rather than just measured up (Jameson 1991). Reading and writing, putting bits and pieces of information together and organizing them in signifying webs of interactions, is the adequate practice to understand and render the cultural production of space.

The turn toward space in this sense not only has its impetus from a fascination with geography and its measuring of the world but also from a critique of the known, traditional maps. The atlas and the globe have been such wonderfully useful instruments that we are prone to take them for objective representations of the world. We easily come to forget that the relation between the map and the territory is always a strategic one, the map being part of a practice of mastering the territory, and consequently that the historical changes to the territories we need to maneuver demand other maps The critique of the old maps and the invention of new ones have gone hand in hand, the gradual deperishment of the first propelling the advent of the latter.

In "The Agency of Mapping," James Corner forcefully argued against the idea of the map as a neutral and transparent recording of space. To map is always precisely a situated agency that stems from precise interests and entails concrete consequences. The Mercator-projection, for instance, as it was devised in the Renaissance to eventually become the predominant technique of mapping, is eminently suitable for navigating the large seas, despite of the evident flaw that it radically distorts the actual sizes of the continents. But we need maps for other purposes too, and thus to also go beyond the Mercator genre. In general, according to Corner, we need to think of the map as a combination of a specific selection of empirical elements to be mapped, a system of salient relations to be marked out between these elements, and finally a specific mode and medium of notation. The medium might be a metrical chart, but it could also be a different distribution of lines, surfaces, and colors, like when the geographer Nigel Thrift once remarked that the best maps, the best renditions of space, to his knowledge were the canvases by the Ethiopian-American painter Julie Merethu (Thrift 2006, 140). By the same token, Irit Rogoff has shown how the social and historical transformations necessitating new ways of representing space have given rise to an intense interest for maps and different techniques of mapping in the art of the twentieth century (Rogoff 2000). The literary experiments conducted by Perec to invent novel strategies for representation of space are affiliated to this endeavor.

When literature takes place

The particular qualities of writing are specifically emphasized by Perec and he amends the series of spaces that ranges from the bed to the entire globe by adding one more: the space of the written page. However counterintuitive this might seem at first glance, the page in a book can arguably be said to have a particular space of its own, already in the way in which letters and words are distributed on the page. And in a few more respects as well: due to the symbolic power of the text, engendering concepts and classifications that allow us to identify and distinguish a variety of spatial qualities, due to the fact that the spaces we live in are themselves imbued with writing of all sorts, ranging from the words and sentences that wrap a huge legible surface around our urban surroundings to the unfathomable mass of code writing that provides the algorithms through which information is funneled, and indeed due to the way in which writing, as Perec cannot mention, might become the home of those that haven't got any other home.

This brings us back to where we started, to the precariousness of place. If the notion of place invariably tags along with it a sense of home, of some primordial intimacy between a body and the surroundings that nurtures it, provides it with protection and support, we are by now equipped to envisage a not less intimate embrace between bodies and their spaces, not in guise of a fundamental unity, but as the continuous metabolism between the practices of our everyday lives and our environments, a metabolism continuously spurred as we breakup from one place to the next. The problem of place is thus eventually not only a matter of nostalgia, it is also a perennial challenge: how are we to go about to take in a place in the world, to inscribe ourselves in the world? Or in Perec's words, toward the end of *Species of Spaces*,

> no longer as a journey having constantly to be remade, not as a race without end, a challenge having constantly to be met, not as the one pretext for a despairing acquisitiveness, nor as the illusion of a conquest, but as the rediscovery of a meaning, the perceiving that the earth is a form of writing, a *geography* of which we had forgotten that we ourselves are the authors. (Perec 1999, 79)

Further reading

Obviously a lot has been written on the notions of space and place, and about what has been alluded to above as "the spatial turn." The literature extends to many different disciplines and even more different traditions within the disciplines.

A good and accessible introduction to theories of space and place can be found in Edward Casey's *The Fate of Place*, which offers a mainly philosophical and historical approach. A classic cultural history of space is provided by Stephen Kern in *The Culture of Time and Space* from 1983, focusing on the dramatic changes in the understanding of time and space in early twentieth century. Other neoclassical works on the spatial turn include David Harvey's *The Condition of Postmodernity* and Edward Soja's *Postmodern Geographies*, both diligently contributing to the rich dialogue between cultural studies and geography in the wake of the spatial turn.

In literary studies, Joseph Frank's 1945 essay "The Idea of Spatial Form" remains an important reference, with its acute sense for the importance of space in modernist texts and the ways in which narrative temporality is attenuated in favor of other techniques that can better be portrayed in terms of spatial distribution than of temporal succession. Although we haven't seen the development of a proper literary topology that can match the strong narratological tenet in modern literary studies, there are a number of important contributions to a spatially oriented methodology. In Germany, a pioneering work has been Elisabeth Bronfen's *Der literarische Raum* from 1986, and among numerous recent publications there is Birgit Neumann and Wolfgang Hallet's edited volume *Raum und Bewegung in der Literatur*. In France, Bertrand Westphal has written extensively about literary space, including the important *La Géocritique*.

References

Augé, Marc (1992) *Non-lieux*, Paris: Seuil.

Bronfen, Elisabeth (1986) *Der literarische Raum: eine Untersuchung am Beispiel von Dorothy M. Richardsons Romanzyklus Pilgrimage*, Tübingen: Niemeyer.

Casey, Edward (1997) *The Fate of Place: A Philosophical History*, Berkeley: University of California Press.

Corner, James (1999) "The Agency of Mapping," in J. Cornes and D. Cosgrove, *Mappings*, London: Reaktion.

Foucault, Michel (1994) "Des espaces autres," I *Dits et écrits IV*, Paris: Gallimard.

Frank, Joseph (1991) *The Idea of Spatial Form*, New Brunswick: Rutgers University Press.

Hallet, Wolfgang and Birgit Neumann (eds) (2009) *Raum und Bewegung in der Literatur: Die Literaturwissenschaft und der Spatial Turn*, Bielefeld: Transcript.

Harvey, David (2004) *The Condition of Postmodernity: An Enquiry into the Origins of Cultural Change*, Oxford: Blackwell.

Jameson, Fredric (1991) *Postmodernism, or the Cultural Logic of Late Capitalism*, Durham, NC: Duke University Press.

Kehlmann, David (2005) *Die Vermessung der Welt*, Hamburg: Rowohlt.

Kern, Stephen (1983) *The Culture of Time and Space*, London: Harvard University Press.

Lefebvre, Henri (1974) *La Production de l'espace*, Paris: Éd. Anthropos.

Perec, Georges (1974) *Espèces d'espaces*, Paris: Galilée.

Perec, Georges (1999) *Species of Spaces and Other Places*, New York: Penguin.

Proust, Marcel (1988) *A la recherche du temps perdu*, Paris: Gallimard.

Proust, Marcel (2015) *In Search of Lost Time: Swann's Way*, New York: Doubleday.

Rogoff, Irit (2000) *Terra Infirma. Geography's Visual Culture*, London: Routledge.

Ropars-Wuilleumier, Marie-Claire (2002) *Écrire l'espace*, St. Denis: Presses Universitaires de Vincennes.

Serres, Michel (1980) *Hermès V. Le passage du nord-ouest*, Paris: Minuit.

Soja, Edward W. (1998) *Postmodern Geographies*, London: Verso.

Thrift, Nigel (2006) "Space," *Theory, Culture & Society*, 23 (2–3): 139–49.

Tygstrup, Frederik (2003) "Espace et récit," in B. Westphal (éd.), *Littérature et espaces*, Limoges: Presses Universitaires de Limoges.

Tygstrup, Frederik (2007) "Still Life. The Experience of Space in Modernist Prose," in A. Eysteinsson and Vivian Liska (eds), *Modernism*, Amsterdam and Philadelphia: John Benjamins.

Westphal, Bertrand (2007) *La Géocritique. Réel, Fiction, espace*, Paris: Minuit.

22

Things

Karin Sanders

Things "endure beyond our vanishing"; Argentinian poet Jorge Luis Borges famously states in his eponymous poem: they "will never know that we have gone" (Borges 1999, 66). They live on; unaware and unconcerned about the human lives they have touched, often quite tangibly. A walking cane, coins, a key ring, notes and cards, a table and a book, a mirror, atlases, wine-glasses, nails, these "many things," he advises: "serve us, like slaves who never say a word,/Blind and so mysteriously reserved" (Borges 1999, 66). But how do blind and silent and mysterious *things* serve us?

Things often carry significance far beyond the apparent value and function they are assigned. They can speak volumes about genre, plot, personification, tropes, and so forth; they can articulate nostalgia for the authentic real or they can become uncanny if we are in doubt as to their status or ontology. They can be made to speak manifestly like anthropomorphic beings or implicitly and metaphorically. When things "come alive" in literature, they can reflect on the nature of writing (pen, ink, book) or they can serve as mnemonics within a given fictional text. Things can form poetic lists, suggest value and commodification, or serve as exotic others. In short, things take on a host of inflections, perhaps because, as Borges laconically notes in his poem, they "endure beyond our vanishing." When we are gone, they can remain, testifying to our lives, or, perhaps more troubling: remain silent about our very existence and our most precious memories, as seen in Borges' mournful suggestion: "A book, and crushed in its pages the withered/Violet, monument to an afternoon/Undoubtedly unforgettable, now forgotten" (Borges 1999, 66). To Borges, then, things become the kind of material metaphors for memory that insinuate our inevitable mortality while insisting on their own obstinate permanence.

Literature can provide material things with agency, give them power as mnemonics. But the use of things in literature also suggests that things can become something ominous and anxiety-filled for humans. When things are made to speak, the human voice is, in some sense, mimicked through them, but also potentially *lost* in them. Therefore anxieties about things' ability to take on a life of their own often make us perceive them as unruly ventriloquisms or uncanny beings. Or, if things insist on being just that, *things*, they can be seen to resist the urge by literature to make them into something else, symbolic vessels for example. As Barbara M. Benedicts has noted, things can "make and unmake themselves" and thus pose a real danger for humans because "of their replicability and fundamental indifference to human possession or loss." Things consequently "embody" the "terrible hazard[s] of living in a world of soulless material powers. They are absolute material: bodies without souls" (Benedicts 2007, 39).

This kind of the anxiety of things is not reserved for modernism, as Borges's poems might suggest, for, as Aileen Douglas has demonstrated, during the eighteenth century: "The displacement of the human voice in this later eighteenth-century fiction expresses fear and excitement [....] that people have become enthralled to things and that therefore objects can explain society as it really is; the excitement comes from the unfamiliarity and novelty of the society that objects reveal" (Douglas 2007, 150–1). But before we can investigate the various functions or meanings of things in literature, we must ask: What do we mean when we use the term *thing*?

Thing theories

The interest in materiality and material culture in literary studies in recent years has prompted the American theorist Bill Brown to coin a literary and cultural subfield called "Thing Theory." Inspired in part by Martin Heidegger, who famously asked if the thing "never yet [has] come near enough for man to learn how to attend sufficiently to the thing as thing?" (Heidegger 1971, 169), Brown posits this distinction:

> We begin to confront the thingness of objects when they stop working for us: when the drill breaks, when the car stalls, when the window gets filthy, when their flow within the circuits of production and distribution, consumption and exhibition, has been arrested, however momentarily. The story of objects asserting themselves as things, then, is the story of a changed relationship to the human subject and thus the

story of how the thing really names less an object than a particular subject-object relation. (Brown 2001, 4)

His argument is that the folding of person and thing into one (such as we see in personification, anthropomorphism, and so forth) produces a potential "unstable ontological status between the animate and the inanimate" that "threatens to transform the human into no more than an object" (Brown 2003, 97).

Another American theorist Jane Bennett's concept of material vitality adds an important facet to this understanding. She notes that when objects appear as things they are "not entirely reducible to the contexts in which (human) subjects set them, never entirely exhausted by their semiotics" (Bennett 2010, 5). In other words, the things we say about things never fully explain them. Furthermore *thing-power*—her term for vibrant matter shared by humans and things—coalesce to an ecological understanding of all things outside of us, nonhuman bodies, animals, minerals, and so on, but also those inside us, like bones. "*Thing-power*," she argues, "has the rhetorical advantage of calling to mind a childhood sense of the world as filled with all sorts of animate beings, some human, some not, some organic, some not," but, as she also acknowledges: "The term's disadvantage [...] is that it also tends to overstate the thinginess of fixed stability of materiality" (20). This means that thing-power bestows to ordinary things, made by man, the power to be themselves; be "alive" and independent outside of the complete control and comprehension of humans. Things, then, signal what W.J.T. Mitchell with Lacan calls: "the moment when the object becomes the Other, when the sardine can look back, when the mute idol speaks when the subject experiences the object as uncanny" (here cited from Bennett 2010, 2).

In some ways the new investigations into the lives of things can be seen as a response to what the French philosopher and sociologist Bruno Latour in *Reassembling the Social* sees as a sidelining of material things that are only allowed to live "like humble servants [....] on the margins of the social doing most of the work but never allowed to be represented as such" (Latour 2005, 73). Therefore, he proposes, "specific tricks have to be invented to make them talk, that is, to offer descriptions of themselves, to produce scripts of what they are making others— human or non-humans—do" (79). One of these tricks, anthropomorphism, is a possible way to explore how things *actually* say something even if, as Latour maintains, the very fact that anthropomorphism define human capabilities projected onto things, often makes us overlook the fact that things "never behave like matter of fact" (255).

Speaking things

The use of anthropomorphic things in fairy tales like Hans Christian Andersen's constitutes a slightly different kind of "trick" to make things talk. Andersen became a master at giving voice to everyday things, as in "The Darning Needle" (1847), "The Silver Shilling" (1861), and "Pen and Ink" (1860), and his virtuosity made him a regular "thing theorist" [Ding-Theoretiker], to borrow a term from the German scholar Klaus Müller-Wille (Müller-Wille 2009, 137). Things, we can add, become things in his fairy tales precisely at the moment when the illusions of straightforward anthropomorphisms are broken; when readers are forced into an experience of aesthetic distance, produced by Andersen's frequent gestures of romantic irony. By pointing to the fairy tale as an artifice ("look I am a tale"), Andersen's works illustrate in many ways what Bennett formulates, as she leans on Latour: "Humans and nonhumans alike depend on a 'fabulous complex' set of speech prostheses" (Bennett 2010, 36). Andersen's tales of anthropomorphized ink and pens and papers are particularly poignant examples of this.

Andersen, of course, did not invent the speaking thing; already in the eighteenth century the booming print culture gave birth to a series of so-called *it-narratives*. Most it-narratives made use of what Russian-American anthropologist Igor Kopytoff has called "thing-biography," a way to narrate a life story of a material entity (Kopytoff 1986, 64).

Favored things in it-narratives were coins or bank notes and this sub-genre of currency stories span centuries, but was particularly popular in eighteenth and early ninetieth centuries as indicated in this shortened list: *The Adventures of a Shilling* (1710), *The Adventures of a Bank- Note* (1770–1771), *The Adventures of a Six-and-Nine-Pence* (1774), *The Adventure of a Silver Penny* (c.1780), *The Adventures of a Rupee* (1782), *The Adventures of a Silver Three-Pence* (1800), *The Adventures of a Bad Shilling* (1805–1806), *A Month's Adventure of a Base Shilling* (1820), *Passages in the History of a Shilling* (1862) (see Bellamy 2007, 135–43). If the thing-narrator is a thing of value, like a coin, the story itself becomes a comment on value, economic as well as literary value.

These narratives often, as Christopher Flint has shown, "foregrounds authorial concerns about circulating books in the public sphere" (Flint 2007, 163). That is to say, if an "author seeks public exposure but frets over its consequences" the use of things as narrators could articulate such anxieties without appearing to "duplicate[s] the author's position" (163). Things, in other words, could serve to mask authorial anxiety, help facilitate potentially dissident voices. From safely behind the cover of an essentially "silent" material object, it was possible to speak against a given "order of things." The genre, also known as circulation novels, were seen as a low form made popular, particularly in Britain, not least among women writers who saw the genre as a way to conceal their identities at a time when potential liabilities of writing publically were acute.

It-narratives also oftentimes made use of items like furniture, clothes, or jewelry, so that, as Christopher Flint explains, the "proximity to human beings [....] invariably evoke[s] physicality, grounding their narratives in the experiences of vulnerable human bodies" (70). Furniture, in fact, has a great deal to say in studies of literary things, and nowhere more conspicuously than in the novel.

Things in novels

The novel, a genre that brings realism to its fore in the nineteenth century, is often stuffed, sometimes claustrophobically, with things. "Realism," as the Swedish literary critic Sara Danius has emphasized, "was accompanied by a historically new emphasis on things: on inert matter, everyday objects, household goods, commodities, kitsch, curiosities, *bibélots*. And because realism wanted to incorporate the thingness of the world into its descriptive discourse, it developed a penchant for the detail—say, blue soap" (Danius 2006, 27). This pendant for details can be found most crowdedly in the Victorian novel. In fact, as the American literary scholar Elaine Freedgood demonstrates in *The Ideas in Things*, the Victorian novel in particular "showers us with things: post chaises, handkerchiefs, moonstones, wills, riding crops [...] instruments of all kinds, dresses of muslin, merino, silk, coffee, claret, cutlets." The list seems endless and, as she succinctly puts it, the "cavalcades of objects threaten to crowd the narrative right off the page" (Freedgood 2006, 1). This crowded narrative space is found not least in the works of Charlotte Bronte, Elizabeth Gaskell, Charles Dickens, and Georg Elliot, and Freedgood demonstrates how Marx's theory of exchange (commodification and fetishization) makes the overflow of things in novels into social hieroglyphs. She concludes that: "Fictional objects become exchangeable figures used in the novel's symbolic system to make a point about the mechanicalness, one-dimensionality, and deadness of industrialized people. Thus, fictional things are themselves commodified" (141).

A different example of the use of things in a novel is to be found at the end of the Danish philosopher Søren Kierkegaard's *The Diary of a Seducer*. Here an arrangement of things is compiled and organized to mimic the seducer Johannes' relationship to a young woman, Cordelia. The room is full of articles that will remind her of their love story; but in reality the staging is a trap meant to induce her to give herself up to his machinations. The seducer describes "the cabinet" (a room) in his diary as "strikingly similar" to the ones Cordelia knows from homes familiar to her: "A carpet woven of osiers covers the floor; before the sofa stands a small tea table with a lamp like the one she has at home. Everything is the same only richer. Surely I must allow myself the luxury of this difference. In the salon stands a piano" and so forth: books of poetry, sheet of music are "opened" to awaken "memories" (Kierkegaard 2006, 148). The compilation of prompts are staged as a premeditated simulacrum; in the end the doors are opened for the female character to step in, as the readers are excluded from witnessing her actual entrapment and seduction, midst the many, by now, sinister things.

Things as mnemonics

An intensely physical way to think about things in novels is found in the Turkish Nobel Prize winner Orhan Pamuk's project *The Museum of Innocence*, conceived simultaneously as a novel and a museum. Pamuk's ambition is bold. Since things play a major part in this project, it will be given some extra attention here. From the inception of the project he set out to "collect and exhibit the 'real' objects of a fictional story in a museum and write a novel based on these objects" (Pamuk 2012, 15). The two projects, the assembly of things and the writing of words about the things, were feeding off each other: "The more objects I collected for the museum, the more the story in my mind progressed" (21). The novel starts with a misplaced earring, lost during secret lovemaking between the novel's protagonist Kemal and his young mistress and distant cousin Füsan. At the end of the novel, after Füsan's (now Kemal's fiancée) violent suicide by car accident, the gravely injured Kemal recasts the painful memories of their story into a tangible plan: "I was at this point—hovering between fact and remembrance, between the pain of loss and its meaning—when the idea of a museum first occurred to me" (490).

Connecting the two, novel and museum, the reader of the novel version of *The Museum of Innocence* is offered an admittance ticket, printed on one of the last pages, to the actual museum located in Istanbul—"single admission only." Although early readers of the novel would have to wait four years from the publication of the book in 2008 to the opening of the museum in 2012, they can now, with the novel in hand, travel to Istanbul as museum goers and contemplate the very earring, lost by Füsan on the first page of the novel, displayed in a glass showcase along with a multitude of other meaningful things belonging to her and described in the novel: a handbag, a belt, a shoe, and so on, physically present and exhibited as fetishistic objects to be gawked at, forcing the reader-turned-viewer to imagine a very physical body of the woman who once wore them and touched them.

In addition to the novel and the museum display, Pamuk published a catalogue in 2012 called *The Innocence of Objects*. Here the novel reader and/or museumgoer can read about the process and the careful curating of the intensely emotional things. As an intermediary between the novel and the museum display, the catalogue tries to offer a poetics, including a manifesto that posits, for example: "National museums, then, should be novels; but they are not" or "If objects are not uprooted from their environs and streets, but are situated with care and ingenuity in their natural homes, they will already portray their own stories" (Pamuk 2012, 56–7).

We could argue that Pamuk's word-thing project muddles Walter Benjamin's distinction between an allegorist and a collector. "The allegorist" Benjamin suggests in a note in his Arcades project, is "the polar opposite of the collector [....] He dislodges things from their context and, from the outset, relies on his profundity to illuminate their meaning. The collector, by contrast, brings together what belongs together; by keeping in mind their affinities and their succession in time, he can eventually furnish information about his objects" (Benjamin 2002, 211). Pamuk, it seems, does both and neither. He is not an allegorist in the sense that the things he describes are not dislodged from their context, in fact he insists on their unbreakable suturing. And he is not a collector in the Benjaminian implication of the term since his museum objects' affinity to time (and the information we have about them) is essentially fictional and fabricated.

While Pamuk's novel/museum is in many ways an unusual enterprise, the project as a whole is beholden to many features of the autobiographical genre (precisely through the insistence of the emotional value of real objects), and we can locate a series of memoirs in recent years that are likewise deeply beholden to the emotive weight of things. In Edmund de Waal's *The Hare with Amber Eyes* from 2010, for example, we follow the author's archaeological digging through the provenance of a collection of 264 Japanese miniatures called *netsuke* that were passed down from generation to generation in his Jewish family, as it went from great wealth to tragic devastation during the Nazi period. When one of De Waal's ancestors, the art connoisseur Charles Ephrussi died, "Proust writes his condolences" (De Waal 2010, 148), a subtle nod to the master of mnemonics, who potentially used Ephrussi as one of the inspirations for Swann in his *À la recherche du temps perdu*. De Waal's memoir, like Pamuk's novel, finds it *modus operandi* in things.

This is also true for Patti Smith's memoir *M train* from 2015; it is full of tings. She acknowledges in its opening line "It's not easy writing about nothing" (Smith 2015, 3), then goes on to write about café chairs and tables, coffee cups and napkins, pens and notebooks, boots and watch caps and old coats, recalling along the way what is lost (a beloved husband). She describes going on pilgrimages to collect stones from the Saint-Laurent prison to give to Jean Genet and tells us how she keeps them in a Gitanes matchbox until she can place them on his grave. Her attachment to things, beholden both to the avant-garde's *objet trouve* obsession and to a melancholic project *à la* Proust, becomes an insistence on the value of the invaluable. "Dried-up ink bottles, encrusted nibs, cartridges for pens long gone, mechanical pencils emptied of lead. Writer's debris" (27). Several photographs in the book show things like a deflating balloon, old ballet shoes, or a common coffeemaker. Memorabilia is everywhere and they summon her. Although "some precious things hold memories too painful to revisit" (37) others, like a fish lure "composed of soft purple transparent rubber, like a Juicy Fruit or a Swedish Fish, shaped like a comma with a spiraled tail" (37), transports her to sweet memories of her husband's fishing skills. Reading Ibsen's *The Master Builder*, she does not notice the symbolism that another reader points out: "I'm not much for symbolism. I never get it. Why can't things be just what they are?" (59). This passage is reminiscent of A.S. Byatt's opening of *The Biographer's Tale* from 2000, where a graduate student, fed up with his critical theory seminars, insists that a dusty windowpane is just that, a dirty thing, not a transparent window to something else. Like Smith, Byatt's graduate student wants to recuperate and restore the thing to itself (Bill Brown also points to this scene from Byatt's book in his article "Thing Theory"). To Smith, however, her resistance to symbolism does not mean that things do not *mean*. But what they mean is not merely a symbolic recuperation of what has been lost, but a way to capture, in the thing itself, a sense of being.

Looming in the annals of many late twentieth century and early twenty-first century fictional and non-fictional works on things, we find Benjamin's ideas (not least from his Arcades project) about modernity and material culture. His memoir *Berliner Kindheit*, published posthumously, however, adds a particularly personal *aura*, to borrow his own term, to his understanding of things. Often seen as a response to Proust's search for lost time, Benjamin's memoir tells of a childhood home abundantly full of stuff. At night in particular, things seem to came alive for the precocious boy, like two basins and two jugs in his bedroom, that "clinked" during a moon-filled night; but "As happy as I was to receive from my nocturnal surroundings a sign of life—be it only the echo of my own—it was nonetheless an unreliable sign, and was waiting, like a false friend, to dupe me" (Benjamin 2006, 116). The young Benjamin felt "effectively unhoused" (115) by such experiences, prompting him to contemplate the very nature of being and nonbeing. In another chapter on "Cabinets," he recounts his pressing anxiety of the power of things vis-à-vis the volatility of humans. In this case a buffet decked and ready to receive guests becomes a cause for concern: "And as I gazed at the long, long rows of coffee spoons and knife rests, fruit knives and oyster forks, my pleasure in this abundance was tinged with anxiety, least the guests we had invited would turn out to be identical to one another, like our cutlery" (158). In this case, things are not just meant as prompts to facilitate memory, but as conduits for grasping the links between house and home, and a sense of alienation and existential anxiety.

Ontological things

This returns us to the anxiety expressed in the opening poem by Borges, about the possibility that things can outlive us. A similar anxiety is fleshed out in Kafka's tale "The Cares of a Family Man" from 1917. The story tells of a "creature" by the name of Odradek and starts with the narrator's aborted attempt of an etymological explanation of the name. Although many literary scholars henceforth have tried to pin one on it, the word itself, Kafka's narrator tells us, has no "intelligent meaning" (Kafka 1971, 428). The creature turns out to be a *thing*: "a flat star-shaped spool for thread" with "broken off bits of thread, knotted and tangled together, of most varied sorts and colors." It has a "wooden crossbar" and "small rod" that allows it to "stand upright as if on two legs" (428). Kafka's thing is both "senseless" and strangely "finished." But more importantly than its semantic inscrutability and functional peculiarity is the fact that the thing, halfway through Kafka's barely two-page short story, turns from an "it" to a "he." He, the thing that looks like a spool of thread and called Odradek, lurks about in eerie ways, not in the center of the house, but in its attics, halls, and staircases, distressing the narrator. "Attics" as Walter Benjamin proposes in his analysis of the tale "are the places of the discarded, forgotten objects" (Benjamin 1968, 133). Indeed, halls and corridors evoke guilt, since this is where one is placed before being summoned to a court of law. "Odradek," Benjamin adds in his discussion of Kafka, "is the form of which things assume in oblivion. They are distorted." What both Benjamin and Kafka are pursuing is to get at a sense of things as ontological multiples (see Bennett 2010, 8). Things, then, are both our tools (slaves) and our rivals; they assist and thwart our ambitions to control the narratives we produce.

If Borges saw things as slaves and Benjamin worried that they were false friends, and Kafka described them as uncanny creatures, a commonality in most of the examples used here is an insistence on the thing-ness of the thing; its relative inability to be broken down to semantic digestibles; or to be mere metaphors for something else. This kind of insistence on the materiality of the thing as valuable in itself has parallels in the historical avant-garde's infatuation with found objects (Duchamp's urinal and so forth). In a sense this infatuation with things-as-things has never left us.

But, as we have also seen, to imagine that thing-ness was a concept born in the twentieth century would overlook important historical inflections of material cultures. Nor are thing studies exclusively part of a conversation across disciplines like literature, art history, philosophy and sociology, covering just the past few centuries.

Archaeological studies, for example, as the Norwegian scholar Bjarnar Olsen establishes in *In Defense of Things*, are rethinking their relationship to the significance of things and the concepts of the real, not least in reconsideration of what is traditionally seen as a "silent prehistory" vis-à-vis a "talkative history" (Olsen 2010, 9). And, finally, yet another modulation of thing studies can be found in so-called object-oriented ontology, which proposes that humans are no longer at the center of *things*. This theory, greatly beholden to Heidegger's ontology, places humans on equal footing with non-human material objects or animals, troubling even further our shared sense of things. With object-oriented ontology, ecocriticism, perhaps most importantly, becomes part of how we can continue to think about things.

Further reading

In addition to the works cited in this article, the reader can consult Jonathan Lamb's *The Things Things Say* about the ways in which "it-narratives" operated in eighteenth-century literature. On the topic of things in the Victorian novel, consult Leah Price *How to Do Things with Books in Victorian Britain*. She discusses how books and other printed material could turn into discarded things within the novel itself. The book as thing is also the topic of Garrett Stewart's *Bookwork. Medium to Concept to Art*. See also Babette Bärbel Tischleder's *The Literary Life of Things* that discusses how things are used in American fiction. Barbara Johnson's *Persons and Things* hones in on the relation between humans and inanimate life in fictions dealing with automatons and dolls, as does Kenneth Gross's *Puppets: An Essay on Uncanny Life*. Also Susan Stewart's *On Longing: Narratives of the Miniature, the Gigantic, the Souvenir, the Collection* offers important insights into the ways in which the scale of things can obfuscate a sense of order. For a discussion of how things and melancholia relate, please see Peter Schwenger *The Tears of Things*, and for an understanding of how a social life of things can "talk back," see Miguel Tamen *Friends of Interpretable Objects*. Finally read about object-oriented ontology in Graham Harman *Tool-Being: Heidegger and the Metaphysics of Objects* and Timothy Morton *Hyperobjects: Philosophy and Ecology after the End of the World*.

References

Bellamy, Liz (2007) "It-Narratives and Circulation: Defining a Subgenre," in Mark Blackwell (ed.), *The Secret Life of Things: Animals, Objects, and It-Narratives in Eighteenth Century England*, Lewisburg: Bucknell University Press.

Benedicts, Barbara M. (2007) "It-Narratives and Circulation: Defining a Subgenre," in Mark Blackwell (ed.), *The Secret Life of Things: Animals, Objects, and It- Narratives in Eighteenth Century England*, Lewisburg: Bucknell University Press.

Benjamin, Walter (1968) "Franz Kafka. On the Tenth Anniversary of His Death," in Hannah Arendt (ed.), *Illuminations*, New York: Schocken Books.

Benjamin, Walter (2002) "The Collector," in *The Arcades Project. Walter Benjamin*, Cambridge, MA and London: Belknap, Harvard University Press.

Benjamin, Walter (2006) *Berlin Childhood Around 1900*, Cambridge, MA and London: Belknap, Harvard University Press.

Bennett, Jane (2010) *Vibrant Matter. A Political Economy of Things*, Durham: Duke University Press.

Borges, Jorge Luis (1999) "Things," Trans. Steven Kessler, New York: *The New Yorker*, March 22, 66.

Brown, Bill (2001) "Thing Theory," in Bill Brown (ed.), *Things*, Chicago: Chicago University Press.

Brown, Bill (2003) *A Sense of Things. The Object Matter of American Literature*, Chicago: Chicago University Press.

Byatt, A. S. (2001) *The Biographer's Tale*, New York: Knopf.

Danius, Sara (2006) *Prose of the World*, Stockholm: Abm Komers.

De Waal, Edmund (2010) *The Hare with the Amber Eyes*, New York: Picador.

Douglas, Aileen (2007) "Britannia's Rule and the It-Narrator," in Mark Blackwell (ed.), *The Secret Life of Things: Animals, Objects, and It-Narratives in Eighteenth Century England*, Lewisburg: Bucknell University Press.

Flint, Christopher (2007) "Speaking Objects," in Mark Blackwell (ed.), *The Secret Life of Things: Animals, Objects, and It-Narratives in Eighteenth Century England*, Lewisburg: Bucknell University Press.

Freedgood, Elaine (2006) *The Ideas in Things. Fugitive Meaning in the Victorian Novel*, Chicago: Chicago University Press.

Heidegger, Martin (1971) *Poetry, Language, Thought*, New York: Harper & Row.

Kafka, Franz (1971) "The Cares of a Family Man," in Nahum Glatzer (ed.), *Kafka. The Complete Stories*, New York: Schocken Books.

Kierkegaard, Søren (2006) *Diary of a Seducer*. Tran. Alistair Hanney, New York: Bloomsbury Academic.

Kopytoff, Igor (1986) "The Cultural Biography of Things: Commoditization in Process," in Arjun Appadurai (ed.), *The Social Life of Things: Commodities in Cultural Perspectives*, New York: Cambridge University Press.

Latour, Bruno (2005), *Reassembling the Social*, Oxford. Oxford University Press.

Müller-Wille, Klaus (2009) "Hans Christen Andersen und die Dinge," in Klaus Müller-Wille (ed.), *Hans Christian Andersen und die Heterogetät der Moderne*, Tübingen and Basel: A Francke Vorlag.

Olsen, Bjørnar (2010) *In Defense of Things. Archaeology and the Ontology of Objects*, Lanham, New York, Toronto and Plymouth: AltaMira Press.

Pamuk, Orhan (2010) *The Museum of Innocence*, New York: Vintage International.

Pamuk, Orhan (2012) *The Innocence of Objects*, New York: Abrams.

Smith, Parri (2015) *M Train*, New York: Alfred A. Knopf.

23

Mobility

Søren Frank

We live in the age of mobility. According to John Urry, movement is not merely an observable fact defining our epoch, it has even developed into an ideology (Urry 2011, 18). We believe we have a right to move, through either physical travel or mental development. But not only that: we are actually supposed to do so. At least this is how everyone around us seem to think, which is why we also feel that we need to think so ourselves. Those of us who might wish to keep still, to remain on the spot, are badly off. As Zygmunt Bauman has remarked, "immobility is not a realistic option in a world of permanent change" (Bauman 1998, 2). Even those who physically stay where they are do not escape movement, partly because their immediate surroundings are being constantly exposed to an inevitable pressure to change, a pressure that ultimately stirs up everything.

"I have traveled a great deal in Concord" (Thoreau 2008, 6), Henry David Thoreau somewhat provocatively remarked in the mid-nineteenth century from his ultra local New England perspective. The statement, which can be found in his *Walden; or, Life in the Woods* (1854), contains a duality: on the one hand, it represents a seriously meant revolt against the American obsession with the western frontier and the transgression of this frontier through physical movement (instead, Thoreau was an exponent of traveling mentally on the spot); on the other hand, it expresses a recognition of the transformative entry of the global in the small town of Concord—not least exemplified by the piece-disturbing (the ruin of the idyll) but also potentially invigorating (the growth of commerce) presence of the railroad in the Walden woods. Thoreau remained on the spot, in a little cottage out in the woods, and tried to find traces of harmony and stasis. However, gradually he realized that life in the woods not only comprised cyclical repetition but also linear movement, and to Thoreau the irreversible change of linearity was ambiguous.

Rather than perceive mobility as something normative, as an unattractive and insurmountable duty, one can also see it as something that involves freedom, openness, and variety. That is partly why mobility, according to Bauman "climbs to the rank of the uppermost among the coveted values—and the freedom to move, perpetually a scarce and unequally distributed commodity, fast becomes the main stratifying factor of our late-modern or postmodern times" (Bauman 1998, 1–2). Whether we associate movement with something negative or positive (and for some it's the first, for others the latter), it is a fact that more people than ever before are traveling greater distances and more often (without necessarily spending more time to travel than before)—and many of them will not return to where they originally came from.

We can discern three types of events as causes behind this accelerating development. Firstly, throughout the twentieth century a series of "political" events meant that millions of people voluntarily migrated or involuntarily were forced to flee. I am thinking especially of the two world wars, the countless regional (and often ethnically or religiously motivated) wars, fascist and socialist dictatorships, the collapse of communism and the creation of the EU, but also the many natural disasters (earthquakes, drought, famine) should be mentioned in this context. Secondly, technological inventions in transport such as the car and the airplane in the twentieth century, but also the steam ship and the proliferation of railways in the early nineteenth century, have, on the one hand, made it possible for humans to overcome the (for some inhibitory, for others reassuring) gravity of the local place, while, on the other hand, and more generally, they have made possible an increased circulation of people, goods, and knowledge. Thirdly, technological inventions in communication such as the (cell) phone, radio, television, the computer, the Internet, and e-mail have only enhanced the ease with which information travels across the globe. In reality, much information has now become totally independent of the friction of local places.

All three types of events, but especially the latter two, mean that we can talk about an accelerating cultural mobility since the beginning of the 1800s. On the one hand. this acceleration is caused by an increased circulation of people, products, information, images, and ideas, and on the other side, it is caused by what we (with David Harvey) could call a general "time-space compression" (Harvey 1990). If the technological developments in transport have "killed space" so that "only time remains" as Heinrich Heine said about the railway in connection with the opening of the lines from Paris to Rouen and Orléans in 1843 (Heine 1890, 360, my translation), then the latest technological developments in communication have completed the job by eliminating time.

Change and continuity

It would be wrong, though, to claim that cultural mobility is a new phenomenon limited to the last two hundred years. On the contrary, as Stephen Greenblatt points out, it has always been an intrinsic part of the world that cultures have been dynamic as a result of exchanges, translations, appropriations, and conquests: "There is no going back to the fantasy that once upon a time there were settled, coherent, and perfectly integrated national or ethnic communities. [...] But world culture does not depend on recent events or on a transient wave of American triumphalism or on recent technological innovations" (Greenblatt 2010, 2, 5). According to Greenblatt, the period from 1800 to the beginning of the twentieth century has only been a sedentary parenthesis (in terms of both our discourse about it and our perspective upon it) in an otherwise fundamentally mobile worldview:

> A vital global cultural discourse then is quite ancient; only the increasingly settled and bureaucratized nature of academic institutions in the nineteenth and early twentieth centuries, conjoined with an ugly intensification of ethnocentrism, racism, and nationalism, produced the temporary illusion of sedentary, indigenous literary cultures making sporadic and half-hearted ventures toward the margins. The reality, for most of the past as once again for the present, is more about nomads than natives. (Greenblatt 2010, 6)

For Greenblatt the world's cultures have always been mobile in some degree. Mobility is the rule, not the exception. Just think of the basic movement dominating the *Odyssey* and the Icelandic sagas. But at the same time he points out that our worldview has changed from a mobile gaze (until about 1800) to a stationary (but illusory) gaze (1800–1945), and that it has now once again become a mobile gaze (1945–). Paradoxically, the stationary gaze dominates precisely at a time when mobility in the world accelerates—or perhaps nationalism and ethnocentrism are just natural reactions of inertia to acceleration?

It is in fact Greenblatt's conviction that the mobility and hybridity fanatics will not succeed easily in getting rid of the old ghosts. Nationalism and identity politics thus live on well in this otherwise global age. If Greenblatt's primary target is to (re-) insert mobility in its proper place in the world historical steamship, that is, in the engine room, it is also his plea and hope that we in the future—with movement as our starting point—will focus on the dialectics between change *and* continuity and thereby recognize the continuous and also partly legitimate presence of inertia:

We need to understand colonization, exile, emigration, wandering, contamination, and unintended consequences, along with the fierce compulsions of greed, longing, and restlessness, for it is these disruptive forces that principally shape the history and diffusion of identity and language, and not a rooted sense of cultural legitimacy. At the same time, we need to account for the persistence, over very long time periods and in the face of radical disruption, of cultural identities for which substantial numbers of people are willing to make extreme sacrifices, including life itself. (Greenblatt 2010, 2)

It is this acknowledgment of *movement* (that illusively has been considered a contingent deviation, but which basically is the world's driving force) as well as *inertia* (that illusively has been considered the world's fundamental modus, but which is in reality a natural, although sometimes problematic, reaction to the inevitability of change and hybridity) that makes Greenblatt's approach both sober and useful in relation to literary and cultural analysis.

In line with Greenblatt's argument, but from a distinctly existential perspective, Hans Ulrich Gumbrecht has characterized globalization as a gradual elimination of man's bodily being and of the local, physical place as the dimension in which the human body articulates itself (see Gumbrecht 2009). At the same time, Gumbrecht designates a series of human reactions of inertia that share the ambition to recuperate the body and the place as natural and not least indispensable parts of human existence. It is Gumbrecht's point that what are in fact metahistorical components in the history of human existence—body and place—have only become truly visible to us the moment we realized that we are about to lose them. It seems that there is a similar acknowledgment of the local place's significance behind Rüdiger Safranski's remark "that mobility and openness to the world need to be balanced by firm local attachments. We can communicate and travel globally, but we cannot take up global residence. We can live only here or there, not everywhere" (Safranski 2005, 12).

The migrant author and Aleksandar Hemon's *The Lazarus Project*

This insight will be transplanted into the dimension of the migrant author since the same duality of *placelessness as a result of uprooting* and *compensation for the loss of place* characterizes much migration literature. It is thus telling that Salman Rushdie has likened the migrant condition with "the conquest of the force of gravity" (Rushdie 1995, 85) and achieved what mankind has always dreamt of, that is, to be able to fly. For Rushdie, as for Gumbrecht, this weightless condition comprises a downside, though, because apart from connoting hope, freedom, and rebirth the migrant has become unstuck "from history, from memory, from Time" (Rushdie 1995, 87). According to

Edward Said, the migrant author reacts to this destructive side of uprooting—that is, to the loss of place, history and past—by "compensating for disorienting loss by creating a new world to rule" and by "efforts meant to overcome the crippling sorrow of estrangement" (Said 2000, 181, 173).

In the following, my focus will be the duality of mobility and inertia that characterizes Aleksandar Hemon's migration novel *The Lazarus Project* published in 2008. I will show that the movement that functions as an underlying condition in the novel, and which potentially results in not only existential homelessness but also in a linear plot (movement connotes a plot driven novel), is being countered by attempts to decelerate. On the existential level, this happens through a recuperation of concrete, physical places and on the narratological level through the creation of a multidimensional and—in terms of plot—fragmented novel. These attempts to decelerate are paradoxical, though, because ultimately they create a new kind of discursive dynamism and formal mobility.

Hemon was born in 1964 in Sarajevo, today part of Bosnia, but then a part of Yugoslavia. His mother is a Bosnian Serb, whereas his father's family came to Bosnia from Western Ukraine before the First World War at a time when both countries were part of the Austro-Hungarian Empire. In 1992, Hemon visited the United States as a tourist, but when the war in the former Yugoslavia expanded to Bosnia while Hemon was still in the United States, he chose to stay in the country and are currently living in Chicago. Hemon, who has a master's degree in English Literature from the University of Sarajevo, had already published a few short pieces before he settled in the United States, but a few years after his arrival, he began to write and publish in English.

Based on his biographical starting point, Hemon is thus a telling example of a mobile author defined by a mishmash of cultural, geographical, and linguistic roots. Mobility seems an inevitable condition of life in Hemon's case, and this is also true of many of the characters in his fiction. However, movement is considered to be an ambivalent condition: "Though immigration has been somewhat traumatic for me, I relish the multiplication of personalities that was its consequence. It's a blessing in multiple disguises for a writer" (Knight 2009, 97). Despite the initial destructive effect of migration—the trauma relates to a split in terms of personal identity—Hemon the author has eventually learned to appreciate its positive aftermath; the split is here replaced by a branching out in terms of personal identity. This is not always the case with Hemon's characters, though. Much more than what is the case with the author himself they seem to suffer under the compulsion of mobility—in the cases of Lazarus Averbuch and Vladimir Brik the recurring post-emigration feeling is alienation and maladjustment, and they both have an urgent need for continuity, placial being, and community.

The Lazarus Project is a two-track novel whose chapters oscillate between the story about the Jewish-Ukrainian immigrant Lazarus Averbuch, who was shot dead by Chicago's anarchism-frightened Chief of Police in 1908, and the contemporary story about the Bosnian immigrant Vladimir Brik, the novel's narrator, who collects material together with his friend, the photographer Rora Halilbašić, for a novel about Lazarus and his gruesome destiny. This story develops into Brik's autobiography and deals with his past life in and his homecoming to Sarajevo, with his and Rora's trip to Chișinău, Moldavia, where Lazarus and his sister Olga fell victims to the anti-Jewish pogrom in 1903 (when the city was called Kishinev and belonged to the Russian Empire), and with his current life in Chicago, not least his marriage troubles and troubles with writing the novel, which the reader holds in her hand.

The first lines of the novel not only thematizes the migrant's schism between living weightlessly in an abstract space and living earth-bound in concrete places, but also the migrant author's challenge when a lost or not-accessible past must be verbally presented (in the sense of brought forth) in all its physicality and placial presence: "The time and place are the only things I am certain of: March 2, 1908, Chicago. Beyond that is the haze of history and pain, and now I plunge" (Hemon 2008, 1). Although the narrator's invocation of a specific date and a specific place apparently points toward placial concreteness, it becomes clear with his next sentence that "March 2, 1908, Chicago" merely represents an abstract container comprising a vague "haze of history and pain." In order to fill this container with concreteness— and Brik's motivation for doing so is his desire "to be immersed in the world as it had been in 1908" and "to imagine how immigrants lived then" (Hemon 2008, 41)— Brik then decides to plunge into this haze. The remaining part of the novel can thus be read as Brik's attempt to transform haze into patterns and forms—that is, into concrete places. His primary tools in this transformational process are imagination, archives, photographs, travels, and, most importantly, language, and the medium through which it happens is place. It is also this list of tools that contributes to making the novel's architecture multidimensional and dynamic.

Immediately following the novel's first lines, the narrator, now plunged into the haze, sets about to concretize and materialize the abstract space of March 2, 1908, Chicago:

> Early in the morning, a scrawny young man rings the bell at 31 Lincoln Place, the residence of George Shippy, the redoubtable chief of Chicago police. The maid, recorded as Theresa, opens the door (the door certainly creaks ominously), scans the young man from his soiled shoes up to his swarthy face, and smirks to signal that he had better have a good reason for being there. (Hemon 2008, 1)

Here, we see the tools of imagination and archives in use, the first indicated by the mentioning of the creaking door and by the need to verify this with "certainly," the latter signaled by "recorded as Theresa" in regard to the name of the maid.

Brik's (and Hemon's) reading of historical sources and their many hours spent in the archives (alluded to by Brik through his meta-comments and by Hemon through paratextual components, for example a bibliography of historical sources and an acknowledgment to libraries in Chicago at the end of the novel) evidently help to ground the novel in concrete space and historical reality, something which entails an attenuation of the placelessness potentially caused by mobility.

The narrator's use of imagination—and his explicit references to the fact that he often relies on this faculty: "I needed to reimagine what I could not retrieve" (Hemon 2008, 46)—would seem to pull in the opposite direction, that is, away from spatial concreteness and historical reality. However, as Hemon emphasizes in an interview, imagination, and storytelling—because they are not mere confirmations of what already exists—have the power, through their evocative and *presencing* nature, to become truth, to become reality: "The beauty of literature is that you [...] know that it's not true in the sense that the street outside is true, but you believe it because it is conceivably human. That is, it could have happened to other people. You believe that, so therefore, it is true. So you add to the world as it is" (Knight 2009, 99–100).

Imagination has its limits, though, like the archive, and this is why traveling becomes a third tool in the attempt to transform haze into form: "I needed to see what I could not imagine" (Hemon 2008, 46), Brik explains in regard to his decision to travel to Kishinev with Rora, a decision which is legitimized by Brik's desire to get closer to Lazarus' and his own history. If imagination and the archive seem unproblematic as tools to counter weightlessness and abstract space, it might seem strange, at first glance at least, to mention traveling in the same category. After all, to travel is to be mobile and therefore potentially placeless, but in *The Lazarus Project* traveling works in a concretizing way on two separate levels: on the one hand, it contributes to the creation of a more authentic and realistic portrait of Lazarus; on the other hand, the journey in Hemon's novel takes place in the opposite of what Gumbrecht in regard to globalization has called the ever increasing "network of channels" (Gumbrecht 2009, 234), which are characterized by being frictionless, air-conditioned, and sterile spaces. Instead the journey of Brik and Rora takes place in an old car smelling of urine and vomit and driven by a chain-smoking chauffeur who practices death-driving, a car that also has a gun in its glove compartment and a victim of trafficking on its back seat. The actual journey, the mobility, is thus anything but placeless, bodiless, and frictionless in Hemon; on the contrary, any translocal dimension is always curbed in local colors, smells, and customs.

In general, the physical-material quality of place in Hemon is not something secondary to the reader, some passive "out there" that is only textually *represented*. Rather, place is produced, *presenced forth*, by language. The semantic and discursive dimensions of language are here superseded by the ability of language to trigger disorganized intensities of sensory experiences and reminiscences of taste, scent, color, touch, warmth, cold, and so on. One example is when the narrator—still in the very beginning of the novel—pauses the plot in order to conjure up (for the reader) a sense (his own and Lazarus's sense) of the Chicago winter: "The late winter has been gleefully tormenting the city. The pure snows of January and the Spartan colds of February are over, and now the temperatures are falseheartedly rising and maliciously dropping: the venom of arbitrary ice storms, the exhausted bodies desperately hoping for spring, all the clothes stinking of stove smoke" (Hemon 2008, 2). The narrator's technique of placial concretization and evocation primarily consists of his use of adjectives and adverbs such as "gleefully," "pure," "Spartan," "falseheartedly," "maliciously," and "arbitrary." The use of these words grounds the fictional universe in a specific locality—and considered as a chronotopic crystallization, the only place (and time) these words make sense together is precisely Chicago, March 2, 1908.

To Hemon, then, literature is not universal; it is always a result of a specific locally and historically determined language and place. Hemon thus attempts to regionalize and localize his stories, but it is then important to bear in mind that these stories are almost always composed of multiple localities and histories—and these localities and histories are for their part always seen through the de-familiarizing, and therefore also intensifying, eyes of the migrant: "it was amazing, she said, how different the things you knew well looked through the eyes of a foreigner" (Hemon 2008, 14).

There is no getting around the fact that *The Lazarus Project*, despite its placial character, is a novel of migration and movement. If Hemon in earlier works "was a bit more interested in the traumatic aspects of immigration, the sense of indelible loss," he now admits that "the transformative aspects have become a bit more interesting: what happens after the loss" (Knight 2009, 86). The point is that Hemon's answer to "what happens after the loss" is closely linked with his obsession with concrete places. Place, or rather the (re-)creation and recuperation of (lost and new-found) places through language (and photographs), is his answer. In a narratological sense, migration and movement imply plot and development. Place, on the other hand, implies pause and fragmentation. Arguably, it would be too simplified to say that the latter is more important to Hemon. Instead, it would be more correct to say that Hemon's obsession with concrete places—with what he himself refers to as "The language. The detail. The absence of the crude come-on" (Knight 2009, 95)—is fused with what seems to be the dominant mode of being in our contemporary world, that is, being on the move, and that this fusion and clash between place and movement constitutes the main, and paradoxical, theme of his works. The paradox can be summed up like this: on the one hand, movement seems to exclude or transcend place, but on the other hand, and as a direct consequence of this exclusion, movement triggers a compensatory urge for re-emplacement and the conjuring up of specific places through specific languages.

However, it is important to emphasize that Hemon's acute placial sensibility is not to be equated with an argument for a monogamous place-boundedness. It goes without saying that every literature of every place is shot through with traces and reminiscences of other places, also in the depths of its language, just as places are never stable and perfectly circumscribed enclosures. This is also the case in the literature of migration in which the presence of several places, past and present ones, helps to intensify the specificities of each of the places.

It is the combination of translocal mobility and local viscosity that places Hemon in-between the low-calorie and tasteless "Euroburger novel" (Patenidis 2010) and the sentimental *Heimatsroman*. In other words, he avoids falling into both the trap of universalism and the trap of nativism. In Hemon, mobility makes identities vibrate, both personal, national and cultural ones, and it does so partly in traumatic ways, partly in enriching ways. With a certain ironic distance and lightness, Brik can thus claim:

> I am a reasonably loyal citizen of a couple of countries. In America—that somber land—I waste my vote, pay taxes grudgingly, share my life with a native wife, and try hard not to wish painful death to the idiot president. But I also have a Bosnian passport I seldom use; I go to Bosnia for heartbreaking vacations and funerals, and on or around March 1, with other Chicago Bosnians, I proudly and dutifully celebrate our Independence Day with an appropriately ceremonious dinner. (Hemon 2008, 11)

The distance to oneself repeats itself when Brik on the one hand sees through the falseness of these yearly get-togethers, for example in relation to the national costumes worn by the girls, while on the other hand he admits that he participates "in that self-deception; in fact, I like to help with it, for, at least once a year, I am a Bosnian patriot. Just like everybody else, I enjoy the unearned nobility of belonging to one nation and not another" (Hemon 2008, 13).

The ironic relationship to double belonging is forced into the background during certain events, though. This happens for example when Brik accidentally meets Rora during one of the annual Independence Day parties. The initial joy at revisiting old friends is for Brik accompanied by "a tide of crushing sadness," not least because "The old film of the common past disintegrates when exposed to the light of a new life" (Hemon 2008, 17, 18). The experience, which Brik is left with, is of "the past embodied in strangers, the present in foreigners" (Hemon 2008, 18).

The novel's ending is open as far as Brik's identity and future are concerned. It does see, though, that there is a slight propensity toward Sarajevo and away from Chicago. "Everybody comes from somewhere," it says earlier in the novel (Hemon 2008, 153), and after having been in Sarajevo for a couple of days Brik realizes that he is at a place and that this place is where he comes from: "I was somewhere; I had finally landed in Sarajevo" (Hemon 2008, 280). When he later strolls around the city and walks in his old neighborhood, Brik admits:

> I relished the Sarajevo pavements under my feet, the asphalt felt softer than on any other street in the world. I walked up to Jekovac to behold the city spreading out of the valley toward the caliginous mass of the Igman mountain. I gorged on myriad sweet pastry all over Baš Čaršija. I quaffed the cold water from the fountain in front of Gazihusrevbegova Mosque. (Hemon 2008, 282–3)

The conclusion thus seems to point at a future in Sarajevo (although we cannot read Brik's remarks as the final truth): "I would always be here, where my heart was" (Hemon 2008, 283).

Does this make *The Lazarus Project* an anti-mobility novel? No, but the ending as well as the entire novel expose a broad spectrum of both problems with and possibilities in the mobile life. Of problems we can mention nostalgia, melancholy, rootlessness, the confrontation with xenophobia and racism—in short, to become a "nowhere man" as one of Hemon's earlier novels is called. In opposition to these problems, the possibilities consist in "the multiplication of personalities" (Knight 2009, 97) and in the simultaneity of worlds that emerge from this—that is, if one knows how to take advantage of or cope with this complexity.

Further reading

Edward W. Said's "Reflections on Exile" demonstrates the increased significance of the migrant in literary history. To Said exile entails a duality of freedom and sorrow: on the one hand, he problematizes the romanticizing of the migrant; on the other hand, he traces the subversive and liberating potentials of exile. In *Imaginary Homelands* and *Step Across This Line*, Rushdie appears as a celebratory voice of migration. Although Rushdie is not blind to the destructive consequences of uprooting he valorizes the individual's right to movement in both essays and novels. Ottmar Ette in *ZwischenWeltenSchreiben* (2005) advocates a new transareal approach to literature focusing on roads instead of spaces, border displacements instead of border demarcations and relations instead of territories. In Søren Frank's *Migration and Literature* (2008), the author shows that migration is not merely a sociological phenomenon that the literature of migration represents on its thematic level but also an aesthetic phenomenon that relates to the linguistic, enunciatory, and compositional dimensions of literature. Sten Moslund's *Migration and Literature and Hybridity* (2010) demonstrates how differently authors react to migration and mobility, and the book develops a conceptual toolbox to capture the nuances between the writers' discursive practices and their view on hybridity, change, and continuity.

References

Bauman, Zygmunt (1998) *Globalization: The Human Consequences*, Cambridge: Polity Press.

Ette, Ottmar (2005) *ZwischenWeltenSchreiben: Literaturen ohne festen Wohnsitz*, Berlin: Kulturverlag Kadmos.

Frank, Søren (2008) *Migration and Literature: Günter Grass, Milan Kundera, Salman Rushdie, and Jan Kjærstad*, New York: Palgrave Macmillan.

Greenblatt, Stephen (2010) "Cultural Mobility: An Introduction," in Stephen Greenblatt (ed.), *Cultural Mobility: A Manifesto*, Cambridge: Cambridge University Press.

Gumbrecht, Hans Ulrich (2009) "A Negative Anthropology of Globalization," Francisco González (ed.), *The Multiple Faces of Globalization*, Madrid: BBVA.

Harvey, David (1990) *The Condition of Postmodernity: An Enquiry into the Origins of Cultural Change*, Cambridge, MA: Blackwell.

Heine, Heinrich (1890) *Lutezia. 2. del. LVII. Bind 6*, Leipzig and Wien: Ed. Elster.

Hemon, Aleksandar (2008) *The Lazarus Project*, London: Picador.

Knight, Lania (2009) "A Conversation with Aleksandar Hemon," *The Missouri Review*, 85: 84–101.

Moslund, Sten Pultz (2010) *Migration Literature and Hybridity: The Different Speeds of Transcultural Change*, London: Palgrave Macmillan.

Patenidis, Andreas (2010) "Interview: Jáchym Topol," *Prague Daily Monitor*, August 9, 2010. Web. January 13, 2012, http://praguemonitor.com/2010/08/09/interview -j%C3%A1chym-topol

Rushdie, Salman (1992) *Imaginary Homelands: Essays and Criticism 1981–1991. 1991*, London: Granta Books.

Rushdie, Salman (1995) *Shame. 1983*, London: Vintage.

Rushdie, Salman (2002) *Step Across This Line: Collected Nonfiction 1992–2002*, New York: Random House.

Safranski, Rüdiger (2005) *How Much Globalization Can We Bear? 2003*, Cambridge: Polity Press.

Said, Edward (2000) "Reflections on Exile," in *Reflections on Exile and Other Essays*, Cambridge, MA: Harvard University Press.

Thoreau, Henry David (2008) *Walden; or, Life in the Woods. 1854. Walden, Civil Disobedience, and Other Writings*, New York and London: W. W. Norton & Company.

Urry, John (2011) *Mobilities*, Cambridge: Polity Press.

24
Memory

Ann Rigney

A common idea about time is that it flows in a linear and inexorable fashion, punctuated by days, weeks, and years that merely succeed each other and never return. The phenomenon of memory complicates this picture, because it folds different moments into each other. Memory is not just about the past, but about the "presence of the past" (Terdiman 1993) or, more specifically, about the multiple ways in which the past is reproduced and recollected by human agents in the present. In the first instance, of course, memory is an individual matter that is embodied in human subjects: it is the mental capacity to recall information, including information about one's own life that is the key to personal identity. In an age when the terms Alzheimer and post-traumatic stress disorder have become common currency, it is not surprising that there has been an enormous body of research into the nature of individual memory, its malleability, and the pathologies that affect it (see, e.g., Schacter 1996; 2001).

Memory is not only an individual matter, however. Societies too have a capacity to recollect and to forget and, as in the case of individuals, this is linked to the shaping of identities. Social remembering, however, is not merely a case of individual memory written large. Society's capacity to remember is not neurologically-based, but cultural. At best we can say metaphorically that stories and the languages we have for telling them are the "brains" of society.

How societies remember: Cultural memory

Social remembering is variously known as "collective memory" (launched by Halbwachs 1997) and "cultural memory" (launched by Jan and Aleida Assmann 1992; 1999). These two terms represent different approaches to the same phenomenon, reflecting the disciplinary backgrounds and priorities of researchers rather than a fundamental lack of agreement. In both cases what is at stake is a common concern with the interplay between social cohesion and shared stories about the past, that is, with the ways in which shared memories can generate the sense of belonging to an "imagined community" in the present (Anderson 1983). Memory is seen as providing imagined roots to contemporary society and to the different groups of which it is composed—be these defined along the lines of family, ethnicity, nationality, religion, class, or political persuasion. The shared narratives that define a group's past, however, are always the outcome, both of remembering and of forgetting. It is neither possible (even in the digital age) nor desirable to retain everything: making sense is predicated on selectivity. So the question then arises which stories are found memorable and which ones are forgotten in a given society? What does this tell us about how a society sees itself and about the power relations at play in defining relevance? When does amnesia with regard to certain topics become recognized and challenged? And how does this influence collective identity?

Social scientists favor "collective memory" as a term to describe how societies remember, since they are primarily interested in *social formations* (Olick et al. 2011). Scholars in literary and cultural studies favor "cultural memory" (Erll and Nünning 2010; Erll 2011) since their priority is with understanding the *narratives* that underpin social formations, and how these are made, circulated, and transformed across multiple media and cultural forms. The central concern of cultural memory studies, as this interdisciplinary field has come to be called, is accordingly with identifying the narratives that are dominant in particular societies and with explaining how they emerged and when they changed. As indicated above, individual (biographical) memory does not automatically provide a blueprint for these complex processes. But biographical memory as such can also be seen as part of the larger cultural dynamic: when individuals tell their own stories in the form of public testimonies and memoirs, they feed into emergent narratives about society as a whole. They may do this in the form of stand-alone texts, such as Frederick Douglass' *The Narrative of the Life of Frederick Douglass* (1845), Siegfried Sassoon's *Memoirs of a Fox-Hunting Man* (1928), and Charlotte Delbo's *Auschwitz and After* (1965–1971), all canonical texts dealing respectively with personal experiences of slavery, trench warfare, and life in a concentration camp. Alternatively, individual stories may be integrated into a synthetic project, such as Claude Lanzmann's documentary *Shoah* (1985) which combines multiple individual testimonies into a larger story about the Holocaust. Through the cultural work of the documentary maker, intensely personal experience becomes entangled with the experiences of other people so as to become significant for the public at large.

Literature as a medium of cultural memory

Traditionally literary criticism has by and large focused on the close reading of discrete texts. In contrast, cultural memory studies positions literary texts within a larger social-cultural dynamic. This is not to say that the specificity of literature, and what Attridge calls the "singularity of literature" (Attridge 2004), becomes irrelevant. Rather aesthetics and literary quality are reframed, providing literary scholars with a new challenge: namely, that of identifying the role of the aesthetic and the imagination, of good writing itself, in the shaping of collective narratives about past, present, and future. Addressing this question calls for a comparative approach that is open to the interplay between different forms of writing but also to the interplay between writing and other cultural practices.

Since the beginning of the nineteenth century, the historical novel (and its offspring, the historical film) has played a key role in producing cultural memory, albeit morphing in the course of its evolution from "classical realist" fiction to more experimental postmodern forms. Thus Tolstoy's *War and Peace* (1869) helped perpetuate, through its many reproductions but also through its many film adaptations, the memory of the battle of Borodino (1812), which historically speaking was not as major as the novelist made it out to be. The case of Tolstoy indicates the power of creative writing to *make* historical events *memorable*, and the power of good storytelling to cross national, linguistic, and generational borders. Some novels and films apparently have the capacity to arouse interest in stories that are not in the first instance "our own," that is, not part of our cultural inheritance and our patterns of identification. Alison Landsberg has written with regard to cinema of its role in producing "prosthetic memory" (Landsberg 2004): an imaginative and empathic involvement with people and events with which the viewers have no prior connection but which then become part of their shared memory. Although "prosthetic memory" was first developed to describe the immersive power of film, the concept can also be applied to literature: it too can draw its reader into the "lives of others" and leave a lasting impact on the individual's memory of historical events.

There is no guarantee, of course, that such prosthetic memory has a basis in documented history. Indeed, in the case of historical fiction, we can assume that a lot of what is depicted is the product of the writer's imagination. The imaginative dimension of literature leaves novelists permanently open to challenges from historians on the grounds of inaccuracy, but at the same time, imagination seems to be the source of literature's public appeal and long-term impact. From the point of view of literary studies, then, imagination is not a bug, but a defining feature. What role, for better or for worse, does creative writing play in linking fictional lives, as experienced by individual readers, to the broader social-cultural dynamic in which collective narratives emerge and change?

Austerlitz

W.G. Sebald's novel *Austerlitz* (2001) provides us with a keyhole perspective on these issues. It was originally written in German, but the fact that it has been translated into nineteen European languages as well as Japanese testifies to its cross-border appeal. Within the relatively short time since its appearance it has also generated a large body of critical commentary. It belongs to the tradition of the historical novel in that it combines fiction with the telling of a story about real events (in this case the Holocaust and the *Kindertransport* that brought Jewish children as refugees from Nazi Europe to the safety of the United Kingdom). However, it is not a "classical" historical novel in the style of Tolstoy, that is to say, presented from a third-person perspective by an omniscient narrator who oversees the development of society as a whole and makes that grand narrative comprehensible by keeping a select cast of fictional characters in the foreground of the story. Scholars have generally agreed that the devastating world wars and genocides of the twentieth century destroyed confidence in the progressive and coherent character of history and in our ability to find words and forms to represent it. In keeping with this, Sebald abandons omniscience. Instead he experiments with new forms for making sense of a history that is construed in terms of suffering and destruction rather than in terms of the redemptive triumph over adversity which is at the heart of *War and Peace*. Specifically, *Austerlitz* combines elements of the classical historical novel with the genre of the testimony, arguably the most important genre to have emerged since the Second World War, fed by the perceived need to have individuals "bear witness" to the Holocaust (Felman and Laub 1992; Wieviorka 2006). Against this background, imagination and creative writing become tools to help represent what is real, but unimaginable in its horror.

Sebald's novel is told from a first-person perspective by an unnamed German narrator who encounters an intriguing and solitary older man called Jacques Austerlitz, a specialist in architectural history. In the course of various encounters over a thirty-year period, the latter gradually unfolds his story to the younger narrator and, through him, to the reader. It is a story of irreparable loss, continuous displacement, and an inability to be happy. As a Jewish child refugee from Europe, Austerlitz is haunted by a traumatic past that increasingly intrudes on his consciousness. Separated from his mother, transported to England as a child, and given a new family, he has buried his memory of the radical disruption that split his life. At the same time, his actions are continuously guided by this blocked memory, in that he restlessly gravitates toward images and buildings that resonate unconsciously with the as yet untold story of his life: railway stations, places of enclosure, images of entrapment, closed off rooms, archives. These trigger his emotions and fix his attention, without his knowing why; they seem haunted. The overall mood is that of the "uncanny," or what Sigmund Freud called the *Unheimlich* (literally: the sense of alienation from the familiar; the sense of not being at home in one's home). During a visit to Prague, Austerlitz learns the basic facts of his story from an old family friend and, from then on, he actively pursues more information about the fate of his parents. He discovers that his mother died in Theresienstadt, but despite his best efforts to track down his father who had escaped to France, the trail runs dry.

A closer reading of the novel would show how it depicts the workings and failures of individual memory in the case of this troubled individual; and how certain objects or even the slope of a hill can trigger involuntarily the memory of earlier moments. In particular, it exemplifies the workings of what is known as "traumatic memory" (Caruth 1995). By this is meant the experience of something so destructive of our worldview that it defies our powers of comprehension. And because we have no words to grasp it, it keeps returning to haunt us in other forms, be this as a nervous tick and compulsive behavior or, as in the case of Austerlitz, in his obsession with particular places and buildings.

Austerlitz of course offers a fictionalized account of the workings of individual memory, not a medical casebook. Its value lies instead in the potential insight it offers into the workings of memory by bringing new aspects to light with the help of language. Like other works of creative writing (Proust's *A la recherche du temps perdu* [1913–1927] is a case in point), its evocative descriptions make the operation of memory observable to readers. Astrid Erll has written in this regard about the distinctive role of literature in what she calls "second-order observations" on lived experience (Erll 2010): literature and the other arts do not only produce memory in the form of new stories but often also reflect on its workings.

An approach to *Austerlitz* from the perspective of cultural memory studies needs to go farther, however, than the story of the individual called Austerlitz. It will want to examine how the novel links the stories of different individuals to each other and, as importantly, to larger trends in society. As the summary of the novel given above indicates, the idea of "transmission" is central to the novel's design: the narrator listens to Austerlitz and passes this on to the reader who by "listening in" acquires a prosthetic memory of personal suffering and dislocation. The novel thus draws our attention to the mechanisms by which stories are transferred from one person to another, specifically how lived experience is transferred from one generation to the next (Hirsch 2008).

Within the novel itself, moreover, Sebald continuously creates connections between Austerlitz's experiences and those of other individuals and groups. His signature fascination with buildings and places is crucial here, and his capacity to evoke the material world with its hidden and dark places using a combination of words and images (photographs and drawings complement the text in often intriguing ways). The physical environment, as mentioned above, triggers Austerlitz's individual memory in the fiction; but since the locations thus evoked actually exist outside the pages of the book, and are known also from other sources, their presence in the novel ensures that Austerlitz's story continuously resonates with the stories associated with those places. Not surprisingly, many of these locations have to do with the Second World War, such as the ghetto of Theresienstadt and the fortress of Breendonk outside Antwerp. But other locations in the novel are associated with different periods and experiences: railway stations, a graveyard, a zoo, a mine. As a result, the world of the novel continuously spills over into our knowledge of the actual world and hence also onto the memories embedded in the urban landscapes where we live our lives.

The novel opens by evoking the extraordinary railway station in Antwerp (which can still be visited today albeit in a renovated form) where the narrator first encounters Austerlitz. On the one hand, Antwerp station is merely a transit zone for passengers waiting for their trains and, within the structure of the story, it is merely the first of many stations to be evoked before Austerlitz finally recognizes Liverpool Street station in London as the scene of his arrival on the *Kindertransport*. On the other hand, as Sebald describes it, the Antwerp railway station is a "fantastical building" (Sebald 2001, 4) that indirectly tells the story of Belgian colonialism: the station's outrageous size embodies Leopold II's wealth and ambition, its castellations the dream of unlimited possibilities; while the environs of the station, including the zoo, present materialized reminders of the colonial exploitation of people and other living creatures: "the verdigris-covered negro boy who, for a century now, has sat upon his dromedary on top of an oriel turret to the left of the station façade [is] a monument to the world of the animals and native peoples of the African continent, alone against the Flemish sky" (2001, 4).

While these locations have a direct role to play in the slow excavation of Austerlitz's story, they also ensure that his story is continuously brought into relation with a larger history of displacement, inhumanity, and injustice that reaches back into earlier periods. The most important framework is that of the Jewish Holocaust but, as the passage quoted above indicates, the latter is also connected through the novel to the larger history of European colonialism and even to the history of cruelty to animals. The material traces of colonialism in the station become an indirect way of telling the story of the Holocaust, while the memory of the Holocaust also opens up a perspective on the inhumanity of colonialism. In this way, the novel exemplifies what Michael Rothberg (2009) has described as the "multidirectionality" of memory: the fact that the memory of one group may provide a model for helping another story to emerge from amnesia into public expression.

Remediation and remembering

Cultural memory is never carried by a single work alone or even by a single medium. It is the ongoing outcome of the reproduction and transformation of stories as they are carried over into different texts and multiple media (Erll and Rigney 2009). It would seem that stories only gain traction in a society when they are subsequently repeated in part or whole across different media platforms and in ever new material forms; in short, when they are not only mediated (that is, brought into circulation using some medium) but also remediated (reproduced in another medium or form). The story of Anne Frank, for example, was mediated in the first instance in her famous diary and then subsequently remediated multiple times as film, as theater, as photographs, and so on. The Anne Frank house in Amsterdam, which is visited by thousands of people every year, was the original site of Anne's imprisonment; since then it has arguably become yet another remediation of the book: visitors physically re-enact the memory of that diary in the form of a pilgrimage to the places it describes so intimately, as they pass one by one through the bookcase into the hiding place of the family. The cultural memory of Anne Frank is thus constituted, not by one single medium but by the ongoing interplay between many different media which both recalls the original text and continuously shifts and disseminates its meaning.

Cultural memory studies will accordingly seek to locate singular literary works within the larger plurimedial dynamic to which they belong. A good starting point is to examine how a particular novel picks up, recycles, and reworks earlier narratives on similar topics, and how it thus contributes to the gradual emergence of knowledge about particular events or developments. Karl Marx once said that people make their own history, but they do not make it under circumstances of their own choosing. This principle also applies to writers of historical novels since, by definition, they do not invent their stories from nothing. Intertextuality is a nonoptional feature. *Austerlitz*, as Sebald acknowledged in an interview, was inspired by a 1991 BBC documentary on the *Kindertransport* focusing on the case of Susi Bechöfer (who later published a written memoir called *Rosa's Child: One Woman's Search for Her Past,* 1996). *Austerlitz* also draws on many among other works and archival materials, including H.G. Adler's *Theresienstadt 1941–1945* [1995]. Where some sources are silently woven into the texture of the novel or enter it in the form of photographs, other sources are explicitly invoked. Most notably at the end of the novel where the narrator dwells on Dan Jacobson's memoir *Heshel's Kingdom* (1996) about the latter's search for his family history in post-Communist Lithuania. Within the context of the fiction, this actual book is presented as a source of information about the precise location of the death of Max Stern, the fictional Austerlitz's purported father. In short, imagination and history are clearly mixed up here, as Sebald's novel "plugs into" stories already in circulation.

The dynamics of cultural memory

In trying to understand the place of literature in the production of cultural memory, it is not enough to look "backwards" toward the stories and images on which particular novels draw. Equally important is to examine the afterlife of a text (Rigney 2012): how do other people re-use it? And what difference, if any, did it make? It is clear that Sebald's novel, when it appeared in 2001, was surfing a wave of emerging interest in the refugee children who had been brought to England at the start of the war and given new identities in British families. This included the BBC documentary mentioned above, but also other documentaries and publications which appeared around the same time, often made by descendants of the refugee children or those who fostered them. These included *My Knees Were Jumping* (dir. M. Hacker, 1996), *Into the Arms of Strangers: Stories of the Kindertransport* (M.J. Harris, 2000), *The Children Who Cheated the Nazis* (dir. S. Read, 2000), and Diane Samuels' play *Kindertransport* (1993). The decade that followed this first wave of interest saw in addition the appearance of several works of young adult fiction and fresh documentaries. It also saw the erection of a series of monuments at various railway stations across Europe associated with the *Kindertransport*, including one at Liverpool Street Station in London in 2006. In 2009, on the occasion of the 70th anniversary, some of the survivors of the *Kindertransport* from Prague physically re-enacted the railway journey that they had taken as children in 1939, a journey which was then televised as a BBC documentary. In short, Sebald's novel was part of the emergence of the memory of the *Kindertransport* into the public sphere and, in the form of monuments, into public space. Did it also have a special role to play in this process? Or in the longer-term dynamics of cultural remembrance?

Only time will really tell in the case of *Austerlitz*. But a number of possible answers can be offered. There is evidence to suggest that literary works and other fictional narratives appeal to a wider audience than nonfiction, and that for this reason they become points of reference for later discussions on particular topics. This was certainly true for historical fiction written in the nineteenth century where literature had no competitors from television and cinema (Walter Scott's *Waverley* [1814], for example, a novelistic account of the failed Scottish struggle for independence in the eighteenth century, was immensely popular at the time). It would be a gross exaggeration to claim that Sebald has achieved mass popularity in the way that Scott's works did or that a Hollywood movie or television series might do today. It is also unlikely, given the complexity of its writing and narrative architecture, that *Austerlitz* will ever become widely popular or the subject of a Hollywood movie. It is nevertheless striking how Sebald is slowly becoming a central point of reference in the public recollections of the *Kindertransport*.

In the first instance, the distinct role of literature in cultural memory can be linked to the capacity of literary works to survive outside the immediate context in which they were produced. It has been argued that the aesthetic properties of literary works gives them a greater "sticking" power in cultural memory than factual works, whose value lies in the accuracy of their information, or first-person testimonies, whose value lies in their authenticity (Rigney 2012). As long as a text is part of a canon, it will be reread and recalled as a voice from another time. It will speak across generations as well as cultures. On this basis, one may predict that in the long term *Austerlitz* will end up being a more important carrier of the memory of the *Kindertransport* to later generations than individual testimonies and memoirs, just as Tolstoy has become our window on the Napoleonic wars. Over a longer period (though there is no predicting how long) it will reach a greater number of people than a more ephemerally popular work.

This still begs the question of what literature "does" that gives it this lasting power. The simple answer might be that creative writing can add memorability to events. It gives us a reason to remember them, and a shape and a form with which to think about their significance. Creative writers, like Sebald, use their mastery of language to make certain types of experiences imaginable to others in ways that may elude actual witnesses; and not only imaginable, but connected to a bigger picture and to fundamental human dilemmas in which we are all implicated. As we have also seen in the case of *Austerlitz*, a novel can use its creative freedom to bring multidirectionality into play, suggestively connecting the dots between different memories—in this case between the Holocaust, colonialism, and the "forgotten" memory of animal suffering. In this sense, literature is not just a medium of memory but also an important antidote to amnesia with its power to make things memorable. As such, it is a valuable resource for critically reflecting on dominant narratives and what they exclude. A more complete survey of historical fiction would show that literature has regularly been a laboratory for new stories, allowing unfamiliar actors and types of experience to become a significant part of cultural memory. Imagination is needed in order to think outside the box, not only in regard to the future but also the past.

Further reading

Olick et al. (2011) offers key texts in the field of memory studies; Erll (2011) gives an introduction to the field of cultural memory studies. Erll and Rigney (2009) examines mediation and remediation in cultural memory. Rothberg (2009) is an important study of the multidirectional entanglements of the memory of the Holocaust and of colonialism; Suleiman (2006) explores the connection between formal experimentations and the difficulties of remembering atrocity. Nalbantian (2003) examines how individual remembering has been thematized in literature, while Rigney (2010) reflects on, and Rigney (2012) offers a case study in, the role of literature in the long-term dynamics of cultural memory. For English-language introductions to Sebald's work, see Long and Whitehead (2006), Schwartz (2010) and Jacobs (2015).

References

Assmann, Aleida (2012) *Cultural Memory and Western Civilization: Functions, Media, Archives*, Cambridge: Cambridge University Press. Originally published in German in 1999.

Assmann, Jan (2011) *Cultural Memory and Early Civilization: Writing, Remembrance, and Political Imagination*, Cambridge: Cambridge University Press. Originally published in German in 1992.

Anderson, Benedict (1991) *Imagined Communities: Reflections on the Origins and Spread of Nationalism*, London: Verso. Originally published in 1983.

Attridge, Derek (2004) *The Singularity of Literature*, London: Routledge.

Caruth, Cathy (ed.) (1995) *Trauma: Explorations in Memory*, Baltimore: Johns Hopkins University Press.

Erll, Astrid (2010) "Literature, Film, and the Mediality of Cultural Memory," in Astrid Erll and Ansgar Nünning (eds), *A Companion to Cultural Memory Studies*, 389–98, Berlin: Walter de Gruyter.

Erll, Astrid (2011) *Memory in Culture*, London: Palgrave Macmillan.

Erll, Astrid and Ansgar Nünning (eds) (2010) *A Companion to Cultural Memory Studies*, Berlin: de Gruyter.

Erll, Astrid and Ann Rigney (eds) (2009) *Mediation, Remediation and the Dynamics of Cultural Memory*, Berlin: de Gruyter.

Felman, Shoshana and Dori Laub (1992) *Testimony: Crises of Witnessing in Literature, Psychoanalysis, and History*, London: Routledge.

Freud, Sigmund (1985) "The Uncanny," in A. Dickson (ed.), *The Pelican Freud Library 14: Art and Literature*. Trans. J. Strachey, Harmondsworth: Penguin Books. Originally published in German in 1919.

Halbwachs, Maurice (1997) *La mémoire collective*, Paris: Albin Michel. Originally published in 1950.

Hirsch, Marianne (2008) "The Generation of Postmemory," *Poetics Today*, 29 (1): 103–28.

Jacobs, Carole (2015) *Sebald's Vision*, New York: Columbia University Press.

Landsberg, Alison (2004) *Prosthetic Memory: The Transformation of American Remembrance in the Age of Mass Culture*, New York: Columbia University Press.

Long, J. J. and Anne Whitehead (2006) *W. G. Sebald: A Critical Companion*, Edinburgh: Edinburgh University Press.

Nalbantian, Suzanne (2003) *Memory in Literature: From Rousseau to Neuroscience*, Basingstoke: Palgrave Macmillan.

Olick, Jeffrey K., Vered Vinitzky-Seroussi and Daniel Levy (eds) (2011) *The Collective Memory Reader*, Oxford: Oxford University Press.

Rigney, Ann (2010) "The Dynamics of Remembrance: Texts Between Monumentality and Morphing," in Astrid Erll and Ansgar Nünning (eds) Erll and Nünning, *A Companion to Cultural Memory Studies*, 345–53, Berlin: de Gruyter.

Rigney, Ann (2012) *The Afterlives of Walter Scott: Memory on the Move*, Oxford: Oxford University Press.

Rothberg, Michael (2009) *Multidirectional Memory: Remembering the Holocaust in the Age of Decolonization*, Stanford: Stanford University Press.

Schacter, Daniel L. (1996) *Searching for Memory: The Brain, the Mind, and the Past*, New York: Basic.

Schacter, Daniel L. (2001) *The Seven Sins of Memory: How the Mind Forgets and Remembers*, Boston: Houghton Mifflin.

Schwartz, Lynne Sharon (ed.) (2010) *The Emergence of Memory: Conversations with W. G. Sebald*, New York: Seven Stories Press.

Sebald, W. G. (2001) *Austerlitz*, Trans. Anthea Bell, London: Penguin.

Suleiman, Susan Rubin (2006) *Crises of Memory and the Second World War*, Cambridge, MA: Harvard University Press.

Terdiman, Richard (1993) *Present Past: Modernity and the Memory Crisis*, Ithaca, NY: Cornell University Press.

Wieviorka, Annette (2006) "The Witness in History," *Poetics Today*, 27 (2): 385–97.

Part III

Practices

25
Archive

Dennis Yi Tenen

Chapter Outline

An archive can be as large as a library or as small as a bookshelf.

What are the minimal requirements to build an archive? How does a pile of haphazardly arranged papers differ from an archive? Look around you and notice the furniture; navigate through your mobile device where you keep your notes and your photos. Think of your social media usage, habits of correspondence, the way you keep in touch with your family and friends, the habits of keeping a journal, taking notes, finding basic facts about the world. All of these involve an archive of some kind. We are surrounded by archives; we live in them and through them. Archives mediate. Like water for fish, they form the medium of our knowledge gathering and finding activity. If, as the headlines tell us, we live in an information age, archives are a way of making sense of that information. More than making sense, they help keep information *at hand*. An archive is a way of ordering things. It is a site of mental as a well as physical activity.

Think of the archive as an interface between internal mental states—what I know now—and the external, physical representation of that knowledge—what I could know at any time. The book on my bookshelf is not just a book; it is a part of my mental furnishings. I may not remember the contents of that book for long, but I know where it is and how to find it. I know I could get to it if needed. It is not as close to me as a memory, accessible immediately and at once, but also not as far as an obscure fact with which I have never had any contact. The book on my shelf, the notebook in a pile on my desk, occupies a space somewhere in the middle of the spectrum, between my rather limited ability to remember a few ideas presently and the unlimited amount of ideas out there. My documents, the ones that belong to me, the ones I organized neatly on my desk and on my virtual desktop, are ideas that I used to have. They are also a part of me, but just slightly further away and outside of myself than my thoughts. I feel safe knowing where they are and how to find them.

Recall Samuel Beckett's play *Krapp's Last Tape*, where the reader encounters Krapp, a "wearish old man," who, every year, on his birthday, records a message to himself and lovingly reviews old recordings as if to enter into a conversation with himself, to encounter himself anew (Beckett 1960). Who is Krapp, the play asks of the reader, if not a collection of these memories and recordings? Krapp is at once an archivist and archive. In this ordinary way—through the continual activity of taking notes, photographs, and recordings of ourselves, our friends, and our families—all of us are implicated in the archival condition. Whatever it means to be someone, a self, involves the enterprise of storage and retrieval. Think of the discomfort we feel when someone disturbs our archives: if someone were to reorganize your music collection for example, or scramble the order of your notes, or rearrange the books on your bookshelf. One feels lost and violated precisely because the archive is so crucial to our ability to find our way through a forest of personal data. The archive, in this sense, is a small, organized vessel of private order adrift in the midst of a vast and turbulent sea of information.

Not all vessels of order are small and private. Some grow into imperial armadas: state archives that project collective power. The aggregate of personal memories gives us our shared, cultural memory, our heritage. That sense of shared culture does not exist in the immaterial ether. It is reflected in publicly and privately supported collections like the Library of Congress and the Guggenheim Museum. These are large public archives, preserving art and books—public in the sense of a collective enterprise (not necessarily funding). They represent a vision of communal remembrance. It is *a* vision, however, not *the* vision. It must not be mistaken for history or reality (LaCapra 1985; Spivak 1985). Someone, somewhere made a decision about what to archive and where. State-sanctioned collections reflect the priorities of a bureaucracy, resulting in archives like the State Archive of the Russian Federation, Ottoman Archives, New York State Archives, West Indies Federal Archives Centre, and China's Central Archives. Smaller, grassroots public archives are often maintained by independent organizations like the *Archiv der Jungendkulturen* in Berlin or the North American Queer Zine Archive Project (QZAP) out of Minneapolis, Minnesota.

Other dynamics come into play when archives grow in size from small vessels to fleets of knowledge. In state archives we begin to think about forces of inclusion and exclusion (Richards 1993; Greetham 1999). Who is allowed to enter and who isn't? Which materials are worthy of preservation and which are relegated to the heap of perishable ephemera? In this way archives can amplify certain historical narratives while suppressing others. By its very design the archive conveys a logic of differentiation. Imperial archives cast divisions between center and periphery. Court archives differentiate between criminals and law-abiding citizens. The archive of the hospital embodies distinctions between the healthy and sick. The archive of peer-reviewed scientific publication separates meaningful knowledge from rumor or mere speculation.

Can there be an archive without records or documents? Do the contents of my pocket—keys, some change, a crumpled receipt, a piece of lint—constitute an archive of a kind? What isn't an archive? I would argue here that an archive requires at least these three components: first, a number of documents or artifacts to be collected; second a place to store them; and third, a system of organization.

An archive without records, documents, or artifacts would be an archive in the name only. We could call it "the library of nothing" but for all purposes it would resemble an empty room; it would be a promise of an archive—that is, the promise of records, documents, or artifacts to come. Could we imagine an archive without space? A virtual collection perhaps? Again, the question seems nonsensical. A virtual archive, a website for example, is still a collection of something occupying the same space, however virtual. An archive of documents on paper, a list of books to be purchased for example, is again only an idea, a promise of an archive. Proximity of material is required. Finally, can an archive exist without a method of organization like a catalog or an index? Again, it seems not. In the Jewish tradition, holy texts like the Torah are not to be discarded. For this reason, special sealed rooms, called the Genizah, have existed to house worn-out documents since the ancient times. The discovery of such rooms has led to important contributions to the study of liturgy and poetry in Judaic studies (Schmelzer 1997; Schechter 1998). But do the Genizah constitute an archive? Or do they become an archive once they are discovered and cataloged? A catalog is what gives the collection its order. Without a catalog the pile of papers on my disk is just a pile. Add a catalog and it becomes an archive. A catalog describes its documents and, most importantly, it tells us how and where to find them. Document, architecture, and epistemic order are all required to constitute an archive. Let us examine each of these archival components in its turn.

Document

The archive is composed of *documents*—that is, physical objects of record. From an infinitude of possible descriptions about reality, records preserve those which are important (I am sidestepping the sometimes important distinction between *documents* and *records* [Vismann and Winthrop-Young 2008, 71–101]). Think of an obvious example, like a police report. A police report captures details relevant to an incident. Police officers who would write a novel at the scene of a crime would be dismissed of their duties. The archiving practice of law enforcement requires records of a particular kind. A literary archive will contain documents drastically different from those of a police report or a medical record. The archive creates answers for questions like "What constitutes an event?" Police reports thus comprise accidents and violations. Medical records consist of symptoms and diagnoses. The literary record contains documents relevant to an author's output. In selecting the important events, or defining what constitutes an event, the archive constructs a sense of time. Archival time is made up of records.

In this disparity between everything that can be recorded and the much smaller subset of details that are actually recorded lies the normative power of an archive. Archives reflect social values by privileging certain facts over others. A collection policy will define the scope of an archive's preservation efforts. The National Archives of the United Kingdom, for example, recommend that collection policies include "information which identifies the repository and the governing body," "information about the legal status of the repository or other source of its authority to collect," "information about the scope of, or limitations to, the [collection] policy," "information about the process of collection," and "information concerning access" ("Archive Collection Policy Statements: Checklist of Suggested Contents" 2004). The collection policy of the National Archives itself defines the role of the institution in terms of collecting and "records from all government departments and bodies whose records are public records under the Public Record's Act" ("Records Collection Policy" 2012, 5). It further identifies an institutional mission to collect "public records of historical value and enduring public interest," which include among other kinds of material "significant records concerning international relations and defence," "records of commissions, tribunals, and inquiries," and "case files, datasets and other records which contain extensive information about the lives of individual or groups [...] which contribute substantially to public knowledge and understanding of the people and communities of the UK" ("Records Collection Policy" 2012, 6–7).

Consider QZAP's collection policy in comparison (QZAP 2016). It includes first, a definition of what a "zine" is: "a self-published, small circulation, non-commercial booklet or magazine, usually produced by one person or a few individuals." Then it narrows that definition to the notion of a "queer zine," a self-published document related to "people's expression of gender and sexuality" in a long list of self-identified categories that include:

> queer, kweer, gay, lesbian, bi, bisexual, fag, faggot, dyke, trans, tranny, queen, king, princess, Nancy boy, Brucey Boy, nelly, femme, butch, bulldagger, bulldyke, polyamorous, pansexual, omnisexual, asexual, homo, Saphist, faerie, and of course Friend of Dorothy.

Materials that the archive is interested in preserving further include a number of themes related to:

> sex, same-gender sex, same-gender love, same-gender attraction/desire, gender, transgender issues, bisexuality, sexual health, HIV/AIDS, STI's (STDs), safer sex, music, popular culture, feminism, activism, politics, racism, classism, fat phobia, ageism, traveling, anti-assimilationism, art, DIY (do-it-yourself), comics/comix, erotica/porn, journaling/diary zines, manifestos, [and] poetry.

Both collection policies identify, in the words of Achille Mbembe, "a process which converts a certain number of documents into items judged to be worthy of preserving" (Mbembe 2012, 20). Because of this selectionally role, archives cannot be treated as neutral sites of knowledge consumption. Rather, as Ann Stoler and others have argued, readers should treat archives as sites of knowledge *production* (Richards 1993; Stoler 2009). In selecting what documents to preserve, an archive makes evidence available to the historical record. Histories are woven from that evidence. Records that do not make it into an archive become less readily accessible to a historian. In a sense, they fall out of history.

Architecture

Space limits the scope of archival activity. The limitation of space is what gives an archive its normative powers. Were an archive to house everything available, its archivists need not exercise their powers of discernment. They would collect it all. The apparent lightness of digital being tempts us to understand digital archives free of space constraints. The mission statement of Google, one of the world's most popular search engines, describes the company's goal to "organize the world's information and make it universally accessible and useful" ("About Google" 2016). Unlike the collection statements we have read above, Google's archiving activity seems to lack the principle of selection. Similarly, a number of people in the so-called life-logging movement believe that technology has enabled us to remember everything and that we are entering the age of total recall. Gordon Bell, an advocate of this movement, writes:

> If you choose, everything you see can be automatically photographed and spirited away into your personal image library within your e-memory. Everything you hear can be saved as digital audio files. Software can allow you to scan your pictures for writing and your audio files for words to come up with searchable text transcripts of your life. If you choose, you can save every e-mail you send and receive and archive every Web page you visit. You can record your location and path through the world. You can record every rise and dip in your heart rate, body temperature, blood sugar, anxiety, arousal, and alertness, and log them into your personal health file. (Bell and Gemmell 2009, 4)

You can begin to understand now why in thinking about archives I evoked not only an obvious few public archives like the state library, but also the numerous small private archives that increasingly house details of our everyday life. A collection of home photographs on a personal computer or mobile phone answers all of our minimal definitions of an archive. It consists of cataloged documents, collected in space especially allotted for them. Such documents are described with meta-data— tags, file names—constituting a method of organized storage and retrieval not so different from your local library catalog. Once the purview of large institutions, archives are now ubiquitous. We are all archivists, in a sense, engaged in the activity of capturing, storing, and sorting documents of record.

One cannot deny that the ubiquity of inexpensive storage media is changing the society's relationship with its archives. If we are to record everything on our own, what role will sanctioned archives play in the formation of collective memory? We cannot forget also that despite evanescent appearances, digital archives too must take up some space. The ephemeral-seeming activity of capturing, sharing, and storing information is grounded in the concrete realities of digital storage. All those photographs, videos, sound files, and texts gain a hefty material presence in aggregate. The very metaphor of "cloud" storage obscures the realities of massive data centers, housed in secure bunkers, under surveillance (Hu 2015). The exclusionary principle returns with a vengeance. In many cases, the digital archive is not a public archive, at least not in the sense of a public library. The public does not usually have direct access to digitally archived information at the site of its inscription, on Google's servers, for example. Law sometimes prohibits even the circumvention of those security mechanisms contained in one's own devices (Ginsburg 2005).

The physical architecture of archives ultimately governs access to information. This holds true for brick and mortar archives just as it does for digital ones. A critical approach to studying archives must include the examination of physical barriers to entry and exit. Under closer examination, we understand the utopian vision of total recall to exclude global populations without access to the Internet and those who access the Internet through low-fidelity connections on tiny screens and in Internet cafés on rented machines (Qiu 2009; Wyche et al. 2013; Mariscal Avilés et al. 2016). The archive does not provide neutral grounds for the storage of and access to information. Because archives cannot be commensurate with the passing reality that they attempt to capture, the idea of archives itself implies something left out.

Catalog

Taxonomies, or ways of organizing information, constitute another axis of exclusion in the archive. What happens to documents archived, but not cataloged? Such documents are lost to time. They are technically in the archive, but practically inaccessible. In this way, a document within the archive relates not only to physical space but also to the epistemological architecture of the catalog. A catalog locates documents in ideational space, just as a building—its stacks and bookshelves—locates it in the physical. To be lost in one is to be lost in the other. Thus in addition to asking What was collected? and How is it accessed? we should also ask, How is it organized? What logics and epistemological regimes govern the order of documents in the archive?

In his short story "The Library of Babel," Jorge Luis Borges imagines the world of an infinite library that contains all possible books:

> *All*—the detailed history of the future, the autobiographies of the archangels, the faithful catalog of the Library, thousands and thousands of false catalogs, the proof of the falsity of those false catalogs, a proof of the falsity of the *true* catalog [...] the true story of your death, the translation of every book into every language, the interpolations of every book into all books [...]. (Borges and Hurley 1998, 115)

A catalog, as we can see, is unlike other books in that it is a map of their location. It is a key to the bibliographic universe. Inhabitants of the infinite library travel on a quest to find "a catalog of catalogs," "the cipher and perfect compendium *of all other books*" (Borges and Hurley 1998, 113, 116). A librarian would find such a book analogous to God, Borges writes (Borges and Hurley 1998, 117). A catalog grows in importance in proportion to the size of the archive.

The advent of powerful computational archive technologies—crawlers, indexers, and classifiers—has transformed the nature of catalogs in our world. Before computers, archivists relied on systems of social filtration to organize their materials. Ask yourself this: How did you find this book and chapter in front of you? Traditionally, search and discovery of new information was facilitated by complex processes of canon formation. One finds a book or film because it is assigned in class, it was advertised, a friend recommended it, or the recommendation came from a critic. These social mechanisms of filtration reify into epistemological categories. Thus a reflection on "genre" by book critics and book sellers results in the isles of a book store dedicated to the genres of fantasy, classics, detective fiction, and so on. In the isles of a book store, we once again observe the close entanglement of document, architecture, and epistemology.

Classification lies at the heart of library science (Robinson and Maguire 2010). The Dewey Decimal Classification system, for example, has guided the organization of libraries by subjects for over a century. This way of organizing material aids in discovery: a library patron looking for a specific book can find a shelf of books on a similar topic. A way of organizing material by alphabet or by size alone would result in different kind of discovery. Classification systems provide the scaffolding for everyday knowledge work. They are difficult to perceive, however, because they are ubiquitous and often invisible (Bowker and Leigh Star 1999). Think of the various classification systems that surround our daily life: physicians classify according to a list of available diagnoses and billable insurance codes, judges classify according to the legal categories, academics classify according to scientific categories, students structure their days according to the course catalog. Not often seen, catalogs are everywhere.

An archivist's job involves classification—an activity that projects order among documents and architectures. One can think of classification as a way of organizing things, or placing documents in accord with the spatial requirements of storage. Classification converts mental, ideational categories into spatial arrangements of things, which together make up the archive. Jacques Derrida has called this organizing activity the power of *consignation*. He wrote:

> By consignation, we do not only mean, in the ordinary sense of the word, the act of consigning residence or of entrusting so as to put into a reserve (to consign, to deposit), in a place and on a substrate, but here the act of consigning and through *gathering together signs* [...] Consignation aims to coordinate a single corpus, in a system of synchrony in which all the elements articulate the unity of an ideal configuration. (Derrida and Prenowitz 1995, 10)

In maintaining order, the archivist imposes a structure onto the world. An archive draws boundaries between the ordered inside and the chaotic (by archival logic), disordered outside. A traditional archive collection thus thrives on the logic of exclusion: some things are in, others are out. In addition to preserving things—documents, artifacts, records, evidence—the archivist preserves a taxonomy—a lexicon, a way of ordering things. Future archivists may wonder at the strange, simplistic perhaps, and alien ways in which we used to organize our stuff (Foucault 1971, xv–xxiv).

The principle of exclusion operates by different logics in the age of ubiquitous connectivity, cheap storage, algorithmic sorting, and social media. The role of culture critics is subsumed by the wisdom of the crowd. Instead of trusting one "expert" opinion, we increasingly rely on the aggregate opinions of many, through reviews and recommendations: if you like this you may also like this, others who liked X also usually like Y. The archive begins to contain multiple logics, multiple systems of classification that compete, undermine, and strengthen each other. Classification systems are no longer the work of a single man like John Dewey; archive dwellers bring with them their own tags and categories. Digital archives encourage their participants to engage in this organizing activity. Archive managers subsequently extract value from such tumultuous social engagement. Digital archives retain the trace of archive dwelling. Inhabitants of the digital archive become archivists themselves. Their searching and organizing activity is further commodified to extract value from the catalog.

The inherently social activity of archive dwelling is also augmented by automated tools. Archivists in their own right, algorithmic crawlers, indexers, and classifiers learn from human behavior to collect, analyze, and catalog data on their own (Gupta et al. 2013). Web crawlers follow links and disperse through the network to search for new material. Indexers begin the task of assigning keywords and categories. Supervised machine-learning classifiers apply existing categories, tagged by humans, to new collections. As the name implies, their task is to classify or sort things into piles. These piles are then assigned labels that help humans sift through vast amounts of data. Unsupervised learning algorithms notice patterns that are not apparent to the human eye and mind. So-called deep learning heuristics mimic the neural structure of human brains to further aid in sorting and classification (Li and Vitányi 2008; Flach 2012; Schmidhuber 2015).

The simple task of using a search engine to find a piece of information belies complex realities of digital archives. Advances in storage media, coupled with novel computational methodologies, have made it possible to imagine a future in which everything can be stored and everything can be organized. A history of archives warns otherwise. The exclusionary principle will continue to operate as long as archives remain instruments of economic and political power. The larger and more inclusive an archive, the more appealing it becomes as an instrument for control and subjugation of its dwellers. Machine intelligence extends and deepens human distinctions. Unlike the archivist who labors in public and follows legible collection policies, the swarm of algorithmic machine archivists operate in the dark, usually without decree or consent. Archive dwellers are moving toward what some have called the "black box society," governed by the "hidden logics of search" (Pasquale 2015). These new computational realities require archivists equipped with the sharp tools of critical theory, information science, and software engineering. The sauntering iron and the binding needle may be needed to occupy free and equitable archives: epistemic structures that are built in the open, dwellings suitable for human habitation.

Further reading

On the power of archives to create and to shelter themselves from memory read Derrida and Prenowitz (1995). Gitelman (2014) and Vismann and Winthrop-Young (2008) examine documents and records from the perspective of media theory. Hamilton et al. (2012) provide an important collection of essays on the archive in and beyond post-colonial studies. On the relationship between the archive and empire, read Richards (1993), Mbembe (2012), and Peterson (2012). Qiu (2009) and Sundaram (2011) give the reader thorough ethnographic accounts of contemporary archival dwelling outside of Europe and North America. Mayer-Schönberger (2009) and Pasquale (2015) explore the social and political consequences of algorithmic archive making.

References

"About Google" (2016) https://www.google.com/about/.

"Archive Collection Policy Statements: Checklist of Suggested Contents" (2004) The National Archives.

Beckett, Samuel (1960) "Krapp's Last Tape," in *Krapp's Last Tape: And Other Dramatic Pieces*, 7–28, New York: Grove Press.

Bell, Gordon and Jim Gemmell (2009) *Total Recall: How the E-Memory Revolution Will Change Everything*, New York: Dutton.

Borges, Jorge Luis and Andrew Hurley (1998) "The Library of Babel," in *Collected Fictions*, 112–18, New York: Viking.

Bowker, Geoffrey C. and Susan Leigh Star (1999) *Sorting Things Out Classification and Its Consequences*, Cambridge, MA: MIT Press.

Derrida, Jacques and Eric Prenowitz (1995) "Archive Fever: A Freudian Impression," *Diacritics*, 25 (2): 9–63.

Flach, Peter (2012) *Machine Learning: The Art and Science of Algorithms That Make Sense of Data*, 1st edition, Cambridge and New York: Cambridge University Press.

Foucault, Michel (1971) *The Order of Things: An Archaeology of the Human Sciences*, New York: Pantheon Books.

Ginsburg, Jane C. (2005) "Legal Protection of Technological Measures Protecting Works of Authorship: International Obligations and the US Experience." SSRN Scholarly Paper ID 785945. Rochester, NY: Social Science Research Network.

Gitelman, Lisa (2014) *Paper Knowledge: Toward a Media History of Documents*, North Carolina: Duke University Press.

Greetham, David (1999) "'Who's In, Who's Out': The Cultural Poetics of Archival Exclusion," *Studies in the Literary Imagination*, 32 (1): 1–28.

Gupta, A., A. Dixit and A. K. Sharma (2013) "Relevant Document Crawling with Usage Pattern and Domain Profile Based Page Ranking," in *2013 International Conference on Information Systems and Computer Networks (ISCON)*, 119–24. doi:10.1109/ICISCON.2013.6524186.

Hamilton, Carolyn, Verne Harris, Michèle Pickover, Graeme Reid, Razia Saleh and Jane Taylor (2012) *Refiguring the Archive*, Springer Science & Business Media.

Hu, Tung-Hui (2015) *A Prehistory of the Cloud*, Cambridge, MA: The MIT Press.

LaCapra, Dominick (1985) *History & Criticism*, Ithaca, NY: Cornell University Press.

Li, Ming and Paul Vitányi (2008) *An Introduction to Kolmogorov Complexity and Its Applications*, 3rd edition, New York: Springer.

Mariscal Avilés, Judith, Sebastián Benítez Larghi and María Angélica Martínez Aguayo (2016) "The Informational Life of the Poor: A Study of Digital Access in Three Mexican Towns," *Telecommunications Policy*, March.

Mayer-Schönberger, Viktor (2009) *Delete: The Virtue of Forgetting in the Digital Age*, Princeton, NJ: Princeton University Press.

Mbembe, Achille (2012) "The Power of the Archive and Its Limits," in *Refiguring the Archive*, 19–27, Springer Science & Business Media.

Pasquale, Frank (2015) "The Hidden Logics of Search," in *The Black Box Society: The Secret Algorithms That Control Money and Information*, Cambridge, MA: Harvard University Press, 59–100.

Peterson, Bhekizizwe (2012) "The Power of the Archive and the Political Imaginary," in *Refiguring the Archive*, 29–35, Springer Science & Business Media.

Qiu, Jack Linchuan (2009) *Working-Class Network Society Communication Technology and the Information Have-Less in Urban China* Cambridge, MA: MIT Press.

QZAP (2016) "Collection Policy," *QZAP*. https://web.archive.org/web/20160402160544/http://www.qzap.org/v8/index.php/about/collection-policy.

"Records Collection Policy" (2012) The National Archives. http://www.nationalarchives.gov.uk/about/our-role/plans-policies-performance-and-projects/our-policies/.

Richards, Thomas (1993) *The Imperial Archive: Knowledge and the Fantasy of Empire*, London and New York: Verso.

Robinson, Lyn and Mike Maguire (2010) "The Rhizome and the Tree: Changing Metaphors for Information Organisation," *Journal of Documentation*, 66 (4): 604–13.

Schechter, S. (1998) "Genizah Specimens," *The Jewish Quarterly Review*, 10 (2): 197–206. doi:10.2307/1450712.

Schmelzer, Menahem (1997) "The Contribution of the Genizah to the Study of Liturgy and Poetry," *Proceedings of the American Academy for Jewish Research*, 63: 163–79. doi:10.2307/3622601.

Schmidhuber, Jürgen (2015) "Deep Learning in Neural Networks: An Overview," *Neural Networks*, 61 (January): 85–117.

Spivak, Gayatri Chakravorty (1985) "The Rani of Sirmur: An Essay in Reading the Archives," *History and Theory*, 24 (3): 247–72.

Stoler, Ann Laura (2009) *Along the Archival Grain: Epistemic Anxieties and Colonial Common Sense*, Princeton, NJ: Princeton University Press.

Sundaram, Ravi (2011) *Pirate Modernity: Delhi's Media Urbanism*, 1st edition, Oxford and New York: Routledge.

Vismann, Cornelia and Geoffrey Winthrop-Young (2008) *Files: Law and Media Technology*, Stanford: Stanford University Press.

Wyche, Susan P., Sarita Yardi Schoenebeck and Andrea Forte (2013) "'Facebook Is a Luxury': An Exploratory Study of Social Media Use in Rural Kenya," in *Proceedings of the 2013 Conference on Computer Supported Cooperative Work*, 33–44. CSCW '13, New York: ACM.

26

Books

Tore Rye Andersen

A text is not an immaterial entity but a tangible thing whose very materiality affects its meaning. To support this somewhat bold statement, I will begin by reading something we usually do not read: the nine blank pages at the end of the American first edition of Thomas Pynchon's short novel *The Crying of Lot 49* (1966). Among other things this postmodern classic is a skewed detective novel that does not behave like most detective novels. *The Crying of Lot 49* tells the story of the young housewife Oedipa Maas who accidentally stumbles upon a vast conspiracy involving the clandestine postal service Tristero. Through centuries this shady organization has fought against various European and American postal monopolies, and welcoming the chance to escape the suburban routines Oedipa throws herself into solving the mystery. As the darkly humorous plot nears its end, she decides to attend a stamp auction where a representative of Tristero will allegedly show up, and where the mystery therefore promises to find its solution. Just as the auction is about to commence, however, the novel abruptly stops. Neither Oedipa nor the reader reaches the desired answer, and the genre expectations that Pynchon has activated through his detective plot are defused in the best postmodern manner. In *The Sense of an Ending* (1967) and *Reading for the Plot* (1984) Frank Kermode and Peter Brooks have discussed our narrative desire for meaningful endings that cause all the elements of the preceding plot to fall into place, but even though it has been strongly titillated throughout the novel this desire is hardly fulfilled in *The Crying of Lot 49*.

The lacking denouement and the resultant exposure of our entrenched genre expectations is still surprising fifty years after the original publication of Pynchon's novel, but the surprise must have been even bigger for readers back in 1966. It is an

Figure 26.1 The front panel of the dust jacket for the first edition of *The Crying of Lot 49* (1966).

integral aspect of the book medium that readers can sense the approaching ending, something Jane Austen famously exploits in the closing pages of *Northanger Abbey*. When watching a movie or listening to a CD or an audiobook, the ending may arrive without warning, but when reading a book, the tactile sensation of weight moving from the right to the left hand as we turn the pages creates a physical awareness of impending closure. When there are no more pages left, the book necessarily ends. Readers of the first edition of *The Crying of Lot 49* would have the same sensation of the novel's approaching conclusion, but when they reached the end of chapter 6—the preparations for the stamp auction that promised the solution to the mystery—they would still sense a number of remaining pages. When they read the famous last words on page 183, "Oedipa settled back, to await the crying of lot 49," they would therefore eagerly turn to page 184, expecting a final revealing chapter, but instead of the solution to the mystery they were met with nine white, silent pages. The novel ends sooner than the physical book lets its readers expect, and the materiality of the book accordingly intensifies the disappointment caused by Pynchon's teasing anti-climax.

The expressive materiality of the book

We rarely pay attention to the fact that books structure our reading experience on a basic physical level. Since the fusion of the codex format with Gutenberg's revolutionary printing technique in the fifteenth century, the book has been so

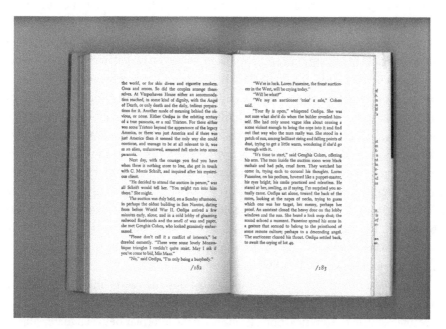

Figure 26.2 The final pages of the last chapter of the first edition.

naturalized a medium for literature that it has practically become invisible. As the American literary scholar N. Katherine Hayles argues, however, the automatic coupling of books and literature has been challenged with the advent of new digital media:

> [T]he long reign of print made it easy for literary criticism to ignore the specificities of the codex book when discussing literary texts. With significant exceptions, print literature was widely regarded as not having a body, only a speaking mind. [...] Rather, digital media have given us an opportunity we have not had for the last several hundred years: the chance to see print with new eyes, and with it, the possibility of understanding how deeply literary theory and criticism have been imbued with assumptions specific to print. (Hayles 2002, 32–3)

In order to address literature's hitherto neglected body language Hayles develops a so-called *media-specific analysis* that discusses "how medium-specific possibilities and constraints shape texts" and supplements our usual text analytical tools with an increased awareness of "literature as the interplay between form, content, and medium" (31).

Hayles's interest in the mediality of literature has been very influential, but she was not the first to investigate the connections between material media and the formation of meaning. In the 1960s Marshall McLuhan discussed the influence of media on the production of meaning in seminal works such as *The Gutenberg Galaxy* (1962) and *Understanding Media* (1964), and in the late 1970s and the 1980s Joshua Meyrowitz elaborated on McLuhan's theoretical groundwork, stressing the necessity of considering "the particular characteristics of each individual medium" when analyzing various communication processes (Meyrowitz 1985).

Concurrently with McLuhan's and Meyrowitz's media theory the discipline of *book history* arose. As the name suggests, this discipline is interested in the role of the book throughout literary and cultural history. In his essay "What Is the History of Books?" (1982) Robert Darnton argues that book history is less an individual discipline than a meeting place for other disciplines, including literary history, sociology, bibliography, economic s, and history, which work in concert to describe the influence of the book on history as well as the influence of history on the book. Darnton's most important contribution to book history is his so-called communications circuit, a model of the many stages and actors involved in the production, distribution and reception of a book. With its emphasis on the complex processes that turn an author's text into a book, Darnton's model has influenced a number of other media scholars and book historians who elaborate on the communications circuit in various ways (see, e.g., Adams and Barker 1993; Murray and Squires 2013).

While Darnton's model and various derivations thereof primarily focus on the institutional and financial contexts surrounding the book, other book historians are more interested in the physical book itself and in the interplay between materiality and literary meaning that informs our reading experience. D.F. McKenzie's article "The

Book as an Expressive Form" (1985) demonstrates how different material features of the physical book affect the meaning of a literary work on a fundamental level. Like McLuhan, McKenzie does not consider the book medium a frictionless channel but a material form with its own performativity. Books come in very different formats and sizes, and each variation sends certain signals that affect our perception of the text they bear. A small, cheap paperback edition and a large, illustrated leather-bound edition of Joseph Conrad's *Heart of Darkness* may contain the same text, but the body language of the two editions creates different expectations for the text.

McKenzie's descriptions of the expressive function of the book challenges our habitual understanding of books as objects carrying texts within them. A book is more than a mere container for a text, and its contents cannot simply be transported to another book like wine poured from bottle to bottle. In the essay "Material Matters" Paul Duguid writes, "Rather than to think of wine in bottles, each of which has a separate identity, it is more useful to consider information and technology [in this case: books] as mutually constitutive and ultimately indissoluble" (Duguid 1996, 501). Duguid accordingly suggests that we conceive of the relation between a book and its contents in terms of the relation between a dancer and a dance: "you don't get one without the other" (1996, 50).

Bibliographical codes

In an attempt to address the coauthoring function of the book medium, Jerome McGann sketches a mode of literary interpretation that he labels "materialist hermeneutics" (McGann 1991, 15). McGann argues that literary criticism has generally paid attention to literature's *linguistic codes* (the purely semantic aspects of literature) while neglecting its *bibliographical codes* (typefaces, bindings, page formats, paper quality, illustrations, etc.). A materialist hermeneutics takes as its premise that literary meaning is a product of the interplay between linguistic and bibliographical codes. In other words, the nine blank pages in the first edition of *The Crying of Lot 49* contribute to the overall aesthetic effect of the novel.

In addition to its significant (and signifying) blank pages, the first edition of Pynchon's novel contains various other examples of the interplay between linguistic and bibliographical codes. The symbol of the secretive Tristero society is a muted post horn—a fitting image of their attempt to obstruct the communication flow of the official postal service. A picture of the muted post horn—drawn in chalk on a sidewalk to emphasize its underground nature—is prominently featured on the front cover of the original dust jacket. The convention that cover illustrations express central aspects of a novel's plot is so dominating that we hardly give it a second thought. Dust jackets without illustrations are fairly uncommon, and cover illustrations play a natural part in our interaction with books. It is worth pointing out, however, that

Figure 26.3 Blank pages following the last chapter of the first edition.

the notion of a natural relation between texts and cover illustrations is somewhat problematical. Authors do not necessarily have a say when the cover illustration is chosen, and the illustration's motif tends to emphasize certain aspects of the story at the cost of others. As in all Pynchon's novels, *The Crying of Lot 49* features a number of themes, including racial politics, gender, economical imbalance, the history of media and the increasing importance of technology in human society. A single cover illustration cannot hope to encapsulate all these themes, and if it tried it would most likely become too crowded and confusing to fulfill its important function as a visual incentive to pick up the book in the bookstore. The necessary decision to single out a certain motif among a welter of possible motifs channels our perception of the work into certain grooves. In principle, cover illustrations and other paratexts are not part of the text itself, but in reality they function as "thresholds of interpretation" (with Gérard Genette's useful metaphor), or as blinkers that focus our attention on certain aspects of the text already before we begin reading. The muted post horn on the cover of *The Crying of Lot 49* emphatically tells us to be on the lookout for this symbol in the text.

The muted post horn is indeed mentioned several times in the novel, and it is even reproduced visually twice (Pynchon 1966, 52, 84). The visual reproduction of the symbol reminds us that printed books can contain much more than merely writing. Writing and literature are of course closely conjoined, but the writing in literary works is frequently supplemented with illustrations and other visual features, and as W.J.T. Mitchell has argued, a notion of text that is purely concerned with the words on the page cannot fully grasp the complex interactions between words and images that often inform literature (Mitchell 1995). Furthermore, it should be stressed that the pictorial aspect of literature is closely connected with the medium of the book. Printed books are eminently suited to handle both words and images, while other media for literature such as audiobooks run into trouble when images are woven into the text. Audiobooks can naturally not reproduce images, and when George Wilson who narrates the audiobook version of *The Crying of Lot 49* encounters the picture of the muted post horn, he has to employ the vague aural simile "like a trumpet"—a pale reflection of the iconic image that interrupts the flow of words so effectively in Pynchon's novel.

The enigmatic symbol not only appears on the dust jacket and in the text itself. Underneath the dust jacket of the first edition three muted post horns are blindstamped into the front board of the hardcover binding. While dust jackets are routinely employed as colorful visual supplements to the text they enclose, the binding beneath the cover is traditionally a more neutral space which besides the name of the author and the title on the spine does not hint at the contents of the book. The three muted horns on the front board of *The Crying of Lot 49* break with this neutrality. Being debossed into the cardboard they assume an almost sculptural quality which can literally be felt by the reader, and therefore they emphatically become part of the book's materiality: a two-dimensional sign that has migrated from the text of the book to its three-dimensional binding.

It is a crucial point in *The Crying of Lot 49* that Oedipa remains uncertain of Tristero's ontological status throughout the novel. Either it is a real organization or else a figment of her imagination: "Either Oedipa in the orbiting ecstasy of a true paranoia, or a real Tristero" (182). From its first to its final page, the novel is shot through with a pervasive ambiguity, and neither the reader nor Oedipa is entirely certain where the border between the real and the imagined should be drawn. This uncertainty is bolstered by the bibliographical codes of the first edition, since the surprising presence of muted post horns on the usually neutral space of the front board creates the sense—and physical sensation—that the story is escaping from the pages of the book and migrating into our own world. (This sense is fuelled further by the many graffitied and tattooed post horns that have been inscribed in our physical space in honor of Pynchon's novel).

The first edition of *The Crying of Lot 49* is an example of a book where the bibliographical and linguistic codes supplement each other well. Since its original publication in 1966 the novel has been published in numerous other editions. Each of these editions constitutes a new material delivery of Pynchon's text, and the connection between linguistic and bibliographical codes is frequently more tenuous in these versions than in the first edition. However, the bibliographical codes need not necessarily harmonize with the linguistic codes to affect our perception of the text they embody. Cover illustrations can guide our attention to minor elements of the plot or marginal characters, and plot descriptions or genre labels can create expectations that are not met by the text itself. At times it is even possible to speak of an outright mismatch between the literary contents of books and their paratexts and material get-up, but even in such cases the body language of the misleading bibliographical codes will influence our initial impression of the work.

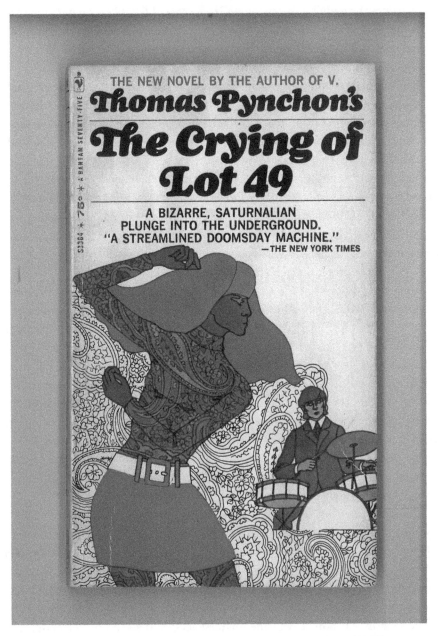

Figure 26.4 The front cover of the first Bantam paperback edition (1967).

When *The Crying of Lot 49* was published as a paperback in 1967 by Bantam, the wasteful materiality of the first edition was replaced with a full utilization of the cheap paper. The broad margins from the first edition shrank an inch, and the sinful use of surplus pages made way for a more economical approach. In the paperback there are exactly zero blank pages at the end of the book. The last page of the novel is also the last page of the book, and as a service to those disappointed readers who may have wondered whether a final chapter had fallen out of the flimsy glue binding, Bantam considerately added the discouraging word END after the novel's last sentence. While the generous materiality of the first edition seemed to promise a solution to the mystery beyond the sixth chapter, the paperback's stingy get-up and explicit closing of the story do not create any false expectations, and the aesthetic experience of reading the novel is thus transformed. At the same time, the cheap price of the paperback (75 cents) brings Pynchon's novel more within the reach of its target audience of young college students who would be less willing to pay for the more expensive hardcover edition. Like other bibliographical codes, prices and formats frame texts in particular ways that appeal to different audiences.

The paperback's appeal to a different audience than the sober first edition is made evident by the new colorful cover illustration. With her paisley-patterned blouse and swirling hair, the mini-skirted dancing hippie girl on the front cover clearly draws on the iconography of the Summer of Love. The dynamic cover would certainly have appealed to American college students in 1967, but Bantam's choice of cover motif simultaneously shows that loyalty to the contents of the book sometimes has to make way for marketing considerations. Bantam's illustration is meant to show the main character (on the back cover the image is accompanied by the phrase "Who is Oedipa Mass?"), but the twenty-eight-year-old housewife Oedipa Maas leads a conventional life in the suburbs, and by her own account she is a Young Republican. The distance between the dancing flower child and the Oedipa depicted in Pynchon's text is in other words significant. With its blatant attempt to address a particular target audience, the picture of Oedipa as a dancing hippie is no doubt motivated by commercial considerations, but this pecuniary motive also has interpretive consequences, since the illustration challenges our perception of the protagonist and creates an expectation that *The Crying of Lot 49* is somehow a novel about the counterculture.

These connotations are not entirely misleading, as Oedipa visits the University of California at Berkeley, San Francisco—the cradle of the Youth Rebellion—to locate a certain book necessary for her detective work. When she walks across the campus, she senses the imminent revolution:

> It was summer, a weekday, and midafternoon; no time for any campus Oedipa knew of to be jumping, yet this one was. She came downslope from Wheeler Hall, through Sather gate into a plaza teeming with corduroy, denim, bare legs, blonde hair, hornrims, bicycle spokes in the sun, bookbags, swaying card tables, long paper

petitions dangling to earth, posters for undecipherable FSM's, YAF's, VDC's, suds in the fountain, students in nose-to-nose dialogue. She moved through it carrying her fat book, attracted, unsure, a stranger, wanting to feel relevant but knowing how much of a search among alternate universes it would take. For she had undergone her own educating at a time of nerves, blandness and retreat [...]. (103)

Toward the end of the passage Oedipa is described as "a rare creature indeed, unfit perhaps for marches and sit-ins, but just a whiz at pursuing strange words in Jacobean texts" (104). Oedipa tangentially touches the burgeoning Youth Rebellion, but the quote also stresses that she is not a part of it. She clings to her fat book and dreams that things could have been different, but at the same time her self-knowledge is developed enough to realize that the revolution will have to unfold without her participation. Bantam's cover activates ideas of the Youth Rebellion, but it does so in a manner that clashes with the text's own portrayal of Oedipa.

Textual events and fluid texts

The portrait of the mini-skirted Oedipa was not a part of the work as it was originally presented to the readers. It was rather a specific event in the novel's long publication history. Jerome McGann describes different editions of literary works as *textual events*, and each of these events materializes the text in a particular way:

> [Texts] are produced and reproduced under specific social and institutional conditions, and [...] every text, including those that may appear to be purely private, is a social text. This view entails a corollary understanding, that a "text" is not a "material thing" but a material event or set of events, a point in time (or a moment in space) where certain communicative interchanges are being practiced. (McGann 1991, 21)

Each actualization of the text in a certain edition is the result of a series of choices made by a number of people, including editors, graphical designers, typesetters, marketing people—and authors. The author's name is usually the only one to appear on the cover of the book, but the book has not been created by the author alone. It is the end product of a collective process that involves various actors, as Robert Darnton's communications circuit clearly shows. In *Merchants of Culture* (2012) the literary sociologist John B. Thompson describes these many production stages as a "value chain" where each stage and each actor adds a certain value to the product.

Besides economical value the choices of the many actors also add nuances of meaning. The American bibliographer John Bryant even argues that their various contributions to the materialization of the text are best described as a set of intentions that affect our perception of the work in certain ways. These intentions change along with the different actors participating in the work's publication history,

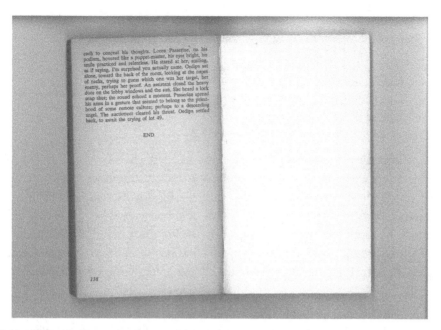

Figure 26.5 The last page of the Bantam paperback.

and different editions thus become "the material evidence of *shifting* intentions" (Bryant 2002, 9). To describe these ongoing changes, Bryant suggests the term *the fluid text*:

> Simply put, a fluid text is any literary work that exists in more than one version. It is "fluid" because the versions flow from one to another. [...] Literary works invariably exist in more than one version, [...] and if we are to understand how writing and the transmission of literary works operate in the processes of meaning making, we need first to recognize this fact of fluidity and also devise critical approaches, and a critical vocabulary, that will allow us to talk about the meaning of textual fluidity in writing and in culture. (Bryant 2002: 1–2)

Literary works are not located in the individual books that bear them but must rather be understood as an intangible sum of different editions, a dynamic accumulation of the transformations undergone by the linguistic and bibliographical codes over time. Joseph Grigely draws on a similar notion of what constitutes a literary work when he describes it as a "nontangible idea represented by a sequential series of texts" (Grigely 1991, 177). Literary works and texts are not stable objects but processual entities, and the person attempting to understand the material and semantic transformations in this process must consult a large corpus of versions rather than just a single edition. Oedipa Maas is also aware of this, and her attempt to solve the mystery of the Tristero involves meticulous studies of various editions of the fictional play *The Courier's Tragedy*. When she sees a performance of the play, she encounters a reference to the

Tristero and its feud against the noble family Thurn and Taxis who held a de facto monopoly of delivering the mail in seventeenth-century Europe:

> He that we last as Thurn and Taxis knew
> Now recks no lord but the stiletto's Thorn,
> And Tacit lies the gold once-knotted horn.
> No hallowed skein of stars can ward, I trow,
> Who's once been set his tryst with Trystero. (75)

Oedipa buys a used paperback edition of the Jacobean revenge play and discovers that the reference to the Tristero only appears in certain editions of the play. In other versions the revealing last line has been replaced with variants such as "Who once has crossed the lusts of Angelo" or "This tryst or odious awry, O Niccolò" (102), and to get to the bottom of the mystery Oedipa contacts Professor Emory Bortz who edited the hardcover edition on which her paperback is based. In his scrutiny of Oedipa's paperback Bortz is just as interested in the bibliographical as the linguistic codes:

> Oedipa showed him the paperback with the line in it. Bortz, squinting at the page, groped for another beer. "My God," he announced, "I've been Bowdlerized in reverse or something." He flipped to the front, to see who'd re-edited his edition of Wharfinger. "Ashamed to sign it. Damn. I'll have to write the publishers. K. da Chingado and Company? You ever heard of them? New York." He looked at the sun through a page or two. "Offset." Brought his nose close to the text. "Misprints. Gah. Corrupt." He dropped the book on the grass and looked at it with loathing. "How did *they* get into the Vatican, then?"
> "What's in the Vatican?" asked Oedipa.
> "A pornographic *Courier's Tragedy*. I didn't get to see it till '61, or I would've given it a note in my old edition." (151)

Bortz then shows her a number of other versions, including microfilms smuggled out of the Vatican, and each edition contains small textual variants. Oedipa's bibliographical quest through various material and textual variations lays bare a *fluid text* that has changed throughout history under the influence of shifting social, political, and religious forces. Such historical transformations work against the attempt to delimit a stable object of analysis, but they should be of interest to any literary historian. The historical context leaves traces in the different material manifestations of literary texts, and reading materially is synonymous with reading historically. As George Bornstein has written in an essay on modernism, "studying texts only in our contemporary reprintings erases the original historicized meanings" (quoted in Young 2003, 389).

The advantages of consulting different material variations of literary texts must necessarily be weighed against pragmatic considerations. It is neither necessary nor feasible to acquire a First Folio from 1623 to analyze *Hamlet*. Still one can profitably maintain an awareness that each particular edition is not a neutral container for the text but a specific textual event in a much longer series of events, each of which bears witness to its historical contexts and is affected by the various actors involved in its production. Books do not merely contain texts, they incarnate them, and each incarnation is part of the ongoing construction of literary meaning that always surrounds the literary work. Yet in spite of its constant wanderings between editions, languages and nations, the work still somehow remains the same. A text is a thing, but in a peculiar fashion it also transcends the object that incarnates it. As Bill Brown puts it:

> For the textual materialist, size matters, style matters, color matters. But despite the fact that readers can only experience a text as it is materialized in one form or another (Chartier), the literary work (like the musical work and unlike a painting or a carved sculpture) can be said to "transcend" the object (Genette 1997, 10–11). The experience of *Great Expectations* is a different experience as mediated by its serial publication in *All the Year Round*, its illustrated serialization in *Harper's Weekly*, its three-volume publication by Chapman and Hall, the six-volume interpoint braille edition, and the most recent Penguin edition, let alone your Kindle, your iPhone, your headphones. But we're still generally willing to say that each experience is the experience of *Great Expectations*. Across those very different mediations, the novel in some sense remains the same […]. (Brown 2010, 25)

If one can retain both perspectives in this paradoxical logic and accept that a novel like *The Crying of Lot 49* has no existence independent of the many editions that incarnate even while it 'in some sense remains the same' across the many different editions, then one is eminently suited to follow Oedipa's bibliographical quest for strange words in Jacobean texts.

Further reading

The field of book history is introduced in the two anthologies *The Book History Reader* (edited by Finkelstein and McCleery) and *A Companion to the History of the Book* (edited by Eliot and Rose). Gérard Genette's seminal work *Paratexts: Thresholds of Interpretation* makes a convincing case for paying attention to the many textual features surrounding and presenting the literary text, and Jerome McGann's *The Textual Condition* and Bill Brown's various writings on objects supplement Genette's theories with discussions of literature's materiality and its influence on the production of aesthetic meaning. D.F. McKenzie's *Bibliography and the Sociology of Texts* focuses on the social processes behind the publication of literary and other texts, and these institutional and economical contexts of literature are further analyzed in Pierre Bourdieu's *The Field of Cultural Production*. Drawing on Bourdieu and others, in *Marketing Literature* Claire Squires investigates how the marketing of books affects their interpretation. John B. Thompson's *Merchants of Culture* provides a valuable introduction to the contemporary publishing business and traces how publishers navigate between the traditional business model of print literature and the new economic logic of digital publishing.

References

Adams, Thomas R. and Nicolas Barber (1993) "A New Model for the Study of the Book," in *A Potencie of Life: Books in Society*, London: British Library.

Bourdieu, Pierre (1993) *The Field of Cultural Production*, Cambridge: Polity Press.

Brooks, Peter (1984) *Reading for the Plot*, Cambridge and London: Harvard University Press.

Brown, Bill (2010) "Introduction: Textual Materialism," *PMLA*, 125 (1): 24–8.

Bryant, John (2002) *The Fluid Text: A Theory of Revision and Editing for Book and Screen*, Ann Arbor: The University of Michigan Press.

Darnton, Robert (1990) "What Is the History of Books?" in *The Kiss of Lamourette: Reflections in Cultural History*, 107–35, New York: W. W. Norton & Company.

Duguid, Paul (1996) "Material Matters: The Past and Futurology of the Book," in G. Nunberg (ed.), *The Future of the Book*, Berkeley: University of California Press.

Eliot, Simon and Jonathan Rose (eds) (2007) *A Companion to the History of the Book*, Oxford: Blackwell.

Finkelstein, David and Alistair McCleery (eds) (2006) *The Book History Reader*, 2nd edition, London: Routledge.

Genette, Gérard (1997) *Paratexts: Thresholds of Interpretation*, Cambridge: Cambridge University Press.

Grigely, Joseph (1991) "The Textual Event," in P. G. Cohen (ed.), *Devils and Angels: Textual Editing and Literary Theory*, 167–94, Virginia: The University Press of Virginia.

Hayles, N. Katherine (2002) *Writing Machines*, Cambridge, MA: The MIT Press.

Kermode, Frank (1967) *The Sense of an Ending*, New York: Oxford University Press.

McGann, Jerome (1991) *The Textual Condition*, Princeton, NJ: Princeton University Press.

McKenzie, D. F. (1999) *Bibliography and the Sociology of Texts*, Cambridge: Cambridge University Press.

McLuhan, Marshall (1962) *The Gutenberg Galaxy: The Making of Typographic Man*, Toronto: Toronto University Press.

McLuhan, Marshall (1964) *Understanding Media: The Extensions of Man*, New York: Signet Books.

Meyrowitz, Joshua (1985) *No Sense of Place: The Impact of Electronic Media on Social Behavior*, New York: Oxford University Press.

Mitchell, W. J. T. (1995) *Picture Theory: Essays on Verbal and Visual Representation*, Chicago: University of Chicago Press.

Murray, Padmina Ray and Claire Squires (2013) "The Digital Publishing
   Communications Circuit," *Book 2.0*, 3 (1): 3–22.
Pynchon, Thomas (1966) *The Crying of Lot 49*, New York: Lippincott.
Squires, Claire (2009) *Marketing Literature: The Making of Contemporary Writing in
   Britain*, Houndmills and Basingstoke: Palgrave Macmillan.
Thompson, John B. (2012) *Merchants of Culture: The Publishing Business in the Twenty-
   First Century*, New York: Plume.
Young, John K. (2003) "Pynchon in Popular Magazines," *Critique* 44 (4): 389–404.

27
Remediation

Kiene Brillenburg Wurth

In *History and Tropology*, Frank Ankersmit defines the term "representation" as substitution (Ankersmit 1994). A representation (cf. a representation of the past) does not resemble or imitate something else, but *substitutes*, that is to say: comes in the place of something else. In children's play, a piece of wood comes in place of a gun, a stick in place of a horse. It is their functional likeness in a specific context—their ability to function *as* something else: a gun or a horse—that makes the piece of wood and the stick into representations. Representations have nothing to do with copying an original. They usurp things and ideas to bring them alive:

> The clay horse or servant, buried in the tomb of the mighty, takes the place of the living. The idol takes the place of the god. The question whether it represents the "external form" of the particular divinity or, for that matter, of a class of demons is quite inappropriate. The idol serves as the substitute of the God in worship and ritual—it is a man-made god in precisely the sense that the hobby horse is a man-made horse .... (Gombrich 1985, 3)

Thus, art historian Ernst Gombrich says, representations create presence-in-absence: the clay horse functions precisely in the absence of the living, the idol in the absence of the god. Representations are not objective or opaque, they are not about seeing through but about seeing *as*—a stick *as* a horse. One could even say, as the philosopher Arthur Danto does, that representations are all about seeing the world in a certain way: about *mediating* the world (Danto 1981). When we say that a clay horse in a tomb represents the living, the clay horse renders the absent present through the viewer's cultural aptitude to see the horse *as* such. Seeing the clay horse means seeing how a sculptor, or even an entire culture, sees the world.

I am reflecting on the concept of representation in such detail here, because it communicates something crucial about the concept of remediation that I will be considering in this chapter. Indeed, the way in which remediation has been used in media theory during the last two decades or so is but a variation on the idea of representation as substitution just considered. Let me try to elucidate this as follows. In the *Oxford English Dictionary*, *remediation* is defined as the remedying or reversing of (mostly environmental) damage. Since 1998, however, with Jay Bolter's and David Grusin's influential article and subsequent book *Remediation*, the term has come to be used as a remedy or redress of a very special kind. Remediation refers to a tendency in contemporary cinema and computer games toward immediacy and total mediation at the same time. Writing on the film *Strange Days*, Bolter and Grusin use remediation to define the paradoxical logic of creating virtual worlds with media technologies (hypermediacy), yet erasing all traces of these media (immediacy):

> In addressing our culture's contradictory imperatives for immediacy and hypermediacy, [*Strange Days*] enacts what we understand as a double logic of "re-mediation." Our culture wants both to multiply its media and to erase all traces of mediation: it wants to erase its media in the very act of multiplying technologies of mediation. (Bolter and Grusin 1999, 312)

Remediation in this sense concerns a double take of presence and absence: a hypermediated presence that creates an illusion of the absence of any mediating interface whatsoever. Remediation, then, is about remedying the presence of technology through its ability to generate immediacy effects. In *Strange Days*, this double logic is exemplified by "the wire": a techno device that captures and records the perception of its wearer, to play them back to her/him. The result is the illusion of an interface without an interface, a mode of mediation to end all mediation, because the wire functions *like* and comes in the place of that which it cancels out: the perception of its wearer. Now it becomes clear that remediation—in the sense of remedying absence—is defined by the same logic of substitution as representation. Remediations take the place of something else by means of a mode of mediation that renders this "something else" present (again) without the sense or awareness *of* any such mediation. However, while representation is a more general concept that could be applied in any time or culture, remediation as a concept is tied to the cultural context of the digital age. In this age, technologies of simulation were developed that apparently rendered remediation visible and significant as a concept in the first place. Remediation is representation plus digital technology—or: representation considered specifically in the context of such technologies.

This statement would end my chapter swiftly. We know what representation is, and now we know what remediation is—how it works. As a media concept, however, remediation also extends beyond this paradoxical play of total immersion and total mediation. It not only has to do with how media create reality effects and thus affect users, but how media relate to each other: about their fundamental *modus operandi*. If remediation tells us something about an illusory game of immediacy, it also tells us something about the illusory nature of what I would like to call medial identity: about the so-called essence of media. The term "media" is a complex one and we will have the time later in this chapter to assess its full complexity. For now, however, it will suffice to point out that according to Bolter and Grusin media in the digital age are never singular entities. They contain other media as well. TV contains film and radio, for instance, just as websites in the early 2000s contained the newspaper, while TV screens began to be restyled in the manner of websites, with multiple screens. This is remediation: the representation of one medium in another medium, old in new, new in old.

In this chapter I will focus on remediation as this "mechanism," this *modus operandi* of media. That is to say, I show how the concept of remediation helps us to make sense of media and how media function and change within society: mediation is always already remediation. To make sense of remediation, we first need to make sense of the concepts of medium and media. I then explore remediation on the basis of the idea of the book in the digital age.

Medium, media

The concept of "medium" is notoriously hard to define. The hardest part for critics has been to differentiate between medium and form—and to determine if and what kind of conceptual differences between medium and form exist. Let me start with "medium." Etymologically, "medium" leads back to the Latin *medium*, meaning *middle, midst, center; interval*. A medium is what comes, lies, or occurs in between; it is an intervening substance or agent. Since around 1600 this sense of an intervening substance is extended specifically to a means or channel of communication. A medium is a vehicle through which messages and meanings are conveyed. Only in the middle of the nineteenth century does "medium" come to be used in the sense that we still often use it today: as the substance or means of artistic expression, the medium of paint, sound, or word that corresponds to specific art forms (painting, music, literature). In that same period, "form" came to be defined as a combination of elements of "medium" to an expressive end: "form" was seen as a particular application of "medium" or "matter." In this definition, "form" is the privileged term, "deciding" or "realizing" the medium, even though precisely in the nineteenth century critics such as Arthur Seidl were already developing an aesthetics of the formless that favored the "medium" and painters like Odilon Redon did the same (Seidl 1887). Like "medium," "form" is a complex concept that I cannot do full justice here as it can be traced all the way to Plato (*eidos*) and ancient Greek philosophy, referring to ideas that can only be conceptually registered. We will therefore leave "form" here as it is, to move on to different meanings of the term "medium" developed in the later nineteenth and twentieth centuries that will eventually help us to get a fuller grasp of the concept of remediation in this chapter.

First, as intervening substance, "medium" corresponds to the presence of technology in the production of immediacy effects that, we have seen, is central to remediation in the later twentieth century. The medium is the vehicle of presentification: a phenomenological concept that refers to a reproduction of perceptions and that, as such, equals the production of presence (through imagination, empathy, simulation, and so forth). Presentification is of course not restricted to the means of new media technologies—though such technologies may simulate presence quite powerfully (as is exemplified by the wire in *Strange Days*). Friedrich Nietzsche, for one, was already aware of the production of presence when he wrote about Greek Tragedy. He thought that the chorus in tragedy was like a wall that tragedies could erect around themselves to create (simulate) a new reality—or what could be felt or experienced *as* the presence of (a) reality. Today we would call such a production of presence *virtual reality*, but such production has always been at issue in art and literature. The painting *Mer orageuse* (*Stormy Sea*) (1869) by Gustave Courbet, for instance, had a striking effect when first displayed in Berlin. Evoking a huge wave that approaches the beach, the painting made people turn round, looking over their shoulder as they kept having the feeling something was approaching them from behind. The image thus created a palpable presence that Paul Cézanne worded as follows: "It as though it [the wave] were coming right at one, it makes one jump back in shock. The whole room is filled with the smell of the foam."

Courbet was able to create this reality effect by means of a radical pictorial method. He did not paint the wave; he only used a spatula and palette to smooth out the pigment, layering paint over paint on the canvas. All this layering created the impression of a wall—which may well have been what materially impressed itself on viewers from behind. This presence of materiality brings me to the second sense of media: the matter or material of different art forms. In this sense, "medium" is often used specifically as an extension of the senses: of smelling, tasting, seeing, hearing, and touching—or a mixture of two or more of them. Medium is what relates to these senses in the form of visual, verbal, sonic, organic, or any other material. For centuries, philosophers and critical theorists have debated the differences between the arts on the basis of the material, the medium, they incorporate and the affordances—the possible uses and effects—of that material. For instance, in the eighteenth century Edmund Burke and, a littler later, Gotthold Ephraim Lessing argued that words and images offer different kinds of affordances: words engage us in a temporal manner, the one after the other, while images engage us in a spatial manner, all at once (Burke 1759; Lessing 1766). In the nineteenth century, writers and painters were rather more interested in the question how media could be mixed. Could painting and poetry become like instrumental music, mimicking its effects or even incorporating compositional methods? Could it be possible for the materiality of paint, or words, to create musical presences? Painters like Odilon Redon or James McNeill Whistler and poets like Stéphane Mallarmé tried to answer these questions in their work.

In the course of the late nineteenth and early twentieth century, this idea of sensuous materiality became more and more prominent in thinking about differences and relations between different art forms. One famous art critic should be mentioned here as he figures prominently in Bolter and Grusin's outline of remediation: Clement Greenberg. Greenberg asserted in a well-known essay "Towards a Newer Laocoön" (1985, the title referring to Lessing's *Laocoön*) that all art forms should retreat into their own sensuous material, rather than being busy depicting certain "subjects." Poetry should be about words, not about people and stories. Painting should be about paint, not about landscapes, historical events, or figures in a real world—as Courbet's wave paintings had already suggested in their thick material layering. Greenberg thought that critics should change their conception of "content" in order to fully grasp the significance of the visual arts (and probably of all other arts): that the *medium* (paint) is the content of art.

This idea of the medium being its own content—and as such being of worthy critical consideration—would become of crucial significance to a twentieth-century media theorist whose work forms the conceptual basis for *Remediation*: Marshall McLuhan. During the latter half of the twentieth century, "medium" more and more became a plural term to refer to the modern means of mass communication (radio, TV, newspapers, magazines, new electronic media): media. McLuhan speculated that media are the extensions of wo/man: the book is an extension of the eye, just as TV is, while radio is an extension of the ear, just as hammers are extensions of the hands and arms. In a way, Greenberg presented a similar argument insofar as he thought that all art forms should bear on—and specifically address—one of the senses.

In *Understanding Media* (1964), McLuhan argued that by extending ourselves again and again with our appliances and communication technologies we are also constantly being reshaped in our thinking, experiencing, and perceiving *through* such media. Our media environments have evolved in the course of thousands of years from extensions of the eye (images, writing) to extensions of the entire nervous system (the Internet). We have to deal with increasingly complex media environments, depending on the means we have ourselves (once) generated. McLuhan captured his assumptions about the reciprocal relations between media and ourselves in the following slogan: *the medium is the message*. In a popularizing publication "message" was playfully changed into "massage": media "massage" or work the senses, our thinking, and our consciousness so that we may sense, perceive, and think differently through our interactions with new media (McLuhan and Fiore 1967). Critics, for McLuhan, should become aware *at all* of the potential of media as an explanatory frame for cultural change. Media themselves, rather than only what we produce with them, should become our critical focus.

A medium, we could say with McLuhan, is that from which change ensues. According to him, cultural change is marked by the transition from one medium environment into another: new media technologies offer new modes and frameworks of presenting, perceiving, experiencing, and remembering the world. We can recognize such transitions by the way in which old media suddenly become visible *as such* in new media—while before, they had been the invisible, unknowable frame or ground from which we approach and understand the world. Thus, early forms of writing on scrolls still contain indicators of oral presentation and reception: these were texts to be read aloud. Likewise, early print books mimic the design and material of handwritten manuscripts, so that the older medium is carried within the new as a visible memory, no longer functioning as a structuring principle or cultural code (a culture's primary information technology), but as an ornament and remnant within a new organizing code: an object, no longer a structuring technology. Indeed, we could say with McLuhan that cultural change is marked by the transition from *ground* to *figure* of a once dominant medium: handwritten manuscripts became *objects*, visible as *figures*, within the new *ground* of print books. Thus, what McLuhan argued for in his theory of cultural change was that *the content of a medium is always another medium*: the former always digests the latter. The fact that, later, handwritten manuscripts started to mimic the Roman type font of print books takes us away from Greenberg and McLuhan back to Bolter and Grusin: to the idea of remediation.

Remediation: The book in the digital age

So far I have addressed three senses of the term "medium" in the service of the concept of remediation. First, we have seen, medium is a means for presentification— the strong sense of presence that remediation (as a mode of substitution) entails. We have also seen that the production of presence is not restricted to new technologies of virtual reality, and not even to hyperrealism: immediacy effects can also be evoked through less accommodating, more robust modes of presentation that emphasize the materiality of a medium (the materiality of paint, or of words or sounds). This presence of materiality led us to a second sense of "medium," namely, that which constitutes the specificity of different art forms. It is very difficult to objectively pinpoint such specificity. What an art form "is" is often also a matter of cultural conventions and traditions. Therefore, I have in the foregoing only pointed to certain Western traditions of thinking *about* the specificity of art forms since the eighteenth century.

From this second sense of "medium" we distilled a tendency in twentieth-century art theory that highlighted the materiality of art: the medium (of paint, word, or sound) was the content of art. Or still: the medium was its own content, for artists as much as for art critics. We learned that this insight constituted one of the basic tenets of Marshall McLuhan's media theory that ultimately formed the starting point for Bolter and Grusin's *Remediation*. With McLuhan, we saw, "medium" gains a third dimension: it refers to modern means of mass communication technology (media). McLuhan argued that media may bring about cultural change, but that they never do so in a vacuum: new media always carry with them the traces of old media.

Bolter and Grusin's theory of remediation emerges out of McLuhan's statement that the content of a medium is always another medium. But they also add something to McLuhan's theory. What they suggest is that old media may not necessarily turn into fossils alone and that we may not be progressing toward ever-newer mediascapes in the future, one medium incorporating and replacing the other. Their idea of remediation is rather one of an ongoing interaction between newer and older media, fashioning and refashioning each other. I aim to explain this in this section on the basis of a contemporary example.

For the last twenty years or so, literary critics have been increasingly concerned with the idea of the death of the book. With the advent of the digital revolution people thought that the print book would not hold as the culturally dominant medium: the medium that allegedly defined the stories that we made, the ways in which we produced and distributed knowledge, the ways in which we read and digested information, and even our relation to the world—our modes of perceiving and experiencing. Some critics already saw the end of the book coming way before. McLuhan, for one, observed in the late 1960s that the book was giving way as an invisible or subliminal *ground* of communication and knowledge distribution to electronic media. It was slowly turning into a *figure*: a medium becoming visible as a fossilized object within the setting of a novel framework of communication and information processing.

However, it was only in the 1990s and 2000s that the effects of electronic media became palpable on a grander scale. This was the era when personal computing became widespread in the Western world and the Internet had begun its ascendency. Critics were speculating on the end of literature as we knew it, as writing and print was now transforming into a technical image, while the format of the book and the paper page gave way to sites and other digital formats. New forms of literature emerged in the 1980s that partly elaborated on concrete poetry—poetry that used words as objects rather than vehicles of linguistic reference—and avant-gardist experiments in visual writing. Such literature made use of the many new possibilities that digital media afforded: texts that could move and flicker, words that could dance, stories made up of fragments to be fused together by a user, flash poetry, or cinepoetry and cinenovels in which text and cinematic images were merged into a new configuration. The recent work *Pry* (2016) exemplifies the full potential of electronic literature. It is a mixture of an app, a novella, cinema, and hypertext: a book to watch and a film to touch. *Pry* is about a character called James, a demolition expert who returned from the first Gulf war six years earlier. James is turning blind and we read his (unreliably narrated) story in a fragmented manner, negotiating our way through the verbal-visual material. Though such active and playful negotiating through a text is nothing new—it is as old as the *I Ching*—the affordances of digital media here do expand the possibilities for narrative and reading, while these media also accommodate an easy mixing of different media. The specificity of media is still at issue in *Pry*, but only within the larger framework of media blended into a digital setup: the novella is charged with cinema, and cinema with dimensions of the touch screen.

Works like *Pry* actively explore the different affordances of digital media. Conversely, e-books that have been competing on the market with print books for the last ten years only *mimic* the print book in a digital setting. They contain and rework (remediate) an image of the book, with pages to be turned on the Kindle: the book has here become a visual remainder, a remnant of the Gutenberg galaxy. For a while people in the book business were concerned that the e-book was going to replace the print book as a new medium. They were especially terrified by the prospect of illegal downloading that had troubled the music industry from the 2000s onward. In a similar vein, some literary critics thought that the future of literature would be electronic. This may be. However, when we consider the production of literary works in print between the late 1990s and the present, we also see a counter development: print books charged with the affordances of the digital. Works like Mark Z. Danielewski's *House of Leaves* (2000), *Only Revolutions* (2006), *The Fifty-Year Sword* (2012) and his recent 26-volume venture *The Familiar* (2016), Grame Rawl's *Woman's World* (2005), Steven Hall's *The Raw Shark Texts* (2007), Anne Carson's *Nox* (2009), or Jonathan Safran Foer's *Tree of Codes* (2010) all indicate how print literature has in its turn been remediating the potentialities of the digital. This ranges from the creative mimicry of code writing in print and handwriting (*House of Leaves*, *The Raw Shark Texts*, *Tree of Codes*), the refashioning of the digital screen (*Nox*), or the blending of visual and verbal media (*Woman's World*), to a thematic reworking of networked identities in a paper-made world (*The Raw Shark Texts*).

It may be that these experimental works of literature—still rather limited in number—will not be the future of the print book. There may be multiple futures for the print book (bearing in mind that the print book is now always already digitally made), as well as for e-books and electronic literature. We cannot say that the new media will survive in a Darwinian struggle, while the old will perish. The relation between literature and digital media today rather suggests a dynamic of remediation that cancels out the idea of the new (as new media consist of old media) and the old (as old media rework new media) at once. Paper-based literature reinvents itself precisely—though never exclusively—in the face of the new digital media that allegedly are about to replace it. One medium never quite erases another. Rather, as the logic of remediation shows, when a new medium becomes dominant, existing media ecologies are rearranged, some media becoming obsolete (or temporarily so, as witnessed in the recent vinyl revival), others refashioning themselves against or merging with the new medium, still others obtaining new significance in a different context (the Xerox machine in zine making). Thus, remediation in turn indicates something else: that time never progresses like an arrow, but rather evolves on multiple levels at the same time—not in a one-directional line, but in loops.

Coda: Remediation and comparative media

I have unpacked the concept of remediation by way of the concepts of media and mediation. I have shown how in the twentieth century a renewed interest in "medium as such" in art criticism is paralleled by media theorists like Marshall McLuhan who wanted to focus attention on the significance of "media in themselves," as agents of cultural change. Interested in media as such agents, McLuhan discovered that the content of a medium is always another medium about to be sidestepped as the culturally dominant medium. Elaborating on McLuhan's discovery, Bolter and Grusin have introduced the concept of remediation to show that there is nothing new under the sun. We have known this for centuries (Ecclesiastes), but Bolter and Grusin made an important contribution to the public debate on digital media when most people believed that these media were about to change our lives forever in an unparalleled way. What they have shown is that new media are never just new, but always consist of and are entangled with existing ones.

For his part, and perhaps unwittingly so, Greenberg showed six decades earlier that the idea of the "medium as such" is the effect of remediation—if not a remediation of "old" and "new," then a remediation of different art forms. Remember that Greenberg's argument was that modern painting retreats into its own materiality, withdraws from figuration. This is how modern painting becomes its own medium, or takes its own medium paint as its subject, as abstract and abstract expressionist art have done. But Greenberg also argues that this "becoming-medium" was an effect of a paradigm change. Painting no longer tried to parallel literature as an art of storytelling and make-believe, but started mimicking the methods of another art form at the dawn of the twentieth century: instrumental music. Ever since the later eighteenth century instrumental music was seen as the most autonomous of art forms. It apparently did not have a "subject matter" as literature had, all it had was (critics believed) its own medium: sounds, tones, tonal form and matter. Instrumental music did not name or depict anything according to critics keen on arguing for the autonomy of art—instrumental music was about…instrumental music. Greenberg thought that abstract and abstract expressionist art adopted this autonomy of instrumental music to discover something essential about painting. Painting too could be about painting alone. However, since this discovery was made with the knowledge of the method of another art form, or how critics conceived of this art form, painting never really became "its own" medium. In becoming "its own," it repeated another medium.

As this example shows, remediation need not just be about the interaction between old and new media—but also just *different* media. Some would call this intermediality: the creative exchange between different media, often resulting in new media forms. This may be. However we call this process, it alerts us to the fact that as literary scholars we cannot turn a blind eye to developments in other media. Literature exists in a media ecology, changing and adapting to changes in that ecology, or interacting with other media, and not only to brand new ones. For instance, important experimental works like James Joyce's *Finnegans Wake* (1939), Virginia Woolf's *The Waves* (1931), or John Dos Passos' *Manhattan Transfer* (1925) emerge in part out of the interaction with instrumental music and the then new medium of cinema. These examples show that as literary scholars we always already need to be comparative media scholars to gauge the depth and significance of the works we teach and research—to situate and localize these works not only in their cultural-historical but also in their complex medial contexts.

Further reading

Jay Bolter and David Grusin's *Remediation* (1999) is an essential text for understanding the conceptual framework of remediation. N. Kathrine Hayles's *Writing Machines* (2002) is focused on the relation between literature and changes in the production of literature since the middle of the twentieth century. Her later book *How We Think: Digital Media and Contemporary Technogenesis* (2012) is a more broad-ranging investigation of the importance of media to humanities with a strong emphasis on literary studies. Marshall McLuhan's *Understanding Media: The Extensions of Man* (1964) is a classic in the field of media studies. For more on adaptation of works into other media, Linda Hutcheon's *A Theory of Adaptation* offers a systematic and highly useful introduction.

References

Ankersmit, Frank (1994) *History and Tropology*, Berkeley: University of California Press.

Bolter, Jay and Richard Grusin (1999) *Remediation. Understanding New Media*, Cambridge, MA: MIT Press.

Burke, Edmund (1990 [1757]) *A Philosophical Enquiry into the Origin of Our Ideas of the Sublime and Beautiful*, Oxford: Oxford University Press.

Burke, Edmund (1998 [1759]) *A Philosophical Enquiry*, Oxford: Oxford University Press.

Danto, Arthur C. (1981) *Transfiguration of the Common Place*, Harvard: Harvard University Press.

Ekman, Ulrik and Matthew Fuller (eds) (2012) *Throughout: Art and Culture Emerging with Ubiquitous Computing*, Cambridge, MA: MIT Press.

Fuller, Matthew (2005) *Media Ecologies*, Cambridge, MA: MIT Press.

Gombrich, E. H. (1985) *Meditations on a Hobby Horse*, Chicago: University of Chicago Press.

Greenberg, Clement (1985) "Towards a Newer Laocooön," in *Partisan Review*, July–August 1940; in Francis Frascina (ed.), *Pollock and After: The Critical Debate*, London: Routledge.

Hayles, N. Katherine (2002) *Writing Machines*, Cambridge, MA: The MIT Press.

Hayles, N. Katherine (2012) *How We Think: Digital Media and Contemporary Technogenesis*, Chicago: The University of Chicago Press.

Hutcheon, Linda (2006) *A Theory of Adaptation*, London: Routledge.

Lessing, Gotthold Ephraim (2012 [1766]) *Laokoon. Über die Grenzen der Malerie und Poesie*, Stuttgart: Reklam.

McLuhan, Marshall (1964) *Understanding Media. The Extensions of Man*, New York: McGraw-Hill.

McLuhan, Marshall and Quentin Fiore (Agel, Jerome) (1967) *The Medium Is the Massage*, New York: Bantam Books.

Seidl, Arthur (1907 [1887]) *Vom Musikalisch-Erhabenen. Ein Beitrag zur Aesthetik der Tonkunst*, Leipzig: Kahnt.

28

Art

Peter Simonsen

Literature is an art form, a special way of using and apprehending language, which is distinct from but also related to other art forms such as music, painting, sculpture, film, or dance. This chapter is not so much about the aesthetic qualities of literature *per se* as about literature's relations to the other art forms. At different moments in the long history of art, literature has been inspired by and taken other art forms as thematic material and sometimes even as formal model and as such aimed to imitate one or more of its sibling art forms—in particular there are rich traditions for literature's dealings with music and painting. Literary criticism and aesthetic theory has at various moments in this history of art held that literature has closer affinities with and should consequently aspire to cultivate its relationship with one rather than another art form. One reason for this may be that literature as an art form explores and takes stock of its own self-identity, its artistic specificity, in the meeting, sometimes friendly, sometimes hostile, and sometimes indifferent, with other art forms. This surely is one good reason why we should always seek to understand and study literature also in relation to other art forms.

The field of comparative art studies has been on the rise since the late 1980s and has branched out into various specialities such as interart studies and intermedial studies (Mitchell 1994; Elleström 2010). This veritable boom is closely related to the multimedia reality we inhabit and the possibilities for remediation and media convergence enabled especially by the arrival of new digital media. Historically literary authors had to seek out art works hidden from public view or to simply make up an imaginary painting or sculpture or piece of music because actual ones weren't at hand. Today, it is hard to escape other media and representations as well as recorded performances of music and dance even if a literary author should wish to do so. Especially the computer and new portable tablets have made possible what Friedrich Schiller envisioned in the *Aesthetic Education of Man* (1793–1795), but never realized:

> it is a natural and necessary consequence of their perfection, that, without confounding their objective limits, the different arts come to resemble each other more and more, in the action which they exercise on the mind. At its highest degree of ennobling, music ought to become a form, and act on us with the calm power of an antique statue; in its most elevated perfection, the plastic art ought to become music and move us by the immediate action exercised on the mind by the senses; in its most complete development, poetry ought both to stir us powerfully like music and like plastic art to surround us with a peaceful light. In each art, the perfect style consists exactly in knowing how to remove specific limits, [without] sacrificing at the same time the particular advantages of the art. (Book 22, bartleby.com)

Schiller imagines an early variant of what Richard Wagner in the middle of the nineteenth century talked about in terms of a *Gesamtkunstwerk* and sought to practice in his own opera with its high degree of confluence between song, music, and drama. This is extremely difficult to realize even as it is an ensnaring and ambitious desire, which still informs a number of artistic strategies. A contemporary artist like Eduardo Kac experiments in the same synesthetic tradition with digital poems coded to move across the computer screen in harmony with music, web 2.0 poems where the reader's input determines the wording and rhythm of the poem, or aroma-poems where Kac uses nanotechnology to store and in a sense "write" with specific smells on the page of the book (http://www.ekac.org/). Through a historical approach to literature's manifold ways of relating to other art forms and media and by analyzing its tendency to appropriate them as artistic material, our understanding of literature's specificity as a verbal art form is enhanced, even as we also reach a better, more nuanced understanding of the historicity of our own epoch's media convergences and the transformation of what we take to be literature.

Aspects of the history of comparative art studies

According to the English aesthetic critic Walter Pater, every art form has its specific "sensuous material," which gives the art lover a specific aesthetic experience that cannot be translated from one art form to another (Pater talks about each art's "untranslatable charm"). The point of departure of aesthetic criticism, as Pater puts it in *Studies in the History of the Renaissance* (1873), is "a just apprehension of the ultimate differences of the arts" (Pater 1901, 133). However, as he continues (in the spirit of Schiller),

> it is noticeable that, in its special mode of handling its given material, each art may be observed to pass into the condition of some other art, by what German critics term an *Anders-streben*—a partial alienation from its own limitations, by which the arts are able, not indeed to supply the place of each other, but reciprocally to lend each other new forces. (133–4)

Pater then provides examples of how literature forges creative alliances with relief sculpture and the art of engraving to conclude that all the arts share in "aspiring towards the principle of music; music being the typical, or ideally consummate art, the object of the great *Anders-streben* of all art" (134–5). All art forms tend toward one another and can provide mutual fertilization and inspiration, yet above all they aspire toward music. Music is for Pater the art form where it is hardest to distinguish between form and content or "matter," and as a true aesthete and supporter of the doctrine of *l'art pour l'art* he believes that distinction should be obliterated: art "should become an end in itself, should penetrate every part of the matter:—this is what all art constantly strives after, and achieves in different degrees" (135).

Pater must be understood in the aesthetic tradition that is typically associated with Kant, which emphasizes art's autonomy and non-instrumental nature and which finds expression in Romanticism's reaction around 1800 to the Neoclassic understanding of art as a mirror whose most important function was the faithful imitation of a nature understood to precede the creative act. If this is the ambition of art, then the pictorial arts will be positioned at the top of the hierarchy of art. Most important poetics from the Renaissance to the Neoclassic age (1500–1750) had in fact supported the famous dictum by Horace in his *Ars Poetica*: *ut pictura poesis* ("as is painting so is poetry"). Horace was taken to mean that poetry should imitate painting and use words to paint pictures. However, Romantics such as Wilhelm Wackenroder, Ludwig Tieck and William Hazlitt opposed this dogma and argued that art, because it expresses the inner life and spirit of the artist rather than something in the visible world, should model itself on music and song.

Horace was not the first to suggest parallels between painting and poetry. Simonides of Ceos, the ancient Greek lyric poet from around 500 BC, had said that poetry is a speaking picture and painting a silent poem. Here we see another hierarchy within the interart relation as poetry both images and speaks, whereas painting cannot appropriate the force of poetry. This is our first example of a long tradition for interart struggle named by Leonardo da Vinci in his treatise, *Paragone*.

In this work Da Vinci favors the art of painting because it can represent a beautiful body in such a way that the viewer comprehends it in a moment, at once. Poetry, on the other hand, has to name each body part one after another which makes it difficult for the listener to apprehend the body as a totality.

The German poet and critic Gotthold Ephraim Lessing is the most influential modern voice in interart studies. In his treatise *Laokoön* (1766), he is concerned to demarcate the boundaries between the art forms and to make sure that there is no miscegenation. He was the first to divide the art forms according to the different semiotic signs they make use of according to whether these signs are temporal or spatial. The signs of painting address the eye and are perceived at once in what he calls a "pregnant moment": they stand above one another and their ideal matter is hence bodies in space. The signs of literature are temporal and address the ear and are perceived one after another: they follow one another and are therefore ideally disposed to render actions in time. Literature, for Lessing, must stop trying to imitate painting through long and detailed descriptions of the kind that dominated much eighteenth-century poetry, and painting must stop trying to imitate literature's narratives. Every art form must maximize its given medium and not aim to transgress its boundaries. Lessing was still theorizing art within a mimetic aesthetics where the role of literature is to render something external to itself rather than aspire for full autonomy, as we find later in Pater. However, Lessing's distinction between plastic art and literature was the condition of possibility for Romanticism's new expressive understanding of literature and its aspiration toward music as the model art form.

Literature and music

The word "music" stems from the Greek "mousike" and means "art of the muses." The position has often been proposed, among other by Nietzsche in *The Birth of Tragedy*, that music in the sense of rhythm and melody predates the birth of poetry. Yet historical research has not been able to confirm the respective origins of song and instrumentation. According to the Greek myth of Orpheus, who was both poet and singer, they co-originated with the power to enthrall nature and awaken the dead Eurydice. Music's overwhelming force and immediate manner of moving us—we cannot close our ears in quite the same way that we can close our eyes and mouths— are brought out in the story of Ulysses who must tie himself to the mast in order to hear the song of the Sirens while the crew put wax in their ears.

Through history poetry and music increasingly move in separate ways. The ode as a genre was originally integrated with song and dance, such as in the work of Pindar (522–442 BC) ("ode" stems from the Greek "aeidein": "to sing"). Later it could be intended for musical accompaniment (e.g., Dryden's odes for St. Cecilia's Day, 1687 and 1697) and later again, in Romanticism, the ode became a purely personal, silent rather than public and performed form as the classic odic forms are dissolved and reconfigured in the odes of Wordsworth, Keats, and Shelley. It might seem paradoxical that this should occur in the Romantic age, where we would expect a *rapprochement* between poetry and music, but it is surely an example of the rather vague and idealized notions they had about music, notions typically very distant from what contemporary composers were attempting.

The poet William Wordsworth was part of this idealization as seen in such poems as "The Solitary Reaper" (1807) and "Power of Music" (1807). Wordsworth opens the latter by daring to locate the rebirth of Orpheus as a blind street musician in the present Oxford Street: "An Orpheus! An Orpheus!—yes, faith may grow bold, / And take to herself all the wonders of old" (Wordsworth 1888, ll. 1–2). This Orphic singer "works on the crowd":

> He sways them with harmony merry and loud;
> He fills with his power all their hearts to the brim—
> Was aught ever heard like his fiddle and him! (Wordsworth 1888, ll. 5–8)

The blind street fiddler brings life to the weary, bliss to the hungry, cheer to the mourner, rest to the anxious, and alleviation to the guilt-burdened soul. He becomes a beacon and is able to make passersby from the lower strata of society (chimney sweeper, baker, apprentice, newsman, lamplighter, porter, cripple) forget their errands while the higher social strata drive by in their "Coaches and Chariots." Music can halt time for the listeners and forge an affective community for them without losing sight of the forces of history.

In *The Renaissance*, Pater does not explicitly address what kind of music all art forms must aspire to emulate. Music is for Pater as for a later aesthetic theorist such as Adorno the place where form and content are most closely related, where the referentiality of art is less evident, and where its status as aesthetic form is most explicit. According to Pater this means that the lyric is the highest form of literature because in the lyric we are "least able to detach the matter from the form […]. And the very perfection of such poetry often seems to depend, in part, on a certain suppression or vagueness of mere subject, so that the meaning reaches us through ways not distinctly traceable by the understanding" (137). Paul Verlaine's ambition in the poem, "Chanson d'automne" (1866), appears indeed to be a certain rhythmical musicality and by implication a coalescence of form and content. The poem heavily foregrounds sound effects. There is a marked alliteration on the "l"-sound in the first stanza whose short lines put increased emphasis on the rhyme words. The poem sounds almost like one long alliterative rhyme. The most pronounced sound, however, is the assonance on the vowel "o":

> Les sanglots longs
> Des violons
> De l'automne

Blessent mon cœur
D'une langueur
Monotone. (Verlaine, ll. 1–6)

The first stanza is about the monotonous painful sound of the violins of fall, which hurt the speaker's heart with a monotonous languor. This content is expressed not least through the intonation and the phonetic modulation of the o-sound (which must be pronounced in three different ways in just this one stanza), which almost reduces the stanza to the pure monotonous and painful emotional outburst, which could have been noted with the semantically pure exclamation "Oh." The poem's aural form here articulates its content and as such supports its semantics and grammar and can be said to tend toward *onomatopoeia*, where a word phonetically suggests its referent or source. The poem emulates the sound of the instrument (violin) it is ostensibly about and gives us the song (chanson) of autumn (d'automne).

Such an almost non-referential sound art is taken toward its extremes in Scottish poet Edwin Morgan's soundpoem, "The Loch Ness Monster's Song" (1973):

Sssnnnwhufffll?
Hnwhuffl hhnnwfl hnfl hfl?
Gdroblboblhobngbl gbl gl g g g g glbgl.
Drublhaflablhaflubhafgabhaflhafl fl fl—
gm grawwwww grf grawf awfgm graw gm.
Hovoplodok-doplodovok-plovodokot-doplodokosh?
Splgraw fok fok splgrafhatchgabrlgabrl fok splfok!
Zgra kra gka fok!
Grof grawff gahf?
Gombl mbl bl—
blm plm,
blm plm,
blm plm,
blp. (Morgan 1996, 248)

If we didn't have the poem's title we would clearly be licensed to say that this is strictly nonsense, a kind of writing that looks like the result of a Dadaist anger attack on a computer keyboard (cf. Hugo Ball's "Karawane" (1917)). Yet in manner similar to the way in which an abstract painting bearing a title is framed and becomes readable, Morgan's poem can be read to suggest the Loch Ness Monster breaking the surface of the lake, asking and interrogating someone or something leading to an angry exclamation ("fok!"), before again diving toward the bottom ("blp"). Our human noncomprehension of the sheer otherness of nature is rendered palpable in this "song." Whatever the Monster's song is about, the poem makes the reader acutely aware of the materially sensual and aesthetic qualities of its language, which cannot be reduced to sense and meaning and which are not necessarily informed by euphonic sonority as in Verlaine, where euphony indeed trumps languor, but can also be informed by cacophonic and nonsensical gargling that tends toward pure noise.

Literature and painting

The relation between literature and painting differs from that between literature and music. Music and language both rely on sign systems that are temporal and arbitrary; painting and the spatial arts on the other hand rely on iconic signs which appear "natural" and seem to render *present* what they represent in a different, more direct manner than the conventional signs of language. However, the sign types of both literature and the plastic arts can be referential in ways not open to music.

Literature can imitate the plastic arts through pattern poems that look like what they are about in the shape of altars, axes, columns, swans, and even a painting of a natural scenery as can be seen in an experiment carried out by Leigh Hunt in the 1820s, where words are typographically arranged on the page to suggest the various positions of the items of a painting imagined in the manner of Claude (Simonsen 2005, 333–8). In a less literal sense we can understand many literary movements especially in the twentieth century as being related to the visual arts in their experiments with different kinds of concretisms: Ezra Pound's notion of the poem as ideogram and the school of *imagisme*, William Carlos Williams' kind of compressed, concrete, and intensely visual short poems, Gertrude Stein's experiments with literary cubism, or E.E. Cumming's typewriter poems. In many ways what is so special about twentieth-century poetry is to be located in the tension between the aural sound of the verse and the visual look of the poem, which is a central aspect of all free verse addressed as much to the eye as to the ear, indicating a departure from Romanticism's valuation of the ear and of music.

There is a long tradition for writing literary texts about paintings in the genre of ekphrasis. The word "ekphrasis" stems from Greek rhetoric where it covers a highly detailed and precise description of something that can lead to the listener's intense visualization of the described (the effect often termed *enargeia*, cf. Krieger). Originally ekphrasis was part of legal rhetoric and used in the courtroom to describe the scene of a crime but from the fourth century its definition was narrowed down and it came to reference the detailed description of a work of art (Webb 2009). Beginning with Homer's description of the Shield of Achilles in the *Iliad* there is a wealth of literary descriptions of works of plastic art in Western literature. These ekphrases can represent actual works or imaginary works, what John Hollander calls "notional ekphrasis" (Hollander 1995). While most ekphrases from before c. 1750 are notional, the period since has seen a continuous increase in actual ekphrases that correspond to the increasing availability of visual art works, both as originals in public museums (Louvre founded in 1793) and as reproductions.

The valorization of music in Romanticism in other words paradoxically coincides with the increasingly public availability of the plastic arts. A poet such as Wordsworth formulates the poetics he is mostly associated with without any real knowledge of the visual arts. This is a poetics that values orality and musicality and devalues visuality. Wordsworth did not leave this point of departure behind but throughout his long career he supplemented it with an increasingly more nuanced understanding and appreciation of the visual arts, which finds expression in a series of ekphrases and in the use of graphic illustrations in his books (Simonsen 2007). Wordsworth's poetry took an ekphrastic turn under the influence of his friend and collaborator, the amateur painter and patron of the arts, Sir George Beaumont (1753–1827), who is the source of most of Wordsworth's documented experiences with plastic art works. Beaumont was part of the founding of the National Gallery in 1824 and he donated 16 masterpieces to the museum, works which prior to their becoming public had been exhibited in his private home and seen by many leading figures of Romanticism, among them Wordsworth.

Wordsworth and other ekphrastic poets such as John Keats in "Ode on a Grecian Urn" (1819) seem to be attracted, partly, by the capacity for the plastic arts to give the sense of having stopped, conquered, or even transcended time, and partly by the quiet stillness of the work that seemingly provokes the poet's speech. Sometimes, as in Keats's "On Seeing the Elgin Marbles" (1817), and even more violently in Shelley's "On the Medusa of Leonardo da Vinci" (1819), the poet can almost feel how his voice and spirit petrify in the overwhelming confrontation with the quietness of art. In Shelley's poem we hear how the poet feels threatened by the grace of the art work: "It is less the horror than the grace / Which turns the gazer's spirit into stone." This is captured with pregnancy in Keats's opening line in "Ode on a Grecian Urn," "Thou still unravished bride of quietness," where the pun on "still" both signals that the bride is quiet *and* fixed as in a still life thus provoking the poet's words. This kind of anxious doubleness in the poetic response to quiet, time-transcending plastic art is also brought out in an ekphrasis Wordsworth wrote on a picture by Beaumonet, the sonnet, "Upon the Sight of a Beautiful Picture" (1811):

> Praised be the Art whose subtle power could stay
> Yon cloud, and fix it in that glorious shape;
> Nor would permit the thin smoke to escape,
> Nor those bright sunbeams to forsake the day;
> Which stopped that band of travellers on their way,
> Ere they were lost within the shady wood;
> And showed the Bark upon the glassy flood
> For ever anchored in her sheltering bay.

Soul-soothing Art! whom Morning, Noontide, Even,
Do serve with all their changeful pageantry;
Thou, with ambition modest yet sublime,
Here, for the sight of mortal man, hast given
To one brief moment caught from fleeting time
The appropriate calm of blest eternity. (Wordsworth 1888, ll. 1–14)

The first eight lines (the octave) represent the motif of the picture by naming a number of specific elements: cloud, thin smoke, sunbeams, travellers, shady wood, and a ship at anchor in a sheltering bay. At the same time the picture is praised for having stopped time and fixed these motifs in the work of art. The last six lines of the sonnet (sestet) reflect on this description and provide an evaluation of the artwork's capacity to soothe the soul by virtue of its ability to capture and visualize a fleeting moment and bestow upon it "The appropriate calm of blest eternity": lift it out of time and render it permanent. The ambition is "modest" in scope and "sublime" insofar as it challenges the great leveler, time.

The painting described seems to have been lost, devoured by time. There are no traces of the original except in the sonnet and in a letter Wordsworth wrote to Beaumont in which he offered the sonnet for the first time. From this letter it is evident that Wordsworth's description of the painting isn't entirely faithful to Beaumont's painting. The smoke and the travelers were in the original, but Wordsworth himself has added the ship that concludes his description, which in effect becomes as much a construction as a reconstruction in words of the painting. Wordsworth says, "The images of the smoke and the Travellers are taken from your Picture; the rest were added, in order to place the thought in a clear point of view, and for the sake of variety" (De Selincourt 1969–1970, 507). Thus when Wordsworth praises the art of painting as an art that can immortalize and visualize something, he also praises his own art. The implications of Wordsworth's supplement is that what appeared to be a straightforward representation of an existing painting in fact becomes a notional ekphrasis of a painting imagined by Wordsworth, who even manages to insult the painter when he points out that the poet improves on the pictorial pretext by introducing variety and claiming a clearer "point of view" through an appropriation of the painter's privilege of vision.

Literature's relation to the other art forms is rarely unproblematic. As in all families conflicts occur about common property and some siblings may forge different alliances at different stages in life. By studying these relations we may become more aware of the different art forms' specificities. And most importantly in terms of this book, we may get a better sense of what it means that literature is mainly a temporal art form addressed to the body in the form of sound for the ear and to the eye as written text on a page or other surface, as well as something aimed for the mind in the form of language shaped into narrative and other meaning bearing forms.

Further reading

A classic study of literature's relations to the plastic arts and pictorialism until the Romantic period is Jean Hagstrum's *The Sister Arts* (1958). James Heffernan reads poetic ekphrasis from Homer through the Romantics and on to John Ashbery in *The Museum of Words* (1993), while W.J.T. Mitchell provides wide-ranging analyses and theoretical frameworks for interart and intermedial studies in his groundbreaking *Picture Theory* (1994), which inaugurated a "pictorial turn" in the humanities. Modernism's various uses of and inspirations from the plastic arts can be studied in Wendy Steiner, *The Colours of Rhetoric* (1982), and contemporary poetry is studied by David Kennedy, *The Ekphrastic Encounter in Contemporary British Poetry and Elsewhere* (2012), which also includes perspectives on poetry and television and the Internet.

References

De Selincourt, Ernest (ed.) (1969–1970) *The Letters of William and Dorothy Wordsworth: The Middle Years, 1806–1820*, 2 vols, Oxford: Clarendon Press.

Elleström, Lars (ed.) (2010) *Media Borders, Multimodality and Intermediality*, Basingstoke: Palgrave Macmillan.

Hollander, John (1995) *The Gazer's Spirit: Poems Speaking to Silent Works of Art*, Chicago: University of Chicago Press.

Krieger, Murray (1992) *Ekphrasis: The Illusion of the Natural Sign*, Baltimore: The Johns Hopkins Press.

Mitchell, W. J. T. (1994) *Picture Theory: Essays on Verbal and Visual Representation*, Chicago: University of Chicago Press.

Morgan, Edwin (1996) *Collected Poems*, Manchester: Carcanet Press.

Pater, Walter (1901) *The Renaissance: Studies in Art and Poetry*, London: Macmillan.

Schiller, Friedrich *Letters Upon the Aesthetic Education of Man*. Project Bartleby, http://www.bartleby.com/32/522.html (web).

Simonsen, Peter (2005) "Late Romantic Ekphrasis: Felicia Hemans, Leigh Hunt and the Return of the Visible," *Orbis Litterarum*, 60 (5): 317–43.

Simonsen, Peter (2007) *Wordsworth and Word-Preserving Arts: Typographic Inscription, Ekphrasis and Posterity in the Later Work*, Basingstoke: Palgrave Macmillan.

Verlaine, Paul (1866) "Chanson d'automne." http://poesie.webnet.fr/lesgrandsclassiques/poemes/paul_verlaine/paul_verlaine.html

Webb, Ruth (2009) *Ekphrasis, Imagination and Persuasion in Ancient Rhetorical Theory and Practice*, Farnham: Ashgate.

Wordsworth, William (1888) *The Complete Poetical Works*. Project Bartleby, http://www.bartleby.com/145/

29
Performance

Claire Warden

What is the difference between attending a committee meeting and starring in William Shakespeare's *Hamlet* on Broadway, between hanging out with friends at a park and improvising in a rehearsal studio? In a sense all these scenarios are forms of performance but some are classified as, borrowing from the title of Erving Goffman's seminal 1959 sociology book, "everyday life" and others are described as "theatre" or "drama" or perhaps, most confusingly, just "performance."

Marvin Carlson notes that "performance" is "an essentially contested concept," a term so full of meaning and potential interpretations that it becomes increasingly tricky to discern quite what it denotes (Carlson 2004, 5). In fact, Richard Schechner concludes that there are eight types of performance from everyday actions (cooking, perhaps), to business, sex or stage, and even then, he admits, he has not covered all possibilities (Schechner 2013, 31). His understanding of performance is embedded in concepts like "play" and "ritual," ancient ideas all rooted in collective traditions and identities in one way or another. Such expansive definitions provide a foundation for the field of performance studies, a discipline characterized by the wide-ranging nature of the concept it investigates.

Performance studies, therefore, brings together aesthetics and anthropology, artistic creativity and sociology; the concept of "performance," according to

Shannon Jackson, has broad implications, potentially providing a "principle for cross-disciplinary binding" (Jackson 2004, 147). "Performance," inclusive and multi-layered as it is, acts as a potential bridge between academic, artistic, and sociological methodological approaches, even if the term is used in very different ways across these disciplines. Due to the term's multifarious characteristics I could viably ask, "how did the footballer perform?" or "did the company's shares perform satisfactorily this month?" or "how well did Laurence Olivier perform in his 1948 film of *Hamlet*?" or "did the schoolchildren perform well in the test?"

Performance, then, is both a specialized event and an act we all engage in every day; it is, in its very broadest sense, an intrinsic part of human experience. Schechner suggests we perform far more than we realize; life largely consists of enacting already behaved behaviors, he says, from brushing one's teeth to attending a rock concert. He calls this "restored behaviour" (Schechner 2013, 28). It is as central to the act of making a cup of tea as it is to the most avant-garde of off-Broadway performance art events: everything human beings engage in is really a combination of already performed actions. Performance in everyday life is, nonetheless, complex. Paul Allain and Jen Harvie, pointing back to the sociologists Henri Lefebvre and Michel de Certeau, suggest that everyday life can be understood as repressive or emancipatory (Allain and Harvie 2014, 181). This umbrella term "everyday life" can, therefore, include the necessary routines of housework or the celebration of carnival, the economically determined clocking in and clocking off of the factory worker, and small everyday acts of resistance such as refusing the allure of an advert. Everyday performance is caught up in economic, social, and psychological systems.

Performing the everyday: From the street to the stage

But how do we make sense of these "restored behaviours"? Goffman suggests that human beings perform in accordance with a "frame" of context. This frame is central to how people (performers, if you will) act. It renders "what would otherwise be a meaningless aspect of the scene into something that is meaningful" (Goffman 1986, 21). We generally comprehend the most suitable performance for the frame without really thinking consciously about it. If I have an audience with the Queen, I do not greet her with a high five; if I attend a tense work meeting I do not (unless I am in a musical—another fascinating frame) burst into song. But there are moments when we approach these frames with a little more awareness. Goffman gives the example of play-fighting, asking how we understand the difference between a real fight and a play-fight. He explains that, although on the face of it similar actions occur (punches are thrown, hair is pulled), these events are keyed differently. When we watch the play-fight we, knowing the primary frame of "fight," ask ourselves, "What is going on here?" By looking at the movements, gauging the atmosphere, understanding the intentions and emotions of the performers we can say, "They're only playing." Here is a primary frame (fight) keyed differently (play-fight) (Goffman 1986, 46). Goffman subsequently transforms everyday interaction into a series of performances with actors, dialogue, scenes, atmospheres, and audiences.

The understanding of "everyday life" as a performative concept is not merely theoretical speculation. Indeed this idea forms the backbone of theater-maker and playwright Bertolt Brecht's practice. He uses what he terms the "street scene" as a foundational moment in the creation of his epic theater. Brecht imagines a traffic incident and proceeds to analyze the performance of the demonstrator, that is the person who witnessed the event and is attempting to tell his friends about what happened. The demonstrator does not aim for a perfect performance and certainly does not attempt to transform himself into somebody else. Rather, he demonstrates the events so his audience can understand. Brecht uses this model as the primary method of acting in his epic theater. By, in his terms, alienating or distancing spectators they are able to make judgments on the scene, decide who caused the incident, recognize the actions of those involved. Such a method enables the audience to identify the political implications of the demonstration: "the object of the performance is to make it easier to give an opinion on the incident" (Brecht 2001, 128). It is clear to see why a figure such as the everyday demonstrator might inspire a politically engaged artist like Brecht.

Other theorists have politicized this idea of everyday performance in different ways, claiming that humans perform because of the pressures or expectations of society. Judith Butler, for example, asserts that "gender proves to be performance," a learned collection of actions that are employed (Butler 1999, 25). Butler points back to the theoretical work of philosopher J.L. Austin who explored linguistic interventions that bring a new state into being or, in Austin's legal terminology, are "operative." Statements like "I do" in the marriage ceremony or "you are sentenced to …" in the courtroom are, according to Austin, "performative utterances" (Austin 1956, 1432). This causes a significant semantic shift from what a certain utterance *means* to what Austin refers to as its "force" (Austin 1956, 1442). So words are far from empty vessels of straightforward meaning; rather they are loaded with intention, action … performativity.

This idea that language *does* something rather than *means* something can be as readily applied to cultural constructs as to spoken words. Butler uses a quintessentially theatrical character in order to illustrate her argument that gender, like language, might be performative: the drag artist. Drag simultaneously disturbs and substantiates the everyday performance of "woman." Butler recognizes this: she understands that drag creates a unified picture of what a woman is (often, extravagant sexualized outfits, makeup, high heels, breasts—think Frank N. Furter in *The Rocky Horror Picture Show* or Edna Turnblad in *Hairspray*) but, in so doing, actually reveals these characteristics as performed, falsely naturalized rather than innately entrenched. These drag figures needn't be as outrageous as Frank N. Furter, of course. In 1899, for example, English actor Sarah Bernhardt performed the central role in *Hamlet*, automatically destabilizing the typical gender identity of the Prince of Denmark and the heternormative relationships of Shakespeare's play simply by her presence on the stage. For Butler, "drag implicitly reveals the imitative structure of gender itself—as well as its contingency" (Butler 1999, 137). Recognizing the performative nature of gender is a political act; gendered identity becomes arbitrary and there is always the possibility of failure or subversion.

Like Butler, many theorists adopt the lexicon of performance as they seek to describe human experience; Luce Irigaray and Homi Bhabha, for example, both employ the term "mimicry," and Frantz Fanon and Michel Foucault use the idea of "masking." Indeed, it has become a central concept in (post)colonial, (post) imperialist, or globalized ways of understanding the world, for performance is a universal concept and yet appears in remarkably different guises depending on where you are in the world. This broad geographical scope invigorates Schechner's understanding of the term. He is as interested in the way performance works in ancient Guinean tribes as in contemporary New York. Indeed, he recognizes "performance" as entrenched in the history and growth of globalization, in the changing stage of world politics, migration, and economic, cultural, and artistic transaction. Culturally embedded performances are consistently influenced by other performances in our increasingly globalized world. In order to understand these events and occurrences he coins the phrase "intercultural performance," that is, a performance that appears between cultures which either emphasizes what is shared or reveals a dissonance (Schechner 2013, 264). This is applicable to ancient religious ritual, tribal dance, or the fusion of European and Japanese cultures and artistic practices in Yukio Ninagawa's 2015 version of *Hamlet*. Understanding the term "performance" in such an expansive way it would seem that Shakespeare was right when he claimed that all the world was a stage. Or perhaps we would do better to follow Goffman's lead and claim "all the world is not, of course, a stage, but the crucial ways in which it isn't are not easy to specify" (Goffman 1959, 72).

In all these theories the human body retains a vital expositional role; it is as central to Butler's understanding of performative gender as it is to Foucault's interpretation of the panopticon prison where convicts perform their incarceration as they never really know when they are being observed. Butler extends her argument about gender performativity by asserting that sex is performed too; there is no body before it is culturally inscribed. Rejecting the traditional Cartesian split between body and mind, she, to borrow the title of her 1993 book, focuses on "bodies that matter." The body is, after all, the material presence of the human, the thing we see performing. In recent years the body has taken a central role in new performance art, particularly in the work of artists such as Orlan, Annie Sprinkle, and Stelarc. Rebecca Schneider coins the phrase "explicit body" to describe their practices (Schneider 1997, 2).

These practitioners muddy the difference between performance as a, for wont of a better word, "real" experience and performance as an onstage construction by letting real blood flow or by opening up their real bodies as a collection of orifices and functions. As Schechner puts it, while in *Hamlet* "no one really dies or is even wounded" the stakes are, in this physical sense at least, considerably higher in contemporary performance happenings, obfuscating the boundaries between the various interpretations of "performance" as concept (Schechner 2015, 154). Suffice to say "performance" as everyday action and as artistic practice can be seen as a complex amalgam, intertwined with embodied human identity.

Performance, theater, and drama: Actors and audiences

But what of those terms associated with "performance" like "theater" or "drama"? Schechner suggests that "performance is an inclusive term" whereas "theater" exists as one node within this broad category (Schechner 2003, xvii). In this sense "performance" is something every human being does, "theater" is a particular, rarefied type of performing. This becomes clearer if we look at Michael Kirby's four types of acting. Kirby suggests an acting continuum which moves from non-acting (where little is feigned or simulated) to symbolized matrix performance (using Kirkby's example, when someone walks down the street in cowboy boots—we know he is not a cowboy but we recognize the connotations of the symbol) to "received acting" (people we recognize as actors on a stage but who fulfill functions, for example, extras). The final points on his continuum are "simple acting" and "complex acting," which Kirkby differentiates by stating "a ballad is relatively simply compared to a symphony" (Kirby 1987, 3–10). Kirby's continuum enables us to identify the scope of acting, for it is as relevant to everyday behaviors as to performances at The Globe.

Acting, like performance, then, is evident in our daily lives and on the stage. One of the liberating and infuriating things about "performance" is its paradoxical nature; it is broadly inclusive and yet seems to exist between other fields rather than providing a way of uniting them. It is, according to Jon McKenzie, "inter-generic, interdisciplinary, intercultural—and therefore unstable" (McKenzie 2001, 50). Mirroring its position in the academy, performance studies place significant emphasis on liminality (or betweeness), particularly when examining rituals and rites of passage. In a sense, the whole field can be read as a liminal intellectual space. Within this impossibly complex concept, there are multiple ways of understanding theater as a type of performance, both as a historical concept to be studied and as a contemporary art to be enjoyed. I started this chapter by asking a question: What is the difference between attending a committee meeting and performing *Hamlet* on Broadway? I have made a case for performance as a defining element of the former (and other everyday actions), so we will turn to the latter to discover how theater is understood in relation to performance.

Shakespeare's play, written at the turn of the sixteenth/seventeenth centuries, looks to ancient Danish storytelling for inspiration. In Shakespeare's day it was performed using the major conventions of Renaissance theater—stock characters, direct audience address, iambic pentameter (mostly)—on the blank stages of the newly built playhouses of England. Since its original production, it has been significantly cut by eighteenth-century Drury Lane producer David Garrick, transformed by the casting of Bernhardt in the central role, and turned into a symbolist monodrama by Edward Gordon Craig (much to the confusion of his Russian collaborator Constantin Stanislavsky) in the early twentieth century. In more recent years, Heiner Müller has written his short, visceral *Hamletmaschine* embedded in a critique of communist politics (1977), the Wooster Group has spliced film and live performance (2007), Femi Osofisan has transported the story to Yorubaland, Nigeria (2003), and Thomas Ostermeier continues to tour a terrifying, bleak version. It has appeared in various film incarnations and has even influenced that most seminal manifestation of globalized popular culture *The Simpsons*, in the final third of its 2002 episode "Tales from the Public Domain." Using the history of *Hamlet* as a guarantor, it would appear that "theatre" is almost as expansive and varied as "performance."

But how do we, as audience members, interpret any of these theatrical reworkings of Shakespeare's play? In his 1985 article "Theatre Analysis: Some Questions and a Questionnaire" Patrice Pavis provides a concise list of techniques, components, and characteristics of theater, specifically the act of watching theater. He asks us as audience members to conduct a general discussion of the given performance, and then concentrate on things like scenography, the text in performance, audience, acting, and pacing. He also suggests identifying the elements that, in his terms, "cannot be put into signs," those aspects that do not make sense or feel awkward (Pavis 1985, 209). Pavis, building on the legacy of Keir Elam's *The Semiotics of Theatre and Drama*, is committed to understanding the theatrical experience as intricately as possible. Ultimately, as Elaine Aston and George Savona have intimated, theater semiotics is about uncovering "*how* drama and theatre *are made*" (Aston and Savona 2013, 5). While theater semiotics and the search for structures and systems have, in some circles, become rather old-hat, the way that Pavis and others break theater down into its constituent parts does engender an appreciation of the complex interweaving of techniques, ideas, objects, and performances that go into making a piece of theater.

Theater semiotics might help spectators understand the varied parts and functions of the stage, but the theatrical event must also be recognized as part of a genealogy and embedded in context. Here lies the importance of theater history, for it is vital, as with all art forms, to understand performances as part of particular historical circumstances. For example, Müller published *Hamletmaschine* in 1977, a period after the death of Stalin when the autocratic communist politics that had gripped much of Eastern Europe were crumbling (Fischlin and Fortier 2000, 209). His version of *Hamlet* is, therefore, a brutal analysis of dictatorial politics, including three naked women representing Mao, Lenin, and Marx who, in unison, pronounce "THE MAIN POINT IS TO OVERTHROW ALL EXISTING CONDITIONS..." before the actor playing Hamlet splits their heads with axes (Müller 1984, 58). The expansive, inclusive terminology of performance has rather overtaken the seemingly more academic, restrictive, or bookish theater history. However, scholars such as Thomas Postlewait and Jacky Bratton have recently encouraged a stronger recognition of theater history as a dynamic field of study, using the term "theater historiography" in order to examine the way theater history has been written, what it has occluded, overlooked, or disregarded. One of the other advantageous by-products of these new ways of understanding theater, and the placing of theater in a multi-layered definition of performance, is, as Schechner notes, that theater is now situated "where it belongs: among performance genres, not literature" (Schechner 2003, 19). Schechner's comment points to the troubled relationship between text and performance, and compels a greater recognition of the interconnected relationship between the two. No longer does the authored script take primacy.

Suffice to say, the history of theater is dynamic and multifaceted, littered with experiments and creativity. There is an astonishing diversity in the history of theatrical performance. Naturalist plays (that present the mimetic real on the stage), pantomime, pageants, musicals are all examples of theater. Theater can take place in a gilded nineteenth-century building or, as with much contemporary site-specific work, on the streets of a city. Theatrical performances can be long, such as the eight and a half hour Royal Shakespeare Company version of *Nicholas Nickleby*, or short like a futurist sketch in which a single protagonist walks on stage, fires a shot, and walks off again. They can include large casts, impressive effects, spectacular dancing, or can simply be centered on a single protagonist telling a story. They can be poetic, didactic, prosaic, comedic.

New terminology has started to deal with such diversity. *Hamletmaschine*, for example, could be described, using Hans-Thies Lehmann's terminology, as "postdramatic theatre." Lehmann's term attempts to infuse theater studies with the dynamism of performance studies, suggesting that contemporary theater increasingly rejects plot or narrative in favor of multimedia expressions of theme that move away from the primacy of the text. Certainly *Hamletmaschine*, with its combination of film and live bodies, its lack of dialogue, and absence of real narrative, exemplifies Lehmann's conclusions.

Lehmann's thesis focuses on a range of performance makers and happenings. It is vital to recognize that a single performance does not exist independently but, like all other artistic media and makers, in relation to other figures and events. This engenders a range of new questions. What is the intrinsic connection, for example, between *Hamlet* and *Hamletmaschine*, or, indeed, between *Hamlet* and the real Kronborg Castle in Elsinore, or the Wooster Group's intertwining of Richard Burton's classic filmed 1964 Broadway production and their own live interpretation, or Agatha Christie's record-breaking thriller *The Mousetrap*? The title of the latter murder mystery play comes from act 3 scene 2 of Shakespeare's original play, in which Hamlet employs a group of players to enact the murder of his father in the hope that the new King will admit his guilt. Lionel Abel uses the scene to illustrate his concept of "metatheatre," or "play within a play." In fact Abel's idea can be extended and used to describe any performance that is conscious of itself as performance. *Hamletmaschine* uses a different technique to produce this effect. Responding to Horatio's entrance, the actor playing Hamlet confirms "HoratioPolonius. I knew [*sic*] you're an actor. I am too, I'm playing Hamlet" (Müller 1984, 54). By, in Abel's description of his term, "drawing attention to the strangeness, artificiality, illusoriness, or arbitrariness," spectators are constantly aware they are sitting in a theater watching a play (Abel 2003, 133).

Performances, therefore, exist in intertextual relationships. In her explanatory note in *Mapping Intermediality in Performance* Sarah Bay-Cheng provides a cogent reading of this term in relation to performance, for, at first, it might seem a little odd to use such an etymologically "textual" word to describe the actions of live bodies in space. But Bay-Cheng returns to Julia Kristeva, the theorist who coined the phrase "intertextuality," and claims that, while the term can refer to written texts, it can also denote other "readable forms of media, such as film texts, visual advertising, and non-verbal performances such as dance and music" (Bay-Cheng 2010, 187). This intertextuality appears in fascinating ways in theater historiography. For example, in 1966 Tom Stoppard's *Rosencrantz and Guildenstern Are Dead*, a comedic take on existential concerns, appeared at the Edinburgh Fringe Festival. Stoppard took his two central characters, of course, from *Hamlet*; they are the protagonist's best friends. While intertextuality can be observed in all artistic works, Stoppard's play is overtly intertextual in its harking back to *Hamlet*. However, this play has been newly theorized in intertextual terms by Martin Esslin who coined the phrase "Theatre of the Absurd" to describe a number of plays that explore existential themes in a tragicomic way, plays like Samuel Beckett's *Waiting for Godot*, Eugene Ionesco's *Rhinoceros*, or Harold Pinter's *The Birthday Party* (Esslin 2014, 366). So, while *Rosencrantz and Guildenstern Are Dead* exists in intertextual webs of meaning simply by existence, and then in light of its indebtedness to *Hamlet*, it also, like all theatrical works, enters new intertextual relationships as soon as we start to make new aesthetic or thematic connections.

But performance intertextuality is even more complex and multifaceted than these initial examples suggest. Elin Diamond claims, "while performance embeds traces of other performances, it also produces experiences whose interpretation only partially depends on previous experience … [it] alters the shape of sites and imagines other as yet unsuspected modes of being" (Diamond 1996, 2). So, performance is about the real and the dream, the familiar and the strange, the new and the remembered, and about the complex interplay of these concepts. Marvin Carlson describes this effect as "haunting," interestingly, using Freddie Rokem's reading of Marcellus's question in *Hamlet*—"what, has this thing appeared again tonight?"—as a catalyst for his study of things that appear again in performance (Carlson 2001, 9). In the case of *Hamlet* the "ghosts" might be nostalgic reminiscences of school plays, Shakespeare's original source material, or standing on the steps of the windswept castle at Elsinore. We might even experience a similar haunting effect when we watch Benedict Cumberbatch perform the title role in the recent National Theatre production; is that Sherlock Holmes, we ask, captivated by the "recycled body of an actor, already the complex bearer of semiotic messages"? (Carlson 2001, 8)

Despite profound differences plays like *Hamlet* and *Hamletmaschine* share a similar issue, one that unites all forms of performance: What do performance scholars study? The performance is surely an ephemeral event, experienced in real time in communion with others. We need to ask, with Erika Fischer-Lichte, "how can we define the *materiality* of performance?" (Fischer-Lichte 2014, 23-4). We could consider the space of the performance—the theater building, the stage—or perhaps the extant script, the leftover costumes, posters, programs, its position in performance history as an origin point for future art, its effect on an audience by engaging in surveys and statistical analysis. If Peggy Phelan is correct in her claim that "performance's being…becomes itself through disappearance" then what are performance scholars left with (Phelan 2004, 146)? What, in Rebecca Schneider's terms, are the "remains of performance" (Schneider 2011, 96)?

Cross-disciplinary performance: The live and the mediated

Perhaps a filmed recording of the live performance might help capture the intricacies of the theatrical event, providing something decisive to study and preserving the nuances of the performance for future generations. But this throws up another set of problems: What is the difference between sitting in the audience at the Royal Exchange (Manchester) watching Maxine Peake as *Hamlet* in October 2014 and visiting one of the two hundred cinemas which showed a recording of her ground-breaking performance in March 2015? Such questions divide performance scholars. On the one hand, Phelan maintains that performance is always defined by its liveness, an essence that is impossible to really capture or repeat. She says, "theatrical performance is always bound to the present. For this reason theatre continually marks the disappearance of its own enactment"(Phelan 2004, 118). For Phelan, theater is defined by its ephemerality. In this way live performance differs from filmed performance. This, according to Phelan, gives live performance a political resonance by "resisting commodification and capitalist appropriation" (Phelan 2010, 522).

In contrast Philip Auslander counteracts this oppositional relationship (live vs non-live). For Auslander, living in the contemporary world means that performance is always already mediatized. It is impossible to escape the mediation embedded in a modern society of film, YouTube, television (although he suggests television has a different relationship with live performance), and the Internet (Auslander 1999, 12). Rather than stand apart as a site of potential political resistance, as Phelan claims, live performance, in Auslander's understanding, exists within a system of unavoidable mediation. His "argument is that the very concept of live performance presupposes that of reproduction—that the live can exist only *within* an economy of reproduction" (Auslander 1999, 54).

Whichever side of the argument you take, there is no doubt that many contemporary performers have explored the relationship between the live and mediatized on the stage. By way of example: from 2008 to the present day Thomas Ostermeier has toured his version of *Hamlet*. It is a strikingly visceral German-language production in which its six actors (playing the twenty parts of Shakespeare's original text) seem perpetually covered in soil and/or blood (Schaubühne 2009). Ostermeier's use of organic materials gives a profoundly disturbing sense of liveness to the piece. And yet, he also utilizes all the techniques and apparatus of the modern stage, including digital projection; in fact, the production begins with Hamlet pondering his most famous line "Sein oder Nicht-sein," his face projected on large screens (Worthen 2014, 151). Certainly many contemporary performers and theater-makers appear to be exploring ways that liveness and mediation could co-exist on the stage.

After watching the play-within-a-play in act 3 of *Hamlet*, Ophelia turns to the protagonist and, in confusion, asks, "will he tell us what this show meant?" (Shakespeare 1993, act 3, sc 2). Ultimately the term "performance" is equally tricky for us to decode. It is an everyday action and an esoteric event, a concept embedded in human experience and yet immersed in complex questions of identity, aesthetics, and mediation. It shares a tricky relationship with its sister terms "theater" and "drama," not to mention other artistic forms such as dance and music. It is liminal and yet inclusive, geographically broad and yet so often firmly connected to specific traditions, national identities, religious beliefs, or cultures. It is both the most useful and universal of theoretical terms, and yet, in its scope, it seems increasingly hard to discern human actions that are *not* performance.

Acknowledgments

I would like to express my thanks to Dr. Andrew Westerside as much of the structure and content of this chapter come directly out of our conversations about undergraduate pedagogy. And thanks to Dr. Alissa Clarke whose comments on the draft of this chapter were so helpful, generous, and encouraging.

Further reading

Richard Schechner's *Performance Studies: An Introduction* (2013) provides a dynamic, practice-led analysis of the field. For clear explanations of concepts and definitions of terms Paul Allain and Jen Harvie's *The Routledge Companion to Theatre and Performance* (2013) is an enormously useful volume. Janelle Reinelt and Joseph Roach's *Critical Theory and Performance* (2010) and Philip Auslander's *Theory for Performance Studies: A Student's Guide* (2008) understand performance studies through the central ideas of modern critical theory and can be read alongside a collection of articles and extracts such as Colin Counsell and Laurie Wolf's *Performance Analysis: Aan Introductory Coursebook* (2011). Other useful introductory books include Tracy C. Davis's *The Cambridge Companion to Performance Studies* (2008), Harry Bial's edited collection *The Performance Studies Reader* (2004), and Erika Fischer-Lichte's *The Routledge Introduction to Theatre and Performance* (2014).

References

Abel, Lionel (2003) *Tragedy and Metatheatre: Essays on Dramatic Form*. Edited by Martin Puchner, London: Holmes and Meier.

Allain, Paul and Jen Harvie (2014) *The Routledge Companion to Theatre and Performance*, 2nd edition, New York: Routledge.

Aston, Elaine and George Savona (2013) *Theatre as Sign-System: The Semiotics of Text and Performance*, London: Routledge.

Auslander, Philip (1999) *Liveness: Performance in a Mediatized Culture*, London: Routledge.

Austin, J. L. (1956) "Performative Utterances," in Vincent Leitch et al. (eds), *The Norton Anthology of Theory and Criticism*, New York: W. W. Norton & Company.

Bay-Cheng, Sarah (2010) "Intertextuality," in Sarah Bay-Cheng, Chiel Kattenbelt, Andy Lavender and Robin Nelson (eds), *Mapping Intermediality in Performance*, Amsterdam: Amsterdam University Press.

Brecht, Bertolt (2001 [1938]) "A Street Scene," (1938) in Bertolt Brecht and John Willett (trans.), *Brecht on Theatre: The Development of an Aesthetic*, London: Methuen.

Butler, Judith (1999 [1990]) *Gender Trouble: Feminism and the Subversion of Identity*, New York: Routledge.

Carlson, Marvin (2001) *The Haunted Stage: The Theatre as Memory Machine*, Ann Arbor: Michigan University Press.

Carlson, Marvin (2004 [1996]) *Performance: A Critical Introduction*, New York: Routledge.

Diamond, Elin (1996) "Introduction," in Elin Diamond (ed.), *Performance and Cultural Politics*, New York: Routledge.

Esslin, Martin (2014 [1961]) *The Theatre of the Absurd*, London: Bloomsbury.

Fischer-Lichte, Erika (2014) *The Routledge Introduction to Theatre and Performance Studies*. Ed. Minou Arjoman and Ramona Mosse, New York: Routledge.

Fischlin, Daniel and Mark Fortier (2000) *Adaptations of Shakespeare: A Critical Anthology of Plays from the Seventeenth Century to the Present*, London: Routledge.

Goffman, Erving (1976[1959]) *The Presentation of Self in Everyday Life*, Harmondsworth: Penguin.

Goffman, Erving (1986) *Frame Analysis: An Essay on the Organization of Experience*, Boston: Northeastern University Press.

Jackson, Shannon (2004) *Professing Performance: Theatre in the Academy from Philology to Performativity*, Cambridge: Cambridge University Press.

Kirby, Michael (1987) *A Formalist Theatre*, Philadelphia: Pennsylvania University Press.

McKenzie, Jon (2001) *Perform or Else: From Discipline to Performance*, London: Routledge.

Müller, Heinrich (1984) "Hamletmaschine," in Heinrich Müller and Carl Weber (ed.), *"Hamletmaschine" and Other Texts for the Stage*, Baltimore: Johns Hopkins University Press.

Pavis, Patrice (1985) "Theatre Analysis: Some Questions and a Questionnaire," *New Theatre Quarterly*, 1 (2), May.

Phelan, Peggy (2004) *Unmarked: the Politics of Performance*, London: Routledge.

Phelan, Peggy (2010) "Immobile Legs, Stalled Words: Psychoanalysis and Moving Deaths," in Janelle Reinelt and Joseph Roach (eds), *Critical Theory and Performance*, Ann Arbor: Michigan University Press.

Schaubühne, Berlin (2009) *Hamlet: Trailer der Schaubühne Berlin*. https://www.youtube.com/watch?v=WvW4sXDBEwI (accessed December 23, 2015).

Schechner, Richard (2003 [1988]) *Performance Theory*, New York: Routledge.

Schechner, Richard (2013) *Performance Studies: An Introduction*, New York: Routledge.

Schechner, Richard (2015) *Performed Imaginaries*, London: Routledge.

Schneider, Rebecca (1997) *The Explicit Body in Performance*, New York: Routledge.

Schneider, Rebecca (2011) *Performing Remains: Art and War in Times of Theatrical Reenactment*, New York: Routledge.

Shakespeare, William (1993 [1603]) *The Tragedy of Hamlet, the Prince of Denmark*, http://shakespeare.mit.edu/hamlet/ (accessed January 21, 2016).

Worthen, W. B. (2014) *Shakespeare Performance Studies*, Cambridge: Cambridge University Press.

30
Translation

Karen Emmerich

Translation and its products are all around us. We use machine translation tools to read our multilingual friends' status updates on social media. We watch movies and sitcoms in dubbed or subtitled versions, or in interlingual remakes that would never exist without the translation of screenplays and scripts, not to mention negotiations between media firms in distant lands. International flights move us from one cultural and linguistic setting to another; on board, the safety demonstrations and in-flight announcements are offered in multiple languages, and passengers often translate yet again for family members or friends who speak languages not accounted for by the airline's translation team. Stores all over the world sell goods made by international companies whose business relies upon written and oral communication conducted in multiple languages; the advertising of these goods involves public relations work whose translation bloopers make for amusing Internet memes, but whose more customary success tends to go unnoticed.

Many of us also read literature in translation, from the high-brow to the popular: the so-called classics of world literature; small-press series of international poetry; contemporary best-selling novels; cookie-cutter mysteries and romances. These texts, distributed in books, magazines, and in online forums, enrich our lives in numerous ways. Some offer insight into other cultures and historical periods. Some simply entertain us on our morning commutes. Many do both. Of course, most works of literature are never translated at all, and many even struggle to find audiences in the languages in which they were first composed. Others have been translated so widely that were we to tally up all the readers of a particular work in the various languages in which it has appeared, those reading translations would far outnumber those reading the "original" (a problematic concept, for reasons I will return to below). Imagine, for instance, all those who have encountered an ancient work such as *The Iliad* in ancient Greek, or even a much more modern work such as *Crime and Punishment* in Russian, standing in a line. Now imagine another set of lines comprised of all those who have encountered these works in the countless translations that have appeared in other languages over the past centuries or (for *The Iliad*) millennia. I suspect that, despite the resurgence of reading in ancient Greek among British schoolboys in the nineteenth century, the lines of readers in translation would stretch far, far longer.

Each reader of a work in translation, each individual in those lines, represents one tiny grain of soil in the enormous mountain of cultural gain that translation provides for the world. Each translation, meanwhile, is a text that never existed before, a new embodied interpretation that allows a new set of readers to encounter a work of literature, or allows the same set of readers to encounter it differently. How, then, has the word "translation" come to be so solidly linked to the word "loss" in popular parlance? Sophia Coppola's 2003 film *Lost in Translation* only brought more attention to the oft-repeated saying attributed to Robert Frost, "Poetry is what gets lost in translation" (a saying that is in fact a pared-down paraphrase, or what Roman Jakobson might call an intralingual translation, of what Frost actually said to Cleanth Brooks in 1959: "I could define poetry this way: it is that which is lost out of both prose and verse in translation" (Brooks and Warren 1961, 200). In academic circles, many professors of literature rely on translations in their classrooms, yet routinely disparage those translations as less interesting, less complex, or less rich than their "originals," or contest a translator's choice of a particular word or phrase, wishing one had been chosen that was more in keeping with their own interpretation of the passage in question. In fact, even translators themselves often gesture in translator's notes and introductions to their inability to "capture" or "reproduce" or otherwise "do justice to" the complexities of the text they have translated.

It is true, of course, that translation cannot capture or reproduce all elements of an original. I would argue, in fact, that it cannot capture or reproduce *any* of those elements, because that is simply not how translation works. When people describe translation as a process that involves loss, they seem to be envisioning translation as a kind of semantic transfer, as if the translator were walking across a language desert carrying a precious cargo of liquid meaning which was steadily dripping from her hands. The rhetoric of loss rests on a mistaken assumption that translation performs a simple transfer of an invariant content—that translation carries meaning across a linguistic divide. But translation does no such thing. Particularly with regard to works of literature, a translation is an embodied interpretation of what an extant work of literature means, and of how that meaning is manifested. This embodied interpretation arises from a particular, usually highly trained, individual's (or group of collaborating individuals') engagement with the work in question. And while these derivative texts do not, and in fact cannot, replicate or reproduce a particular text for a work, they continue the life and growth of that work in a new textual manifestation, which can be equally rich and exciting.

Some interpretations of texts are more compelling than others. Some translators are also better writers than others, and create translations that are more interesting or beautiful than others, at least according to some readers' understanding of what is interesting or beautiful. But regardless, when we read a translation, we are reading a text that has come to us through multiple processes of mediation. This accretive progression of rewriting is precisely what keeps a work of literature living and growing in space and time. We could, then, see this process not as a chain of losses, as in the children's game of telephone, but as a chain of incremental and sometimes astonishing gains.

What is *translation?*

I've said a fair bit about what translation *isn't*, and described literary translation as an embodied interpretation of a work of literature in a different language. But is that as specific as we can get? Could we say, once and for all, what even just literary translation is, or what it should be, in a broad definition that will cover all cases of literary translation in all linguistic and cultural contexts?

The answer to this question is probably a resounding no, despite the efforts of many translators and scholars to do so. Part of the difficulty arises from the cross-linguistic and cross-cultural nature of translation itself. If translation is a process that negotiates linguistic difference, it follows that "translation" is only one of many, many words in many, many languages that describe the process(es) to which that word refers, just as what counts as "literature," too, will change from place to place and time to time. Any serious consideration of translation therefore needs to take into account the understandings of it operative in other languages, places, cultures, and times. In the English-language scholarly context, some of the most widely quoted texts about translation—Jerome's "Letter to Pammachius," Freidrich Schleiermacher's "On the Different Methods of Translating," Walter Benjamin's "The Task of the Translator," Derrida's "Des Tours des Babel"—are texts we read and discuss *in* translation. We operate, that is, as if Jerome, Schleiermacher, Benjamin, and Derrida were all talking about "translation." But were they? As Robert Young has pointed out, much translation theory "assumes that there is a unitary global concept for practices called (in English) translation": the field proceeds as if "there is in fact an equivalence among the terms 'translation,' 'traduction,' 'Übersetzung,' and so on" (Young 2014, 51). If even the words "Brot," "bread," and "pain" each, as Paul De Man once said, "has its set of connotations which take you in a completely different direction" (De Man 1963, 87), so too do these presumed equivalents for "translation." "In order for 'translation' to have any meaning at all," Michael Emmerich has suggested, "it must be translatable into other languages, but the moment it is translated, it is swept up in a system of differentiations different from the one in which it is enmeshed in English" (Emmerich 2013, 47).

In Emmerich's view, translation cannot therefore be seen as a narrowly defined enterprise of assigning equivalents; on the contrary, it "must be viewed as a node within which all the ideas of translation in all the languages there ever have been or could ever be might potentially congregate, intersect, mingle" (Emmerich 2013, 47). Maria Tymoczko has similarly spoken of translation as a cross-cultural "cluster concept" comprised of a "wide range and variation of conceptualizations, ideas, norms, practices, and histories" that, she hopes, will "[begin] to open up the domain of translation far beyond the ideas of transfer, fidelity, and so-called equivalence that have been valorized in Eurocentric cultures" (Tymoczko 2014, 168). Indeed, for a field putatively concerned with cross-linguistic networks of meaning, translation studies as practiced in English, for instance, has done a particularly poor job of accounting for the fact that many of its key terms may not resonate in places where translators and scholars speak not of "translation" but of "μετάφραση" (Greek), "oversættelse" (Danish), "käännös" (Finnish), "अनुवाद" (Hindi), "fordítás" (Hungarian), "翻訳" (Japanese), "ترجمہ" (Urdu), and so on. I do not mean by this to suggest that there is only *one* term in each language that could be translated as "translation"; in fact, Greek Nobel laureate poet and translator George Seferis famously used the terms "αντιγραφή" and "μεταγραφή," in addition to "μετάφραση," to refer to intralingual and interlingual rewritings of texts, while Emmerich lists over thirty terms in Japanese that denote activities we might refer to as forms of "translation." And of course even the English word is used to refer to a range of different activities and products.

Indeed, at the same time that popular culture refers to translation as unavoidable loss, the word is used in countless contexts to refer, in a positive sense, to processes of mediation and interpretation *within* a language, or between different media. This popular, perhaps metaphorical use of the word dovetails with Jakobson's widely quoted "On Linguistic Aspects of Translation," in which he famously identifies three kinds of translation—interlingual (between languages), intralingual (within a language, discussed above as a form of paraphrase), and intersemiotic (an "interpretation of verbal signs by means of signs of nonverbal sign systems," Jakobson 2004, 139). The last of these three assumes that there are modes of meaning that are not strictly linguistic, but that we can still translate both into and between. I myself have conflicting responses to this expansive understanding of "translation," since I see value in reserving a way of speaking specifically about interlingual translation. By the same token, thinking about other semiotic systems helps us recognize that texts, and particularly literary texts, *mean* in ways that go beyond simply the words on the page—or screen, or scroll, or clay tablet, or parchment roll, or cassette tape, or digital voice recording, and so on. To put it otherwise, literature isn't just about words and text, it is also about their material manifestation.

Consider, for instance, the poems of Emily Dickinson. Most American students encounter Dickinson's poetry in high school, or even earlier: "I'm Nobody! Who are You?" and "Because I could not stop for Death" appear in textbooks across the country, usually printed in edited forms and appended with discussion questions, vocabulary lists, and brief biographies of the poet. But students usually learn about Dickinson's reclusive life and the fact that almost none of her poems were published during her lifetime. But they may not realize that the nearly two thousand poems in manuscripts she left behind in states of varying legibility, many bristling with variants, were subsequently introduced into the American literary scene by a string of editors who regularized Dickinson's punctuation, spelling, line breaks, and even syntax, and sometimes assigned the poems titles they did not have in the poet's handwritten drafts. Then, in the 1980s, spurred in part by the publication of a facsimile edition that made images of her manuscripts widely available for the first time, many scholars began to argue that these early editions had done an injustice to Dickinson's mode of meaning: the variants were not options between which the poet hadn't yet chosen, but an indication of her "choosing not choosing" (Cameron 1992); others even saw the curves of her script and the upward or downward tilting of her dashes as bearers of meaning. Some scholars, including Jerome McGann, suggest that any print transcription of her work should be considered a "translation" or "type-translation" (McGann 1993), which negotiates not between languages but between media, or different ways of presenting the same words; print, they say, isn't just incidental but in fact radically changes how we view and understand Dickinson's poetry. If this is true—if, indeed, these (and other) poems' visual and material form matter to our understanding of them—the question arises of how those who hope to translate Dickinson's poetry into languages *other* than English are to grapple with those additional layers of meaning.

With the recent turn to book history and material culture, more and more literary scholars are recognizing the importance of the visual and material aspects of textual presentation—page design, the incorporation of illustrations or images, binding, page size, paper weight, and so on—to a reader's experience of a work. After what some might call a "Gutenberg moment," in which Western readers came to think of texts as paradoxically fixed (just as we refer to Homer's *Iliad* as if there were a single original text we could all turn to) and independent of the material on which it was inscribed (second-century BCE papyrus in Alexandria, sixteenth-century parchment in Europe, or twenty-first-century acid-free paper anywhere in the world), we now seem to be entering a period in which works are coming to be understood once again as radically *un*stable, capable of existing in different versions, in different media, and even in different languages. This is, of course, an argument that translators have been making for a long time, if only implicitly, in the form of their translations. Any time we sit down to translate a Czech play into French, or a Bengali novel into Japanese, we are operating on the assumption that the work is more than its "original" textual manifestation—and perhaps also recognizing that the "original" was not a sui generis creative product, but one that itself drew on prior works, generic conventions, and even the grammatical potential of a particular language. All texts, whether translations or not, depend on existing materials for their own innovations and departures. The very notion of intersemiotic translation can, in turn, help us think about those aspects of textual production and reproduction that go beyond the merely linguistic.

So what, then, *is* translation? It may be that we can only answer this question provisionally, in the context of the particular linguistic and cultural situations we are translating both into and from. Gideon Toury, the father of a branch of translation studies known as "descriptive translation studies," proposed that the field avoid proscriptive pronouncements and concern itself instead with descriptive accounts of whatever a particular culture or literary tradition *treats* as translation—or as μετάφραση, oversættelse, käännös, and so on (Toury 2011). Toury's proposal helps us reconceptualize translation as an accretive concept; it can also help us recognize the contingency of our own, local definitions of what translation is. For instance, I am writing here for an English-reading audience interested enough in translation to read these pages, and therefore likely with some knowledge of a different language in which what we call "translation" might be conceptualized very differently. For my purposes, translation is an interpretive activity that takes one textual manifestation of a work as the basis for assisting the growth of that work in a different language. As a reader, just as I consider a fairly wide range of products acceptable as editions of works in the "original" language, I also consider a fairly wide range of products acceptable as translations: scholarly translations; abridged versions and partial translations; translations of poetry that prioritize meter, rhyme, sound, or the visual aspect of the text on the page; bilingual editions; interlingual translations that take the word as the primary unit of meaning and consequently may, at times, wreak havoc on the syntax and sense of the resulting text. I am certainly willing to accept as translations texts that cross generic boundaries, particularly as languages and cultures distant from one another may also have distinct categories and genres of cultural production: I can enjoy a prose translation of Homer, or a seventeenth-century translation in iambic pentameter, just as I can enjoy a translation of Murasaki Shikibu's eleventh-century *Genji Monogatari* that adopts many of the conventions of the English-language novel, a genre that took shape several centuries later. Translation is, in fact, one way that literary traditions renew themselves, through contact not only with works but with genres from other times and places.

Just as a work of literature is a quasi-organic entity that keeps growing with each new textual manifestation, so too do the forms of rewriting we refer to as "translations" (or any of that word's interlingual translations) continue to multiply and complicate one another, forming an accretive, ever-growing conceptual whole.

But what is a good translation?

Most people would agree that there are better and worse translations. But how, really, are we to judge a translation's success or failure, particularly if we can't access the language of the "original"? Certainly translators make mistakes, and some make more than others. It is easy to know when a technical translation fails: the machine doesn't start, the piece of furniture remains stubbornly unassembleable. In oral interpreting contexts, diplomats may storm off in a huff rather than shaking hands. In the realm of translated literature, too, mistakes are often made: a translator can misread or misunderstand a word or phrase, or confuse tenses or cases, positives for negatives. As a reader, however, it can be difficult to tell when a mistake is actually a mistake. In fact, this sort of identification of mistakes rests both on a comparison of translation and "source" and, in part, on an understanding of translation as transfer that leaves little room for the complexity of translation as an interpretive process. Moreover, there are some contexts in which "mistaken" translations can actually be quite useful. I would suggest, then, that judging the quality of a translation is really a matter of determining its appropriateness to a given context of reading. A translation is good if it helps us achieve what we are hoping to achieve.

Take the example of the work we have come to know as the epic of *Gilgamesh*, considered one of the oldest works of literature—though the concept of "literature" may be anachronistic in the case of a work that began to take shape in the second millennium BCE, in a society whose conception of texts, writing, leisure time, religion, and so on were all quite different from ours (and even our conceptions of these things are plural rather than singular, as we ourselves are plural). *Gilgamesh* has been the object of a century and a half of decipherment, scholarly reconstruction, and translation, involving fragments found all over the Near East, written in several historical stages of the Sumerian, Hittite, Assyrian, and Babylonian languages. Most current-day readers encounter *Gilgamesh* in editions based on the so-called Standard Babylonian version, which was redacted at some point between the twelfth and tenth centuries BCE and circulated in fairly stable textual form throughout the Middle and Neo-Assyrian Empires. Gilgamesh, a formerly unruly leader, has been broken and tamed by the loss of his friend Enkidu and his subsequent soul-searching wanderings in distant lands. He has returned to Uruk with a "message from the antediluvian age" (in one of Andrew George's two translations, George 2003a, 539), learned in part from Uta-napishti, survivor of a great flood, and in part from his confrontation of the inescapable fact of human mortality. Gilgamesh returns, rebuilds the "ramparted walls of Uruk" and "Engrave[s] all his hardships on a monument of stone" (in Benjamin Foster's translation, Foster 2001, 3), a story that then finds its way onto the tablets in the box of cedar (or, depending on the translation, of copper), where it waits to tell its cautionary tale for the benefit of future generations.

This is the story as it has arrived to us after nearly two centuries of decipherment, which involved an incremental fixing of modern-day lexical equivalents for ancient words written in cuneiform scripts. Since no one on the planet still speaks any of the languages in which these ancient texts were composed, there is no "native informant" around to help us in this endeavor. Yet that has not stopped many translators from trying their hand—and in fact, it may have opened the door to individuals who might otherwise have hesitated to tackle such a project: some translators of *Gilgamesh* have no knowledge of the languages of ancient Mesopotamia at all, and base their work on pre-existing translations by scholars. In English alone, over twenty-five versions of this work were produced in the twentieth century, ranging from metered verse translations to prose translations to illustrated versions for children to very differently illustrated versions for scholars: the academic translations that include hand-drawn images of the fragmented clay tablets on which bits of the epic are recorded. There are translations into many, many other languages as well, including the invented language of Klingon. And the translations differ from one another not only in how they choose to render particular passages or elements of the text but also in what they treat as their "original." Since new fragments of text in the various languages in which it was circulated continue to be found, and new progress continues to be made in the decipherment of those languages, any translator of the work has to decide which text(s) to use as her basis.

Imagine you are a university professor or high school teacher (which in fact you may be!) trying to decide which English-language version of the Gilgamesh tale to assign to your students. Let's put aside considerations of cost and availability for the moment. How do you determine which is the best translation to assign? The best translation depends, I suggest, on what it is you want that translation to do. Translations, like any other text, may be informative, instructive, persuasive, beautiful, entertaining, challenging, or all of the above. In this instance, you may want your students simply to enjoy the story, to learn the same lessons as Gilgamesh about human mortality and the importance of ethical leadership, without getting bogged down in discussions about the textual conditions of the "originals" of this work. In that case, David Ferry's or Stephen Mitchell's translations are two good options, since they both present the epic as a unified whole. Both are written in verse, and you may have an aesthetic preference for Ferry's well-turned, two-line stanzas or Mitchell's less poetic presentation of the story's narrative elements; you may either appreciate or be annoyed by Mitchell's explicitly political presentation of the poem in his introduction, which places it in the context of US military engagements in the Middle East. If you wish to avoid both poetry and contemporary politics, you may choose N.K. Sanders' version from the 1950s, which presents the story in prose, and whose introduction focuses on the international literary company in which *Gilgamesh* now travels.

Or, if you want your students to have some awareness of the fragmentary nature of the texts we now have at our disposal, you might choose Andrew George's 2003 Penguin edition, which includes lines like "[My son, *in the city of*] Uruk [*go, seek out*] Gilgamesh! /... in his presence" (George 2003b, 6) thus giving some indication of just how difficult it is ever to *find* Gilgamesh, or arrive at a textual presence one can trust. George has also prepared a two-volume scholarly edition which includes hand-drawn images and transliterations of all extant cuneiform witnesses to the Standard Babylonian version, as well as composite texts and translations for three previous historical stages of the epic's evolution. The translations offered in this edition are far more focused on word-level meaning and syntax than those in the Penguin edition, presumably in keeping with George's intended audience of scholars, for whom this focus on the level of the word is more useful than translations aimed at an overall plot.

In other words, Mitchell will give us one *Gilgamesh*, one set of solutions, while George will give us another, or indeed multiple others, and Ferry and Sandars others still. Each will be based on profoundly different assumptions about what that work is and the mode of its meaning—and the divergence between the interpretations these translations offer illustrates some of the fundamental lessons translation can teach us about how texts come to be, about the force of rewritings, about the makeshift nature of interpretive work. These lessons can be as general or as specific as we want them to be; sometimes they may *feel* like genuine, final answers, like books being closed. But the strongest ethical claim for translation both as an activity and as a teaching tool may be that it demands of us a willingness to inhabit an open book, to maintain a sense and an attitude of uncertainty, and to welcome the endless provisionality of our answering. Rather than choose one version to assign to your students, you may, for instance, decide to allow a multiplicity of versions to enter the space of your classroom—a daring move, given instructors' more customary desire for some amount of control over a classroom. And yet translation *and* the teaching of translations are both all about risk-taking and entering the uncertain space of otherness. The *why* of translation, as of translation pedagogy, may be answered with a *because* that has everything to do with opening up spaces of reflection and of difference in our stubbornly complex world.

Further reading

For an excellent introduction to Translation Studies and an overview of past and current research in the field, see Bassnett (2014). Venuti (2004) offers a fine selection of key texts in the history of thinking about translation, while Bermann and Porter (2014) include a number of exciting new pieces that push the field in important directions. Venuti (1995) has now become a classic in the field of Translation Studies, changing the way we talk about the many actors involved in the process of translation, and encouraging a nuanced understanding of translation as an interpretive act; Venuti (2013) both builds on and revises the thinking in that earlier volume. For further thinking on the role of the translator and the metaphors that inform our understanding of the process of translation, see Robinson (1991) and (2001).Apter (2015) has proven very significant to recent discussions of "untranslatability," which has become a key concept for much new writing in the field though some, including Venuti (2016), would consider this topic to fall outside the realm of Translation Studies *per se*.

References

Apter, Emily (2015) *Against World Literature: On the Politics of Untranslatability*, Princeton: Princeton University Press.

Bassnett, Susan (2014) *Translation*, Oxon and New York: Routledge.

Benjamin, Walter (2004) "The Translator's Task," in Michael Emmerich, "Beyond Between: Translation, Ghosts, Metaphors," in Lawrence Venuti (ed.), *The Translation Studies Reader*, 2nd edition. Trans. Stephen Rendall, 75–83, London and New York: Routledge.

Bermann, Sandra and Catherine Porter (eds) (2014) *A Companion to Translation Studies*, West Sussex: John Wiley & Sons.

Brooks, Cleanth and Robert Penn Warren (1961) *Conversations on the Craft of Poetry*, New York: Holt, Rinehart, and Winston.

Cameron, Sharon (1992) *Choosing Not Choosing: Dickinson's Fascicles*, Chicago: University of Chicago Press.

De Man, Paul (1963) "Conclusions: Walter Benjamin's 'The Task of the Translator'," in *The Resistance to Theory*, 73–105, Minneapolis: University of Minnesota Press.

Derrida, Jacques (1985) "Des tours de Babel," in Joseph F. Graham (ed.), *Difference in Translation*. Trans Joseph F. Graham, 165–248, Ithaca, NY: Cornell University Press.

Emmerich, Michael (2013) "Beyond Between: Translation, Ghosts, Metaphors," in Esther Allen and Susan Bernofsky (eds), *In Translation: Translators on Their Work and What It Means*, 44–57, New York: Columbia University Press

Ferry, David (trans.) (1992) *Gilgamesh: A New Rendering in English Verse*, New York: Farrar, Strauss, and Giroux.

Foster, Benjamin (trans.) (2001) *The Epic of Gilgamesh*, New York: W. W. Norton & Company.

George, Andrew (trans.) (2003a) *The Babylonian Gilgamesh Epic: Introduction, Critical Edition and Cuneiform Texts*, 2 vols., Oxford: Oxford University Press.

George, Andrew (trans.) (2003b) *The Epic of Gilgamesh: The Babylonian Epic and Other Texts in Akkadian and Sumerian*, London: Penguin Classics. [Reprint with minor revisions from 2002 edition.]

Jakobson, Roman (2004) "On Linguistic Aspects of Translation," in Lawrence Venuti (ed.), *The Translation Studies Reader*, 2nd edition, 138–43, London and New York: Routledge.

Jerome (2004) "Letter to Pammachius," in Lawrence Venuti (ed.), *The Translation Studies Reader*, 2nd edition. Trans. Kathleen Davis, 21–30, London and New York: Routledge.

de Man, Paul (1983) "Conclusions: Walter Benjamin's 'The Task of the Translator,'" in *The Resistance to Theory*, 73–105, Minneapolis: University of Minnesota Press.

McGann, Jerome (1993), *Black Riders: The Visible Language of Modernism*, Princeton, NJ: Princeton University Press.

Mitchell, Stephen (trans.) (2004) *Gilgamesh: A New English Version*, New York: The Free Press.

Robinson, Douglas. (1991) *The Translator's Turn*. Baltimore: Johns Hopkins University Press.

Robinson, Douglas. (2001) *Who Translates? Translator subjectivities beyond reason*. Albany: State University of New York Press.

Sandars, N. K. (trans.) (1960) *The Epic of Gilgamesh*, London and New York: Penguin.

Schleiermacher, Freidrich, "On the Different Methods of Translating," in Lawrence Venuti (ed.), *The Translation Studies Reader*, 2nd edition. Trans. Susan Bernofsky, 43–63, London and New York: Routledge, 2004.

Toury, Gideon (2011) *Descriptive Translation Studies and Beyond*, Amsterdam: John Benjamins.

Tymoczko, Maria (2014) "Cultural Hegemony and the Erosion of Translation Communities," in Sandra Bermann and Catherine Porter (eds), *A Companion to Translation Studies*, 165–78, West Sussex: John Wiley & Sons.

Venuti, Lawrence (1995) *The Translator's Invisibility: A History of Translation*, London and New York: Routledge.

Venuti, Lawrence (ed.) (2004) *The Translation Studies Reader*, 2nd edition, London and New York: Routledge.

Venuti, Lawrence (2013) *Translation Changes Everything: Theory and Practice*. London and New York: Routledge.

Venuti, Lawrence (2016) "Hijacking Translation: How Comp Lit Continues to Suppress Translated Texts," *Boundary 2*, 43 (2): 179–204.

Young, Robert J. C. (2014) "Philosophy in Translation," in Sandra Bermann and Catherine Porter (eds), *A Companion to Translation Studies*, 41–53, West Sussex: John Wiley & Sons.

31

Creative Writing

Kiene Brillenburg Wurth

In 2015, Will Self gave a talk at Arnhem, the Netherlands. Sketching an outline for the future of literature in a digital age, he began to criticize creative writing programs in the United Kingdom. Creative writing programs, Will Self argued with the cynicism of a great experimental writer who did not sell , at best produced teachers of creative writing. This is, indeed, what D.G. Myers already claimed in 1996: creative writing programs are "elephant-making machines": such programs are arguably taught by authors who cannot make a living, and produce authors who likewise cannot make a living that then go on teaching creative writing (Myers 1996, 168). Yet, in the United States, post–Second World War creative writing programs in universities across the country also produced writers like John Irving, Larry McMurtry, and Joyce Carol Oates. Authors like Will Self may cherish the model of an individual and autonomous author-genius that typified the late eighteenth and nineteenth centuries. But in the later twentieth century, originality and individual expression were, as Mark McGurl has shown, precisely also the effect of institutionalization: of academic writing programs built on progressive educational systems and ideals (McGurl 2009).

In this chapter, I focus on the surge in creative writing programs in the United States (and, later, in Europe) as part of a reconceptualization of the idea of "creativity" after the Second World War. This is a different take than most accounts of creative writing. Such accounts zoom in on the schism between creative writing programs and literary studies. Literature, one might think, is the common focus of both creative writing- and literary studies. As has often been observed, though, literary studies train *readers* of literature who have had a historically and theoretically oriented education, while creative writing programs train *writers* of literature who have been taught in the tools of literature, rather than in the conservation of its past through critical interpretation. A lot has been written about this schism. A lot has also been said about mending this schism in the newly created academic field of creative writing *studies* that critically reflects on creative writing as a practice (Leahey 2016). Here, I open a different perspective on creative writing *as part of the wider democratization of "creativity" in the United States after the 1950s*. I start with a brief history of creative writing in the academia. I then unpack the concept of "creativity" to reassess the meaning of creative writing to post-war fiction as institutionalized practice.

A brief history of creative writing

In his *Introduction to Creative Writing* (2007), David Morley argues that creative writing is as old as Aristotle's *Poetics*. Aristotle teaches about the do's and don'ts of writing, the structure of dramatic composition, and why certain dramatic structures succeed and others fail. Writing has always been a matter of instruction and imitation rather than inspiration and invention alone. More than that, Aristotle's *Poetics* is not just an instruction for playwrights, as we started to call them later on, but also for civic and human conduct (Morley 2007, 16). He was eager to show how and why drama benefited people: how they could feel very strongly vicariously, leading to that culmination and ritual cleansing of emotion called *catharsis*, and how they could be uplifted morally.

There are many other famous precursors to the modern invention of creative writing programs, chief among them the eighteenth-century Scottish tradition of rhetoric and belles-lettres that connected literary tradition with the production of new work long before the Americans invented creative writing on the graduate level (Crawford 2001, 223). However, what concerns me here is the development of such programs in the modern universities. For a long while, this was an American development, fuelled by a growing trend in education at the beginning of the twentieth century to foster creative learning (Myers 1996, 36). Iowa already offered a course on Verse Making in the spring semester of 1897. But Iowa calls itself the writing university because of the famous Iowa Writer's Workshop that was launched there in 1936, for both poetry and fiction. As of 1922, Iowa had been the first university in the United States to accept creative work for a graduate thesis, in the form of fiction, poetry, painting, or a musical composition. Creative writing was developed as an academic program in the Workshop, attracting prospective writers from all over the world. The setting of the workshop was like a group therapy session: "Creative writing programs," Louis Menand has put it, "are designed on the theory that students who have never published a poem can teach other students who have never published a poem how to write a publishable poem" (Menand 2009, n.p.). An established author would guide a discussion about the written work of one of the students to which the other students responded critically. Alumni spread the format.

Significantly, the Pulitzer Prize has been awarded to forty Iowa graduates, while Orhan Pamuk—the 2006 Nobel prize winner—has been a fellow of the 1985 International Writing Program established at Iowa in 1967 to foster global exchange. You name it and Iowa has grown it. In 2008, UNESCO designated Iowa the third city of literature (with Edinburgh and Melbourne), as part of is Creative Cities network—not in the least because of its impressive list of alumni that features, among others, Flannery O'Connor, David Milch, Bharati Mhukerjee, T. Coraghessan Boyle, and James Tate.

As Eric Bennett has pointed out, the boom in creative writing programs after the Second World War cannot be seen apart from the G.I. Bill (the Title II of the Servicemen's Readjustment Act) of 1944. This Bill granted veterans forty-eight months of tuition in colleges and universities (McGurl 2009; Bennett 2015). Eventually, with over two million veterans taking up on the offer, the bill helped to change the demographics of education and increase the number of colleges and universities. At Stanford, Wallace Stegner (coming from Harvard) started leading writing seminars on the graduate level in 1946. The seminars accommodated a select number of master degree students and five writing fellows—sponsored by scholarships for war veterans. The significance of the G.I. Bill to creative writing programs like those at Stanford and Iowa was profound, but part of a larger picture of cold war concerns and politics. In the cold war climate, Bennett argues, "creativity" and "literature"—with their aura of particularity and individuality—were perceived with a strong urgency (Bennett 2015, 8). In the period after the Second World War, anxieties about totalitarianism, dehumanization, and mass culture were vividly felt. As academic disciplines, Stegner (like Paul Engle, leading the workshop at Iowa during the cold war) believed, literature and creative writing were strong counterweights to the bureaucratic, statistical logic that had informed the Nazi regime and was then still informing the Soviet Union: a logic reducing the individual to an anonymous part; a number of, or outside, the whole (Stegner 1950, 512–23). In this view, the "institutional flowering of creative writing was inextricably associated with [a] strident veneration of the personal. The impulse was political and ideological, the expression belletristic" (Bennett 2015, 5). Creative writing thus served American dreams of freedom and individuality well.

All this suggests that creative writing programs were deeply embedded in the cold war effort, and some (like Iowa) were even sponsored by the CIA to collect international "left-leaning" writers to receive a good American writer's education (Bennett 2014). It can also be determined with some amount of certainty that, from the 1950s onward, creative writing programs flourished in the wake of an appeal to creativity as a means for—what Arthur Cropley half-seriously calls—"national survival" (Cropley 1997, 73). In the 1960s and 1970s, Cropley reminds us, the need to keep ahead of the Russians led to concrete "attempts to reform the education system in order to foster creativity" (Cropley 1997, 73). We can now put two and two together: in the post-war era the urgency of individual expression was given voice in creative writing programs. In turn, creative writing was part of a larger, post-war effort to restyle education in such a way so as to facilitate the "systematic reproduction of original persons" (McGurl 2009, 83). These programs occupied a space within the universities where learning could be consensually de-standardized as it *was* learning on the job in a workshop setting.

In this setting many new creative programs on the graduate level were founded in the United States in the late 1940s and after (Bennett 2014, 32–54). Johns Hopkins started its writing seminars in 1947, as did the graduate program in Denver; Cornell followed in 1948, Indiana in 1949. Brown, Columbia, Boston University, the University of Virginia, University of Michigan—all would establish their own prestigious programs in creative writing and creative arts. By 1975, there were fifteen Master of Fine Arts (M.F.A.) programs in the United States; by now there are more than 125 (Menand 2009). Despite, or precisely because, of the spirit of new humanism, many such programs remained largely insensitive to issues of gender, race, and ethnicity until the recent past. Now, staff members are often of a more diverse background, while initiatives like the Asian-American Writers' Workshop (AWW) accommodate cultural diversity in writing. The problem still remains that for many, M.F.A. programs are way too expensive.

Creative writing programs were exported to the United Kingdom after some skepticism about their academic validity. Sir Malcolm Bradbury and Sir Angus Wilson founded creative writing courses on MA level at the University of East Anglia in 1970. Other programs followed, inside and outside the United Kingdom, from continental Europe to Australia, Canada, New Zealand, and South Korea (McGurl 2009). The European Association of Creative Writing Programmes (EACWP) was founded in 2005, organizing members from the United Kingdom, France, Germany, the Netherlands, Norway, Portugal, Italy, and the Czech Republic. However, writing programs in these countries do not compare to M.F.A. programs in the United States as they are often only offered in art colleges or private agencies (as in the Netherlands).

Creativity as a concept

Now that I have outlined the institutional history of creative writing as a twentieth-century American educational re-invention, this section is devoted to the concept of creativity in research. As I show, creativity, as a new philosophical and scientific concept of the twentieth century, is shot through with contemporary Western cultural assumptions about novelty, innovation, democracy, and progress. Unpacking this concept provides a deeper understanding of the significance of creative writing in the cold war and digital era's.

Creativity is a recent term. It seems, Raymond Williams has pointed out, that *creation* as a concept is much more associated with the kind of mysterious and divine inspiration animating high art in the eighteenth and nineteenth centuries, while *creativity* began to be used in the twentieth century as a human cognitive ability to invent things, to generate new ideas (Williams 1983, 82–5). Accordingly, "creative" began to be used as an adjective for learnable skills in the 1920s and 1930s, such as creative learning and writing, and much later for computer programs and AI's (Boden 2004). Scholars in English, Comparative literature, and aesthetics often consider it a major achievement that Roland Barthes, Michel Foucault, Pierre Bourdieu, and others have debunked the myth of the artistic genius in the later twentieth century. However, what they do not realize—apart from the fact that Roland Barthes wrote his piece on the death of the author specifically for a special issue on conceptual art in the magazine *Aspen* (1967)—is that the myth of artistic genius had already been debunked in the more craft-oriented notion of *creativity* that became dominant in psychology, pedagogy and the cognitive sciences in the early and mid-twentieth century. Differently put, if we, in Comparative literature, continue to think in terms of (and to challenge) *creation* alone, we miss an important development in thinking about the production of literature, art and literary or artistic identities in the twentieth century.

Most scholars in the field of psychology agree that Charles Darwin's *The Origin of Species* (1859) has played an important role in the shift from divine-like *creation* to teachable and programmable *creativity*. The idea that nature itself (rather than the metaphysical presence of an omnipotent God) is creative, because every species is constantly adapting and reinventing itself to changing circumstances to survive and reproduce itself, may well have formed a basis for future scientific theories of creativity: the ability to produce novelty. Does not creativity in artists and writers and composers, too, revolve around an ability to adjust oneself again and again to different contexts, challenges, and options—around being *inventive* and *resourceful*? For that matter, Darwin would famously speculate in *The Descent of Man and Selection in Relation to Sex* (1871) that the arts—the domain of creative expression—are a remnant of the flirting or seducing that is part of sexual reproduction. One way or another, Darwin's theory brought the ability to produce novelty down to earth and into an ability that could be seen as *common,* not unusual.

The adjective "creative" (as in: the creative imagination) became current in a much wider context than the arts alone in the earlier twentieth century. Mary Parker Follett's *Creative Experience* (1924) and John Dewey's *Creative Democracy* (1939) are a case in point. The first is a plea for the productive integration of knowledge and experience of people from different backgrounds and professions in organizations to solve societal problems; the second advocates the task of democracy as infinitely and jointly producing a better human experience for all: "the creation of a freer and more humane experience in which all share and to which all contribute" (Dewey 2008, 233). This emphasis on *creation* is inextricably intertwined with the fact that democracy was perceived as being originally *created* in the US constitution. Writers like Follett and Dewey approached this creation as a progressive task: as constantly being invented.

Creative learning in America, we have seen, became an issue in progressive education in the 1920s. Carl Seashore, the multidisciplinary scholar who started the Iowa graduate program in the arts, also was the psychologist who researched the measurement of musical, creative aptitude in the 1910s. He published his Seashore Tests of Musical Ability in 1919, and, together with Norman Meier, the Meier-Seashore Art Judgment Test in 1929. These tests, we will presently see, significantly predate post-war efforts to measure what then would be called creative cognition as a mode of problem solving.

It was in this same era between the wars that the concept of creativity gained currency. Apparently, "creativity" had no particular meaning in the English language before Alfred North Whitehead coined it as a term in *Religion in the Making* (1926). Very broadly conceived, creativity refers to an innovative capacity that in Whitehead's philosophy specifically bears on productive nature. Nature encompasses everything we live in, from the physical world on earth to the outermost galaxies of the universe. In *Process and Reality* (1929), Whitehead's use of the term becomes more specific as a natural principle of novelty that animates reality as being ever in movement rather than static or given. For him, creativity could never bear on a *human* cognitive ability alone, because (recalling Darwin somewhat) creativity propels nature as ever-shifting movement.

Some twenty years later, however, creativity precisely came to mean that in psychology: a specifically human cognitive ability. In his famous 1950 address to the annual American conference of psychologists, Joy Paul Guilford urged his colleagues to take creativity as their new point of focus. He approached creativity as a cognitive ability to produce novelty that was common in all people and (therefore) was not restricted to the creation of "high" art, literature, sculpture, or music. Guilford laid a basis for creativity as a specific and measurable way of thinking that was perfectly ordinary and essential to our everyday dealings with reality. Thus, as a twentieth-century term, creativity was projected back onto history: *then* it was exclusive, a matter of genius, *now* it was democratized.

When Guilford made his address, the cold war was already in full swing and the race for space would follow at the end of the 1950s. Guilford thus opened up the field of creativity research within an ideological space and out of an ideological urgency: developing creativity in schools, at colleges, and universities was part of a larger necessity to keep ahead of the Soviets in science, art, and war. Remarkably, this repressive age (under the reign of terror of senator McCarthy) was also an innovative one, due to an increasing interaction between arts, and arts and new media. As Arthur Koestler later observed, creativity is the unusual and innovative *combination* of existing elements—as in metaphor, which became a defining figure of creativity, but also as in *remediation* or the interaction between old and new media (Koestler 1964).

Guilford developed a model for measuring creativity as a cognitive ability by differentiating between convergent and divergent thinking. Divergent thinking is an open way of thinking that explores many different solutions to a problem or many different associations evoked by an image. It is a horizontal, rhizomatic way of thinking without hierarchic structure. Conversely, convergent thinking is finding the right answer to a question—a more directed way of thinking leading to a set target, always already known. Guilford supposed that creative thinkers are strong divergent thinkers and that divergent thinking can be measured. How many different solutions can one invent for a problem? How many ideas does an image generate, and how valuable and useful are such ideas? Tests like the Torrance test for Creative Thinking were developed in the 1960s to measure how inventive and resourceful children were in solving problems. Other versions of the Torrance test, and other tests, were to follow, though testing in education is still dominantly focused on convergent rather than on divergent thinking.

Since the 1960s, and especially in the last decades, psychological, sociological, and cognitive research on creativity has exploded. Many of the insights established back then (such as the chiasm between divergent and convergent thinking) are now outdated. Here, however, I have merely wanted to show how profoundly the meaning of "creative" and "creativity" transformed in the twentieth century when psychologists started to redefine the latter as a common cognitive ability that could be measured, learned, developed—and that was *necessary* to be learned and developed to meet societal challenges. Then, it was the Soviet Union or the race for space, now it is our rapidly changing digital present.

As research in creativity progressed, and scholars like Melvin Rhodes, Teresa Amabile, and Vlad Glaveanu established the complexity of creativity as a cultural and social rather than only psychological phenomenon (Rhodes 1961; Csikszentmihalyi 1996; Amabile 2005; Glaveanu 2014), the concept of creativity entered the domain of organizational psychology and management in the late 1960s and 1970s. Defined as the successful implementation of creative ideas, innovation and innovative work forms became the new expression of creativity as a cultural concept in the United States and Europe. Indeed, Western economies were to evolve from industrial- to knowledge- to creative economies in a matter of decades. While once creativity had been the defining feature of a space for art to be kept apart from the commercial needs of everyday life (the aesthetics of Immanuel Kant), creativity now thoroughly pervaded that life. As Andreas Reckwitz has shown in *Die Erfindung der Kreativität* (2012), we have now all become obliged to be creative. This is not just a matter of commercial life thoroughly pervading the arts—we know all that—but of the "methods" of art and creative thinking pervading our societies, institutions, and businesses, and the ways in which we organize them. This begs the question: if everyone is or can be creative, what then is the distinctive value of the arts?

Creative writing and post-war American fictions

In *The Program Era*, Mark McGurl quotes Clark Kerr—one of the twentieth-century leaders in American higher education—from *The Uses of the University* (1963) when the latter reflects on the new (and to many problematic) presence of creative arts in the universities: "In the arts the universities have been more hospitable to the historian and the critic than to the creator .... *Yet it is the creativity of science that has given its prestige in the university.* Perhaps creativity will do the same again for the humanities, though the tests of value are less precise" (McGurl 2009, 42, McGurl's emphases). For Kerr, McGurl observes, creative writing—like all creative arts—is associated with "the modern Cold War laboratory" that served the larger purpose of cultural and scientific innovation (42). What happened within these laboratories? Bennett, we have seen above, argues that the felt urgency of distinct, individual expression informed the writing programmes at Stanford and Iowa after the Second World War. Sponsored by businesses, foundations, and organizations engaged in the defeat of communism, creative writing programs, Bennett shows, adopted and imposed aesthetic standards cunningly serving that same defeat (171–2).

These standards converged on the idea of sensuous, concrete reflection—to show, not to tell—and were ingeniously presented as universal literary values and timeless criteria for good fiction (Bennett 2015, 172). Learning to write at Stanford or Iowa thus involved learning to write on the basis of minute observation: how things were felt, seen, heard, touched, or recollected. It meant learning to be precise and to consider things in their thingness as they appeared to you as a writer. Famous Stanford alumni like Larry McMurtry are indeed noted for their fresh conveyance of physical experience, the ability to render things palpable as if they were perceived in a direct encounter. Yet of course, the same can be said of Gustave Flaubert, Thomas Hardy, or Marcel Proust. An aspiring writer with a little more curiosity and a wider horizon than the American present could have gleaned these lessons from earlier European literary traditions as well. All that can be claimed, therefore, is that workshop directors like Wallace Stegner and Paul Engle—convinced that creative writing had something valuable to offer to society—shaped the poetics of creative writing in a way that served their purposes best (Bennett 2015, 172). This is apparently how they intended to forge a post-war canon of American literature.

While "show, don't tell" remained at the basis of many creative writing programs, gradually losing its specific legacy of the veneration of the particular in the post-war era, other ways of writing literary fiction were forged at the universities as well. As a graduate from the Writer's Workshop, Bennett in "How Iowa Flattened Literature" (2014) lists three tastes to be chosen from at Iowa. First was a minimalist, modernist style that can be traced to Flaubert, the early Joyce and, famously, Raymond Carver as a teacher at Iowa. Recent alumni like Justin Tussing, Bennett points out, master this style. Second was a charismatic, radiant style that goes back to the likes of Scott Fitzgerald and John Irving that can be recognized in the more recent work of Marilynne Robbinson, a teacher at the workshop. Third was the way of magical realism in the European (Kafka, Bruno Schulz) and the Latin American traditions that, Bennett explains, we encounter in the work of alumni like Sarah Shun-lien Bynum and Paul Harding. It remains to be empirically assessed what the risks would have been of falling outside these categories: of not being published and anthologized, of failing to get prizes or sponsorships.

Taking a broader view than the Writer's Workshop at Iowa alone, McGurl has also identified three "brands" of literary fiction that were dominantly (re-)produced from within the American universities after the Second World War: first, the kind of virtuoso writing McGurl calls technomodernism, associated with the likes of John Barth; second, the kind of minimalist modernism Bennett identifies as well but that McGurl specifies as lower-class modernism to single out the strands produced by Carver and Joyce Carol Oates; third, high cultural pluralism that McGurl uses to refer to Native American, American-Asian, African-American, or Jewish writers (McGurl 2009). Still it remains to be seen how useful McGurl's categories really are, as literary realities often confound and muddle theoretical distinctions: high cultural pluralist writers could, for instance, be lower-class modernist writers as well (if such writers in fact still existed during the post–Second World War era). What can, however, be noted in conclusion is that the establishment of creative writing programs at the American universities will have informed modern conceptions and values of literary fiction in the academia, just as academic conceptions and values of literary fiction will have tripled down into the workshops of creative writing. McGurl calls this circulation *autopoetics*, with the New Criticism as a case in point (McGurl 2009, 32).

Conclusion

In this chapter, we have seen how the institutions of creative writing have significantly transformed modern literature and our idea of literary writing and literary history. In the wake of Pierre Bourdieu, and of the canon wars, critics have for a long time focused on the impact of publishers, and changes in publishing strategies, the power of critics and bloggers, and of cultural binaries in the creation and institution of the literary. To represent authors as disparate as Ken Kesey, Kurt Vonnegut, Flannery O' Connor, Toni Morrison, Sandra Cisneros, and Kiran Desai as being involved with American writer's workshops on the graduate level reveals as much about the unsuspected critical significance of these workshops as about the mournful gap that has hitherto existed between creative writing and literary studies. Yet to fully understand the transformations of creative literacy after the Second World War, I have tried to show, we need to insert another piece of the puzzle: the surge in creativity research initiated in the United States with the work of Guilford, Rhodes, Torrance, and others. Taking stock of the insights produced in psychology, sociology, educational, and cognitive sciences, as well as of developments in management theory, it can be concluded that creativity became—aesthetic theories to the contrary—purposive *with* a purpose in the twentieth century. One field of academic pursuit has illustrated this development fully, if inadvertently: the writer's workshop.

Further reading

An extended presentation of the subject can be found in David Morleys *The Cambridge Introduction to Creative Writing*. Among the numerous handbooks listing exercises in creative writing one might pick Julia Bell and Paul Margi's *The Creative Writing Coursebook*. In *Three Steps on the Ladder of Writing* Hélène Cixous, in, digs deep into the processes and states of mind that is involved in writing literature. One classic text on creativity is Arthur Koestlers *The Act of Creation*. For a discussion of the role of creative writing in education and at the universities, read Paul Dawson's *Creative Writing and the New Humanities*.

References

Amabile, Teresa et al. (2005) "Affect and Creativity at Work," *Administrative Science Quarterly*, 50: 367–403.

Bell, Julia and Paul Margrs (2001) *The Creative Writing Coursebook*, London: Macmillan.

Bennett, Eric (February 10, 2014) "How Iowa Flattened Literature," in *The Chronicle of Higher Education*, http://chronicle.com/article/How-Iowa-Flattened -Literature/144531/ (accessed July 21, 2016).

Bennett, Eric (2015) *Workshops of Empire: Stegner, Engle and Creative Writing During the Cold War*, Iowa City: University of Iowa Press.

Boden, Margaret (2004) *The Creative Mind: Myths and Mechanisms*, London: Routledge.

Cixous, Hélène (1993) *Three Steps on the Ladder of Writing*, New York: Columbia University Press.

Crawford, Richard (2001) *The Modern Poet. Poetry, Academia, and Knowledge Since the 1750s*, Oxford: Oxford University Press.

Cropley, A. J. (1997) "Creativity: A Bundle of Paradoxes," *Gifted and Talented International*, 12: 9–15.

Csikszentmihalyi, M. (1996) *Flow and the Psychology of Discovery and Invention*, New York: HarperCollins.

Darwin, Charles (1998) *Origin of Species*, London: Wordsworth Editions.

Darwin, Charles (1871) *The Descent of Man and Selection in Relation to Sex*, London: Wordsworth Editions.

Dawson, Paul (2005) *ECreative Writing and the New Humanities*, New York: Routledge

Dewey, John (2008) "Creative Democracy," in Jo Ann Boydston (ed.), *John Dewey: The Later Works 1925–1953. Vol. 14: 1925–1941*, 224–31, Carbondale: University of Illinois Press.

Follett, Mary Parker (1951 [1924]) *Creative Experience*, New York: Peter Smith.

Glaveanu, Vlad (2014) *Distributed Creativity. Thinking Outside of the Box of the Creative Individual*, Cham: Springer.

Koestler, Arthur (1964) *The Act of Creation*, London: Hutchinson & Co.

Leahey, Anna (ed.) (2016) *What We Talk About When We Talk About Creative Writing*, Bristol: Multilingual Matters.

McGurl, Mark (2009) *The Program Era. Postwar Fiction and the Rise of Creative Writing*, Harvard: Harvard University Press.

Menand, Louis (June 8, 2009) "Show or Tell. Should Creative Writing Be Taught?" *The New Yorker*, http://www.newyorker.com/magazine/2009/06/08/show-or-tell (accessed July 20, 2016).

Morley, David (2007) *The Cambridge Introduction to Creative Writing*, Cambridge: Cambridge University Press.

Myers, D. G. (1996) *The Elephants Teach*, Englewood Cliffs, NJ: Prentice hall.

Reckwitz, Andreas (2012) *Die Erfindung der Kreativität. Zum Process gesellschaftlicher Ästhetisierung*, Berlijn: Surhkamp.

Rhodes, James Melvin (1961) "An Analysis of Creativity," *The Phi Delta Kappan*, 42 (7): 305–10.

Stegner, Wallace (1950) "Variations on a Theme by Conrad," *Yale Review*, 39, 512–23.

Williams, Raymond (1983) *Keywords. A Vocabulary of Culture and Society*, Oxford: Oxford University Press.

Whitehead, Alfred North (1926) *Religion in the Making*, New York: Macmillan.

Whitehead, Alfred North (1929) *Process and Reality. An Essay in Cosmology*, New York: Macmillan.

32
Critical Writing

Gloria Fisk

When it comes to following street signs and texting friends, literary critics know as well as anybody else what it means *to read* and *to write*: We can define those verbs in opposition to each other and in sequence, understanding that a writer precedes a reader with the same necessity that a baker precedes an eater. The clarity of those definitions muddies notably for us, however, when we sit down to work. Our species of scholarship entwines reading literature with writing about it, so the difference becomes hard to see. Reading with a pen in hand and writing with a book nearby, literary critics say that we have written "a reading" of a literary text when we mean that we have put words on a page. This usage reveals an assumption that structures our field, where reading and writing become less oppositional and sequential than synonymous and simultaneous. And that has import beyond the obvious for any student in a literature course.

The best works of literary criticism yield an interpretation of a text—or two, or three, or ten—that proves broadly useful for other readers, too, because it answers some interpretive questions that readers persistently ask, like, *what does this seemingly inexplicable thing mean*, or *how does this text fit into some larger context?* The best student essays also answer those kinds of questions, too, by engaging with a scholarly conversation that began decades if not centuries ago. By learning what other readers have already written, the student develops her ability to glean more from the literature she encounters. And as she learns to read better, she learns to write better, too, so she can interject in the conversation. By adding her voice to it, she becomes a critic.

This is both easier and harder than it sounds. To contribute meaningfully to the discussion among literary scholars, the nascent critic doesn't need to be a solitary genius with an intellect that is rare. Every reader comes to literature with an ability to read it with a constellation of interests and experiences that are unique to her, because they are formed over the course of her life in school and elsewhere. By bringing that intellectual framework to bear on the work of literary interpretation, the student makes her insights useful to other people who also care about the best ways and reasons to read. If university students knew in advance—but how could they?—what they could add to the scholarly traditions that precede them, they would arrive with the authority they need to write literary criticism professionally. They would falter less at the questions that every blank document poses to every writer: Where should I begin, and what should I say next? How can I make it interesting; and how can I make it good?

Those are the right questions to ask. To begin to answer them, a reader creates a written record of what happens in her mind as she turns the pages, documenting the steps she takes through the text so she can retrace them later, when she begins *to write* in the more general sense of the word. Scribbles in the margins become available for translation out of the private language the critic speaks with herself for extension into an argument that has more general significance. And the beginning of that writing process does not mark the end of the work of reading. On the contrary, it entails rereading the text, inevitably, and writing more, and reading more, and so on. Pushing past easy questions toward harder ones, the critic makes a place for herself in a field of inquiry that already exists. She demonstrates the value of reading literature as she reads it, with a focus on some features of it among others. She makes a case also for the method she uses to interpret the text as she does, highlighting these features and examining them in this way. But, again, the student of literature might ask: How?

How and what to read

The answers to that question shift with the topics of scholarly conversation in the field. A student of literature a half-century ago would have been taught "close reading" as the primary tool for critical writing, which restricted its terrain tightly to the literary text under discussion. The New Critic I.A. Richards instructed his students to read every poem without "peeping to see who the author is," and to extricate textual analysis from the messiness of the world that contains it. Anglo-American critics of this era read literature by the same logic that a scientist takes a bug out of the field and puts it under a microscope. Constructing a library that transcends history, this method makes sense retrospectively as an artifact of its time. In this moment when literary critics were relatively likely to be white men who came to the university with degrees of class privilege, they expressed little interest in the ways that their work was shaped by differences among readers and writers, texts, and contexts. And when historical forces colluded to make literary critics less homogenous, the conditions of race, class, and gender elicited more interest as categories for literary analysis.

That interest grew in the latter half of the twentieth century, when women and people of color gained more access to the public sphere, including but not limited to higher education. Scholarship flourished in the emergent fields of gender studies, Marxist theory, postcolonial studies, and critical race theory. In 1990, the African-American critic Cornel West attributed the new vitality of these areas of research to the "new kind of cultural worker [that was] in the making, associated with a new kind of difference" (West 1990, 93). The critical vocabulary of difference took hold in this more heterogeneous university, where literary critics recuperated the traditions they inherited to interpret literature in ways that did not take whiteness, maleness, and the transcendent meaning of the text for granted. Close reading became one method among many.

It remains essential in that context, as a tool that works in tandem with a broad array of others. The critic's challenge now is to choose the right tool for the task she has in mind. A scholar who wants to think critically about the ways that literature advances capitalist logics might use close reading alongside Marxist theory; her colleague who wants to think about literary engagements with the human brain might read through the lens of new evidence gathered by neuroscientists. When the critic Franco Moretti wanted to study the patterns that emerge among a lot of texts in the same genre or field, he argued for the utility of "distant reading." Against I.A. Richards and company, he devised new ways of writing about texts from far away, not close, in the plural rather than the singular (Moretti 2004; Moretti and Piazza 2007). And new methods for literary study generate new bodies of evidence, as the scholar Timothy Aubry discovered when he wondered what a literary critic could learn from the massive success in the United States of Khaled Hosseini's *The Kite Runner* (2003) during the years that witnessed the beginning of the war in Afghanistan. He studied reviews that readers posted on Amazon.com to see what they revealed about the politics of the novel's reception, and he devised a method to understand it critically.

Across all of these modes of analysis, literary critics choose the theories, methods, and texts they need to generate the "readings" that interest them most. And interestingness in this context does not lie wholly in the realm of opinion and subjective experience. Two different readers may reasonably disagree about whether a text is good or enjoyable, but any critic should be able to convince another that the intellectual project he undertakes is worth the effort. This quality of critical writing is nearly as ineffable as it is essential. It provides an answer to the question that every critic should ask after writing a thesis statement: So what? If this thesis is true, what good is it? What interpretive problem does it address, and why should other critics take the time to read it? Why should it be interesting to anybody else, besides me?

These can be hard questions to ask and answer, but they work, because they point the way toward the element of academic writing that Gordon Harvey calls "motive." In his list of the elements of academic writing that every student at Harvard University should learn, Harvey places motive second only to an arguable thesis, and he asserts its necessity to good work in every field. Motive is for Harvey "the intellectual context" that gives a writer authority to exceed the rhetorical position of a student by addressing a scholarly audience as a peer. Through motive, Harvey argues, a student can

> suggest why someone, besides your instructor, might want to read an essay on this topic or need to hear your particular thesis argued—why your thesis isn't just obvious to all, why other people might hold *other* theses (that you think are wrong). Your motive should be aimed at your audience: it won't necessarily be the reason you first got interested in the topic (which could be private and idiosyncratic) or the personal motivation behind your engagement with the topic. Indeed it's where you suggest that your argument *isn't* idiosyncratic, but rather is generally interesting. (Harvey, n.d.)

The generality of that interest is broad but not universal, and its lack of universality is crucial; nobody can write an essay that is interesting to everybody. The fantasy of that possibility is implied every time a student writer begins an essay with the assertion that something—racism, perhaps, or the interpretation of Shakespeare's plays—has been a problem "since the beginning of time." That opening suggests a misapprehension of scale. A literary critic is not curing cancer or generating world peace, and we need not assert our motive in those grand terms. On the contrary, we diminish the real contributions we can make whenever we posit false ones. The essays that literary critics write are, like all essays, boring to most people on the planet. But they are good whenever they confront a problem that is interesting to other literary critics in the contemporary period. Anybody who is wholly uninterested in the best ways and reasons to read literature is excluded from our audience from the start, just as people who don't care about neuroscience are excluded from the audience for recent studies of the brain. As experts in our field, we present our research to our colleagues by saying, in effect, a lot of you have studied this particular question or body of evidence, but none of you have read it in quite this way. I have, and here's what I have found.

Those thesis statements work by the same logic in different fields and sub-fields, but they take different rhetorical forms. A historian motivates the analysis of ancient evidence by saying that debate about it persists, and this scholar can contribute an insight that promises to move the conversation forward. Literary critics work by the same logic to write in conversation with others about the texts that we read. We say, in effect, there is something about this text or body of texts that demands interpretation, because it isn't clear, and it seems important. We identify some new question to ask, or a new way to confront an old question, and we lay it out to show you how it works. But, again, the student might ask: How?

Identify an interpretive question

It's impossible to write a good essay without a problem to solve, so the first thing to do is to find one that is worthy of your attention. This is why literary critics read with a pen in hand. Without good notes, it's hard to remember which features of the text provoke readerly wonder: What does this ambiguous passage mean; how does the newsworthiness of this Dickens novel translate into contemporary television; what does Claudia Rankine accomplish by inserting this photograph of a Danish tennis player into her "American lyric"? Some of the questions that yield strong motives are locally focused, because they're answerable with nothing other than the evidence in the text. Others are more theoretical, historical, or intertextual, enabling the critic to understand this text in a new way by reading it in relation to some other body of evidence—an article, perhaps, or a poem, a film, a theory, a song, a book.

Consider, for example, how the critic Sianne Ngai asserts her motive for the thesis she argues about Juliana Spahr's experimental novel, *The Transformation* (2007). Ngai shows how she can draw more meaning out of Spahr's text by reading it through the lens of Bruno Latour's actor-network theory, which she summarizes briefly in the opening paragraphs so she can hold it, as the metaphor implies, like a *lens* through which to read. Magnifying some features of Spahr's novel and diminishing others, Latour helps Ngai think about the aesthetics of "the network," which gains power as a "normative concept" in Western cultures at the turn of the twenty-first century. From that premise, Ngai asserts her motive clearly enough that her reader doesn't need prior knowledge of either of these texts to understand why it might be valuable to think about them at the same time: "Read together," Ngai argues, they "give us a sense of what an aesthetics or discourse of pleasure and evaluation based on networks might feel like and look like, as well as a sense of the poetics of connexionism's limits" (Ngai 2012). The reader knows that this article is going someplace, and its reader will learn something.

This is a good illustration of what motive can do: It makes the case that the analysis of this particular body of evidence—whether it is a novel, a poem, a hundred novels, or the collected works of Geoffrey Chaucer—has more general significance. Ngai says, in effect, that her article might be worth your time even if you don't particularly care about the interpretation of *The Transformation*. If the idea of a network seems promising to you as an analytical tool, *or* if you'd like to know more about the poetics of connection in the contemporary world, then you might want to read on. That's a motive.

And it is worth noting in this context that motive is, as Harvey contends, "aimed at your audience." Some critics are interested in neither networks nor "connexionism," nor Spahr's novel, nor Latour's theory. Those critics will prove unlikely to find Ngai's argument useful, because they have different interests so they need different theoretical tools. But they can recognize the value of Ngai's argument to their colleagues whose interests are different, because she has made that value easy to see. With motive, the critic answers the question that every critic writer should pose rhetorically in response to her thesis: So what? Why should this observation interest anybody else, besides me?

Good critical writing always provides a strong rationale for its relevance, which is why literary criticism is a matter of interpretation without being wholly subjective. Scholars debate the merits of our work analytically by considering what a work of criticism tries to do, and how nearly it achieves its goal. To write well as a literary critic then demands the articulation of a goal that is worth achieving and a path toward its achievement. It demands the formulation of an arguable thesis and a motive that is appropriately ambitious. With those "elements of academic writing," as Harvey calls them, a student of literature develops the authority she needs to confront an interpretive problem that is real. She writes for an audience that is implied in her writing even though the overwhelming likelihood is that nobody will read it except her professor. That is, she uses the rhetorical moves that address her argument to readers beyond the classroom: to literary critics who arrived to the university before she did, so they are already busy talking to each other. By addressing this scholarly community, she develops the authority she needs to join it.

Engage with a scholarly conversation

The critic Mark Gaipa uses the metaphor of the ballroom to list eight strategies that students can use to achieve this effect in academic writing across the disciplines. Gaipa makes the case that scholarly authority is "less a characteristic" that is inert in a piece of critical writing "than a relationship that a writer has with other authors, measuring how powerfully his or her work affects theirs" (Gaipa 2004, 419). To teach his students how to construct that kind of relationship rhetorically in their essays, Gaipa imagines with them a ballroom where the scholarly critics they have read are talking about Ernest Hemingway's *The Sun Also Rises*. The class draws the

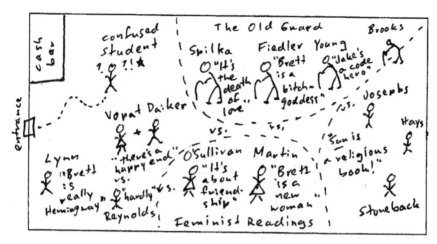

Figure 32.1 A conversation students have had about Ernest Hemingway's *The Sun Also Rises*.

conversation on the board (Figure 32.1), mapping out who is talking with whom, agreeing or disagreeing with whom, on what grounds:

The "confused student" stands eavesdropping near the cash bar, emitting question marks and exclamation points. Gaipa normalizes those affects of frustration and confusion with the observation that all of the critics in the ballroom had to enter through the same door at some point. They had to orient themselves from that oblique angle, too, in conversations that were already well underway. The question, again, is how.

Gaipa answers that question by diagramming the strategies that student writers can use to "make room for their arguments amid this crowd" (Gaipa 2004, 425). The first is "Picking a Fight" (Figure 32.2), which enables the student to challenge a theoretical Goliath as an upstart David:

This strategy is by Gaipa's reckoning appealing in its simplicity but hard to do well, because students tend to do battle with "a straw man they have concocted by reducing a complicated argument to a level where they can finally knock it down" (Gaipa 2004, 426–7). Newcomers to the ballroom have greater success, Gaipa observes, with strategy number four, "Leapfrogging," or "Biting The Hand that Feeds You." It represents a more qualified way to pick a fight by enabling the student to "agree with a scholar (i.e., kiss ass), then identify and solve a problem in the scholar's work—for example, an oversight, inconsistency, or contradiction." That even-handed strategy looks like that depicted in Figure 32.3.

By leapfrogging, the emerging critic expresses admiration for his more established colleague and, at the same time, disputes or supplements her findings in a specific way. As Gaipa observes, this strategy proves indispensable to student writers, who can use it to demonstrate their ability to learn from their elders while they also alter substantially the scholarly conversation they enter.

Figure 32.2 Picking a fight.

What to add to the conversation

To enter it with authority, the critic has to have something arguable to say. A student of Shakespeare who chooses to argue the thesis that Hamlet is indecisive, for example, makes a choice that severely limits her potential for success, because nobody would disagree. It is a fact of the text that Hamlet *is* indecisive; that quality of his character is captured succinctly but not singularly in his self-questioning, "To be or not to be?," and it is reiterated throughout the play. A paper that assembles quotations that illustrate that fact is *descriptive* rather than *analytical*, which is to say that it stops short of doing the work of literary criticism. It may provide a good summary of the

Figure 32.3 Leapfrogging.

text and express a literary appreciation of it, but it has no motive. Likewise, a reader who chooses to argue that Ngũgĩ wa Thiong'o's *The River Between* (1965) is legible through the lens of postcolonial theory will find that hard, not because it is not true, but because it is so clearly true that the thesis needs no argument. Set in Kenya in the wake of British colonialism, *The River Between* represents precisely the same variety of crises that scholars like Gayatri Spivak and Edward Said describe, so it is too easy to apply those theories to this text. The critic gives herself too little work to do.

But these observations are useful, nonetheless, because they can be refined and revised into more arguable claims. A critic can strengthen an insufficiently debatable thesis by subjecting it to the "so what" question, asking: Why does it matter to the form of Shakespeare's play, for example, that Hamlet is indecisive, and what does his indecision accomplish for the play as a whole? How can contemporary theorists reread Ngũgĩ's work in light of new ways of thinking about imperialism on a global scale? These are hard questions, with answers that aren't obvious, which means that they give a critic ample interpretive work to do. To generate them, the critic looks for resonances and dissonances, for things that don't make sense, and for things that make sense in ways that come as a surprise. She asks how the text is generally understood by other critics, and what can be learned by reading it in a new way. And she pays close attention to her own responses to the text, noticing what interests her, and what she wants to know. Her readerly experience dictates her writerly choices, prescribing a text and a method for its interpretation.

Gaipa's strategies describe eight different ways that a literary critic can accomplish that effect, representing and satisfying her curiosity about literature. As the student builds that authority, she can go farther afield, perhaps with strategy eight, "Crossbreeding with Something New." Timothy Aubry used it to good effect in his proposal that scholarly critics should study reviews on Amazon.com as "a remarkable source of information about contemporary critics, which has thus far received scant scholarly attention" (Aubry 2009, 25). With this rhetorical gesture, Aubry argued for the utility and the newness of his research as a source of insight that is hard to get any other way (Figure 32.4).

Likewise, Sianne Ngai leaves the ballroom where *The Transformation* is the dominant subject, and she returns to show her "fatigued colleagues" what Bruno Latour's actor-network theory can do: "Hey, look what I found!"

Such a clear thesis and motive never falls from the sky, and it rarely comes quickly or without research. It happens slowly through the recursive process of writing, reading, rewriting, and rereading. A reader who is assigned Virginia Woolf's *Mrs. Dalloway* (1925) might begin on the very first sentences of the very first page, asking: What strategies of form and content does Woolf use to draw the reader in and set the plot in motion? "Mrs. Dalloway said she would buy the flowers herself. For Lucy had her work cut out for her. The doors would be taken off their hinges; Rumpelmayer's men are coming. And then, thought Clarissa Dalloway, what a morning—fresh as if issued to children on a beach" (Woolf and Howard 1990, 3). A reader who comes to Woolf with an interest in her representations of class and the domestic will notice that the novel opens with a temporary disruption of the hierarchy between the lady of the house and her maid, followed by a dismantling of the entry to the house itself. But what does this mean, and how could a critic use it to make sense of the novel as a whole?

Those questions prompt the beginning of the process by which an observation about a text grows into an essay. They enable critics to gather our notes and revise our drafts, to construct a portrait of *what is happening* in the text as we read it. We identify what we find worth noticing here, and we test our hunches and hypotheses with literary analysis. Oscillating between closeness and distance from

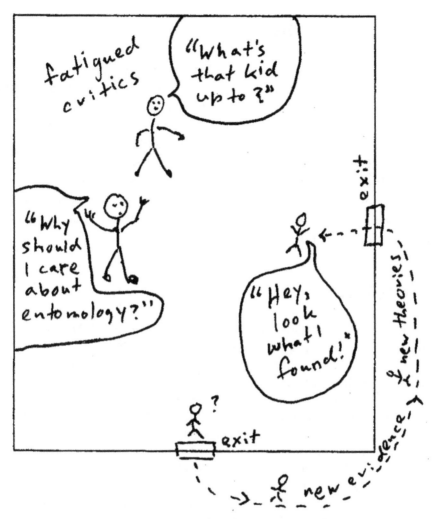

Figure 32.4 The crossbreeding strategy.

the text, we make our experience of reading it available as a source of insight to ourselves and others. And, every time, we lodge an argument about *how, what,* and *why to read.* Professors don't always say that this is what they want from student writing, but the goal is implicit in the assignments we give: We want our students to meet us as colleagues and engage in this scholarly conversation with us. We want our students to build on what we have learned, much the same way that a scientist generates new insights by building on an existing body of research. With that kind of engagement, our best students read and write, sharpening their understanding of literary texts and their place in the world. In all likelihood, they delete much of what they have written as they read and reread. They write and rewrite, and so it goes.

Further reading

To practice the rhetorical moves that work best for scholarly writers, many students refer to Gerald Graff's *They Say, I Say: The Moves That Matter in Academic Writing* (2008). Eric Hayot's *The Elements of Academic Style: Writing for the Humanities* (2014) shows advanced students how to write more persuasively at the level of the sentence, paragraph, and essay. Writers in literature courses also benefit from thinking about the difference between symptomatic reading and surface reading, which are described clearly in *Surface Reading: An Introduction* (2009) by Stephen Best and Sharon Marcus. Every writer also needs to make regular use of a reference text like *The MLA Handbook* (2016) or *OWL Purdue* (https://owl.english.purdue .edu/) for matters of style, citation, formatting, and usage.

References

Aubry, Timothy (2009) "Afghanistan Meets the Amazon: Reading *The Kite Runner* in America," *PMLA*, 124 (1): 25–43. doi:10.1632/pmla.2009.124.1.25.

Gaipa, M. (2004) "Breaking into the Conversation: How Students Can Acquire Authority for Their Writing," *Pedagogy: Critical Approaches to Teaching Literature, Language, Composition, and Culture*, 4 (3): 419–37. doi:10.1215/15314200-4-3-419.

Harvey, Gordon (n.d.) "A Brief Guide to the Elements of the Academic Essay," *Harvard Writing Project*, https://writingproject.fas.harvard.edu/files/hwp/files/hwp_brief _guides_elements.pdf.

Moretti, Franco (2004) "Conjectures on World Literature," in Christopher Pendergrast (ed.), *Debating World Literature*, 148–63, New York: Verso.

Moretti, Franco and Alberto Piazza (2007) *Graphs, Maps, Trees: Abstract Models for Literary History*, London and New York: Verso.

Ngai, Sianne. (2012) "Network Aesthetics," in Cindy Weinstein and Christopher Looby (eds), *American Literature's Aesthetic Dimensions*, 367–92, Columbia University Press, http://columbia.universitypressscholarship.com/view/10.7312/ columbia/9780231156172.001.0001/upso-9780231156172-chapter-17.

West, Cornel (1990) "The New Cultural Politics of Difference," *October*, 53: 93–109. doi: 10.2307/778917.

Woolf, Virginia and Maureen Howard (1990) *Mrs. Dalloway*, 1st edition, San Diego: Mariner Books.

33
Quality

Susan Bassnett

The question as to what constitutes literary quality has been hotly debated over the centuries, going back as far as Plato's famous criticism of poetry and Aristotle's subsequent defense. For Plato, poetry was less desirable that philosophy, hence poets, carried away by the irrationality of their inspiration would not be fit citizens for his new Republic. Centuries later, Shakespeare played ironically with that notion of the poet as madman in the last act of *A Midsummer Night's Dream*. Duke Theseus, alone briefly with his bride, Hippolyta, opines that "the lunatic, the lover and tube poet/ are of imagination all compact," since all see things that do not exist. The madman sees "more devils than vast hell can hold," the lover "sees Helen's beauty in a brow of Egypt," while the poet's pen turns unknown things into shapes and "gives to airy nothing/a local habitation and a name." Madness, passion, and poetry are presented as manifestations of unstable elements of human existence.

Shakespeare was not being serious, of course, being a poet himself, and there has been a great deal of time spent arguing over quite what Plato's view of poetry actually was and whether it was really so negative. Nevertheless, what both Plato and Shakespeare were inviting us to consider was the question of how to see the role of literary creativity in society, a question that inevitably takes us along the path of evaluation. For those of us who work with literature, whether as students, teachers, university professors, literary critics, reviewers, publishers, literary agents, or any of the people who earn their living from books, that is, those people André Lefevere defined as "professional readers" (Lefevere 1992), the task of determining quality is by no means an easy one.

In the late nineteenth and early twentieth centuries, when programs in national literatures were being established in schools and universities, most notably in Europe and the English-speaking world, decisions were taken about which texts to include in a curriculum on the basis of their "greatness," that is the quality that had enabled them to continue to be appreciated through the ages. Such an idea followed logically from the long-established teaching of the Ancient Greek and Latin foundational texts of Western culture, though it has to be noted that the classical works most studied included both historical and philosophical writings, alongside epic poetry and Ancient Greek tragedies. Just as a canon of ancient works was established for students, so with the development of programs of study in modern languages and literatures the emergence of a vernacular canon followed on logically. Included in such a canon were those writers deemed to have made the greatest contribution to the national literature, writers such as Dante, Chaucer, Petrarch, Boccaccio, Shakespeare, Rabelais, Cervantes, Montaigne, Tasso, Milton, Camoens, and so forth through into the nineteenth century.

At the same time, the rise of literacy, which was leading to an increase in book production generally to accommodate new readers, saw the growth of publishing projects that offered readers a chance to encounter great works from around the world. The 51-volume Harvard Classics series first appeared in 1909, while in 1906 the English bookbinder turned publisher, Joseph Dent, launched his Everyman series, with an edition of Boswell's *Life of Dr Johnson*. Dent, who came from a humble background in the North of England, is renowned for the phrase he coined to appeal to readers, offering them "infinite riches in a little room," the infinite riches being their discovery of great writers from around the world.

To bring to all readers cheap versions of the work of great writers from around the world, this was Dent's very laudable objective, but it is the adjective "great" that today has become problematic. For although it is indeed the case that some works have continued to be read throughout centuries, we need to ask questions about their survival as "great" works, about who decides on what constitutes a "great" work, we need to consider how the quality of a work is determined, given that tastes and aesthetic norms change constantly. Dr. Johnson declared that Alexander Pope's translation of the *Iliad* would endure forever; fifty years later the English Poet laureate, Robert Southey dismissed it as a corruption that would offend public taste. Writers have also been subject to ideological constraints too. Heinrich Heine, today regarded as a major poet, was removed from the official German canon during the Nazi period on account of his Jewishness. In the former Soviet Union, when Boris Pasternak was awarded the Nobel Prize for Literature in 1958, he was forced by the Soviet authorities to turn it down. His novel, *Dr Zhivago*, was banned in the Soviet Union and had to be smuggled out of the country, to be published in 1957 in Italy.

This article starts, therefore, with the premise that "quality" is a slippery, fluid notion, which varies across time and cultures, and is subject to all kinds of fluctuations, some material, some aesthetic, some ideological. That is not to say that literary quality does not exist, rather that it is not a constant and has been determined according to ever-changing criteria. As Jorge Luis Borges famously pointed out, the concept of the definitive text belongs only to religion or exhaustion.

Changing taste

A good example of how tastes change is the case of William Shakespeare, renowned Renaissance writer, translated into over eighty languages, including Klingon, the invented language of the villains in the TV series *Star Trek*, and the only writer that all English pupils are obliged to study in school. We know little about Shakespeare's life, doubtless because its details were not worth recording in his own time, since he was not considered a major writer by his contemporaries, who ranked Ben Jonson as far superior. After his death in 1616, his plays went out of favor and it was not until the 1740s that the actor David Garrick began a Shakespeare revival. However, Shakespeare's plays were reconfigured according to the norms of the age, and Garrick had no qualms about rewriting them, taking out scenes considered too violent, and amending plot lines to appeal to the growing vogue of sentiment. Shakespeare on the French stage, where the classical unities of Racine and Corneille continued to prevail, was even more radically revised. Jean-Francois Ducis, whose translation of *Hamlet* came out in 1770, wrote to Garrick, explaining that he had been compelled to make a new play entirely, removing the Ghost, the traveling players, the final combat scene and some fifteen of the original twenty-three characters so as to conform to the French tragic blueprint and avoid offending audiences.

The German translation team of August Wilhelm Schlegel and Ludvig Tieck, working in the late eighteenth and early nineteenth centuries proved so successful that Georg Brandes, the Danish critic declared that it was as if Shakespeare had been born in Germany, "at the side of Goethe and Schiller" (Brandes 1966). Shakespeare, in effect, became a canonical German writer through those translations, to the extent that Leo Tolstoy declared in his essay on Shakespeare, published in 1906, that Shakespeare's fame originated in Germany and was only then transferred back to the

English. Certainly Shakespeare enjoyed a huge reputation across Europe in the Age of Revolutions, and plays that dealt with the struggle against political oppression and tyranny, such as *Macbeth*, *Hamlet*, *Julius Caesar*, and *Richard III*, were as frequently translated and performed as the tragedies that appealed to Romantic sensibilities such as *Romeo and Juliet*, *Othello*, and *King Lear*. Such was the influence of the German versions, that they were more frequently translated into other European languages than the English originals.

When we consider the fortunes of Shakespeare in Europe, several significant issues arise: firstly, Shakespeare's reputation in his own country fluctuated considerably and it took some 150 years after his death for his reputation as an important writer to be established. Secondly, the fame Shakespeare came to enjoy in other European countries was as a result of translations of specific plays. Thirdly, that choice of plays tended to appeal to the rising wave of political unrest across Europe, so that Shakespeare came to be seen as a revolutionary writer, while in his own country he was increasingly seen as an English patriot and as the writer of delightful comedies and plays about English history. *King John*, which today is rarely performed and regarded as one of the lesser plays, was enormously popular throughout the nineteenth century in England, though not elsewhere.

Translation

It is impossible to underestimate the role of translation as a shaping force in literary history, though the question of quality becomes even more clouded when we consider the movement of texts across linguistic and cultural frontiers. Through translation, some writers and their work acquired a much higher status in the target culture than they did in their own language. Good examples are Jack London, the American Socialist writer who was translated into Russian just before the October Revolution and whose work was published in millions of copies. London's narratives combined with his socialist idealism appealed to the *zeitgeist* of the age, to such an extent that today Jack London is regarded in Russia as a canonical writer, and is well-known throughout the former USSR countries and in China. In the English-speaking world he is considered as a children's author, best-known for *The Call of the Wild* and certainly not viewed as a major figure. The novel *Vendetta*, by Marie Corelli, the pot-boiling English novelist beloved of Queen Victoria was the first novel to be translated into Thai, with the consequence that Corelli's work is still highly regarded in Thailand, while in her own country she has vanished into oblivion.

Political events have epistemological consequences, and the production of translations is linked to wider social changes. In the 1920s, following the founding of the new Republic in Turkey under the leadership of Kemal Ataturk, part of the program of Westernization was the systematic translation of "great works" by Western authors, considered to be both foundational texts and classical works of more recent origin. In the early nineteenth century, the poetry of Lord Byron was translated extensively across Europe, with Byron seen as the revolutionary poet *par excellence*. His work strongly affected both Pushkin and Karel Hynek Macha, so that Byron can be seen as having had a major impact on Russian literature and on the Czech Revival movement. Yet Byron today is rarely studied in English-speaking schools and universities, and has all but disappeared from the curriculum of Romantic literature. Charles Baudelaire's translations of Edgar Allen Poe not only had an impact on his French contemporaries but became the channel through which Poe's work became popular in many other languages, so it could be argued that Baudelaire "discovered" Poe and boosted his reputation as an important writer.

Translations that are successful in the target culture can introduce new ideas and new forms and so change expectations and affect judgments on literary quality. The sonnet as a new form spread across Europe through translation, as did the haiku several centuries later. The Arabic novel, which has developed in the Arab world since the first translations in the nineteenth century, combines elements of Western literary traditions with local traditions, resulting in new literary forms.

However, some writers who have enjoyed high status in their own language may fail to reach new readers in another language. Dante Alighieri, regarded as the father of Italian poetry, did not have any significant impact in English until the twentieth century, seven hundred years after his death. It was T.S. Eliot who began the reappraisal of Dante, and the Irish Nobel prize-winning poet, Seamus Heaney, who used Dante's *Divina Commedia* in his own writing, notably in his long poem, *Station Island*. This lack of interest in Dante was not due to the absence of potential translators, given that a great deal of Italian literature was translated into English from the Middle Ages onward, but can be attributed to problems of religious doctrine. The Reformation and subsequent anti-Catholic sentiment that remained a powerful force in England for centuries meant that Dante's panoramic view of Hell, Purgatory, and Paradise was unacceptable.

Censorship and social change

As noted already, much of Shakespeare in the eighteenth century was viewed as violating good taste, while Pasternak was banned in his own country. In some places, censorship controls literary production in all fields, with quality being determined by a committee that puts ideological issues before anything else. Even in Britain, censorship of the theater was only abolished in 1968. Censorship has led to the persecution of writers, who have been exiled, imprisoned, or even executed for having violated expected social or aesthetic norms. Quality issues are subject to political expediency.

There are many cases of writers whose work offended public taste when it first came out, but who have since been considered as major innovators. There was a riot in Rome in 1921 at the Teatro Valle when Luigi Pirandello's play, *Six Characters in Search of an Author* was first performed, as the plot was considered obscene. Henrik Ibsen's *A Doll's House*, which premiered in Copenhagen in 1879, had to be rewritten for English audiences and was first performed in that new version in 1884 entitled *Breaking a Butterfly*. Ibsen was required to write a different ending for the first German version, which outraged him. Both those plays, which scandalized contemporary audiences have since become totally acceptable. What shocks one generation may have little impact on another generation.

It is also the case that within a literary system the status of texts that initially shock or surprise can gradually alter. When Jonathan Swift's *Gulliver's Travels* was first published in 1726 it was read as a savage satire on human expectations, and as an ironic response to Daniel Defoe's optimistic account of human ingenuity and endurance, *Robinson Crusoe*, that had come out in 1719. Both books remained popular, but their status shifted, so that by the late nineteenth century both had come to be regarded as preeminently children's literature. Editions of *Gulliver's Travels* were abridged, so that the focus was on the lighter-hearted Lilliput and Brobdingnag voyages, and not on the much darker third and fourth voyages. Today, following the Disneyfication of Swift's work on film, all trace of social satire has vanished. In a similar vein, the Disneyfication of Hans Christian Andersen's dark tale of hopeless love and masochism, "The Little Mermaid" has led to its filmic rewriting for small children. The happy ending of the Disney film can be compared to the happy ending of the eighteenth-century performances of *King Lear* in London, that is, a complete rewriting to accommodate the taste of a designated public.

The unpredictable

By the eighteenth century there were other significant factors that affected the quality debate. Increased public literacy meant a greater demand for books; traveling libraries for the general public expanded, there was an increase in newspapers and journals and all the commercial aspects of publishing became more important. This led, inevitably, to the commercial promotion of writers, with book reviewers playing a powerful role. Charles Dickens, who arguably became the most famous novelist in the world during his lifetime, understood from the start of his career the importance of writing for magazines, and his novels were published in monthly installments before being issued as volumes, which ensured a very large audience. Dickens is today one of those figures who has become canonized in the literature of many nations, but whose prose style is too convoluted for most modern readers. Today, people are more likely to have seen the musical *Oliver* or a film of one of novels than to have read one. Like Byron, Dickens is no longer seen as an essential writer to be read by English literature students, though his reputation as a major nineteenth-century novelist continues.

Part of the difficulty of assessing "quality" is the unpredictability of readers' responses to some texts. The first of the Harry Potter novels by J.K. Rowling was rejected by several publishers, since it was generally agreed by publishers, pedagogues and anyone with an interest in writing for children that there was no longer any interest in school stories, especially fantastical school stories about boy wizards, because children wanted to read books that reflected aspects of their own, sometimes difficult, lives. The global success of J.K. Rowling's novels shows how wrong that estimate of readers' tastes could be. Indeed, such has been the success of the Harry Potter books with readers of all ages, that they have been marketed in many countries in two formats with different paratexts, one aimed at children, the other at adult readers.

Similarly, when the Brazilian writer Paulo Coelho published *The Alchemist* in 1988, with a small Brazilian publisher, the print run was only a few hundred copies. When it came out in English in 1994 it became a best-seller, and today Coelho is the most successful Portuguese language writer of all time, having sold some 200 million books around the world. His success, like that of J.K. Rowling, defied expectations.

Such unexpected successes inevitably result in imitations by other writers that are then marketed extensively, and global success today is also linked to social media and the Internet. Coelho has millions of followers on Twitter, for example, and writes regular blogs. The Internet has also led to the rise of fan fiction, whereby readers write their own stories about characters from novels they have read and enjoyed. Self-publishing is another popular development, with E.L. James' soft-porn novel, *Fifty Shades of Grey* as the best example of how a self-published e-book could go on to become a global best seller. In terms of literary quality, however, the success of *Fifty Shades of Grey* returns us to the core of the debate, for despite the millions of copies sold, the language is clumsy, the dialogues stilted and the descriptive passages so florid as to verge on the comic.

But if we say this about that novel, then it means that a judgment about stylistic quality is being made, and the question then to be asked is on what basis such a judgment is founded.

Challenging the canon

In the 1970s, the idea of a canon of great books came under attack from several directions as new approaches to the study of literature and culture emerged that focused on gender, race, ethnicity, and class. The 1960s was the decade that saw civil rights marches in the United States, demonstrations against the American war in

Vietnam and against the Russian suppression of the Czech uprising in 1968, political protests across Africa, Central, and Latin America, and student unrest globally on an unprecedented scale. As ever, political events began to have epistemological consequences. As feminist criticism became established in academia, critics attacked the absence of women writers from the literary canon, which they perceived as symptomatic of the pervasive power of patriarchy. The canon, it was argued, consisted of nothing but dead white males. Feminist criticism, as Toril Moi has pointed out, came into being as a specific kind of political discourse (Moi 1985), and the canon began to be revised in consequence, as more and more women writers were discovered, reappraised, republished, and included in literature curricula.

In the United States, attempts to face up to the history of slavery as one of the least palatable foundation myths of the republic led to the inclusion of many more black writers in the curriculum, further altering the selection of texts for use in schools and universities and raising serious doubts about the objectivity of white literary historiographers. Questions began to be asked about the criteria for inclusion and exclusion from the canon, along with questions about its relevance for the twentieth century. Many traditional literature degrees had a heavy philological component, and the time frame studied tended to stop in the middle of the nineteenth century, which meant that the emphasis was mainly on poets and essayists rather than on novelists. Yet the novel, it could be argued, had come into its own in the twentieth century and deserved serious attention. Moreover, the novel was the genre more likely to engage with contemporary concerns.

The advent of postcolonial criticism brought about a major shift in categorizing literary production. English Literature was redefined as Literatures in English, to include the many writers from around the world who wrote in English, but for whom England was a foreign country and whose work had been ignored. Wole Soyinka, the Nigerian Nobel-prize winning writer, recounts how in the 1970s, when a Visiting Fellow at the University of Cambridge, he was obliged to give his lectures on African literature in the Department of Social Anthropology, since African literature was not recognized in the English Department (Soyinka 1976). Derek Walcott, the St. Lucian Nobel Laureate, wrote passionately about what he defined as the New World servitude to the muse of history, and offered an alternative reading of both Shakespeare's *The Tempest* and *Robinson Crusoe*, viewed from the perspective of Man Friday and Caliban (Walcott 1974, 370). Ngugi wa Thiong'o proposed that the English Department in his home university should be abolished and replaced with a Department of African Languages and Literatures (wa Thiong'o 1972).

Challenges to the canon also came from the growth of film, media and cultural studies. Robert Scholes, the American critic, proposed that no text was so trivial as to be outside the bounds of humanistic study, a view shared by British Cultural Studies theorists such as Stuart Hall. Such an idea did not altogether demolish the notion of "quality," but took away the special position of "high" literature as more deserving of critical attention. Literary critical methods could still be applied, but applied equally to *Paradise Lost* or to an advertisement. But perhaps the death blow to the idea of a canon of works whose intrinsic "quality" had led to them being read for centuries came from Roland Barthes, with his seminal 1968 essay "The Death of the Author," which opened the way for the surge of interest in post modernism that endured until well into the 1990s. Barthes's essay sought to shift the emphasis from the figure of the author onto the reader; henceforth it was to be the reader who "constructed" a text, bringing his or her individuality into the construction of the meaning of that text. Barthes does not mention quality, but it is clear that if it is the reader who assumes power over the text, then quality will be determined by the reader in whatever way he or she chooses (Barthes 1968).

Since the 1970s, the map of literary history has changed radically, not only with the inclusion of many writers whose work had been marginalized or completely forgotten but also with a reappraisal of writers from the past whose works no longer conform to the acceptable norms of the present. There has been a long-standing debate in the United States about Mark Twain's *Huckleberry Finn*, published in 1884 and initially condemned by some as vulgar and unsuitable for young readers. More recently, the novel has been at the center of heated arguments about whether it is racist, and in some editions language deemed offensive has been replaced. Since the novel revolves around the relationship between Huck and the escaped slave, Jim, race is a central issue, and Twain's irony does not, for some, compensate for the language he gives to his characters.

Judging quality

The twenty-first century is seeing a proliferation of literary prizes. It is also an age of mass marketing of books, through advertising, book fairs, literary festivals, and reviews. Although there is clearly a commercial dimension to all this, it is nevertheless the case that there have to be criteria for awarding prizes, and the language used is always qualitative: judges select "the best," "the outstanding" of the works sent to them to read. Sometimes the judges fail to agree; when the Man Booker International Prize was awarded to Philip Roth in 2011, one of the three judges, Carmen Calill withdrew in protest saying she did not rate him as a writer at all. Also in 2011, the judges of the IMPAC Dublin prize failed even to put Hilary Mantel's Booker prize-winning novel, *Wolf Hall* onto the longlist. There has not always been consensus about the Nobel Prize either, as the Secretary to the Swedish Academy Horace Engdahl has pointed out (Engdahl 2008).

It is worth bearing in mind that there is considerable variation in how the books to be judged are selected. In some cases, publishers put books forward, the IMPAC prize entries are selected by librarians around the world, in other cases sales figures, readers' nominations, reviewers, and others have an input into the nominations. Judges are for the most part writers and academics, but the Booker Prize judges have increasingly been selected from the world of entertainment, to add a more "popular" note to a prize that is now televised in the United Kingdom in a similar way to the Oscar ceremony. The selection and judging of literary prizes around the world does not demonstrate a coherent idea of quality criteria.

Alongside the proliferation of literary prizes are websites, television programs, and published lists advising readers on the 50 best books to read in a lifetime, or the 100 best books ever written and so forth, a variant on the old canonical approach to literature but generally more populist now and more international. The lists are complied by journalists, though occasionally a named academic or writer is listed as one of the selectors. What such lists show, however, is that there seems to be a desire on the part of the public to have some sort of guidance about what to read, and sales figures for prize-winning books confirm, for a short period after the announcement at least, that there are readers actively seeking what is branded as "quality" writing.

The turmoil of the three decades from the 1960s to the end of the last century resulted in radical changes as to which writers are taught in schools and universities, and marked the end of attempts to define "quality" in absolute terms. Yet clearly there is qualitative difference between writing: *The Da Vinci Code* may have sold millions of copies, but it is a formulaic book written like the steps in a computer game, and once read can be instantly forgotten. In contrast, novels like Alexandar Solzhenitzin's *The Gulag Archipelago* or J.M. Coetzee's *Waiting for the Barbarians* or Gabriel Garcia Marquez' *One Hundred Years of Solitude* open up great vistas in the mind and stay with us long after we have closed the pages. A production of *Medea* or *The Trojan Women* can still shock and move audiences, the linguistic brilliance of poets like Dante, Wang Wei, Rilke, or Machado continues to astound new generations of readers.

Quality, as stated at the outset, is a slippery notion, but although the concept of a universal canon may have been deconstructed, and although there is always a readerly, individualistic dimension to assessing quality, nevertheless some writers manipulate language and their material more skillfully than many of their peers. A simple suggestion for determining quality might be the following: does the text I am reading take me to new places, either inner or outer, through a combination of the writer's use of language, that is, the form, and the content? And when I have finished reading, are there elements that remain with me—ideas, words, images, sounds, characters, scenes, in short, have I been taken out of myself, even if only for moments, even if I have had to struggle to understand, even if I have not enjoyed the text, even if I have been disturbed by what I have read? For the determination of quality as we understand it today lies in the relationship between the writer, the text and the reader. Of course the author is not dead, but neither is the author all-powerful, for the author creates in his or her own time and context, and the reader then engages with the text in another time and context entirely, often in another language altogether.

Further reading

John Guillory's *Cultural Capital and the Problem of Literary Canon Formation* and Dean Kolbas' *Critical Theory and the Literary Canon* provide both provide wide-ranging discussions of valuation and canon formation with reference to theory of sociology. Harold Bloom's *The Western Canon* is an idiosyncratic but passionate defense of the values of literary form and strangeness. In *The Making of the Modern Canon,* Jan Gorak presents the processes of canonization of different eras. Terry Eagleton's *How to Read Literature* is an accessible introduction that deals with literary values through numerous examples. Cathrine Belsey's and Jane Moore's *The Feminist Reader* is a rich resource to understand the role gender plays in appreciation of literature, while Susan Bassnett's *Translation* focusses on the challenges of conveying cultural values in translations.

References

Barthes, Roland (1977 [1968]) "The Death of the Author," in *Image, Music, Text,* London: Fontana.

Bassnett, Susan (2014) *Translation,* London and New York: Routledge.

Belsey, Catherine and Jane Moore (eds) (1997) *The Feminist Reader: Essays in Gender and the Politics of Literary Criticism,* London: Blackwell.

Bloom, Harold (1994) *The Western Canon: The Books and School of the Ages,* New York: Harcourt, Brace and Co.

Borges, Jorge Luis (2002) "The Homeric Versions," in Daniel Balderston and Marcy Schwartz (eds), *Voice-Overs: Translation and Latin-American Literature,* Albany: State University of New York Press, 15–20.

Brandes, Georg (1966 [1898]) *Hovedstrømninger i det nittende Aarhundreds Litteratur,* 6 vols, Copenhagen: Gyldendal, 1872–90, 56–7.

Ducis, Jean-Francois (1770) cited in Romy Haylen (1993) *Translation, Poetics and the Stage. Six French Hamlets,* London and New York: Routledge.

Eagleton, Terry (1983) *Literary Theory: A Critical Introduction,* London: Blackwell.

Eagleton, Terry (2014) *How to Read Literature,* New Haven and London: Yale University Press.

Eliot, T. S. (1950) "Dante," in *Selected Essays,* New York: Harcourt, Brace and Co.

Engdahl, Horace (2008) "Canonization and World Literature: The Nobel Experience," in Karen-Margrethe Simonsen and Jakob Stougaard-Nielsen (eds), *World Literature World Culture,* Aarhus: Aarhus University Press, 195–214.

Gorak, Jan (2013) *The Making of the Modern Canon: Genesis and Crisis of a Literary Idea*, London: Bloomsbury.

Guillory, John (1993) *Cultural Capital and the Problem of Literary Canon Formation*, Chicago: University of Chicago Press.

Heaney, Seamus (1984) *Station Island*, London: Faber.

Kolbas, E. Dean (2001) *Critical Theory and the Literary Canon*, Boulder, CO: Westview Press.

Lefevere, Andre (1992) *Translation, Rewriting and the Manipulation of Literary Fame*, London and New York: Routledge.

Moi, Toril (1985) *Sexual/Textual Politics: Feminist Literary Theory*, London: Methuen.

Ngugi wa, Thiong'o (1972 [1995]). "On the Abolition of the English Department," in Bill Ashcroft, Gareth Griffiths and Helen Tiffin (eds), *The Post-Colonial Studies Reader*, London and New York: Routledge, 285–90.

Scholes, Robert (1998) *The Rise and Fall of English*, New Haven: Yale University Press.

Soyinka, Wole (1976) *Myth, Literature and the African World*, Cambridge: Cambridge University Press.

Tolstoy, Leo (1906 [2014]) *Shakespeare: A Critical Essay*, Create Space Independent Publishing Platform.

Van Peer, Willie (ed.) (2008) *The Quality of Literature*, Amsterdam: John Benjamins.

Walcott, Derek (1995 [1974]) "The Muse of History," in Bill Ashcroft, Gareth Griffiths and Helen Tiffin (eds), *The Post-colonial Studies Reader*, 370–4, London and New York: Routledge.

An Overview of Schools of Criticism

Formalism

Formalism is generally divided into early Russian formalism (1914–1927) and later Czech formalism (1928–1948). The formalists focused on formal devices and functions. They considered art a field with specific laws that can be described and that have an effect on the reader, with a particularly divergent use of language.

Formalism is an aesthetics, in the word's original meaning of sensory learning, and not a hermeneutics, that is involving learning through interpretation. Here Viktor Shklovsky's (1893–1984) concept of defamiliarization is central. Our perception of the world is automated, which means that we do not see the world, but our expectations of the world, and art should therefore defamiliarize by expressing things in an alternative and apparently strange way. It leads us via detours to see the world in a different light. This is generally done by breaking the automatic and pragmatic connection between language and the world. In terms of language, this break is seen on a literary historical level as a break with tradition. Art is conditioned by history, but it evolves through breaks where the new does away with the old.

In Roman Jakobson's concept of the poetic function, signs refer to the world, but first and foremost to themselves and thus to the difference between themselves and the world. Furthermore, by entering into patterns conditioned by other signs, they indicate that meaning emerges between signs, and not just between signs and things. Here and in Vladimir Propp's investigations of plot structures in folk tales, formalism anticipates structuralism. It has also had a major influence on New Criticism. Formalism shared the joy of facts and method with the futurists and the Russian avant-garde, cf. Shklovsky's manifesto from 1914. Russian literary philosopher Mikhail Bakhtin (1895–1875) criticized formalism for its consideration of language and art in isolation and outside the context of society. He did this among other ways through his concepts of polyphony and the carnivalesque, which he developed in the latter half of the 1920s.

DR

New Criticism

New Criticism is related to formalism. This movement arose in the 1920s and 1930s in the US South. It was never a formally organized movement, but represented by number of independent critics, such as John Ransom Crowe (1888–1974), Allen Tate (1899–1979), Cleanth Brooks (1906–1994), and Robert Penn Warren (1905–1989), who were often practising poets. They read and analyzed contemporary literature, primarily poetry, and came up with a text-focused approach: "close reading." The movement emphasizes the notion of the *autonomous* literary text, inspired among others by the poet and critic T.S. Eliot (1888–1965). The text is considered a structural unity that works independently of the author and the context, but in timeless dialog with other texts. It constitutes one coherent whole. From this it follows that nothing in the reading should be considered in isolation. Everything should be read as integrated elements of the textual unity—a unity that often depends on ambiguity, paradox, or irony. New Criticism's notion of the literary text as a unity of opposites is underlined by Cambridge professor I.A. Richards' (1893–1979) concept of the *inclusivity* of poetic language. Poetic language is considered a unique form of expression that brings together apparently incompatible elements in a charged and thus particularly meaningful unit.

The heyday of New Criticism was over by the 1950s and 1960s, when it had to make way for structuralism, psychoanalysis, and ideological criticism among others. But its significance cannot be underestimated. New Criticism is the dominating modern literary theory in relation to which the other theories define themselves. The new critical "close reading" is still a key aspect of teaching wherever literary texts are studied.

ST

Structuralism

Structuralism represents a scientific theoretical paradigm within a number of disciplines rather than an actual school of criticism. What these disciplines share is the notion of basic structures or systems organizing phenomena. Structuralism is often more specifically linked to a group of theorists in France around 1960 who expanded linguistics' concept of language as structure to the study of social and cultural phenomena. In linguistics, structuralist analysis is often concerned with structures in the text, and based on this tries to understand general, conventional patterns as well as linguistic and cognitive models that make the individual text possible.

Structuralism has its origins in linguist Ferdinand de Saussure's (1857–1913) series of lectures (1907–1911) that were recorded by his students and published in 1916 under the title *Cours de linguistique générale* (*Course in General Linguistics*). Here

Saussure outlines a study of signs, a *semiology*, that replaces a diachronic historic-causal analysis method (words, etymologies, language families) with a synchronic analysis method (language here and now). Saussure argued for a differentiation between actual language use (*parole*) and the abstract, underlying language system (*langue*), a differentiation that involves a division of linguistic signs into expression and content, signifier and signified. The relationship between the two is arbitrary and conventional rather than naturally given. Access to the language system is only gained through language use, in which the language system manifests itself, and linguistic signs can only be studied in relation to other signs.

Saussure's linguistics in combination with Russian formalism became an important model for the development of structuralism as cultural and literary criticism, as practised by Claude Lévi-Strauss (1908–2009), Roman Jakobson (1896–1982), Algirdas Julien Greimas (1917–1992), Roland Barthes (1915–1980), and Gérard Genette (b. 1930), among others. Structuralism is also considered the basis of Jacques Lacan's (1901–1981) psychoanalysis, Louis Althusser's (1918–1990) Marxism, and Michel Foucault's (1926–1984) discourse analysis.

AMKL

Post-structuralism

Post-structuralism is a designation for a number of French intellectuals who emerged during the 1960s and 1970s and made a name for themselves in literary theory as well as in, for example, political theory, gender studies, and cultural studies. The avant-garde journal *Tel Quel* (founded 1960) is considered a central hub for the movement. Post-structuralists often mentioned include among others Jacques Derrida (1930–2004), Roland Barthes (1915–1980), Michel Foucault (1926–1984), Gilles Deleuze (1925–1995), and Julia Kristeva (b. 1941). However, most of the theorists themselves reject the designation. Post-structuralism is thus not a self-aware, organized group, but refers to a number of independent thinkers who in various ways are critical of structuralism in particular, but also phenomenology—two dominating schools of thought in the twentieth century that both seek to achieve certain knowledge by focusing on fixed structures and real "phenomena" respectively.

The basis is a destabilization of notions of knowledge, meaning, and truth that is experienced as liberating. In relation to textual analysis and literary criticism, this leads to a movement away from a focus on the author (biographical criticism) or the text as an independently meaningful structure (New Criticism) toward the reader. A post-structuralist approach to textual analysis will thus often focus on the reader as a source for creating meaning. Doing away with one authoritative interpretation of a text opens it up to many different perspectives. The basis for a post-structuralist reading is often the theory of deconstruction. However, post-structuralism is a broader designation than deconstruction, and certain elements in the movement focus on desire, the body, and subjectivity rather than deconstruction's core concepts of textuality, rhetoricity and intertextuality. In this sense, there are also interfaces with, for example, psychoanalysis, feminism, queer theory, and postcolonialism.

ST

Deconstruction

Deconstruction (sometimes called *deconstructivism* or *deconstructionism*) is a direction within post-structuralism. Deconstruction arose as linguistic philosophy and literary theory in France and the United States at the end of the 1960s. Deconstruction really means a certain way of reading that French philosopher Jacques Derrida (1930–2004) instigated. Deconstruction does away with Western thinking's metaphysics of presence and logocentrism, that is the notion of an original, irreducible truth that exists in itself, regardless of language. Deconstruction is a criticism of binary and hierarchic contrasts—for example, spirit/body, content/form, nature/culture—that Derrida considered repressive power hierarchies restricting meaning's free play (what Derrida calls *jeu*). Deconstructing means demonstrating how the binary contrasts are constructions themselves, not ahistorical or eternal models.

In terms of linguistic philosophy, deconstruction is based on a criticism of Saussure's notion of a division of signs into *signifiant* and *signifié*. For Derrida, language will never grant access to the extratextual, and signs can never refer to anything other than several signs, which is why meaning is always displaced. Derrida calls this phenomenon *différance* in his major work *De la grammatologie* or *Of Grammatology* (1967). Derrida's ideas have influenced the Yale school, including Paul De Man (1919–1983), Geoffrey Hartman (1929–2016), and J. Hillis Miller (b. 1928), who developed an American variant of deconstruction as literary criticism. Paul De Man undertakes detailed close readings that show how literary texts destabilize their own message by introducing an *aporia*, that is an impasse. For the American practitioners of deconstruction, it is a central point that literary language in itself is deconstructive and that deconstruction is therefore not a method of analysis but a precondition that can be observed in the text.

AMKL

Discourse analysis

Discourse analysis was originally a linguistic discipline that focused on the structure and function of spoken texts. In the mid-1980s, under the influence of post-structuralism and particularly French theorist Michel Foucault (1926–1984), discourse analysis became a key designation for a number of different approaches to spoken or written language use within the arts and social sciences.

A discourse is any form of written or spoken text or conversation. The concept encompasses the notion that these texts are time and place-bound phenomena that shape and limit thoughts and actions. Discourse exercises power in that it limits how we perceive the world. Foucault presents discourse as a system built on the relationship between knowledge and power. The analysis aims to uncover this system: how knowledge is generated through discourse. Discourse analysis is based on a basic socio-constructivist understanding: that reality and truth are social constructions. Discourse analysis is therefore the only approach to knowledge of the world.

Discourse analysis is a tool for investigating how meaning is found socially. It is not really a method but more of an approach that relates critically to any method that aims to achieve certain knowledge—in this sense, it might be called "anti-scholarly," if not "anti-research." It is used in widely differing ways within different disciplines: in social science, discourse analysis is social analysis in that there is a focus on uncovering the power structure behind specific discourses while history, cultural and literary studies have used discourse analysis to investigate the relationship between text and context, language and reality. Discourse analysis as textual analysis often coincides with deconstruction, while the overall perspective also links to post-structuralism, postcolonialism, feminism, and so on.

ST

Biographical criticism

Biographical criticism considers literary texts an expression of the author and his or her life and times. The father of biographical criticism is French critic and literary historian C.A. Sainte-Beuve (1804–1869), who in a positivistic spirit wrote a number of author portraits and biographical essays based on the notion of *tel arbre tel fruit*—that the relationship between the author and the text corresponds to the relationship between the tree and its fruit. French literary historian and philosopher Hippolyte Taines' (1828–1893) historicist literary criticism was also central to biographical criticism, and Germanist Wilhelm Scherer (1841–1886) contributed to its development as a scholarly method. Biographical criticism was based on the notion of a causal relationship between the author and the text, and the aim of the analysis was to recreate an original and authentic authorial intention.

New Criticism was at odds with biographism. In connection with the emergence of New Criticism's ideas of literary autonomy, critics M. C. Wimsatt (1915–1985) and W.K. Beardsley (1907–1975) launched the term *the intentional fallacy* to characterize what they saw as a misreading of literature based on the notion of retrieving the author's intention behind the text. This led to a theoretical degradation of the author in literary criticism, where many inspired by Wayne C. Booth (1921–2005) instead preferred to talk about the *implicit author*. In recent years, there seems to have been a shift in discourse on the author. Serge Duobrovsky (b. 1928) introduced the term *autofiction* in the 1970s to signify a deliberately complicated relationship between autobiography and fiction. Séan Burke's *The Death and Return of the Author* (1998) is a seminal contribution in recent years.

AMKL

Sociology of literature

Sociology of literature is a discipline that looks at the dynamics between literature and society and considers the literary text as a junction in a wider social network. Historically, sociology of literature has its roots in a positivistic view of science and in Marxist criticism and critical theory among other things. Sociology of literature became an internationally recognized designation from around the 1960s, when theorists such as Robert Escarpit (1918–2000), Lucien Goldman (1913–1979), Pierre Bourdieu (1930–2002), Robert Darnton (b. 1939), and Raymond Williams (1921–1988) developed it as a trend. Sociology of literature partly investigates the social conditions for the origin and spread of literature, and partly its function in a wider social context or system.

The discipline covers both the study of social issues in literature and the study of literature's production, distribution, and reception in relation to, for example, publishers, book markets, libraries, teaching, the press, literary politics, technology, and other media. Sociological analyses of literature are typically interested in the interplay between intratextual strategies and extratextual conditions for literature. Within sociology of literature, the discipline *history of books* is a central field that brackets New Criticism's prohibition of intention and context and instead focuses on sociology, media, and materiality with inspiration from bibliography among other forms. Here mention may be made of Darnton's model for the book as a commodity and its life cycle in a *communications circuit*, D.F. McKenzie's (b. 1931) concept of the book as an *expressive form* and Jerome McGann's (b. 1937) concept of texts' *socialization*. Sociology of literature approaches are generally all interested in agencies beyond the literary text that influence how the text is produced, distributed, consumed, and received.

AMKL

New Historicism

New Historicism emerged during the 1980s as a result of various attempts to further develop and re-evaluate Marxist reading strategies. The designation thus does not refer to a specific school of thought, but to many different reading strategies that relate to literary texts as historical documents originating from specific social, cultural, and political contexts. This thus marks a departure from New Criticism's and deconstruction's formal, decontextualized analyses among other things. Louis Montrose describes the movement as an expression of a post-structuralist turn toward history, which in literary studies means an immersion in "texts' historicity and history's textuality" (1992). The text is considered on the basis of its historical specificity and social and material embedding, and history is read as a textual entity rather than the authentic past.

The designation New Historicism was introduced by American renaissance specialist Stephen Greenblatt (b. 1943), who is also a key figure in one of the two marked directions within the movement. Greenblatt analyses the Renaissance and its literature, including Shakespeare in particular, based on key words such as circulation, negotiation, energy, and power, inspired by post-structuralism and Foucault in particular. The other direction was developed by Marjorie Levinson (b. 1951) among others, in studies in Romanticism based on a basic Marxist or materialistic understanding. She thus expanded on Marxist reading strategies, inspired by Louis Althusser (1918–1990), Raymond Williams (1921–1988), and Fredric Jameson (b. 1934) among others.

New Historicism has interfaces with both cultural studies and cultural materialism, but differs due to its insistence on a historical basis. Criticism of New Historicism is often based on the approach reducing the literary text to a testimony of the specific historical context and thus ignoring the potential of literature as an existential and aesthetic statement.

ST

Cultural studies

Cultural studies is an interdisciplinary academic field that focuses on the study of cultural phenomena. The field investigates all aspects of what we designate culture with a view to understanding how meaning is produced and disseminated within a given culture through various forms of practices, beliefs, and institutions as well as political, economic, or social structures.

Cultural studies emerged as a field in the 1960s in connection with the Birmingham Centre for Cultural Studies. The starting point was classic Marxist analysis, but the field evolved, inspired among other things by the Italian theorist Antonia Gramsci (1981–1937) and his key concept of cultural hegemony where culture is considered a central tool in exercising political and social control. Cultural studies is based on this perspective among others and investigates how culture in all forms permeates everyday life. The field distinguishes itself by focusing on popular and mass culture over elite and high culture. It draws on the work of numerous theorists from the Marxist and post-structuralist tradition in addition to Gramsci including Walter Benjamin (1892–1940), Theodor W. Adorno (1903–1969), Raymond Williams (1921–1988), Roland Barthes (1915–1980), Terry Eagleton (b. 1943), and Pierre Bourdieu (1930–2002). In the analysis, several different methodological approaches are used, of which two can be highlighted as particularly characteristic: institutional analysis and ideological criticism. Institutional analysis investigates institutions' role in creating, maintaining, and making use of cultural discourses. This perspective is often combined with ideological criticism, which reveals how ideas, emotions, beliefs, values, and representations are present in various cultural phenomena.

Cultural studies has been criticized, partly because the field replaces the traditional canon of "great" works with popular and mass culture, and partly because an aesthetically oriented close reading is replaced by sociological analysis and ideological criticism. The field has been criticized for politicizing culture with its focus on conflict, dominance, class struggle, and so on. Nevertheless, cultural studies' agenda has made headway within literary studies, among other things in the form of New Historicism, which uses this approach in historical studies of literature.

ST

Phenomenology

Phenomenology is the study of phenomena as they register to a consciousness. As a philosophical discipline, phenomenology was founded at the beginning of the twentieth century by philosopher Edmund Husserl (1859–1938). For Husserl, phenomenology was a fundamental concern that tried to circumvent the separation of subject and object, consciousness and the world. Phenomenology concerns the sensual experience of the world within a world imbued with conceptuality— phenomenology involves looking beyond science and examining actual acts of consciousness. A key point here is that consciousness has an *intentionality*, that is it is never void, but directed at the world. As a philosophy, phenomenology was further developed by German philosopher Martin Heidegger's (1889–1976) concept of a being's being and French philosopher Maurice Merleau-Ponty's (1908–1961) body philosophy, among other things.

As a method of literary criticism, phenomenology is generally linked to the Geneva School, a group of critics inspired by phenomenology consisting of Georges Poulet (1902–1991), Jean-Pierre Richard (b. 1922), and Jean Starobinski (b. 1920), among others, who in the 1950s and 1960s developed a textual approach that did not analyze the text as an object, but considered the literary text a structure of consciousness, an articulation of the author's particular way of orientating himself or herself sensually in the world. Key to the development of phenomenology as a form of literary criticism within a German-speaking tradition is Polish philosopher Roman Ingarden (1893–1970), who put forth two theories regarding literary texts: first a theory of the literary text as an intentional and functional whole comprised of four *layers*—a phonetic layer, a meaning units layer, a represented objects layer and a schematized aspects layer—and later a theory of *phases* in the cognition of a literary text. Especially where the latter is concerned, Ingarden's phenomenology points toward the reader-response theory practised by Stanley Fish (b. 1938) and Wolfgang Iser (1926–2007), among others.

AMKL

Reader-response theory

Reader-response theory or *reception aesthetics* focuses on the reader as an active party who contributes to creating meaning in the text. It thus represents a departure from focusing on the origins of the text, the author (biographical criticism) or the text as an independent structure (New Criticism, formalism, structuralism). Early studies of the relationship between the reader and the text were conducted by American teacher of literature Louise M. Rosenblatt (1904–2005) as early as in the 1930s. However, reception research had its first serious breakthrough in the 1970s in Germany, where a group of researchers associated with the University of Konstanz made their mark with Wolfgang Iser (1926–2007) and Hans-Robert Jauss (1921–1997) at the forefront. In the last twenty-five years, reception research has played a key role in France, Italy, and the Anglophone countries, among others.

Reception research is located between text-oriented and reader-oriented interpretations. Within the field, a distinction can be made between *interaction theories* that focus on interaction between the text and the reader and *socialization theories*, which focus on the behavior of the reader. Among the socialization theorists we can name Norman Holland (b. 1927), who sees reading as an expression of the reader's personal experiences, and Stanley Fish (b. 1938), who points out that the reading also depends on the reader's expectations and *interpretative communities*. Both consider reading highly subjective. The interaction theorists focus to a greater degree on the reading conditions that the text presents. Iser's theory of the text's indefiniteness is key here. With inspiration from Gestalt psychology, the reader is presented as the entity who creates meaning in the text, which is full of "empty spaces" (*Leerstellen*). However, the creation of meaning does not only depend on the individual reader. Jonathan Culler (b. 1944) points out how the reading of a text "as literature" is governed by literary conventions.

Reception aesthetics focus on the reader not dissimilarly to how constructivism focuses on the reader, but is more accessible and has led to a rethinking of the teaching of literature in primary and secondary schools.

ST

Psychoanalysis

Psychoanalysis was founded as an analytical practice around 1900 by Austrian physician Sigmund Freud (1856–1939). Freud's psychoanalysis and theories on the unconscious and infantile sexuality among other things are central to psychoanalytical theory and literary criticism. For Freud, the psyche is powered by unconscious forces that are separate to or *displaced* from the conscious, because sexual or aggressive notions are not compatible with the subject's rationality or cultural norms, for example. In Freud's dream analyses from *The Interpretation of Dreams* (1900), the latent dream thoughts behind the manifest dream content are projected, whereby the unconscious structures are made conscious in analytical practice. In particular, it is the close link between dream analysis and textual analysis that made Freud's ideas interesting from a literary critical perspective.

Freud's ideas evolved in different directions: his student, Carl Gustav Jung (1875–1961), broke away from Freud's notions of the significance of sexuality and introduced the term *the collective unconscious* for a shared collection of mental images that link people across countries and ages, including the images that Jung calls *archetypes*. Freud's ideas also evolved into so-called object relations theory in the work of Melanie Klein (1882–1960) and Donald W. Winnicott (1896–1971), among others. French psychoanalyst Jacques Lacan (1901–1981) emphasized the formalistic aspects of Freud's ideas and put language in focus for psychoanalysis by claiming among other things that the unconscious is structured like a language.

In literary criticism, psychoanalytical concepts have often been used as a technical vocabulary in the study of literary language and as a "meta-language" in order to understand the literary text's basic creation of meaning. Several different schools of literary criticism have appropriated aspects of psychoanalysis' *practice of interpretation*, including biographical criticism, ideological criticism, and feminism, just as one might highlight a methodological relationship to New Criticism and deconstruction.

AMKL

Feminist literary criticism

Feminist literary theory rests on the basic assumption that notions of gender contribute to structuring literary texts and that, conversely, the texts contribute to structuring notions of gender. As its starting point, feminism is interested in the notions of woman inherent in the production and reception of the texts as well as in their internal form and themes, but the field covers ideas about gender, the relationship between the genders, and the correlation between gender and other markers of difference.

Feminist literary analysis is not in itself a method of analysis, but a fundamental lens that, since it emerged in the 1970s, has developed its methods in line with general literary theory. Two traditions dominated during the 1980s in particular: the Anglo-American culturally and historically oriented *gynocriticism* and the French, language-oriented *écriture féminine*. Gynocriticism, represented by Elaine Showalter (b. 1941) among others, tries to write women's literary history by focusing on texts written by female authors, among other methods. It builds on the idea of a particularly female experience that is expressed in certain literary themes, but also on the idea of an idiom that differs from that of men. This focus on female idiosyncrasy also characterizes the French écriture féminine, represented by Julia Kristeva (b. 1941), Luce Irigaray (b. 1930), and Hélène Cixous (b. 1937), who focus on the relationship between language, writing, and the body. A female language thus emerges that emphasizes fluidity and ambiguity.

Gynocriticism and écriture féminine are criticized for an inherent notion of difference that makes female literature divergent. Post-feminism, represented by Judith Butler (b. 1956), breaks away from this focus on female idiosyncrasy and instead emphasizes a performative gender concept. This approach has had an impact on the development of queer theory. Feminist literary theory and analysis also has links to post-structuralism, discourse analysis, and deconstruction in particular.

AMKL

Queer theory

Queer theory designates a theoretical perspective in gender criticism that criticizes cultural constructions of heterosexual normativity. Queer theory falls within post-structuralism, and more specifically, it has its roots in social constructivism, discourse analysis, and—not least—in feminist literary criticism. "Queer" is another word for "homosexual" that really means "strange" or "different." At the beginning of the 1990s, queer theory emerged in connection with social movements and debates concerning homosexuals' political projects (*queer politics*). Later the framework of the concept was expanded as theory on the historical, cultural, and discursive construction of gender, the body, and sexuality, with a focus on criticizing heterosexual sexism.

In particular, it was American philosopher and rhetorician Judith Butler's (b. 1956) gender concept from *Gender Trouble* (1990) that contributed to establishing the category of queer as a theory. Based on J.L. Austin's theory of *speech acts*, she deems gender—both biological and social—*performative*. For Butler, gender identity is thus a construction that is effectuated through rituals and appellation. Eve Kosofsky Sedgwick (1950–2009) is another central critic in the field whose interest in literary sexual politics, particularly in relation to homosexuality and homosociality in male literature, has contributed to the shaping of queer theory as a reading strategy.

AMKL

Marxism and ideological criticism

Marxist literary criticism relates to the literary text in its historical and social context. Its starting point is German philosopher and economist Karl Marx's (1818–1883) representation of the correlation between a society's *base*, the production-related conditions, and the cultural and idea-related *superstructure*. The literary text is part of a superstructure determined by social and economic conditions. The perspective is superindividual: the text is considered an expression of values and attitudes in society rather than an independent aesthetic expression.

There are many forms of Marxist literary criticism. Ideological criticism tries to uncover ideological content in literature. It emerged, particularly in its early form, as a criticism of literature that by virtue of its seductive, mystifying, and myth-creating properties keeps the reader in a state of "false consciousness" and supports a capitalist social order. Another approach that was particularly well represented by the so-called Frankfurt School focused on the critical potential in literature itself. The Frankfurt School practiced criticism of culture in the interwar years with Theodor W. Adorno (1903–1969), Max Horkheimer (1895–1973), and Walter Benjamin (1892–1940) as central figures. As opposed to early ideological criticism, Adorno emphasized aesthetic expression: good texts offer resistance through their form.

Marxist literary criticism has interfaces with many other theories including feminism and structuralism. An important and newer approach to Marxism was developed by French philosopher Louis Althusser (1918–1990), who links Marx's social theory with Lacan's psychoanalysis. Other key rethinkings of Marxism in an aesthetic and cultural-analytical context are featured in Althusser's student Jacques Rancière (b. 1940) and Slovenian philosopher Slavoj Žižek (b. 1949). Marxist thinking and ideological criticism has also had a very important role in the development of more recent movements such as New Historicism and cultural studies.

ST

Postcolonial theory

The concept of postcolonialism or postcolonial theory is generally associated with a number of theories and methods of analysis taken from, for example, sociological and critical theory that emerged in the 1980s. The concept is used partly for analyses of literature from former colonies where the imprint of the colonial power can be detected in the literary text and partly for wider theoretical discourses about literature's connection with the effects of European imperialism and colonialism. With their slogan "the empire writes back," postcolonial critics drew attention to cultural relations of dominance, particularly between the East and the West.

A chief work within postcolonial theory is American literary theorist Edward W. Said's (1935–2003) *Orientalism* (1978), which investigated the discursive construct of the Orient as the cultural "Other" in Western science, art, and literature. Orientalism is a construct in relation to which Europeans have been able to define themselves. It exercises dominance through a number of institutional literary bodies and constitutes a self-corroborating system that is immune to criticism. Marxist-inspired critic Gayatri Spivak's (b. 1942) focus on the *subaltern's* (i.e., a person from a former colony) lack of opportunity to express himself or herself and Homi K. Bhabha's (b. 1949) concepts of cultural hybridity and mimicry have also been central to the establishment of the field.

Postcolonial theory's *center–periphery* distinction and its focus on relations of dominance and marginalization indicates a wider minority discourse about literature from ethnic, religious, economic, and gender minorities. Minority discourses arise in relation to debates about cultural diversity and in connection with the study of literature's role in the creation of cultural identity, among other things.

AMKL

Cognitive poetics

The study of human intellect, cognitive science, is an interdisciplinary field that has also had an impact on the study of literature. The obvious fact that literature is given meaning during reading through a mental process gives rise to the investigation of how this creation of meaning takes place and whether the way in which a person creates meaning is reflected in their aesthetic preferences.

The cognitive approach to literature has been most influential in the study of metaphors and imagery. George Lakoff (b. 1941) and Mark Johnson's (b. 1949) *Metaphors We Live By* and George Lakoff and Mark Turner's (b. 1954) *More Than Cool Reason* argued for number of apparently innocent, "dead" metaphors being taken seriously as imagery that reveals how meaning is created. Since then, Mark Turner and Gilles Fourcournier (b. 1944) have developed a theory of *conceptual blending* that demonstrates structures in the creation of new metaphors through mixing expressions from various domains in language use. While there are difficulties associated with applying the cognitive approach to studies of literature's often very complex expression, there is in principle no limit to what parts of literature the cognitive approach can be applied to. Peter Stockwell's (b. 1967) *Cognitive Poetics* and *Texture: A Cognitive Aesthetics of Reading* were inspired by Gestalt psychology and look at topics such as voice, empathy, identification, style, and prototypes.

The approach tries to give a better scientific basis for the understanding of literature, but cannot be said to have had a major influence on literary criticism, among other reasons because of an absence of concrete analyses to demonstrate insights that are significantly different from other literary criticism.

MRT

World literature

The concept of world literature is attributed to German poet Johann Wolfgang von Goethe (1749–1832), who in 1827 predicted that the time of national literature would soon be over and that the future belonged to cosmopolitan literature. However, the national anchoring of literatures has proved to be more robust than he thought, something that Georg Brandes (1842–1927) stated in an article on the topic from 1899. World literature was long considered either an excellent and universal literature or just all the literature that did not belong to one's own nation. As such, the concept was of no further significance to literary criticism until the end of the 1990s, when it gained new significance in light of cultural globalization.

Franco Moretti (b. 1950) indicated a need to develop new methods of studying the development of genres across cultures, where not least the novel's ability to change national literary history has been significant. David Damrosch (b. 1953) pointed out the importance of the translator to the study of world literature and appealed to not define world literature as universal literature but as an approach to literature that emphasizes meetings between texts from different cultures. In an approach inspired by Pierre Bourdieu's (1930–2002) sociology, Pascale Casanova (b. 1959) argued that literature circulates internationally based on a different logic compared to that which applies to a national market. World literature can also be considered in relation to other paradigms within literary studies, particularly comparative literature, which historically developed in a Eurocentric manner, and postcolonial literary criticism, which has to some extent integrated itself with the canon that represents comparative literature.

MRT

Interdisciplinarity

Literary criticism has always been influenced by other disciplines. The most influential have been linguistics, psychology, history, and philosophy. However, in recent decades there has been a shift from these traditional auxiliary discourses to a number of others such as medicine, biology, archaeology, geography, and law. This area and kind of research might be dubbed literary interdisciplinarity and understood as an investigation of literature's interfaces with other discourses in the sense of the mutual influence between literature and the discourse in question. On the one hand, how is disease or evolution or law and order or how are tangible historical findings or maps or places depicted in literature? On the other hand, how are the discourses in question characterized by, for example, narrative, or metaphorical organizational structures?

One example is the research field Law and Literature. Its prima facie comes from literary masterpieces such as, for example, Shakespeare's *The Merchant of Venice*, Dostoyevsky's *Crime and Punishment*, Kafka's *The Trial*, and Camus' *The Stranger*. On the basis of this we can differentiate between *law in literature*: how are legal processes, legal concepts and issues, and more general ethical questions about justice, guilt, judgment, and punishment used in literature?—*law as literature*: can literary-scientific knowledge of, for example, interpretation, narration and rhetoric say anything about legal theory and practice?—and *literature as law*: can literature in itself be considered a field that makes laws and judgments that have an impact on society? (Simonsen, Porsdam, and Nielsen, 2007). The field was opened up in 1971 by James Boyd White's (b. 1938) *The Legal Imagination*. Richard H. Weisberg's (b. 1945) books have had a major impact, Peter Brooks' (b. 1938) *Troubling Confessions* is a key text within the field where Jacques Derrida's (1930–2004) *Force de loi* is also important.

DR

Compiled by *Ane Martine Kjær Lønneker, Dan Ringgaard, Lilian Munk Rösing, Sara Tanderup*, and *Mads Rosendahl Thomsen*.

About the Authors

Jan Alber is Professor of English Literature and Cognition at RWTH University Aachen (Germany). He used to work as Marie Curie Research Fellow at the Aarhus Institute of Advanced Studies (Denmark) looking at the negotiation of Aboriginal identities in recent Australian narratives. He is the author of *Narrating the Prison* (Cambria Press, 2007) and *Unnatural Narrative: Impossible Worlds in Fiction and Drama* (University of Nebraska Press, 2016). Alber received fellowships and research grants from the British Academy, the German Research Foundation (DFG), and the Humboldt Foundation. In 2013, the German Association of University Teachers of English awarded him the prize for the best Habilitation written between 2011 and 2013. Alber is currently First Vice President of the International Society for the Study of Narrative, and he will be the Society's President in 2017.

Tore Rye Andersen is Associate Professor of Comparative Literature at Aarhus University, Denmark. He is the director of the research centre Literature Between Media and the editor of the literary journal *Passage*. He is the author of the book *Den nye amerikanske roman/The New American Novel* (2011), and he has published a number of articles on American and British fiction and on the materiality and mediality of literature in journals such as *Critique, English Studies, Orbis Litterarum*, and *Convergence*.

Eva Hättner Aurelius is Professor (em.) of Comparative Literature at Lund University, Sweden. Her research comprises pre-twentieth-century women's literature, primarily in the form of autobiographies *(Inför lagen,* 1996) and letters *(Women's language. An Analysis of Style and Expression in Letters Before 1800,* 2012), genre theory ("Att förstå och definiera genrer: ett semantiskt perspektiv på genreteori" in *Genrer och genreproblem,* 2003), performativity *(Performativity in Literature. The Lund-Nanjing Seminars,* 2016) and the work of Swedish author Birger Sjöberg. She is a member of The Royal Swedish Academy of Letters, History and Antiquities.

Susan Bassnett is Professor of Comparative Literature at the University of Glasgow, UK, and Professor Emerita at the University of Warwick, UK. She has published extensively in Translation Studies, comparative literature, women's theater history and is also a poet and journalist. She is a Fellow of the Royal

Society of Literature, a Fellow of the Institute of Linguists, and a member of the Academia Europea. In 2016, she was elected President of the British Comparative Literature Association.

Christoph Bode is Chair of Modern English Literature at LMU Munich and was Visiting Professor at UCLA, UC Berkeley, Tsinghua University Beijing, and the University of Sichuan at Chengdu. He has published twenty-four books (e.g., *The Novel*, 2011) and some eighty scholarly articles, mostly in Romanticism, Travel Writing, Poetics, and Critical Theory. A permanent Fellow of LMU's Centre for Advanced Studies and member of the Academia Europaea, Bode is also the recipient of various research grants, among them an *Advanced Investigator Grant* from the ERC. Order of Merit of the Federal Republic of Germany in 2013.

Kiene Brillenburg Wurth is Professor of Literature and Comparative Media at the University of Utrecht, The Netherlands. She has been Director of Graduate Studies since December 2013. She is the author of *Musically Sublime* (2009), and (with Ann Rigney) *Het leven van teksten. Een Inleiding in de literatuurwetenschap* (2006, 2008) used throughout the Netherlands. Her new monograph *Back to the Book: Fiction and the Future of Writing* is due in 2017 with the MIT Press.

Karen Emmerich is Assistant Professor of Comparative Literature at Princeton University, United States, and a translator of modern Greek poetry and prose. Her translations have received grants and recognitions from the National Endowment for the Humanities, PEN America, the National Book Critics' Circle, and the Modern Greek Studies Association. Her monograph, *Literary Translation and the Making of Originals*, is forthcoming from Bloomsbury Academic.

Gloria Fisk is Assistant Professor of English at Queens College of the City University of New York (CUNY). Her essays have appeared or are forthcoming in *The American Reader, Comparative Literature, Contemporary Literature, MLA Approaches to Teaching Orhan Pamuk, n+1*, and *New Literary History*. Her first book, *Orhan Pamuk and the Good of World Literature*, is forthcoming in the *Literature Now* series at Columbia University Press.

Winfried Fluck is Professor (em.) of American Culture at the John F. Kennedy Institute for North American Studies of Freie Universität Berlin and Co-Director of the "Futures of American Studies"-Institute at Dartmouth College. His most recent book publications are *Romance with America? Essays on Culture, Literature, and American Studies* (2009), and, as editor, *Re-Framing the Transnational Turn in American Studies* (2011), and *American Studies Today. New Research Agendas* (2014). He is a member of the Academia Europaea.

Søren Frank is Associate Professor in Comparative Literature at the University of Southern Denmark. He is the author of *Migration and Literature* (2008), *Salman Rushdie: A Deleuzian Reading* (2011), *Standing on the Shoulders of Giants: A Cultural Analysis of Manchester United* (2013), and the editor of three anthologies. He is chair of the Hans Christian Andersen Literature Award's academic advisory board and a member of the Young Academy of Europe.

Elisabeth Friis is Associate Professor in Comparative Literature at Lund University, Sweden. She has written several books on the aesthetics of Greek myths and the erotics of archaic poetry. Current research interests include ecofeministic and posthumanistic readings of contemporary poetry. Most recent publication in English (with Stefan Herbrechter) is *Narrating Life: Experiments with Human and Animal Bodies in Literature, Science and Art* (2016).

Jesper Gulddal is Senior Lecturer in literary studies at the University of Newcastle, Australia. A specialist in European literature of the eighteenth and nineteenth centuries, his publications have focused particularly on the literary history of anti-Americanism (*Anti-Americanism in European Literature*, Palgrave-Macmillan 2011), and the nexus of mobility and movement control in the modern novel. Recent essays have appeared in *New Literary History*, *Comparative Literature*, *German Life and Letters*, *Nineteenth-Century Contexts*, and *Comparative Literature Studies*.

Jon Helt Haarder is Associated Professor of Danish and Nordic literatures at the University of Southern Denmark. He has written extensively on various topics within his field, in recent years specializing in autofiction and literary self-fashioning in general. His latest book is *Performativ biografisme. En hovedstrømning I det senodernes skandinaviske litteratur* (Performative Biographism. A Main Trend Within Late Modern Scandinavian Literature, 2014).

Isak Winkel Holm is Professor of comparative literature and co-founder of the excellence research project *Changing Disasters*, University of Copenhagen, Denmark. Author of *Tanken i billedet. Søren Kierkegaards poetik* (Thinking in Images: The Poetics of Søren Kierkegaard, 1998), and *Stormløb mod grænsen: det politiske hos Franz Kafka* (Assault on the Border: The Political in Franz Kafka, 2015); articles on Rousseau, Schlegel, Kleist, Hegel, Nietzsche, Dostoevsky, Musil, Kundera, DeLillo, Sebald, McCarthy, zombie movies, and so on. Translator of Franz Kafka, *Fortællinger* and *Efterladte fortællinger* (Stories and Posthumous Stories, 2007), and Friedrich Nietzsche, *Tragediens fødsel* (Birth of Tragedy, 1996).

Stefan Iversen is Associate Professor at the Department for Communication and Culture at Aarhus University, Denmark. He has co-edited the anthologies *Why Study*

Literature? (2011) and *Strange Voices in Narrative Fiction* (2011) and is the author and co-author of articles and books on subjects such as unnatural narratives, narrative rhetoric, fictionality, and literature of testimony. Iversen leads the PhD program "Summer course in Narrative Studies" and is a member of the steering committee for the European Narratology Network.

Tabish Khair, Ph. D., D. Phil., is Associate Professor at Aarhus University, Denmark. His studies include *Babu Fictions: Alienation in Contemporary Indian English Novels* (2001), *The Gothic, Postcolonialism and Otherness* (2009), and *The New Xenophobia* (2016). He has edited or co-edited several anthologies, including *Other Routes: 1500 Years of African and Asian Travel Writing* (2005) and is also an award-winning and widely translated poet and novelist. His latest novel, published in 2016, is titled *Just Another Jihadi Jane*.

Lasse Horne Kjældgaard is Professor of Danish Literature at Roskilde University, Denmark. He is a member of the Danish Academy of Letters and former Director of the Danish Society for Language and Literature. He has authored several monographs on Danish literary and cultural history, including Meningen med velfærdsstaten: Velfærdsstatsdebat og dansk litteratur 1950–1980 [*The Meaning of the Welfare State: Welfare State Debate and Danish Literature, 1950–1980*] (2017), Sjælen efter døden: Guldalderens moderne gennembrud [The Soul after Death: The Modern Breakthrough of the Golden Age] (2007), and *Mellemhverandre: Tableau og fortælling i Søren Kierkegaards pseudonyme værker* [Between-Each-Other: Tableaux and Narrative in Søren Kierkegaards Pseudonymous Works] (2001), as well as being a contributor to a general history of Danish Literature, *Dansk Litteraturs Historie* [A History of Danish Literature] (2006–2009).

Jakob Ladegaard is Associate Professor in Comparative Literature at Aarhus University, Denmark. His main research interest is the relation between literature and political and economic history. Recent publications include *The Book and the People: The Politics of Romanticism* (in Danish, 2013) and "The Comedy of Terrors— Ideology and Comedy in Marlowe's *Doctor Faustus*," *Textual Practice*, 2016. He is the director of the research project "Unearned Wealth—A Literary History of Inheritance, 1600–2015" funded by the Danish Research Council.

J. Hillis Miller is UCI Distinguished Research Professor of Comparative Literature and English Emeritus at the University of California at Irvine. He has published widely on nineteenth- and twentieth-century literature and on literary theory. Recent books are *Communities in Fiction* (2015); *An Innocent Abroad: Lectures in China* (2015); *Twilight of the Anthropocene Idols*, with Tom Cohen and Claire Colebrook (2016). Miller is a Fellow of the American Academy of Arts and Sciences and a member of the American Philosophical Society. J. Hillis Miller and Ranjan Ghosh's *Thinking Literature Across Continents* (2016), Duke University Press.

Lis Møller is Associate Professor of Comparative Literature at Aarhus University, Denmark. She is the author of *Erindringens poetik: William Wordsworth, S.T. Coleridge, Thomas De Quincey* (2011) and *The Freudian Reading: Analytical and Fictional Constructions* (1991; republished as eBook 2016) and co-editor since 2012 of *Romantik. Journal for the Study of Romanticisms*. She is the editor of several volumes including a textbook in literary analysis, *Om litteraturanalyse* (1995).

Peter Mortensen, Ph.D. (The Johns Hopkins University, 1998), is Associate Professor of English at Aarhus University, Denmark. He is the author of *British Romanticism and Continental Influences* (2005) and many essays on nineteenth- and twentieth-century literature and culture, and he is the editor (with Hannes Bergthaller) of *Framing Nature: Explorations in the Environmental Humanities* (forthcoming). He is currently working on an ecocritical study of life reform and *askesis* in the twentieth-century novel.

Ann Rigney is Professor of Comparative Literature at Utrecht University, The Netherlands, and convenor of the Utrecht Forum for Memory Studies. She has published widely in the field of cultural memory studies, narrative theory, and romanticism. She is the author of *The Afterlives of Walter Scott* (2012), *Imperfect Histories* (2001), and *The Rhetoric of Historical Representation* (1990). She recently co-edited *Transnational Memory* (2014) and *Commemorating Writers in Nineteenth-Century Europe* (2014).

Dan Ringgaard, Dr. Phil., is Professor at School of Communication and Culture, Aarhus University, Denmark. He is the author of a number of books on poets, poetry and poetics, and, more recently, books on place, on creativity, and on the postliterary and co-editor of *A Literary History of Nordic Literary Cultures 1–3*.

Lilian Munk Rösing is a Ph.D. in comparative literature and an Associate Professor at the Department of Arts and Cultural Studies, University of Copenhagen, Denmark. She has published four books (three in Danish, one in English) and a large number of articles combining psychoanalysis with literary and cultural criticism. Latest publication is *Pixar with Lacan: The Hysteric's Guide to Animation* (2016).

Karin Sanders is Professor of Scandinavian Literature at University of California-Berkeley, US. She is the author of *Konturer* (1997) and *Bodies in the Bog and the Archaeological Imagination* (2009), and co-editor of *Litteratur Inter Artes* (2016) and

A History of Nordic Literary Culture. Volume III. Figural Nodes (forthcoming). She is member of The Royal Danish Academy of Sciences and Letters.

Peter Simonsen is Professor of European literature at the Department for the Study of Culture at the University of Southern Denmark. He is the author of *Wordsworth and Word-Preserving Arts* (2007) and several related articles on Romanticism, ekphrasis, and textual materiality. In 2014, he published (in Danish) *Lifelong Lives*, a study of fiction about old age and the welfare state. Currently he is writing a book about the precariat in contemporary British fiction provisionally titled *Precarious Literature*.

Dennis Tenen is Assistant Professor in the Department of English and Comparative Literature, Columbia University, USA. His teaching and research happen at the intersection of people, texts, and technology. A former software engineer at Microsoft and currently faculty associate at Columbia's Data Science Institute, he is the author of *Plain Text: The Poetics of Computation* (2017) and a co-founder of Columbia's Group for Experimental Methods in the Humanities. His most recent work concerns the limits of algorithmic imagination.

Mads Rosendahl Thomsen is Professor with Special Responsibilities in Comparative Literature at Aarhus University, Denmark. He is the author of *Mapping World Literature: International Canonization and Transnational Literature* (2008), *The New Human in Literature: Posthuman Visions of Changes in Body, Mind and Society* (2013), and the editor of several volumes, including *World Literature: A Reader* (2012), and *The Posthuman Condition: Ethics, Aesthetics and Politics of Biotechnological Challenges* (2012). He is a member of the Academia Europaea.

Lilla Tőke is Assistant Professor at CUNY, LaGuardia Community College, USA. She obtained her Ph.D. in 2010 from Stony Brook University in Comparative Literary and Cultural Studies. She also has an M.Phil. degree in Gender Studies from the Central European University, Budapest, Hungary. Her research interests revolve around film and literature, feminist theory, and cultural studies. She has wide experience teaching various levels of academic composition, literature, and film courses.

Frederik Tygstrup is Professor of Comparative Literature at the University of Copenhagen, Denmark and founding director of the Copenhagen Doctoral School in Cultural Studies. Originally specialized in the theory and history of the European novel, his present work evolves around the changing nature of fiction on twenty-first-century culture, socio-aesthetics, cultures of Big Data, and studies of affect. Recent publications include *Structures of Feeling* (with Devika Sharma, 2015), and *Socioaesthetics* (with Anders Michelsen, 2015).

Claire Warden is Reader in Drama at De Montfort University, Leicester, UK. Her primary research interests include modernism, performance, and popular culture. She is the author of *British Avant-Garde Theatre* (2012), *Modernist and Avant-Garde Performance: An Introduction* (2015), and *Migrating Modernist Performance: British Theatrical Travels Through Russia* (2016). She is also co-editor of *Performance and Professional Wrestling* (2016).

Karen Weingarten is Associate Professor of English at Queens College, City University of New York. She is the author of *Abortion in the American Imagination: Before Life and Choice, 1880–1940* (2014) and has published articles in the journals *Literature and Medicine, Feminist Formations, Feminist Studies, Radical Teacher*, and online through *Avidly* and *Somatosphere*. She enjoys collaborative writing.

Index